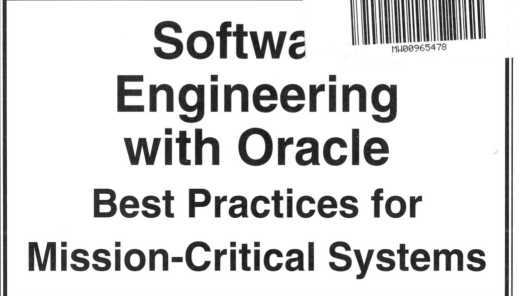

Softwa
Engineering with Oracle
Best Practices for Mission-Critical Systems

Elio Bonazzi

Prentice Hall PTR
Upper Saddle River, NJ 07458
http://www.phptr.com

Acquisitions editor: *Tim Moore*
Editorial assistant: *Bart Blanken*
Cover designer: *Talar Agasyan*
Cover design director: *Jerry Votta*
Manufacturing manager: *Alexis R. Heydt*
Marketing manager: *Bryan Gambrel*
Project coordinator: *Anne Trowbridge*
Compositor/Production services: *Pine Tree Composition, Inc.*

Prentice-Hall, Inc.
Upper Saddle River, New Jersey 07458

Prentice Hall books are widely used by corporations and government agencies for training, marketing, and resale.

The publisher offers discounts on this book when ordered in bulk quantities. For more information contact:

Corporate Sales Department
Phone: 800-382-3419
Fax: 201-236-7141
E-mail: corpsales@prenhall.com

Or write:

Prentice Hall PTR
Corp. Sales Dept.
One Lake Street
Upper Saddle River, New Jersey 07458

Printed in the United States of America
10 9 8 7 6 5 4 3 2 1

ISBN 0-13-020091-3

Prentice-Hall International (UK) Limited, *London*
Prentice-Hall of Australia Pty. Limited, *Sydney*
Prentice-Hall Canada Inc., *Toronto*
Prentice-Hall Hispanoamericana, S.A., *Mexico*
Prentice-Hall of India Private Limited, *New Delhi*
Prentice-Hall of Japan, Inc., *Tokyo*
Prentice-Hall (Singapore) Pte. Ltd., *Singapore*
Editora Prentice-Hall do Brasil, Ltda., *Rio de Janeiro*

This book is dedicated to

my son George, who redefined my notion of love,
and
to my wife Marcia, the person who dared to share my dreams.

CONTENTS

Acknowledgments **xi**

1 Software Engineering in Oracle Projects **1**

1.1 Mid-Range: The Domain of Rightsizing 1

1.2 Typical Mistakes to Avoid 3

1.3 How This Book is Structured 5

1.3.1 Design and Documentation 6

1.3.2 Establishing a Development Environment 8

1.3.3 Oracle and Third Party Development Tools 9

1.3.4 Putting it Into Practice 9

2 The Software Development Life Cycle **11**

2.1 The Traditional Approach 11

2.2 The Waterfall Model 12

2.3 Entrenched in the Large Corporations 14

2.4 Issues and Problems Associated to the Waterfall Model 15

2.5 Risk Analysis, Prototyping, and the Spiral Model 19

2.6 Different Methodologies, Same Development Paradigm 22

2.7 Object Orientation and the Fountain Model 24

2.8 Software Development Life Cycle in Oracle Projects 27

Summary 28

3 Documentation as an Integral Part of Software Projects **30**

3.1 Three Fundamental Requisites 30

3.2 Traceability 32

3.3 Traceability through SGML 34
3.4 XML 38
3.5 Traceability Through HTML 39
3.6 Using Oracle ConText to Manage Project-Related Documentation 41
3.7 Oracle ConText: Text Retrieval Features 42
3.8 The Oracle ConText Option in Action 43
3.9 Synchronization 44
3.10 Synchronization Through Change Management 46
3.11 Project Deliverables: They Are All Documents! 47
Summary 48

4 Designing an Oracle Application 49
4.1 The Intellectual Tools in the Software Engineer's Bag 49
4.2 Design for Flexibility 53
4.3 Design for Performance 59
4.4 Design for Scalability 62
4.5 Design for Reliability 70
4.6 Design for Distribution and Replication of Data 72
4.7 Design for Very Large Database/Data Warehouse 81
Summary 86

5 Detailed Design 88
5.1 Choosing a Development Environment/Language 89
5.2 Application Architecture Paradigms 90
5.3 Rapid Application Development Tools: Compatibility and Performance Issues 94
5.4 Detailed Design Issues 96
5.4.1 Null Values and Indicator Variables 97
5.4.2 Referential Integrity 102
5.4.3 Bind Variables 104
5.4.4 Host Arrays 108
5.4.5 Char and Varchar2 data types 109
Summary 111

6 Data Modeling and CASE Tools 113
6.1 Data Modeling Methodologies 114
6.2 The Role of Domains 118
6.3 The Importance of a Repository 120
6.4 CASE Tools 121
6.4.1 Oracle Designer 122
6.4.2 Oracle ODD 128
6.4.3 ER/Win 129
6.4.4 PowerDesigner 131
6.4.5 ER/Studio 135

6.5 Design Deliverables 138
Summary 140

7 How to Structure the Server Code 141
7.1 Beyond the Oracle Manuals 142
7.2 Procedural Code LIs the Error Handler Function 143
7.2.1 Business Logic Layer 143
7.2.2 Logical Data Access Layer 143
7.2.3 Physical Data Access Layer 143
7.2.4 Communication Between Layers—Parameters and Return Values 145
7.2.5 Procedural Code Layering—An Example in "C" 146
7.2.6 Automatic Code Generation 159
7.3 Using Composition in OO 160
7.4 Error/Exception Handling 168
7.4.1 Error Handling in "C" 170
7.4.2 Exception Handling in OO languages 173
7.5 Application Event Logging 175
7.5.1 Application Monitoring—Operator Alerts 179
7.5.2 Problem Escalation 180
Summary 180

8 Software Engineering Essentials 182
8.1 Version Control 183
8.1.1 File Management 184
8.1.2 Products and Bundles 186
8.1.3 Promotional Group Models 188
8.2 Release Building 190
8.2.1 Source Code Keywords 191
8.2.2 Trouble Shutting Faulty Builds 192
8.3 Tools for Better Code 193
8.3.1 Internal Debuggers 193
8.3.2 Disabling Instrumentation in Production Code 200
8.3.3 Profilers 202
8.3.4 Test Coverage Monitoring 205
8.3.5 Run-time Error Detection 208
8.3.6 Oracle Trace 210
8.4 Writing Performance Conscious SQL Statements 211
8.4.1 Explain Plan 215
8.4.2 Trace and TkProf 225
8.5 Testing Strategies 233
8.5.1 Test Techniques 234
8.6 Internationalization Issues 237
Summary 241

9 Managing Multiple Environments **242**
9.1 Development, Test, Production 242
9.2 Synchronizing the Environments 247
9.3 The Oracle Security Model 262
9.4 Application Objects Owner 269
9.5 Environment Setup 272
Summary 274

10 Developing the Client **276**
10.1 There is No Such Thing as the "Best Tool" 276
10.2 The Major Players in the Client-Server Arena 279
10.2.1 Oracle Corporation 280
10.2.2 Microsoft 291
10.2.3 Inprise/Borland.com 296
10.2.4 Sybase/Powersoft 304
10.3 Connecting to Oracle 313
10.3.1 Native Drivers / Third Party OCI Drivers 314
10.3.2 Microsoft Connectivity 317
10.3.3 Inprise BDE/SQL Links 323
10.3.4 Oracle Objects for OLE 324
10.4 The Software Engineering Focus 328
Summary 330

11 Oracle Tools: Pro*C/C++ **331**
11.1 Error Handling in Pro*C 332
*11.1.1 Building an Error Handler in Pro*C 340*
11.1.2 The Oracle Communication Area (ORACA) 361
11.2 Host Array Processing 365
11.3 Pro*C and PL/SQL 372
11.4 Support for C++ 394
11.5 Precompiler Options 399
11.6 Dynamic SQL in Pro*C 401
11.7 Interfacing Pro*C to OCI 409
*11.7.1 Interfacing Pro*C to OCI Release 7 409*
*11.7.2 Interfacing Pro*C to OCI Release 8 411*
11.8 Developing Multi-Threaded Applications 415
11.9 Handling LOB Types in Pro*C 427
11.10 The Object-Relational Paradigm 428
11.11 Oracle Type Translator (OTT) 434
11.12 The Object Navigational and Associative Interfaces 437
Summary 444

12 Beyond Pro*C: The Oracle Call Interface **445**
12.1 OCI release 7 446
12.1.1 OCI Data Structures 446

12.1.2 In OCI release 7 everything is a cursor! *447*
12.1.3 Error Handling in the OCI *449*
12.2 The OCI release 8 456
12.3 The OCI Advantage 467
12.3.1 Schema Metadata Querying and Reverse Engineering *468*
12.3.2 Dynamic SQL processing *470*
12.3.3 Large Object Management *472*
12.3.4 DML Statements with a RETURNING Clause *473*
12.3.5 Advanced Queuing *474*
12.3.6 Object Navigation *475*
12.3.7 The Best of the Two Worlds *476*
12.4 The OCI: Best Companion for C++ 476
Summary 477

13 Oracle Trace **479**
13.1 Oracle Trace Components 479
13.1.1 Server Side Components *480*
13.1.2 Client Side Components *481*
13.2 Using Oracle Trace—Deciding What to Sample 487
13.3 Oracle Trace APIs 490
13.4 Formatting and Analyzing Oracle Trace Data 493
Summary 494

14 Procedural SQL **496**
14.1 Oracle Extension to ANSI SQL 497
14.2 Business Logic and PL/SQL 498
14.3 Database Triggers 504
14.4 PL/SQL as a Query Helper 510
14.5 Packages 515
14.6 Supplied Packages 516
14.6.1 DBMS_SQL *517*
14.6.2 DBMS_JOB *520*
14.6.3 DBMS_SESSION *523*
14.6.4 DBMS_SHARED_POOL *524*
14.6.5 DBMS_OUTPUT *525*
14.7 External Procedures 526
14.8 Hiding PL/SQL Code 533
14.9 Third Party Tools 534
Summary 540

15 Getting Data In/Out of Oracle **541**
15.1 Communicating with the External World 542
15.1.1 Oracle Pipes and Alerts *542*
15.1.2 An External Procedure Ancestor: PLEX *547*

15.2 Oracle Advanced Queuing 553
15.2.1 Using Oracle AQ 556
15.3 Perl—OraPerl/PerlDBI 564
Summary 566

16 Communicating with the Server 567
16.1 SQL*Net/Net8: The Main Road To Connect to an Oracle Server 567
16.2 When SQL*Net Is Not To Be Used 570
*16.2.1 SQL*Net Alternatives 571*
16.3 Middleware and ACID Messages 572
16.3.1 Middleware Paradigms 573
16.3.2 BEA Systems TUXEDO 577
16.3.3 IBM MQ Series 597
Summary 610

17 Client Development Tools: Putting Them Into Practice 611
17.1 ShrPool, An Oracle Shared Pool Browser 612
17.2 ShrPool Source Code 616
17.3 ShrPool in Visual Basic 618
17.4 ShrPool in Oracle Developer 640
17.5 ShrPool in Delphi 659
17.6 ShrPool in Powerbuilder 680
Summary 702

18 Oracle Performance Tuning 703
18.1 Two Areas Where Oracle Performance Can Fail 704
18.1.1 Poorly Formulated SQL Statements 704
18.1.2 Engine Poorly Configured 705
18.2 The Tool DBAs Need 707
18.2.1 OPERA and its Tuning Method 707
18.3 OPERA Design 710
18.3.1 A Three-Tier Architecture 711
18.4 The OPERA Java Client 723
18.5 OPERA Server Source Code 728
18.5.1 OperaSvr Source Code 729
18.5.2 Extending OPERA: An Example 747
Summary 751

Index 766

About the CD-ROM 772

ACKNOWLEDGMENTS

This book would not have been possible without significant contributions from several colleagues and friends. First of all I would like to thank Guy Harrison, my friend, master, and mentor, who supported me in many occasions during the recent years. He has always been available for advise, even after hours, and helped me while sorting out several problems in my role of Oracle DBA of large, mission-critical systems. I also feel I owe Nick Goldsmith a great deal. He has been one of my technical reviewers for the book and, as usual, he did an excellent job. The other reviewer, Arch Murphy, demonstrated patience and dedication, spending a considerable part of his spare time proofreading my chapters, making sense out of what I was trying to convey to the readers. His corrections and advise have definitely improved the final quality of this book.

This book includes a great deal of source code examples and analyzes many software products. While I am thoroughly responsible for any error in inaccuracy inadvertently slipped through the final version, several people provided me with code snippets and samples. Tony Castley wrote the Delphi version of ShrPool, Glenn Stokol wrote the Oracle Developer version of ShrPoor (Chapter 17). Their contribution is very much appreciated. David Ninnes wrote the Perl/DBI example shown in Chapter 15.

Several people made possible this book, by allowing me to use the various software products presented in the chapters ahead. Brett Hannath, the Australian marketing manager for the Oracle database server, provided me with all the software I needed—quite a lot! Gary Lloyd of Sybase Australia sent me Powerbuilder

Enterprise, and Di MacDonald, of BEA Systems Australia, allowed me to use TUXEDO. Dennis Carmody, of IBM Global Services, activated his own network inside IBM and was able to provide me the MQ Series of Solaris and NT for one entire month (!), enough for me to write the MQSeries section that appears in Chapter 15.

I would also thank Peter Bennett, a very competent Oracle DBA, who put up with my unsolicited book-related "progress reports" during the many times we had lunch together. I hope I did not bore him too much; from my perspective it has been great discussing the topics of the various chapters, before writing about them, with someone really competent and willing to share his knowledge. Peter definitely helped me to "fine tune" the content of the most difficult chapters.

Ideas, concepts, opinions, and views expressed in this book are the result of interactions with many IT professionals I was lucky to work with in the course of my career. I would like to mention Luigi Porro, Mario Bocca, Gaetano D'imprima and Roberto Agliani from the initial part of my career in IT in Italy, and Australian professionals such as Nick La Frenais, Simon Jackson, Yuri Budilov, Robert Germech, Jim Paradies, and Peter Wallace, who in more recent years contributed in making me not only a better IT professional, but above all a better person.

I also want to thank my initial Executive Editor, Mark Taub, who made possible this book, and Tim Moore, who replaced Mark half way through, catching up quickly and competently, and Anne Trowbridge, the Production Coordinator.

A particular thank to Patty Donovan, my Project Editor. She has been really great, demonstrating true professionalism, improving with her editing the overall readability of all chapters. I would really like to know English the way she does! It would greatly simplify my life.

Finally, many thanks to Richard Wagner (1813–1883) the German composer who lifted my spirits up during my long nights spent working at the book. If it wasn't for "Prelude and Death of Isolde" to give me the necessary strength, I would have probably given up before completing my project.

Elio Bonazzi

Chapter 1

Software Engineering in Oracle Projects

This chapter introduces the topics that will be discussed throughout the rest of the book. While the market offers a large variety of publications focused on Oracle technologies, very little has been said so far on the software engineering framework that is the basis for a successful implementation of projects that make use of Oracle servers and tools. This book is about best practices, useful third party tools that facilitate development and management of Oracle applications and tips and tricks learned during several years of hard work and many nights spent on solving practical problems that commonly affect Oracle based projects.

This first chapter will introduce the basic idea that triggered the realization of this book and will offer an overview of the rest of the chapters, highlighting the main thread shared by almost all the remaining pages of the book. The common thread can be identified in *good software engineering practices* that guarantee scalability, easy maintenance, and rapid development of applications that use Oracle technologies in mission critical environments.

1.1 Mid-Range: The Domain of Rightsizing

The Oracle database is available on virtually all commercially supported hardware platforms, from PCs running MS Windows 3.1 to IBM mainframes running MVS. This book focuses on mission critical applications, which tend to exclude the use of PCs to store data that is crucial for conducting the business of large corporations. MS Windows NT release 4.0 is still a bit immature and unstable to be considered a viable solution, especially in environments that must support more than two hundred users on a 24-hour, 7-day basis.

The large IBM mainframes typically run the IBM proprietary database, DB2, or legacy systems such IMS or ADABAS. While Oracle is available for MVS, it is definitely not a major player in that arena.

Oracle is the king in the mid-range environments. In practice this means Unix, given that OpenVMS is in sharp decline and that the IBM mid-range offer, the AS400, is shipped with a database integrated in the operating system that basically precludes Oracle from seriously competing.

Oracle is also number one in the MS Windows NT environment, but, as pointed out above, we cannot yet consider NT ready for mission critical applications serving hundreds or even thousands of concurrently connected users.

If this analysis is correct, and I believe it is, its major implication is that building a new Oracle based mission critical application means choosing the Unix operating system in 90% of the cases. Furthermore, the so-called Oracle appliances, the servers that are shipped by a few major vendors with a pre-installed version of the Oracle database, run a thin variant of the Unix operating system that provides very basic services. The file system is built in the Oracle 8i database, and it can store ordinary files that can be optionally included in transactions, ensuring commit/rollback capabilities.

The bottom line is that at the end of the nineties and beginning of the new century IT professionals using Oracle to build mission critical applications must be familiar with a set of tools, attitudes, and habits typical of the Unix environment. Traditionally, the Unix world has been one of the most prolific sources of good and freely available software engineering tools. To be able to proficiently exploit the great potential offered by the Unix operating system, IT professionals working with it must become intimately familiar with its philosophy, its way to accomplish tasks, and even with its idiosyncrasies. While Oracle remains the main topic of this book, a few sections are focused on tools provided by Unix (or by third party in MS Windows NT platforms) that facilitate the development or management of applications that do not necessarily use Oracle.

Does this mean that OpenVMS or MS Windows NT users can disregard this book? Well, the main focus throughout the book is on best practices and scalability, and the techniques used to achieve these goal's can be successfully applied to all computing environments. Even if your present domain is a LAN of several connected PCs with a server running Novell or MS Windows NT, if you code your application using the techniques explained in this book, you leave your door open to scalability. This ability can become a major asset in the future, if the company grows from a few to a few hundred users or if you can sell the same application to a larger company.

While the focus of this book is on large applications accessed by hundreds of users, the best practices illustrated in the chapters ahead can also be implemented in smaller environments, in the case of PCs running Microsoft software, or in different environments, in the case of OpenVMS running on Alpha servers.

Several tools, which were originally born under Unix, have been ported to MS Windows NT, and are commonly used by programmers who come from a pure Microsoft background. I am thinking, for instance, of profilers, now available with MS Visual Studio, or version control systems such as RCS, today available for MS Windows NT, or Perl, which has a large population that uses the language under NT. The same applies to OpenVMS, which nowadays offers most of the Unix tools to its loyal customers. Very few sections of this book are relevant only in a Unix environment. Most of the topics covered in the chapters to come are operating system "agnostics," and source code examples and tips can be used in the majority of the computing environments.

1.2 Typical Mistakes to Avoid

As an independent Oracle consultant, I came across several projects, sometimes in advanced stages, for which the design and most of the implementation were already done. Occasionally, I have been called in to "rescue" projects, or to "fix" performance problems. In many cases I have seen the same recurring mistakes made in different environments by different people. A careful analysis of the mistakes, and the people who made them, identified "patterns" of errors made by professionals sharing the same background. For instance, developers from an MVS background who work in an Oracle/Unix environment are likely to try forcing an MVS philosophy into Unix, with potentially disastrous consequences. Once, in an MVS shop that had only one Oracle application, designed and implemented by people mainly familiar with MVS, all Oracle tables were named "T0001456," "T0005678," and the like. This is because in DB2 a table is a file, and the naming convention of MVS file provides eight characters for the volume name, eight characters for the file name, and three characters for the extension. DB2 users can set only the file name, which is eight characters long. The tool used to design the application had been tailored for MVS/DB2, and the maximum length allowed for a table name was eight characters. It was necessary to use a dictionary to map the absolutely meaningless table names to business entities. Luckily, DB2 allows for longer column names, so at least the columns had meaningful names, which helped keep my sanity.

This wasn't the only mistake made by these MVS engineers. Security is managed in DB2 in a totally different manner from that of oracle. Authentication is done only through the operating system: When you invoke the interactive SQL environment in DB2, you don't provide username and password. The engineers who designed that application were unfamiliar with the Oracle concepts of schema, schema owner, synonyms, roles, and profiles. They admitted that they were sloppy at the beginning of the project, creating only one Oracle account and regularly defining application objects in the schema owned by that account. For the entire duration of the development phase, all developers shared the same account, freely accessing the database objects created in that schema.

The day before deploying the application in a production environment, they created several user accounts, and to their surprise, they realized that the new accounts could not see the objects created by the schema used up to that moment by all developers. It was a moment of panic. The deadline was rapidly approaching and Oracle manuals were not readily available, so the night before the deployment they implemented a "workaround." They built a security system from scratch, based on an Oracle table that stores username and password for each user. The client application written in Powerbuilder connects to the account that is the owner of all objects. A connection form requires the users to input username and password, which are checked via a table lookup performed against the security table using a stored procedure. The username and password of the schema owner of all application objects are hard-coded in the Powerbuilder executable. It now sounds horrific, but that application is still in production at the moment of this writing.

Different, but no less dangerous mistakes are made by professionals with a PC background. The two recurring mistakes in this "pattern" are the use of literal strings or numbers in the where clause of SQL statements, which forces Oracle to re-parse the statement each time it is executed, and the inadvertent exclusion of indexes from columns appearing in the where clause because SQL functions are performed against the values contained in the columns (i.e., *where upper(surname) = 'SMITH';*).

Although the Oracle application implemented in the MVS shop suffered from a few major mistakes, nevertheless it was scalable, because the basic performance-boosting techniques in Oracle and DB2 are similar. All where clauses coded in SQL statements contained bind variables, and no inadvertent index exclusion was performed by the application built in the MVS shop. The same cannot be said for application ported from MS Access to Oracle, or for application coded natively in Oracle by professionals who previously worked solely with PC-based database systems. Inadvertently excluding indexes, or using literal strings in the where clause of SQL statements submitted to an Oracle engine are problems that infallibly destroy the potential scalability of applications.

The idea behind this book is simple. To be able to build successful applications in mission critical environments, sound software engineering practices must be known, applied, and enforced by designers and developers. The rapidly increasing popularity of Oracle technologies produced a shortage of Oracle professionals in the market. More often, professionals with experience in different technologies are employed in Oracle projects, sometimes in senior roles. In most cases they are not novices to the IT industry, but they don't have any previous exposure to Oracle, and they are likely to make mistakes such as those described above. This book has been conceived to fill this gap, and to allow professionals who already know SQL and relational concepts and theories to rapidly become proficient in Oracle without painfully learning through the hard way of trial and error.

This book also represents an attempt to provide a systematic coverage of Oracle best practices, tricks of the trade, third party tools, tips, and a lot of common sense. Professionals who already know Oracle may find this book useful as a sort of cookbook of recipes that can be used to implement an Oracle development environment from scratch. Universities and other academic institutions that offer Oracle courses in their curriculums can also benefit from this book and its strong focus on software engineering.

1.3 How This Book is Structured

The book comprises four sections. The first, Design and Documentation, is dedicated to high-level application design and documentation production and keeping. The first two chapters of the section are very generic, applicable not only to Oracle based projects, but virtually to all software projects. Starting with Chapter 4, Oracle becomes the focus of the discussion, and strictly Oracle-related topics and issues dominate the rest of the chapters.

The second section, Establishing a Development Environment, introduces software engineering fundamentals, or basic concepts and techniques that all IT projects should adopt to ensure maintainability and manageability of software applications. Both generic tools, such as profilers and version control systems, and Oracle specific tools, such as SQL Trace/Tkprof and Explain Plan, are adequately introduced and their uses explained.

The third section, Oracle Development Tools, offers a detailed analysis of Oracle specific tools for application development, such as Pro*C, OCI, and PL/SQL. Middleware technologies such as TP monitors and queuing systems are also covered towards the end of the section.

The final section, Putting into Practice, comprises two chapters, which focus on pure application development, illustrating and analyzing the source of two applications. Readers are welcome to use the applications presented in the chapters and to extend their functionality, to fulfill their needs and esthetical preferences.

Basic prerequisites for a proficient reading of this book are a strong knowledge of SQL, a basic-to-intermediate knowledge of "C", and an exposure to OO concepts. Optionally, a basic knowledge of Java would be beneficial for the use of the Oracle performance monitoring tool presented in Chapter 18.

This book is not intended to be a surrogate of Oracle manuals or a summary of SQL syntax. This book implies that all readers have access to Oracle manuals as a reference for a better understanding of the concepts presented in the chapters ahead. No single book can completely replace Oracle documentation, and this definitely is not the goal of "Software Engineering With Oracle," which rather strives to offer a consistent and systematic approach to best practices for successful implementation of IT projects based on Oracle technologies.

1.3.1 DESIGN AND DOCUMENTATION

This section includes Chapters 2 through 7. Chapter 2, The Software Development Life Cycle, discusses various types of Software Development Life Cycle (SDLC). After an initial introduction to the Code-and-Fix model, just to demonstrate its unsuitability for large-scale mission critical environments, the chapter examines the Waterfall model, the influence it exercised upon the entire IT industry, its merits and also its limits. After a brief overview of the Waterfall model sub-variants, Chapter 2 continues analyzing the Spiral model of SDLC and its strong focus on prototyping. With the advent of Object Oriented design and languages, which represent a true technological quantum leap, the traditional models of SDLC struggle to demonstrate their suitability in event-based, rather than function-based, environments. A serious and coherent attempt to categorize an SDLC model specifically tailored for OO has been made by Professor B. Henderson- Sellers [1995]. His model of SDLC, called fountain model, strives to capture the essential elements of the OO methodology, with its focus on component reuse, generalization, and abstraction of classes and milestones based on delivery of classes, rather than conclusion of phases as in the Waterfall model.

The direction recently taken by Oracle Corporation, with a new emphasis on the Internet and Java, is likely to shift the focus from more traditional development environments to Object-Oriented methodologies and languages. The fountain model offers a model of SDLC that seems more appropriate than the Waterfall or the Spiral models.

Chapter 3, Documentation as an Integral Part of Software Projects, deals with project documentation. In several projects where I worked I had to fight fierce battles against the tendency to use PC based word processors to produce and keep project-related documentation. A word processor is probably the perfect tool for secretaries writing business letters, but it is not appropriate for documentation redaction and keeping, especially when the files are saved in the internal format supported by the word processor of choice. Mission critical environments need industrial-strength searching and retrieving capabilities, which are outside the domain of PC based solutions. An ideal solution proposed in Chapter 3 is the adoption of an SGML-based environment, where documents are in ASCII format with relevant sections of the text wrapped within SGML tags. An SGML-based Document Management System offers excellent storing and retrieving capabilities. When SGML cannot be adopted, an alternative solution proposed in Chapter 3 uses word processors to produce documentation in HTML format. The files containing HTML tags can be stored in version control systems, thus ensuring traceability of documents, which can be searched and compared using utilities such as *grep* and *diff*. Project-related documentation can also be kept in Oracle, using the ConText cartridge, which allows for powerful searches using sophisticated linguistic methods.

Chapter 4, Designing an Oracle Application, introduces the intellectual tools commonly used to design software applications, such as abstraction, coupling/de-coupling, information hiding, cohesion, and complexity reduction. Progressively refining the models of the problem domain (analysis) and the proposed solution (design), by using the intellectual tools described above, designers and architects are able to build applications useful for supporting the business that requires them.

Relational-specific design techniques based on *metadata* (or data about data), which allow achieving flexibility and de-coupling of table physical structure from business entity organization, are presented in Chapter 4, together with Oracle-specific features, which ensure increased performance, redundancy, and scalability. The chapter also focuses on data replication and distributed databases, as well as Oracle extensions and advanced features, the use of which must be carefully evaluated during the design phase, and not simply superimposed during the implementation phase. The last part of the chapter deals with Very Large Databases (VLDB) and data warehousing, illustrating particular database configurations such as star queries, which use a nonrelational approach to perform Decision Support System (DSS) analysis of business facts.

Chapter 5, Detailed Design, delves into detailed design issues, such as the choice of an application architecture, which can be dumb terminal based, client/server, or WEB based, and a development environment. Choosing third party products, such client side IDEs as Visual basic or Delphi involve incurring risks that must be identified and managed. The chapter also discusses Oracle specific low-level design issues, such as the treatment of NULL values and indicator variables, referential integrity, bind variables, host arrays, and the use of CHAR and VARCHAR2 datatypes.

Chapter 6 deals with data modeling and CASE tools. First the three most popular data modeling notations are introduced (E-R, Information Engineering, and IDEF1X), then the abstraction level of data models is discussed. Data modelers produce conceptual, logical, and physical models. Each abstraction level is defined and clearly differentiated using examples to better convey concepts. The chapter then focuses on the important role played by domains and by repositories, which give persistence to domain definitions across different design sessions. The last part of the chapter analyzes the market offer for CASE tools that can be used with Oracle, starting with Oracle Designer and Oracle ODD, and also considers third party tools such as Logic Works ER/Win, Powersoft PowerDesigner, and Embarcadero Technologies ER/Studio.

The final chapter in this section, Chapter 7, How to Structure the Server Code, introduces a very important technique that helps ensure modularity and control over large and complex projects. This technique, called "software layering," involves separating business programs in four distinct layers: control, business logic, logical data access, and physical data access. A few examples illustrate this technique applied in different contexts and to different languages, including object-oriented languages such as C++. Another important aspect covered by Chapter 7 is that of error handling, strictly related to application run-time monitoring and problem escalation. Again, examples illustrate how to proficiently monitor mission-critical applications once they are in production, and how to deal with problems when they occur.

1.3.2 ESTABLISHING A DEVELOPMENT ENVIRONMENT

This section includes Chapters 8, 9, and 10. Chapter 8, Software Engineering Essentials, focuses on the fundamentals of software engineering, providing detailed information about tools and techniques that must be used together with Oracle tools and technologies to achieve the best possible results in Oracle based projects. Tools usually bundled together with the operating system, or alternatively shipped with development environments, are introduced and their usefulness explained. The chapter considers and evaluates tools such as internal debuggers, profilers, test coverage analyzers, and run-time error detection packages. Oracle specific tools for SQL statement analysis and performance improvement, such as EXPLAIN PLAN and SQL Trace/Tkprof, are also discussed in this chapter, which ends by considering software localization issues, which can help developers who use Oracle to produce software sold internationally.

Chapter 9, Managing Multiple Environments, deals with consistency and synchronization issues brought about by developing projects that use several environments, such as development, test, staging, and production. Ensuring that all environments define the same number and type of object involves using reverse engineering techniques, which can be facilitated by appropriate tools. The chapter considers TOAD and SQL Navigator, by Quest Software, DB Artisan, by Embarcadero Technologies, and the Change Management Pack, add-on to the Enterprise Manager, by Oracle.

Also discussed are testing techniques applied to custom software that makes use of Oracle servers and tools, deployment of applications to different environments, usually accomplished to enforce migration paths during the SDLC, and related issues such as object sizing and tablespace fragmentation.

While Chapters 7, 8, and 9 deal mainly with server-related environments and issues, Chapter 10, Developing the Client, is dedicated entirely to client side development environments and tools. The chapter considers four major players in the client/server market: Oracle Developer, Microsoft Visual Basic, Inprise/Borland.com Delphi, and Powersoft Powerbuilder, highlighting strengths and weaknesses of each tool. Low-level connectivity to Oracle databases plays a crucial role in ensuring adequate levels of performance in mission critical environments, so several connectivity solutions are evaluated in Chapter 10, such as MS OleDB/ADO and ODBC, Powersoft low-level Oracle access drivers, Borland.com BDE, and third party solutions such as Allround Automation Direct Oracle Access (DOA) and Sylvain Faust Inc. SQL Sombrero. Oracle Objects for OLE (OO4O) is also briefly mentioned in the chapter, which concludes suggesting that real scalability and performance issues really pertain to the server domain, rather than the client domain.

1.3.3 ORACLE AND THIRD PARTY DEVELOPMENT TOOLS

This section includes Chapter 11 through Chapter 16. Chapter 11, Oracle Tools: Pro*C/C++, covers several key aspects of Pro*C, suggesting useful techniques for a better use of the pre-compiler. The main topics of the chapter are error handling, host arrays, interfacing Pro*C with PL/SQL and OCI, dynamic SQL, threads, and the object-relational interface.

Chapter 12, Beyond Pro*C: The Oracle Call Interface, explains the use of the Oracle Call Interface, first introducing OCI7, which offers an older but simpler programming model. Once the reader has been eased into OCI concepts, the chapter steps up and presents OCI release 8, providing a few good reasons for a wider use of this powerful API. OCI calls can be intermixed with Pro*C embedded statements, making the best use of both technologies available to Oracle developers.

Chapter 13, Oracle Trace, illustrates the use of Oracle Trace, highlighting its advantages and drawbacks.

Chapter 14, Procedural SQL, covers the Oracle proprietary extension to SQL, PL/SQL. A few powerful techniques are introduced in this chapter, such as user defined functions that act as SQL query helpers, increasing query performance, or a customized trigger implementation that avoids errors such as "ORA-04091, table is mutating, trigger/function may not see it." Also covered are recently introduced and advanced features provided by PL/SQL, such as external procedures.

Chapter 15, Getting Data In/Out of Oracle, deals with esoteric and unorthodox ways to store data into Oracle or to retrieve data from it. Event based programming implemented through database pipes and alerts is explained, as are Advanced Queuing and data extraction through Perl/OraPerl/PerlDBI.

Chapter 16, Communicating with the Server, explores the improvements introduced by Net8, which allow for greater scalability and better performance, and delves into middleware concepts, presenting BEA Systems TUXEDO and IBM MQ Series as examples of sophisticated middleware tools that can be proficiently used together with Oracle to ensure limitless scalability and improved performance.

1.3.4 PUTTING IT INTO PRACTICE

This section includes Chapters 17 and 18. Chapter 17 is an ideal continuation of Chapter 10, as it shows the implementation of a useful tool, an Oracle shared pool browser, in all four client application development environments presented in

Chapter 10. The tool I developed in 1997 in Borland C/C++ version 5, called ShrPool and freely available through the Internet, originally used the OCI7 primitives to connect to Oracle. ShrPool is now available in four reincarnations, one per each client side RAD tool. The source code of each implementation is explained in Chapter 17 and is available from the companion CD.

Chapter 18 explains the concepts behind OPERA, or Oracle Performance Evaluator and Real-time Analyzer, a tool I built to monitor Oracle databases in order to pinpoint performance bottlenecks. The tool is extensible, thanks to its architecture and to the availability of its source code, also discussed in Chapter 18. OPERA is a three-tier tool, where the presentation services are implemented in Java and the middle tier uses "C" and OCI7 to implement a socket server that connects to Oracle and provides the connected Java client with engine statistics. Chapter 18 provides useful guidelines for readers who want to extend the functionality of the tool to better fulfil their needs with minimal efforts.

1.4 Living Appendix

In the world we live in today, the web offers the author and the publisher a wonderful opportunity to interact with you, the reader, to exchange additional information that will help you in your career and the author and publisher to publish better books. The web has become, for many books, a sort of "living appendix" for the book.

In that spirit, this book is supported by the author via the web. You will find that support at: www.appsoft.com.au/sewo.html.

Software bug fixes and text corrections can be found at that page. It is also possible to give feedback to the author, who will include significant suggestions in future editions.

Chapter 2

THE SOFTWARE DEVELOPMENT LIFE CYCLE

2.1 The Traditional Approach

It can start as a hobby, developed while you are a teenager, and then evolve into a career path, or it can be a well thought plan for a future professional life in one of the most wanted careers of our times. You decide to be involved in computing and to become "a programmer." You discover what can be done with a computer language, and how to dominate the machine. You are thrilled by the sense of power given by your achievements while getting acquainted to "the art of programming."

You write programs, gradually refining your techniques, until you master the language and the operating system or the environment. You can be either a self-taught programmer writing simple programs (200 to 300 lines of code) to keep track of your personal collection of CDs, or an undergraduate student in Computer Science working at assignments which require writing programs.

In both cases, you attribute a great importance to the code. All your efforts are initially put in getting the code right by applying the correct algorithm. Later on you will pay more attention to efficiency and you will try to optimize your code. Still, the code appears to be the only goal of your efforts. You are given the problem, to be solved by the means of computer science, and you start by launching either the editor or the RAD prototyping tool and you delve straight into writing code. You compile your code, which is likely to contain defects—at least at the first pass. The compiler flags the problems, you re-edit the code, fix the problems and try to compile again, until an executable is produced. You launch the program, and you test the application. If it contains logical errors, you re-edit the code, and you fix the logical mistakes in it.

You edit the same file and you modify it, overriding the previous version of your code. Sometimes, in the iterative process of editing–compiling–fixing, you introduce more defects than fixes, and you would like to be able to un-do the latest changes. Unfortunately, the previous version of your code is gone forever, overridden by the current version which has been saved. You learn the lesson the hard way, and, next time you significantly modify your code, you save the file with a different name (maybe by using a number as the file name suffix, like myfile_1, myfile_2, etc). If you are not satisfied with the modifications in myfile_2, you can always re-edit myfile_1 and try another alternative, saving the file as myfile_3.

Very soon your directory will be plenty of junk, and, if your application requires more file to be compiled and linked together, you will have to identify, among tenths of files, the "right" ones. That manual process will be slow and painful.

Yet, you are developing software. And, consciously or unconsciously, you are well into the SDLC (Software Development Life Cycle). The model of SDLC just described is known as "Code-and-Fix." It is definitely code-centric, and is applicable only (with very limited usefulness) to tiny projects (a few hundred lines of code) managed by junior programmers.

The code-and-fix model does not have any administrative burden/overhead: no planning, no documentation, no quality assurance, and extremely limited testing. No other activities but pure coding. Clearly, it is not suitable for complex systems, which require a close interaction between different teams often located in different buildings and possibly in different countries. The code-and-fix model is not suitable for planning, estimating, controlling, and managing the resources participating in a project; it is not suitable for creating and keeping the documentation required to maintain the system once in production, or to comply with Quality Assurance parameters. Since the early days of the computing era, the software engineers realized that, in order to manage the intrinsic complexity associated to a software project, a more formalized and articulated model of SDLC was necessary.

2.2 The Waterfall Model

The domain of the software engineers is technology. They master the technological side of the computer operations, but they usually don't excel in the business side. It is not their job; even if they are designing a general ledger application, they are not accountants. They cannot have a thorough understanding of all the minor details and nuances associated to the double entry method. Yet, if well directed by the business analysts, they can produce a successful application.

The point, here, is that, generally speaking, a software engineer is a specialist who must serve, in the course of his/her career, different and varied business domains. A software engineer uses a specific terminology, understood by his/her pairs, sometimes a specific jargon, commonly used within the restricted circle of colleagues.

When a corporation decides to implement a new computerized system, it is primarily a business decision, and, as such, business indicators determine the success or failure of the operation. The business specialists gather in meetings to specify the requirements for the new system. Being specialists themselves, they will use their own terminology (sometimes jargon) to express their needs. Eventually, after the business has sorted out the initial doubts and has a clear vision of the project requirements, the computer experts become involved. They have to re-interpret the business problem in computer terms in order to formulate a plan which will materialize in a document (or a set of documents). That plan states the business requirements and what the information technology support can do to fulfil the business expectations.

The initial phase of the project is concluded. Now, the leading thread is in the hands of the Information Technology specialists, who start the Design Phase.

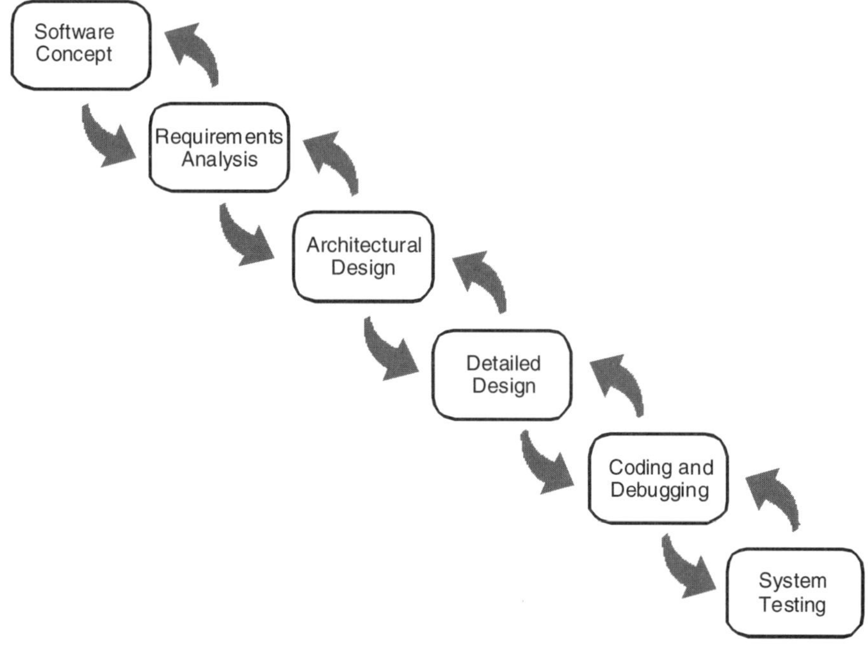

FIGURE 2.1 The Waterfall Model

They spend long hours sketching strange symbols on whiteboards, sometimes involving the business specialists to clarify obscure points stated in the requirements analysis. Eventually, another set of documents is produced, this time concluding the Architectural Design phase.

The subsequent phase is dedicated to the detailed design; every aspect of the system being built is broken down in smaller, more manageable units, and a software solution is carefully crafted for each of them. The Detailed Design phase is accompanied by a massive production of documents; each goes to different stages and reviews, until the editor of the document and the senior designers/architects are satisfied with the content. Notice that up to this point not one line of code has been produced. It is only after the Detailed Design phase that, finally, programmers are hired to cut code, in the Construction phase. Once the construction phase is completed, the testing phase begins. At the end of the tests, the system is ready to be implemented in production.

2.3 Entrenched in the Large Corporations

The waterfall model is by far the most widely used form of SDLC today. The focus is definitely on the documents rather than on the code. From a managerial perspective, the waterfall model offers many and distinctive advantages, primarily control over the various phases and clear scope over resources and results. Every intermediate phase has a clearly defined start and end, each milestone produces concrete and quantifiable outcomes (the related documents).

In large corporations and governmental departments, the financing of the IT projects strictly follows the waterfall model. It isn't uncommon to have the initial design phase budgeted with the time and material method, and, once the overall efforts of the project have been defined, the subsequent phases are offered to the customer on a fixed price basis. The cost controller knows in advance that, at the beginning of the project, the budget must cover the expenses for the remuneration of a few (and expensive...) senior designers and architects (and possibly a few electronic whiteboards). Further down the track, the budget to be set aside will increase to allow for more analysts programmers (during the Detailed Design phase). The financial peak will be reached during the construction phase, when hordes of programmers will join in the project to cut code. Finally, the financial burden will decrease, when the new system makes to production and goes into the maintenance phase.

The tenderers for software bids are supposed to follow the waterfall model and to bid accordingly. It would be difficult to present a plan for a tender advertised by a major governmental department which does not reflect in some way the waterfall model, mainly because that plan couldn't be consistently compared against the ones put forward by the competition.

Undoubtedly, the waterfall model has been very successful. It is also very old (at least in the computer realm, where one generation lasts for eighteen months . . .). In fact, the waterfall model was born in the late sixties as a more articulated and enhanced extension of another model, called "stagewise development." The latter was initially presented in a paper by H. D. Benington at a Symposium on Advanced Programming Methods for Digital Computers in June 1956. Since the very beginning of the computer era the software engineers were struggling to find a way out of the code-and-fix model, and, by that year, they had come to the conclusion that it would have been better to develop software in successive stages (operational plan, operational specifications, coding specifications, coding, parameter testing, assembly testing, shakedown, system evaluation).

The waterfall model, presented formally for the first time in 1970 by W. W. Royce, enhanced the stagewise development in two directions:

- addition of a "feedback loop" between contiguous stages. An emphasis was put in the effort to confine the loop to successive stages, rather than across many stages, to minimize the rework needed.
- addition of prototyping in the form of a "build it twice" step to be conducted in parallel with the Requirements Analysis and Design phases.

A crucial factor which contributed to the progressive success of the waterfall model was its intimate consistence with the programming paradigm which, in the same period, was establishing itself as the winner: the top-down structured programming model. The code-and-fix model was perceived as the natural precursor of the "spaghetti-like code," and, together, they played the part of the "bad guys" in the industry. On the other extreme, the "good guys" were the waterfall model and Algol-68 (the programming language popular at that time), which were promoting themselves as the examples of the raising software engineering discipline that finally defeats the craftsman approach represented by the code-and-fix model.

In spite of its wide acceptance and success, the waterfall model has been held responsible for some of the major software disasters in the history of computing.

2.4 Issues and Problems Associated to the Waterfall Model

The basic assumption intrinsic in the waterfall model is that the iterations are confined to successive steps. The model allows for two-way interactions between, for instance, Requirements Analysis and Architectural Design. They are contiguous phases, and it is possible, though difficult, to realize at the design stage inconsistencies belonging to the requirements analysis phase and to retrofit the documentation produced at the end of that phase with corrections and refinements. The real problem becomes apparent when the system testers find logical errors in one of the last phases of the life cycle. Fixing a design defect which slipped through the various phases and reached system testing is enormously expensive.

Furthermore, it is very easy to overlook design details, or not to consider in the right perspective real issues at the beginning of the SDLC. The business specialists often take for granted key aspects of the business procedures they try to capture on paper to explain the system designers. The system designers often lack a sufficient grasp of the business practices to realize that something is either implied and not sufficiently explained, or even totally forgotten. We have pointed out that the terminology used by the business specialists rarely coincides with the terminology used by the software specialists. There is an *impedance mismatch* between the language spoken by the business specialists and the language understood by the software engineers, and vice-versa. This easily leads to oversights and omissions which can go undetected until late in development.

While the waterfall model offers good scope from a managerial point of view, it gives little visible progress feedbacks from a technical point of view. The

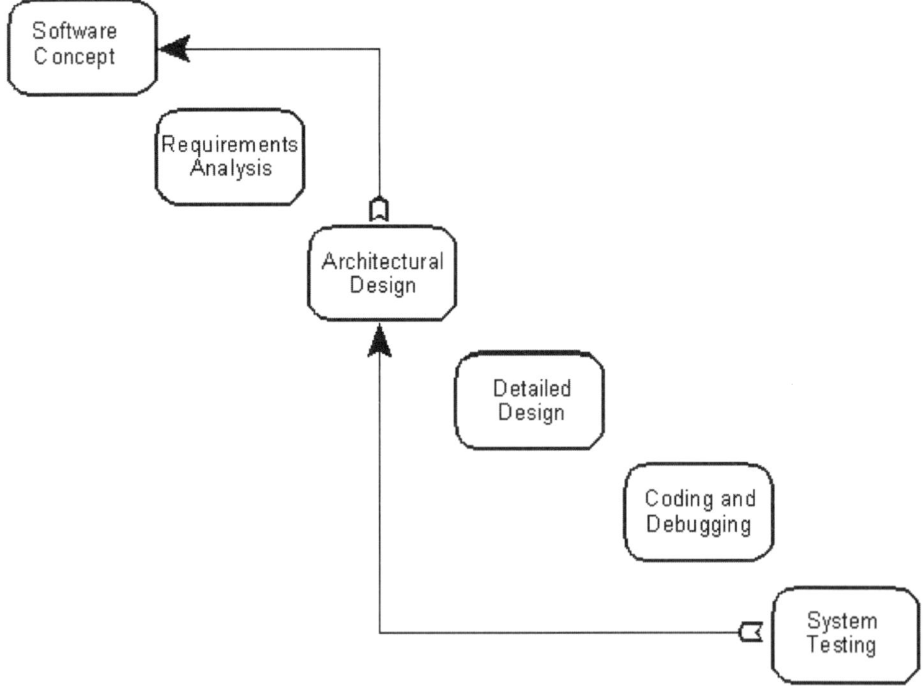

FIGURE 2.2 It is often necessary to skip entire phases and fix problems in non-contiguous stages

major risk associated to a blind adoption of a pure waterfall model is to produce elaborate and over-sophisticated specifications of inconsistent and poorly understood business requirements. The net effect of this mistake, further down the development phases, is the design and development of entirely useless sections of code, which have to be completely reworked, if the project is not halted because of the costly mistakes made.

The advocates of the waterfall model may object at this point that what said is not true, because the model allows for prototyping, through the "build it twice" step, included in the waterfall model since its early conception. The reality is, as some authors demonstrated (primarily Brooks, [1975]), that the "build it twice" step is the entire process done in miniature, bringing about the side effect of the "second system syndrome." The latter is the tendency to overcharge the second system (the one which eventually makes to production) with "baroque embellishments."

Other authors (see Royce [1970]), estimate the required time for the pilot system in up to one-third of the total development effort. The critics of the waterfall model point out that:

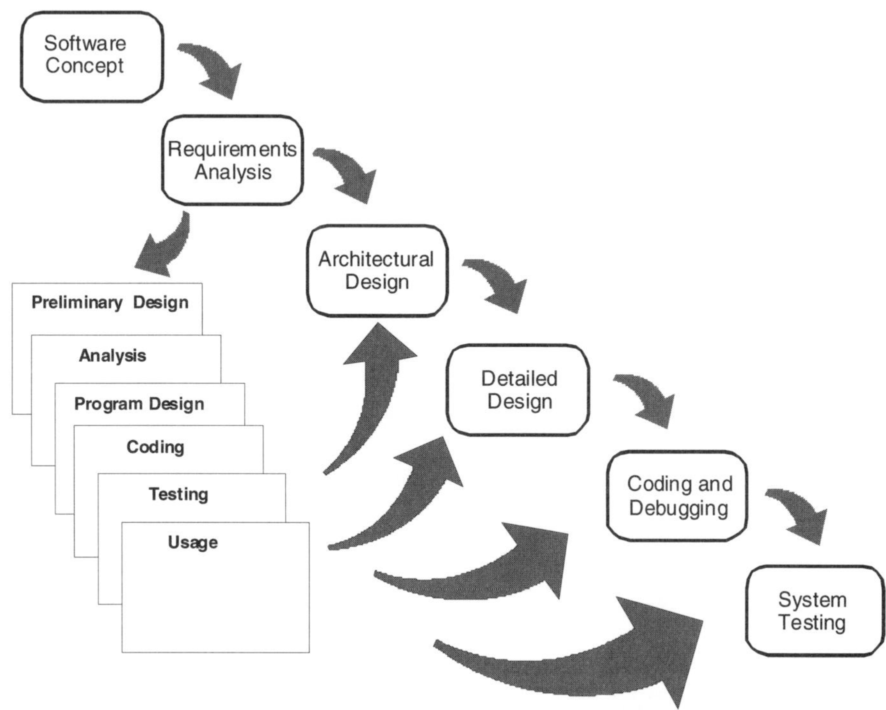

FIGURE 2.3 The "build it twice" process included in the waterfall model

- The build it twice step is unnecessary in applications where the design issues are well understood and thoroughly accepted
- The pure waterfall model does not sufficiently cater for risk analysis and management

The second point is particularly important. In the recent years, most of the research and the debate on software engineering and project management focused on risk analysis. A few attempts to enhance the waterfall model to include an adequate stress on risk analysis have been made. It is indicative that the author who best elaborated on this subject, B. W. Boehm, finally walked away from the waterfall model, giving birth to a totally different model for the SDLC, the Spiral model (explained in the next section).

The software-related activities identified in the waterfall model are unavoidable. One cannot design a software system if an adequate Analysis of Requirements has not been carried out. The Architectural Design must precede the Detailed Design, and so on so forth. The real weakness of the waterfall model is in its rigid and absolute sequentiality and its considering each phase as totally disjoint from the predecessor and the successor.

A number of extensions and modifications to the waterfall model exist to overcome this basic weakness. Few are worth of mention:

1. Sashimi (Waterfall with Overlapping Phases)
2. Staged Delivery
3. Evolutionary Prototyping

The Sashimi model (DeGrace-Stahl, [1990]) takes its name from the Japanese way to present raw fish, where the raw fish slices overlaps each other. According to this model, the traditional waterfall phases can be stretched to include activities and procedures belonging to successive phases. For instance, the Requirements Analysis phase not be concluded until the completion of the Detailed Design, with continuous feedback and retrofitting of the early phases documentation with refinements and tuning operated in later phases. What is gained in flexibility, through the use of this model, is lost in control. In fact there are no clearly defined milestones and the tracking of the activities becomes problematic. Furthermore, when multiple activities are conducted in parallel, it is easy to have lack of communication and to operate on the basis of false assumptions, specially in large projects. The sashimi model works well in small scale project, where the software domain is clearly defined, for instance where a new system, using up to date technology, replaces an old one because the underlying technology is not longer supported.

In the Staged Delivery model (also more informally called incremental development) the software to be built is subdivided in separate stages. At the completion of each stage, the software is delivered to the customer. This model avoids the "big-bang" approach of the pure waterfall model, in which no software is available until the very last phase, and then delivered in block. In the staged delivery model every stage goes through the traditional waterfall phases, but since the customer can evaluate the software delivered, all the basic design mistakes can be gradually caught before their effect becomes a compounding negative effect. Among the drawbacks of this model one can list the overwhelming managerial difficulties of planning the subsequent stages. Every stage must be atomically self-contained, and not be depending in any way on modules scheduled for any successive stages. Yet, it must be fully functional, so that the customer can still work with a subset of the final product. In projects with a very high module interdependence staged delivery is an almost impossible goal.

The Evolutionary Prototyping model prescribes a life cycle in which the target system moves together with the project steps. The most interactive parts of the system are developed first (horizontal prototyping), the customer evaluates the prototype and according to the feedbacks received, functionality is put behind the visible options, or, in other words, the system expands vertically. The customer eventually agrees that the prototype is satisfactory; at that point in time no more functionality is added to system, and the remaining efforts are put in completing every single part of the final product, increasing its robustness. The problem with this approach is its total lack of predictability and control. One never knows in advance how long the project will take to complete. Furthermore, the model implies an impeccable relationship with the customer, who must be understanding and willing to collaborate. What if the customer is never satisfied with the proposed prototype? There are no agreed terms established at the beginning of the project, and the risk of litigation is high. For this reason this model is confined to software developed within the boundaries of one company, where eventual arguments between the IT department and the function requesting the software product can be settled by involving the top management across the various departments.

2.5 Risk Analysis, Prototyping, and the Spiral Model

In the spiral model, the SDLC is seen as a sequence of cycles, which include the same sequence of steps, that evolve from the most internal and small ring through the larger, external rings. It is difficult to describe the spiral model without referring to its pictorial representation:

Every cycle of the spiral is an SDLC in miniature, where the crucial aspect is risk evaluation. In fact, first the objectives of the portion of the software being built are carefully drafted, and then all possible alternatives weighted and considered, together with their constraints. The purpose of this exercise is to identify since the beginning potential areas of risk, and to act consequently, in order to

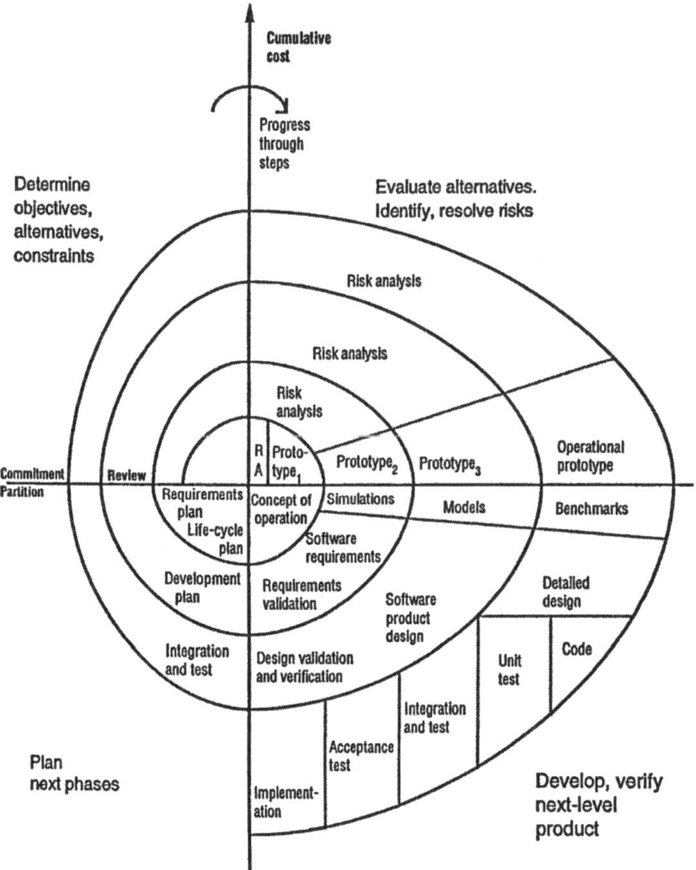

FIGURE 2.4 The Spiral model

minimize and control (and possibly avoid) the identified risks. The risk-reduction activities usually performed in this phase are:

1. prototyping
2. simulation
3. analytical modeling
4. administering questionnaires
5. market research

As Dr. Boehm, the creator of the Spiral model, suggests:

> If performance, or user-interface risks strongly dominate program development or internal interface-control risks, the next step may be an evolutionary

> development step: a minimal effort to specify the overall nature of the product, a plan for the next level of prototyping, and the development of a more detailed prototype to continue to resolve the major risk issues.
>
> [. . .]
>
> On the other hand, if previous prototyping efforts have already resolved all of the performance or user interface risks, the next step follows the basic waterfall approach.'
>
> *Barry W. Boehm "A Spiral Model of Software Development and Enhancement" [1987]*

The intrinsic flexibility of the spiral model accommodates for a mixture of software development techniques; more than one technique can be used within the same project, even within the same cycle. The goal, here, is to identify and resolve the risks associated to the project as early as possible, and not to proceed until they have been brought under control.

Every cycle of the spiral begins with the determination of objectives, alternatives, and risks; it then continues with specific and concrete actions, which help resolving risks and constraints, developing adequate deliverables (prototypes, models, statistical analysis, etc). A crucial point is the verification of the correctness of what stated/proposed. The cycle ends with the identification of the next iteration and a plan for it.

The real breakthrough introduced by the spiral model is that the early iterations are the cheapest, and the gradual cost increase, associated to the larger spiral circles, is counter-balanced by a reduced risk. Also, the spiral model guarantees the same level of managerial control as the pure waterfall model. But it goes much further, including risk analysis and resolution as a crucial ingredient of its recipe.

The spiral model has been successfully applied at TRW Software Information Systems by Dr. Boehm, where he was Chief Engineer. Among its merits, the spiral model can ascribe the definitive status attributed to prototyping, which becomes an integral and crucial part of the SDLC. Furthermore, it brings the advanced managerial conceptions of risk identification and planning into software development.

The major issue associated to the spiral model is that it relies on highly competent people, both on the technical and the managerial side, to be successfully implemented. In fact, using Dr. Boehm own words, "The spiral model places a great of reliance on the ability of software developers to identify and manage sources of project risk."

The risk, here, is that a team of inexperienced developers could focus on well understood and low risk elements, producing a detailed and as voluminous as useless analysis on something which is falsely perceived as important, neglecting the real risks and issues. On the other side, it also requires knowledgeable management. It is not simple to define objectives and determine milestones that pave the way for the next iteration. To the contrary, the managerial action must be exercised attentively and constantly, and has to be able to capture any premature sign of uncertainty or "grey area" in the technical analysis performed by the software engineers during the successive iterations.

2.6 Different Methodologies, Same Development Paradigm

Undoubtedly, the spiral model represents a breakthrough with regard to the waterfall model. Yet the two model have in common the underlying programming paradigm under which they have both been conceived: the procedural (or functional) approach to problem solving, applied to software modules. Within this paradigm, the main way to solve or to reduce the intrinsic complexity of the real life problems to a manageable dimension, is by functional decomposition.

The model of the surrounding reality that the software engineer depicts in his/her efforts to capture the underlying relationships between the objects of the problem domain, heavily relies on the identification of the functions, needed by the system being built, to work correctly and to provide the requested functionality. The perfect design tool for this approach is the data-flow diagram. The data being accessed and manipulated by the program, in the traditional, functional approach, is disjoint from the process which actually performs the various operations on the data. Since they are two separate entities, information hiding becomes a difficult, though not impossible, goal.

Another distinctive characteristic of the paradigm built around the functional decomposition approach is sequentiality. The user interaction with the system is carefully shaped by the software designers so that the flow of operations allowed by the program follows only specific paths, in a strictly sequential way. Again, the data-flow diagram perfectly describes the universe defined by functional decomposition.

In mid-eighties, the Object Oriented approach gained momentum. The Object Oriented (OO) paradigm represents a totally different and new mind set in software development. The qualifying points of the OO paradigm are four:

- **Identity:** Data is quantized into discrete distinguishable entities called objects.
- **Classification:** Objects with the same data structure (attributes) and behavior (operations) are grouped into a *class.* A class is an abstraction that describes properties important to an application and ignores the rest. Any choice of classes is arbitrary and depends on the application. Each class describes a possibly infinite set of individual objects. Each object is said to be an instance of its class. Each instance of the class has its own value for each attribute, but shares names and operations with other instances of the class.

- **Polymorphism:** The same operation may behave differently on different classes. An operation is an action or transformation that an object performs or is subject to. A specific implementation of an operation by a certain class is called a *method.* Since an object-oriented operator is polymorphic, it may have more than one method implementation it.
- **Inheritance** is the sharing of attributes and operations among classes based on a heirarchical relationship. A class can be defined broadly and then redefined into successively finer *subclasses.* Each subclass incorporates (or inherits) all of the properties of its superclass and adds its own unique properties.

Source: Rumbaugh et. al. *Object-Oriented Modeling and Design,* Prentice Hall 1991, pages 2–3.

One of the several reasons which contributed to the success of OO as a software development paradigm is that it gives the perfect framework for the design and development of graphical user interfaces. After the Athena project, which gave birth to a graphical interface standard across many hardware platform, and the concurrent success and wide acceptance of MS Windows, the way users interact with a computer has radically changed. The GUI environment is fundamentally event-driven, and it is convenient to consider every element of the graphical interface as an object, with its own particular characteristics and behavior.

Another important factor, which determined the success of the OO paradigm, is that it promotes a concept of global re-usability across all the phases of the project. It is in the very nature of a class to be extensible by refinement (through the inheritance mechanism). The important point to underline, when considering OO re-usability, is that it affects not only the code, but the design as well. Limited forms of software re-use were possible also while operating within the functional paradigm. One does not need OO to produce software libraries or components which can be re-used in different projects and environments. That kind of re-usability is severely limited, though, by the absolute absence of extensibility. A software component written in traditional computer languages can be re-used only in the way its designer allowed for. An OO software component can be extended and adjusted to new problem domains even when the source code is not available, thanks to inheritance. And this applies to design too. In the last few years there has been a great interest in design re-use, culminated in the appearance of object-oriented design patterns, or elements of re-usable software design (see Gamma et al. [1995]).

Naturally, the OO paradigm brings about new issues and problems, which cannot be resolved using the tools and techniques created and refined for the functional paradigm. Both the spiral and the waterfall model, with all its subvariants, fail to capture the distinctive elements of the object-oriented software development life cycle. While the applicability of the spiral model to object-oriented development is still under investigation, a number of concerns emerged towards its real effectiveness in an OO context (see Berard [1992] and Henderson-Sellers and Edwards [1994]).

2.7 Object Orientation and the Fountain Model

The very nature of object-oriented development is highly iterative and highly recursive, where iteration spans over analysis and design. A common criticism of the spiral model among the OO community is that in spite of being depicted as a spiral, in reality it describes a linear succession of events, where some activities are repeated. The activities *must* be repeated, because the spiral model is of an intimately prescriptive nature, which makes it not perfectly suitable for an OO environment.

According to Henderson-Sellers and Edwards [1993], the real essence of an object-oriented development is captured in the fountain model. The fountain model takes into account that some activities cannot start before others, for instance design must precede coding, and before design can start, the requirements of the system being built should be defined through some sort of analysis. At the same time though, the fountain model stresses the considerable overlap and merging of activities common of an object-oriented approach. Like in a fountain, where water rises up the middle and falls back in the pool at the bottom of the fountain, or it is re-entrained at an intermediate level, so in an object-oriented development the general flow from analysis, to design and to implementation is overlaid with re-iterative cycles across all phases, where software elements are created, modified, re-engineered and discarded or re-used in successive phases.

In an object-oriented software development life cycle the emphasis is on classes, rather than systems or subsystems. For this reason it seams more appropriate not to consider the system in its totality at every stage of its life, but rather to focus on specific classes or cluster of classes, to monitor and control how they go through their own cluster life cycles.

It is likely that the clusters of classes being developed will be out of phase with each other, for instance while cluster n. 2 is beginning the specification phase, cluster n.1 has already been promoted to design.

In an object-oriented software development environment, it is possible to retrofit the requirements with potential improvements, which originated from a more detailed analysis of the problem performed while refining a design abstraction during the life cycle of a cluster of classes. This happens because in the worst case scenario only a class or a cluster of classes must be thrown away; it is very unlikely to scrap the entire design of the system. Furthermore, even if one class or cluster is judged not suitable and has to be replaced, it can be always re-utilized in other similar projects. The benefits of the objected-oriented software development life cycle, as proposed through the fountain model, are:

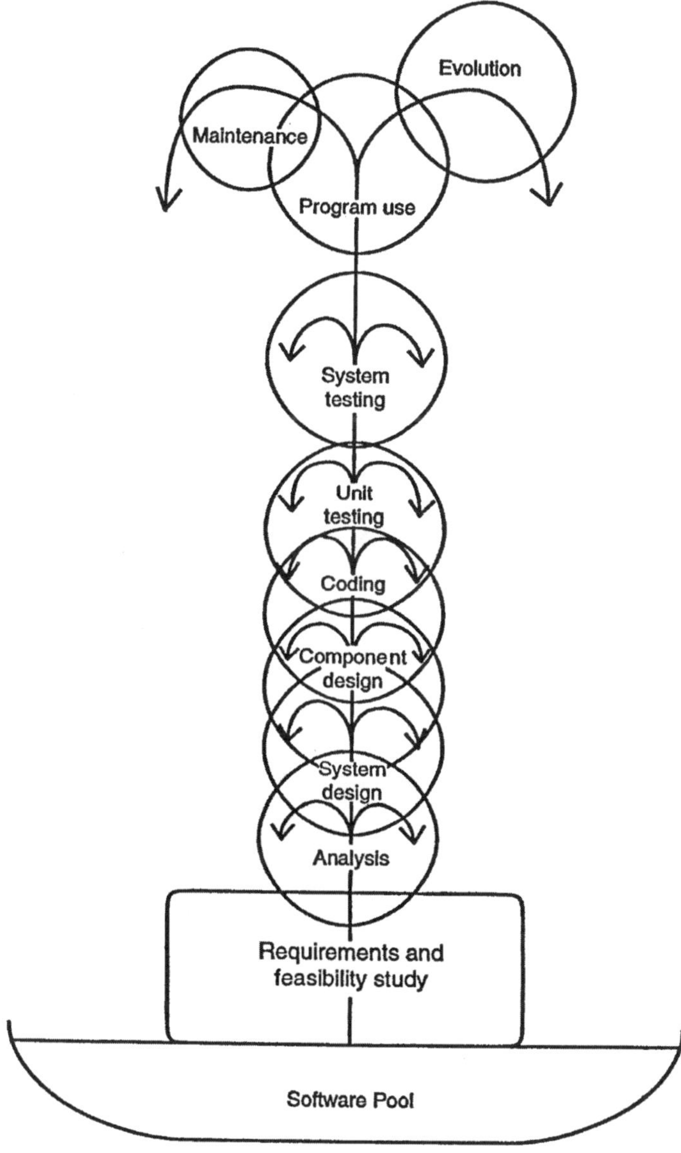

FIGURE 2.5 The Fountain model

1. The requirements don't have to be frozen very soon in the life cycle; but they can reasonably evolve with the project
2. The iterative process includes requirements, design, and early implementation, allowing greater interactions among these three phases than in the traditional waterfall model

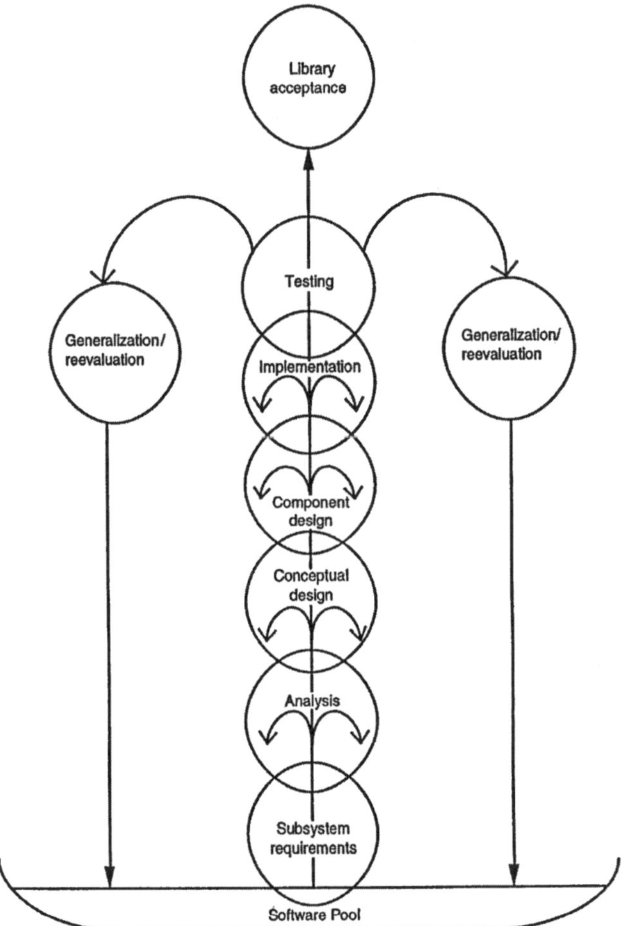

FIGURE 2.6 The fountain model for an individual class or cluster of classes

3. The coding of software elements can start earlier than in the traditional model, often overlapping the design phase.

The following diagram gives a pictorial representation of the overall object-oriented software development life cycle.

In Figure 2.7 time is shown on the ordinate. The two triangles representing the requirements and design phases are overlapping, and the first cluster of classes, Cluster 1, starts at the beginning of the design phase. When it is completed, it becomes part of the library of classes, which together participate in the bottom-up construction of the overall system.

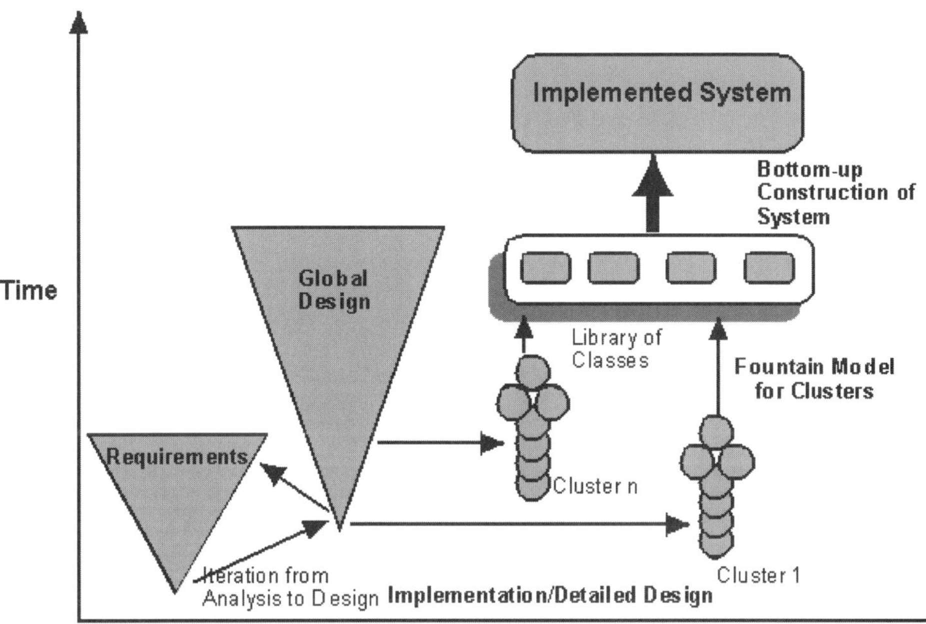

FIGURE 2.7 Interaction Between Requirements Analysis, Design and Implementation. (*Source:* Adapted from "A Book of Object Oriented Knowledge", Henderson-Sellers, Prentice Hall, 1992)

2.8 Software Development Life Cycle in Oracle Projects

The first commercial version of Oracle to hit the market was Oracle release 2, in 1979. Oracle became increasingly popular during the eighties, before the big shift of the IT industry towards object-oriented methodologies and languages. The Oracle Corporation started supporting C++ relatively recently (the Pro*C precompiler began to understand C++ syntax only with release 2.1, shipped in 1994). The usual technique implemented in projects which wanted to use C++, prior to Pro*C 2.1, was to wrap a C++ class around the Oracle OCI APIs.

Most of Oracle application, however, were implemented in traditional environments, where design was following the functional decomposition model and the coding was carried out using traditional languages, such as COBOL and C. Such environments were the absolute domain of the waterfall model of software development life cycle. The major obstacle to a wider use of OO languages in application having a relational engine in the back-end was the impedance mismatch between the basic Oracle data types and the richness of user defined data types typical of an object-oriented environment. Most of today's mission critical applications built around an Oracle database still use either C or COBOL, perhaps both languages together, for back-end processing and interfacing to legacy systems. The front-end is the domain of Oracle Forms, both character-based and GUI, together with other popular GUI client-server RAD tools (MS Visual Basic, Borland Delphi, Sybase PowerBuilder, etc). The client-server RAD tools all offer more or less limited object-oriented capabilities (in Chapter 10 we will examine the above mentioned tools in details), which had to be sacrificed to better fit in a relational environment, strongly focused on traditional technologies, methodologies, languages, and tools.

The release of Oracle 8 put the premise for a major change in attitude, towards object-oriented environments and technologies. The support for objects in Oracle 8.0x is far from ideal, but it represents the first solid step of Oracle Corporation in the OO direction. The inclusion of a Java Virtual Machine into the Oracle kernel in Oracle 8.1, allowing the interchangeability of Java with PL/SQL as Oracle native languages, represents another milestone towards a more integrated object-oriented environment built around an object-relational engine. Java is a pure object-oriented language, and not a hybrid like C++. Adopting Java means automatically a strong commitment to OO. Java does not support nonmember functions, or global variables. Every method or attribute can only exist within a class, which means that designing a Java applications implies designing classes.

The fountain model of software development life cycle undoubtedly provides a development framework in which object-orientation plays a crucial role in achieving benefits such as true iteration and better overlapping between analysis of requirements, design, and implementation. Oracle Corporation is doing its best to marry the absolute reliability, generally associated to traditional and mature technologies, typical of mission critical applications, with newer technologies which lure their adepts with enticing promises, such as shorter time to market and more profitable ROI. It is likely that object-orientation will play a major role in future Oracle projects; the emphasis put on Java as the backbone of the Network Computing Architecture tells us that Oracle Corporation is betting part of its future on Java and object-oriented environments and tools. SDLC models like the fountain model will increase in popularity, as soon as the software designers and project managers will realize that the traditional waterfall model is unsuitable and inadequate to support object-oriented development environments.

Summary

We started the chapter by describing the "code-and-fix" model of software development, focusing on its inadequacy to support large and complex software projects; we introduced the traditional waterfall model, highlighting its merits in planning and controlling software development. We also analyzed its limits and deficiencies, evaluating the various extensions operated to the original model with the goal of overcoming its problems. The introduction of the spiral model represented an initial breakthrough in the theory of software engineering, with its greater emphasis on iteration and risk analysis. We considered that the common origin of both the waterfall and the spiral models to be the functional decomposition approach in software design and development, and we pointed out the inadequacy of models elaborated within one software paradigm (functional decomposition) for a totally different software paradigm (object orientation). We then introduced the fountain model, one of the best efforts currently undertaken for building a software development life cycle model for object-oriented environments. Finally, we analyzed the evolution of the Oracle technologies, in transition from their traditional roots to the leading edge of the current object-oriented languages and environments (Java and the Network Computer Architecture).

Chapter 3

Documentation as an Integral Part of Software Projects

3.1 Three Fundamental Requisites

Irrespective of the model of software development life cycle chosen, documentation plays a crucial role in determining the success of a project. The state of the project documentation is an indicator of how well the project has been conducted. Generally speaking, if documentation is out of control, it means that the entire project is out of control. Unfortunately, a common attitude among programmers and software engineers is to consider documentation as an unnecessary burden which distracts from the main goal, which is to write defect-free code. This problem can be addressed by integrating technical writers in the development teams. Initially, the technical writer principal role was to produce the end user written documentation, the manuals. More recently, this role evolved into a more sophisticated one, where the technical writer is much closer to the developers, keeping the technical documentation in order; in some cases, where quality assurance standards are in place, the technical writer is also responsible for the compliance to the quality assurance practices and procedures.

As a general rule, poor documentation is worse than no documentation at all. This could seem like a very strong statement, and it is. But it is justified by the sad sense of frustration that affects the software engineers who design an extension to a current system only to realize, during the implementation phase, that much of the design was based on wrong assumptions, based on out-of-date design documentation. This usually leads to massive rework of both design and code, and, ultimately, to financial losses.

Too often the software engineers have to verify the design documentation against the code implemented in production, to figure out whether they can trust the documentation which was written by someone else. Again, this is a costly exercise, and should be avoided. A software engineer who joins a project in maintenance state should be confident about the documentation he/she finds, because he/she should rely on it to maintain and enhance the system. The issue is how to ensure synchronization between the documentation and the software. This must be automated as much as possible and not left to the good will of the programmers, who have the tendency to focus on writing code and to postpone indefinitely the housekeeping tasks ancillary to the production of code, such as upgrading documentation.

Documentation should be readily accessible, and browsing through the various documents, looking for specific topics, should be easy and simplified by search engines or tools. Finally, it should be possible to trace the various modifications applied to a document, in order to follow the changes that the document went through in its lifetime.

In other words, it should be possible to recognize the modifications done to the sections of a document during the editing of it. For instance, a design document is drafted and then submitted for a formal review. It is likely that the review process will force the author of the document to change parts of it, to reflect the suggestions made by the panel of reviewers. The documentation keeping system should record a version of the draft document, and a version with the changes made after the review.

Also, it should be possible to automate the process of flagging the differences in the two documents, so that at a glance, by using a tool, one can visualize the various modifications made to the document.

We have just highlighted the three fundamental requisites of good software related documentation. They are:

- Traceability
- Easy Retrieval
- Synchronization (with the software system currently running)

3.2 Traceability

In order to achieve traceability, the documents should be stored in plain ASCII. It is not a good idea to store the project documentation in the Microsoft Word proprietary format. To be fair, it is worth to add that this applies also to the other binary formats used by the commonly used word processor packages, such as Corel WordPerfect, Lotus WordPro, and Adobe FrameMaker.

To be traceable, a document should be stored (with all its versions) into a version control system, such as SCCS, RCS, CVS, PVCS, DEC CMS, or MS Visual Source Safe. Chapter 6 will cover these software tools in detail, at the moment we can anticipate that their goal in life is to maintain and track changes made to source code or documentation. They are basically file custodians. Under a version control system, whenever changes are made to a file, those changes are recorded and the original maintained. A version control system can:

- store text files
- retrieve specific versions of files
- control updating access to files
- identify the version of a retrieved file
- record when, why, and by whom changes are made to a file

Even if the more recently conceived tools, such as MS Visual Source Safe, can store binary files, the version control tools are designed to work with text files. It is very useful, specially under the typical stress experienced while trying to fix a production problem, to perform the *diff* command against the current and the previous versions of a document to visualize the changes and, possibly, to map the cause of defect found in production to a design glitch. To achieve this, the document format must be carefully chosen.

Developers keen on using a PC word processor to create documentation often store the file saved in the internal format used by the word processor package in the version control system. So, the file with its characteristic extension (DOC, WPD, etc.) is either checked in the version control system that supports binary files (such as MS Visual Source Safe), or converted into ASCII using, for instance, *uuencode,* and then checked in the more traditional version control tools, such as RCS.

Using this method it is still possible to retrieve previous versions of a document. The problem is that looking for changes across different versions becomes laborious and cumbersome. In fact, one should check out the versions of the document to be verified, perhaps reconvert them in the internal format, then open them in the word processor, save them in ASCII, and then use the diff command to expose the differences between the versions of the document being checked. Diff can be either the standard Unix command or an equivalent visual tool used under MS Windows to achieve the same thing; the concept common to both environments is that storing documents in a proprietary format (non ASCII) in a version control system leads to unnecessary administrative burdens when comparing different versions.

A common suggestion, made in development environments where MS Word is used to produce software related documentation, is to save the documents in Rich Text Format (RTF), and to store the RTF files in the version control system, because they are ASCII files.

Unfortunately, this is also a bad idea. In an RTF file the real document content is surrounded by an impressive amount of procedural markup instructions, which makes it difficult to recognize the "real" text. The following is an RTF example of the last sentence, the one which start with "Unfortunately":

```
{\rtf1\ansi \deflang1033\deff0{\fonttbl
{\f0\froman \fcharset0 \fprq2 Times New Roman;}{\f1\fswiss
 \fcharset0 \fprq2 Arial;}}{\colortbl
  \red0\green0\blue0;}
{\stylesheet{\fs20 \snext0 Normal;}
}\margl1440\margr1440\ftnbj\ftnrestart\aftnnar \sectd \sb
 knone\endnhere
{\*\pnseclvl1\pndec\pnstart1{\pntxta .}}
{\*\pnseclvl2\pnlcltr\pnstart1{\pntxta .}}
{\*\pnseclvl3\pnlcrm\pnstart1{\pntxta .}}
{\*\pnseclvl4\pndec\pnstart1{\pntxtb (}{\pntxta )}}
{\*\pnseclvl5\pnlcltr\pnstart1{\pntxtb (}{\pntxta )}}
{\*\pnseclvl6\pnlcrm\pnstart1{\pntxtb (}{\pntxta )}}
{\*\pnseclvl7\pndec\pnstart1{\pntxta .}}
{\*\pnseclvl8\pnlcltr\pnstart1{\pntxta .}}
{\*\pnseclvl9\pnlcrm\pnstart1}
\pard \sl0
{\plain \f1\lang3081 Unfortunately, this is also a bad idea.
 In an RTF file the real document content is surrounded by
  an impressive amount of procedural markup instructions,
  which makes it difficult to recognize the \'93real\'94
  text. }}
```

Most of the bytes are taken by the procedural markup, and, in a complex document, it becomes difficult to recognize the meaningful text. Furthermore, even a small change to the document is reflected exponentially in the procedural markup. The net effect of this shows up when one uses the diff command to visualize the differences between two versions of the same document: ninety percent of the output is useless, because the procedural markup changes are flagged together with the text changes, making the output unreadable. What said for the RTF format is also valid for Postscript.

How to achieve document traceability, then? Well, I can provide two solutions, one ideal and one of compromise. The ideal solution is to use a document management system based on SGML/XML. The second solution is a reasonable compromise between the ideal, SGML-based solution and no or very little traceability, and it is based on HTML.

3.3 Traceability through SGML

SGML stands for Standard Generalized Markup Language. SGML is an international standard for the definition of device-independent, system-independent methods of representing texts in electronic form. Basically, SGML is a *metalanguage*, or a way for formally describing a language, specifically a *markup language*. It provides the constructs to create an infinite number of descriptive markup language. The most notable example of an SGML-derived language is HTML (HyperText Markup Language). SGML became an ISO standard in 1986, with the official designation of ISO-8879-1. SGML is characterized by five basic principles:

1. It allows to create descriptive markup languages
2. It is hierarchical, with interconnected elements and components
3. It does not have any implied markup conventions; therefore supporting any sort of tag sets
4. It is completely and formally defined
5. It is human-readable and machine-readable at the same time

A recurring word, while speaking about SGML, is "descriptive," referred to a markup language. Descriptive is used to differentiate SGML (and its derivatives) from the *procedural* markup languages, such as *troff*, RTF, Postscript, etc.

A *descriptive* markup language is concerned with the role played by a specific sentence, or set of words, in a document, rather than its esthetical appearance. SGML disregards the formatting overhead usually imposed by procedural markup languages. In SGML it is important to identify a set of words as being part of a paragraph, or a footnote. The typographical formatting is totally disjointed from the editing of the text, and it is left to external and separate procedures or programs.

SGML introduces the notion of a document type, and hence a document type definition (DTD). A DTD is a set of rules that describe how a document that claims to be compliant with that specific DTD is structured. The task of a special purpose program, called SGML *parser*, is to verify that all required parts of a document are really present, and that they are correctly ordered. The parser is given two file names as parameters, the file name corresponding to the document containing SGML tags and the file name corresponding to the DTD that the document is to be verified against. The parser then checks that the document complies to the SGML rules specified in the DTD file.

A qualifying point of SGML is its absolute data independence from any specific either hardware or software platforms. It is possible to port SGML documents to virtually all platforms without loss of information, thanks to a basic mechanism of string substitution, which is a simple machine-independent way of stating that a particular string of characters in the document should be replaced by some other string when the document is processed.

Several optional software components participate in making up an SGML environment:

1. Parser
2. SGML Editor
3. Formatter
4. DTD Editor
5. SGML-based retrieval system

We already know what an SGML parser does. An SGML editor is an editor which knows about the DTD that has to be used and helps the author to write a compliant document. A formatter is an interesting piece of software which gives typographical formatting to SGML documents, interpreting the various document elements and formatting them according to the typographical conventions of a specific target. If the same document content has to be made available in different formats, for instance in Postscript, in Unix *man* pages, and in HTML, the author is not forced to produce three different documents. From only one source, a formatter can produce three outputs which preserve the look and feel of the target environment, so that the same version of the document does not look either different or unnatural if seen from a WEB browser rather than by invoking *man* under a Unix system.

A DTD editor is a specialized editor that "knows" about the SGML syntax used for the Document Type Definition. The most sophisticated DTD editors allow for visual building of DTDs.

The most advanced document management systems built around the SGML technology offer text retrieval facilities. The underlying SGML philosophy extremely simplifies searching for text. In fact, having the text structured in homogeneous categories clearly delimited by tags, makes it easy to look for particular keywords or topics appearing in specific portion of a document. This concept is better illustrated via an example. Let us take a DTD which defines an e-mail message, specifying, by the means of the SGML syntax, that we consider an e-mail to be made up by a header and a body; the header contains a mandatory "to," "from," and "date" elements and an optional subject. The body of the message contains at least one paragraph and optional attachments. Our over-simplified DTD follows:

```
<!DOCTYPE email [
<!ELEMENT email       - - (header, body)>
<!ELEMENT header      - - (from, to, date, subject?) >
<!ELEMENT from        - - (#PCDATA)>
<!ELEMENT to          - - (#PCDATA)>
<!ELEMENT date        - - (#PCDATA)>
<!ELEMENT subject     - - (paragraph+) >
<!ELEMENT paragraph   - - (#PCDATA)>
<!ELEMENT body        - - (paragraph+,attachment*) >
<!ELEMENT attachment - - (#PCDATA)>
]>
```

Just a few words to explain the SGML DTD syntax. The three symbols I have used in the above DTD have the following meaning:

?	=	0 or 1 occurrence
+	=	1 or more occurrences
*****	=	0 or more occurrences

The DTD defines the DOCTYPE, in our case "email," and a few elements, which can or must appear in a document that complies with our e-mail DTD. An example of a document, e-mail DTD compliant, follows:

```
<email>
<header>
<from> Nick Souris</from>
<to> Elio Bonazzi </to>
<date>17-Apr-1998</date>
<subject>
<paragraph> I wish you luck! </paragraph>
</subject>
</header>
<body>
<paragraph> Hi Elio!

I hope you know what you are doing!

</paragraph>
<paragraph>

Writing a book about Oracle is a very demanding task!
Good luck, and please, be technically accurate!
```

```
Regards, Nick
</paragraph>
</body>
</email>
```

The SGML shown above is an example of "pedantic" SGML. It is possible to offer shortcuts and abbreviated syntax to an Author writing in SGML. The double minus, which follows the element definition in the DTD, means that both the opening and the closing tags are mandatory. Sometimes this is not strictly necessary. If in one section of my document, for instance, I can only have one or more paragraphs, then the closing tag is superfluous, and can be omitted. The DTD would be modified as follows:

```
<!ELEMENT subject  - o (paragraph+) >
```

The double minus is replaced by a minus and an o, which means optional, and the subject element can contain paragraphs which are only delimited by the opening tag, as in:

```
<subject>
<paragraph> Account Overdue
<paragraph> Last notice !
</subject>
```

The tag which defines the element "paragraph" is a little long, and can be shortened to "p," for example, making the SGML document much more legible. We can appreciate the difference in the following, re-worked example:

```
<email>
<header>
<from> Nick Souris
<to> Elio Bonazzi
<date>17-Apr-1998
<subject>
<p>
I wish you luck!
</subject>
</header>
<body>
<p>
Hi Elio!

I hope you know what you are doing!

<p>
```

```
Writing a book about Oracle is a very demanding task!
Good luck, and please, be technically accurate!

Regards, Nick
</body>
</email>
```

The "from," "to," and "date" elements have been modified, making the closing tag optional. The paragraph element is now defined by the "P" tag, and the overall legibility of the SGML document has improved.

I hope that this brief digression on the SGML syntax has been useful to clarify why an SGML-based text retrieval system offers a finer granularity, in terms of search capabilities, when compared with other text retrieval systems. SGML is all about the function that a word or a set of words accomplish within the document. Thanks to the tag marking, a human or an automated tool can realize straight away if a word or a sentence appears in a paragraph, or in the subject, or any other document element defined by the accompanying DTD. This characteristic makes it possible to limit the scope of a text search to a specific element in the document. I could have hundreds of thousands of e-mail documents stored in my SGML document database, and search for all the occurrences of the word "luck" in the subject element. I am not interested in the simple occurrence of the word "luck." I want to confine the search to only one specific element of my text, the subject. In an SGML text retrieval system, this is not only possible, but also easy to implement. Other (non-SGML) text retrieval tools don't have the ability to discriminate against specific portions of text appearing within a document. They usually use very sophisticated indexing algorithms to perform quick searches, but they cannot narrow down their search on specific text elements.

3.4 XML

XML stands for Extensible Markup Language, and is a subset of SGML, or a simple SGML dialect. It has been developed under the auspices of the World Wide Web Consortium, with the clear goal of enabling generic SGML to be served, received, and processed on the Web in the way that it was previously possible with HTML.

HTML shares with XML a common ancestor, SGML, and it excellently fulfilled its original purpose to make possible and to promote the expansion and the wide acceptance of the WEB. Unfortunately, the HTML DTD loses much of the SGML descriptive nature, by being concerned with the rendering of the text, instead of its function in the document. HTML has tags like <b> and </b> to specify that the text contained between the two tags has to be visualized in bold; or tags like <i> and </i>, which make the text italicized. XML, by contrast, is a purely descriptive markup language. It is interoperable with both SGML and

HTML and it is primarily intended to meet the requirements of large-scale Web content providers for industry-specific markup, vendor-neutral data exchange, media-independent publishing, one-on-one marketing, workflow management in collaborative authoring environments, and the processing of Web documents by intelligent clients.

The XML Working Group comprises representatives from the major companies in the industry, most notably Sun, Netscape and Microsoft (plus many others). MS Internet Explorer supports XML in version 4, Netscape supports XML in Netscape 5. XML is destined to play a major role in the future development of the WEB.

In development environments where SGML has been already adopted, it should be relatively easy to embrace XML. It should be noticed that the two standards are not in opposition, but they can co-exist; XML is a restricted subset of SGML, with limitations and unsupported features such as tag omission. Nevertheless, it should be easy to create an automated tool that translates pure SGML into simpler XML, to WEB-enable documentation previously available only in an SGML environment.

There are no technical drawbacks to SGML/XML. It is definitely the best choice for creating, keeping, and searching for documentation produced to support a software project. The only obstacle to its adoption is that it requires a big commitment by the organization which wants to implement it. SGML is not something that can be informally adopted by a few senior developers in a team and then spread gradually to the other developers. SGML requires specific tools, dedication, and training. If you joined an Oracle project conducted by a large organization, chances are that SGML is already used. If you joined the project in an early phase, and SGML has not yet been adopted, try to investigate about a possible adoption of SGML by other departments of the same company or institution. It is usually much easier to convince the managers in charge of the project to embrace a technology that has been already successfully adopted by someone else in the company.

What if you are working on Oracle project already in an advanced phase, where SGML is an unknown acronym and a PC word processor is used as the primary tool for creating software-related documents? Well, do not abandon all hopes. There is still something that can be done to impose sound software engineering principles upon documentation creating, keeping, and deploying. Here is where our solution of compromise comes handy.

3.5 Traceability Through HTML

The word processor packages sold today all support the creation of HTML documents. This is definitely true for MS Office 97, Corel WordPerfect 7/8, and Lotus WordPro. Many corporations did not yet complete the transition to Win32, and are still using MS Windows 3.1 or 3.11 and, consequently, older releases of word processors. There are available MS Word macros which allow for editing and saving of HTML documents in Word for Windows release 2 or 6 (releases appeared before MS Office 97, that supports HTML natively).

The bottom line is that it should be possible and relatively easy to create HTML documents from word processors running under MS Windows, no matter what release. Once again, the recommendation is to avoid using the word processor proprietary internal format to save the documents produced, but to save them in HTML and to store HTML files in the version control system.

Sharing documents in HTML format becomes very effective when they are made available through a WEB browser. The development team can use the development machine and an HTTP server to access the project documentation. If security is a concern, or if the development machine cannot be loaded with an HTTP server, then a small PC running inexpensive or free software (Linux and Apache for instance) can easily be set up to become the HTTP host for the team. The PC can even be located in proximity of the development team to further reduce the strain put on the network.

The development team can easily access the current version of the software documentation using a WEB browser in an intranet environment. By using this method, together with a version control system, tracking changes across different releases is simplified, because one can perform the diff command, supported by the specific environment, against ASCII files containing HTML tags. So, if the

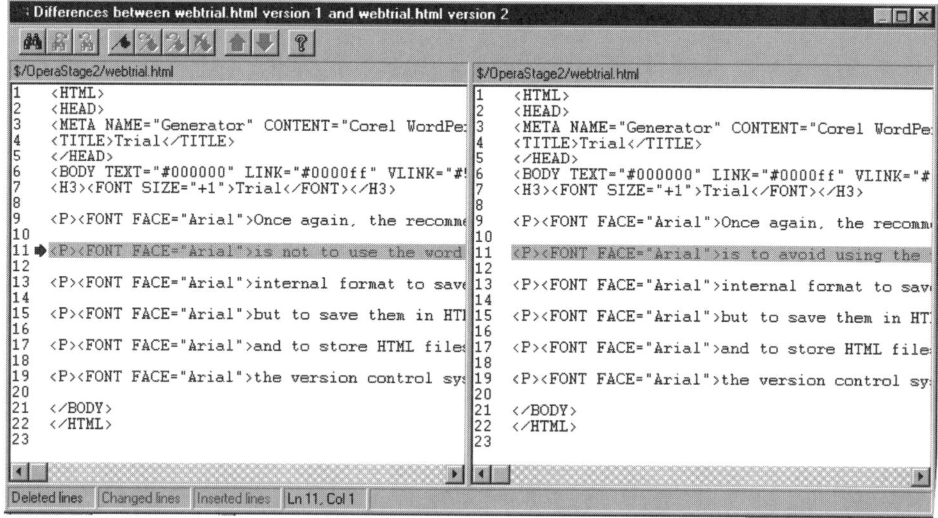

FIGURE 3.1 MS Visual Source Safe highlighting the lines of the HTML file which changed from one version to the other

version control system used offers a visual interface, tracking differences across multiple revisions of the same file becomes as simple as highlighting the wanted revisions and clicking on the diff button (in MS Visual Source Safe or Intersolv PVCS, for example). Otherwise, in character based environments, the diff command has to be explicitly invoked from the shell prompt.

By using HTML, instead of proprietary document formats, we achieved document traceability. How can easy retrieval be achieved? Oracle can help us with its text engine, called Oracle ConText.

3.6 Using Oracle ConText to Manage Project-Related Documentation

The ConText option allows advanced text management tools to coexist with the relational engine and SQL, combining the best of the two worlds.

A part from the academic research for efficient text retrieval engines, which failed to deliver so far a satisfactory fall-out in terms of industrial-strength products, the large corporations needing text management followed typically two paths which can be summarised as follows:

1. Text stored in flat file systems and accessed via specialized standalone tools. A pioneer in this field was Ize, by Persoft Inc., appeared in mid-eighties. It was able to search and retrieve text from files written by the most common PC tools at that point in time (MS Word, WordPerfect, IBM Display Write, dBASE, Lotus 123, Excel, etc). Ize supported queries in networked environments, scanning through directory trees. Another good example of this technology is the Australian made ISYS, which represents a technological leap if compared to Ize, because of a state-of-art indexing algorithm. In spite of its improvements, this technology suffers from major drawbacks, which make it not viable for large corporations. First it lacks of scalability; the domain of ISYS is a PC lan, and the size of the document repository is measured in megabytes or hundreds of megabytes. The requirements of a large corporation are today measured in gigabytes and terabytes. Second, it lacks of any replication capability.
2. Small amount of text stored in relational databases. The classical example is the resume stored as unformatted text in the Employee table. The weak points of this approach are, again, poor scalability and insufficient query capabilities. Looking for a specific word in the resume field would mean searching sequentially the entire table. In addition, it is not possible to use advanced characteristics typical of search engines, such as proximity searching, multilingual stemming, etc.

Another interesting point to consider is that the same corporation which maintains data as text in file systems searched through search engines, usually also has a relational database for more structured data. The two systems coexist within the company but are incompatible with each other.

The Oracle ConText option brings advanced text retrieval functionalities into the standard relational world. The ConText option is fully integrated with the Oracle server. In technical terms, ConText servers are simple background processes which cooperate with the other background processes making up an Oracle instance. Any text updates are handled by the engine with the same degree of data integrity reserved to the other relational information is.

Any efficiency gains obtained through parallel, multiprocessor, and distributed architectures are propagated automatically to text management via the ConText option. Scalability applies to text as well as other more structured data within the Oracle architecture. Text retrieval and management becomes an integrated part of Oracle to an extent such that it is possible to text-enable client-server applications implemented using standard client tools like Powerbuilder and Visual Basic.

3.7 Oracle ConText: Text Retrieval Features

Oracle ConText offers advanced and sophisticated text oriented capabilities, such as text reduction and automatic classification.

The standard text retrieval feature includes:

- Multilingual Stemming
- Proximity Searches
- Relevance Ranking
- Boolean Logic
- Term Weighting
- Thesaurus Support
- Soundex/Fuzzy Matches
- Stop Lists

The text reduction feature condenses large documents to smaller and reduced versions, which respect the original framework. The users can search the reduced version before or instead of the original version, in order to be quicker.

ConText can make use of the text classification feature to automatically categorise documents according to main themes. The technique used to accomplish that is not word-counting and statistics, but advanced linguistic. Customised user dictionaries are also supported, in order to deal with specific jargons.

ConText can access text stored in Oracle (typically in LONG columns, LONG being a standard Oracle data type supporting variable length character strings up to two gigabytes), but also stored in external files. Text or documents in a standard Oracle column can be in standard word-processing format (MS Word, WordPerfect, etc), HTML, PDF or ASCII.

If the text or the document are stored in external files, then the text column in the Oracle table identifies the path name of the external file.

3.8 The Oracle ConText Option in Action

Within the Oracle ConText domain, a text query is submitted as a standard SQL query, which can contain both text and nontext fields. The text engine will separate the text part of the query and will operate the text search operation.

Let us imagine to have the following Oracle table:

```
Table:                  DOCUMENT_TEXT
fields:
     DOC_KEY            number (unique primary key)
     DOC_DATE  date
     DOC_AUTHOR         varchar2(60)
     DOC_TITLE          varchar2(150)
     DOC_TEXT           LONG  (direct text storage up to two
                               gigabytes)
```

There are two basic methods to perform a query using the ConText option. One is called One-Step Query and requires Oracle version 7.3 or higher. If one wants to look for "Java threads" in the text field DOC_TEXT, then he/she might issue the following query:

```
select DOC_DATE, DOC_AUTHOR, DOC_TITLE
from DOCUMENT_TEXT
where contains
(DOC_TEXT,'java and threads') > 0
and DOC_DATE >'01-FEB-98'
```

The above query has extended SQL syntax (CONTAINS) and includes a textual part as well as a standard relational part. The query is split in two and the part containing the text search is passed to the text engine. The result of the query is combined and presented to the user.

The second option available to the user is called Two-Step Query and uses the CONTAINS stored procedure. This method works irrespective of the version of Oracle (must be 7.0 or higher). The results of the text search are stored by the stored procedure in a temporary table, the user than displays all the fields from that temporary table.

Oracle ConText provides query operators for advanced text retrieval. For instance the NEAR operator (;) is used to perform a proximity query as in "contains (DOC_TEXT, 'java; threads)." The FUZZY operator (?) is used in fuzzy matches, such as "contains (DOC_TEXT,'?(java & jakarta')."

Oracle ConText was initially implemented as an "option," but after the architectural changes introduced to harmonize the Oracle components with the WEB Server, ConText is now offered as a "cartridge," so that the text retrieval capabilities can be fully exploited also in a WEB environment.

The ConText cartridge is available with both Oracle8 and Oracle8 Enterprise Edition, at an additional cost. When evaluating the cost effectiveness of the ConText cartridge, one should consider the undoubted benefits related to the ability to browse and scan through the documentation of one or more projects, specially if the documentation produced is voluminous. The IT department of a large corporation that makes extensive use of the Oracle technology, or a software house that builds solution around the Oracle server should seriously consider using Oracle ConText as the preferred way to deal with software related documentation, if an alternative SGML-based text system is not already implemented.

3.9 Synchronization

Documentation can be well written and well managed, using the techniques explained in the preceding paragraph, and yet useless if left out of date. Keeping documentation synchronized with the current release of software which runs in the production environment is a complex and demanding task. Nevertheless, there is something which can be done to make this task easier and to detect divergences between the software and its related documentation.

Fundamentally, documentation can go out of sync in two occasions:

1. After the initial implementation. The developers implement the software according to the detailed design document which they are given. It is very likely that, while crafting the code, a few inconsistencies and small design defects emerge. They are fixed in the code, which successfully goes through the test phase, but the documentation is not retro-fit the fixes applied to the code.
2. While the system is already in production, and in maintenance mode. A defect is found and the fix involves re-working a few routines. The pressure is high, everybody would like to keep the down-time to a minimum, the code is modified, and the parts changed don't behave any more like the documentation say.

I have seen a great deal of efforts put in design reviews at the end of the design phase. The goal is to catch as many inconsistencies and defects as possible, before they are allowed to slip through the subsequent phases. Usually, the author (or authors) of a design document signals that the draft copy is ready. The senior designers working in the project collect the draft copy, assess it, and mark any ambiguities or points that require further discussion.

After a few days, the author and the designers get together in a room and go through all the points marked. After the resolution of all ambiguous or erroneous points, the document is compared against a walkthrough checklist, which usually takes into account characteristics like completeness, cohesion, coupling, testability, consistency, etc. At the end of the first review, the author implements all changes agreed upon during the first meeting. A second meeting verifies the correctness and consistency of the document after it has undergone the modifications. If everybody is happy, the document ceases to be a draft and becomes an officially endorsed design document. Otherwise, the process is repeated until a satisfactory document is produced. Academic research and experience have proven that design walkthrough are very effective for early detection of defects.

I have rarely seen the same efforts put in making sure that the documentation produced during the design phase remains consistent with the software implemented. Towards the end of a project, the team is either in "celebration" or in "frantic" mode. If the project proceeded smoothly, and the deadlines are basically respected and no major problems arose, then, after the tension of the recent months, the team tends to relax and become sloppy about procedures and standards. If the project is encountering difficulties, running late, requiring consistent overtime, then the principal goal is to "get it done," even by using dirty tricks; documentation has a very low priority under these circumstances. If the project avoids cancellation, and something is finally delivered, usually is late and over budget; so it becomes difficult to set aside money to finance a second round of design walkthrough to verify that the documentation produced reflects what implemented in the final system.

Given the importance of up to date and proper documentation, especially when the software system will be maintained for a few or several years, it is essential to conduct a design walkthrough round after the coding of the software has been completed. The purpose, here, is to reconcile the software with its specification, making sure that there are no divergences between the two.

In Oracle-based projects, I would make sure that all tables specified in the design documents are effectively implemented in production; all fields in the tables should have the same name and the same data type as per design specifications; the routines specified should be the same as the ones used in the code, and their parameters the same in number, type, and order; the class interfaces, in object oriented projects, should be the same as specified. Other areas of analysis can be the sequential order of operations, the number and purpose of the processes used in the system.

3.10 Synchronization Through Change Management

In order to maintain an up to date documentation during the entire lifetime of a software product, a proper change management system should be implemented. Bug track tools and change control systems are available on the market, for virtually all development platforms. They help managing the changes to be applied to running systems, categorizing the change requests by assigning them a priority level and a change identifier (usually an alphanumeric code). A change can be originated either by a bug fix or by enhancements required by the business. The change identifier should appear in a comment in the code and in the message typed in by the programmer at the moment of the check-in of the software module in the version control system. If what said is not clear, please see Chapter 6, where version control is covered exhaustively.

If the change made to the code affects the way a function behaves, then the related documentation should be corrected to reflect the modification to the code. The same change identifier should appear in the text of the document. If the document is saved using a proprietary format, then the change identifier should be in hidden text. If the document is in SGML or HTML format, then the comment tag can be used. It is helpful to make the change identifiers meaningful, by using prefixes and suffixes and attributing precise meanings to them. An example better clarifies this point.

If a software defect is due to incorrect coding (an array that is allowed to exceed its boundaries, as the classical case), then the change request identifier should specify that design is not involved; in an over-simplified convention, the identifier could be CCC-XXXX, where XXXX is a progressive defect number, and CCC means that the change affects only the code.

An identifier the prefix of which is CCD means that the technical design documentation is affected and has to be changed. A "B" in the second position of the identifier prefix, as in CBD, means that the business related documents have also been affected, because the changed functionality modifies the way the business operations are conducted.

If an identifier convention has been adopted, and if the change codes have been used consistently in both software modules and documents, and if the documents are stored in ASCII format, then it becomes quick and easy to scan through both software modules and documents to verify that the same change identifiers have been used, and, ultimately, that documentation has been updated with the latest changes. The change management system should be flexible enough to allow the change of the identifier after the identifier has been assigned to a change request, to allow for those circumstances where, after an initial assessment, a change is judged to affect only the code, and in a second moment it is discovered that also design documents have to modified. The change identifier prefix should be changed wherever it appears (software modules and documentation).

3.11 Project Deliverables: They Are All Documents!

Irrespective of the SDLC chosen, every project conducted according to sound software engineering principles produces a great deal of documents. The more senior a software engineer becomes, and the more he/she deals with documents, rather than code.

Traditionally, the waterfall model has been the model of SDLC which favored the largest production of documents. But even when operating in a spiral model, at the end of every iteration, the risk assessment and the commitments formulated for the subsequent iteration are written in documents. The class documentation, which allows the software components to be used in the current project, and possibly re-used by other developers in future projects, is an integral part of the software production process also in an object oriented environment using the fountain model as SDLC.

Until the final delivery of the working system, which is undoubtedly the delivery of software, documents represent the milestones of a project during its lifetime. The documents produced vary according to their scope and intended audience, but they should all be connected and consistently traceable to each other. The quality measurements, when applied to software related documents, insist on traceability as principal requirement for a document to be considered acceptable.

The documents specifying business requirements should be consistent, complete, correct, unambiguous, understandable, feasible and modifiable; they should specify constraints and discuss/assess usability. Their intended audience comprises business analysts, business managers, and IT specialists, such as senior software designers and systems architects. The business requirement documents represent the bridge between the business and the IT professionals implementing the system to provide a solution for the business.

The documents specifying business requirements are crucial to the success of the project. They represent the starting point, so all the other and more specific documents descend from them and are or should be traceable to them. The fundamental metrics used to judge the quality of a design document specifying the software architecture is its traceability to the business requirements. Consequently, the metrics used to judge the quality of a detailed design document is its traceability to the software architecture document. This way all documentation is connected in a consistent and cohesive chain, where every ring plays a specific role.

Internal coherence and consistence of documentation is an important indicator of the health state of a project. In the course of my career as a software specialist, I have joined many different projects at different stages of their life. Unfailingly, where I could find good documentation, showing well connected and up to date design documents, the project progressed smoothly to its conclusion; conversely, where documentation was poorly written and maintained, the project encountered major obstacles and, in a couple of occasions, it was cancelled half way through.

The importance of producing, keeping, and maintaining good documentation to the final success of a project is never stressed enough. The ultimate responsibility for keeping a good standard in software-related documentation lies on management. Generally speaking, programmers see documentation as a tedious burden, which they try to postpone indefinitely.

The senior designers usually are more aware of the importance of well kept documentation, but often they lose control over the code, which is the domain of the programmers. Ensuring synchronization between code and documentation has to be carefully orchestrated by the team leader, who has to put in place verification procedures to be strictly observed. In environments where software engineering is well implemented, the developer checks in the modified or the newly created code. That code is not yet accepted as part of the current build until the team leader has conducted basic unit testing. If the team leader is satisfied with the tests, then the code is promoted to be part of the next build. Is at that point in time that the accompanying documentation should be checked.

Summary

In this chapter, we examined the various aspects of software-related documentation, highlighting three crucial characteristics that good documentation must have in order to comply with sound software engineering principles: traceability, easy retrieval, and synchronization with the software it specifies.

We also have indicated how traceability can be achieved, stressing the point that the format chosen for the documents plays an important role in their management and administration; an ideal solution for documentation producing, keeping and retrieving is the implementation of an SGML-based system.

When the ideal solution cannot be implemented, we proposed an alternative, but yet effective, solution based on the Internet standard way to deploy documents (HTML).

A complete text management solution based on SGML generally includes a text retrieval component. Where such a solution is not implemented, we suggested an alternative way to ensure easy retrieval of documentation, based on Oracle technologies (ConText).

Finally, we faced the issue of ensuring synchronization between the documentation describing and specifying the software, and the software itself. The solution to this problem is neither simple nor unanimous, but we strove to put the matter in the right perspective, giving possible solutions, and stressing the point that the project managers are responsible for establishing the correct procedures and to maintain the focus on proper documentation keeping.

Chapter 4

Designing an Oracle Application

This chapter focuses on intellectual and software tools commonly used during the design process. Initially, generic intellectual paradigms such as cohesion, coupling, information hiding, and complexity reduction will be examined, to demonstrate their usefulness in the context of software design. Subsequently, more Oracle specific tools and configurations will be discussed, exploring the rich set of options made available by Oracle Corporation to designers and architects to facilitate their tasks during the design phase.

4.1 The Intellectual Tools in the Software Engineer's Bag

Many IT professionals share the opinion that programming, more than a scientific discipline, is an art. Computer science is a very young discipline, and, as such, still lacks a widely accepted scientific method, or paradigm, endowed with a universal and repeatable approach to the solution of the problems. Many IT theoreticians are convinced that we still lack an established software engineering discipline, and that specific IT solutions are crafted ad hoc for each contingent situation, rather than the result of a well structured and organized method. Mary Shaw, of the Software Engineering Institute, states that: "The phrase *Software Engineering* is more of an aspiration than a mature discipline of software development."

There is some truth in these common feelings of the more theoretical section of the IT community. But this is a book aimed at software practitioners, who must implement software solutions for the good of the companies they work for. We, as practitioners, are looking for workable and available solutions to make our job easier, and to increase our chances of success. The pessimism spread throughout academia is probably a bit exaggerated, because in reality we can recognize scientific knowledge systematically applied to the crafting of IT solutions. This is particularly true with respect to software analysis and design, where several practices and techniques have been successfully and repeatedly used for the solution of IT problems.

Specifically, a set of intellectual tools has been refined and systematically used to model the various problem domains in the realm of Computer Science, in order to dominate their intimate and intrinsic difficulty. The natural approach of the human mind, which strives to comprehend the surrounding reality, is to build a small-scale version of reality, or a model. In the progressive refinement of the model, redundant and inessential attributes are dismissed, while essential traits and characteristics are kept, until the model built is simple enough to be comfortably analyzed, and complex enough to capture the basic elements of the problem being studied.

We usually build a conceptual model of the problem we want to solve, and we call it analysis; the conceptual model of our solution is generally referred to as design. The principal intellectual tool we use to refine our models is abstraction, a logical process that recognizes similarities and commonality between objects, processes, and activities and focuses upon the attributed commonality, neglecting peculiarities and differences. The ultimate goal of abstraction is the creation of a model or a subcomponent of it. There are different levels of abstraction, and we generally use the term *generalization* to mean a higher level of abstraction, and *specialization* to mean a lower level of abstraction. The model built by applying abstraction comes near to reality through progressive rounds, becoming increasingly specialized.

As software designers, we usually begin the study of our solution by building and agreeing upon a generic model, called high-level design. When we are satisfied with the high-level design, we specialize the various components, lowering the abstraction level into the so-called low-level design. A programmer is not supposed to cut code by interpreting a high-level design document. This would mean skipping one ring in the chain.

It is important not to mix different levels of abstraction in the same context. If one reads a software architecture specification document, which is a high-level design type of document, one doesn't expect to find a list of routines and relative parameters. Conversely, a low-level design document should be detailed enough for a programmer to start writing the code. In an object-oriented development environment, the high-level design of a class is not overburdened with all methods supported by the class; only the crucial ones are listed, the ones which denote the specific behavior of the class being built.

Abstraction is definitely the queen of our intellectual tools; there are also a few knights who play an important role in the definition and refining of our software models:

- ❑ Coupling/De-Coupling
- ❑ Information Hiding
- ❑ Cohesion
- ❑ Complexity Reduction

Coupling is the degree to which a software entity is connected to other entities. A strong association of one software entity/module to another module means that they become intimately connected, or that one knows specific details about the implementation of the other, and it relies on that knowledge to work properly. In this case, we say that the two software entities are strongly coupled. The main disadvantage of strong coupling shows up when one of the two modules is modified to reflect, for instance, a change in the business practice. The second module must also be modified, to adjust to the modification implemented in the first module. If strong coupling is cascadingly propagated throughout many modules comprising the application, then a small change risks having a major impact on the code to be modified.

A software designer applies de-coupling to his/her design after the initial cut. Usually, the first abstraction attempted to build a model for the proposed solution defines an incorrect or unsatisfactory grouping of the basic design elements in design entities.

The successive refining of the initial design strives to identify those elements that were mistakenly grouped together, and to reorganize them in new decoupled aggregations. The best known example of design de-coupling is probably the Model/View/Controller (MVC) architecture pioneered by Smalltalk, where the user interface is conceptually divided into an underlying application model, one or more views over the application model, and one or more controllers, which synchronize the views with the state defined by the model. The MVC architecture is definitely an example of de-coupling applied in an object-oriented context; nevertheless, coupling is a notion introduced by structured design, and widely used and applicable to non object-oriented environments.

Information hiding is the process that makes elements and operations of a software entity inaccessible to other entities of the same system. Using global variables, which can be accessed and modified by all modules, exposes the program to the risk of unwanted modifications that are very difficult to debug and track. Constraining the change of the state of a variable to one function, and one function only, and hiding the variable from all modules but the function allowed to modify the variable in question, minimizes the risk of inadvertent modification. Information hiding is possible, although difficult to implement, in traditional programming paradigms; object-oriented languages allow for very natural and easy to implement information hiding.

Cohesion is the degree to which a software entity homogeneously includes related software elements and excludes the unrelated ones. A module is said to be cohesive if its attributes and methods (or functions and variables) are intimately connected with each other, and no elements extraneous to purpose of the module are present. The exact opposite is called *coincidental cohesion*, and describes the case of totally unrelated software elements included together in a module.

Cohesion and coupling are often mentioned together. Academic research and practical experience show that it is highly desirable for a module to be strongly cohesive and loosely coupled. This is a recurrent concept in software design, and it means that a properly designed software module should accomplish one only function, hiding the implementation details, and offering to its users few consistent and well defined interfaces. The initial implementation of a module can change during the progressive refinement and specialization, typical of an iterative software development life cycle. As long as the interface does not change, all the other modules interacting with the one being changed should be unaware of such implementation changes.

Cohesion and coupling play a crucial role in this book. In Chapter 7 we will analyze in detail how to de-couple the data-access logic from the business logic, in both traditional and object-oriented environments. These concepts will recur many times throughout the book, and will be applied and used to evaluate the various technologies and components comprising the overall Oracle development environment.

Complexity reduction is the computer science re-edition of the ancient Latin motto *divide et impera* (divide and conquer). If a model, which is the result of an abstraction, becomes too complex to be comfortably managed in its first conception, then it should be broken down into smaller and simpler subsystems in the following refining stages. If, after having sketched the first release of your entity–relationship diagram, you realize that the core tables are more than 25–30, then you should break the system down into two subsystems and build interfaces between them. I used the phrase *core table*, meaning the tables that grow consistently, are heavily accessed, and are crucial to the functioning of the application, not the tables used as a reference or to normalize data, which are relatively static and rarely accessed in update or insert mode. I have seen mission critical applications in large companies built around 10 to 15 core tables, which end up having more than 200 tables in total. Yet, they are workable, because the underlying complexity of the model is still manageable. If the basic entity–relationship diagram of an application being built in a project is of a difficult reading, spans over many pages, shows lines which connect almost all tables with each other to the point of becoming illegible, then disaster is only a question of time.

A word of caution about the classification here proposed. I feel that coupling and de-coupling are real intellectual tools, which imply well-defined intellectual procedures for their accomplishment. Other authors, for example Booch [1994], consider cohesion and coupling, together with sufficiency, completeness, and primitiveness, as mere metrics useful to judge the quality of an abstraction. When, after having revised a design document of a fellow colleague designer, I advise to de-couple an operation from a module into a module of its own, I am advising my colleague to use a specific and well-defined intellectual technique, the result of which will hopefully be a better design. For this reason I consider coupling/de-coupling something more than useful design metrics.

The intellectual techniques seen so far are of general applicability to all software design, irrespective of the underlying technology used. We are about to explore design techniques and concepts that are specific to the relational database theory and applicable to Oracle in particular.

4.2 Design for Flexibility

There are applications that are built on very dynamic data models. The designers know in advance that it is impossible to predict all possible combinations of relationship between specific entities, or that they are not in a position to predetermine all attributes of an entity. This kind of application is the perfect candidate for the use of a technique called *metadata* (or data about data). Instead of establishing fixed data access paths, which require code changes whenever a relationship is either added or removed, the relationship model is stored together with the application data, and queried by the application, which finds out about the underlying rules which govern the data relationship at run-time. As usual, an example helps clarifying the concept. Let us take a common military structure and an administrative application that helps manage a battalion. Our classical (and static) ER diagram would look like this:

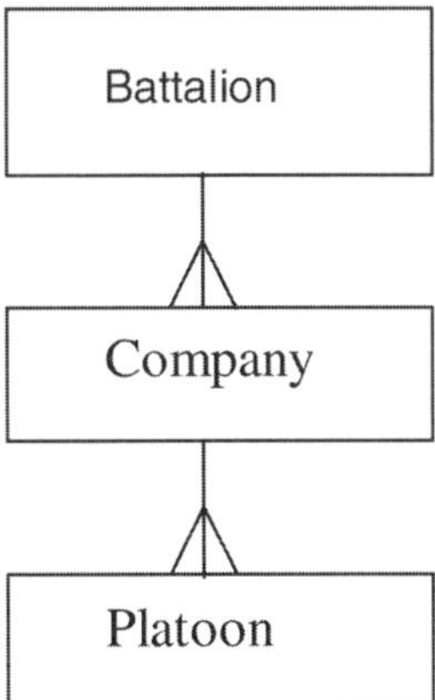

This model holds for a while, and then a new directive comes from the High Command, which requires the administrative personnel to record administrative facts at a squad level. The new ER model would look like this:

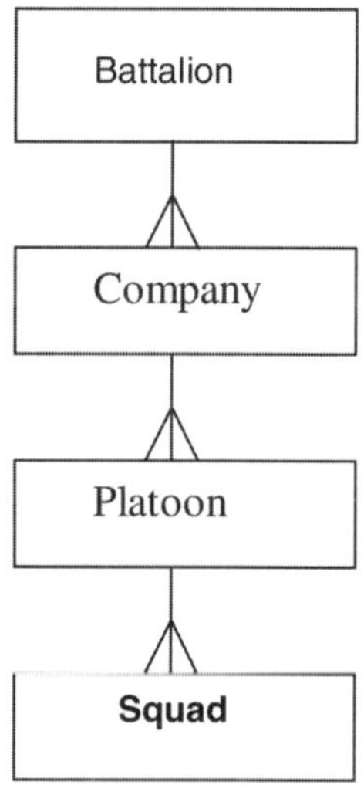

A new entity is added to the model, the data-entry screens must change, and new SQL statements must be implemented to allow for the new entity. A change in the data model implies a corresponding change in the application level code.

Later, a new change has to be introduced to the model. A company is usually organized in one or more platoons. Generally, a platoon reports to a company, but, in the case of an infantry battalion, there is one anti-tank platoon, which normally reports to the headquarters company, and which in special occasions (for instance a N.A.T.O. maneuver) becomes part of a specific Tactical Group, and reports directly to the battalion, bypassing the company level. The new ER model must be modified in this way:

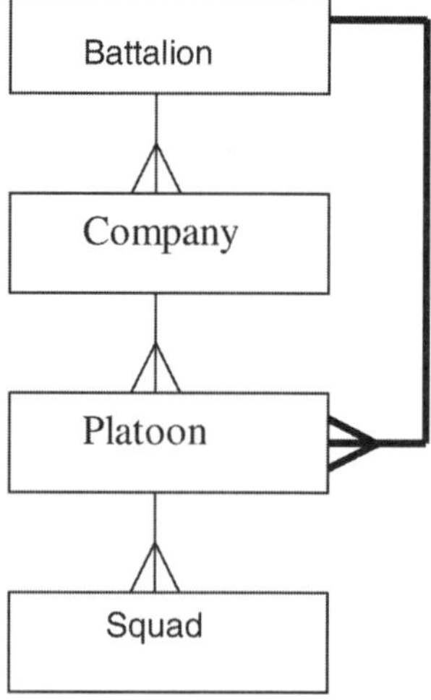

Again, a change in the data model has to be reflected in the code, because a new attribute is needed, and several to many SQL statements need to be modified to take into account the new attribute, and new ones have to be coded.

Now, let us take a different approach: We want to describe the hierarchical structure in a way such that an organizational change simply adds or removes records in tables, rather than requiring structural modifications to our data model. To this purpose, we need to use four tables:

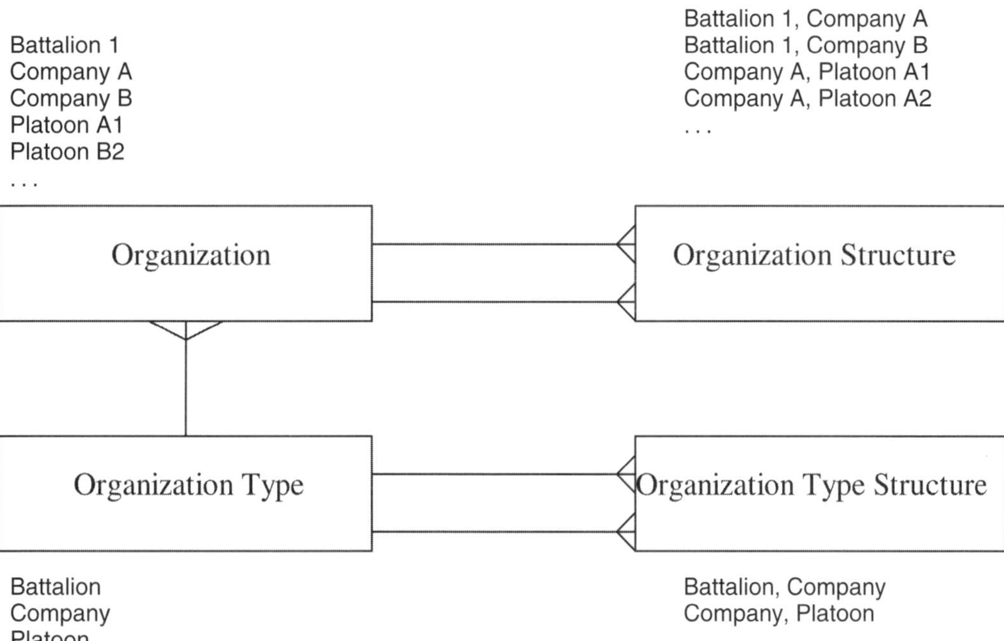

This new structure allows for maximum flexibility, because we can now capture every organizational change in our model, without modifying the data manipulation statements when new organizational entities are introduced, or when the relationship between organizational elements changes.

Through our metadata structure, we defined the basic organizational entities of the battalion appearing in the preceding example. When we receive the directive that forces us to include the squads in our administrative application, we simply add the new entity in our tables, with no underlying changes to the data model.

The new diagram shows the introduction of the squad:

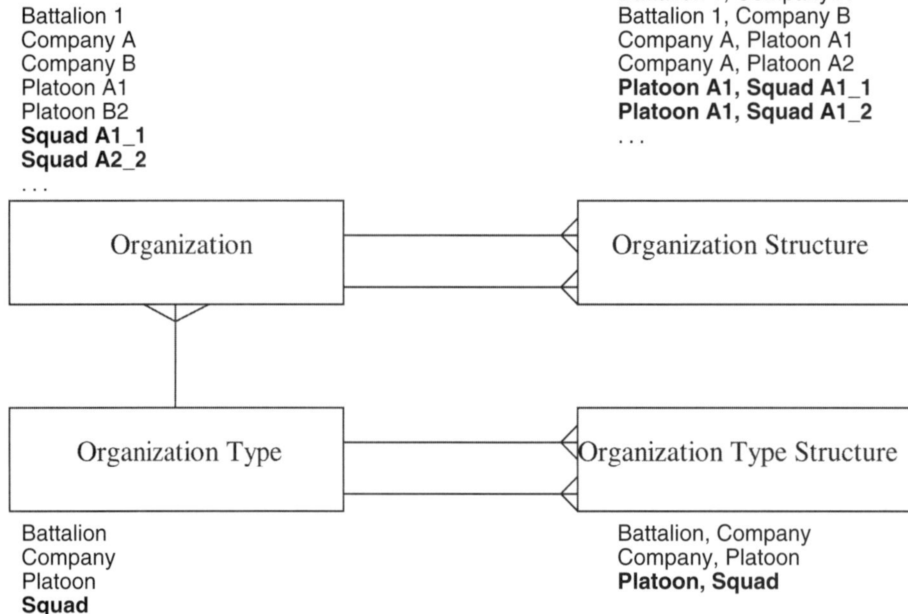

This model allows us to cope with hierarchical changes as well, for instance, the anti-tank platoon reporting directly to the battalion, instead of the company:

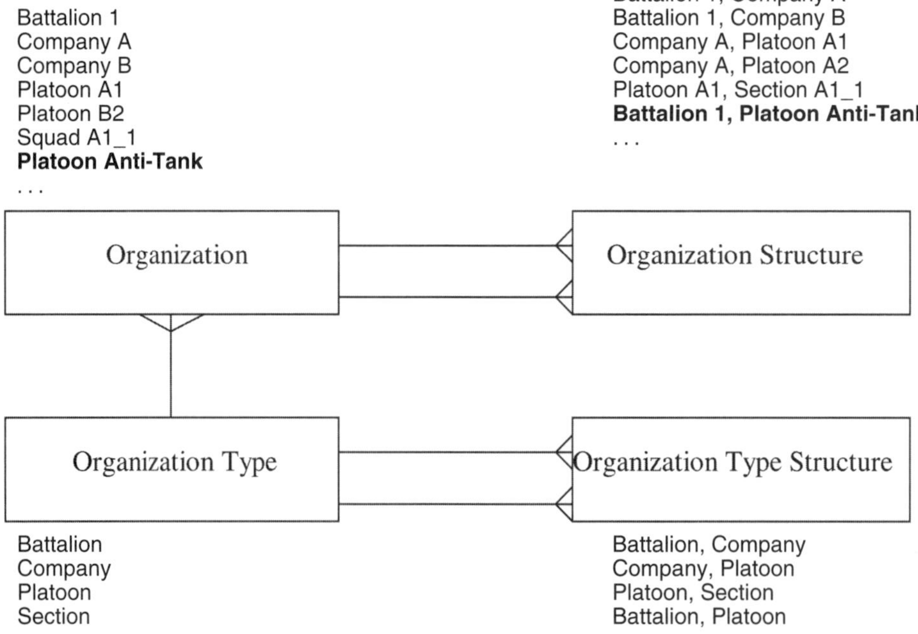

Metadata can also be successfully used in bill-of-material kind of applications, where the part explosion can have alternative components depending on the availability of the single item. Nothing comes for free, though, and always in software design one should consider the trade-off that every choice brings about. In this case we are giving away efficiency to gain flexibility, because the application must perfom one more query to find out at run-time about the underlying structure of the data model, before being able to perform any of the requested operations. In a client-server environment it would be wise to store the data model query either in a stored procedure or, in the case of a multi-tier model, in the third tier, in order to avoid multiple round trips over the network.

If flexibility is of paramount importance, then it must be designed for from the beginning; it simply cannot be superimposed on an existing model that wasn't originally designed with flexibility in mind. This is because, as we have seen, flexibility is normally accompanied by performance issues, which need to be solved to allow the application being built to run at acceptable levels.

Metadata is not the only technique that can be used to achieve flexibility. Storing business rules in tables has been a common practice since the beginning of the relational era. It is the extent to which this technique can be used that deserves our attention.

The simplest degree of flexibility is given by parameters that drive the behavior of an application. For instance the interest rate or the Value Added Tax are classical values that by their very nature are volatile and likely to be stored in tables where they can be updated frequently. It is possible, though, to extend this technique to achieve much greater flexibility.

For example, a few years ago I had the privilege to work on a project for one of the major telecommunication companies. I will use a fictitious name for the company (IperTelX) and for the project (SwitchX). That project achieved something really remarkable in the area of table-driven business rules; it deserves to be presented here as a case study.

SwitchX is a data driven, real time service activation system, capable of automatic provisioning and activation of single line subscribers on the Public Switched Telephone Network. SwitchX supports three major telephone switch hardware technologies, each comprising different software releases for the supervision of the switch operations and service provisioning. When an IperTelX customer wants a telephone service, a Customer Sales Representative handles the call and records in a computerized system the customer request. All possible products and services grantable to a customer are cataloged in the Product Code Maintenance System. Not all range of products is available for all switch technologies. If a customer is physically linked to an old technology switch, and the requested service is not available on that particular switch technology, then a manual intervention is required to re-link the telephone line of the customer to a more modern switch, so that the service can be granted. SwitchX is designed to perform automatic activation, but in case of problems like the one just described, or in case of errors during the dialog with the switch, it is able to generate a worksheet detailing the type of intervention required; the worksheet is forwarded to the switch technicians who carry out the job.

SwitchX maintains a table that lists all the incompatibilities and prerequisites for Product Code Maintenance System product codes. For example: The product named "WA0" is incompatible with "WA1," "WA2," "WA2," and "WA3"; or the product named "YHCC" has a prerequisite of either "OP000," "OP1," "OP2," "OP3," "OP4," or "OP5." For each software version, the Product Code Maintenance System product code is listed as either "Automatic," "Manual," or "Not Available." For example, the product named "YHCW" is "Automatic" in two of the three switch hardware technologies, and "Not Available" in the third switch technology, which is the oldest. This allows SwitchX to verify the Customer Sales Representative entered data. Any inconsistencies are returned to the Customer Sales Representative for correction. For each telephone switch owned by IperTelX, SwitchX stores the number range, software version type, and X25 address. When an order arrives from the system used by the Customer Sales Representatives, the National Service Number (NSN) is used to determine the software version type and X25 address. SwitchX uses three tables for product provisioning. These are "tsk_generation_rule," "tsk," and "tsk_instruction_rule."

The "tsk_generation_rule" table maps the software version type plus Product Code Maintenance System product code plus the product action type into one or more tasks. The "tsk" table stores the priority of the task, used to sequence the tasks. The "tsk_instruction_rule" table maps each automatic task into a single instruction for that software version type. The "tsk_instruction_rule" table also records which response rules are to be used to interpret the switch response.

SwitchX communicates with switches via the Man Machine Language (MML) interface. A state engine is used for each software version type. Each state engine is subdivided into three parts; the logon engine, command engine, and logoff engine. The state engine does not contain any intelligence except for start and end prompt character recognition. Once a command has been processed, the entire switch response string is passed to the Response Rule Engine to determine command execution status.

For each command, SwitchX stores Regular Expressions. Each switch response string is parsed against the regular expressions for a match. When a match is found, the "Response Type," "Destination," and "Problem Text" determine the next action to be taken by SwitchX. The switch vendor companies continuously ship new software versions for their telephone switches; very often a new software release implies a different and new syntax to be used to drive the switch. It would be simply unfeasible to hard-code the switch syntax in SwitchX, which would be in constant maintenance mode. Furthermore, multiple different software releases must be concurrently supported, because switches of the same technology can have different software releases. By storing the switch syntax needed to establish the dialog between SwitchX and all the telephone switches in Oracle tables, the designers achieved maximum flexibility. Whenever a new software release comes out, or new products or services are introduced, it is sufficient to add a few records in the reference tables accessed by SwitchX to make SwitchX fully aware of the newly introduced features and capable to handle them. The SwitchX source code is never or very rarely touched, yet the business rules change almost daily.

4.3 Design for Performance

Data modelers strive to capture in a model the often complex data needs of an application. Their job is to apply a well-defined methodology while solving data-related business problems. A methodology is used for a few purposes, for instance, being able to share the model with other designers familiar with the same methodology, or to re-use or re-adapt other models, developed for similar business problems, using the same methodology.

While it is up to the single designer to adhere more or less strictly to the rules and prescriptions imposed by the methodology followed, it is true that every methodology brings about biases and deficiencies, as well as points of strengths. The Standard Information Engineering is the methodology commonly used today for designing relational databases. It is supported by all major design tools currently available on the market (for instance, Oracle Designer).

The most visible outcome of this methodology is the Entity–Relationship diagram, which is the design document used by the software specialists and database administrators to actually implement the database using specific SQL syntax. The Information Engineering method makes a very clear distinction between a more abstract level of data design, called logical design, and a more low-level abstraction called physical design.

The two different design domains use different terminologies, but there is usually a one-to-one relationship between a design element defined at a logical level and a corresponding design element defined at a physical level. So, a logical entity (which is an object defined in the system, about which one wants to store information) becomes a table in the physical model; a logical attribute (which is a data item attached to an entity, to specify entity's characteristics) becomes a column in the physical model.

The data modeler is usually concerned with the logical level, because it is at that level that the real business analysis is conducted, and the data needs of the problem domain are determined. A good logical model is *normalized*, that is, redundancy and repeating groups have been eliminated, and the key attributes are properly defined to uniquely identify the entity recurrences. The intellectual effort put into the definition of the logical model is considerable; unfortunately, too often the transformation of the logical model into a physical model is overlooked. This is partially due to the automatic conversion facility provided by most database design packages, which allows it to generate a physical model by a click of the mouse on a visual control.

Automatically generated physical models are exact replicas of the logical model, with the terminology changes described above. If they are implemented without any further analysis and adjustments, the resulting application is not only not optimized for performance, but at risk of upsetting the users for unacceptable response time.

Performance is a goal which has to be taken into consideration at design time, and not something achievable through tuning once the application is already deployed in production. Performance is also a vague concept, which must be carefully analyzed and considered by the designers. The modern theory of systems teaches us that the optimization of a single subsystem does not necessarily imply an improvement of the entire system; to the contrary, the optimization of a subsystem is usually to the detriment of the other participating sub-systems.

The same applies to applications that use Oracle as the back-end database. Let us imagine the following scenario:

An important financial application requires the main data forms to be displayed within three seconds (a common requirement), because the operators use the application while speaking over the phone with the customers. The financial accounts are reconciled by a long and resource-intensive process that runs every night. The window of time available for the batch, overnight process is approximately four hours. The designers study the data model, compute the necessary projections to figure out the approximate number of records and size of the tables involved in the reconciliation process, perform a benchmark, and determine that after the database has been fully loaded, and after a period of six months of growth, the available window of time for reconciliation is not long enough. To speed up the reconciliation process by an order of magnitude, information has to be stored redundantly. The trade-off, here, is between better performance for the batch process and slower updates and insertions, because the same information has to be stored in multiple tables.

Specific and precise performance targets have to be set at design time, since it is impossible, as we have seen, to optimize every single performance aspect of an application. Choices operated at design time privilege specific aspects or parts of an application and penalize other aspects or parts. One of the tasks of the designer is to identify precisely the various trade-off points and take careful and well-informed decisions, either knowing or estimating costs and benefits associated with each decision.

Most importantly, the physical data design of an application has to be pedantically revised and reviewed to make sure that elegance at a high-level logical design does not translate into inefficiency at a low-level physical implementation.

There are a few techniques commonly used to modify a physical data design with the purpose of enhancing the potential performance of the application being built:

1. De-normalization
2. Precalculated fields
3. One-to-one relationship consolidation

De-normalization is the process of re-introducing redundant data in specific tables in order to achieve a better response time for queries accessing those tables. For instance, storing logical children in parent tables so that only one table instead of two, is accessed, is a common de-normalization technique.

The purpose of de-normalization is to avoid joining two or more tables together by duplicating columns. A join is an expensive operation, the complexity and the response time of which increase as the number of tables joined increases. At the same time joining tables is the core, the essence of the relational model, and it cannot simply be avoided. The point, here, is that a reasonable balance must be reached between relational elegance achieved through formal correctness, and acceptable performance and response time. Striving to achieve performance cannot become an excuse for poor relational design. The starting point must *always* be a normalized and correct model.

De-normalization is not the *panacea* for all evil in relational performance, because it introduces an entire new category of issues and problems, which have to be evaluated to make sure that the benefits associated with de-normalization really outweigh the costs. De-normalizing means introducing redundant information; the query response time increases at the expense of insertions and updates. Furthermore, duplicated information can easily go out of synchronization, becoming inconsistent and contradictory. While an automatically generated physical model is not to be accepted passively, but questioned, criticized, and improved, at the same time every de-normalization must be carefully considered before being introduced.

Another common technique used to achieve better performance is to store precalculated fields, to avoid costly SQL operations such as SUM, AVG, MIN, MAX, etc. This makes sense, because if a statistical computation is consistently requested by hundreds of concurrent users, then it is better to compute it only once, store its result, and allow the concurrent users to fetch a precalculated result. This effect is usually achieved through the use of database triggers, which fire at any insertion or update and do the requested computation storing the result in the field hosting the precalculated amount. This technique is also not immune to problems, though. The risk of contention on the precalculated field is very high if, for instance, the core table of an application is heavily accessed in insert or update mode, and a trigger updates the value of only one field hosting a precalculated sum or average in another table. The contention for accessing in update mode the field holding the precalculated amount can become a real bottleneck, slowing down the response time for the insertions or updates of the core table of the application. Again, storing precalculated values in redundant fields is not a recipe good for all seasons and all problems, but its applicability has to be determined evaluating the specific case and the specific environment.

It is perfectly legitimate for a data modeler to sketch entities in a one-to-one relationship. At a physical level, though, this is not always a good idea, because a join is required. For this reason, it is a common practice to consolidate two tables in a one-to-one relationship into one larger table containing the combined columns. As usual, there is an exception to be considered. If a table contains a LONG (an Oracle specific data type, holding character data of variable length up to two gigabytes), together with other data columns, then it is better to keep the LONG column in a separate table linked to the other related columns in a one-to-one relationship, to avoid costly full table scans of unstructured data.

4.4 Design for Scalability

Oracle Corporation has constantly improved the scalability features of its flagship database over the recent releases. Nevertheless, scalability must be designed for from the early stages of the architectural design, because the degree of achievable scalability does not depend on the Oracle software alone, but on the hardware configuration as well. If the number of concurrent users, including a conservative expected growth, does not exceed the few hundreds, then a single machine with SMP capabilities can be enough. If high reliability were also part of the requirements, then a combination of two smaller machines in a cluster configuration, with an Oracle parallel server, would be a better solution.

If the application needs to support thousands of concurrent users, then parallelism is the only option able to ensure an adequate scalability. In this context, parallelism does not imply the use of the Oracle Parallel Server, but parallel hardware architecture. Before delving into parallel architecture concepts, we should familiarize ourselves with the terminology commonly used by the architecture designers:

- **Massively Parallel Processing Hardware (MPP):** Parallel hardware configuration where every processor (or node) has its own portion of memory.
- **Symmetric MultiProcessing Hardware (SMP):** Multiple processors share the same memory resource.
- **Interconnect:** Communication facility between the various nodes in a MMP or clustered environment. Typically implemented through Ethernet, FDDI, or other proprietary protocols.
- **Bandwidth:** Total size of messages that can be sent per second through the Interconnect.
- **Latency:** Time (in seconds) it takes to put a message through the Interconnect. It indicates the number of messages that can be placed on the Interconnect per second.
- **Tightly Coupled Systems:** Parallel configuration that share memory. They are characterized by having multiple CPUs sharing memory, each CPU having full access on shared memory through a common bus.
- **Loosely Coupled Systems:** Parallel configurations that share disks. They are characterized by having one or more CPUs, which do not share memory between them. Each node shares disks (and possibly other resources) with the other nodes. Communication occurs over high-speed Interconnects.
- **Distributed Lock Manager (DLM):** Locking facility that coordinates resource sharing between nodes in a parallel configuration.
- **ScaleUp:** Factor that expresses how much more work can be done in the same time period by a larger (i.e., parallel) system.
- **SpeedUp:** Extent to which more hardware can perform the same task in less time than the original system.

Oracle offers two different kinds of parallelism: the Parallel Server (OPS) and the Parallel Query Option (PQO). They are similar but different, and it is important to highlight their difference. The fundamental prerequisite to the use of the PQO is an architecture with multiple CPUs. By using the PQO the work required to satisfy a single SQL statement can be split and performed in parallel by the different CPUs. The engine takes care of the required synchronization and a single result is presented back to the user who submitted the SQL statement. The user can influence the way the engine deals with parallelism by setting appropriate degrees of parallelism through specific Oracle SQL syntax. The PQO can be used in a single instance environment, provided that the hardware used is configured with at least two CPUs.

The Oracle Parallel Server implies a hardware configuration with at least two nodes, each running an Oracle instance sharing the same database files with the other Oracle instances running on the system. It should be noted that while the PQO undoubtedly offers increased performance for queries that require full table scans, it does not provide any additional reliability. If the single instance crashes, the entire Oracle system is down. By using the OPS, a system does not necessarily improve its performance (if its SpeedUp factor is equal to zero), but it definitely increases its reliability, because if an engine crashes, the database is still accessible through the working engines located on different nodes. If the nodes where the OPS is being implemented have multiple CPUs, then the PQO can also be used, cumulating the two parallelisms together, in a very reliable and performant environment. By combining together the Oracle configurable options for scalability with appropriate hardware configurations, the architecture designers have a very rich set of possibilities to choose from, able to satisfy every budget and need.

In a *continuum,* which goes from the least to the most scalable architecture, we can identify several possible configurations:

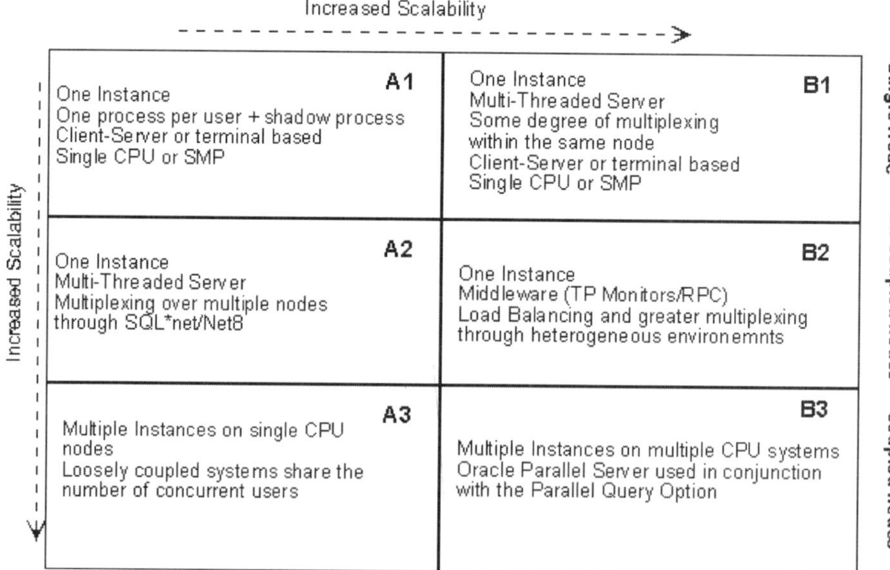

FIGURE 4.1 Oracle Architectures for Scalability

The configuration described in cell A1 is at the same time the least scalable, and probably the most common, in the real world. A commonly accepted absolute top limit in such a configuration is in the neighborhood of one thousand users, on a very powerful multi-processor server. The problem with this configuration is the accumulation of one oracle shadow process per connected user. In particular hardware configurations (typically DEC machines running OpenVMS), the Oracle single-task mode can be enabled, so that the application executable is linked directly against the Oracle shareable image, providing single-task connections to Oracle. In such a software configuration the Oracle shadow process is not needed, unless the connection happens through SQL*Net; however, this is the exception rather than the norm, because all Oracle implementations under the Unix operating system usually require a two-task connection. In a traditional character and server based application, this implies having two processes per user: the application process and the Oracle shadow process, which accesses the database on behalf of the application process, guaranteeing memory protection and security.

In a client-server environment running over SQL*Net/Net8, only the shadow process is needed, because the client takes care of the other end of the SQL*Net connection.

The amount of memory required by each Oracle shadow process is not negligible (typically at least two megabytes). In order to lessen the amount of memory

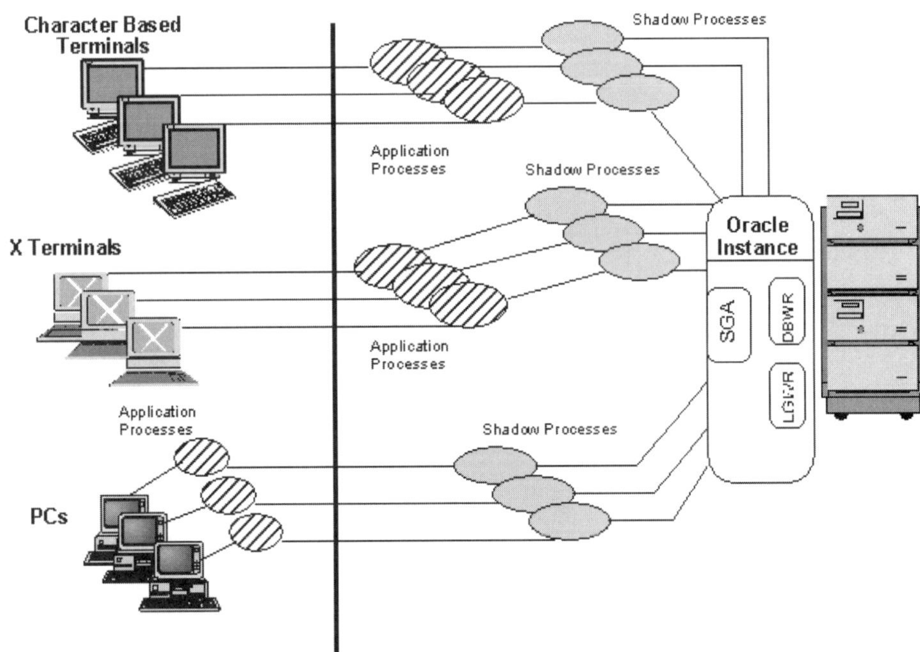

FIGURE 4.2 The Oracle Architecture Corresponding to the Cell A1 of Figure 4.1

required by hundreds of shadow processes running concurrently, Oracle offers the MTS (Multi-Threaded Server) option. In a MTS configuration, multiple client (or application) processes are connected to a limited number of dispatchers, which in turn dialog with shared servers through the Oracle System Global Area. The typical user to server process ratio is between 1:5 and 1:10. One has also to allocate an adequate number of dispatchers (again, a possible ratio is one dispatcher per 5–10 servers). Not all applications are suitable for a multi-threaded server configuration; in fact, multiplexing is made possible by using the idle time of a client process for the benefit of the other processes. The basic assumption, here, is that an application user spends 80% of the time looking at the screen, assimilating the information just displayed, deciding the next course of action, perhaps questioning a customer over the phone. Only 20% of the time the user process is actively fetching data from the database server. If an application is not substantially interactive, and of the type just described, then implementing a multi-threaded server is not likely to improve the performance, or to increase the potential number of users.

Figure 4.3 shows an architecture where the Oracle engine is accessed through a multi-threaded configuration. The larger server hosts the single Oracle instance, while two smaller servers help off-loading the character-based application. The application processes (one per user) are run on the front-end servers,

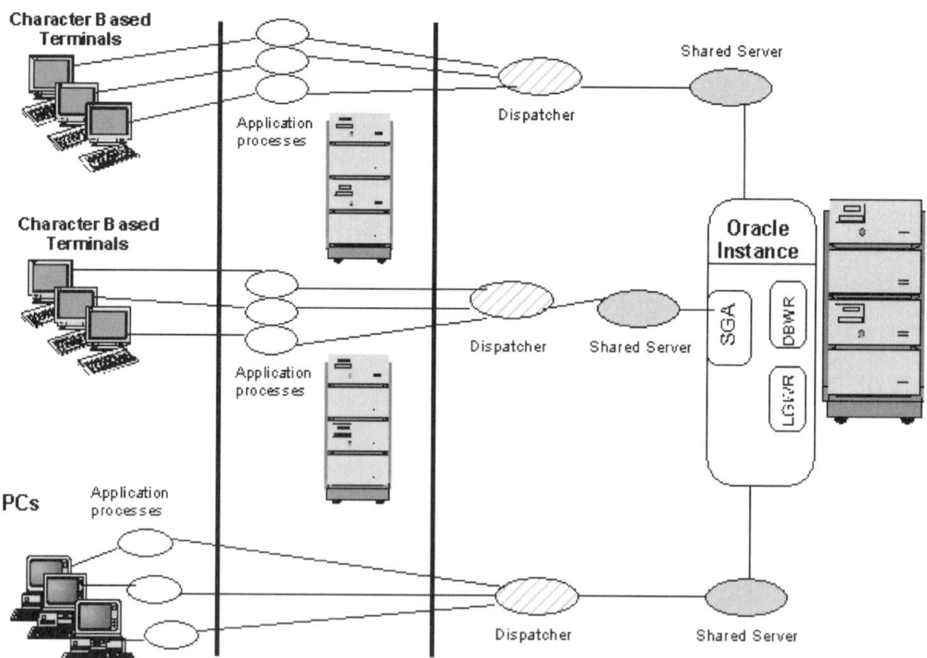

FIGURE 4.3 The Oracle Architecture Corresponding to the Cell A2 of the Diagram in Figure 4.1

which are connected through SQL*Net to the back-end server. The multi-threaded option lessens the number of server processes required to access the data stored in the Oracle database; multiple processes running on the front-end server share a much smaller amount of Oracle server processes (as we have seen, the ratio is between 5 :1 and 10 :1), running on the machine hosting the Oracle instance. This is possible thanks to the dispatcher processes, to which the user processes are connected by the SQL*Net listener. When a user submits a request, the dispatcher stores it in the request queue located in the instance SGA. The first available shared server finds the request and processes it, storing the result in the response queue, also located in the SGA. The dispatcher then finds the result of the request in the response queue and sends it back to the requestor process.

Figure 4.3 shows a common configuration where a typical OLTP application, implemented using character-based terminals, coexists with a client-server user population, which accesses the same database using personal computers or workstations.

A wise use of the multi-threaded option helps extending the potential number of users on one single Oracle instance running on a single node. As noted before, however, not all applications are suitable for a multi-threaded configuration. Furthermore, even if an application is highly interactive, and therefore theoretically suitable for Oracle MTS, an extremely large user population can preclude its use. To achieve the goal of a scaleable architecture, one should consider implementing an Oracle Parallel Server. The hardware architecture that gives the best result, when coupled with Oracle OPS, is the one based on loosely coupled systems, typically a cluster of two or more servers sharing disks and other resources over high-speed interconnects. In such a configuration, critical factors are high bandwidth and low latency, but above all, proper application design that allows for logical partitioning of the application units of work.

This is a crucial concept, which deserves particular attention for a correct and proficient use of the Oracle OPS. In an OPS configuration, the main issue is synchronization, which can become expensive to the extent of making OPS a not viable option. When two or more Oracle instances share the same datafiles, they rely on a distributed lock manager to regulate the access to the single data block. OPS in Oracle 7 uses the distributed lock manager (DLM) provided by the operating system (typically Unix or OpenVMS). Oracle 8 provides the internal distributed lock manager, bundled together with the Oracle Server, which is generally more performant than the generic lock manager shipped with the operating system. Irrespective of the efficiency of the DLM, if two users connected to two different instances are updating the same row contained in the same data block, they incur a large overhead, due to network round trips to synchronize and release the lock between the two instances. If thousands of users concurrently access a limited set of data blocks in update mode, the overhead required to synchronize the locks among the various instances makes the scaleup factor negative, and, ultimately, the OPS option unviable.

Ideally, each instance should update data blocks that are not shared with any other instance. This implies the concept of data ownership, and opens the way to application partitioning, which is the real clue to an efficient use of Oracle parallelism. Once again, application partitioning can happen only at design time, because it is very difficult to super-impose a partitioned architecture over an existing application designed according to other criteria.

There are applications that show a natural predisposition to be partitioned. For instance, the ones that carry an intrinsic notion of geographical subdivision in regions are the best natural candidates for partitioning. Let us take, as an example, a mail-order company that accepts orders nationwide, and is organized in three regions, each having a warehouse. In the company headquarters, a cluster runs one Oracle instance per region, plus an additional instance implementing a Decision Support System. Every region normally accesses its own instance to process its business. Under a few circumstances, a region is authorized to query, and eventually update, data stored in other regions' partitions, for instance, when a requested good is not in stock, and the time required to re-order it exceeds the shipping time the company is committed to with the customers. In this case a region is allowed to move the good from the warehouse of another region, provided it carries out all administrative procedures associated to it. The DSS application helps the managers to assume the correct decisions, and it mainly accesses data in read-only mode, to produce the required reports.

It is not enough to buy expensive clustered hardware and make Oracle Corporation happy by paying the expensive Parallel Server license to achieve true scalability. Most of the burden is on the designers' shoulders, who have to "think parallel" in every important design decision.

A certain degree of parallelism can also be achieved with single instances running on SMP machines, if the application design allows for it. At one stage I was involved in a project dealing with workflow management. The system, built on an Oracle database, used to receive requests for tasks to be carried out by the company's workforce, regionally distributed across the country (Australia). The system's main purpose was to split the tasks into activities, according to specific business rules, to be dispatched via middleware to the distributed workforce. The tasks were either manually created via a client-server interface, or received from other computerized systems through RPC mechanisms. A background process operated the task splitting into activities, stored in a table acting as output queue. A second process scanned the table, fetching the queued activities, and sending them through a commercial messaging product (IBM MQ Series) to external systems. Complex business logic was used to determine the recipient of the single activity. This caused the process to perform slowly, to the extent of producing a real bottleneck. I was requested to investigate the possibility of doubling the processing power by running a second background process in parallel, to speed up the queueing of the activities to the MQ Series queue. A quick look at the design documentation and source code of the de-queueing process determined that unfortunately that system component wasn't designed with built-in parallel capabilities. In fact, the algorithm used for accessing the activities stored in the table acting as the output queue was like the one that follows:

```
Loop Forever
        Access the output queue table
        Declare cursor:
                Select all fields from output queue
                where SENT = 'N'
                for update
        Open cursor
        Until no rows found
        Begin
                Fetch all fields into activity host variables
                Process activity
                Update output queue
                        Set SENT = 'Y'
                where current of cursor
        End
        Close cursor
        Sleep for a few seconds
End loop
```

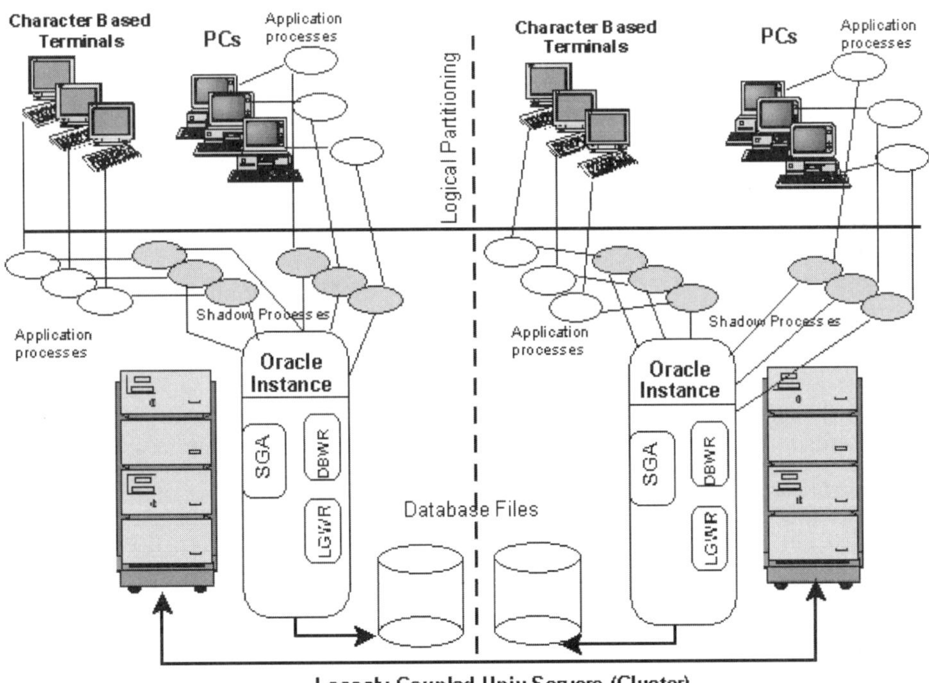

FIGURE 4.4 An Oracle Parallel Server Architecture Implemented on a Cluster

This algorithm prevents a second background process from accessing any activity stored in the output queue because the Oracle pessimistic locking strategy is being used. Until all entries in the output queue have been processed by the first background process, the second background process is in idle state, waiting for the lock to be released. This is a clear example of inflexible design, which doesn't take into consideration the possibility for parallelism. Furthermore, it is not an efficient algorithm, because the Oracle host arrays capabilities are not being used. A much better algorithm would be the one that makes one process fetch a small lot of entries from the output queue (possibly a configurable number), updates their status to something like "BEING PROCESSED," closes the cursor releasing the lock and then processes them, one by one. The second background process would do the same, fetching all entries that are not "BEING_PROCESSED" or "COMPLETED." This way the two processes can cooperate in speeding up the de-queueing of the activities by exploiting the SMP capabilities of the host. Again, good design is worthy more than expensive hardware and software.

4.5 Design for Reliability

Mission critical applications often require a high degree of continuous availability. If the business requires an Oracle application to be up and running *always*, then an adequate budget needs to be set aside to provide for absolute redundancy. By always I mean 24 hours per day, 7 days per week, 52 weeks per year. This kind of requirement cannot be met by a single Oracle instance. It is unthinkable never to bounce[1] an instance for an entire year. It simply doesn't happen. And even if it could be theoretically possible, it definitely wouldn't be desirable because of the problems and side effects associated to it. For instance, the internal counters kept by Oracle in the memory structures known as the dynamic V$ tables are generally 32 bit integers. After the instance has been actively accessed for a few days or weeks, those counters overflow, biasing all performance statistics and figures which are so useful to maintain an instance under control. From an administrative point of view it is much more flexible to have the option of bouncing an instance without causing a major disruption of the normal operations.

To accomplish this, an Oracle parallel server is the only architecturally sound solution. Absolute reliability means systematically avoiding all possible single points of failure, at both hardware and software levels. An Oracle parallel server running on a multi-node cluster that uses a RAID 0+1 configuration for its disks is a good starting point. RAID means Redundant Array of Independent

[1]In the Oracle DBA jargon, to bounce means to shut an instance down and to re-start it.

Disks and is a popular hardware technology designed to provide better I/O performance and fault tolerance for the I/O subsystem. There are several different levels of RAID, but the most common are:

1. RAID 0. It is also known as "disk striping." A logical disk is built by joining together multiple physical disks. Data is spread across the different devices, so that reading and writing are done concurrently on multiple disks via several I/O channels, increasing the overall I/O throughput.
2. RAID 1. It is also known as "disk mirroring." A logical disk of the size of, say, four gigabytes is built from two physical disks, each as big as four gigabytes. Data is written twice, once per disk. In case of disk failure, the faulty disk is replaced on the fly, without requiring any down time, and the RAID firmware copies the content of the disk that didn't crash to the new disk.
3. RAID 3 – RAID 4 – RAID 5. They are variations on the same theme, basically writing parity data on a dedicated disk of the RAID set and striping all data across the RAID set. If one disk in the set fails, data can be rebuilt from the parity information. The disadvantage with this type of configuration is that generally the recovery phase requires down time. The most recently introduced RAID configurations (RAID 6 and 7) allow for redundancy based on data striping that doesn't require down time during recovery.

RAID 0 and RAID 1 can be combined to provide excellent reliability. This configuration requires double disk capacity to accommodate the mirroring needs, so it is generally more expensive than the other RAID options. If absolute reliability of the system is of paramount importance, then redundancy must be implemented at any level, including the network. It is pointless having a perfectly accessible Oracle database if the users cannot connect because of a network failure. The nodes where the mission critical application resides have to be accessible via different network paths, and the network administrator has to be able to interchange segment access on the fly, in the event of hardware failure of one or more routers or repeaters.

When the requirements for reliability are not that strict, and a down time in the order of one or two hours is tolerable, or when the hardware configuration used does not support the Oracle parallel server, then an option is the setting up of a *hot standby* database. The latter is a backup copy of the production database that is kept on an identical, separate machine. Identical means same number and configuration of disks, (in Unix, same mount points), same directory paths, etc. The standby database is maintained almost in sync with the primary database by continuously applying the redo log files copied from the primary database, at regular intervals. In case of failure of the primary database, the standby database can be opened and used while the primary database is being recovered. The hot standby database is a good solution to minimize the down time in case of a sudden failure of the primary database.

It should be noticed that a longer down time is only postponed, and not avoided, because it is not possible to switch back and forth between the two databases. To reach again the initial situation, after having enabled the standby database, it requires a database re-synchronization, that is, the standby database has to be copied over the primary. In sites where the DBA can have a long window of time for administration (typically during weekends), the hot standby technique can be applied with success. If the primary database failure happens on Tuesday, the DBA can enable the hot standby database and use it until the next weekend. On Saturday, both databases are shut down, a cold backup of the standby database is performed, and the datafiles are then copied over the datafiles of the primary database. The next Monday the database is again running in "normal" mode.

Even if reliability is not in the top list of requirements, it is wise to use at least the Oracle built-in redundancy capabilities. Oracle can maintain multiple copies of the control files and multiple threads of redo log files; it us up to the DBA to spread the redundant control files and redo log files across different disks.

In the context of an Oracle project, reliability does not apply only to the production instance. The source code of the application must be reliably kept and organized, so that accidental loss of files is prevented. In Chapter 9 we will examine common software engineering techniques for a well organized software development environment.

4.6 Design for Distribution and Replication of Data

A distributed database is a collection of two or more databases physically residing in different nodes of a network, connected in such a way that they appear to be one database to users and applications accessing them. A single transaction can refer to tables and views residing in different nodes, and still maintain data integrity in case of failure. This is possible thanks to a specific protocol, called *two-phase commit protocol*, which splits the transaction in two phases. In the first phase the committing of a transaction is *prepared*, that is, the global coordinator (or the initiating node) establishes a dialog with all participating nodes asking them to prepare to commit. In the *commit* phase, if all participant nodes responded that are willing to commit, the transaction is committed at the commit point site. The transaction is considered to be committed when all participant nodes respond with an OK to commit, and the transaction is actually committed at the commit point site. The commit is then eventually propagated to all nodes. The recoverer background process (RECO) looks after potential failures and discrepancies that can arise in distributed committing of transactions.

The two-phase commit mechanism couples all updates to all locations participating in an update. In practice, it accomplishes a synchronized locking of all pieces of a transaction, with the net effect of an atomic action performed upon multiple locations and processors. Data integrity is preserved across several, different machines and locations.

The limit of the above described architecture resides in imposing a rigid data integrity primacy even when this is not required. Let us imagine the following scenario:

> A large corporation has hundreds of branches worldwide, including developing countries, which do not offer highly reliable network backbones. In a distributed database context a transaction is basically at least atomic (if not also consistent, isolated, and durable). Being atomic, it updates successfully either all the sites or none of them. If the branch in Zambia is suffering from network problems, then the transaction will not succeed in any of the remaining countries. Also, one has to consider the network traffic associated with an update that spans over hundreds of machines located in different countries. If a transaction must be secured over hundreds of nodes, the response time of the system can soon become very frustrating for the users.

The distributed database technology, in its "pure" form, is today impractical for many of the business applications that work in a wide, cooperative environment, often operating in several, if not many, different countries.

While absolute data synchronization is required for applications dealing with financial trading and banking funds transfer, there are also a lot of applications that don't need the features offered by the two-phase commit protocol. Order processing, for instance, together with hotel and airline reservations, might be handled using Data Replication. Airlines and hotels usually overbook intentionally, and then solve the problems at a second stage, when data has been stabilized and reconciled. In this case, Data Replication is even more in line with the way the business proceeds.

Data replication can be defined as the copying of data in databases to multiple locations to support distributed applications. Replication provides users with their own local copies of data. These local, updatable data copies can support increased localized processing, reduced network traffic, easy scalability, and cheaper approaches for distributed, nonstop processing. The real challenge, for Oracle, DBAs and IS managers is to reach the same level of integrity offered by the systems that follow the central, monolithic model supported by the two-phase commit protocol. Given the intrinsic nature of Data Replication, when one speaks about integrity, he/she refers to a concept of "deferred integrity," meaning an integrity which is eventually reached at a postponed point in time (i.e., when data across the various sites become reconciled).

Data Replication is a very young discipline, but there exist already many different approaches to it, each aimed at solving different classes of problems. To begin with, there are two fundamental categories of replication supported by Oracle: basic replication (Master/Slave approach) and advanced replication (Peer-to-Peer, Update Anywhere).

The Master/Slave approach eliminates transaction collisions, but is more rigid and less generic than the second approach, called Peer-to-Peer Update Anywhere. In the master/slave model, only one site (the master) can update a table, which is later replicated to the slave site (or sites). The latter sees the table in a read-only mode. In the Peer-to-Peer model, on the other hand, all the sites can update the same table, which is later reconciled against all sites. A collision occurs when the same record, which is physically replicated at two or multiple sites, is updated during the asynchronous latency period. In other words, after the time a first update has happened, a second update occurs, which is processed at one site before the propagation of the first update has been completed. So although a peer-to-peer approach provides the most general solution for transaction distribution, it requires policies for collision resolution.

One can identify at least three different types of data replication, within the master/slave model, from an application point of view:

1. Data Dissemination
2. Data Consolidation
3. Workload Partitioning

The *Data Dissemination* approach defines only one master site empowered to access the tables to be replicated in read/write mode. All the other sites participating in the replicated database are prevented from updating the replicated tables, which are refreshed periodically from the master to the slaves. This is the simplest form of data replication, implemented by all the major database vendors. The tables in common between the master and the slaves are called "Snapshots."

An example of applied Data Dissemination is a computer store chain whose headquarters sends updated price lists of available computer components overnight. The stores have read-only access to the prices, while the headquarters can modify them.

The *Data Consolidation* model implements an opposite philosophy, where each peripheral site updates each either a separate table or nonoverlapping records within one table, and then the central server receives the consolidated data from all the sites. The central server cannot update the snapshots, but simply queries the replicated tables to produce reconciled reports from all sites.

An example of Data Consolidation is a retail store chain that gathers point-of-sale information throughout the day. Each store must supply a copy of this information to headquarters on a daily basis. At the end of the day, this information is transmitted to headquarters and consolidated into the central data warehouse, which management can use to perform trend analysis on its business.

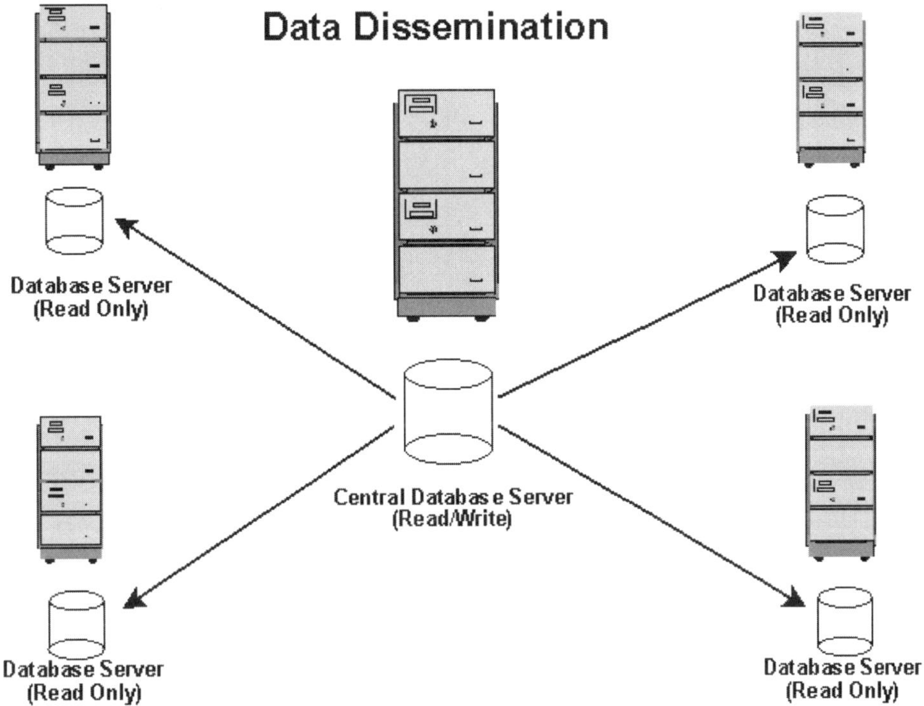

FIGURE 4.5 Basic Replication through Data Dissemination

The *Workload Partitioning* model introduces yet another important concept, widely used in Data Replication: ownership of data. A perfect example of Workload Partitioning is given in Figure 4.7.

The replication schema matches the partitioning schema for the order entry tables. The Australia-based server has ownership of its partition and can therefore update, insert, and delete order entry records for orders in its region. The changes are then propagated to the U.S. and New Zealand regions. Australia can query or read the other partitions locally, but will not be able to update those partitions. This strategy applies to other regions as well.

The methods illustrated so far all have in common the goal of avoiding data collision. They are relatively easy to implement and to administer. Unfortunately, the trade-off here is between simplicity and flexibility. The master/slave approach is not flexible enough for specific needs. Organizations also require the ability to support updates at multiple sites, working independently from each other. Every local branch can function autonomously, irrespective of the availability of other systems or network participating in the distributed environment. In a peer-to-peer environment it is not possible to avoid data collisions. One has

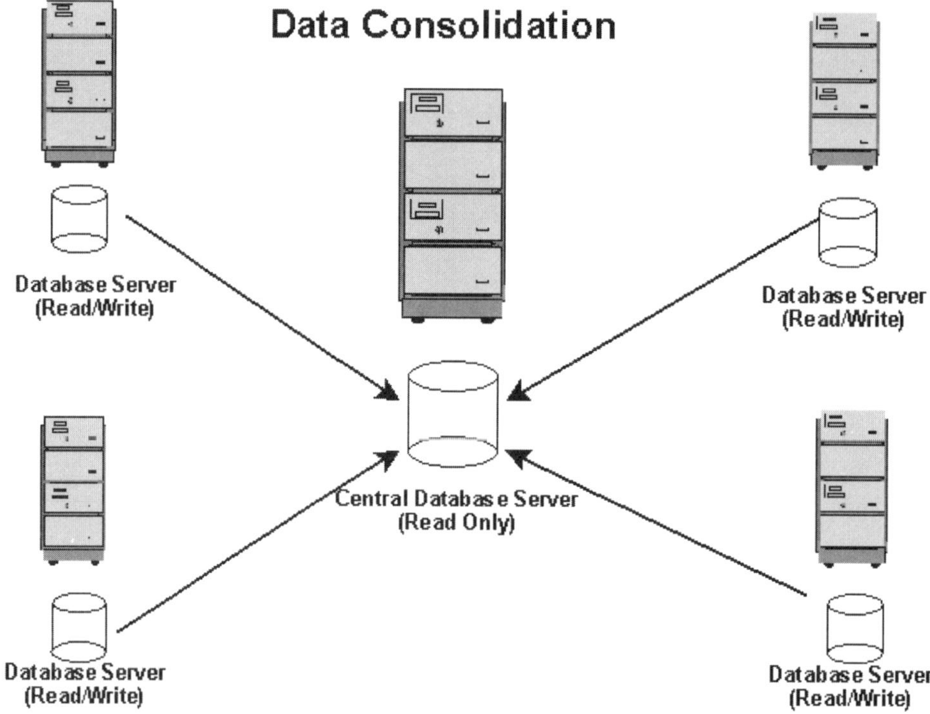

FIGURE 4.6 Basic Replication through Data Consolidation

simply to live with them, but the software provided by Oracle can help in detecting and resolving them.

The peer-to-peer model supports disconnected environments; for instance, the salesman who records all sales made during the day in a notebook and then synchronizes the central company database at the end of the day, connecting from home or from the telephone line of a hotel. Another possible use of this technology is to provide a completely replicated failover site, in case the principal site is down following a crash or for maintenance reasons. Oracle supports both synchronous and asynchronous replication. In an environment replicated synchronously, data collision does not happen, because all transactions are propagated atomically. The synchronous replication model overlaps with the more traditional distributed model, which makes use of the two-phase commit protocol. The drawback of such a model is that it requires all participating nodes to be up and running to allow a single transaction to succeed. Furthermore, performance can become an issue if many different nodes, geographically dispersed, participate in the same transaction.

Most of replicated applications use the asynchronous mechanism for change propagation. Oracle offers different options, suitable for the implementa-

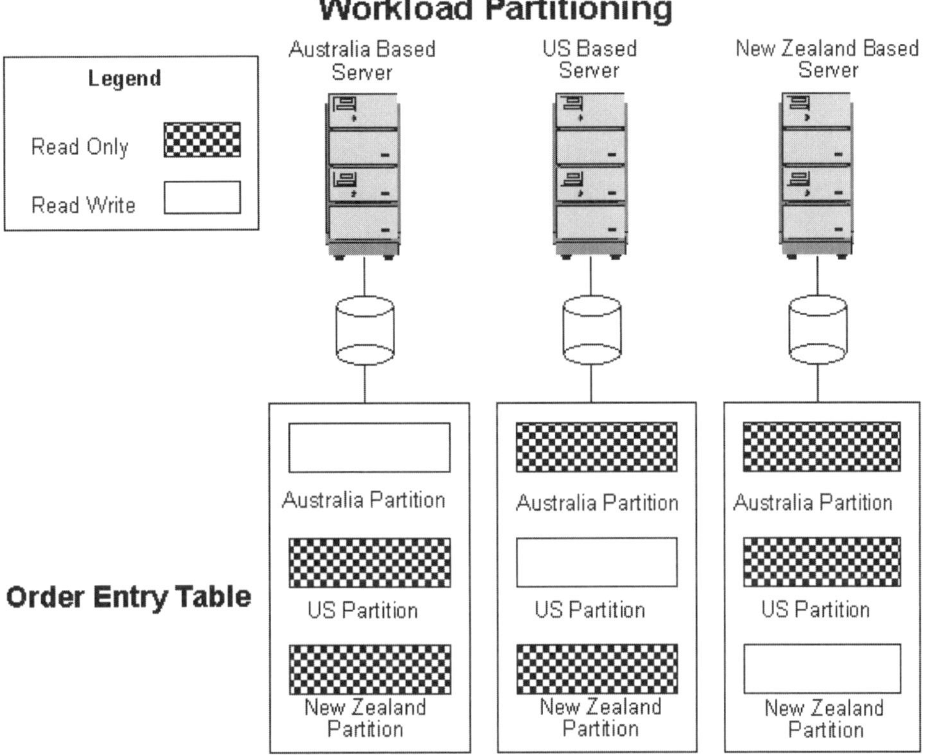

FIGURE 4.7 Workload Partitioning

tion of heterogeneous replicated environments, where different replication models can coexist and cooperate in hybrid configurations. In a multimaster configuration, for instance, multiple sites are equals and manage groups of replicated database objects. This means that applications are able to update any replicated table in any participating site. A different configuration sees a master site managing data propagation through the use of updatable snapshots. The two configurations can coexist in the same replicated environment.

The main difference between a multimaster configuration and a configuration based on updatable snapshots is that the first forces the replicated tables to be identical in all sites, while the second allows for an updatable snapshot to be a subset of the master table. With updatable snapshots, propagation happens in both senses, that is, a change operated on a table in the master site is replicated in all snapshots; conversely, a change operated on a remote updatable snapshot is replicated to the master and to all remaining snapshots. The Oracle replication option offers a fine granularity, allowing for a row-level propagation. To effectively design and manage an Oracle replicated environment, designers must familiarize themselves with the terminology used in this context.

> **Replication Object:** a database object existing on multiple servers in a replicated database system.
> **Replication Group:** a set of related replication objects that are grouped together to facilitate administration and management. A replication object can be a member of one replication group only.
> **Replication Site:** a database node participating in a replicated database environment. There are two different types of replication sites: a *master site* maintains a complete copy of all objects in a replication group, while a *snapshot site* supports read-only and updatable snapshots of the table data residing in an associated master site.
> **Replication Catalog:** a set of data dictionary tables and views that maintains information about replicated objects and replicated groups at every site.

Oracle 8 uses internal triggers to support replicated tables. In previous releases, Oracle used PL/SQL p-code triggers to do the same. Internal triggers are more reliable and more efficient because they are run within the Oracle kernel. They build remote procedure calls with the purpose of propagating data changes made at the local site to all remote replication participating sites. The automatically generated RPCs are stored by Oracle in its *deferred transaction queue*, which is implemented in every site. To manage propagation, Oracle uses its own *job queue mechanism*, implemented as a table holding data about what PL/SQL procedures have to be invoked to incur propagation, when to apply them, to what sites, etc.

Designers have further options to choose when determining the replication configuration of the architecture being built. They can decide to implement serial propagation, where Oracle replicates transactions one at a time, using the same order of commit observed at the originator site. If the nodes participating in a replicated environment are SMP machines, then Oracle offers parallel propagation, where multiple transit streams are open and used concurrently in a parallel environment, exactly like what happens when the Parallel Query Option is used. Oracle replication allows designers to choose either a pull or a push model for data propagation. When a master site table is modified, the changes are asynchronously pulled from the table to the snapshots. When an updatable snapshot is changed at a remote site, the changes are pushed to the master site table.

The main issue, when dealing with asynchronous replication, is data collision. We have seen how to avoid any potential collision by using techniques such as data dissemination, data consolidation, and workload partitioning. If a true peer-to-peer model needs to be implemented, then a conflict resolution policy has to be designed.

There are three types of replication conflicts:

1. Uniqueness conflicts
2. Update conflicts
3. Delete conflicts

A uniqueness conflict occurs when the replication of a row violates a referential integrity constraint. An update conflict materializes when an update to a row conflicts with another update to the same row performed during the latency period.

A delete conflict appears when a transaction originated in one site deletes a row updated in another site during the same latency period. Oracle organizes every column in a replicated table in *column groups*. The DBA can assign conflict resolution methods to each column group.

Oracle has prebuilt mechanisms for update collision detecting and resolving, but does not offer any prebuilt mechanism for the resolution of delete collisions. The prebuilt methods are:

1. Overwrite and discard value
2. Minimum and maximum value
3. Earliest and latest timestamp value
4. Additive and average value
5. Priority groups and site priority.

To understand how these methods work, the notion of data convergence is a prerequisite. Data convergence is the goal of the replication process. It means that ultimately all sites will have the same content for any given row. Every conflict resolution strategy or policy must guarantee data convergence. If an administrator does not assign conflict resolution methods to the columns of replicated tables, Oracle will simply log conflict data at the sites where those happened. This forces the DBA to resolve all conflicts manually, a task that can soon become overwhelmingly complex. A better solution is to use the Oracle prebuilt methods, or to create customized methods if the basic ones are not sophisticated enough. Notice that customized methods have to be used to resolve delete collisions. Multiple conflict resolution methods can be applied to the same column. Oracle will try to resolve the conflict by applying all defined methods in succession, until either the conflict is resolved or an error has to be logged, and manual resolution is required to ensure data convergence.

The Overwrite and Discard methods can be used with single master sites, because they don't guarantee data convergence in multimaster configurations. Basically, the overwrite method replaces the current value at the destination site with the new value from the originating site. The opposite is true for the discard method, which ignores the new value inserted or modified at the originating site.

With the minimum (or maximum) conflict resolution method, if the new value at the originating site is less than the value at the master site, then the new value is propagated. If the new value is greater than the current value, the conflict is resolved by leaving the value unchanged. The counter-intuitive part of this kind of conflict resolution is that if the new value at the originating site is the same as the current value, then the conflict is not resolved. An alternative, backup conflict resolution method has to be defined for the column in question.

In order to use the earliest (or latest) timestamp method, a date column must be part of the replicated column group, and that column must contain the system date and time taken at the moment when the transaction happened. When two transactions that occurred during the latency period affect the same row, the DBA can choose to keep the one that happened first (or last).

The additive method for conflict resolution adds the difference between the old and new values at the originating site to the current value at the destination site, as in the following formula:

```
final value = current value +
              (new value from originating site - old value
               in replicated column)
```

The average conflict resolution method averages the new column value from the originating site with the current value at the destination site, as in the following formula:

```
final value = (current value + new value from the originat-
               ing site)/2
```

It should be noticed that in a multimaster replication configuration, the additive method provides data convergence, while the average method does not. The average method provides data convergence only in configurations supporting one only master site, and updatable snapshots.

The DBA can define a priority group of columns, assigning priority levels to every possible value allowed in a specific column. This method works only for columns with a restricted set of possible values (cities, ZIP codes, etc). When Oracle detects a conflict, it keeps the value that has the highest priority associated to it. A slightly different scheme allows the DBA to assign specific priorities to particular sites, forcing data convergence on the value issued by the site with the highest priority.

If the prebuilt methods offered by Oracle Replication are not sophisticated enough, then customized methods can be built and assigned to column groups. Custom methods are PL/SQL functions, which return either TRUE (the function resolved every pending conflict) or FALSE (the function could not resolve the conflict). The replication option offers a programmatic interface to define column groups and to assign conflict resolution methods. It is a set of APIs to PL/SQL packages, and it is of not simple or immediate use. For this reason, Oracle provides the Replication Manager, a client application that provides a visual interface to the complex set of APIs. A user can record in a file the PL/SQL statements

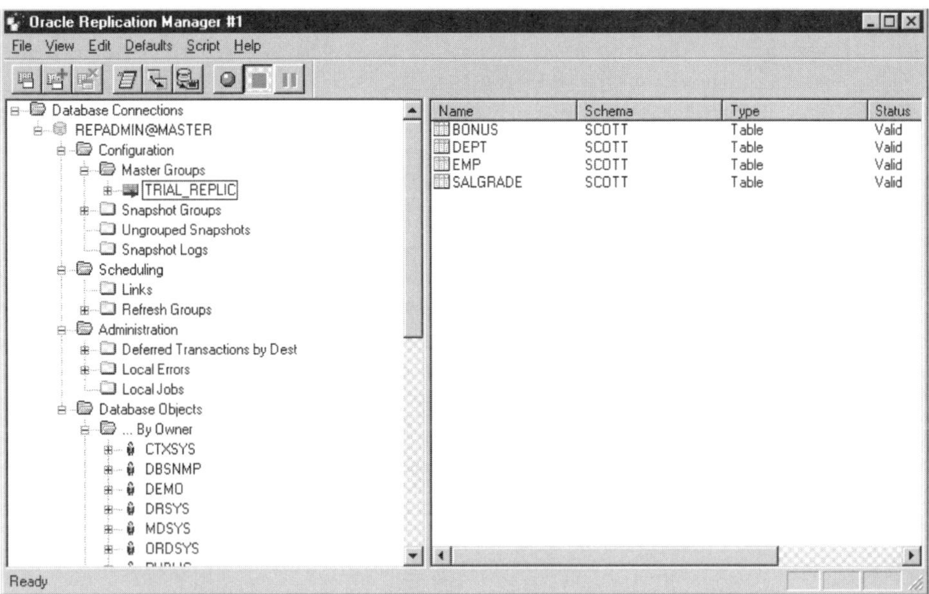

FIGURE 4.8 The Oracle Replication Manager at Work

generated by an interactive session with the Replication Manager, making it possible, for the same commands, to be repeatedly executed in different sites by running the automatically generated script.

Distributed databases and synchronous replication avoid data collision by definition, but the apparent administrative simplicity has a high associated cost, in terms of higher availability of the overall system. If only one component of the system is suffering from an outage, the potential is there for the entire system to be severely limited in its functionality. The peer-to-peer asynchronous replication model carries a big administrative burden in terms of data conflict detection and resolution. The most effective data replication approach is the one that is asynchronous and avoids data collision. We have examined three commonly used paradigms (data consolidation, data dissemination, and workload partitioning); others can be designed and implemented.

4.7 Design for Very Large Database/ Data Warehouse

It is not uncommon nowadays to find Oracle sites supporting very large databases, especially after the wide acceptance of the data mining and data warehouse paradigms. We have already considered the support that Oracle offers for scalability. When "large" refers to the user population, then the easy answer is parallelism. Unfortunately, there is no easy answer for the issues brought about by databases that store a huge amount of information. Luckily for designers, in general the databases huge in volume have a restricted number of users. Nevertheless, they represent a good challenge for designers and administrators, because of the number and the variety of variables to be considered and kept under control.

Ensor and Stevenson, in their "Oracle 8 Design Tips" book state that "if size alone requires the designer to take some special action in order for the enterprise to cope with the application, then it is big."

Several years ago, I joined a project that was building a database which, at that moment, was considered very large (little less than 100 gigabytes). It was my first experience with problems and issues related to the database size. I remember clearly I was impressed by the restrictions imposed by the designers and team leaders on the allowed SQL constructs. The DISTINCT and ORDER BY clauses were banned for SQL statements issued against the core tables. The application was mainly of the OLTP type, but management also required a few reports to be run overnight. We used all sorts of tricks to emulate more efficiently in Pro*C the banned SQL constructs.

We discovered that it was much more efficient to fetch all rows in one pass (obviously using host arrays), compute a 32 bit checksum of the string that we wanted to select distinctly, store the checksum in a hash table, discarding the checksums that were already in the hash table to eliminate the duplicates, rather than submitting the simple DISTINCT clause in a SQL query. The drawback of such an approach was that every simple report required an ad hoc Pro*C program, exactly like in the "good old days" of hierarchical databases. No flexibility whatsoever, we could use neither SQL*ReportWriter nor any of the third party tools that allow for a visual creation of reports and automatic generation of the SQL required. We were using Oracle 7.0, and we were rapidly approaching the top edge of the technology available.

Since then, Oracle greatly improved the support of very large databases. Two powerful weapons are now in the hands of designers and administrators to defeat the complexity and performance issues associated to the size of huge databases:

1. Partitioning
2. Parallelism

To a limited degree, partitioning is available in Oracle 7.3, in the form of *partitioned views*. Multiple tables are logically grouped in views by the means of the set operator UNION ALL. This is good enough for queries, but unfortunately it introduces other issues when inserts and updates have to be performed, because views obtained by joining multiple tables are not updatable.

Real partitioning has been introduced with Oracle 8. It is an optional component, which means it is available at an additional cost, and only if the Enterprise Edition has been purchased. If the database being implemented is very large, then the partitioning component is definitely worth the money, given the benefits it gives. Partitions, under Oracle 8, are *transparent*, because they are physically distinct but held and managed independently, and referred to transparently in the application code; they are also *independent*, which means that data can be accessed and modified in one partition even if other partitions of the same object are momentarily unavailable.

The big advantage offered by partition transparency, over the partitioned views of Oracle 7.3, is that the application code can refer to the same object in both queries and inserts or updates. In Oracle 8, code refers to the name INVOICE when it selects all the invoices from the four partitions INVOICES_QUARTER1, INVOICES_QUARTER2, INVOICES_QUARTER3, and INVOICES_QUARTER4; it also refers to INVOICE when it inserts invoices sent during the third quarter. Oracle understands what partition to use to store the invoices by looking at the partition key (in this case, the period of the year). The partitioning option allows for indexes to be partitioned as well as tables, which gives designers even more flexibility in laying down the physical structure of a very large database.

The Parallel Query Option (PQO) is the other Oracle feature commonly used to speed up data manipulation in a VLDB context. We have already encountered the PQO while examining the options that Oracle offers for scalable architectures. On multi-CPU platforms, the PQO allows for splitting of the work required to satisfy a query in multiple units of work, each carried out by a distinct CPU. Oracle transparently synchronizes every sub-task participating in the query, and a single result is presented back to the user. The PQO is effective only when a query performs a full table scan, at least partially. For this reason, the PQO is much more effective in data warehousing than in OLTP. In OLTP, every query should be highly optimized for users who interact with an application that follows strictly predetermined paths to access data. Every query can be supported by an index, for quick retrieval of selected data.

In data warehousing, it is not possible to support with indexes every possible query potentially submitted by a user. A data warehousing or DSS application, by its very nature, is likely to perform full table scans regularly, therefore exploiting the PQO capabilities. The PQO can also be effectively used for very large database administration, for instance, to create indexes in parallel and to load data into a table using the parallel feature provided with the Oracle utility that loads external data into a database, called SQL*Loader.

In recent years there has been a growing interest in Data Warehousing and in the various techniques used to provide the business operators with analytical data describing behaviour and trends associated with consumers of particular market segments. The focus of data warehousing is on large volumes of historical data, for quantitative analysis. The data needed for the analysis is generally already present in the company, perhaps scattered across different departments, gathered via different applications. A large part of the data warehousing effort is devoted to collecting and consolidating the required information, because the source data pre-existed in a variety of forms in the company well before the introduction of analysis based on data warehousing.

New OLTP applications should be designed with data warehousing in mind, by enabling, for instance, easy transfer of on-line data from the OLTP engine to the engine used for Decision Support analysis. Good software designers have to be able to predict the needs of the business, even before the business realizes the opportunities given by the availability of new technologies.

In business environments where data warehousing has been already introduced, it is very likely that the business specifications for a new or enhanced OLTP (or, more generically, operational) application will define adequate automated mechanisms to guarantee the feeding of the data warehouse with OLTP (or operational) data. If this is not the case, designers working at a new OLTP application should strive to leave the door open to possible links to data warehouses, likely to be implemented in the future.

We have introduced data warehousing without giving, so far, an appropriate definition. By data warehousing we intend a collection of corporate information, tools and techniques the purpose of which is to support business decisions. A common implementation of data warehousing is through the use of *star queries*. In a star query, there is one central table holding data related to a fact of interest for the business analysts (*fact table*). The fact table uses a set of ancillary tables, called *dimension tables*, which help gathering data about all entities participating in a fact. Let us take the example of an insurance company analyzing the car incidents where drivers holding a policy were involved:

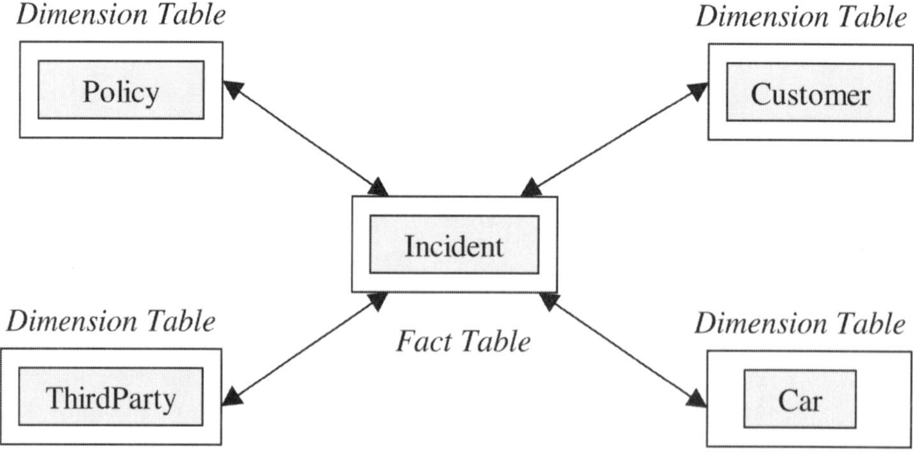

The management wants to restructure the discount policy, rewarding those drivers who are less likely to be involved in car accidents. The star configuration of the example provides all wanted data. With a few properly formulated queries, it would be possible to isolate the categories of cars, policy types, and people less likely to provoke incidents. Let us imagine that the same insurance company is investigating insurance frauds; it would be interested in knowing potential relationships between claimants, lawyers, and doctors involved in claims for accidents.

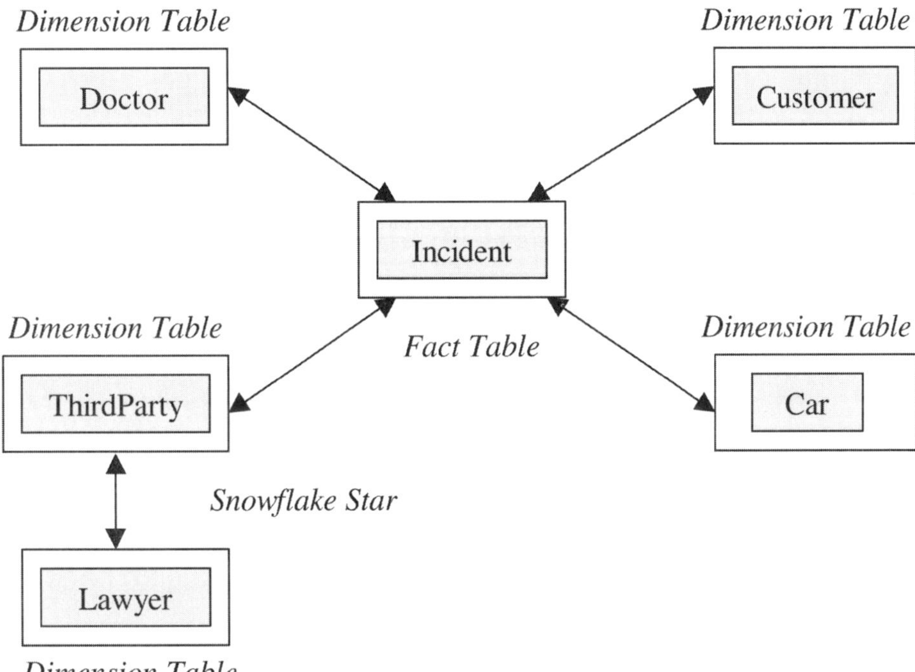

The star configuration shown in the new example is slightly different from the previous one. The fact table doesn't contain a direct reference to the lawyers involved in the incidents. To include that information in the query, an extended star query has to be used (it is also called *snowflake* star).

The structure of a star configuration is characterized by de-normalization. For this reason the normal table structure, typical of operational databases, is not suitable for data warehousing. It is common to use dedicated architectures for the implementation of data warehousing, which is a perfect candidate for data replication. An operational, OLTP database can be replicated asynchronously in tables stored in a DSS database. The structure of those tables can be a mirror image of the OLTP normalized structure. A background process, running on the DSS machine, can consolidate the normalized data into the de-normalized structure typical of a data warehousing configuration.

Designing operational tables with the possibility of an easy replication to a DSS database should be considered by architects and designers of new operational applications, even if an explicit specification has not been included in the official business requirement specification document. In other words, *don't build today what tomorrow could be considered as a constraining legacy: leave your doors open.*

The star configuration is typical of data warehousing, but data warehousing doesn't coincide with star queries; it is, in fact, a much wider discipline. A star query is only a basic technique that offers little sophistication, if compared with the more advanced options offered under the umbrella of data warehousing. To appreciate the magnitude of what can be achieved through the state-of-the-art data warehousing today, the notions of knowledge verification and knowledge discovery have to be considered. Knowledge is verified by proving or disproving well formulated hypotheses. Knowledge is discovered when trends and patterns in raw data are organized and grouped to flag unusual and potentially significant information.

Considering again the insurance company example, one is verifying knowledge when he/she submits a query to find out if young singles owning sport cars are more likely to cause accidents than middle aged married people owning family cars. Data discovery is one step forward, because it allows for identification of previously unidentified factors or intervening variables. Using the means made available by *data mining*, a user can instruct the data mining tool to identify the best predictors of accidents. The result of the query can be a set of well defined patterns, identifying precise categories of people who provoked in the past a statistically significant high percentage of accidents. The company can then decide not to take the risk of insuring the categories of people identified by the data mining query.

The Oracle offer in the data warehousing arena is very strong. Above all, Oracle Corporation offers the database server, powerful and scalable enough to satisfy the demanding needs of designers and architects opting for a data warehousing solution. It offers the distribution and replication features, which prove very useful for the automatic uploading of DSS databases. In addition, the Parallel Query and the Partitioning options simplify by a great deal the life of database administrators looking after very large databases.

Oracle also has specific products for the implementation of data warehousing solutions, most notably Oracle Express, a tool which offers On-Line Analytical Processing (OLAP) capabilites, gathering data stored in heterogeneous environments.

Summary

The main goal of the chapter has been to familiarize the reader with the rich set of options offered by Oracle to designers and architects. We examined the intellectual process commonly used to deal with real life business problems, in order to design and implement effective solutions. We considered the intellectual tools used to build the model of the problem (analysis) and the solution (design). They are above all abstraction, but also cohesion, coupling/de-coupling, information hiding and complexity reduction.

After the generic introduction to application design, we identified specific areas where Oracle, if properly used, gives its best: flexibility, performance, scalability, reliability, distribution/replication of data, and support for very large databases/data warehousing.

For each identified area, we examined potential issues and ways to avoid or ease them. After having read this chapter, the reader should have a reasonably precise idea on the points of strength of Oracle, and on how to utilize the more advanced features to design applications and architectures that exploit the rich set of options made available by the market leader in the database field.

Chapter 5

DETAILED DESIGN

This chapter focuses on aspects and issues that can potentially arise in the detail design phase of projects based on Oracle technologies. Once the back-end database has been chosen and its purchase approved, architects and designers must make important software engineering decisions that will have a considerable impact on the overall success of the final product. When the information stored in an Oracle database must be made accessible to interactive users, designers must choose from several communication models, such as traditional client/server, WEB enabled client/server, multi-tier client/server and dumb terminals. The number of potential concurrent users is an important factor that influences the overall architecture of an application.

The chapter discusses various client/server models commonly used in Oracle projects, focusing on business requirements, rather than technical sophistication, to provide optimal solutions that take into account the pre-existent culture of the company implementing the IT project. Many projects fail not because of technical inadequacy, but because the final product doesn't fulfil the end-user expectations, or because it forces business practices perceived as unnatural or cumbersome by the employees who ultimately interact with the application.

Finally, the chapter delves into Oracle-specific detailed design issues, which must be solved very early in the design phase, in order not to become serious problems further down the software development lifecycle. Issues like referential integrity, use of host arrays, and bind variables in SQL statements are dealt with in the final part of the chapter.

5.1 Choosing a Development Environment / Language

Once the architecture of the application has been determined, it is time to specify and adopt a development environment before delving into design details. The environment chosen plays an important role in determining the future directions of the design process that will follow later in the project. Both technical and business requirements must be taken into consideration when choosing the development environment. Sometimes, a product technically superior has to be sacrificed in favor of a product that offers better long term stability. At the beginning of the nineties, the Gartner Group correctly predicted that Borland would experience financial difficulties. Choosing Borland technologies for a new project would have increased the project risk. Sometime after the Gartner Group prediction, Borland was effectively in trouble and on the verge of collapse, and was financially saved by Novell, which bought the spreadsheet QuattroPro, injecting enough cash to allow Borland to overtake the financial crisis.

Soon after Delphi was released, and the company flourished. It is currently doing well, by embracing the enterprise market and becoming a leader in middleware and development tools. This example shows the importance of business related factors in determining the technology used in a project. Today, it would be advisable to chose Borland/Inprise technology, especially to implement CORBA based projects.

Sometimes, regulatory bodies impose legally binding requirements for archiving data and transaction information maintained by a computerized system after the system has been decommissioned. If that period is very long, say seven or even ten years, then the designers must ensure that the archiving technology will survive the test of time. This can have an impact on today's design decisions, perhaps limiting the range of acceptable options. The point is that a number of intervening factors, such as business requirements, legal requirements, available personnel, company's culture, etc., determine the technology adopted.

Every IT project has associated risks, which must be carefully managed to minimize their impact on the project. Adopting one technology in preference to another has above all a business impact. It may also have technical implications, but the business priority must not be overlooked.

A company implementing a major mission critical application using Java in early 1996 would have taken huge risks. Currently, at the time of this writing, the technology built around Java appears to have matured to the extent that makes it a sound business option for mission critical implementations. The culture present in the company wanting the new software product also plays a significant role. The company culture has to be compatible with the technology proposed. It would probably be hard to justify adopting Java enthusiastically, with a big-bang type of approach in a software development environment consisting only of COBOL and mainframes. A much softer approach to such a transition should be prepared and implemented.

One of the principal tasks faced by designers of a new system is to understand the pre-existing company's culture. This understanding is fundamental to the choice of a technology compatible with attitudes, habits, and even idiosyncrasies present in the business environment. Failing to do so introduces further risks for a project, which may well be successful from a technical point of view, but *de facto* rejected by the workforce. A typical example is imposing a GUI interface in environments where it is not appropriate. Working people don't look for esthetically appealing forms. They are more concerned with easy and productive ways to accomplish their tasks. For example, a mouse requires more space on the desk and forces the operator to move a hand from the keyboard to the mouse pad. In environment mainly dedicated to data entry, this translates to a loss of productivity.

5.2 Application Architecture Paradigms

There are several different models governing the interaction between users and an application. A well known paradigm is the client-server model, which emerged towards the end of the eighties. With this model, computing power is off-loaded from the server to intelligent devices (PCs and workstations), which handle the presentation logic locally, freeing precious resources on the server.

The client-server model was initially extended and then re-invented to fit the new interactive capabilities offered by the WEB. Most of the computer magazines' and the general IT debate focuses on the client-server paradigm, either in its pure form or adapted for the WEB. The more traditional server-centric model is largely neglected, having lost momentum and appeal.

Nevertheless, mission critical business applications supporting large corporations still make good use of the server-centric, dumb terminal based architecture. This model undoubtedly offers significant advantages in the area of centralized administration, easier scalability and network bandwidth. In spite of not being fashionable, the server-centric model is still effective in specific environments, typically with a large volume of data entry, mainly through the numeric keypad, as in the customer account keeping applications commonly used by bank tellers. Another common application of this model is where input devices are positioned in computer-hostile environments, typically close to assembly lines in factories, where dust and grease are part of the environment. Dumb terminals are likely to have a longer lifetime in hostile environments than the more fragile PCs.

Several variations of the client-server paradigm exist. The qualifying aspect of a specific client-server model type is the method by which various components of an application are grouped together and coupled. One can identify three main components that are always present in a traditional database-centric application:

- ❑ Presentation Logic
- ❑ Business (or application) Logic
- ❑ Data Logic

In a two-tier client-server implementation, designers are forced to fit three components into two tiers. The presentation logic definitely belongs in the first tier, the client. The data logic definitely belongs in the second tier, the server. The problem is fitting the business logic into the model. There are three available options:

1. Business logic on the client side (fat client syndrome)
2. Business logic on the server (fat server syndrome)
3. Business logic split between the two tiers

In the fat client model, the server is seen a black box, which receives SQL statements and gives back result sets. Data validation and business logic are coded in the client application, which usually requires a reasonably sized client device, typically a PC with adequate processing capabilities and large amounts of memory. In spite of being generally criticized by the IT press, this option presents a few advantages, mainly simpler design efforts, and less development costs. Young graduates on low salaries and with little experience can code such an application. Few or no skills are required on the server side. The typical case is an MS Visual Basic or MS Access application that accesses an Oracle database through a Jet Engine-ODBC connection. Among the drawbacks are absolute lack of scalability and underutilization of the server resources.

In the fat server model the business logic is implemented in the server, usually in the form of database stored procedures. This approach offers better scalability and slimmer clients but requires either multi-skilled people or a larger team, including client specialists and PL/SQL programmers.

By adopting the third approach, designers strive to achieve better scalability by balancing the computational needs between the client and the server. Usually data validation is implemented in the client, while more complex business logic is embedded in stored procedures. The drawback with this approach is more complex maintenance.

Because of its relative simplicity, the two-tier client-server model was widely adopted at the beginning of the client-server revolution. It is also called the *first generation* client-server model to identify its age and its intimate association with the first wave of client-server computing.

Enthusiasm for the new client-server paradigm was soon mitigated by the problems encountered by designers and IT professionals adopting client-server solutions, mainly in the area of scalability. The two-tier model, irrespective of whether it is implemented through a fat client or a fat server, is not really scalable. It cannot support thousands of concurrent users. To achieve a high level of

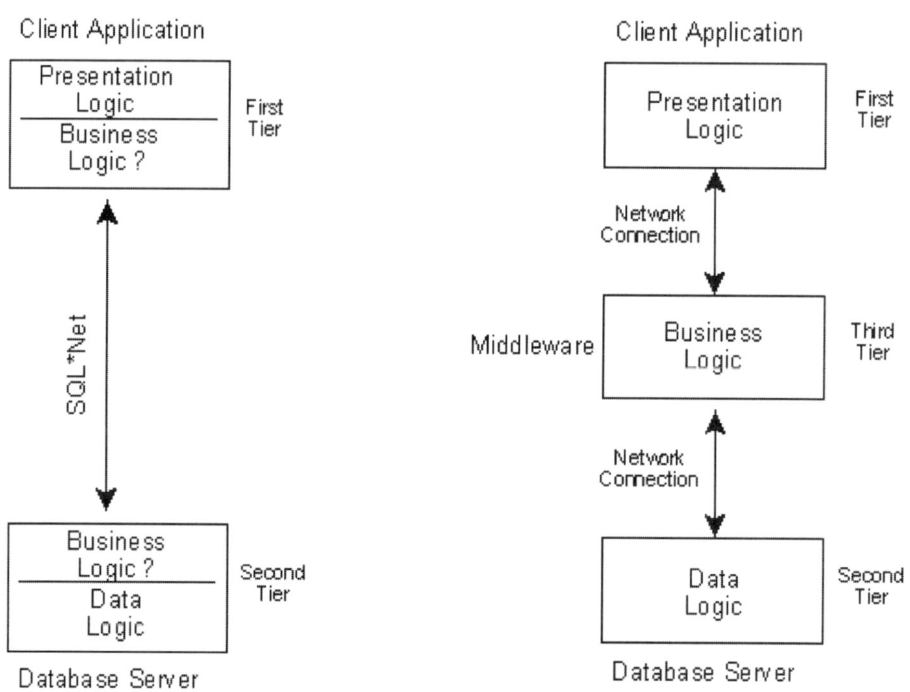

FIGURE 5.1 Two-tier and three-tier client-server models

scalability, one more tier is needed in the model to resolve the conflict between three application components and only two tiers. In a three-tier client-server model, the business logic resides in a separate tier. This approach simplifies both the presentation logic and the data logic and provides a clear-cut distinction between the various components of the application.

In a two-tier implementation, the client application has to use SQL*Net to connect with the Oracle database on the back-end. In a three-tier implementation SQL*Net is not usually needed, because the middleware products provide an alternative connection method between the client and the server. Chapter 16 will cover the middleware products in depth. In this context it is enough to say that middleware represents the backbone for the implementation of the third tier.

By switching to a three-tier model, designers can definitely achieve the wanted increased scalability.

Unfortunately, one fundamental problem, which has plagued the client-server model since its appearance on the IT scene, still persists: the *deployment nightmare*. Real life business applications change regularly, in line with business requirements. Consequently, the application's business rules must also change. New database fields have to be created, and sometimes destroyed. A change performed to the database structure implies modifications to the forms displayed by the client application. The forms must be modified and deployed to allow the users to see and modify the new fields or hide the obsolete ones.

In a small departmental environment, this is not a serious problem. If a few tens of users load the client application from a shared disk, it is enough to store the new application executable in only one location. This allows all users to load the upgraded application the next working day. When the user population includes a few thousand entities, physically scattered across a large country, as in the case of the United States or Australia, the magnitude of the problem becomes apparent. Synchronizing the massive deployment of an upgraded client application is the single most important environmental criterion that can rule out the client-server model for supporting a very large user base.

One solution is to make the client application both aware of its own release number and able to detect an upgraded database release. The client can then automatically download a new version of itself when a discrepancy between the release number of the client and the release number of the client is detected at application startup.

There are two problems with this approach. First, large corporations have very strict policies regulating security. An automatic download triggered and managed by software is unlikely compatible with policies enforcing high security. Second, one can imagine the strain put on the network by thousands of users who concurrently download a few hundred kilobytes to several megabytes of new client software when the upgrade is released.

The traditional methods for client application deployment have been a major obstacle, which prevented the client-server model from achieving true scalability. At the beginning of the nineties, while the IT community was struggling to resolve client-server deficiencies, two major external influences surfaced. Their initial development occurred independently from one another, but an intimate relationship evolved. Together they contribute to revitalize the client-server paradigm. The first was the sudden success and proliferation of the Internet. The second was the birth of Java. The Internet provided a simple, low-cost infrastructure to support information flows. Java was initially conceived as a small footprint language to drive appliances of mass production like microwaves and washing machines. It became the "language of the Internet" overnight, thanks to its ability to run from a WEB browser.

The model inaugurated by the coupling of Java with the Internet represented an immediate solution for the typical client-server deployment problem. A Java applet is downloaded from the server *on the fly*, before interacting with the user. A single copy of the client application resides on the server, which is accessed by all users to download the Java byte codes. An application change is not deployed any more. It doesn't need to be propagated to the users. It is sufficient to put a new Java class in the shared directory accessed by the client. The next downloading operated by the client's browser will fetch the upgraded release. The idea of using the protocols and the apparatus of the Internet as a means for internal corporate networks generated the concept summarized by the word *Intranet*. Marc Andressen, Vice President for technology at Netscape Corporation, announced to the world that "client-server was dead." In reality, the client-server paradigm was simply being redefined and extended to include the WEB model.

The "deployment nightmare" was finally over, but the issue of scalability to meet the needs of mission critical applications for a large user base, was still unresolved. Oracle Corporation has been among the first vendors to understand the WEB revolution, offering WEB based solutions for publishing information stored by Oracle servers. The first wave of products and solutions strove to simplify access and publishing of information stored in Oracle databases. It didn't really focus on scalability. It is only with Oracle Web Server release 3, appearing in late 1997, that a complete and scalable solution for the implementation of mission critical applications over the Internet/Intranet was finally available to designers and IT professionals.

Another component, which initially followed a parallel development path totally disjointed from the Internet, now provides the scalability desperately needed by designers to develop mission critical Internet applications. That component is the Common Object Request Broker Architecture (CORBA). The CORBA standard, initially acclaimed as the panacea for every facet of distributed computing, suffered slower acceptance and growth than expected. Nevertheless, it progressed through various releases and achieved stability and maturity. In the same way Java was promoted as the "language of the Internet" for its small footprint, CORBA was adopted as the backbone for integrated application communication over the Internet. Oracle Web Server 3.0 provides a CORBA cartridge that finally integrates CORBA in the Oracle architecture.

Has the WEB model totally supplanted the more traditional two- and three-tier client-server model? Not at all. The two will coexist for a long while, one being the complement of the other.

5.3 Rapid Application Development Tools: Compatibility and Performance Issues

Once the architecture of the back-end server has been decided, and the application model defined, the next important choice is the development environment. Technical IT magazines contain plenty of advertising extolling the virtues of products that supposedly can cut the development time down to only one-tenth by allowing "point and click," instantaneous creation of the most complex applications. The crude reality is that, to use the words of F.P. Brooks Jr. [1987], there are no *silver bullets* individually capable of providing the magic to produce such great gains.

Last time that happened was with the move from assembler to high-level languages, which resulted from a shift in the programming paradigm rather than the introduction of a single product. The appearance of visual programming environments, such as Visual Basic, Delphi and Powerbuilder, produced a large increase in productivity, but the increase was less significant than the shift to third generation languages.

If the application being built is large and mission critical, using the client-server paradigm is very likely to require two distinct development environments: one for the server, typically based on either Pro*C or Pro*Cobol and PL/SQL, mainly dedicated to batch jobs, reporting processing and interfaces with legacy systems; a second, mainly devoted to handling data input and display of data for the user.

When choosing among competing products for a development environment, especially in a mission critical context, the following essential selection criteria should be observed:

- Vendor stability
- Estimated and effective gain
- Maturity
- Learning curve
- Future development

The producer of a development tool, on which the designers of a system bet their credibility, becomes a sort of *de facto* partner in the venture. This very fact reduces the possible options to a few vendors. Chapter 10 will examine the most commonly used development environment and tools suitable for interacting with Oracle as a back-end database. The vendors producing them are likely to still be in business five years from now. Making predictions for longer terms is virtually impossible in the IT field.

The real gain obtained by the adoption of Rapid Application Development (RAD) tools should be carefully measured, perhaps by building a prototype before delving into production code. One cannot estimate time for client application construction on vendor's claims, 90 percent of which are highly inflated.

In order to judge the maturity of a product, one should look at the history of the vendor. Microsoft, for example, is known to "get it right at the third attempt." It happened with MS-Windows, Visual Basic, and other products. In contrast Inprise (Imprise/Borland.com) is known to provide very stable first release products. Delphi release 1, for example, needed only minor patches; it didn't require a major rewriting and is still Inprise's offer for applications in a 16-bit environment years after its first appearance.

Every new product has an associated application developer learning curve that should be carefully evaluated, to establish its impact on development time estimates. This is particularly true for products that are really revolutionary and, by their very nature, off the well beaten track in software development terms. A user interface different from those consolidated by Visual Basic or Delphi, for example, would require a higher learning curve, simply to acquaint developers with the new environment.

The future directions planned by a vendor for its product may also have a major impact on designers' choices. A product is often chosen because it supports a specific platform, say OpenVMS, for example. After the product's second release, the OpenVMS support is discontinued due to a drop in OpenVMS popularity. A project built around that technology instantly suffers from a major drawback. This usually implies completely rewriting for the client with another tool. Another example is choosing a product for its very fast performance, to realize that the third or fourth release shifted the focus from performance to portability. Suddenly, the number of supported platforms increases significantly, but performance is likely to decrease on all of them.

As a rule of thumb, development tools that support only an ODBC connection to Oracle are not suitable for mission critical applications serving a large user base. In addition, the adoption of development tools that cannot be used, or are very difficult to use with middleware, should be carefully evaluated and possibly avoided. Usually, the low-end version of a development tool is shipped with ODBC drivers. The corresponding enterprise edition usually provides native Oracle drivers which support direct connection to Oracle SQL*Net. The most commonly used development tools, produced by the major vendors, all support native drivers and middleware. This is not usually the case for leading edge products just released by start-up companies. Products that allow only dynamic SQL to access the back-end database should not even be considered. They cripple any hope for even minimal scalability, as we will see further ahead in this chapter.

5.4 Detailed Design Issues

After selecting the application development environments for both the server and the client components, the detailed design phase can start. There are a few recurring design issues that an application developer should be aware of when designing an application that interacts with an Oracle database.

Designers who neglect to resolve those issues early in the design phase will confront them sooner or later. At that point in time resources required to resolve the consequent problems may have escalated to an unacceptable level. It is therefore better to sort these issues out at the beginning, to avoid problems later. The Oracle related design issues are:

- ❑ Treatment of NULL values and indicator variables
- ❑ Referential integrity
- ❑ Bind variables
- ❑ Host arrays
- ❑ Char and Varchar2 data types

5.4.1 NULL VALUES AND INDICATOR VARIABLES

The treatment of null values has implications and consequences, which must be evaluated and dealt with by establishing policies and guidelines early in the design phase. An Oracle database can be configured to reject insertions or updates that would result in certain columns not receiving a value, that is, being set to null. A column can be forced not to be null by using the canonical ANSI SQL syntax:

```
CREATE TABLE CUSTOMER
(
        Surname       VARCHAR2 (30) NOT NULL,
        Name          VARCHAR2 (25) NOT NULL,
        ...
        ...
);
```

Oracle prevents columns being left blank by creating—behind the scenes—a constraint with a meaningless name, as in "SYS_C00123." If absolute ANSI portability is not of paramount importance, and a sensible naming convention is in place, it is better to use an Oracle specific syntax to define a not nullable column, as in the following example:

```
CREATE TABLE CUSTOMER
(
        Surname       VARCHAR2 (30)
              CONSTRAINT CUSTOMER#SURNAME_1_NN NOT NULL
              CONSTRAINT CUSTOMER#SURNAME_2_UC CHECK
                    (SURNAME=UPPER (SURNAME)),
        Name          VARCHAR2 (25)
              CONSTRAINT CUSTOMER#NAME_1_NN NOT NULL,
        ...
        ...
);
```

By following the convention <table_name>#<field_name>_<constraint_number> _constraint_type, as in CUSTOMER#SURNAME_1_NN, the DBA has better control over the data dictionary. The following query:

```
Select constraint_name from user_constraints
where table_name = 'CUSTOMER'
```

displays a much more human readable constraint list, rather than a series of meaningless constraint names like SYS_C00232, SYS_C00233, etc,:

```
CONSTRAINT_NAME
------------------------------
CUSTOMER#SURNAME_1_NN
CUSTOMER#SURNAME_2_UC
CUSTOMER#NAME_1_NN
...
```

When the time comes to drop a not null constraint, it is easy to identify it:

```
alter table customer drop constraint CUSTOMER#NAME_1_NN;
```

Oracle does not store null values in the corresponding column index. This implies that Oracle doesn't use an index when searching for null values, even if the only column in the where clause is indexed. The net result of a query like:

```
select surname from customer where name is NULL;
```

will always be a full table scan, that is, Oracle will sequentially scan all blocks containing rows belonging to the customer table, storing them in its own global memory, the System Global Memory (SGA), to provide the calling program with the result set. Oracle would perform a full table scan even if an index on the column "name" was available.

A better way to treat null values is to prevent their occurrence by defining a not null constraint for the column, together with a default value:

```
CREATE TABLE CUSTOMER
(
      Surname     VARCHAR2 (30)
            CONSTRAINT CUSTOMER#SURNAME_1_NN NOT NULL
            CONSTRAINT CUSTOMER#SURNAME_2_UC CHECK
                  (SURNAME=UPPER (SURNAME)),
      Name        VARCHAR2 (25) DEFAULT 'UNKNOWN'
            CONSTRAINT CUSTOMER#NAME_1_NN NOT NULL,
      ...
      ...
);
```

Allowing nulls can occasionally be a specific design decision. The main reasons are:

1. The column is almost always NULL.
2. The column selection criterion is never NULL.
3. The search criteria for the column will always be IS NOT NULL.
4. One wants to save space, and an index on a column that contains almost entirely null values is very small in size.

In all other cases, designers should define not null constraints and default values rather than null values for columns containing strings, unless business rules dictate otherwise.

A different approach is required for the treatment of numeric columns. If any of the statistical functions will be used to perform calculations on a numeric column, the use of nulls is unavoidable. A null value in a numeric column is considered as a *missing* value. Statistical group functions disregard the null value when performing a computation. Therefore, it is not possible to define a default value for a null entry in a numeric column without the results of statistical functions applied to the column being biased.

If a numeric column stores a nominal scale, as in the case of codes that are simply placeholders for strings, a not null constraint can be defined. The default value can define the residual category, e.g., the typical *99 –other*. From a statistical point of view, it is meaningless to use nominal scales in any numerical computation. If, on the other hand, a numeric column stores true numbers and there is even the smallest likelihood of statistical computations against it, null values must be allowed.

Why is so much emphasis placed on minimizing the number of nullable columns present in the database? The reason is that nullable columns require particular care by programmers, resulting in more code and complexity. Fetching a null value in a program that incorporates embedded SQL, such as Pro*C or Pro*Cobol, causes Oracle to return an error:

```
ORA-01405: fetched column value is NULL
```

Oracle stops processing and returns as soon as it encounters the null value. There are three ways to prevent ORA-01405 from occurring:

1. Applying the NVL function against the nullable column
2. Using Indicator Variables
3. Setting the compatibility mode of the pre-compiler (DBMS) to V6[1], or
4. Enabling the UNSAFE_NULL pre-compiler option

---

[1]The Oracle pre-compilers offer a set of options that alter the default behavior of the executable code. The options can either be activated on the command line, when invoking the pro-compiler, or they can appear in the code, in the form of *inline statement* (EXEC ORACLE OPTION (option_name=value)).

Options (3) and (4) are not really viable. The V6 compatibility mode has other unwanted side effects. The UNSAFE_NULL is valid only when the precompiler option MODE is set to Oracle and the DBMS option is set to V7 or V6CHAR. UNSAFE_NULL is also ineffective on PL/SQL blocks contained in Pro*C.

The NVL function forces Oracle to return a predefined value instead of a null when it finds null values in a column:

```
select cust_name, NVL(age,-99) from CUSTOMER;
```

In the above example, if age is null, the value –99 is returned, and the query returns successfully. The NVL function can also be used for null strings:

```
select cust_name, NVL(SUBURB,'Unknown') from CUSTOMER;
```

It should be noted that NVL coerces an arbitrary value into a variable that, in theory, should contain the corresponding database value. This is due to the impedance mismatch between Oracle's treatment of a null value, and the high level computer languages notion of a null value.

Using indicator variables provides a more effective way to handle null values. An indicator variable is a numeric variable, typically a 2-byte integer, that can be associated with a host variable for the purpose of monitoring what happens when Oracle interacts with the host variable. Oracle stores a numeric code in an indicator variable:

- -1 means that the column value is null and the value of the host variable is indeterminate
- 0 means Oracle assigned a column value to the host variable
- >0 means Oracle assigned a truncated column value to the host variable. The length of the host variable was shorter than the effective column length and Oracle removed the characters in excess.

The indicator variable mechanism allows programmers to monitor and check for null values in host variables without coercing arbitrary values into them.

The next example shows how to use indicator variables in Pro*C code:

```
main()
{
        char  customer_name[31];
        int   customer_name_ind;
```

```
        EXEC SQL
        SELECT CUST_NAME into
              :customer_name:customer_name_ind
        WHERE CUST_ID='12567';

        if(customer_name_ind == -1)/*CUST_NAME is null, stop
        processing */
        {
              ...
              ...
        }
        else
        {
              /* Process the entry, a customer name has been
                 found */
              ...
              ...
        }
}
```

Indicator variables are also used to insert null values in Oracle columns. Instead of hard coding the insertion of a null value by using the keyword NULL in the insert statement, as in the following example:

```
EXEC SQL
INSERT INTO CUSTOMER (CUST_NAME) VALUES (NULL);
```

an indicator variable provides a more flexible method to accomplish the same result:

```
customer_name_ind = -1;
strcpy(customer_name,"\0");

EXEC SQL
INSERT INTO CUSTOMER (CUST_NAME)
VALUES (:customer_name:customer_name_ind);
```

To summarize, our recommendations about null values:

1. Establish a comprehensive naming convention for all objects in an Oracle database, including constraints—specifically, NOT NULL constraints.
2. Name constraints explicitly; do not rely on the name automatically assigned by Oracle to unnamed constraints.
3. Minimize the definition of columns that accept null values. Use a default value and a NOT NULL constraint in preference to null columns.

4. Oracle cannot use indexes to search for null values. Every query that has an IS NULL construct in the where clause produces a full table scan.
5. When nullable columns are unavoidable, *always* use indicator variables to access them in preference to the NVL function. When inserting null values, use indicator variables instead of hard coding the NULL keyword in the SQL statement.

5.4.2 REFERENTIAL INTEGRITY

Referential integrity is an essential part of the relational theory because it assists in achieving data consistency and is extensively supported by Oracle. Referential integrity ensures that no orphan rows are left when a parent row is deleted and that no children can be inserted in absence of a parent row in a parent table. This is automatically carried out by the database engine, without the intervention of user code. Unfortunately, Oracle's implementation of referential integrity requires designers to be aware of its potential serious side effects. Let us take a close look at how referential integrity is handled by Oracle:

```
TABLE CUSTOMER               parent table
(CUST_ID            NUMBER(5)        PRIMARY KEY,
 ...
 ...)

TABLE CUSTOMER_CONTACT              child table
(
 CONTACT_NAME       VARCHAR2(30)      PRIMARY KEY,
 CUST_ID            NUMBER(5)   REFERENCES CUSTOMER(CUST_ID)
      ON DELETE CASCADE,
 ...
 ...)
```

In the example above, the CUSTOMER table contains data about customer companies and CUSTOMER_CONTACT table stores data about people working for those companies who have relationships with our company. In CUSTOMER_CONTACT, one finds the names of the relevant people to be contacted, for example, in case of dispute. It doesn't make sense to store an entry in CUSTOMER_CONTACT without a corresponding entry in CUSTOMER. Constraints prevent the insertion of a record for Mr. Johnson in CUSTOMER_CONTACT if the column CUST_ID either is NULL or specifies a CUST_ID number that does not exist in CUSTOMER. In this case Oracle would issue the following message:

```
ERROR at line 1:
ORA-02291:  integrity constraint (SYSTEM.SYS_C00941)
            violated - parent key not found
```

The field CUST_ID in CUSTOMER_CONTACT was created with the "on delete cascade" clause in the referential integrity definition. The effect is that an automatic deletion of all customer contacts referring to a company occurs when the company is deleted from the CUSTOMER table. This makes sense; if one removes a company from the customer table it is likely that no further relationship will be maintained with people working for that company. It is good practice to avoid having names in CUSTOMER_CONTACT corresponding to people who won't be contacted any longer; such would waste space in the database and confuse the users.

Referential integrity (RI) doesn't come free. To work properly, RI requires an index on the foreign key in the child table, that is, such as in the example above, the field CUSTOMER_CONTACT.CUST_ID should be indexed. To ensure RI, Oracle must be able to scan both parent and child tables. When a row is deleted from the parent table, or a primary key is modified, Oracle scans the child table to delete all children or verify that there are no orphans left. Conversely, when a record is inserted in the child table, Oracle scans the parent table to ensure that a parent exists. When an index supports referential integrity on the child table, only the child rows affected by the check or deletion are locked. If the foreign key is not indexed, Oracle places a share lock on the entire child table for the duration of the transaction. With a share lock, other sessions can access the rows in the tables in read-only mode, but they cannot update or insert. Since the transaction can last for many seconds, locking becomes an issue for applications with hundreds of concurrent users.

The easy solution is to index every foreign key present in a table. Unfortunately, this method is often impractical; many mission-critical applications are built around a few core tables, each comprised of many columns. If a table contains 20 or even 30 foreign keys, creating indexes to support all of them is definitely out of the question. Inserting rows in such a table would have a tremendous impact on performance, causing Oracle to update 20 or 30 indexes in one transaction.

How can this problem be solved? Sorry, but there is no unanimously agreed solution. The following is a simple recipe that has been successfully used at several sites:

1. For each of the core tables, perform an ABC categorization in order of importance for the columns that need referential integrity. Strive not to have more than four or five columns in category "A," and not more than ten columns in category "B."
2. Build the indexes required to support referential integrity for the columns included in category "A."
3. Put the logic to enforce referential integrity in stored procedures for all fields included in category "B". Enable triggers that invoke the stored procedures at a row level, for insertion, deletion, and updating.

4. There are two options for dealing with the fields included in category "C." One can simply disregard referential integrity during the normal database activity, and use batch procedures incorporated in the database housekeeping tasks to clean any inconsistencies. The second option is to leave referential integrity to the application code.

In summary, use the Oracle built-in features to enforce referential integrity. If a table contains too many foreign keys, enable the Oracle enforced referential integrity sparingly on a selected set of fields. Use triggers to invoke PL/SQL and programmatically check referential integrity for less important fields. For the unimportant foreign key fields, leave the RI checks in the application code, or use housekeeping procedures to reestablish referential consistency.

5.4.3 BIND VARIABLES

Every SQL statement arriving at the Oracle server is compared against the SQL statements already processed and stored in a sub-area of the Oracle System Global Area (SGA), called the shared pool. If a match is found, the SQL statement is not parsed by the engine before processing. Oracle identifies the blocks containing the wanted data. If the wanted blocks are already in memory—in a sub-area of the SGA called buffer cache—physical I/O is not necessary, and the data can be immediately sent back to the requesting application. If the wanted blocks are not in the buffer cache, then physical I/O is performed to load the requested blocks into the buffer cache, before the rows are sent back to the requesting application.

On the other hand, if the SQL statement sent to the engine is not in the shared pool, the statement is parsed by Oracle. That is, the statement is verified to make sure that the tables referred actually exist, that all columns mentioned in the statement exist in their respective tables, and that the user has the appropriate privileges.

Parsing a statement is quite an expensive operation. Parsing statements that do not perform full table scans can take more than half of the CPU time required to fetch the data. The expensive parsing step should therefore be avoided whenever possible, or at least minimized. Consider the following Oracle trace report from a session that submitted only SQL statements that didn't use bind variables:

```
OVERALL TOTALS FOR ALL NON-RECURSIVE STATEMENTS

call      count     cpu  elapsed disk  query  current   rows
----      ----   ------  ------- ----  ------ -------  -----
Parse     28566  161.55  201.11     0       3       0      0
Execute   14283    3.41    3.48     0       0       0      0
Fetch     14283   90.75   96.94     4  187212       2  13412
----      ----   ------  ------- ----  ------ -------  -----
total     57132  255.71  301.53     4  187215       2  13412
```

The report shows that approximately 63% of the CPU time was spent parsing SQL statements! Which is not necessarily the worst case scenario.

Every SQL statement is parsed at least once: the first time that it is sent to the engine. *Bind variables* should be used to avoid subsequent re-parsing. A bind variable is like a query parameter. It is a placeholder for a real value, which can vary every time the statement is executed. As usual, an example better clarifies the concept:

1. ```
   Select * from CUSTOMER where CUST_NAME='Taylor';
   Select * from CUSTOMER where CUST_NAME='Jones';
   ```
2. ```
   my_cust = "Taylor";
   Select * from CUSTOMER where CUST_NAME=:my_cust;
   my_cust = "Jones";
   Select * from CUSTOMER where CUST_NAME=:my_cust;
   ```

In (1) bind variables have not been used. The value of the where clause is specified literally, surrounded by single quotes. In (2) the bind variable my_cust has been used. Before invoking the first select statement, the content of the bind variable is set to "Taylor," causing Oracle to select all rows from CUSTOMER in which the customer name is equal to "Taylor." Before invoking the same statement again, the content of the bind variable has been changed to "Jones." The same statement is invoked, and this time all records where cust_name is equal to "Jones" will be returned.

The significant difference between (1) and (2) is that in (1) the same statement is re-parsed, while in (2) no re-parsing is performed by Oracle when the statement is executed the second time. The SQL syntax in (1) is generally referred to as "dynamic SQL,"[1] while the SQL syntax of (2) is known as "static SQL".

Now, imagine the CPU resources wasted by the Oracle engine when hundreds of clients all submit the same dynamic SQL statement. Oracle compares the literal string containing the SQL statement against all SQL statements already stored in the shared pool. Oracle cannot determine that

```
Select * from CUSTOMER where CUST_NAME='Taylor';
```

and

```
Select * from CUSTOMER where CUST_NAME='Jones';
```

---

[1]It is not accurate to define SQL statements that don't use bind variables as dynamic SQL. SQL statements dynamically processed by Oracle through PL/SQL packages (DBMS_SQL) or pre-compilers can contain bind variables. Since most of the first-wave visual query builders used to produce SQL statements dynamically, storing literal strings or numbers in the where clause, instead of bind variables, it is still common to refer to SQL statements that use literals instead of variables as "dynamic" SQL.

are basically the same statement. It considers them different, re-parsing the statement over and over. The shared pool has a finite size. It cannot contain all SQL statements ever sent to the engine. When the space for new SQL statements is exhausted, the oldest statements are discarded to allocate space in the shared pool for the new ones.

Let us imagine the following scenario:

An application has approximately 500 concurrent users, all of them actively fetching data from a database with SGA space for 300 statements. The application sends a total of 260 static SQL statements to the engine, which are parsed once and re-executed many times per day. The response time is satisfactory and nobody complains to management about the application.

Suddenly, after a new release has been deployed, the response time drops dramatically; sometimes a form displaying customer data which used to appear after 1 second takes 20 or more seconds to be displayed.

The IT department is informed and, during investigation, discovers that one statement, executed several times per connected user, was mistakenly coded using dynamic SQL. A new release is built after fixing the SQL syntax, and released the same day. The next day the application response time is back to normal.

How can only one dynamic SQL statement cripple an entire application? The diagnosis is simple: the statement in question was being executed several times, each with different where clause values. Multiplying the number of users (500) by the number of times the statement was executed shows that Oracle was being "bombarded" by thousands of "different" SQL statements, each requiring to be parsed. The shared pool could "only" contain approximately 300 parsed statements. Oracle was discarding static SQL from the shared pool, to accommodate the incoming dynamic SQL. This progressed to the limit of continuously re-parsing both static and dynamic SQL statements.

Is it enough to use bind variables to avoid re-parsing? Unfortunately not. The two following SQL statements are both using bind variables:

```
Select * from CUSTOMER where CUST_NAME=:my_cust;
Select * from CUSTOMER where CUST_NAME=:my_customer;
```

Nevertheless, the second statement will be re-parsed because the two bind variables are named differently, causing Oracle to consider that the two statements are different.

The standard Oracle development tools favor the use of bind variables. In Pro*C, using dynamic SQL cannot be unintentional, because sending dynamic SQL to the engine requires specific complex syntax. A Pro*C programmer needs to know what he or she is doing, before being able to use dynamic SQL. The same can be said for Oracle Forms or Developer/2000. In PL/SQL, which is used to interact with the database, variable binding is automatic. Dynamic SQL can be generated only by using the complicated advanced dynamic SQL features introduced in ORACLE 7.1 (the DBMS_SQL package).

The danger of unintentionally creating and sending SQL statements that contain literal strings or numbers in the where clause increases when third party tools are used as Oracle clients. Most of the MS-Windows based form painters and RAD tools use the ODBC APIs for accessing database services. Those tools are able to support a variety of file managers or even database engines using ODBC. Unfortunately, software vendors often compromise performance for portability when developing and commercializing ODBC database access modules. The same RAD tool generally allows interacting with the traditional PC-based file managers such as dBASE or Paradox, as well as real databases like Oracle or Informix.

Bind variables are not supported by the PC-based file managers. Using bind variables for one category of databases and not for the other forces vendors to have different code versions, and more expensive development and maintenance programs. If the software company providing the ODBC-based solution is not large, it is likely that it will standardize on dynamic SQL, the common denominator between the file managers and the back-end engines.

This is not to say that every ODBC-based solution necessarily ends up sending dynamic SQL to Oracle; the market offers excellent ODBC based client tools. The ODBC specifications fully support bind variables. It is up to the software vendor to make proper use of them while developing middleware on top of the ODBC layer. When selecting client tools for an application being built, designers and IT managers should carefully evaluate bind variable handling capabilities of the competing tools.

In summary, two kinds of SQL statements can be sent to an Oracle engine, dynamic SQL and static SQL. Dynamic SQL is characterized by having literal string values enclosed in single quotes describing the where clause of a Data Manipulation Language (DML) statement. Static SQL is characterized by the presence of variables, prefixed by a colon, instead of literal values. Dynamic SQL must always be parsed, while static SQL is parsed only the first time. It then resides in an area of the Oracle SGA, the shared pool, and it is re-used without being re-parsed. Parsing is a very expensive operation that should be minimized. By using bind variables, in preference to dynamic SQL, performance is significantly improved.

5.4.4 HOST ARRAYS

Oracle allows for data retrieval either by fetching one row at a time, or by fetching a set of rows in a *batch*, or an *array*. It is possible to modify or retrieve multiple rows in a single operation using this mechanism, to minimize database calls and reduce network traffic.

Host arrays can be used for both bulk insert and bulk retrieval of multiple rows. The network performance gain obtained by the use of host arrays is very significant in any kind of Oracle architecture, especially two-tier client-server. The efficient data retrieval on the server side is compounded by an even more efficient use of network resources.

Designers should consider organizing coding guidelines or standards and code walkthrough to make sure that host arrays are consistently used in preference to single row insertion and selection. An example of Pro*C code using host arrays follows:

```
char    customer_name[20][31];     /* the rows will be filled */
char    customer_address[20][51]; /* in batches of 20 */
int     customer_code[20];

int     cust_id_par;

memset(customer_name,'\0',sizeof(customer_name));
memset(customer_address,'\0',sizeof(customer_address));
memset(customer_code,0,sizeof(customer_code));

cust_id_par = 145;

EXEC SQL DECLARE CustCurs1 CURSOR FOR
SELECT CUSTOMER_NAME,CUSTOMER_ADDRESS,CUSTOMER_ID FROM
CUSTOMER
WHERE CUSTOMER_ID > :cust_id_par;

...
...
EXEC SQL OPEN CustCurs1;
...
...
EXEC SQL WHENEVER NOT FOUND DO BREAK;
...
...
for (; ;)
{
```

```
   EXEC SQL FETCH CustCurs1 INTO
  :customer_name,
  :customer_address,
  :customer_code;

  /* Process the fetched rows */
       ...
       ...
  /* etc, etc */
}
```

5.4.5 CHAR AND VARCHAR2 DATA TYPES

Oracle provides two datatypes that provide storage for alphanumeric data, CHAR and VARCHAR2. The difference between the two datatypes pertains to comparison semantics and storage mechanism. Strings stored in a CHAR column are fixed length. That is, in a CHAR(60) column, a 20-byte string is blank-padded and occupies 60 bytes of space. Conversely, a string stored in a VARCHAR2 column occupies a variable number of bytes, depending on its length. The dimension parameter of a VARCHAR2 datatype specifies only the maximum number of characters allowed in that column. So, the following declaration:

```
CUSTOMER_NAME        VARCHAR2(30)
```

means that the column *customer_name* is alphanumeric and contains strings of up to a maximum length of 30 characters. When a string shorter than 30 characters is stored, Oracle allocates only the space required to store the string's contents. It should be noted that 30 characters correspond only to 30 bytes for Western languages. Other languages, such as Asian languages, Arabic, and Hebrew often require more than one byte per character.

CHAR and VARCHAR2 have different comparison semantics. Oracle compares CHAR values using blank padded comparison semantics. If the two values being compared are of different lengths, Oracle appends blanks to the shorter one, until the same length is reached for both strings; then it performs the comparison. The tricky part is that Oracle considers two strings equal when they differ only in the number of trailing blanks. This semantic is ANSI standard.

Conversely, VARCHAR2 values are compared using non-padded comparison semantics. That is, two strings are considered equal only if they have the same characters and are of the same length. The VARCHAR2 comparison semantics are not ANSI standard, and the VARCHAR2 datatype is supported only by Oracle. VARCHAR2 shouldn't be used if portability to databases offered by other vendors is required. Oracle allows the definition of VARCHAR columns. Internally that datatype currently equates to VARCHAR2. Oracle Corporation warns that the semantics associated with VARCHAR columns can change, in the future if VARCHAR is implemented as a specific dataype, different from both CHAR and VARCHAR2.

Another significant difference between the CHAR and VARCHAR2 datatypes is that the maximum length of a CHAR is 255 bytes, while VARCHAR2 allows a maximum length of 2000 bytes (4000 in Oracle 8). Consistently using VARCHAR2 strings saves space and can improve the performance of full table scans. It is likely that fewer data blocks would be fetched for VARCHAR2 strings than fixed-length CHARs.

Does this mean that opting for VARCHAR2 strings is always better? Not necessarily; there are circumstances for which using CHAR strings could be a better alternative.

Oracle stores all data in blocks. The block is the atomic unit of space used by Oracle for its data operations. The Oracle engine moves physical blocks stored on disk into the SGA, where they are accessed and sometimes modified. Eventually they are returned to disk by an Oracle background process. The database block size is determined by the DBA when the database is created. The default size of a block is two kilobytes. Larger sizes are more commonly used, typically four or eight kilobytes. One block can thus contain multiple rows.

A block could be almost full when one of its rows is updated by inserting long strings VARCHAR2 columns. If those columns were previously empty, it is likely that the new size of the updated row will exceed the space available in the block.

The row no longer fits in the original block so Oracle migrates the entire row to another block with sufficient space. In the process, a pointer to the new block will be inserted in the original location of the migrated row.

This condition, known as *block chaining*, is detrimental for performance. Block chaining forces Oracle to fetch two blocks instead of one when loading a row. If a large table has hundreds of chained blocks, a full table scan runs the risk of being very inefficient.

The nature of some applications, for instance, those that allow a user to save an empty row in a table, makes them susceptible to block chaining. This technique is sometimes used to allocate the next number in a sequence, or to store the creation date and time. Storing the remaining data in the row is postponed, in line with business requirements.

A typical example would be an invoice processing system, where new invoices are partially entered every working day. The system generates *a receive* sequence number and stores an entry timestamp in the invoice row. The data entry operator records only the name of the company that sent the invoice. Once a month, the remaining details are entered, just before the accounting department begins processing payments.

If the invoice details were kept in VARCHAR2 columns, every row in the invoice table would expand considerably when the invoice details were entered. The potential for generating block chaining in invoice table rows is very high. In this case, designers could consider using CHAR columns to avoid row expansion by pre-allocating a fixed number of bytes within the invoice table blocks.

Given the different comparison semantics between CHAR and VARCHAR2 datatypes, it is best to standardize on one datatype and use it consistently. There is nothing worse than having to continuously query the database for the datatype of a column so that the correct comparison semantics can be chosen, while coding an application. To avoid any potential for confusion, only one string datatype should be allowed throughout the entire database.

In summary, Oracle provides two datatypes for strings storage in the database, CHAR and VARCHAR2. They are not easily interchangeable, due to their different semantics. Their storage mechanisms also differ, making a VARCHAR2 defined column a better solution for space saving. Sometimes using CHAR columns is also a sensible option in situations where block chaining could become an issue, or where the ANSI standard comparison semantics are required. Avoid programmer confusion and improve consistency by standardizing on one datatype for alphanumeric columns in the database.

Summary

The chapter covered aspects of detailed design related to Oracle projects. We started by examining business impacts on technical choices, recognizing that business factors take priority over technology factors, in a business context. We analyzed the various application architectures commonly implemented today. We focused on the problems associated with the client-server architectures, showing how the goals of scalability and easy application deployment can be achieved using the latest WEB technology. Finally, we considered five recurring issues that must be confronted while designing Oracle based applications. The issues are:

- ❑ NULL values and indicator variables
- ❑ Referential integrity
- ❑ Bind variables
- ❑ Host arrays
- ❑ Char and Varchar2 datatypes

Each of these design issues must be carefully evaluated by designers and architects. Their directions and recommendations must be documented for the guidance of team leaders and programmers. Neglecting to do so can lead to a scenario where the same field is defined as CHAR in some tables and as VARCHAR2 in others. Redundant or unrelated information can be left in the database due to a lack of referential integrity. Oracle array processing capabilities can be inadvertently neglected by application programmers, with a detrimental impact on the overall performance of the application. Clear coding guidelines and appropriate training for newcomers to the project are the key for avoiding the potential pitfalls presented above.

Chapter 6

DATA MODELING AND CASE TOOLS

This chapter will examine the data modeling methodologies and CASE tools commonly used in environments where a database management system plays a fundamental role in the economy of an IT project.

When an RDBMS is used to support applications that implement sophisticated business rules, involving a large number of business entities, it is likely that the complexity of the supporting data model will require some form of management, to allow designers, data modelers, and architects to be in control.

Data modeling methodologies provide the intellectual framework that allows designers and data modelers to consistently apply the same design techniques to different problem domains, thereby achieving a high degree of standardization and communality. Designers and data modelers can therefore share common methods, languages, and notations, and then focus on adopting common strategies for the resolution for the problem domain.

Several CASE tools are available on the market to help data modelers increase their productivity while using standard methodologies, such as Information Engineering or IDEF1X. Oracle Corporation ships Oracle Designer, arguably the most comprehensive tool for business information engineering. Its completeness is accompanied by a steep learning curve, and when a data modeling tool is required for a project more limited in scope, Oracle Designer can be an overkill. Designers can look at other "pure" data modeling tools of more modest ambitions, but that are as effective in increasing productivity and control over complex data models.

The chapter will also examine the important role played by domains, which allow key formatting characteristics for attributes to be consistently applied across different entities. When a repository is used to store metadata information, domains can be used even across different projects, helping designers to achieve overall consistency at an enterprise level, which becomes very useful in data warehousing projects.

The last topic in the chapter concerns the deliverables of the design process. Data models are created to be shared among designers and developers, who regard them as an important tool for the creation of good quality code.

6.1 Data Modeling Methodologies

The relational theory grew in popularity outside academia towards the end of the 1970s, thanks to the work of Codd and Date. While the relational model was gaining wider acceptance, database theoreticians started working towards the creation of methodologies capable of providing IT professionals with design tools operating within a relational framework.

One of the earliest and most successful attempts was the Entity Relationship (ER) Model, by Chen [1976]. The ER model advocates a strong distinction between entities, defined as things or objects of significance about which information must be known or held, and relationships between entities, which define the network of interactions that links entities together.

The initial ER model was conceived with simplicity in mind, yet soon its creator, trying to capture the inevitable complexity of real life systems, started adding complexity to the model, introducing, for example, attributes to better qualify relationships. The net effect of this addition was the creation of a great deal of confusion between entities and relationships. What to one designer is an entity in the context of a specific problem domain, can legitimately to another designer be a relationship in the context of a different problem domain.

Both Codd [1990] and Date [1995] have pointed out this lack of clarity in the definition of the basic building blocks of the ER model. The latter defines the ER model as "essentially just a thin layer on top of the basic relational model."

One of the drawbacks of the ER model is that it strives to capture all potential types of relationship between entities, neglecting the same level of detailed analysis for entities, which ultimately should be more important in the economy of a database design methodology. Consider the toolbar of the Entity-Relationship Diagrammer provided by Oracle Designer, shown here.

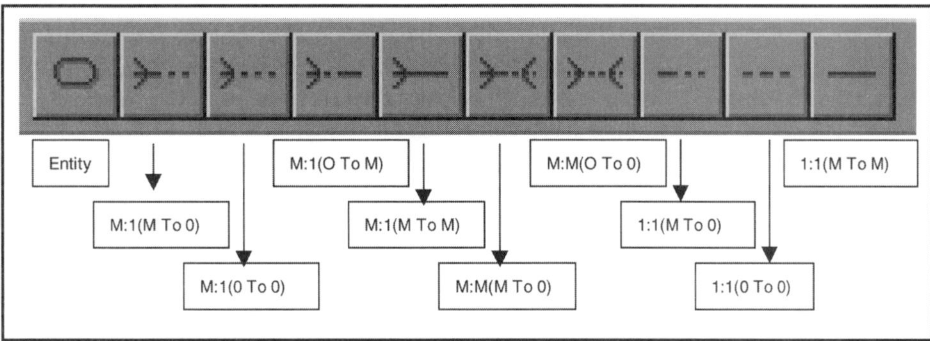

The ER Diagrammer toolbar displays one icon for entity creation and nine icons for creating all possible relationships between entities. The reason so many combinations are possible is that one entity can be in one-to-one, one-to-many, and many-to-many relationships. Furthermore, the ER model tries to capture further details, such as the mandatory or optional nature of the relationship being established between entities. According to the ER model, it is important to distinguish between relationships that link zero, exactly one, or many instances of one entity with zero, exactly one, or many instances of another entity. The ER notation captures the subtle difference between zero or more, and at least one or more.

The Information Engineering (IE) methodology, conceived by James Martin and presented to the public through his book (Martin [1990]), and extremely successful in the community of data modelers, gently simplifies the relationship complexity of ER models. In IE every relationship is binary and involves either two entities or one only entity if the relationship is reflexive. The graphic notation is simpler than that of ER diagrams, yet it maintains its expressive semantics power.

One more modeling technique deserves to be mentioned because of its popularity, the IDEF1X methodology, developed by Robert Brown in the late 1970s and described by Bruce [1992]. The graphic notation introduced by this methodology is less strict and precise than that of either ER or IE, but more easily mastered by modelers. In spite of being semantically less powerful than the other methodologies, IDEF1X has been adopted by the U.S. Air Force as the required methodology for their projects, *de-facto* promoting IDEF1X to be a major player in the modeling industry.

The common trait of the methodologies examined so far is that they strive to translate business requirements, initially expressed in plain English, into formal symbols and equations. The diagrams created by the modelers will be used to generate the code understood by the database for the definition of tables, indexes, and constraints. In other words, methodologies are intellectual tools that force designers and modelers to formalize business concepts, rules, and practices in an

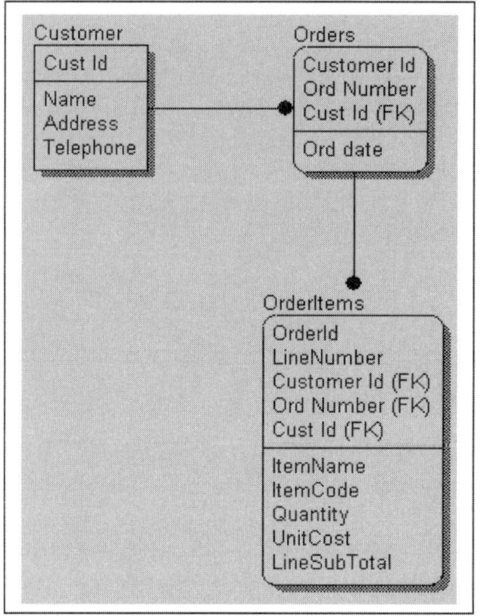

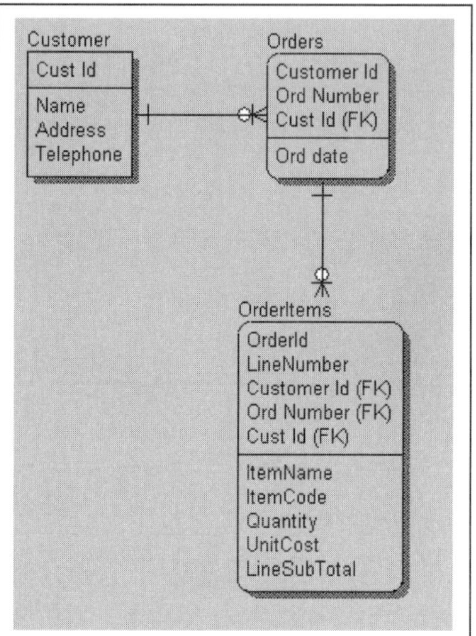

FIGURE 6.1 The IDEF1X notation (left) and IE notation (right)

unambiguous manner, avoiding the imprecision and ambiguity inherent in all natural languages.

An initial sketching of business practices cannot avoid the use of natural language, because business analysts and data modelers usually understand the problem domain by interviewing the key people involved in the business processes. Data modeling methodologies show their usefulness in a second stage, when the result of the interviews must be formalized into diagrams and documents for the analysis by IT professionals such as designers and architects. Inconsistencies and "gray areas" are usually exposed in the translation process between natural language and formalized notation.

The level of abstraction of the models sketched by data modelers evolves through progressive refinements from a conceptual stage at the highest level, to a physical implementation of records and fields at the lowest level.

Data modelers produce conceptual, logical, and physical models. At present there is no clear definition unanimously accepted for any of the three abstraction levels; however, in very broad terms it is possible to border the scope of each level.

A conceptual data model captures the big picture of the business domain, focusing on a few key entities that broadly describe crucial aspects involved in the business information flow. The relationship that links the entities is also defined in the conceptual model, usually at a high level of abstraction, that is, avoiding the complex identification of the cardinality between entities. In other words, at this level of abstraction, it is important to show that two entities are linked by some sort of relationship, rather than specify exactly the type of relationship.

The conceptual diagram includes only those attributes relevant to an understanding of the business process. For instance, if a conceptual diagram identifies the CUSTOMER entity, it is likely that the surname and address attributes won't appear in the diagram. But if a conceptual diagram is drawn for a company that deals with international customers, and an important part of the pricing policy affects the geographical location of the customers, the attribute that identifies the customers' country can be included in the conceptual diagram.

A logical data model is much more detailed and contains all attributes for both entities and relationships. A complete logical model shows fully normalized entities with candidate keys and their propagation into correspondent foreign keys, thus identifying the hierarchy that links the entities participating in the model. The logical datatypes of the attributes are indicated in the model. Logical datatypes are char, date, number, blob, etc. It is important to note that logical data models are so generic that they can be implemented in different target databases, even nonrelational.

A physical data model represents the instantiation of a logical model into a specific database management product such as Oracle. The datatypes of the attributes reflect the database specific implementation; for instance, the Oracle supported VARCHAR2 or ROWID datatypes can legally appear in a physical model that describes an Oracle implementation of a logical model.

A physical data model must describe every aspect of a database implementation, including physical storage entities like tablespaces, clusters, or hash clusters. When CASE tools are used for logical and physical models, the SQL DDL scripts that physically create all database objects are usually automatically generated from the physical model. The physical model must therefore provide a very fine-grained description of all objects that will constitute the database schema.

An example of a logical model for a movie rental business is shown below.

The logical data model shown in Figure 6.2 uses the Information Engineering notation to display the entities identified in the model together with their relationships. From the model, it is possible to generate the physical data model, shown in Figure 6.3.

The definition of the physical model is one of the most delicate tasks performed by the designers of an application. This is the crucial passage that will determine the overall performance and usability of the system. Most CASE tools can automatically generate a physical data model out of a logical model. This is definitely a good feature, but it must be intended only as a starting point. Switching from a logical data model to a physical data model doesn't mean the mere resolution of many-to-many relationships with the automatic creation of a supporting table. This is easily implemented by all good CASE tools available on the market. A good physical data model also implements de-normalization and other

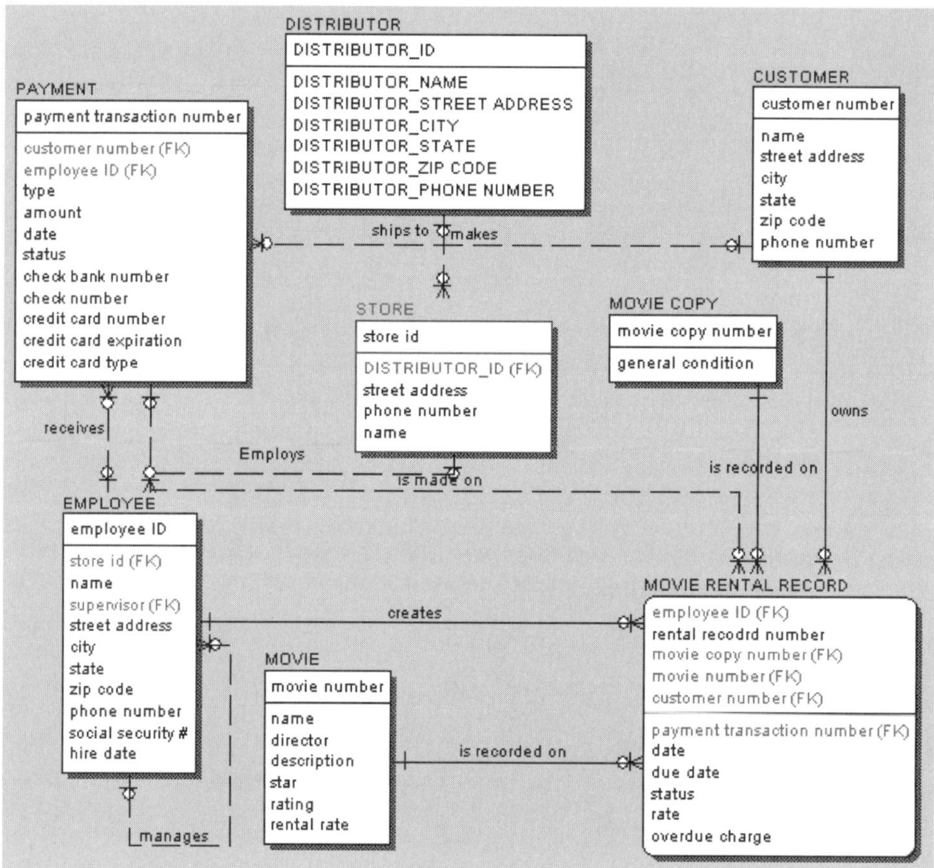

FIGURE 6.2 A logical data model for a movie rental business[1]

performance-increasing artifices described in Section 4.3. These activities cannot be automated, because they depend more on a thorough comprehension of the business domain rather than on generic rules of universal applicability.

6.2 THE ROLE OF DOMAINS

Often, attributes defined in different entities share the same formats or the same properties. Consider for example the SURNAME attribute, which can be defined in the customer entity as well as in the employee entity. The same can be said for currency attributes, such as PRICE, which can appear in both order items and inventory entities.

---

[1] Source: *Logic Works*, together with the ER/Win package ships this example.

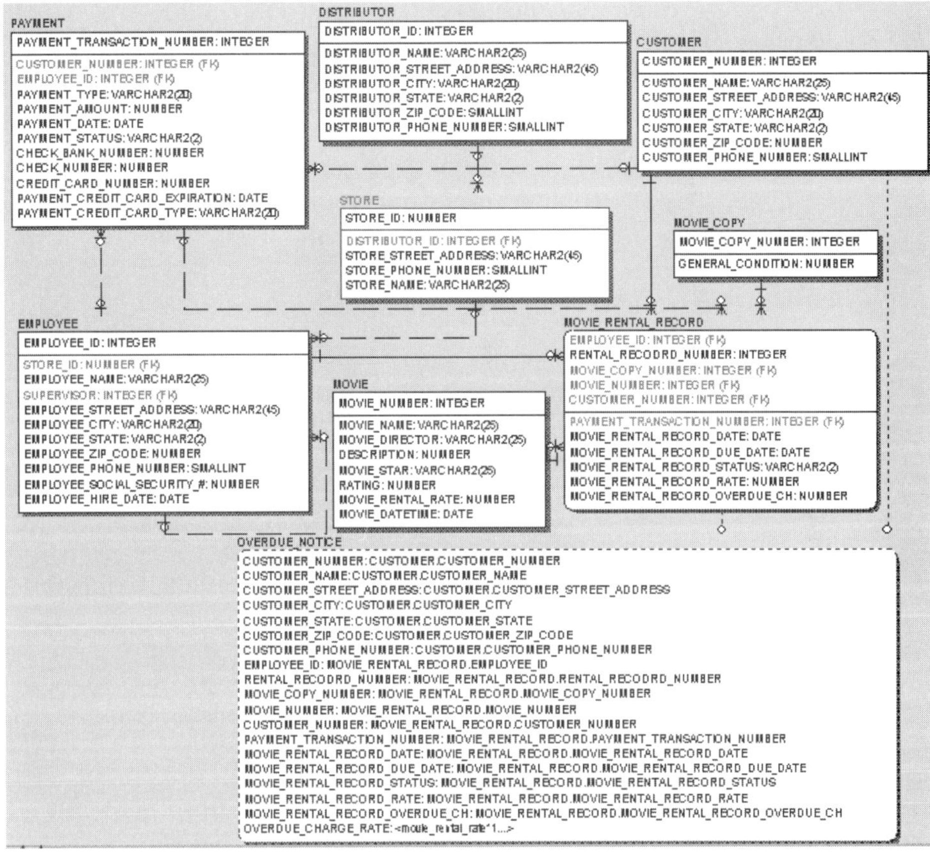

FIGURE 6.3 The physical data model for the movie rental business

Individual definitions of datatype formats for attributes appearing in multiple entities can lead to redundancies and inconsistencies. That is, discrepancies between similar but not identical datatype definitions would be inevitably introduced into the system by designers who don't coordinate their efforts while defining entity attributes.

The net result could be the definition of the SURNAME attribute in the customer entity as CHAR(30) and in the employee entity as VARCHAR2(25). To avoid introducing inconsistent datatype definitions into the system, the notion of domain was introduced as a fundamental concept of the relational model. In its purest definition, a domain is essentially a set of values that an attribute may legitimately assume. The domain of a foreign key will be determined by the domain of the corresponding primary key. Nonnumeric descriptive attributes, such as sex gender or accepted credit card, will take a list of allowable values as their domain.

While this definition of domain is useful at a conceptual or logical level, it is a little ambiguous when applied to a physical level, where the list of allowable values can be implemented using both the CHAR datatype for one attribute and the VARCHAR2 datatype for the same attribute included in a different entity. For this reason the notion of domain has been refined and further specified to include physical attributes such as datatype and length definitions. Most CASE tools, if not all, allow for domain definition by the user, who can create new domains or edit and assign attributes to existing domains.

Designers can create a NAME domain, defined as a VARCHAR2 and having a maximum length of 30 characters. The SURNAME column defined in both the employee and customer tables can inherit its attributes from the NAME domain. Two currency domains can be defined, one to hold small amounts of money (up to a three digit number plus two positions for cents), named SMALL_MONEY, and one to hold large amounts of money (up to six digit numbers), named LARGE_MONEY. The PRICE column defined in the LINE_ITEM table, child table of ORDER, can inherit its attributes from SMALL_MONEY, while the INVOICE_TOTAL column defined in the INVOICE table can inherit its attributes from the LARGE_MONEY domain.

Using domains improves consistency across different tables including columns that share meaning and attributes with corresponding columns in related tables. The productivity gain introduced by an extensive use of domains becomes even greater when data must be gathered and consolidated from many different sources within the same enterprise, as in the case of data warehousing. One of the most time consuming tasks usually performed by data warehousing architects is to harmonize the different datatypes that represent the same attribute across different applications running in the same enterprise.

6.3 The Importance of a Repository

In order to implement domains, some degree of persistence must be given to the user-defined objects. In other words, the domains defined by the users must be stored somewhere, in order to be retrieved during later sessions. The logical and physical models produced by designers during many hours of hard work must also be stored, to be subsequently retrieved when the design sessions are resumed. There are usually two options for storing user defined repository objects, such as domains, or model diagrams, such as the physical model. One option is to use the file system of the supporting platform where the CASE tool runs. The other is to use the target database to define metadata tables that will be used as a repository for the model being built. The second option is arguably a better solution, especially when the repository format is open and published, freely accessible, and even extensible by the users of the CASE tool.

Implementing the repository in Oracle allows for easier and centralized backups, and encourages sharing the same standards across multiple applications, when they coexist in the same repository.

6.4 CASE Tools

When Oracle is used for database-centric applications, the complexity of which exceeds 20 or 30 tables, a CASE tool should be used to manage the creation of the data models and the generation of the SQL scripts that create the application schema. A CASE tool is also very useful to progressively refine the initial data models during the development phase. It is likely that before "freezing" a database schema definition to allow developers to start coding the application, database designers and data modelers will produce several releases of their models. They will be reviewed, discussed, and modified in a common effort shared between business analysts, user representatives, application designers, and architects. It is therefore crucial to be able to verify the changes introduced in the latest version against an older version, or to revert back changes that were mistakenly introduced by newer releases. In other words, a good CASE tool should implement some form of version control, either internally or by allowing the users to interface with standard version control systems, such as PVCS or Visual Source Safe.

A CASE tool is also useful during the maintenance phase, when the database schema must be changed to keep the application synchronized with the inevitable changes that affect the business rules. The market offers different tools that can help designers and data modelers to define conceptual, logical, and physical models using standard methodologies and notations. Most tools also implement version control and allow for DDL script creation that automates the database schema definition. Only a few allow for code generation, usually targeted at client RAD tools such as Powerbuilder, Visual Basic, and Delphi.

Automatic code generation is a very ambitious goal that is either achieved completely or not achieved at all. If the CASE tool I am using generates "only" 90% of my application, but the effort required to understand the code automatically produced by the tool is big, I won't be able to code the remaining 10% until I have intimately understood the concepts behind the code generator engine. This could be a very challenging task, the cost of which could nullify the benefits of an automatic generation of the code.

Automatic generation of electronic forms that allow users to query and update database entities, even complex master-detail relationships, is nowadays quite common. It is indeed useful for building prototypes that can be used as proof of concepts, or to test the usability of user interfaces. When an application relies on complex business logic to accomplish its tasks, even the most sophisticated CASE tools show their limits.

In Chapter 4 we examined the intellectual tools commonly used by IT professionals to do their job. We learned the importance of building a small-scale version of the surrounding reality, or a model, which can be easily understood by the human mind. The model of the problem is called analysis, and the model of the proposed solution is called design. Most CASE tools take analysis for granted, and are useful only for the design of the solution. Only a few CASE tools are really complete, allowing designers to model both the problem domain and the proposed solution in one integrated environment.

6.4.1 ORACLE DESIGNER

Oracle Designer, formerly called Designer/2000, is the Oracle offer in the field of database oriented CASE tools. Oracle Designer is a repository-based tool that requires an Oracle database to store its repository. While Oracle Designer offers limited support for databases of different vendors, not only is a working Oracle database required, but also strong DBA skills are needed during the installation of the repository.

Oracle Designer is a client-server tool that runs only under MS Windows (9x or NT), interacting with an Oracle database that can be installed either on a back-end computer or locally in the same client computer, as in the case of Personal Oracle.

Oracle Designer is huge. To give an idea of its size it is enough to quote the disk space required, approximately half a gigabyte. It is a multifaceted product that provides a set of tools helpful at any stage of the information systems design lifecycle. Oracle Designer is definitely not just a data modeling tool to produce logical and physical data models that can generate a database creation script. Oracle Designer provides data modeling diagrammers, but its real strength is in the holistic approach that starts with strategic business planning, continues with business process engineering, and finally proceeds towards the implementation of Information Systems solutions to the business requirements identified during the preceding stages.

This is not all. Oracle Designer includes code generators for C++, Visual Basic, and WEB-enabled applications. Theoretically, it is possible to use Oracle Designer to produce a complete application, generating the source code directly from the design diagrams stored in the repository.

Given its complexity, Oracle Designer is a product that has a steep learning curve and requires a strong commitment by professionals considering its adoption. If you are looking for a tool that allows you to reverse engineer an existing schema to create a data model that can be edited and extended, Oracle Designer is not the best option. Its forte is not in this area; several competing tools offer more powerful and easier to use features for pure data modeling and are less expensive. But if you are a senior designer or architect involved in business process re-engineering, interacting with business analysts to define or re-define the information flow of an enterprise or one of its departments, then Oracle Designer is the tool that fits all requirements.

Oracle Designer is not a single tool, but a set of integrated tools that offer different scope over the same problem domain. The centralized repository that provides the single common point for all views makes possible this high level of integration. Figure 6.4 shows the Oracle Designer launch pad, which organizes all tools comprising the product in broader categories, to help novice users better understand the purpose of each component.

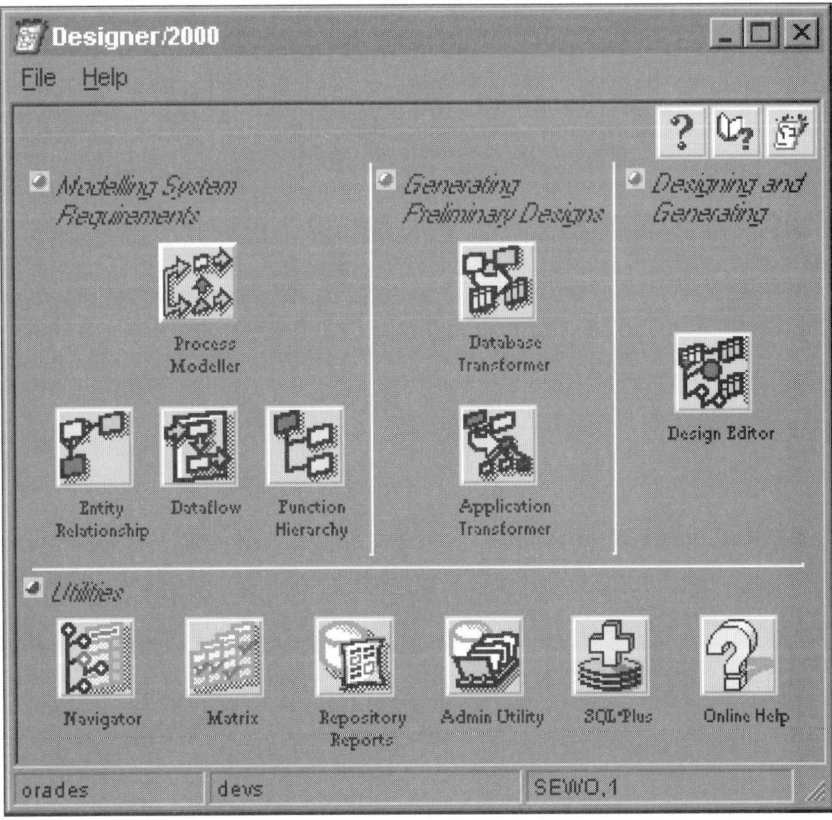

FIGURE 6.4 Oracle Designer launch pad

The picture shows the four functional areas provided by the tool:

Utilities	Object Navigator, Matrix Diagrammer, Repository Administration Utility, Repository Reports
System Requirements Modelling	Process Modeller, Entity Relationship Diagrammer, Dataflow Diagrammer, Function Hierarchy Diagrammer
Preliminary Design Generation	Database Transformer, Application Transformer
Design and generation	Design Editor

Designers are free to choose the tools appropriate to their tasks. Oracle Designer doesn't enforce a mandatory sequence that must be followed to obtain specific results. On the contrary, one can freely decide to use a small subset of the provided tools. For instance, it would be possible to focus on logical and physical data modeling only, using the Entity Relationship Diagrammer, the Database Transformer, and the Design Editor, totally bypassing a business engineering analysis, based on tools like the Process Modeller or the Function Hierarchy Diagrammer.

Oracle Designer is definitely repository-centric. The repository contains both the elements introduced by the designers using the various tools and the logic used by the system to verify data consistency, generate diagrams, and automatically produce code for the target applications.

Given the importance of the repository in the Oracle Designer architecture, the tool allows for fine-grained management of all facets of the repository/data dictionary. It is even possible to extend the repository, choosing between two options. The so-called "user extensions" can be entered via a simple user interface and saved on the fly. Alternatively, for more low-level tasks, a set of repository APIs is published and available to developers.

All information required to conduct a detailed business analysis can be entered in the Oracle Designer repository, using the system modelling tools. For instance, it is possible to record all business functions, storing the location details and the personnel working in the various departments in the repository. A top-down approach can be taken to analyze the business processes of a company. The mission statement can be entered in the repository, together with a detailed analysis of the current processes, which can be nonautomated and paper-based. With Oracle Design it is not only possible, but also encouraged, to start from a model of the problem, rather than from the solution. The effort required in formalizing the business processes being re-engineered forces designers and data modelers to catch early on the design stage discrepancies and inefficiencies that can alternatively go undetected.

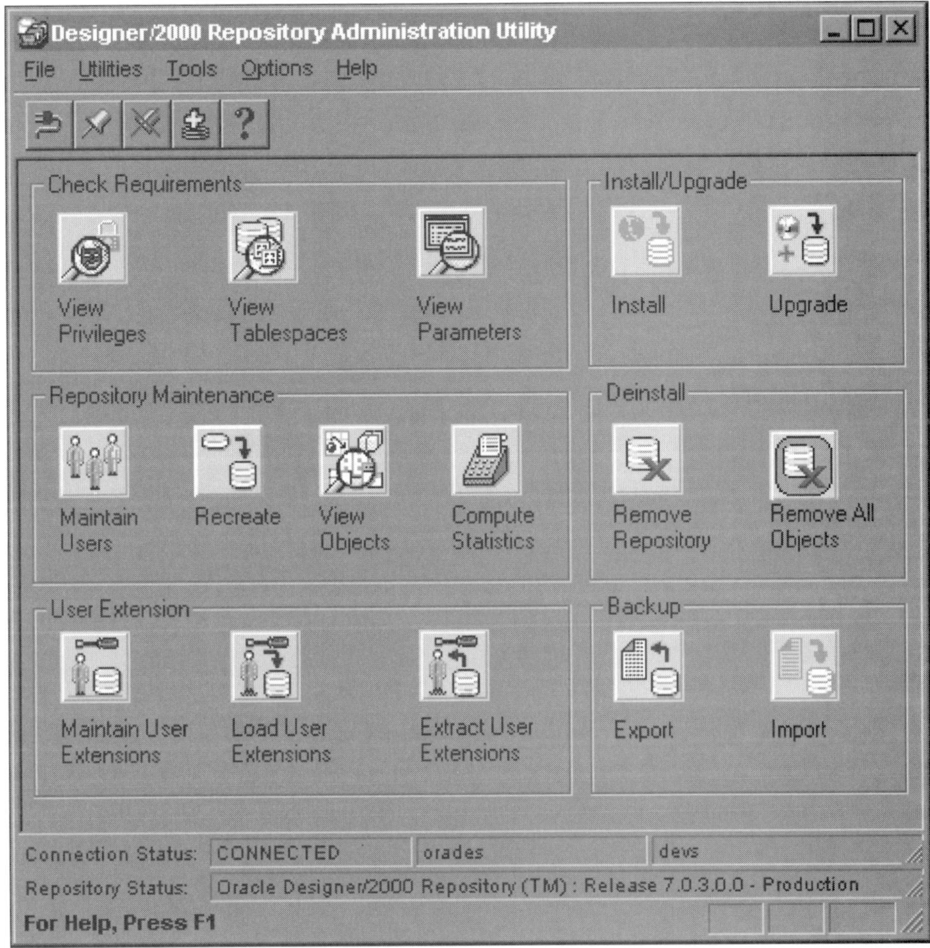

FIGURE 6.5 The Repository Administration Utility

The repository-centric nature of Oracle Design is well suited for business process re-engineering. The same data is entered once, but is accessed from different tools, assuming different shapes and meanings according to the different contexts, allowing data modelers to view the same design issue from different angles and perspectives.

An example better clarifies the concept. One can define one process, say an Order Process, using the Dataflow Diagrammer. The following picture shows the Order Process entered into the repository using the Dataflow Diagrammer.

Once the process has been defined, one can launch the Function Hierarchy Diagrammer and load the just entered Order Process as a function hierarchy diagram, without duplicating the effort.

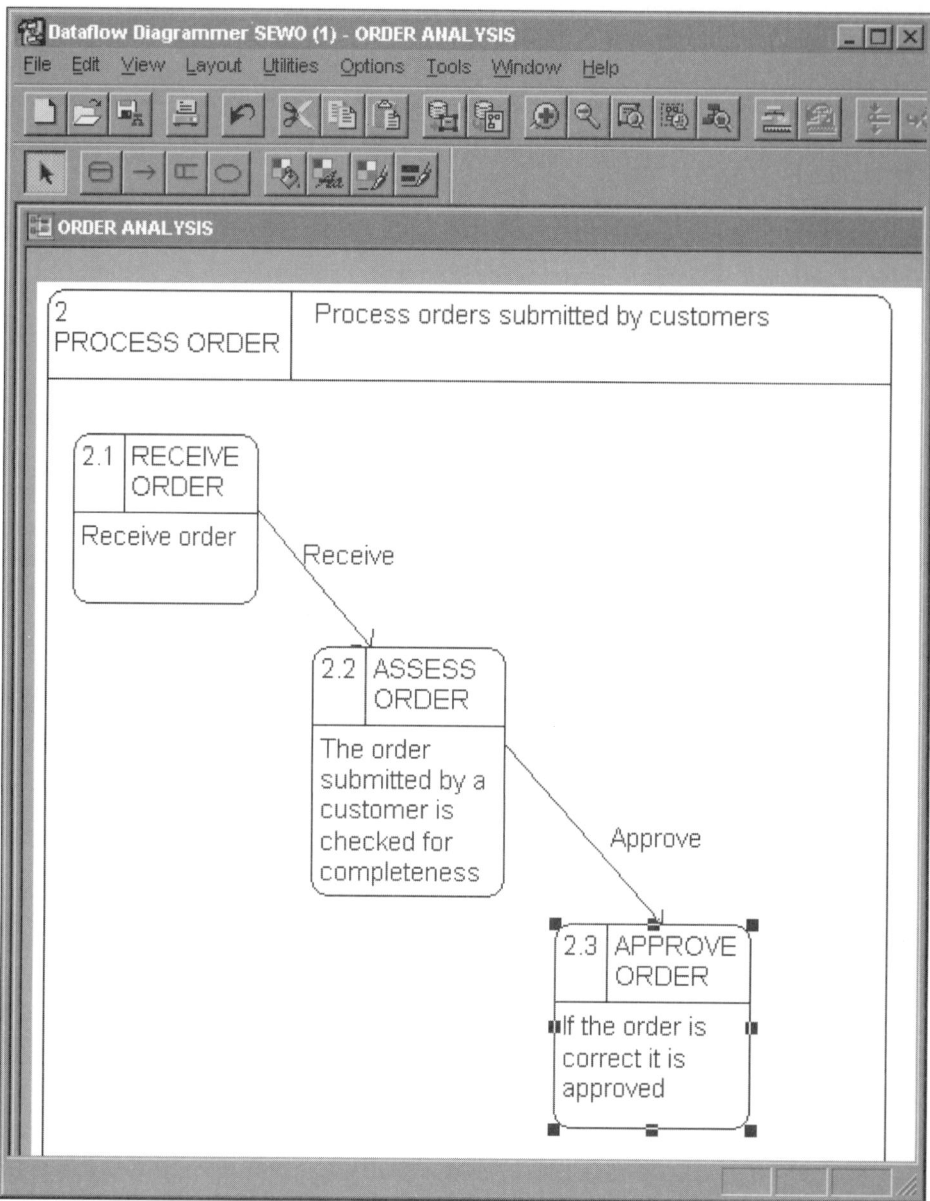

FIGURE 6.6 The dataflow Diagrammer at work

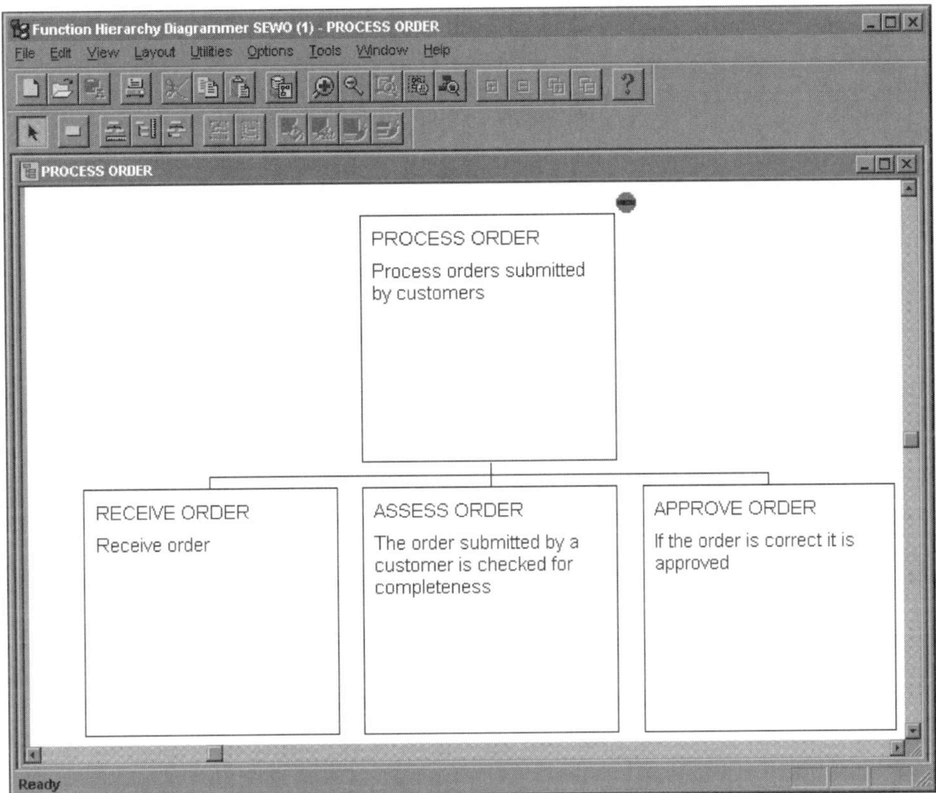

FIGURE 6.7 The Order Process is loaded into the Function Hierarchy Diagrammer

Figure 6.7 gives the view over the same data changes with different context, and the diagram can be embellished and integrated with details more specific to the new context, but the important point is that the raw data is entered only once.

Designers new to the package are usually confronted with the dilemma of choosing the best possible tool to enter specific data into the repository. Choosing the "wrong" tool simply means giving up on flexibility and being forced to enter more data later on, when the right tool is identified. Throwing away complete data entered into the repository is a rare event for data modelers using Oracle Designer. Experience soon teaches the users of this complex tool what tasks are best suited for each tool comprising the package.

Oracle Designer, unlike other competitors, uses a pure ER diagrammer for an initial sketch of the entities and their relationships. The database logical model is generated with the help of the Database Transformer, which guides the user to the mapping of entities to tables and attributes to columns, resolving the many-to-many relationships, defining the primary keys, and migrating the foreign keys to all affected tables.

Data modelers control the automatic generation of the code constituting the application through the Design Editor tool. An option of the same tool assists data modelers with the creation of a physical model for a database logically defined in previous steps. Oracle Designer can automatically generate the DDL scripts that create the database.

In summary, Oracle Designer is the king among the Oracle-centric data modeling tools. It can be used at different levels of complexity, allowing for really complex business engineering analysis, or simply as a pure data modelling tool, to reverse engineer existing databases and automatically convert the schema objects into entities and relationships. Given its steep learning curve, its power, and its price, it is clearly more indicated for sophisticated tasks performed by sophisticated users.

6.4.2 ORACLE ODD

Oracle Corporation realized that a product like Oracle Designer was an overkill for somebody who wanted simply a data modeling tool of limited scope, enough to be capable of reverse engineering database schemas, as well as creating DDL scripts for database/scheme definition. At the end of 1997, Oracle Corporation shipped Oracle Database Designer (ODD), an MS Windows tool capable of running under both 16- and 32-bit Windows environments. In order not to cannibalize the much more lucrative potential market for Oracle Designer, ODD is very limited in its capabilities. For instance, it only allows physical data modeling, requiring 16 bit SQL*Net drivers to connect to an Oracle instance. This forces 32-bit MS Windows users to install on the same workstation both SQL*Net versions, for 16 and 32 bit, in two separate directories.

ODD is definitely less powerful than other data modeling tools but can find its place in shops where basic data modeling capabilities are required, for instance, to maintain a mature application that only occasionally needs limited database changes.

Figure 6.8 shows the reverse engineering wizard that allows ODD users to create a physical data model from an existing database schema. Oracle native drivers are supported, together with ODBC data sources. This feature allows ODD to reverse engineer schemas stored in databases different from Oracle. A DDL script can also be used as a source for reverse engineering.

ODD provides a schema generation wizard that creates a DDL script containing the SQL commands required to generate the database schema objects defined in the physical data model.

ODD is a stable tool that doesn't bother its users with sudden and inexplicable crashes, as other more expensive competitors do, and delivers what is in the reach of its limited capabilities. If Oracle Designer can be an overkill, ODD probably doesn't offer enough features to lure a professional data modeler.

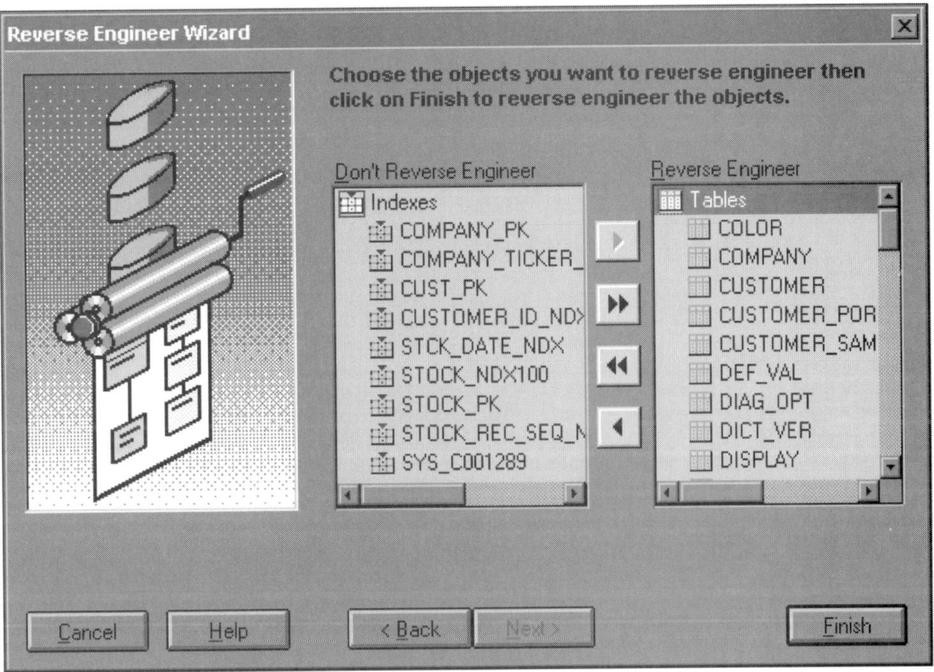

FIGURE 6.8 The reverse engineering wizard in ODD

6.4.3 ER/WIN

ER/Win by Logic Works is one of the oldest and more popular data modeling tools. The user interface provided by this tool shows its age and its pre-Windows 95 origin. Nevertheless, the overall usability of the product is quite good. In line with the basic features offered by most competitors, ER/Win operates a clear-cut distinction between logical and physical definitions of the same data model. While ER/Win was born as a IDEFX1-based tool, its latest incarnation also implements the Information Engineering notation. The user can switch freely between the two notations simply by ticking a checkbox.

One of the useful features offered by the separation between logical and physical diagrams is the automatic resolution of the many-to-many relationships with the introduction of a supporting table. In Figure 6.11, the customer and the incident entities are linked by a many-to-many relationship. Simply by clicking the combo box displayed at the top of the diagram and selecting "physical," the user of this tool resolves the many-to-many relationship.

We have mentioned several times that designers cannot rely on the automatic conversion operated by the design tool at the moment of the generation of

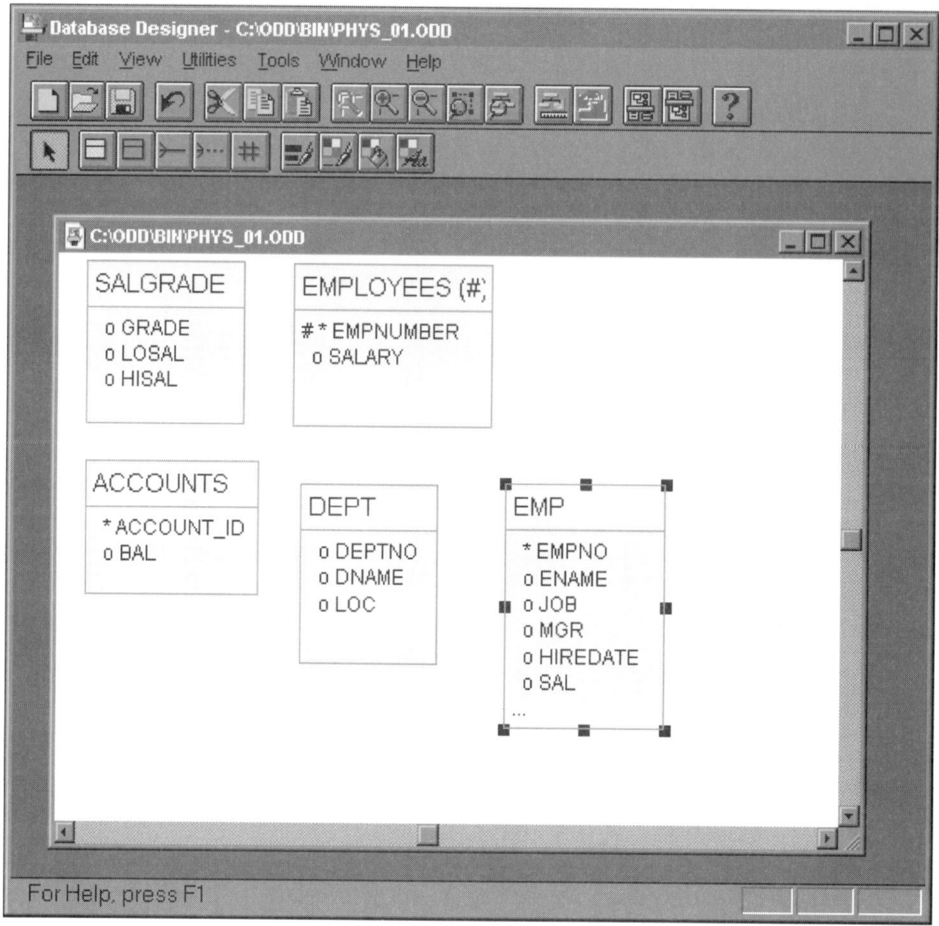

FIGURE 6.9 ODD at work. Only physical data models are supported

the physical model. ER/Win supports "Physical Only" and "Logical Only" properties for entities/tables, attributes/columns, and relationships. An entity marked as "Logical Only" in the logical model won't be considered when the physical model is generated. Conversely, a physical relationship marked as "Physical Only" won't be displayed by the logical model.

Designers who manipulate the physical diagram automatically generated by the tool can mark as "Physical Only" the de-normalized tables and the additional foreign key relationships, preventing them from appearing in the logical model.

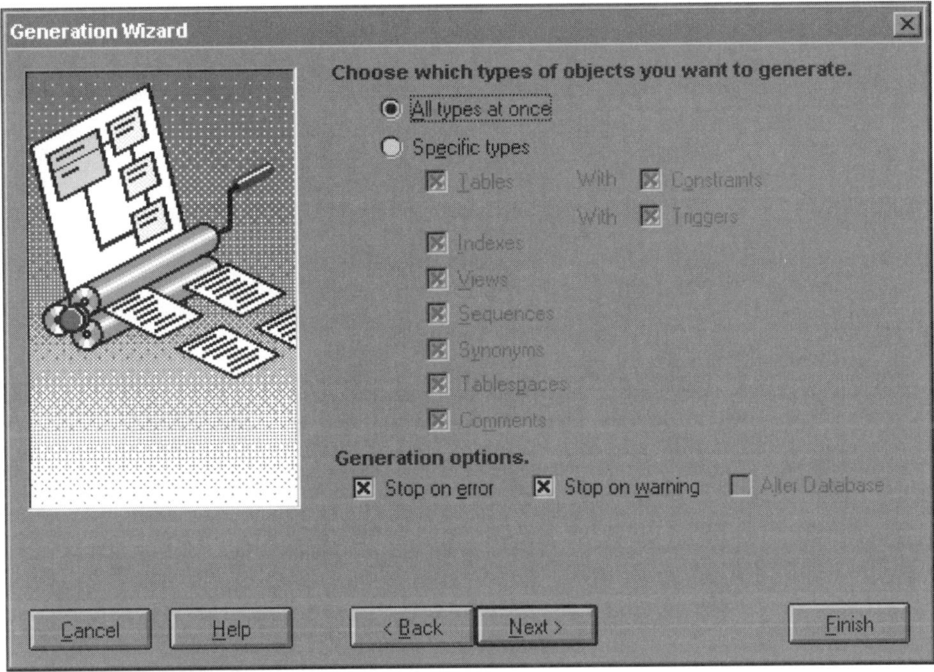

FIGURE 6.10 The ODD schema generation wizard at work

ER/Win connects to Oracle using native drivers and can optionally use the back-end database as a repository. Furthermore, ER/Win allows the physical attributes such as tablespace name and storage parameters to be synchronized directly from the database.

Users can check out the diagrams stored in the repository during previous sessions, apply changes to the diagrams, and check them back in under control by the ER/Win data dictionary manager. Multiple versions of the same diagram are kept in the dictionary, available to users through the "History" button.

ER/Win can import and export Oracle Designer repository definitions. This promotes ER/Win as a candidate to replace the Oracle Designer data modeling capabilities, which are not as powerful and easy to use, allowing designers to keep using the other tools provided by Oracle Designer.

6.4.4 POWERDESIGNER

PowerDesigner, formerly S-Designor, by Powersoft, a Sybase division known for being the maker of Powerbuilder, is the market leader in its sector. PowerDesigner includes a family of products that cover a very broad area, from data dis-

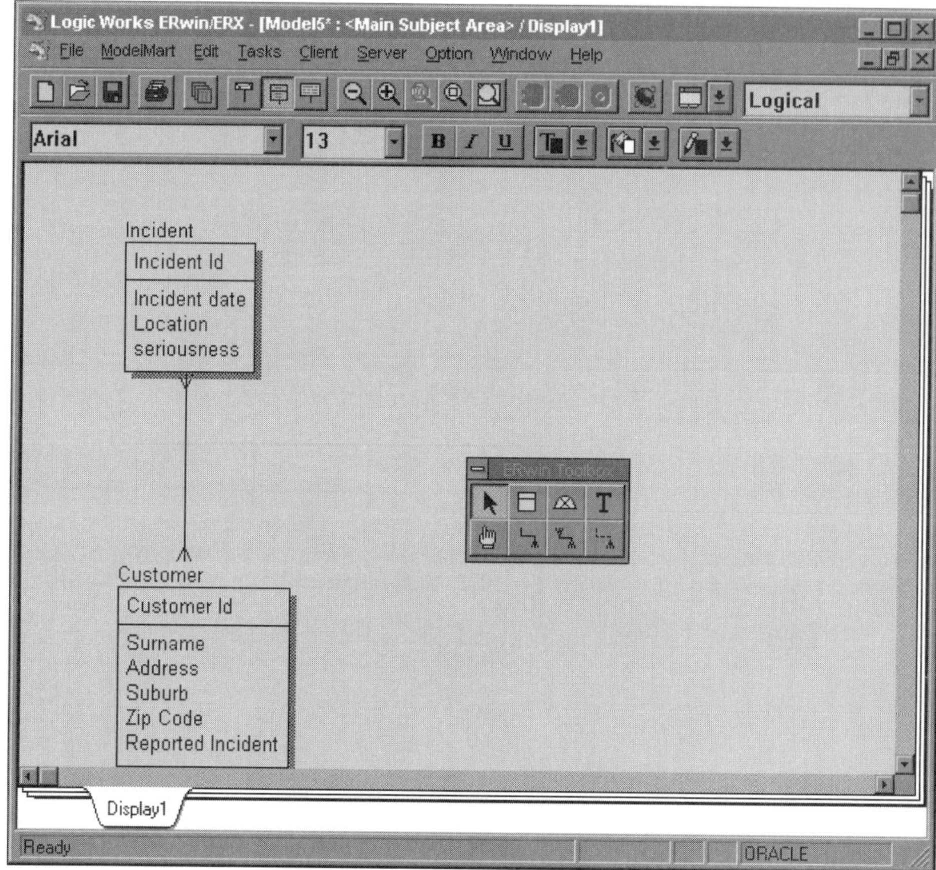

FIGURE 6.11 ER/Win Logical modeling

covery and process definition (*ProcessAnalyst*) to physical data modeling and application generation (*AppModeler*), through logical data modeling and database generation (*DataArchitect*).

PowerDesigner is not as complete and integrated as Oracle Designer, but it supports virtually all relational databases existing in the market. All major players appear in the list of supported databases (Oracle, DB2, ADABAS, Sybase, Informix, Ingres, Progress), together with less common products, such as Oracle RdB, ALLBASE/SQL, Teradata, Omnis 7, etc.

ProcessAnalyst, the most recent addition to the PowerDesigner family, is not, as its name would suggest, a tool that can compete with the Oracle Designer Process Modeler. It is a mere data flow diagrammer, which has been recently con-

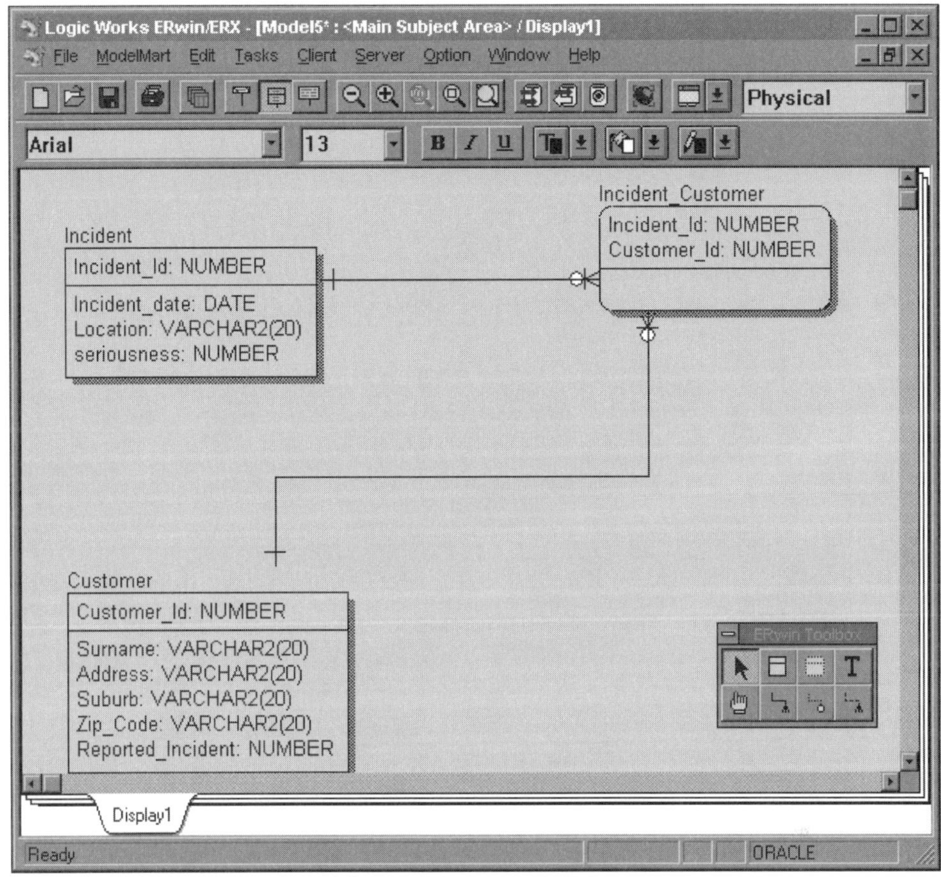

FIGURE 6.12 The ER/Win physical diagram creates the supporting table for a many-to-many relationship

ceived to be simple and flexible, usable by designers familiar with data flow diagram and methodologies based upon them with no training at all.

DataArchitect and AppModeler, on the contrary, are a very powerful pair that determined the fortune of PowerDesigner, which has become in a few years the market leader.

PowerDesigner not only supports many, if not all, relational databases, but also offers a broad support for the RAD tools commonly used today in client-server applications such as Delphi, Powerbuilder, VisualBasic and Power++, the Powersoft C++ IDE.

The reverse engineering capabilities of PowerDesigner are somehow limited by its ODBC interface, which is the only supported communication layer used by

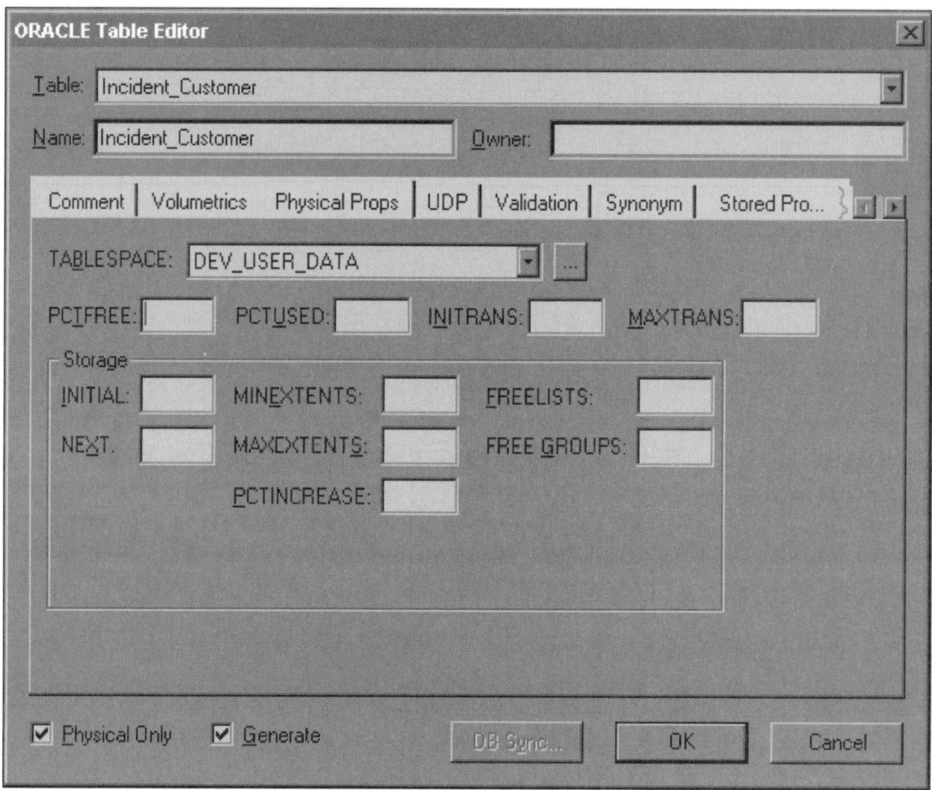

FIGURE 6.13 ER/Win allows attributes to be "Physical Only"

the tool. No native drivers are supported, not even to connect to a Sybase database.

One of the best features of PowerDesigner is its capability to generate triggers that support referential integrity when designers opt to avoid the use of foreign keys. This can prevent the definition of many supporting indexes, one for each foreign key, necessary when a core table contains tens of foreign key columns.

The PL/SQL code automatically generated by PowerDesigner is of good quality, making extensive use of exceptions to report referential integrity violations. Designers have fine-grained control over the number and the type of triggers generated by PowerDesigner.

Unlike ER/Win, PowerDesigner doesn't make use of the back-end database to store its repository. The models generated by the tool are saved in the local filesystem. A good aspect of this arrangement is that the files are in ASCII format, easily handled by version control systems, which must be used externally from

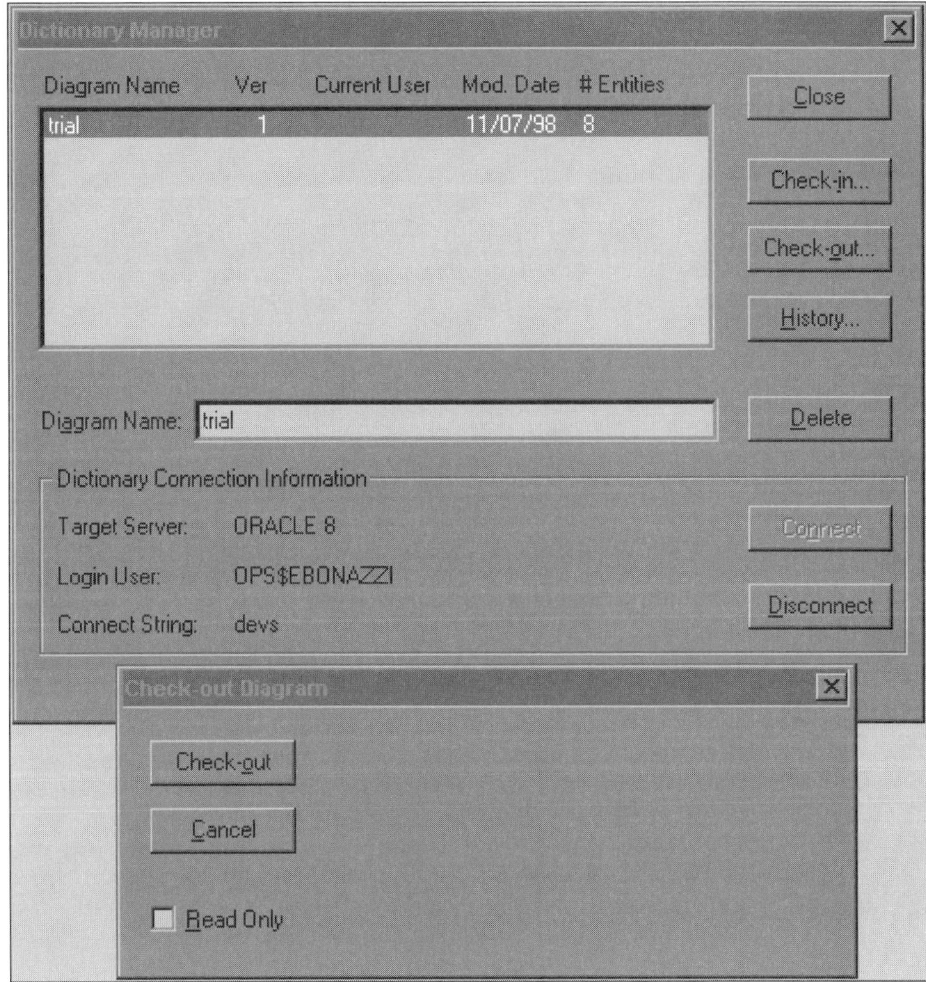

FIGURE 6.14 The ER/Win Data Dictionary Manager at work

PowerDesigner to guarantee an adequate level of control over the production of models.

6.4.5 ER/STUDIO

ER/Studio, by Embarcadero Technologies, is a relative newcomer in the data-modeling arena, yet it appears to have plenty of features and capabilities able to make it one of the strongest competitors. Its modern conception shows off in its

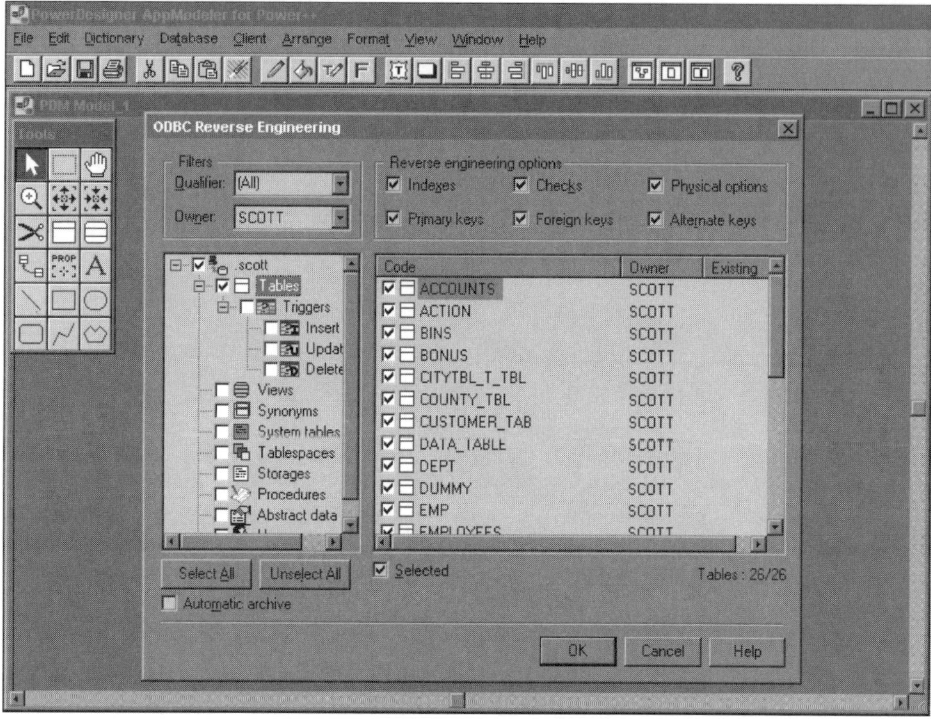

FIGURE 6.15 PowerDesigner only supports ODBC connections

extremely usable user interface, completely in line with the latest trends and standards established by the most recent releases of MS Windows.

The main innovation introduced by this tool is the division of the modeling framework in two panes; the left pane implements a tree control where the two topmost nodes are the logical and the physical models. By expanding the tree, the next node shown, in both logical and physical models, is the so-called main view, which contains the model in its entirety. Designers can organize sets of entities into sub-views, which become child nodes of the main view in the tree. The use of the tree control soon becomes like a second nature, allowing for quick navigation among the various models, views, sub-views and entities. The tree control in the left pane drives what the tool displays in the larger part of the desktop, but repainting the right pane takes virtually no time, so the overall impression is of an extremely well engineered interface.

Its powerful GUI is not the only point of strength of ER/Studio, which allows multiple physical data models to be attached to a single logical model, so that in one project file the logical diagram coexists with the physical models for all target databases.

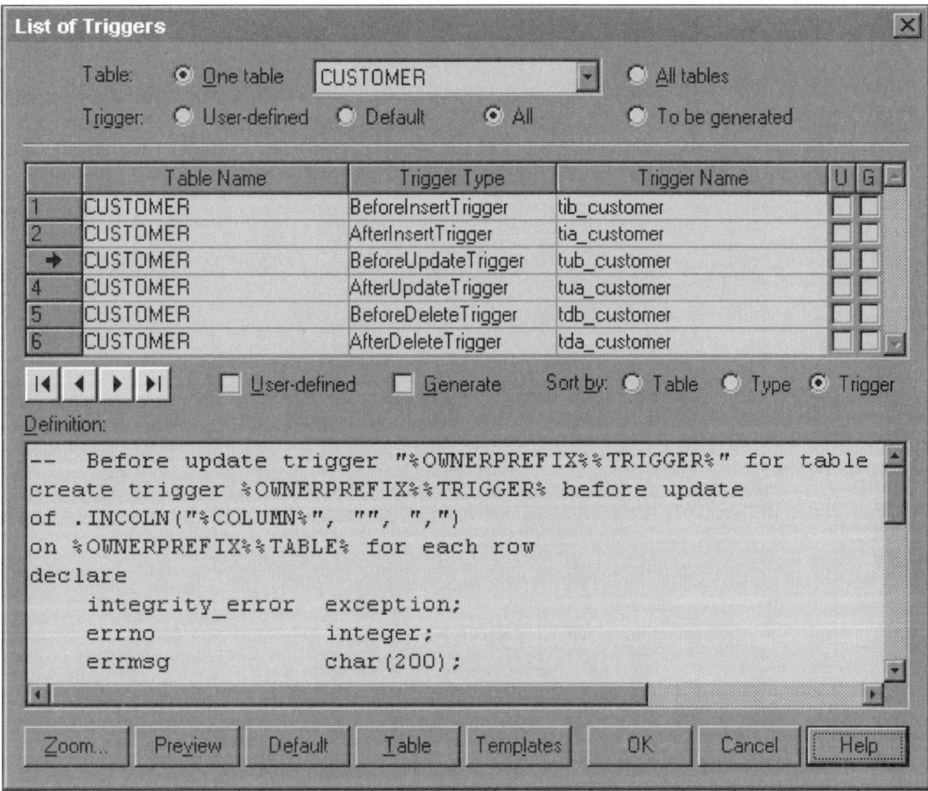

FIGURE 6.16 PowerDesigner supports a strong trigger definition facility

Drawing entities and linking them with relationships is an area in which ER/Studio sets new standards for usability. These tasks are performed in this environment much more easily and more effectively than in all other competing tools.

The data dictionary in ER/Studio is locally defined, as in PowerDesigner; nevertheless, it shows powerful features combined with above average usability.

Unlike PowerDesigner, ER/Studio uses native drivers to connect to Oracle. Like most competing tools, ER/Studio supports both the IDEF1X and IE modeling notations.

ER/Studio is set to rapidly become one of the major players in the data modeling market, thanks to its innovative approach and its stability. To appeal even more to the community of database designers who make an extensive use of Oracle technologies, ER/Studio should emulate ER/Win in its implementation of the repository directly into Oracle, possibly with version control capabilities.

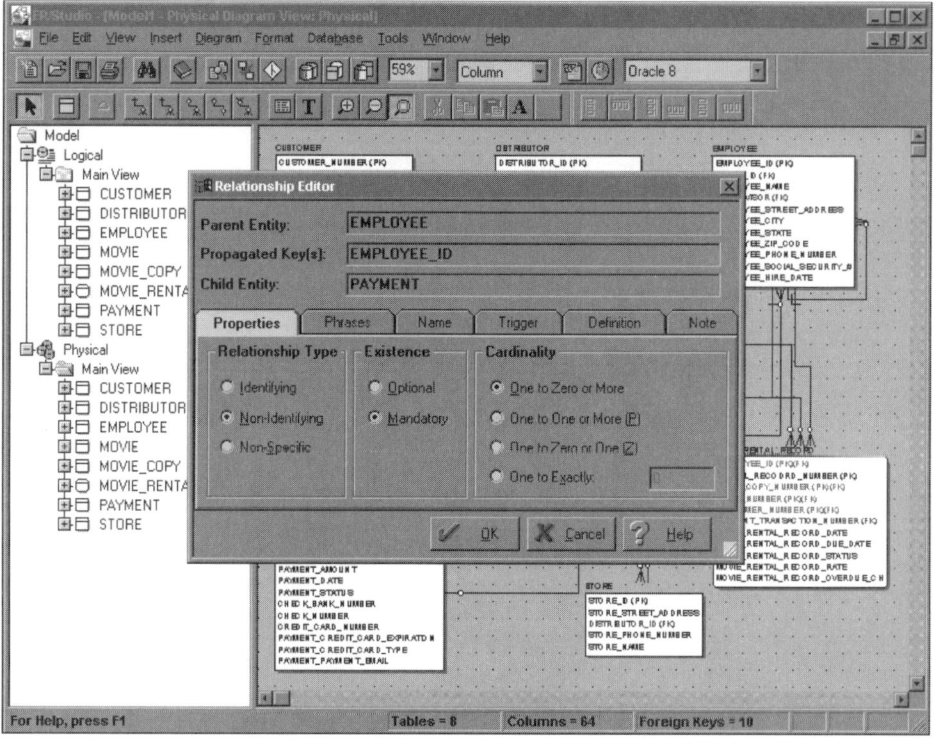

FIGURE 6.17 ER/Studio allows for fine-grained definition of relationships

6.5 Design Deliverables

Irrespective of the tool used, the final outcome of the database design phase is a database schema that will be used by the application in its interaction with the database management system. While conceptual and logical data models must be readily available to designers and architects for further refinements and reviews, the physical data model is particularly important because it becomes the main source that drives the creation of the SQL statements required to access the data stored in the database.

Developers must be intimately confident with the physical data model that represents the current definition of the schema objects. The diagram representing the physical model must be clear, visible without the need for a magnifier, and consistently kept up-to-date. The physical data model of an application of moderate complexity usually contains a number of tables and relationships that hardly fits in a single sheet of paper (letter or A4 format).

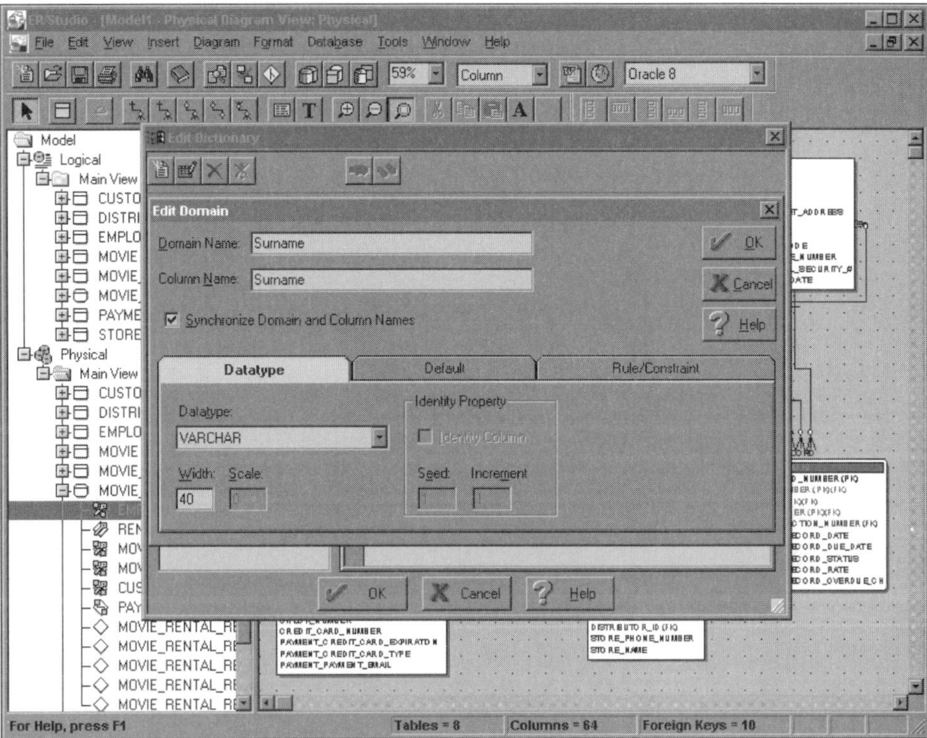

FIGURE 6.18 Data dictionary manipulation in ER/Studio

Since the physical data model is an indispensable tool used by SQL developers to produce their code, it should be delivered on large sheets of paper, such as the A3 format. Ideally, larger formats should be available in meeting rooms and in common large areas shared by the components of the team working on the project. It is not uncommon for start-up IT projects to spend a large amount of money in the very first week to buy electronic boards and plotters capable of handling large sheets of paper.

The data modeling tools presented in this chapter all provide sophisticated drawing capabilities that should be exploited while creating the data models delivered to developers. For example, colors can be used to visually identify sets of related tables. Dotted lines can divide the model in logical sub-models, and different implementations of referential integrity can be identified by lines marked with different colors or drawn using different patterns.

This point is particularly important. When referential integrity is implemented using foreign keys the data modeling tool clearly indicates the relationship between the parent and the child tables. When referential integrity is implemented programmatically, usually the data modeling tool doesn't display a linking line between the related tables. Designers should manually draw the missing lines using a convention (either color-based or pattern-based) to emphasize that referential integrity is supported programmatically. When referential integrity is implemented via reconciliation procedures executed in batch, yet another convention should be used to inform developers using the diagram that they cannot rely on real-time referential integrity mechanisms.

Summary

This chapter examined the common methodologies and CASE tools available to designers and data modelers to accomplish their tasks in the most productive possible manner. Three methodologies have been taken into consideration, together with their distinctive notation:

- ❑ Entity/Relationship (ER) model
- ❑ Information Engineering (IE)
- ❑ IDEF1X

The role of database domains has been highlighted, together with the importance of sharing common definitions across different views of the same project, or even across different projects. This goal is generally achieved through the implementation of a repository. A few data modeling tools—most notably Oracle Designer and ER/Win—store their repository in Oracle. Other tools, such as PowerDesigner and ER/Studio, rely on files stored in the local filesystem. Irrespective of the method used, most data modeling tools considered in this chapter provide a repository, demonstrating how important this feature has become.

An overview of some of the most commonly used data modeling tools has been presented in Section 6.4. The tools are:

- ❑ Oracle Designer
- ❑ Oracle Database Designer (ODD)
- ❑ Logic Works ER/Win
- ❑ Powersoft PowerDesigner
- ❑ Embarcadero ER/Studio

The final part of the chapter focused on the outcomes of the design process. Particular care must be taken in the delivery of data models, especially the physical data model, to SQL developers who must rely on an accurate picture of the database schema objects in order to write SQL statements both semantically correct and performance conscious.

Chapter 7

HOW TO STRUCTURE THE SERVER CODE

This chapter focuses on code practices and techniques that help ensure modularity and control over large and complex projects. Structuring the code in layers and isolating each layer, defining interfaces to facilitate communication and parameter passing, are key elements for the implementation of good and sound software engineering practices.

Code layering techniques are initially shown using traditional procedural languages, such as "C." Further ahead in the chapter the same modular approach is applied to object-oriented environments. The purpose is to show how the same philosophy, based on the separation of the business logic from data access, can be used in different contexts, irrespective of the language adopted.

Another crucial element in the implementation of server-side software components is the error handler, which is often overlooked. The chapter covers error handling in detail, illustrating the basic characteristics that a good error handler should have to assist developers and maintainers in their defect hunting efforts.

A working system, especially in mission critical environments, requires constant monitoring and prompt intervention by the administrators when a problem occurs. The last part of the chapter deals with system monitoring, error logging and event alerting, exploring automated techniques such as e-mail alerting and operator paging triggered by software. Advantages and drawbacks of automatic alerting techniques will be analyzed in the final part of the chapter.

7.1 Beyond the Oracle Manuals

The Oracle manuals provide plenty of examples on how the use of the various pre-compiler features. They use minimal code to provide working examples of the specific syntax or feature being explained. This is good enough for educational purposes, but the same style cannot be used for industrial strength applications.

The main problem with the example-like coding style is that the program logic is mixed with embedded SQL, that is, there is minimal separation between business logic and the various database access functions. In most database-centric applications one can distinguish four separate main functions, which can easily translate into the following four layers:

- control
- business logic
- logical data access
- physical data access

Physically separating the various layers into different files offers several advantages. The most evident is that only the physical data access layer modules need to use embedded SQL. All other modules can be coded using either plain "C" or Cobol.

This enormously simplifies debugging, by isolating the incomprehensible pre-compiled lines of code in the physical data access modules. De-coupling the data access from the business logic makes it easy to modify the physical structure of the database, without reworking the business logic code. Data gathering from the database may be initially implemented via embedded SQL called from Pro*C or Pro*Cobol, and later modified and re-implemented as a database stored procedure. Only the physical data access layer would change; all other layers would remain the same.

Another distinct advantage of program decomposition is the separation between SQL and other language coding. A team can specialize in SQL coding and testing to make data access functions available as libraries for use by other teams. In smaller projects, one programmer can take responsibility of SQL coding and provide the other team members with libraries of SQL functions.

In Chapter 5, while considering the issues related to the Oracle bind variables, we noticed that Oracle re-parses the statements when bind variables are used with different variable names. Centralizing SQL development using one person or one small team can avoid the use of similar but not identical SQL statements in different sections of the program, ultimately providing performance gains.

7.2 Procedural Code LIs the Error Handler Function

Non-fatal errors can be handled in any layer, by calling the error handler.

7.2.1 BUSINESS LOGIC LAYER

The business logic layer modules have the following characteristics:

- Perform the processing necessary to meet the business needs
- Never make database calls nor communicate with the outside world
- Make calls to logical data access layer modules in the majority of cases
- All database accesses made via calls to a logical data access layer module

7.2.2 LOGICAL DATA ACCESS LAYER

The logical data access layer modules have the following characteristics:

- Called by business logic modules and other logical data access modules
- Used to provide independence between the business logic and actual database organization
- Used for each logical unit of work
- Provide validation for database changes, e.g., referential integrity checks that are performed by the program and not by Oracle
- Concurrency checks, e.g., handling of the optimistic locking strategy

7.2.3 PHYSICAL DATA ACCESS LAYER

The physical data access layer provides one module to perform each physical database action, e.g.,

DBFetchTransactionsFromOutQueue()
DBInsertExternalTxn()
DBDeleteWithdrawnTxn()
DBSelectTxnsCount()

It also performs preliminary error checking via the error-handling module, that is, for completely unexpected SQL return conditions like "Oracle not running." All module names in this layer start with "DB." This naming convention makes it easy for a developer to avoid stepping into a physical data access function when using a debugger, and thus avoids accessing multiple lines of meaningless, automatically generated code.

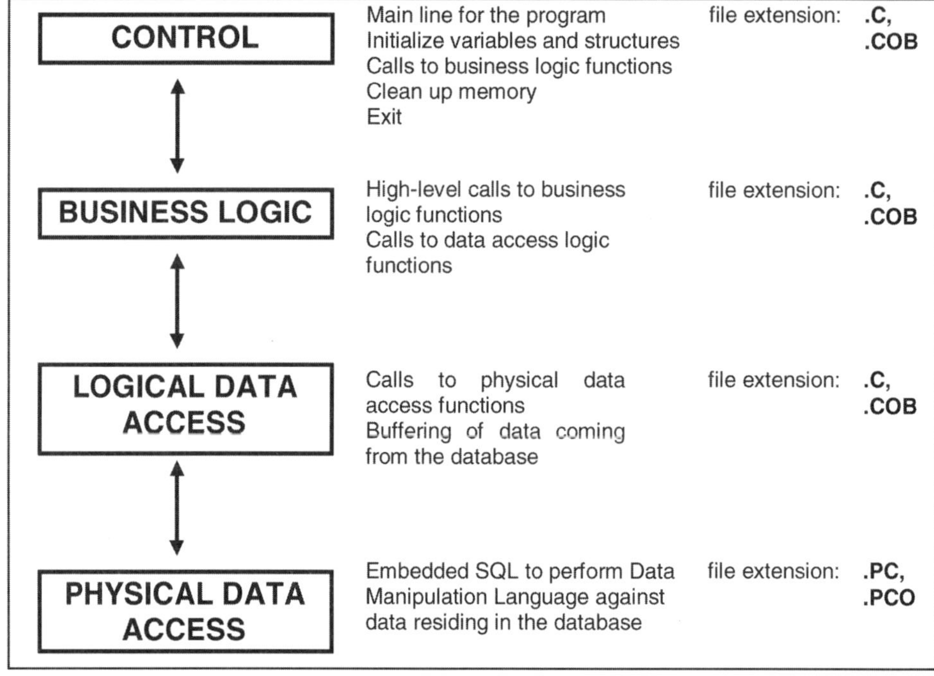

FIGURE 7.1 The different code layers

The following example illustrates the relationship between the physical and logical data access layers:

LOGICAL *RecordIncomingTxn()*

⇓

PHYSICAL *DBInsertTxn()*

Later on, as a result of analyzing the processing efficiency, it is decided that the running total of transactions for the day would be better stored separately. The logical and physical layers are modified as follows:

LOGICAL *RecordIncomingTxn()*

⇓ ⇓

PHYSICAL *DBInsertTxn() and DBUpdateTxnTotal()*

No changes to the business logic layer are required.

7.2.4 COMMUNICATION BETWEEN LAYERS—PARAMETERS AND RETURN VALUES

All modules within a layer receive in and out parameters and return a status to signal the successful or unsuccessful completion of the module. Non-error return values must be handled in the functions parameter list, as demonstrated by the following examples:

Example a)

```
dCircumference = 2 * dRadius * dCalcPi();                INCORRECT!


double dPi;
if (dCalcPi(&dPi))
    dCircumference = 2 * dRadius * dPi;                  CORRECT!


 else
      return(FALSE);
```

Example b)

```
....
if (DoTheFirstBit(Param1, Param2))
    if (DoTheSecondBit(Param3, Param4))
      ....
  else
        return(FALSE);
else
     return(FALSE);
     ....
 int DoTheFirstBit(char cArg1,
                   int  iArg2)
 {
     ... doing something ...
     if (an error found)
         return(FALSE)
     else
         return(TRUE)
 }
```

In the above examples, the return value of all functions is always a success code. If the caller needs to receive the result of a computation performed by a routine, the variable used to store the computed value must be passed as a parameter in the parameter list.

7.2.5 PROCEDURAL CODE LAYERING - AN EXAMPLE IN "C"

What follows is a complete example of an application that is coded according to the layering rules. The example comprises four "C" files, three files containing embedded SQL (characterized by the .pc extension), and seven"C" that include files (extension .h). This simple example application uses two tables for storing information about companies and the value of their stocks. The application performs a query on the stock value of a specific company by providing the ticker I.D.

In spite of its simplicity, the application demonstrates the distinctive traits of a typical database-centric application.The control layer is coded in "CodeLayerExample.c," the business logic can be found in "FetchStock.c," the logical data access layer is coded in "LDFetchStock.c," and the physical data access appears in "DBFetchStock.pc." The database connection logic is provided by ConnectDb.pc and the disconnection from the database is coded in DisconnectDb.pc.

The structure of the database tables is shown in Figure 7.2.

In this first example, the business logic is represented by only one function call (at line 23). In a real life program, the business logic section can comprise many calls, possibly several hundred. Accordingly, the start-up section of a real program that runs in the background collecting messages from a queuing system would be much more complex than our example. It would require logic to open the input queue, obtain the queue handle and connect to the Oracle database before passing control the business logic.

```
            TABLE COMPANY
Name                              Null?    Type
 ------------------------------- -------- ----
 COMPANY_NAME                     NOT NULL VARCHAR2(30)
 TICKER_NAME                      NOT NULL VARCHAR2(12)
 TICKER_ID                                 NUMBER
            TABLE STOCK
Name                              Null?    Type
 ------------------------------- -------- ----
 TICKER_ID                        NOT NULL NUMBER
 DATE_VALUE                       NOT NULL DATE
 LOW                                       NUMBER
 HIGH                                      NUMBER
 CLOSE                                     NUMBER
 VOLUME                                    NUMBER
 REC_SEQ                          NOT NULL NUMBER
```

FIGURE 7.2 The database tables used in the example

Control Layer

```
#include <stdio.h>
#include <string.h>
#include "base.h"
#include "error_handler.h"
#include "ConnectDb.h"
#include "DisconnectDb.h"

int main()
{
     ERROR_DETAILS            structError;
     DB_CONNECT_STRUCT        structConnect;
     int                      nSts;

     memset(&structError,'\0',sizeof(structError));
     memset(&structConnect,'\0',sizeof(structConnect));

     if((nSts = nDBConnectDb(&structConnect,&structError))!=
     SUCCESS)
     {
         ProcessError(&structError,"Connection Failed");
         fprintf(stdout,"Could connect to Oracle.
         Aborting...\n");
         exit(ERROR);
     }

     if ((nSts = FetchStocksById(&structError)) != SUCCESS)
     {
         ProcessError(&structError,"Fetch Stock");
         fprintf(stdout,"Error Fetching Stocks\n");
         exit(ERROR);
     }
     if ((nSts = nDBDisconnectDb(&structError)) != SUCCESS)
     {
          ProcessError(&structError,"Disconnecting
          from Oracle");
          fprintf(stdout,"Error disconnecting from
          Oracle");
     }
     exit(SUCCESS);
}
```

FIGURE 7.3 The CodeLayerExample.c program, containing the control layer

Initialization

10–15 The data structures needed by the program are defined and initialized.

Database connection

17–22 The physical data access function nDBConnectDb is called to establish the database connection, and its return value is checked. Graceful program termination is handled, when the connection attempt fails.

Business logic

24–29 The business logic entry routine is called, and its return value checked. In case of failure, the program can determine if it makes sense to continue anyway, or an exit is the only possible alternative.

Database disconnection

30–34 The program detaches from the database.

Business Logic Layer

```
 1: #include <stdio.h>
 2: #include <string.h>
 3: #include "base.h"
 4: #include "stock.h"
 5: #include "error_handler.h"
 6: #include "GenericFetch.h"
 7: #include "DBFetchStock.h"
 8:
 9: int FetchStocksById(ERROR_DETAILS *pErr)
10: {
11:
12:     STOCKS   **ppStocks=NULL,
13:              *pStockCur=NULL;
14:     int      nTickerId;
15:     int      ii=1;
16:     int      nSts;
17:
18:     nTickerId = 87;
19:     ppStocks = (STOCKS **) malloc(sizeof(char));
20:    if((nSts=nLDFetchStocks(ppStocks,nTickerId,BUILD, pErr))!=SUCCESS)
21:     {
22:          ProcessError(pErr,"Error returned from nLDFetchStocks");
```

FIGURE 7.4 The FetchStock.c program, containing the business logic

```
23:         return (ERROR);
24:     }
25:     for(    pStockCur = *ppStocks;
26:             pStockCur != NULL;
27:             pStockCur = pStockCur->pNext)
28:     {
29:             printf("%d: %-30s %15s %d %d %d %d\n",ii++,
30:                    pStockCur->Stock.szCompany,
31:                    pStockCur->Stock.szDate,
32:                    pStockCur->Stock.nLow,
33:                    pStockCur->Stock.nClose,
34:                    pStockCur->Stock.nHigh,
35:                    pStockCur->Stock.nVolume);
36:
37:     }
38:     if((nSts=nLDFetchStocks(ppStocks,nTickerId,DESTROY, pErr))
        !=SUCCESS)
39:     {
40:         ProcessError(pErr,"Error returned from nLDFetchStocks");
41:         return (ERROR);
42:     }
43:      free(ppStocks);
44:     return(SUCCESS);
45: }
```

FIGURE 7.4 *Continued*

Function definition

9 The function receives an error handler structure.

Data structure definition and initialization

12–13 The program defines two pointers to the structure STOCK. They will be used to build and traverse a linked list containing the stock values fetched from the database.

Logical data access function call

18 The ticker id of the wanted stock is hard coded. In real life application, this value could be either interactively entered by a user, or the computational result of a preceding function.

20–24 The logical data access function LDFetchStocks is called, passing the root pointer to the stock linked list, the wanted stock ticker and the error handler structure. If the called function returns an error, the error is logged by calling the error handler and control is passed back to the control logic. The return status signals that the business logic function did not succeed. The function is called passing the BUILD mnemonic as the third parameter. This means the linked list has to be built by LDFetchStocks.

Data displaying and clean-up

25–37 If the logical data access function returned successfully, the stock linked list is traversed and all stock data displayed on the screen.

38–42 LDFetchStocks is called again, this time passing the DESTROY mnemonic as a parameter. LDFetchStocks will free all memory allocated to each node belonging to the linked list and will return.

Logical Data Access Layer

```
#include <string.h>
#include "base.h"
#include "stock.h"
#include "error_handler.h"
#include "GenericFetch.h"
#include "DBFetchStock.h"

int nLDFetchStocks(STOCKS ** pIn, int nTickerId,
          int nAction,  ERROR_DETAILS *pErr)
{
    HOST_ARR_PARM   structStockParm;
    HOST_ARR_STRUCT structStock;
    int             ii;
    BOOL            boolFirstTime=TRUE;
    STOCKS         *pStocks=NULL,
                   *pStockCur=NULL,
                   *pStockLast=NULL,
                   *pStockPrevious=NULL;
    BOOL           bFirstTime = TRUE;

    memset(&structStockParm,'\0',sizeof(structStockParm));
    memset(&structStock,'\0',sizeof(structStock));
    if (nAction == DESTROY)
    {
       bFirstTime = TRUE;
       for(    pStockCur = (*pIn);
```

FIGURE 7.5 The LDFetchStocks.c program, with the logical data access logic

```
                    pStockCur != NULL;
                    pStockCur = pStockCur->pNext)
        {
                if (bFirstTime)
                {
                    bFirstTime=FALSE;
                    pStockPrevious=pStockCur;
                }
                else
                {
                    free(pStockPrevious);
                    pStockPrevious=pStockCur;
                }
                pStockLast=pStockCur;
        }
        free(pStockLast);
        return(SUCCESS);
    }

    structStockParm.CommonStruct.chWhatToDo = OPEN_CURSOR;
    structStockParm.CommonStruct.nMaxRowsToFetch = 30;
    structStockParm.nTickerId = nTickerId;

    for(;;)
    {
        if( (nDBFetchStock(&structStockParm,&structStock,
                                pErr)) != SUCCESS)
        {
                return(ERROR);
        }
      if ( structStockParm.CommonStruct.nNbrRowsFetched == 0)
            break;
        structStockParm.CommonStruct.chWhatToDo =
        FETCH_AND_CLOSE;
        for (   ii=0;
                ii<=structStockParm.CommonStruct.nBuffCardinality;
                ii++)
        {
```

FIGURE 7.5 *Continued*

```
         if (boolFirstTime)
         {
            if( (*pIn = (STOCKS *)
                  malloc(sizeof(STOCKS))) == NULL)
            {
               pErr->nFatal = TRUE;
               strcpy(pErr->szCoreErr,"MEMORY EXHAUSTED");
               return(ERROR);
            }
            pStockCur = (*pIn);
            memset(pStockCur,'\0',sizeof(STOCKS));
            boolFirstTime = FALSE;
         }
         else
         {
            pStockCur->pNext =
              (STOCKS *) malloc(sizeof(STOCKS));
            if (pStockCur->pNext == NULL)
            {
               pErr->nFatal=TRUE;
               strcpy(pErr->szCoreErr,
                    "MEMORY EXHAUSTED");
               return(ERROR);
            }
            if (ii > 0)
                pStockCur = pStockCur->pNext;
            memset(pStockCur,'\0',sizeof(STOCKS));
         }
         strcpy(pStockCur->Stock.szCompany,
               structStock.szCompany[ii]);
         strcpy(pStockCur->Stock.szDate,
               structStock.szDate[ii]);
         pStockCur->Stock.nLow = structStock.nLow[ii];
         pStockCur->Stock.nClose = structStock.nClose[ii];
         pStockCur->Stock.nHigh = structStock.nHigh[ii];
         pStockCur->Stock.nVolume = structStock.nVolume[ii];
      } /* End for ii */
      if (structStockParm.CommonStruct.chFlowIndicator ==
```

FIGURE 7.5 *Continued*

```
102:            MORE_ROWS_TO_BE_FETCHED)
103:                 continue;
104:         else
105:                 break;
106:     } /* End for ;; */
107:     return(SUCCESS);
108: }
```

FIGURE 7.5 *Continued*

Function definition

8 The function receives the doubly indirected root pointer to the stock linked list, the ticker id of the wanted stock values, the action mnemonic (either BUILD or DESTROY) and the error handling structure.

Data structures definition and initialization

11 `HOST_ARRAY_PARM` is a protocol structure used by the logical data access function to communicate with the physical data access function. The caller uses the structure to specify the host array dimension, and if the cursor has to be opened. The callee stores the cumulative number of rows fetched, the rows fetched in the last batch and whether there are more rows to be fetched. The same structure is used to pass the where clause variables to the physical data access function.

12–15 The other data structures provide a structure to receive the Oracle array data, a pointer to a structure of type STOCK, used to traverse the stock linked list, and a boolean flag used to indicate if the linked list is traversing the first node.

Linked list de-allocation

23–44 If the requested action is to destroy the linked list, the linked list is traversed and all nodes de-allocated. The function then returns to the caller.

Populating the "protocol" structure

46–48 The structure used to support the communication protocol between the logical data access layer and the physical data access layer is populated with the relevant fields.

Getting the data

50 The endless outer loop is initiated. The program flow will interrupt the loop when all data has been fetched from Oracle.

52–56 The physical data access function is called with 3 parameters: the "protocol" structure, the structure to be populated by Oracle and the error handler structure.

57–58 If the cumulative number of rows fetched from Oracle is 0, then exit the main loop.

59 The cursor was opened during the first call to the physical data access function. From this point onwards the caller only wants to fetch new batches of data coming from Oracle, without opening the cursor.

60–62 The inner loop is started. It iterates from 0 to the number of rows fetched in the current batch. If there are 49 rows to be fetched from the database, and the host array is dimensioned to 30, the first batch would contain 30 rows. The cumulative number in the protocol structure would be 30, the buffer cardinality would also be 30. After the second call to the physical data access function, the cumulative number of rows fetched would be 49, and the buffer cardinality would be 19.

64–91 The linked list is extended.

92–100 The data fetched by the Oracle batches is stored into the linked list.

101–106 The protocol structure is queried to determine whether Oracle reached the end of the cursor, or if more incoming rows are expected. If Oracle exhausted all rows the program exits the outer loop.

The business logic routine is unaware of the physical structure of the data in the database. The data requested by the business logic function requires a join between two tables. If the implementation of some other business change forces a physical restructuring of the database, for instance collapsing the two tables into one, the business logic function remains untouched.

The logical data access function follows:

When fetching data from Oracle, the logical data access function usually needs to call the corresponding physical data access function repeatedly, until all rows have been fetched. The database cursor holding the rows is opened only once and the logical data access function must cease calling the lower-level function when no more data is expected from the cursor. In other words, the two functions need a two-way communication mechanism, to synchronize their efforts. The protocol structure pointer passed to the physical layer routine allows the two routines to communicate the relevant information between the various calls. The structure is defined in GenericFetch.h.

```
#ifndef GENERIC_FETCH_H
#define GENERIC_FETCH_H

#define INPUT
#define OUTPUT

#define OPEN_CURSOR_FAIL       110
#define CLOSE_CURSOR_FAIL      111
#define FETCH_ROW_FAIL         112

#define OPEN_CURSOR 30
#define FETCH_AND_CLOSE 40

#define NO_MORE_ROWS_TO_FETCH  10
#define MORE_ROWS_TO_BE_FETCHED 20

typedef struct
{
INPUT   int  nMaxRowsToFetch;/* Number of rows to fetch
                                at once              */
INPUT   char chWhatToDo;     /* OPEN_CURSOR or
                                FETCH_AND_CLOSE      */
OUTPUT  int  nNbrRowsFetched;/* Number of rows which
                                have been            */
                             /* fetched              */
OUTPUT int  nBuffCardinality;/* Number of rows fetched
                                in                   */
                             /* the current buffer   */
OUTPUT char chFlowIndicator; /* NO_MORE_ROWS_TO_FETCH
                                                     */
                             /* or MORE_ROWS_TO_BE_
                                FETCHED              */
}FETCH_COMMON_STRUCT;

#endif
```

FIGURE 7.6 GenericFetch.h

Input values

19–20 The two structure fields nMaxRowsToFetch and chWhatToDo are received by the physical data access function. They specify the dimension of the host array and if the cursor has to be opened.

Output values

21–26 The output values from the physical data access function tell the calling function the cumulative number of rows fetched after the last call, the number of rows fetched by the last call, and if the cursor has been completely filled with data, or whether further calls are needed to fetch the remaining rows identified by the SQL query.

The physical data access function follows:

Physical Data Access Layer

```
EXEC SQL INCLUDE SQLCA;

#include <string.h>
#include "base.h"
#include "error_handler.h"
#include "GenericFetch.h"
#include "DBFetchStock.h"


GLOBAL int nDBFetchStock(  HOST_ARR_PARM          *pIn,
                           HOST_ARR_STRUCT        *pOut,
                           ERROR_DETAILS          *pErr)

{
    static int      MaxRowsIn1Fetch;
    BOOL            nEndOfSet;
    BOOL            boolErrorOccurred = FALSE;

    int             nTickerId;
    int             sts;
    int             nSqlErrdCount=0;


    if ( pIn->CommonStruct.chWhatToDo == OPEN_CURSOR )
    {
```

FIGURE 7.7 DBFetchStock.pc, containing embedded SQL

```
        pIn->CommonStruct.nNbrRowsFetched      = 0;
        sqlca.sqlerrd[2]                       = 0;
        MaxRowsIn1Fetch          = pIn->CommonStruct.n MaxRow-
        sToFetch;
        pIn->CommonStruct.nBuffCardinality     = 0;
        nEndOfSet                              = FALSE;

        nTickerId = pIn->nTickerId;

        EXEC SQL DECLARE StockArrCurs CURSOR FOR
        SELECT
             COM.COMPANY_NAME,
             TO_CHAR(STK.DATE_VALUE,'DDMMYYYY HH24MISS'),
             STK.LOW,
             STK.CLOSE,
             STK.HIGH,
             STK.VOLUME
        FROM
             COMPANY COM, STOCK STK
        WHERE
             COM.TICKER_ID = STK.TICKER_ID
             AND
             STK.TICKER_ID = :nTickerId;

        EXEC SQL OPEN StockArrCurs;

        if (sqlca.sqlcode != 0)
        {
           pErr->sqlcode = sqlca.sqlcode;
           strncpy(pErr->szSqlErr,sqlca.sqlerrm.sqlerrmc,
                   sqlca.sqlerrm.sqlerrml);
           return(ERROR);
        }
    }
    nSqlErrdCount = sqlca.sqlerrd[2];
    EXEC SQL
    FOR  :MaxRowsIn1Fetch
    FETCH StockArrCurs
    INTO :pOut;

```

FIGURE 7.7 *Continued*

```
    pIn->CommonStruct.nNbrRowsFetched = sqlca.sqlerrd[2];
    pIn->CommonStruct.nBuffCardinality=sqlca.sqlerrd
    [2]-nSqlErrdCount;
    if (sqlca.sqlcode == NO_MORE_DATA )
    {
        nEndOfSet = TRUE;
    }
    else if (sqlca.sqlcode < 0)
    {
        nEndOfSet = TRUE;
        boolErrorOccurred = TRUE;
        pErr->sqlcode = sqlca.sqlcode;
        strncpy(pErr->szSqlErr,sqlca.sqlerrm.sqlerrmc,
                sqlca.sqlerrm.sqlerrml);
    }
    else if (sqlca.sqlcode == 0)
    {
        nEndOfSet = FALSE;
    }
    if ( nEndOfSet)
    {
       if (boolErrorOccurred == TRUE)
       {
          pIn->CommonStruct.chFlowIndicator = NO_MORE_ROWS_TO_FETCH;
          EXEC SQL CLOSE StockArrCurs;
          return(ERROR);
       }
       EXEC SQL CLOSE StockArrCurs;
       pIn->CommonStruct.chFlowIndicator = NO_MORE_ROWS_TO_FETCH;
    }
    else
       pIn->CommonStruct.chFlowIndicator = MORE_ROWS_TO_BE_FETCHED;

    return(SUCCESS);
}
```

FIGURE 7.7 *Continued*

SQL Communication Area

1 The Oracle SQL Communication Area structure is included in the file, so that the various fields contained in the sqlca structure can be accessed by the program.

Cursor opening

24 If the caller function specified that the cursor has to be opened, then declare the cursor.

48 Execute the SQL command to open the cursor.

51–56 Check the value returned by Oracle in the sqlca structure to verify that the cursor has been successfully opened. If an error occurred, populate the error handler structure and return to the caller with an error status.

Cursor fetching

The nSqlErrdCount variable returns the number of rows stored in the last batch returned by Oracle.

60–63 The rows are fetched into the structure received from the caller.

65–66 The protocol structure is filled with information related to the cumulative number of rows fetched and the number of rows fetched in the last batch.

Error checking

67–90 The sqlcode field of the sqlca structure is accessed to check for errors during the last fetch. Oracle stores the return code in that field. If it is 0, everything was OK and more rows have to be fetched. If the value stored in it is less than 0, an error occurred. If the number stored in that field is 1403, then all data has been fetched and the cursor can be closed. The magic number 1403 has been made equal to the mnemonic NO_MORE_DATA in the error handler include file.

Cursor closing

83–90 If the end of the set of rows identified by the SQL query has been reached, then the cursor can be closed.

95 The closure of the cursor and the finishing of the fetch operations are communicated to the caller function by storing the mnemonic NO_MORE_ROWS_TO_FETCH in the appropriate field of the protocol structure.

7.2.6 AUTOMATIC CODE GENERATION

It should be noted that the structure of the physical data access function is almost entirely fixed and predetermined. The only variable part is represented by the names of the fields and the tables in the SQL statement used to query the database, or to insert, update, or delete rows. This characteristic makes it easy to automate the generation of code required to interact with the database.

Tools like Perl, OraPerl or awk can be used to automatically produce all of the physical data access functions and most of the logical data access functions. Using OraPerl, it would be possible to query the Oracle data dictionary for the precise table configuration. The next step would be to generate on the fly the "C" file containing the embedded SQL for the required DML statements.

Alternatively, Oracle Sql*Plus can be used to describe the various tables and capture the output in a file. An awk script can then be launched to loop through every field in the file automatically generating the physical data access logic.

It is easy to automatically generate the physical data access logic for individual tables. These files should be edited only for a manual insertion of the where clause fields and logic. The generation of the DML statements for joining tables is a little more complex. The automated process used for single tables can still be used, but the manual intervention is more demanding. Alternatively, more sophisticated code generators that are able to understand more complex SQL syntax, including joins, can be built.

The real value of a database-centric application resides in the business logic. The initial design efforts strive to capture the business flow and business rules to be enforced and followed by the application. Database access is of minor importance, compared to the business logic, and is a tedious, yet defect prone process, potentially capable of disrupting the project schedule. Enforcing a rigid separation between business logic and database access helps to achieve three major goals:

- Independence of business logic from data structure
- Automated generation of database access code
- Centralization of database access code

Maintaining the business logic independent from the data structure of an application allows database objects to be physically restructured without a corresponding change in the business logic code. In addition, an application can be initially implemented using a two-tier architecture and later extended by introducing a TP monitor without a major re-writing of the code.

Automatic code generation means the production of less error prone code modules and productivity gains. Finally, centralizing the database access code produces better control over the SQL statements sent to the Oracle engine, avoiding the re-parsing of similar but not identical SQL statements.

7.3 Using Composition in OO

The goal of de-coupling the data access logic from the business logic can be achieved, probably even more elegantly, in object-oriented environments. The mechanism used to achieve this is called composition. The operation being "delegated" is caught in one class and forwarded to another class for proper execution. The tension, here, is between encapsulation, typical of object-oriented languages, and de-coupling database access from the business logic.

Let us take the class "customer" as an example. Encapsulation dictates that all attributes and methods pertaining to the entity "customer" should be captured in the customer class definition. Attributes and methods can be inherited by child classes that further qualify the specificity of a customer.

OverseasCustomer, for instance, can be a class inherited from *Customer* with additional attributes and methods dealing with currency exchange, international fund transfer, etc. One option for the implementation of Oracle database access is the definition of a *Connection* class holding a connection context. An instance of the connection class can be passed as a parameter for the customer class constructor. The latter can then use the received connection context to fetch the customer data while creating an instance of the class customer, the customer *object*. An example in pseudo-code (a little cplusplusish!) follows:

```
class Connection
{
        public:
        Connection(char * szUsername, char * szPassword);
        ...
        private:
        Lda_def loc_lda; /* Oracle OCI Structure */
        unsigned char hda[256]; /* Oracle OCI Structure */
        ...
};

class Customer
{
        public:
        Customer(Connection OC, int cust_id);
        protected:
        char szCustName[31];
        char szCustAddress[51];
        ...
        ...
};

Connection::Connection(char * szUsername, char * szPassword)
{
        /* Connecting using the Oracle Call Interface (OCI) */
        orlon(&loc_lda,had, szUsername, -1, szPassword, -1,0);
        ...
        ...
};
```

```
Customer::Customer(Connection OC, int cust_id)
{
      Cda_Def      loc_cda; /* Oracle OCI Structure */
      char *       szSQL = "select customer_name,
                            customer_address from
                            customer where cust_id = :1";
      from oopen(&loc_cda,OC.loc_lda,(text *) 0,-1,-1,(text
      *) 0, -1,0);
      oparse(&loc_cda,szSQL,,-1,1,2);
      odefin(&loc_cda,1,szCustName,sizeof(szCustName),
      CHAR_TYPE,
             -1, 0, 0, -1, -1);
      odefin(&loc_cda,1,szCustAddress,sizeof(szCustAd-
      dress),CHAR_TYPE,
             -1, 0, 0, -1, -1);
      obndrn(&loc_cda, 1, &cust_id, sizeof(int), 3, -1,0,0,-
      1,-1);
      oexfet(&loc_cda,1,0,0);
      oclose(&loc_cda);
      ...
      ...
}
main()
{
      Connection OC ("scott","tiger");
      Customer CUST (&OC,257);
      ...
      ...
}
```

The example uses the Oracle Call Interface to access the Oracle database. If the *oopen, odefin, obndrn* calls look like hieroglyphics, go to chapter 12 for a detailed explanation. The example shown above is a poor implementation because the customer class is intimately dependent on the physical structure of the data defined in Oracle. A modification to the customer table implies re-working the code for the customer class.

The structure that a relational engine imposes upon object-oriented languages differs from the more "natural" approach typical of the object-oriented databases. In a pure object oriented database, the objects are given "persistence" more or less transparently, so a programmer can freely encapsulate all attributes and methods in one class. The object is stored in its entirety and does not need to be re-assembled when the customer information stored in the database is retrieved.

Customer.h, definition of the classes used in the example

```
#ifndef CUSTOMER_H
#define CUSTOMER_H 1
class customer;
class ora_customer
{
public:
   ora_customer(void) {}
   void cust_fetch(const customer * cust);

};

class customer
{
   friend ora_customer;
public:
   customer(int nCustCode);
   char * get_cust_name(void);
   char * get_cust_address(void);
   char * get_cust_telephone(void);
   char * get_cust_fax_number(void);
protected:
   char    szCustName[31];
   char    szCustAddress[51];
   char    szCustTel[16];
   char    szCustFax[16];
private:
   ora_customer OC;
   int          nCustCode;
};

class Connection
{
public:
   Connection(char * szUsername, char * szPassword);
};

#endif
```

FIGURE 7.8 Class definition

Class definition

3 Forward declaration of the customer class. Necessary because ora_customer refers to customer prior to its definition.

4–10 ora_customer class definition. Only two public methods are defined, the constructor and the method that operates the SQL fetch.

12–29 customer class definition. Customer is declared to be *friend* of ora_customer so that ora_customer can access all customer attributes. Also, customer uses *composition,* that is, it defines ora_customer in the private section to which it will "delegate" the Oracle operations.

31–35 An ancillary class is needed to manage a connection to the database. The connection class only has one method, the constructor, which receives username and password as parameters.

Connection class implementation

```
#include <iostream.h>
#include <string.h>
#include "customer.h"
extern struct sqlca sqlca;
connection::connection(char * szUsername, char * szPassword)
{
        EXEC SQL BEGIN DECLARE SECTION;
        VARCHAR username[20];
        VARCHAR password[30];
        EXEC SQL END DECLARE SECTION;
        username.len = (unsigned short)strlen (strcpy((char *)
                       username.arr,szUsername));
        password.len = (unsigned short)strlen (strcpy((char*)
                       password.arr, szPassword));
        EXEC SQL CONNECT :username IDENTIFIED BY :password;
        cout << "Connected to ORACLE as user: "
       << (char *)username.arr << endl << endl;
}
```

FIGURE 7.9 Connection class implementation

Connection class

6	The only method defined in Connection is its constructor.
8–11	Embedded SQL commands to define Oracle host variables.
13–16	The constructor parameters are copied into the Oracle host variables.
19	SQL statement to request a connection to Oracle.

Ora_customer class implementation

```
#include <string.h>
#include "customer.h"

extern struct sqlca sqlca;


void ora_customer::cust_fetch(const customer *cust)
{
   EXEC SQL BEGIN DECLARE SECTION;
   int nCustId;
   struct Cust
   {
        VARCHAR CustName[30];
        VARCHAR CustAddress[50];
        VARCHAR CustTel[15];
        VARCHAR CustFax[15];
   }CustRec;
   struct CustInd
   {
        short int NameInd;
        short int AddressInd;
        short int TelInd;
        short int FaxInd;
   }CustRecInd;
   EXEC SQL END DECLARE SECTION;

   memset(&CustRec,'\0',sizeof(CustRec));
   memset(&CustRecInd,'\0',sizeof(CustRecInd));
   nCustId = cust->nCustCode;

   EXEC    SQL SELECT CUSTOMER_NAME,CUSTOMER_ADDRESS,
               CUSTOMER_TELEPHONE,CUSTOMER_TELEFAX
               INTO :CustRec INDICATOR :CustRecInd
               FROM CUSTOMER
```

FIGURE 7.10 ora_customer class implementation

```
35:                WHERE
36:                CUSTOMER_ID = :nCustId;
37:
38:     strcpy((char *)cust->szCustName,(char *) CustRec.CustName.arr);
39:     strcpy((char *)cust->szCustAddress,(char *)
40:              CustRec.CustAddress.arr);
41:     strcpy((char *)cust->szCustTel,(char *) CustRec.CustTel.arr);
42:     strcpy((char *)cust->szCustFax,(char *) CustRec.CustFax.arr);
43: }
```

FIGURE 7.10 *Continued*

Implementation of the ora_customer class

7	The cust_fetch method receives an instance of the customer class as a parameter.
9	Pre-compiler instructions to define Oracle host variables.
10	nCustId will be used as the where clause variable.
11–17	Definition of a host variable structure to receive the data stored in the Oracle customer table.
18–24	Definition of corresponding indicator variables structure.
27–28	Initializing the host variables within the structures.
28	The where clause variable receives the input from the variable initialized by the constructor of the customer class
31–36	SQL statement to fetch one complete row from the customer table.
38–42	The attributes of the instance of the customer class get the values fetched from Oracle. This is possible because ora_customer has been declared as a friend of the Customer class.

The relational nature of the Oracle engine forces designers and programmers of object-oriented applications to compromise, giving up OO purity in exchange for more scalability and reliability. An Oracle based application using object-oriented languages cannot rely on the elegant concept of "object persistence." While this may change in future Oracle releases, some steps can be taken to achieve modularity and flexibility while using OO languages.

Let us re-work the previous example, this time trying to de-couple the Oracle access logic from the customer class implementation. The new example uses Pro*C release 2.2 to pre-compile the embedded SQL code.

The advantage provided by the previous example is the de-coupling achieved between the customer class and run-time gathering of the attribute values from Oracle. As long as no new columns are added or dropped, the customer

Customer class implementation + program main line

```
#include <string.h>
#include <stdio.h>
#include <stdlib.h>
#include <sqlca.h>
#include "customer.h"

char * customer::get_cust_name(void)
{
    return szCustName;
}

char * customer::get_cust_telephone(void)
{
    return szCustTel;
}

char * customer::get_cust_fax_number(void)
{
    return szCustFax;
}

char * customer::get_cust_address(void)
{
    return szCustAddress;
}

customer::customer(int nCode)
{
    nCustCode = nCode;
    OC.cust_fetch(this);
}



int main()
{
    char * szName;

    Connection Conn("ebonazzi","oracle8");
    szName = (char *) malloc(31);
    customer OC(1);
    szName = OC.get_cust_name();
    printf("Customer: %s\n",szName);
    return 0;
}
```

FIGURE 7.11 Customer class implementation

Customer class and main program

- *7–25* Methods to return the class attributes are defined.
- *27* The class constructor receives the customer code as a parameter.
- *30* The cust_fetch method of the ora_customer instance is called, passing the entire customer object as a parameter.
- *39* The main program instantiates the connection class into a connection object, passing username and password as parameters.
- *41* An instance of the class customer is instantiated, passing the customer code to the class constructor. The customer class constructor automatically fetches the data from the Oracle customer table.
- *42* The customer object has retrieved the values for all its attributes. They are now accessible through the set of get methods.

class doesn't have to be modified if the physical structure of the customer table changes. The customer table can be split in two and the same fields retrieved a table join. This can be achieved by modifying the ora_customer class only. The customer class and the business logic implemented in its methods would not change. This implementation represents an improvement over the first example but is not the best possible solution. Chapter 12 will provide a better implementation, using the Oracle Call Interface.

7.4 Error/Exception Handling

The stock example application shown in Section 7.2.5 used a rudimentary error handling mechanism. The error handler shown in the example is good enough for educational purposes, but it cannot support a mission critical, industrial strength application.

In real estate, a property evaluator carefully examines the toilets in order to judge the quality of the material used to build a house. The quality of the material used for the sinks and water closets, not to mention the toilet tiles, tells a lot about the overall quality of the house. In software engineering, the quality of the error handling of an application tells a lot about the overall intrinsic quality of all application components.

The time and money invested in building a high quality error handler at the beginning of the project pays big dividends towards the end of the project. When project deadlines are approaching and the last remaining defects have to be found and fixed before going to production, a precise and accurate error handler can be invaluable.

The information recorded by the error handler can be very helpful to a developer investigating a software defect. A good error handler should record the following information:

1. The application facility that produced the error
2. An extended message, possibly able to handle parameters, explaining the nature of the error
3. The exact timestamp of when the error occurred
4. The error number, if a numeric convention is in use
5. The severity of the error (informational, warning, fatal, etc.)
6. The username of the application user when the error occurred
7. The process id of the process that produced the error

If the errors being recorded are produced by applications running on the server, typically Pro*C or Pro*Cobol executables, then the following information should also be recorded:

1. The filename of the file containing the application source code that produced the error
2. The code line number in the source file which produced the error

If the errors are produced by client applications, typically MS Windows based applications, then the following information is also useful.

1. The window name of the active window when the error occurred
2. The name of the object which produced the error
3. The active window event when the error occurred

Since an Oracle based application has the luxury of being supported by a database, it is a good idea to store the errors in database tables. This simplifies the production of detailed error reports for error pattern analysis. It also facilitates ABC categorizations of the errors to establish priorities for allocating resources to bug fixing.

There are two components of an error handler that can proficiently use the database services. One is the expansion of the error number into meaningful error messages. The other is the storage of information pertaining to error occurrences for statistical analysis.

Usually, the application code deals with error codes or mnemonics. This is a good practice because it reduces the size of the executable and minimizes the run-time memory needed by the application. In addition, it simplifies dealing with internationalization issues. The error is the same in all languages; it is the text associated to the error which varies with the language. The various error messages can be stored in a database table so that the error handler can expand an error number to produce the text associated by performing a table lookup when an error occurs at run-time. The error handler should be smart enough to store the error code in an error log file in the file system, if the database is inaccessible.

A sophisticated error handler should allow for parameter expansion. The error text can contain placeholders, which can be replaced by expanded parameters at run-time as shown in the following example.

```
Error text:  "File {FILENAME} not found."
Error handler expansion: "File APPLICATION.INI not found."
```

The error handler should be called with the error number of the error being recorded. It should try to expand the error number into a meaningful message, including eventual parameter expansion, by looking up the database table containing the error messages. The error number should be the key for the error message search. If the database lookup operation is successful, the error handler can try to record the expanded error in a database table devoted to error capturing. Otherwise, the error handler should record the unexpanded error in an error log file in the file system. In some instances the error handler may successfully retrieve and expand the error message, and then fail to store the error message in the database. In that case the error handler should record the fully expanded message in the file system.

The golden rule of error handling, which is often overlooked, is that there is a one-to-one correspondence between an error and its related entry into the error log table. This seems so natural that it shouldn't even need to be mentioned. Unfortunately poorly implemented error handling routines provoke error storms, which rapidly populate the error log table with hundreds of error messages. The difficult part is to identify the initial error that triggered all the others. The error timestamp is usually not enough to establish the correct error sequence as the default granularity of the Oracle time stamping is seconds. This is not adequate for most computer architectures, as tens of messages could be recorded in a single second.

7.4.1 ERROR HANDLING IN "C"

In spite of the great popularity achieved by the object-oriented languages in recent years, most of the Oracle-based mission critical applications running today are still coded in "C". Unfortunately, error handling is definitely not the strong point of procedural languages such as "C". In a procedural language, error handling must be implemented using a daisy chain mechanism. The error information must be passed back and forth between routines from the most deeply nested level to the least nested level.

It is easy to lose control and fail to keep track of error information when an error occurs in a routine five levels down the code main line. The error information has to be preserved while going through four levels of routine calls without being changed or inadvertently lost. This situation resembles that game usually played by children called "wireless telephone" or simply "the telephone". A large group of people stand in a circle and the master of the game starts by whispering something to the person standing at his or her immediate left. That person whispers the message to the person standing close at the left. The game continues until all participants have whispered the message. Invariably, the message received by the last person is radically changed and has very little in common with the original message.

Following the same principle, the error finally logged in the database can be very misleading if it is modified several times while being passed along the chain. Structuring the server code in distinct layers can help enforce an error handling discipline. Designers can easily establish error handling rules, such as, "The physical access layer only populates the error-handling structure, and is never allowed to call the error handling routine," or "The business logic layer is in charge of recording all errors encountered by routines in the lower levels."

The SQL Communication Area (SQLCA) plays an important role in the interaction between a pre-compiled high-level language and Oracle. The SQLCA structure is populated by Oracle every time an SQL statement is executed. A few fields within the SQLCA contain very important information such as the return error code stored by Oracle, and the associated error message. Another field stores the number of rows processed by the most recently executed SQL statement. For an SQL statement involving host arrays, this field signals which element in the array caused the error.

This kind of information is very useful and should be captured by a sophisticated error handler. It is a good idea to have an SQLCA replica defined in the structure used by the error handler. It can be populated by the physical data access layer routines when an Oracle error occurs. An example of an error handling structure, suitable for use by a server program written in "C", is shown below.

```
…
#include "sqlca.h"
…
#define ProcessError(pstructError,nErrNum,szErrString)\
 { nErrorHandler(__FILE__,__LINE__,pstructLocalError, nErrNum,\
    szErrString); }
...
#define CONTEXT_MSG_SIZE              101
#define UNAME_LEN                     30
#define EH_MAX_FILE_NAME_LEN  255
...
typedef struct error_info
{
            SQLCASTR        structSQLCA;
            int             nReturnCode;
            int             nApplMsgNbr;
            char            szApplContMsgText [CONTEXT_MSG_SIZE];
            pid_t           nProcessId;
```

```
19:              char           szUserName[UNAME_LEN + 1];
20:              BOOL           BoolStop;
21:              char           szFileName[EH_MAX_FILE_NAME_LEN + 1];
22:              long           lLineNumber;
23:              int            nNumberOfArgs;
24:              char           **ppchMsgArgs;
25: }ERROR_DETAILS;
26:
27: GLOBAL int nErrorHandler(char *,int ,ERROR_DETAILS *,int,char *);
```

Error handler include file

2 Inclusion of sqlca.h. sqlca.h is provided with the Pro*C installation.

4–6 Definition of the ProcessError macro. The error handler routine will always be called through the macro, to obtain the expansion of the C compiler constants __FILE__ and __LINE__.

12–25 Error handler structure. It includes a copy of the Oracle SQLCA, and other relevant fields which are populated by either the macro expansion (source filename and line number) or the error handling routine (process ID, username, etc.). The two last structure fields hold the number of arguments passed to the error text (nNumberOfArgs) and an array of strings, holding the arguments for the error message.

27 Definition of the error handler function. It receives 5 parameters: source filename and line number (through macro expansion), a pointer to the error handler structure, the error number and an optional context string.

The error handler structure is allocated by the main program, in our case by the control layer, and passed as a parameter to all routines and modules comprising the application. The error handler routine receives a pointer to the error structure and other parameters, the most important being the error number.

The error handler that we will implement further ahead in this book fills in all error structure fields, using Unix system calls to get the Process Id and the process username. It then tries to access the database table to fetch the error message associated with the error number. If the operation is successful and the error message contains parameters, the error handler expands the parameters and replaces the placeholders in the error text. Finally, it records the message with all the relevant information collected in the process in a database table. The database table is an exact copy of the error structure. In other words, it contains all fields found in the error structure. If Oracle is not available, the error text cannot be retrieved and expanded. The other relevant fields are dumped in an error log file. The application developer investigating the error can still count on most of the relevant error related information being stored in the error log. Only the error message text must be looked up manually.

7.4.2 EXCEPTION HANDLING IN OO LANGUAGES

Among the advantages introduced by the object-oriented paradigm, exception handling has been welcomed by programmers for the following two major features:

- Cleaner code
- Error handling removed from the program's main flow

The use of exception handlers makes the code cleaner by removing the error processing code from close proximity to the code that could potentially provoke the error. The program is not continually interrupted by error handling code, resulting in improved overall program readability. In addition, exception handlers can be combined with inheritance, allowing for polymorphic processing of related errors. This characteristic makes the granularity of an exception handler even finer.

The two most popular object-oriented languages used in Oracle-based applications are probably C++ and Object Pascal. Given their current popularity, they still deserve our attention, even if Java soon will probably outpace them.

Traditionally, C++ applications have communicated with an Oracle database using two methods. Until the release of Pro*C 2.1 (March 1995) a C++ wrapper around the Oracle Call Interface was the only viable solution. Pro*C release 2.1 understands C++ keywords and can be used to pre-compile embedded SQL calls in C++ programs.

Irrespective of the solution adopted, the only way to find out about an error occurred in the database processing is by using the means made available by Oracle. Oracle Pro*C provides either the SQLCA structure or the SQLSTATE and SQLCODE variables to communicate the exit status of the most recently executed SQL statement (see Chapter 11 for the details of error handling in Pro*C). Every OCI API communicates the Oracle status through its return value.

In either case, an exception can be thrown when an Oracle anomaly is detected. The advantage over procedural error handles is the immediate execution of the error processing code, bypassing the daisy chain mechanism where several modules pass around an error structure before any action is taken.

The following is an example of Oracle based exception handling in pseudocode.

```
class OraError
{
	public:
	OraError(struct sqlca * sqlca);
};
```

```
ora_customer::cust_fetch(const customer *cust)
{
       ...
       ...
       // Host variable declarations, etc …
       ...
       EXEC SQL SELECT CUSTOMER_NAME,CUSTOMER_ADDRESS,
              CUSTOMER TELEPHONE,CUSTOMER_TELEFAX
              INTO :CustRec INDICATOR :CustRecInd
              FROM CUSTOMER
              WHERE
              CUSTOMER_ID = :nCustId;


       if (sqlca.sqlcode != 0)
       {
              throw OraError(&sqlca);
       }


       strcpy((char *)cust->szCustName,(char *) CustRec.CustName.arr);
       // all customer object attributes are set …
       ...
       ...
}
int main()


{
  ...
  Connection Conn("ebonazzi","oracle8");
  try
  {
      customer OC(1);
  }
  catch OraError;
  ...
}
```

The OraError exception class constructor contains the logic to derive all error handler parameters, such as process Id, username, etc., and to record an error entry either in the log file or in the database.

The same concept applies to Object Pascal, with slightly different syntax; *except* is used instead of *catch*, and *raise* replaces the C++ counterpart *throw*.

7.5 Application Event Logging

An application should log all events that can assist with trouble shooting. There are no clear cut recipes on what events should be captured in a log. It depends on the nature of an application.

Avoiding a single point of failure is one of the reasons for using an external log file. If an application completely trusts Oracle for all I/O operations, it runs the risk of missing important information in case Oracle fails to record data; it may exhaust all available free table space.

The other extreme of duplicating all information in both Oracle and a log file is not always a good idea. If the log information in Oracle tables can be easily rebuilt after an Oracle logging problem, then a log file can be used to record just a few essential details. The information captured in the log file should be enough to identify the records to be re-processed.

On the other hand, if the log information is lost forever during an Oracle logging failure, the log file must be an exact replica of the original log data collected. In this case, the format of the log file is important. It should be designed to simplify the job of tools like SQL*Loader, which can be used to insert the data into Oracle once the logging problem has been fixed. Consider the following two scenarios.

1) A background process is responsible for de-queuing messages accumulated in a commercial messaging queue, and storing them in an Oracle database. An acknowledgment mechanism ensures that all received messages originate an acknowledgment transaction, which is sent back to the source system using an output queue. Occasionally, a message is skipped and it mysteriously disappears. The maintenance team of the source system blames the receiving system for the "vanishing" messages. The maintenance team for the receiving system swears that the message has not been recorded because it was never sent.
2) An on-line financial databank receives all stock values in real-time from the Tokyo stock market via an X.25 connection to Japan. The X.25 packets are read by a background process, which assembles all information related to the stocks and stores it into an Oracle database. Each stock value is sent only once. Sometimes the information is lost because of abnormal overnight activity that fills Oracle tablespaces.

In the first scenario the source system stores the messages in an output queue and does not delete them until an acknowledgment is received from the remote system. In this case, the background process running on the receiving system should record the message Id and a read timestamp in the log file, before attempting record insertions in Oracle. This makes it easy to track down what happened when a message "disappears."

If the log file shows an entry for that specific message Id, and a corresponding entry is not found in the Oracle table, the message was effectively received. Either a business logic error caused the database insertion to fail or a space-related problem prevented the message from being stored in Oracle.

Recording the timestamp and the message Id only keeps the log file growth to a minimum yet maintains full effectiveness in case of trouble shooting. The message could be several hundred bytes (or even kilobytes) in length, but the only relevant part, in this context, is the message Id. The source system can use the Id to identify messages that must be resent, once the initial problem has been resolved.

A different approach must be chosen to solve the problem presented in the second scenario. In this situation it is crucial to checkpoint everything received from the X.25 channel in a log file before anything gets lost. The log file must be an exact replica of the Oracle table and the information must be duplicated to guarantee redundancy in case of record insertion failure. Furthermore, the layout of the log file should be simple and well structured, so that Oracle SQL*Loader[1] can use a simple script to load the financial data into the appropriate table.

Producing a log file implies an administrative overhead, which cannot be underestimated or neglected. Procedures have to be put in place to monitor log file(s) growth as well as purging policies for the log entries that are no longer needed.

Event logging can be achieved through different levels of sophistication. In its simplest form, logging is operated by appending data to a file using a single routine, which keeps the log file open for the duration of the application. A more sophisticated event logging mechanism is the one that allows the multiple processes comprising an application to append event messages to the same log file. Record locking issues have to be accommodated, and the log file must provide concurrent access to the various event-logging routines. An example of event logging code which allows several processes to queue event messages to the same log file is shown below.

```
#include <fcntl.h>
#include <stdio.h>
#include <stdarg.h>
#include <stdlib.h>
#include <string.h>

#define SUCCESS 0
```

[1] SQL*Loader is the Oracle utility designed to allow data from different sources to be inserted into an Oracle database.

```
#define ERROR 1

#define GLOBAL  extern
#define LOCAL   static

GLOBAL   FILE * LogFile;

LOCAL int nLockRegister ( int , int , int , off_t, int, off_t);
LOCAL int nPerformWriting (const char * , va_list );
GLOBAL   int nWriteToLogFile ( char * fmt, ...);

GLOBAL   int nWriteToLogFile ( char * fmt, ...)
{
   va_list         argptr;

   va_start(argptr,fmt);
   if ( (nPerformWriting(fmt,argptr)) != SUCCESS)
   {
          va_end(argptr);
          return(ERROR);
   }
   va_end(argptr);
   return(SUCCESS);
} /* end function */

LOCAL int nLockRegister ( int fd, int cmd, int type,
                          off_t offset, int whence, off_t len)
{
   struct flock lock;       /* From fcntl.h */

  lock.l_type = type;      /* can be F_RDLCK, F_WRLCK, F_UNLCK*/
  lock.l_start=offset;     /* byte offset relative to l_whence */
  lock.l_whence = whence; /* could be SEEK_SET, SEEK_CUR, SEEK_END */
  lock.l_len= len;        /* number of bytes (0 means to EOF) */

   return( fcntl(fd,cmd,&lock));

} /* end function */

LOCAL   int nPerformWriting (const char * fmt, va_list argptr)
{
   int              nByteCnt;
   /* lock the entire file */
   nLockRegister(fileno(LogFile),F_SETLKW,F_WRLCK,0, SEEK_SET,0);
```

```

    nByteCnt=vfprintf(LogFile,fmt,argptr);
    fflush(LogFile);
    /* unlock the entire file */
    nLockRegister(fileno(LogFile),F_SETLK,F_UNLCK,0, SEEK_SET,0);

    if (nByteCnt == EOF) /* this means we could not */
                         /* write to the log file   */
        return(ERROR);
    else
        return(SUCCESS);
} /* end function */
```

The logging routine nWriteToLogFile in the example above receives a variable number of arguments, starting with a format string, mimicking the behavior of "printf". To log a message in the global log file used by all application components the function could be called as shown below.

```
nWriteToLogFile("%s: Process %d wakes up\n",ctime
(&lTimestamp),getpid());
```

An even more sophisticated logging system can use dedicated background process, or daemon, which receives messages through operating system mechanisms. They can be OpenVMS mailboxes, Unix IPC message queues, or pipes or MS Windows NT OLE.

A centralized logging facility is very useful when a single logging console controls multiple applications, running on large, clustered machines. This situation commonly occurs when the computing facilities of one or more corporations are concentrated in one large data center. Operators working in shifts constantly monitor the logging console. All applications running in the same cluster are required to log their events using the centralized facility so that one operator can easily supervise all applications. Multi-tier event logging products are available to allow for inter-node logging on a single control console.

Event logging plays an important role in the normal daily operations of production applications. It plays an even more important role during the development phase when application anomalies are being investigated.

Debugging a complex application, with many interacting processes requires a much finer event capture granularity than the normal logging. The verbosity of the event logging should therefore be configurable.

SQL*Net/Net 8 provides a good example of configurable event logging verbosity of the logging facility. SQLNET.ORA is one of the configuration files read by the SQL*Net listener at startup. The TRACE_LEVEL_CLIENT parameter can accept several values to control logging. OFF means that client SQL*Net connections won't generate any logging. When TRACE_LEVEL_CLIENT is set to USER, a minimal logging will be produced by SQL*Net. Setting the parameter to ADMIN produces a much more verbose output. Net8 introduced an additional parameter, SUPPORT, which generates even more output information than ADMIN. It is normally used by Oracle World Wide Support to troubleshoot serious networking problems.

Well-designed applications allow administrators to influence the verbosity of the logging facility. An even more sophisticated logging system allows administrators to switch logging on and off and to change the verbosity levels, without shutting down any application processes. In ninety percent of the cases, shutting down a process that behaves erratically "fixes" the problem. At the next startup of the process in question, the chances of behaving erratically again are often very slim. Process monitoring should therefore be switchable while a process is running. Administrators should not be forced to shut down a process to change logging verbosity. This facility simplifies the identification of those software defects that show up only under specific and unusual conditions that are easily repeatable.

In Unix, switching logging on and off and changing logging verbosity on the fly can be achieved by sending the application process a signal. The application process can re-read logging flags from a configuration file.

7.5.1 APPLICATION MONITORING—OPERATOR ALERTS

In the last section we considered error handling and event logging. They provide the application maintainers with precise and accurate mechanisms for dealing with errors, defects, and application related problems. The attention of system administrators must be directed to important events when they are detected. Mission critical applications requirements usually specify very little or no down time. Immediate corrective action by competent supervisors can reduce the impact of potentially more serious side effects. Operator alert generation can be automated using technologies such as e-mail systems and pagers. When an application comprises several processes running in the background, a "watchdog" process can monitor the presence of all other background processes. If one of the application processes dies, the "watchdog" will alert the system maintainers. A pager can be carried by the person on duty, to display messages automatically generated by the application. This allows the system administrators to immediately assess the area of the application requiring attention, if not the exact problem.

Electronic mail systems can also be used for error alerting, but with care. An e-mail message automatically created by the error handling routine of a client application can reach the help desk very quickly, even before a telephone call from the user. When this occurs, the user is usually delighted to realize that his or her problem is already in hand. Undoubtedly, this gives an impression of efficiency and professionalism.

The down side of automatic error alerting by e-mail is error storms. The entire network gets bogged down with hundreds, if not thousands, of e-mail messages all reporting the same error. If electronic mail systems are used for automatic error alerting, the error handling routines should be coded in a way that limits the likelihood of error storms. One way to achieve this is by limiting the number of messages that can be sent in a given interval of time.

7.5.2 PROBLEM ESCALATION

The appropriate person must be called once an application problem has been detected either automatically, by alert instrumented software monitors, or manually, by operators monitoring output consoles. Problem escalation procedures must be established and documented to minimize the potential down time incurred by a fault condition.

One doesn't want to call the most senior designer in the team to resolve simple problems. When operators monitoring application consoles detect the problem outside office hours, the key issue is to determine the application area responsible for the problem. This is crucial for selecting the appropriate person to contact. If an overnight housekeeping process fails due to Oracle space allocation problems, the Oracle DBA should be contacted. If the same process crashes due to a high level language related bug—typically mismanagement of dates, array boundary exceeded, etc.—the developer on duty for that specific application should be called.

The solution is to educate operators in error classification so that they can contact the correct person. Those who have carried a pager to provide after-hours support can testify to the annoyance caused by overnight callouts for problems that fall within someone else's area of competence.

The text of the error message printed on the logging console must be clear, concise, and unambiguous. Events and errors should all be given a priority level, such as warning, error, fatal error, etc. The error escalation policy should be based on the category of the error occurred.

If error alerting is done automatically, the person on duty should be in a position to divert the call to the other maintainer with the appropriate discipline to solve the problem without any further help.

Summary

In this chapter we learned how to structure the code in layers, separating business logic from logical and physical data access. We applied the same techniques to both traditional and object-oriented languages. The basic idea behind code layering is that having business logic concentrated in one layer independent from data access improves modularity and minimizes code reworking. This can be appreciated either when the physical data structure of the database changes or when the application model is migrated from a two-tier organization to a three-tier organization. De-coupling data access from business rules simplifies the introduction of middleware and keeps code reworking to a minimum.

A significant part of the chapter focused on error handling, highlighting its crucial importance for the production of quality software. We considered the basic ingredients of a good error handler, implementing a few examples in "C" and object-oriented languages.

The last topic discussed in the chapter is about event logging and problem escalation. We analyzed software techniques for automatic error alerting and policies for escalating problems when they occur, affecting production systems and potentially provoking down-time. We looked at error prevention policies, and we considered measures to be taken to minimize the risk of unscheduled outages.

Chapter 8

SOFTWARE ENGINEERING ESSENTIALS

In this chapter we will consider the software engineering tools that are essential for the success of IT projects. Initially, we will analyze tools and techniques common to generic IT projects to focus, and further ahead in the chapter, we will discuss Oracle specific facilities and tools.

Every single project I have ever been associated with was implemented with a few mistakes, omissions, and things that could have been done better. It is easy to retrospectively recognize the mistakes made. It is much more complicated not to make any mistake while designing and implementing a project, always under constant pressure to deliver on time and on budget. No project is immune to mistakes. The projects that end up in disaster and are abruptly cancelled are usually the ones that lack software engineering *fundamentals*. Among these fundamentals, software productivity tools are essential elements for a correct implementing of good software engineering practices.

The tools examined throughout the chapter are:

- source code control related tools
- internal debuggers
- profilers
- test coverage analyzers
- run-time error detection tools

The Oracle specific tools covered in the chapter are:

- ❑ Oracle trace
- ❑ SQL optimization tools (Explain plan and SQL tracing/TkProf)

Software testing is an important discipline of software engineering, and therefore, a significant section of this chapter is devoted to it, with a specific focus on Oracle related problems and issues.

The final section in the chapter is about internationalization. Several hints are given to designers and programmers who must produce easily customizable software in order to simplify the software localization process.

8.1 Version Control

Version control is an essential part of software engineering. It can be said that without version control, there is no software engineering at all. Development environments operating without version control systems are environments where software is handcrafted. The craftsman approach is definitely not applicable to serious software development. The source code comprising an application, even of moderate complexity, cannot be kept under control relying on the memory of the single developer and on quick fixes when something goes wrong and the source code build fails.

Keeping the source code under strict control and surveillance is a full-time job for a developer, whose task is mainly to coordinate development, test teams, and release building. The job title of such a developer is generally known as Configuration Manager. Configuration Management is a generic term, which usually includes source code control, version control, and deployment control. The typical activities conducted under the configuration management umbrella are source control, dependency checking, bug tracking, automated testing, and customer installation.

Source code control pertains to the control activities operated against source code while being produced. Version control groups together all those activities required to produce a software release, including the identification of all compatible modules, eventual creation of build scripts, maintenance of make files, etc. Deployment control occurs when different releases are concurrently supported for different operating environments that require particular customizations.

Source code control is generally implemented with the help of specific tools. They differ in price and features, but they all have in common the ability to keep track of different versions of files, in order to avoid clashes between developers modifying the same file. Source code control tools also restore previous releases of the same file.

The source code control tools use specific terminology, which is generally the same across the various tools. Below is a glossary of the terminology used in source code control.

Source Code Control Glossary

Archive: A single archive containing the revision history of a single managed file

Branch: A separate line of development consisting of one or more revision

Promotional Group: Promotion is the process of moving software forward from one stage of its life cycle to the next. Each stage is represented by a promotional group

Revision: Each configured change to a managed file is referred to as a revision

Tip: The most recent revision of a branch

Trunk: The main development branch

Historically, source code control tools have been included in most of Unix flavors. The Source Code Control System (SCCS) is generally part of the Unix distribution kit. Other commonly used Unix source code control systems, such as Revision Control System (RCS) or Concurrent Versions System (CVS), are available as GNU tools. Having so many options available at no extra cost contributed to the general diffusion of source code control mentality among the community of Unix developers. In OpenVMS, DEC made available, at additional cost, the Code Management System (CMS); in MS Window NT, Microsoft offers Visual Source Safe, integrated into the Visual Studio development environment. A very popular suite of tools dedicated to configuration management is the one offered by Intersolv (PVCS). The points of strength of the Intersolv package are a common visual interface across all supported platforms, such as MS Windows 3.x, Win95, NT, OS2, and the major Unix flavors, and a complete set of tools for configuration management. Not only PVCS includes the basic source code control system, but also Tracker, a system change request tracking tool, and Configuration Builder, a tool that replaces and extends the make facility. It allows for extraction of revisions from the common repository and automates the release building.

8.1.1 FILE MANAGEMENT

Developers are requested to store into the common repository new files produced during development sessions, commonly referred to as "checking in" a file. The opposite action, that is, extracting a file from the repository into a directory is commonly referred to as "checking out" a file. Each time a file is checked out and then checked back in, a new revision of the file is created. The most recently created revision is referred to as the *tip* revision.

The set of revisions originated by the modifications made to a file, considered in its entirety, is called trunk. During concurrent development, a trunk is often needed to allow two or more developers to work on the same file. One developer can work at a new release, while another one maintains an old release, which needs a defect to be fixed. In this case, the modifications made to a file that is checked in last do not override the modifications made to the same file, checked in earlier. Instead, a branch is created. A branch is a separate line of development consisting of one or more revisions that diverge from one revision on the trunk. The following diagram illustrates the concept of trunk and branch:

The process of reconciling the branches originated from a revision is called *merging*. Several source control tools provide an automatic merge facility, which operates the merging of multiple revisions into one. Conflicting or incompatible

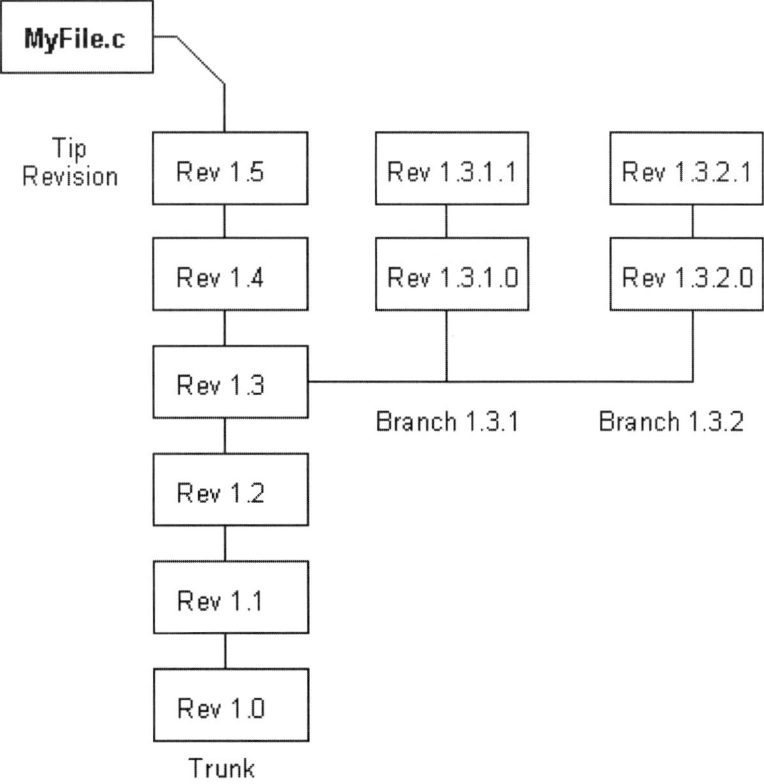

FIGURE 8.1 Trunk, Branch, Tip Revision

lines of code, when detected, are flagged and the developer's intervention is required.

DEC CMS, RCS, PVCS, and MS Visual Source Safe allow a name, or a label, to be associated with a revision. This feature is very important because it allows the Configuration Manager to extract from the common repository only those revisions that are compatible with a specific release. In this way, it is possible to selectively extract and build specific releases, even old releases, at any time. Most source code control systems by default extract the tip revision if a version label (or a name) is not given through the check out command.

A very important concept in source control, especially for large development teams, is "promotion" or "promotional group." Promotion is the process of moving software forward from one stage of its life cycle to the next. Each stage is represented by a promotional group. Promotional groups are hierarchical and generally follow the revision they are assigned to. This means that branches originated from revisions in the trunk are by default assigned to the promotional group of the parent revision.

Not all source code control systems support promotional groups natively; nevertheless, through interfaces wrapped around source control systems, it is possible to emulate this important feature.

Developers usually don't interact with the source code control system. This is particularly true in environments supporting several teams developing concurrently large applications. In those environments, a set of scripts is available to simplify and automate as much as possible the interaction of the developer with the source control system.

8.1.2 PRODUCTS AND BUNDLES

Large systems usually consist of several components, which often share common modules. For example, an application STK_MAN, which stands for Stock Manager, comprises an interactive part that allows remote users to access the database in a client-server configuration, and an interface to legacy systems running under IBM MVS. Another interface is supported, to an OpenVMS system, which controls several Programmable Logic Controller (PLC) devices in a factory.

To be able to test the complex system, each release includes two simulators, one for each of the interfaces to the external systems. If these interfaces are implemented through the same messaging system, then software modules can be shared across the OpenVMS and IBM MVS interfaces. Each new software release includes several components, which must remain synchronized with each other. In this environment, it would be convenient to think of each component in terms of a "product," which comprises a collection of individual files, and to introduce the concept of a "bundle," comprised by a collection of products.

Promotional groups can be established for each of the products included in the bundles, so that multiple versions of the system can be built in a controlled manner, to simplify the tracking and managing of each release. In operational terms, one could imagine the product as a file, listing all revisions connected to the product, each with an associated version label. The same product could exist in several versions. In this case, the product file would be recognizable by a meaningful suffix included in the file name. The same applies to the bundle file, which lists all products included together to produce a release. The suffix appended to the bundle file makes it immediately recognizable.

Figure 8.2 shows the STK_MAN bundle, which includes five products. The bundle reached release n. 1.7. Each product has an associated release number. All revisions associated with a product are extracted from the repository, compiled, and, where necessary, linked to produce executable images. Products can share revisions. In Figure 8.2 there are two examples of shared modules, `MQ_Intfc.h` and `Sim_Intfc.h`. A formal build is performed by the Configuration Manager on a regular basis, and provides all developers with a consolidated and current software release. In the figure, the label "1.7," which corresponds to the release number of the bundle, can be associated with all revisions included in all products, to simplify the extraction of all revisions from the repository. The extraction of the single revision, its compilation, and its eventual linking is performed by the build script; there exists one build script per bundle.

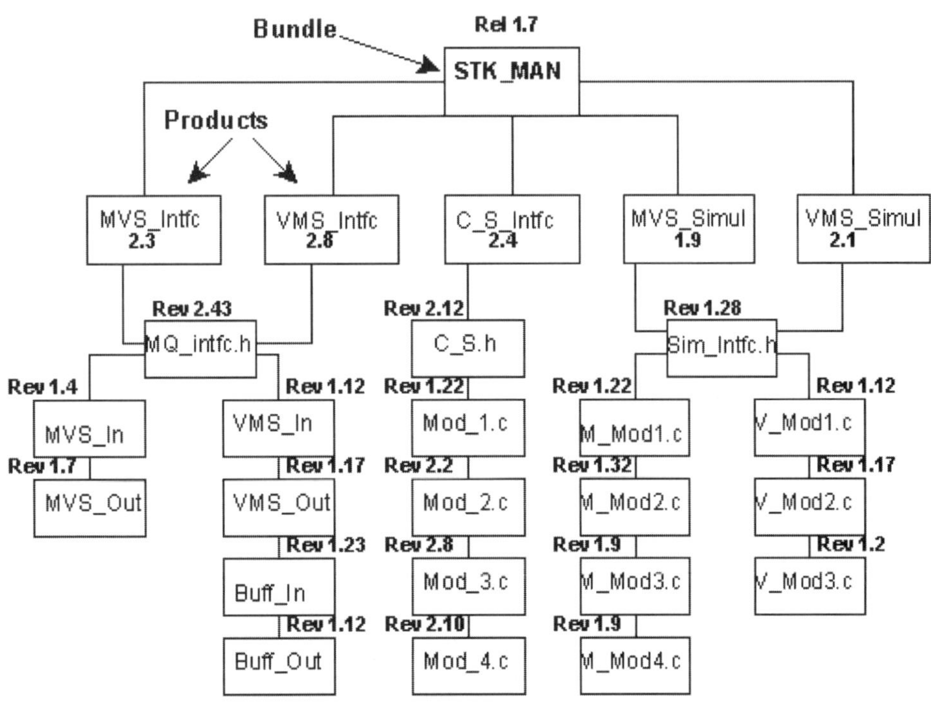

FIGURE 8.2 Products, Revisions, and Bundle

A developer operating in a source controlled environment needs to be able to modify source code revisions, compile, and link without affecting other developers. This is commonly achieved by using logical names (in OpenVMS) or file links (under Unix). All source code of a release is extracted from the source control repository and kept in a common directory. Each developer has access to a local directory, which is a mirror image of the common one. The local directory doesn't contain the source code files of the release, but links to the files stored in the common directory. The only real files in the directory are the ones being modified by the developer.

When a build is performed, the executable image is partially produced from the common files residing in the shared directory, and partially produced from the local files. This happens transparently, without any modification required to the script that performs the build, thanks to the link mechanism. This method allows developers to modify the source code and to unit test each module without forcing other developers to use and rely on code just created and not yet tested. This would happen if all developers would be allowed to modify the source code in the shared directory.

Once a software module has been adequately tested and released by the developer, it is ready to be deployed in the common directory, to be used by the other components of the development team.

8.1.3 PROMOTIONAL GROUP MODELS

In complex development environments the promotional model chosen can considerably influence the way each developer interacts with other developers, with the source control tool, and with the team leader. Consequently, the productivity of the single developer is directly affected by the procedures designed to enforce source code control.

Unfortunately, there does not exist an infallible recipe good for all development environments. The nature of the application being built should drive the decisions leading to the implementation of the version control system. In development environments where a revision is rarely concurrently modified by two or more programmers, sophisticated merging features are not needed. It would probably be better to prevent any potential collision by locking each checked out revision, so that only one developer at any one time can modify a revision. Conversely, in environments where continuous branching is a necessity, an adequate policy for revision reconciliation has to be formalized.

In the model characterized by "one promotional group, shared source," a single promotional group is set up per release, and source code is shared between the various products. Whenever a file is checked out, it is checked out using the version of the file associated with the promotional group. If work is being performed concurrently on shared files, then as soon as a file is checked in, the new version of the file is available to all developers. Essentially, the check-in becomes the formal promotion point.

The advantage of such a model is the automatic update of all dependent source code, without the need for an intervention by the Configuration Manager. No intermediate formal builds are required. The significant disadvantage is that each developer cannot check in incomplete or nonworking revisions; otherwise, other developers could incur faulty builds. Developers usually intentionally want to check in nonworking revisions, in order to be able to undo changes, while in the process of finding the best way to implement algorithms.

In the model characterized by "one promotional group, no shared source," sharing of source code is accomplished through the use of libraries. The output of every product making up the bundle is a library. In order to make new versions of shared source available, the library to which the revision belongs must be formally built. Among the advantages of such a model, the developers can check in intermediate versions of source code without influencing the common build.

The formal build makes the promotion of shared source files a widely known event for all developers. Changes can only be made to shared source code by modifying the library in which it is contained. By using this model, the Configuration Manager intervention is required more often, and it is theoretically possible to miss a promotion (e.g., to change a library forgetting to promote it).

A more complex promotional model advocates the use of multiple promotional groups for a release. Each time a new product is added to a release, a new promotional group is generated for the product. This mechanism of multi-step promotions within the products allows for greater flexibility, because the source is still shared between products, but clashes are avoided by implementing protections based on promotions. Needless to say, flexibility is paid for in the form of a more demanding administration.

The promotional model is a function of the nature of the application, the size of the development teams, and the overall complexity of the development environment.

As stated, usually developers don't interact directly with the source code control tool, but with a set of scripts made available by the Configuration Manager. This is generally true in character based environments, where the Unix standard tools are used, typically RCS and "make." In this case, the interaction with source control happens through shell scripts, invoked by developers from the operating system prompt.

In environments where a visual tool is available, typically PVCS in Unix and either PVCS or MS Visual Source Safe in MS Windows NT, a visual interface is provided. Graphical interfaces, usually coded in Tcl Tk, are also available for the Unix traditional tools such as RCS and CVS.

PVCS allows the administrator to set up the triggering of specific actions following the happening of predetermined events, like checking in, formal builds, etc. For example, an e-mail message could be automatically sent to all developers as soon as a formal build has been successfully completed. Even if a visual interface to the source control tool is available, the need for specific scripts to accomplish the most complex tasks doesn't disappear.

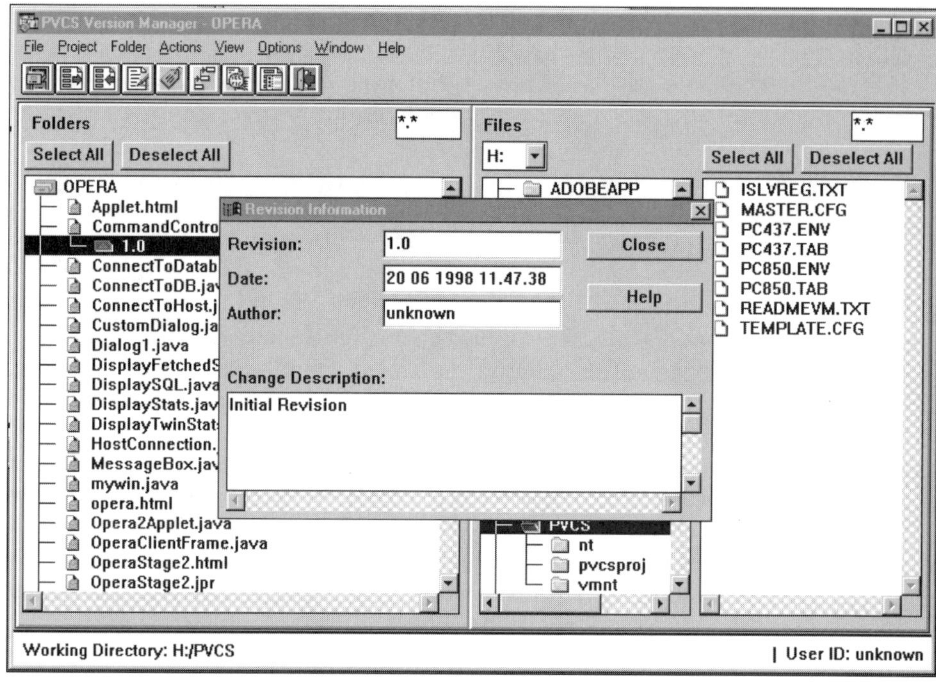

FIGURE 8.3 PVCS Version Manager

8.2 Release Building

In order to produce the executable file or the set of executable files comprising the application, all revisions must be extracted from the common repository, and all source code files must be compiled. According to the rules specified in the bundle and product files, compatible modules have to be linked together to generate the final executable file. This is usually accomplished by the use of tools like make (in the Unix and MS-DOS/Windows worlds), or Module Management System (MMS) in OpenVMS. Make or MMS opens a file which lists the rules that govern and supervise the build, and performs a selective compilation and linking based on each file timestamp and the specified rules. PVCS offers a module called Configuration Builder, which replaces and enhances the make utility. The file listing the rules for the build, usually called *makefile*, should be kept in the source code repository, exactly like any other source file, and checked out at the moment of the build.

8.2.1 SOURCE CODE KEYWORDS

Most source code control tools support the use of keywords. These are words with a specific meaning in the context of the source control environment. They are used to place source control related information directly into the text file being source controlled. At the moment of checking out, the keywords are expanded, and the result of the expansion is shown in the text file. Let us imagine we are using RCS; we want to add a new revision to the RCS repository, a "C" file called main.c:

```
/*************************************************************
* File:     $RCSfile$
* Purpose: to illustrate to use of rcs keywords
* Author:   $Author$
* History:
* $Log$
*************************************************************/
#include <stdio.h>
static char main_c_rcs[]="$Header$";
int main(int argc, char **argv)
{
        int ii;
        for(ii=1;ii<argc;ii++)
                printf("Argument %d: %s\n",ii,argv[ii]);
}
```

The keywords are shown in bold in the example. The marker `$RCSfile$` will be expanded with the file name of the revision. `$Author$` will be replaced by the login name of the developer checking in the file. The marker `$Log$`, placed inside a comment, accumulates the log messages that are requested by rcs at the moment of checking in the file. Next time one checks the revision out, the source file shows the expansion performed by the system against each keyword:

```
/*************************************************************
* File:     $RCSfile: main.c,v $
* Purpose: to illustrate to use of rcs keywords
* Author:   $Author: ebonazzi $
* History:
* $Log: main.c,v $
 * Revision 1.2  1998/06/19  23:30:05  ebonazzi
 * This is an example. It shows the use of the rcs keywords
 *
*************************************************************/
```

```
#include <stdio.h>

static char main_c_rcs[]="$Header:   /u2/usr/ebonazzi/example/
main.c,v 1.2 1998/06/19 23:30:05 ebonazzi Exp ebonazzi $";

int main(int argc, char **argv)
{
        int ii;
        for(ii=1;ii<argc;ii++)
                printf("Argument %d: %s\n",ii,argv[ii]);
}
```

The keyword mechanism is very useful when tracking revisions in occasion of formal builds. The configuration manager can reconcile the revision number stamped on the file by RCS with the revision number listed in the build script for the product.

8.2.2 TROUBLE SHUTTING FAULTY BUILDS

The `$Header$` keyword is used to track single modules within executables. `$Header$` is supported by RCS, PVCS, and MS Visual Source safe. In SCCS, the corresponding keyword is `%W%`. In main.c, the static string `main_c_rcs` receives the result of the expansion of `$Header$`. That string will be included in the executable. Source code control systems usually provide a utility that scans through executable files looking for specific keywords, printing the expanded text either to the screen or to a file. In SCCS that utility is called *what;* in RCS it is called *ident.* If each source file included in an application is marked with the appropriate keyword, then the result of *ident* or *what,* launched against the executable file, will be a list of strings. Each string will show the module name and the revision number associated to every single module. If a formal build skipped a promotion, and the application is behaving erratically, the Configuration Manager can verify that the wanted modules are effectively included in the executable file. A simple check can detect inconsistencies or discrepancies in the build mechanism. In the following example, the SCCS what command, issued against the OperaSvr binary file, produced the output:

```
OperaSvr:
    OperaStg2.h       1.9
    AncillaryFunctions.c     1.4
    OperaStg2.h       1.9
    DictSts.c         1.1
    OperaStg2.h       1.9
    ...
    ...
```

```
...
FileStats.c      1.1
OperaStg2.h      1.9
LatchStats.c     1.1
OperaStg2.h      1.9
LockSql.c        1.1
OperaStg2.h      1.9
SqlInteract.c    1.1
```

The include file `OperaStg2.h` appears several times in the listing. This is desired, because that file is included by many modules. Each time it appears, it should show the latest revision number, in our case 1.9. If, during the build, the previous revision had been erroneously checked out while compiling one module, the listing would display that revision number, therefore flagging the inconsistency.

Source code control, version control, formal builds, and proper keyword use are crucial to sound software engineering practices. Without them, control over development teams is difficult, if not impossible. Oracle development tools like Developer/2000 offer integration with third party source code control systems (in general, PVCS is one of the most supported tools).

8.3 Tools for Better Code

Writing software has become increasingly complex, to the extent that it is no longer possible to simply rely on human capabilities to manage and supervise the production of complex applications. More and more software developers make use of tools that help in producing, debugging, testing and maintaining source code. These tools all have one thing in common: increasing the developer's productivity.

Some tools, such as debuggers and profilers, have been around for a long time. A few have been brought to the market more recently. The latter category includes test coverage analysis tools and run-time error detection tools.

8.3.1 INTERNAL DEBUGGERS

All developers, including hobbyist programmers, know what a debugger is and make use of it regularly. Not as much known and used are internal debuggers, which can be very useful in tracking down defects not otherwise detectable by the interactive debuggers. This mainly happens when software defects manifest themselves in specific and rare occasions, difficult to be artificially re-created during debugging sessions. It is difficult to emulate, by using interactive debuggers, events that have to happen synchronously, such as inter-process communication events. It is virtually impossible to manually trigger events the life of which is measured in milliseconds.

The disadvantage associated with the use of internal debuggers is that the source code must be *instrumented*. This means that specific instructions for the activation and capturing of debugging information must be inserted into the source code.

An internal debugger is not a substitute for an interactive debugger. It is normally used as an additional aid for debugging sessions. If properly used, an internal debugger can also provide basic profiling and regression testing capabilities. Several internal debuggers are available on the market, and a few are offered as freeware. For the purpose of illustrating how an internal debugger works, I will use DBUG, a freeware utility that can be easily found through the WEB. The DBUG package will be used by most "C" code examples throughout the book. I have slightly modified the original source code to include time stamping up the hundredth of second. Time stamping can be optionally enabled by setting a global variable.

A few macro commands are needed to activate the DBUG package. The source code of an application is instrumented by using these macros. DBUG works with "C" programs, and all instrumentation can be filtered out simply by re-compiling the source code with the variable DBUG_OFF enabled. A simple "C" pre-processor substitution will cause all instrumentation not to be included in the object file. The macros commonly used to instrument the code are:

DBUG_ENTER: used to communicate to the run-time support the name of the function being entered. It requires a matching DBUG_RETURN macro to signal the run-time support that the function has finished execution.

DBUG_RETURN: exists in two flavors, DBUG_RETURN and DBUG_VOID_RETURN. The argument to the function is the value to be returned. In case the function doesn't return any value, dbug_void_return has to be used. This macro cannot appear in the code without a corresponding DBUG_ENTER macro; the compiler will complain if this happens.

DBUG_PUSH: determines the debugger features to be activated. Its argument is a string containing a debug control string. The latter is a set of characters that are interpreted by the run-time support system.

DBUG_PRINT: used to print to the standard output meaningful debugging strings determined by the developer. The first argument is a debug keyword; the second argument is a format string followed by a set of parameters, as in "printf()".

The output provided by DBUG can be regulated by a debug control string, which is interpreted by the run-time support. This allows a great deal of flexibility, because the debug string can change the behavior of the internal debugger at run-time. The debug control string can be passed to the program via the command line, or alternatively read from a configuration file.

Useful options passed to the debugging package as debug control strings are:

d [,keywords] enable selective output from macros containing the listed keyword. The macro DBUG_PRINT has, as its first, parameter, a keyword. By using the "d" option, the output of the DBUG_PRINT macro can be either included or excluded. A null list of keywords means that all output will be printed.

f [,functions] limit debugging actions to those functions that are specified in the list of functions. An empty list means that all functions are selected and consequently debugged.

T enables time stamping for the selected functions.

t [,N] enables function control flow tracing. The nesting depth is specified as a parameter. A null parameter means a nesting depth of 200 levels.

A colon is used as a separator between the options in the debug control string, as in: `"d,info,err:f,nDBFetchRecord,nLDFetchRecord:t:T"`.

It is time to put all in practice. We are going to build a small application that uses the DBUG package. It will fetch stock related data from Oracle, displaying the company name, the date of trading, and the usual stock data (low, high, close, volume). It will accept three parameters, passed from the command line. The first is a number between 1 and 600,000, and is a record identifier. The second is the debug control string, and the third is a code, either 0 or 1, which is used to enable time stamping up to one-hundredth of second. A value of 0 means time stamping with one second precision; 1 will enable the more precise time stamping. The small application follows the code layering rules. It includes a control layer, a business logic layer, and the logical and physical data access layers. The source code of all modules can be found on the "Chap08" directory of the companion CD-ROM. The source code of the main module follows:

Using the DBUG package

```
#include <stdio.h>
#include <string.h>

#include "base.h"
#include "error_handler.h"
#include "ConnectDb.h"
```

```
#include "DisconnectDb.h"
#include "dbug.h"

int Micro = 0;

int main(int argc, char **argv)
{
    ERROR_DETAILS           structError;
    DB_CONNECT_STRUCT       structConnect;
    int                     nSts;
    int                     nOraSeq;
    DBUG_ENTER("main");
    DBUG_PROCESS(argv[0]);
    DBUG_PUSH(argv[2]);

    nOraSeq = atoi(argv[1]);
    Micro = atoi(argv[3]);
    memset(&structError,'\0',sizeof(structError));
    memset(&structConnect,'\0',sizeof(structConnect));

    if ((nSts = nDBConnectDb(&structConnect,&structError))
            != SUCCESS)
    {
            ProcessError(&structError,"Connection Failed");
            DBUG_PRINT("Info",
                    ("Could not connect to Oracle. Aborting..."));
            DBUG_RETURN(ERROR);
    }

    if ((nSts = FetchRecordBySeq(nOraSeq,&structError))
                    != SUCCESS)
    {
            ProcessError(&structError,"Fetch Stock");
            DBUG_PRINT("Info",("Error Fetching Stocks"));
            DBUG_RETURN(ERROR);
    }
    if ((nSts = nDBDisconnectDb(&structError)) != SUCCESS)
    {
            ProcessError(&structError,
                    "Disconnecting from Oracle");
            DBUG_PRINT("Info",
                    ("Error disconnecting from Oracle"));
    }
```

```
50:     DBUG_RETURN(SUCCESS);
51: }
```

Initialization

10 Micro is a global variable used by DBUG. If it is set to 1, function time stamping is enabled with a granularity of hundredth of seconds.

18–20 The DBUG macros are used to tell the run-time support that we are entering the main function and the program used (in argv[0] one can find the program name), and communicate to the run-time support the debug control string (through DBUG_PUSH).

Connection to Oracle

27–28 The physical data access function responsible for the connection to Oracle is called.

31–33 DBUG_PRINT is used to print a message to the user; DBUG_RETURN is needed to gracefully exit from the run-time debug support.

Business logic function call

36–42 This is the call to function residing in the business logic layer. The function will print to video the stock values related to the record identifier passed from the command line. If the function fails, the macro DBUG_PRINT is called to display a message to the user, and the macro DBUG_RETURN is called to terminate gracefully.

Disconnection and exit

43–49 The physical data access function supervising the disconnection from Oracle is called. Should an error occur, the two DBUG macros called will print a message and terminate gracefully.

After having instrumented our code, we are now able to see the internal debugger in action. Initially we are not interested in time stamping the functions; we only want to verify the correct behavior of the program. The command line follows:

```
268$ DbugExample 27 "d:t" 1
```

The following is the video output:

```
|   >nDBConnectDb
|   <nDBConnectDb
|   >FetchRecordBySeq
|   |   >nLDFetchRecord
|   |   |   >nDBFetchRecord
```

```
|   |   |   <nDBFetchRecord
|   |   <nLDFetchRecord
Pharmacia Upjhon          07091997 225536 1 30 53 43489
|   <FetchRecordBySeq
|   >nDBDisconnectDb
|   <nDBDisconnectDb
<main
```

The indentation operated by the DBUG printout is very effective in showing the hierarchical relationship between the various functions. The four layers used by the application are visible at a glance. nDBFetchRecord, the physical data access routine, is the most indented function, called by nLDFetchRecord.

The logical flow of the program appears to behave correctly; it is now time to investigate the performance of our program. The new debug control string will enable function time stamping:

```
282$ DbugExample  27 "d:t:T" 1
```

The capital "T" inserted in the debug control string enables function time stamping:

```
980620 234043.96: |   >nDBConnectDb
980620 234045.45: |   <nDBConnectDb
980620 234045.46: |   >FetchRecordBySeq
980620 234045.46: |   |   >nLDFetchRecord
980620 234045.46: |   |   |   >nDBFetchRecord
980620 234045.84: |   |   |   <nDBFetchRecord
980620 234045.85: |   |   <nLDFetchRecord
Pharmacia Upjhon              07091997 225536 1 30 53 43489
980620 234045.85: |   <FetchRecordBySeq
980620 234045.85: |   >nDBDisconnectDb
980620 234045.86: |   <nDBDisconnectDb
980620 234045.87: <main
```

The output shows that our program takes a little more than 1.5 sec to connect, and only .38 sec to fetch the wanted record from Oracle. Disconnecting from Oracle is a fast operation, which takes only .01 sec.

An internal debugger that provides features similar to the ones available in DBUG can be used as a basic regression-testing tool. The output of an entire session can be captured in a file, becoming the baseline. Successive runs are expected to produce the same debugging output, which can be verified by performing a *diff* command against the two ASCII files containing the output captured in different runs. Any discrepancy found by diff in the two output files means that the program is behaving differently from the baseline.

Internal debuggers can also be used as basic profilers. The time stamping functionality is very useful in determining the time taken by the execution of each routine called by the program. Let us take the program used as an example to show the DBUG features. The database table accessed is the STOCK table, which contains 600,000 records. We fetch a record using the record identifier, stored in the REC_SEQ field. That field is indexed, to allow a fast retrieval of records based on the Oracle sequence used to uniquely identify each record stored in the STOCK table. This explains why it only takes .38 sec to fetch a record (see the previous DBUG output).

If we drop the index on REC_SEQ and we try our program again, we are expecting very different results, because now Oracle has to perform a full table scan of a table containing 600,000 records.

We initially drop the index:

```
SQL> drop index stock_rec_seq_ndx1;

Index dropped.

SQL>
```

We then invoke `DbugExample` again, not before having bounced the Oracle instance to flush the SGA. This is necessary to avoid biasing the statistics on the time required to fetch a record. We need to be sure that the record in question is not already cached in the SGA; otherwise, Oracle will be very quick to retrieve the record, even in absence of an index.

```
Oracle Server Manager Release 2.3.2.0.0 - Production
Copyright (c) Oracle Corporation 1994, 1995. All rights re-
served.
Oracle7 Server Release 7.3.2.3.0 - Production Release
With the distributed, replication and parallel query options
PL/SQL Release 2.3.2.3.0 - Production
SVRMGR> connect internal
Connected.
SVRMGR> shutdown immediate
Database closed.
Database dismounted.
ORACLE instance shut down.
SVRMGR> startup open
ORACLE instance started.
Total System Global Area        7929208 bytes
Fixed Size                        41832 bytes
Variable Size                   4602384 bytes
Database Buffers                3276800 bytes
```

```
Redo Buffers                          8192 bytes
Database mounted.
Database opened.
SVRMGR> exit
```

When the instance is up again, we can launch DbugExample again, giving the same command line parameters as before:

```
292$ DbugExample  27 "d:t:T" 1

980621 001940.58: |   >nDBConnectDb
980621 001940.69: |   <nDBConnectDb
980621 001940.70: |   >FetchRecordBySeq
980621 001940.70: |   |   >nLDFetchRecord
980621 001940.70: |   |   |   >nDBFetchRecord
980621 001956.12: |   |   |   <nDBFetchRecord
980621 001956.12: |   |   <nLDFetchRecord
Pharmacia Upjhon                 07091997 225536 1 30 53 43489
980621 001956.12: |   <FetchRecordBySeq
980621 001956.12: |   >nDBDisconnectDb
980621 001956.13: |   <nDBDisconnectDb
980621 001956.13: <main
```

The output confirms our expectations. Without an index, Oracle takes little more than 15 seconds to return the row. If the index was dropped inadvertently, or was not correctly re-created while moving the application to the production environment, the internal debugger can be used to pinpoint the problem. One doesn't need to be an Oracle guru to understand that something has gone wrong, simply by looking at the statistics produced by the internal debugger. The Oracle DBA can be called in to further investigate what happened and find a good starting point for the troubleshooting exercise.

8.3.2 DISABLING INSTRUMENTATION IN PRODUCTION CODE

Internal debuggers usually offer the ability to disable the instrumentation of the code. The DBUG package offers the DBUG_OFF macro, which helps to limit or avoid the expansion of all other macros provided by the package. DBUG_OFF allows developers to switch off the instrumentation just before releasing the code to the production environment.

There is a small price to be paid in performance when the internal debugger is left active in the final build. Each call to an application function produces two more calls, one at the moment of entering the function, triggered by the DBUG_ENTER macro, and one at the moment of exiting the function, triggered by the DBUG_RETURN macro. The two functions called by the internal debugger do not perform any I/O operation, and they execute very quickly. Nevertheless, they are repeatedly invoked, and in the economy of an entire program run, the accumulated time spent by the instrumented code can become significant. The temptation to remove the instrumentation from the code is very strong for programmers who care about program performance.

In some cases, however, it is better to be able to activate the debug output while the program is running. A mission critical system usually runs in a strictly controlled environment, where every change has to be scheduled well in advance, sometimes even weeks in advance. In these contexts, leaving a back door open for debugging activated on the fly can prove very useful.

The Mars Pathfinder mission is one of the best examples of a critical system saved by its internal debugging capabilities left active by the engineers when the spacecraft was launched. The Pathfinder was initially a great success. The most delicate moment of the mission was the landing on the Martian surface. The smallest mistake at that moment could have jeopardized the entire mission. Luckily, everything went fine, and the Pathfinder, after a successful landing, started sending data back to Earth. The panoramic pictures taken by the Pathfinder became an instant hit on the WEB.

A few days into the mission, however, the spacecraft started experiencing system resets, each causing total loss of data. The gathering and transmitting of the meteorological data was identified as the area provoking the system resets. On Earth, the engineers driving the mission were frantically working on a Pathfinder replica, trying to re-create in the laboratory the conditions under which the system resets were happening. They were finally able to isolate the problem, caused by an unwanted priority inversion on the priorities associated with different threads.

The meteorological data gathering subsystem ran infrequently, carried out by a low-priority thread. To publish its data, it used the "information bus," a sort of shared memory area used by the various components of the spacecraft to exchange data. Access to the information bus was regulated by mutexes, to be acquired and released by the various components. The priority inversion bug provoked a deadlock situation, constantly resolved by a watchdog timer, which used to clean everything up by triggering a system reset. The solution to the problem was simple; the low-priority meteorological thread should have acquired the mutex inheriting the higher priority level from the information bus. Because of the extremely well-engineered architecture of the Pathfinder, a boolean variable should have been set to TRUE to force the meteorological thread to acquire the mutex, performing priority inheritance.

The real-time embedded system kernel of the Pathfinder included a "C" language interpreter that allows developers to insert "C" expressions and functions to be executed on the fly. This feature was conceived to simplify system debugging, but the Pathfinder engineers decided to leave the interpreter enabled for the entire mission. The mutex initialization parameters were stored in global variables, whose addresses were in symbol tables accessible by the "C" interpreter.

A "C" program was uploaded to the spacecraft. When that program was interpreted, the values of the initialization parameters were changed from false to true. This fixed the problem, and no more system resets occurred. It must have been a rather thrilling experience starting an "FTP session" with a host residing on Mars, to upload the fix. Leaving the debugging facilities enabled in the system saved the mission. Without the ability to modify the Pathfinder software on the fly, the problem could not have been fixed.

The Pathfinder mission is definitely an example of extreme criticality of a system. Nevertheless, the lesson learned could well apply to business systems. Sometimes losing 5–10% of run-time performance, due to enabled debugging facilities, can be considered as an investment. In the economy of a project, it pays out well when trouble shooting is needed to fix a problem that can potentially provoke downtime.

8.3.3 PROFILERS

Profilers help identify where the program spent its time. Traditionally, they have been part of the Unix distribution kit at no additional cost. Profiling is enabled by including an appropriate parameter in the command line that invokes the "C" or "C++" compiler. Alternatively, the source code can be instrumented to reach a finer level of control over profiling. Profilers have not been standardized by the various international committees, so each Unix variant implements them slightly differently. A common trio of profiling utilities is *monitor, profil,* and *prof*. monitor() is used by default if the program is compiled with the option that enables profiling. Developers can exclude specific functions from being profiled by using monitor() directly. After a program has been instrumented for profiling, it can be run. Profiling statistics are accumulated by default in the mon.out file, unless an environment variable (usually PROFDIR) has been defined. The prof utility can be used to produce a human readable format of the statistics accumulated in the profiling output file. An example of function profiling follows:

```
%Time Seconds Cumsecs  #Calls   msec/call  Name
 44.1    0.15    0.15                      _r_write
  8.8    0.03    0.18    2611      0.011   _idoprnt
  5.9    0.02    0.20                      _r_read
  2.9    0.01    0.21     824      0.01    _tz_int
  2.9    0.01    0.22                      _r_open
  2.9    0.01    0.23                      _mcount
  2.9    0.01    0.24                      nsprecv
  2.9    0.01    0.25     824      0.01    _tz_hms
  2.9    0.01    0.26       4      2.      nDfileStats
  2.9    0.01    0.27                      nsgblini
  2.9    0.01    0.28                      nsdo
```

```
   2.9     0.01     0.29                         _fdopen
   2.9     0.01     0.30                         lnxnur
   2.9     0.01     0.31                         __lxstat
   1.7     0.01     0.32                         nlfncons
```

The tabular six-column report shows the number of calls for each routine, together with the time and the cumulative time spent executing. Some Unix variants allow for line profiling. A different switch is used while invoking the compiler to enable line profiling. The utility that formats the profiling data is often called *lprof*. The command-line parameter accepted by lprof is the name of the instrumented program. Profiling information at line level is displayed on the standard output, which can be redirected to a file. An example of line profiling information extracted using lprof follows:

```
int nDictSts(void)
   10 [32]      {

/**********************<DICT_STS>***********************/
/*   Dictionary Cache statistics                        */
/*   array size: 83 bytes                               */
/*******************************************************/
                char    szSqlStmt[212];
                char    szParameter[10][33];
                float   fMissRatio[10];
                int     nGets[10];
                int     nMiss[10];
                int     nCount[10];
                int     nUsage[10];
                char    szRowNum[5];
                static  char OP2_DictSts_c[]="@(#)DictSts.c
                        1.1";
                int     nn,
                        nRowsDone,
                        ii,
                        sts,
   10 [50]              nStatementsProcessed=0;

                typedef struct tagDictSts
                {
                        char    szLine[84];
                        struct  tagDictSts *pNext;
                }DICT_STS;
   10 [56]      DICT_STS *pDictSts=NULL, *pDictStsCur=NULL,
```

```
                              *pDictStsPrevious=NULL,
 10 [57]                      *pDictStsLast=NULL;
 10 [58]        BOOL          bFirstTime=TRUE;

 10 [60]        DBUG_ENTER("vDictSts");
 10 [61]        strcpy(szSqlStmt,"select parameter, gets,
                getmisses, \
                decode(getmisses,0,0,round((getmisses/
                (gets+getmisses)
                                                  )*100,2) ),\
                count,usage from sys.v_$rowcache");
 10 [65]        if (oparse(&CursCda,(text *) szSqlStmt,-
                1,1,2))
                {
  0 [67]
            DBUG_PRINT("ORA_ERR",("%s",GetOraMsg(&CursLda,
            CursCda.rc)));
  0 [68]                    if( (sts=SendToClient("ERROCI",6))
                            == -1)
                            {
  0 [70]                        DBUG_PRINT("SND_ERR",("Could not
                                send message through sockets"));
  0 [71]                        DBUG_RETURN(-1);
                            }
  0 [73]                    DBUG_RETURN(0);
                }
```

The report shows the line number, as seen by the compiler, surrounded by brackets. The number on the left-hand side of the line number is the number of times the statement appearing in the line has been executed. Line profiling provides program coverage analysis. Coverage data can be merged so that multiple runs don't overwrite profile information previously accumulated. A satisfactory level of coverage can be the result of progressive refinements. Being able to keep the previous results, and to merge the accumulated data during the latest run with all previous runs, helps to achieve the desired coverage threshold.

Profilers have the advantage of being offered with the operating system, usually at no additional cost. They are often included in the Unix standard distribution, no third party involved. They do well at what they were designed to do, which is mainly producing statistics on the time spent by each routine. This is useful to identify bottlenecks and to pinpoint those parts of a program that should be optimized.

A profiler is not included in MS Windows NT, but it is available in the professional and enterprise editions of MS Visual Studio. When profilers offer coverage analysis, through line profiling, they cannot usually compete with third party specialized tools, like Rational Pure Coverage (see next section). When third party coverage tools are not available, the line profilers can provide the basic coverage analysis features. Profiling should be a standard part of every software development life cycle. Program optimization is often overlooked and one of the first activities to be sacrificed when a project schedule has to be compressed as a result of budget cuts. This is comprehensible if the software product being built will be in the "good enough" category. When striving to build a product for the "best" category, profiling becomes an essential activity.

8.3.4 TEST COVERAGE MONITORING

In a software development environment operating within strict quality control procedures, a great deal of coding efforts is put in to the creation of test harnesses. Their purpose is to exercise most, and possibly all, the instructions contained in a program. The program flow can follow a different path while the program is running. This path is determined by user options and other factors, including errors due to unavailability of peripheral devices, network failures, etc. While it is possible, though tedious, to write comprehensive test harnesses that test the behavior of the program under all possible options chosen by the users, it is generally difficult to test for all potential external failures. This is because it is also generally difficult to artificially re-create in experimental conditions certain categories of errors, which in real life are possible.

Exhaustive test coverage is hardly, if ever, achieved. It has been mathematically demonstrated that the CPU time required to exhaustively test a very simple program consisting of three or four iterations and several "if" conditions enclosed in a loop is measurable in terms of thousands of years. This is not to say that testing is a useless exercise. A reasonable and commonly accepted coverage goal is 80% of the code. Commercially available test coverage tools, like PureCoverage by Rational Software Corporation, use 80% as a default value.

The test coverage tool works by instrumenting the code of the program being analyzed. This type of instrumentation is very low-level and happens in the object file produced by the compilation of the source. That is, the source code remains untouched, and no additional high-level language instructions need to be added. This is an advantage over internal debuggers, where the source code has to be instrumented. Commercially available tools optionally allow developers to use coverage-oriented APIs for a better control of data gathering for test coverage.

After the executable binary file of a test harness program has been instrumented, the program is run and the coverage statistics are accumulated in a file. They can be displayed by an interactive tool after the test harness has completed. When the interactive tool that interprets the coverage statistics offers a visual interface, developers can visually identify the areas of the program that are not sufficiently covered by the text harness.

The more sophisticated test coverage tools allow developers to selectively exclude lines of code that cannot be tested, so that they don't bias the overall statistics. This makes sense, because sometimes the only way to test the behavior of an error handling routine is to force the return value of a function using the debugger. A developer could simulate an error condition returned by a function by changing the returned value of the function, using the appropriate debugger command. If this is done before the variable is checked, then the flow of the program can be manually forced and the behavior of the program under error condition tested. Clearly, this test has to be performed interactively, and cannot be continuously replicated in experimental conditions. Developers can flag the

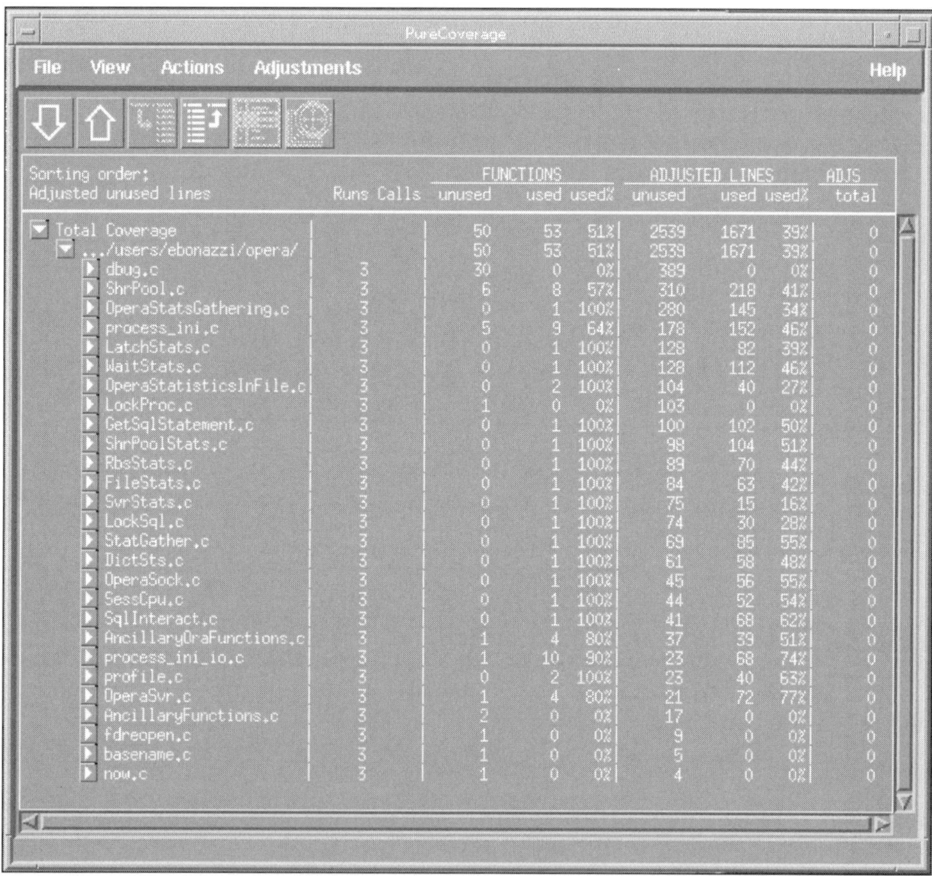

	Runs	Calls	FUNCTIONS unused	used	used%	ADJUSTED LINES unused	used	used%	ADJS total
Total Coverage			50	53	51%	2539	1671	39%	0
.../users/ebonazzi/opera/			50	53	51%	2539	1671	39%	0
dbug.c	3		30	0	0%	389	0	0%	0
ShrPool.c	3		6	8	57%	310	218	41%	0
OperaStatsGathering.c	3		0	1	100%	280	145	34%	0
process_ini.c	3		5	9	64%	178	152	46%	0
LatchStats.c	3		0	1	100%	128	82	39%	0
WaitStats.c	3		0	1	100%	128	112	46%	0
OperaStatisticsInFile.c	3		0	2	100%	104	40	27%	0
LockProc.c	3		1	0	0%	103	0	0%	0
GetSqlStatement.c	3		0	1	100%	100	102	50%	0
ShrPoolStats.c	3		0	1	100%	98	104	51%	0
RbsStats.c	3		0	1	100%	89	70	44%	0
FileStats.c	3		0	1	100%	84	63	42%	0
SvrStats.c	3		0	1	100%	75	15	16%	0
LockSql.c	3		0	1	100%	74	30	28%	0
StatGather.c	3		0	1	100%	69	85	55%	0
DictSts.c	3		0	1	100%	61	58	48%	0
OperaSock.c	3		0	1	100%	45	56	55%	0
SessCpu.c	3		0	1	100%	44	52	54%	0
SqlInteract.c	3		0	1	100%	41	68	62%	0
AncillaryOraFunctions.c	3		1	4	80%	37	39	51%	0
process_ini_io.c	3		1	10	90%	23	68	74%	0
profile.c	3		0	2	100%	23	40	63%	0
OperaSvr.c	3		1	4	80%	21	72	77%	0
AncillaryFunctions.c	3		2	0	0%	17	0	0%	0
fdreopen.c	3		1	0	0%	9	0	0%	0
basename.c	3		1	0	0%	5	0	0%	0
now.c	3		1	0	0%	4	0	0%	0

FIGURE 8.4 PureCoverage at work. The viewer interprets the statistics accumulated in a .pcv file and displays them in an easy to use form

"manually tested" lines of code to prevent the reporting tool from considering those lines as not covered by the test harness.

Tools like PureCoverage allow developers and administrators to run periodical batch reports on coverage-instrumented files. Developers can be automatically e-mailed when the coverage of files being tested falls below a certain threshold.

The test coverage tool can be configured such that a single program can accumulate coverage statistics of multiple runs in one file. Alternatively, each program run generates a different coverage file. In the first case, the coverage file will show cumulative statistics for all runs. In the second case, the coverage file contains statistical information about the most recently executed program. The most sophisticated test coverage tools allow programmers to discard data from the cumulative coverage file if a specific test harness fails, in order not to bias the overall statistical indicators.

PureCoverage is also available for the MS Windows NT platform. The NT version is called Visual PureCoverage, and is well integrated with Microsoft Developer Studio.

Test coverage tools are extremely useful for test monitoring and controlling. They can improve all administration tasks associated with the testing activities, as well as detect areas of the program being developed not properly tested.

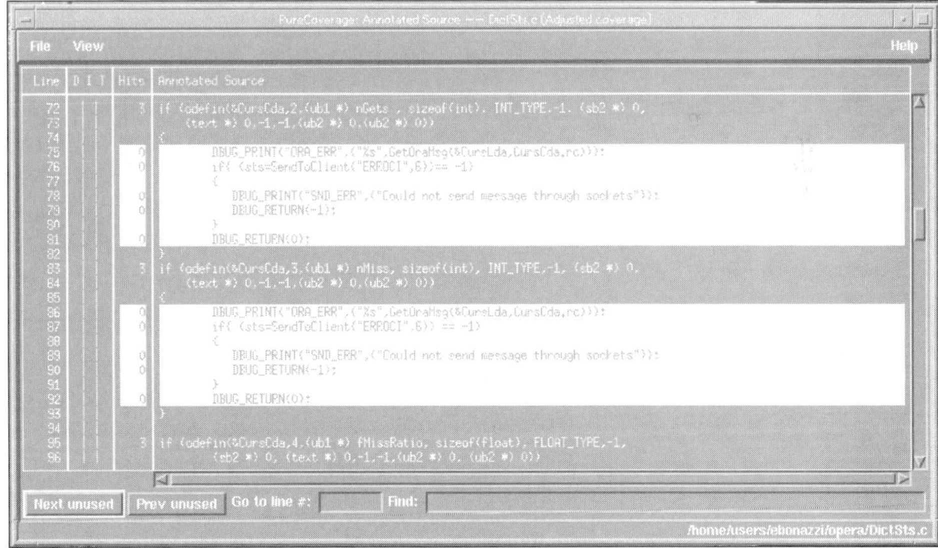

FIGURE 8.5 From the main window, by double clicking on a module name, a user can access a secondary window that displays lines of code not covered by the test harness. In this figure, these lines of code are the ones in white.

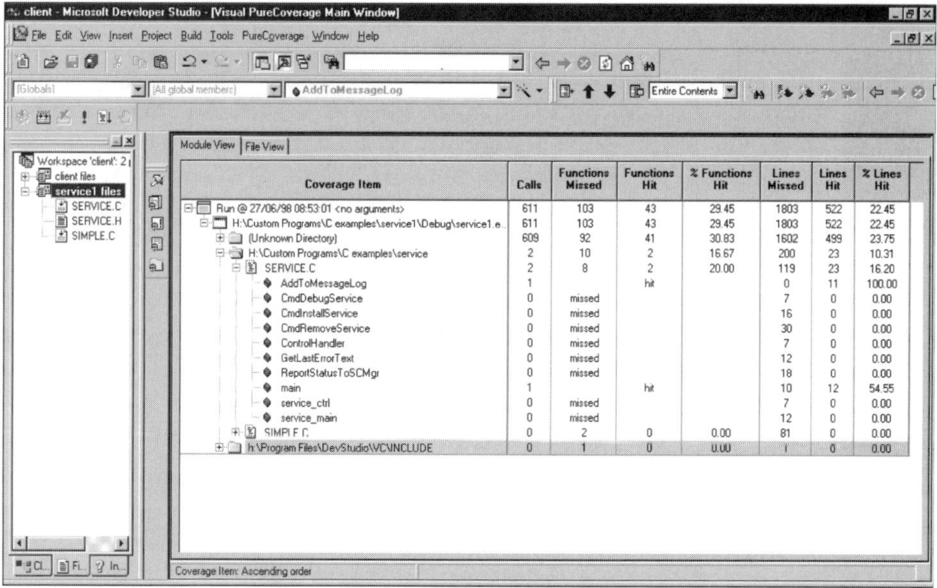

FIGURE 8.6 Visual PureCoverage for Windows NT. The product is well integrated into the Microsoft Developer Studio.

8.3.5 RUN-TIME ERROR DETECTION

Languages such as "C" and "C++" leave the responsibility of making good and safe use of memory resources to the programmer. A "C" programmer is not restricted in any way from accessing directly memory locations. However, such freedom is paid dearly in terms of more error prone coding. Typical categories of errors in accessing memory resources include:

- wild pointers
- incorrect pointer arithmetic
- memory allocated and not released
- accessing of uninitialized memory

Object-oriented languages, such as Smalltalk, Eiffel, and Java, implement a garbage collector directly in the run-time system. Memory is under direct control of the garbage collector. Programmers can neither interfere with the run-time system nor access memory locations directly. The garbage collector takes care of releasing the memory that was allocated and is no longer needed by the application. In the above mentioned languages, memory is never directly accessed by the programmer. For this reason programs written in Smalltalk, Eiffel, or Java are shielded against memory related problems. The garbage collector mechanism is one of the recent great advancements in software technology.

Unfortunately, many large and mission critical systems still use traditional languages that do not provide garbage collecting capabilities. Among them, "C" and "C++" are particularly exposed to memory related defects. While no available tool can help prevent programmers from introducing memory related software defects, run-time error detection tools can be used throughout the entire SDLC to pinpoint memory related bugs.

With respect to test coverage tools, run-time error detection tools instrument the object files produced during the compilation phase. This kind of instrumentation does not usually affect the source code. Running an executable file that has been instrumented results in the run-time error detection support to flag memory related errors. In order for an error to be found, the program must run the routine containing the error. This implies that the test harness for the program in question has to exhaustively check every routine comprised in the program.

The market leader for run-time error detection tools in the Unix environment is Purify, by Rational Software. Purify can be used together with Rational

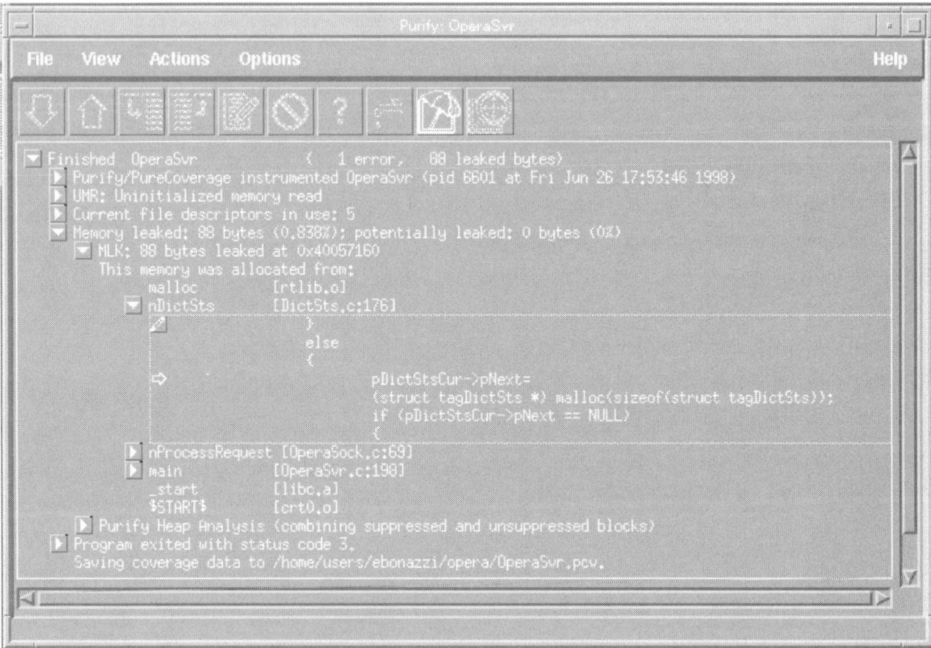

FIGURE 8.7 Rational Software Purify at work. In this figure, Purify flagged a memory-leaking problem. By double clicking on the module name, the Purify viewer shows the line of code that originated the error.

Software's PureCoverage to provide a comprehensive test bed for concurrent test coverage and run-time error detection. Purify has also been ported under MS Windows NT. Under NT Purify shows its nonnative origins and lacks sufficient integration with Microsoft Developer Studio. In addition, it does not support other development environments, such as Inprise Delphi or C++ Builder. The market leader for the NT platform is BoundsChecker by NuMega Technologies Inc., which is able to detect more MS Windows NT specific run-time errors than Purify for NT. It is also more integrated with the standard development tools used in the NT platform and supports the Inprise development tools.

8.3.6 ORACLE TRACE

Internal debuggers are generic tools, enabled at a language level, useful when used in conjunction with Oracle-based programs, as we have seen in Section 8.3.1. Their usefulness stops as soon as the Oracle sub-system takes control of the program. Sure, they can still provide the total time taken by an Oracle task to exe-

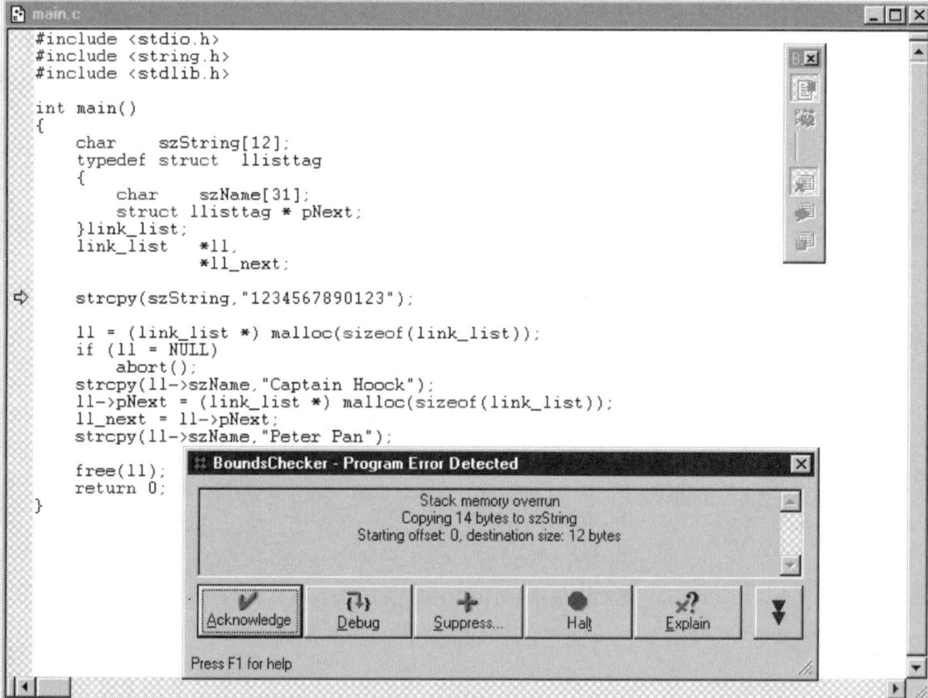

FIGURE 8.8 NuMega BoundsChecker at work. When debugging in Visual Studio, stepping through a line of code that contains a memory-related error triggers an immediate feedback from the run-time error detection tool.

cute, but they cannot "look inside" Oracle to determine where the time is spent. The most recent releases of Oracle (7.3x and 8.x) provide a facility called Oracle Trace, the purpose of which is to gather performance information directly from the Oracle kernel. The performance data is written to an external file, in order not to influence the database performance while monitoring it. Oracle Trace provides a utility that reads the trace file and stores the performance data into Oracle, to simplify the analysis of the data using standard database browsing tools. See chapter 13 for a detailed explanation on the use of Oracle Trace.

8.4 Writing Performance Conscious SQL Statements

Programmers with a background in PC based file managers and databases, such as products of the xBase family (Borland dBASE, CA Clipper, CA VisualObjects, etc.) or MS Access, usually tend to apply functions to the columns appearing in the where clause. This is done to force exact comparisons between the operands of the where clause. For example, if you want to avoid any confusion with strings that contain both lowercase and uppercase characters, you can use the SQL UPPER function in both sides of the where clause, as in

```
where upper(surname) = upper(:my_surname);
```

xBASE dialects go even further, allowing programmers to embed the function in the index when the index is initially created, as in

```
create index cust_surname on upper(surname)
```

This technique doesn't work with Oracle. An index cannot be created with an embedded function.

Oracle allows programmers to apply functions to columns appearing as operands of the where clause. Unfortunately, there is a major side effect associated with this technique. If the column in question is indexed, the function coercing the column prevents the index from being used. This applies only to the columns appearing in the where clause, and not to the values they are compared against. An SQL function can be used to coerce the value appearing on the right side of the comparison operator, as in

```
where surname = UPPER(:var_surname)
```

In this case, the index on the surname column can be used by Oracle to retrieve the rows.

There are occasions when calculations have to be performed to identify the value needed to select the wanted rows. In the following example, we want to select all employees who are older than 40. The date of birth of each employee is stored in the employee table. Our query can be as follows:

```
select surname from employee where DOB +(365 * 40) > SYSDATE;
```

Our query is syntactically correct, but unfortunately, an index on the DOB column cannot be used. Functions and calculations performed against the column appearing in where clause disable the associated index.

We can obtain the same result, but this time allowing Oracle to use the index on the date of birth column, by rewording the SQL statement in this way:

```
select surname from employee where DOB > SYSDATE - (365 *
40);
```

In chapter 4, when we considered how to deal with null values and columns that allow the insertion of NULL values, we found out that Oracle cannot use indexes when looking for rows using NULL keys. The SQL statement

```
select surname from employee where dob is null;
```

will always use a full table scan to return the requested rows.

In order to retrieve the rows requested by the user in the most efficient way, Oracle uses a *query optimizer*. Older releases of Oracle used a rule-based optimizer, which ranks every possible access path for each table. The access path with the lowest ranking is preferred and chosen supposedly as the most efficient. The ranking of the access paths follows mechanical rules that are applied without taking into consideration the size of each table.

According to the rule-based optimizer:

- Indexes are preferred to table scans
- Unique indexes are preferred to nonunique indexes
- Concatenated indexes are preferred to single column indexes (if the entire concatenated index is used)
- Single values are preferred to ranges
- Bounded ranges (e.g., BETWEEN) are preferred to unbounded ranges (e.g., GREATER THAN)

If access path rankings are equal, the order in which the tables are listed determines the access path. The table specified last in the from clause becomes the first table in the join order. In other words, the rightmost table in the from clause is the *driving table* of the join operation. In the old days of Oracle SQL optimization, determining the driving table was very important. The *position* of the table in the wording of the SQL statement made a significant difference. The driving table was chosen based on its size. The smallest table should have been the last in the "from" clause.

The problem of the rule-based optimizer is that its analysis is hopelessly static. That is, the same optimization pattern will be repeatedly chosen by the optimizer for the lifetime of the application, without taking into consideration the size of the tables. The smallest table at the moment of the initial optimization—the one chosen to be the driving table for the core joins performed by the application—can have faster growth than the other tables. After a while, that table would no longer be the best candidate for being the driving table. Yet, unless the application maintainers rework the SQL statements, the table continues to stand in the position of the driving table, causing degrading performance and worsening with time.

In addition, the Oracle rule-based optimizer requires human intervention, at least initially, to study and determine the best combinations and the best wording of the SQL statements. When an application is comprised of relatively few and well-known data access paths, as in the case of OLTP applications, a rule-based optimizer can successfully be used. In decision support environments, such as data warehousing, the designers are not in a position to predetermine all potential data access paths that will eventually be required by the users.

In these contexts, a rule-based optimizer is definitely not an option. For this reason, starting with release 7.0 of the database server, Oracle Corporation introduced the cost-based optimizer. After two or three minor releases, Oracle 7.3 was introduced, which performs better than the rule-based optimizer in most cases. The two optimizers today coexist in the database server, but Oracle Corporation warned that the rule-based optimizer will eventually be phased out. In addition, while the cost-based optimizer has been constantly improved, the rule-based technology has not been further developed. The cost-based optimizer is rapidly becoming the only reasonable option.

What is a cost-based optimizer and why it is better than the rule-based alternative? A cost-based optimizer compares possible execution plans by estimating the amount of I/O required to satisfy each. This estimate is based on statistics periodically generated on the database. The execution plan for the queries is *dynamically adjusted,* taking into account the varying size of the tables. The position where the tables appear in the SQL statement is irrelevant. The driving table automatically chosen by the cost-based optimizer is guaranteed to generate the most efficient data retrieval, the one that has less cost associated to it.

By using the cost-based optimizer, the SQL queries are, to a certain degree, self-tuning. The cost-based optimizer receives its input from the statistics on the database objects stored in the data dictionary. Gathering those statistics doesn't happen magically, but just be arranged by the Database Administrator. Most sites run the statistics generation as a batch job that is performed overnight, together with other housekeeping tasks. Up-to-date statistics on the database objects accessed by the SQL queries are crucial for a correct functioning of the cost-based optimizer.

To populate the data dictionary with the relevant statistics for the database objects, which are necessary for the cost-based optimizer to work properly, the DBA uses the ANALYZE command. ANALYZE serves several purposes, for instance, for checking the integrity of tables and indexes, by using the VALIDATE STRUCTURE clause. When used to produce the object statistics, ANALYZE provides two options, ESTIMATE and COMPUTE. When ANALYZE is used with ESTIMATE, as in:

```
analyze table customer estimate statistics;
```

Oracle samples up to 1064 rows and projects the statistics for the table. It is possible to choose a larger sample, by issuing the ANALYZE command with the following syntax:

```
analyze table customer estimate statistics sample 20 percent;
```

Absolute precision is achievable by using the COMPUTE clause, instead of ESTIMATE, as in:

```
analyze table customer compute statistics;
```

The trade-off is between precision and table availability. Computing statistics is a very expensive operation that forces Oracle to access each row contained in the table. Computing statistics on very large tables (a few million rows) can bring an engine to its knees. Furthermore, Oracle places several locks while scanning the table, so other users can be prevented from changing data on the table while the statistics are being computed.

On the other hand, 1064 rows are too small a sample when the table contains a few million rows. The statistics projected from such a small sample can be distorted. The best compromise is to run a statistics estimation on a significant sample (20–30%) while the database is not heavily accessed, typically overnight.

Irrespective of the optimizer used, we have pointed out that using functions on where clause columns disables their indexes, and the same happens if the where clause columns are included in a computation. We also considered the case of the index not being used by Oracle when looking for NULL values.

How do programmers know when an SQL statement is likely to perform satisfactorily? Oracle provides two methods to facilitate the optimization of SQL statements. The first relies on the EXPLAIN PLAN Data Manipulation Language (DML) command, is simpler to use, and can be easily operated by client-server programmers who don't have access to the back end machine. The second method forces Oracle to trace the execution of the SQL statements into a file, which is saved in the file system of the host machine. That file, produced by the internal Oracle trace facility, is of very difficult interpretation, unless it is filtered through a utility, called TkProf, to produce a human-readable output. In order to proficiently use the Oracle trace facility and TkProf, a programmer must be granted access to the host computer, that is, must have a host account and appropriate privileges.

8.4.1 EXPLAIN PLAN

The EXPLAIN PLAN command instructs Oracle to place the execution plan for a SQL statement into a table in the schema of the user who requested it. By default, EXPLAIN PLAN looks for a table called PLAN_TABLE; it is possible to name explicitly the table other than PLAN_TABLE. The PLAN_TABLE, or the user-defined alternative, has a specific structure. If you try to explain a command without having the PLAN_TABLE in your schema, Oracle will complain by issuing the following message:

```
SQL> explain plan for
  2  select table_name from user_tables;

select table_name from user_tables
                       *
ERROR at line 2:
ORA-02402: PLAN_TABLE not found
```

Oracle provides a PLAN_TABLE creation script that is installed by default. That script is called UTLXPLAN.SQL. In a Unix environment, it can be found in $ORACLE_HOME/rdbms/admin. In OpenVMS, it resides in the directory pointed to by the ORA_RDBMS logical name. In MS Windows NT, it is found in \ORANT\RDBMS80\ADMIN. All users should have read-only access to that file, so that they can run the script to create the PLAN_TABLE in their own schemas.

Another option allowed by EXPLAIN PLAN is to name the statement to be explained explicitly. This is useful if you want to explain multiple statements in your session. You can extract the SQL statistics from the PLAN_TABLE referring to each statement by its statement Id. Another option is not to name the statement, invoke EXPLAIN PLAN, and truncate the PLAN TABLE right after having extracted the SQL statistics.

A common mistake is to run the same statement twice without truncating the PLAN_TABLE between the two runs, or to run EXPLAIN PLAN twice forgetting to name the two statements differently. Oracle will append the statistics of the two runs without complaining, but you will encounter problems when extracting the SQL statistics.

In order to interpret the statistics stored by Oracle into the PLAN_TABLE, a hierarchical query must be issued against that table. That is, Oracle specific syntax, not standard ANSI, must be used. A commonly used SQL script to extract the SQL statistics from the PLAN_TABLE follows:

```
select lpad(' ',2*level)||rtrim(operation)||'
     '||rtrim(options)||' '||object_name query_plan
from plan_table
connect by prior id=parent_id
start with id=0;
```

It is time to put all into practice. We want to verify what has been previously stated about indexes that are supposedly excluded by the optimizer when an SQL function is issued against the column appearing in the where clause.

We use the STOCK table, which is indexed on rec_seq, the Oracle generated sequence that uniquely identifies all our records in the table. The statistics extraction script shown above has been saved to disk with the name EXPLAIN.SQL. The STOCK table and all scripts are in the companion CD-ROM, under the directory chap08.

We invoke SQL*Plus and we create the PLAN_TABLE in our schema:

```
SQL> @$ORACLE_HOME/rdbms/admin/utlxplan

Table created.
```

We issue the query using EXPLAIN PLAN:

```
SQL> explain plan for
  2  select * from stock where rec_seq = 234898;

Explained.

SQL> @explain

QUERY_PLAN
-----------------------------------------------------
  SELECT STATEMENT
    TABLE ACCESS BY INDEX ROWID         STOCK
      INDEX UNIQUE SCAN          STOCK_REC_SEQ_NDX
```

The execution plan displayed by the explain script is, in this case, easy to interpret. The most indented row is the one performed first. In our case, the unique index REC_SEQ_NDX is scanned. The identification number (ROWID) of the wanted row is found, and then the row is retrieved.

We now try to use a function against the rec_seq column, to see if it is really true that Oracle excludes the index:

```
SQL> explain plan for
  2   select * from stock where ABS(rec_seq) = 234898;

Explained.

SQL> @explain

QUERY_PLAN
------------------------------------------------------
  SELECT STATEMENT
    TABLE ACCESS FULL   STOCK
SQL>
```

As we expected, the execution plan shows that Oracle will perform a full table scan to fetch the requested row. The ABS function didn't do much, because the number stored in REC_SEQ is a positive number by default. The net effect of applying the ABS function to the REC_SEQ column has been the exclusion of the index.

Unfortunately, it is not always that simple to interpret the output of the hierarchical query performed on the PLAN_TABLE. The queries issued against Oracle data dictionary views are generally more complex, because of their deeply nested structure. Let us show the execution plan of a query that lists all tables owned by the user's schema:

```
SQL> explain plan for
  2  select table_name from user_tables;

Explained.

SQL> @explain

QUERY_PLAN
------------------------------------------------------
  SELECT STATEMENT
    NESTED LOOPS
      NESTED LOOPS OUTER
        NESTED LOOPS OUTER
          NESTED LOOPS
            TABLE ACCESS BY INDEX ROWID         OBJ$
              INDEX RANGE SCAN  I_OBJ2
            TABLE ACCESS CLUSTER        TAB$
              INDEX UNIQUE SCAN         I_OBJ#
          INDEX UNIQUE SCAN     I_OBJ1
        TABLE ACCESS CLUSTER    SEG$
          INDEX UNIQUE SCAN     I_FILE#_BLOCK#
      TABLE ACCESS CLUSTER      TS$
        INDEX UNIQUE SCAN       I_TS#

14 rows selected.
```

The first rule is to try not to be overwhelmed by the output. Proceed sequentially, and identify the most indented part of the statement. In our case, we should start by the unique index scan of the I_OBJ# index and progress towards the less indented parts of the plan. To interpret an execution plan, one should be familiar with the common execution steps performed by Oracle when processing an SQL statement.

An explanation for the execution steps listed in the above query plan follows:

INDEX UNIQUE SCAN	An index lookup that returns the ROWID of only one row.
INDEX RANGE SCAN	An index lookup that returns the ROWID of multiple rows. This can happen because the index is nonunique or because the query contained a range operator (BETWEEN, GREATER THAN, etc.).
NESTED LOOPS	A nested loop is being performed on the preceding step. For each row in the parent result set, the child set is scanned to find a matching value.
NESTED LOOPS OUTER	This is an outer join imposed upon a nested loop join.
TABLE ACCESS CLUSTER	An index cluster key is used to access data in the table in question.
TABLE ACCESS BY ROWID	The ROWID of a row is used to access data in a table. This is the fastest way to retrieve data in Oracle. Usually the ROWID is found by using an index lookup in a preceding step.
TABLE ACCESS FULL	This is the full table scan. Oracle reads every block containing data associated to the table being accessed.

The access steps listed above are only a subset of all access paths supported by Oracle. The best way to get acquainted to SQL optimization is by experience. After having explained the execution plan of a few tens of queries, and understanding each access step performed by Oracle, everything will start making sense. There is no substitute for experience. Every programmer working with Oracle should become familiar with SQL optimization through the standard Oracle tools.

We stressed several times that, under a few circumstances, Oracle is unable to use an associated index. A programmer should be aware when he or she is excluding an index from the query. Sometimes one wants to intentionally force Oracle not to use the index associated to a column, to *increase* the efficiency of a query. This statement appears counterintuitive, but it is in line with the behavior of Oracle and its architecture. How can a query that excludes an index be more efficient than a similar query that uses the index?

The answer is that it depends on the number of rows returned by the query. If the query returns a small number of rows, then an index significantly improves the overall performance. If the query returns a large number of rows, typically more than 20–30% of the rows contained in the table, then a full table scan becomes more efficient.

Index traversal in Oracle begins with the index root node access, and reads the subsequent nodes via direct I/O to fetch exactly the wanted block. Each block read requires a single read call. When Oracle is requested to perform a full table scan, it uses a smart look-ahead algorithm, which fetches multiple blocks at once, up to the number defined by the DB_FILE_MULTI-BLOCK_READ_COUNT parameter. This is a database parameter read by the engine at boot time. In most Oracle installations, it is by default set to eight blocks, but it can be increased if an application is expected to often perform full table scans.

To fully understand how a full table scan becomes more efficient than index retrieval, consider the situation where a database has been built with a block size of four kilobytes. The average row length of a table we are accessing in our query is 300 bytes. The table has been created with a PCTUSED parameter of 60%. In average, it will have eight records per block. When Oracle performs a full table scan of the table in question, the engine will read 64 records per read (eight records per block multiplied by eight blocks per read). If the table contains 1000 rows, Oracle will take 15 or 16 reads to move all blocks from the disk to the SGA. If a query against the same table uses an index, and fetches, say, 20 rows, the requested I/O operations are 40, many more than the full table scan.

To simplify the process of explaining the SQL statements submitted to the engine, the most recent releases of SQL*Plus Oracle offer the AUTOTRACE system variable. To analyze the SQL statements, the AUTOTRACE variable can be set to OFF (the default), which means no execution statistics, or ON, which produces a report on the execution plan.

When AUTOTRACE is set to ON, there are further available parameters:

ON STATISTICS	The AUTOTRACE report shows only the SQL statement execution statistics.
ON EXPLAIN	The AUTOTRACE report shows only the optimizer execution path.

AUTOTRACE can be enabled with the TRACEONLY parameter, which suppresses the output of the query.

We are going to use AUTOTRACE to test the different execution plan taken by Oracle when the same query is submitted to the engine, but the two different optimizers are used. When using the rule-based optimizer, the engine cannot use an index if the value of the where clause is compared for inequality. In other words, a query will exclude the index if the operator used is "!=" (not equal).

To force Oracle to use the index, the statement must be reworded. For instance, if we want to select all records where the column age is different from 21, instead of submitting the following where clause

```
where age != 21;
```

we should use:

```
where age < 21 or age > 21;
```

We are interested in analyzing the behavior of the cost-based optimizer, to verify if it actually improves the execution plan.

The test will be performed using our customer table, which contains 23 records. Each record has two fields, CUSTOMER_ID and CUSTOMER_NAME. We want to select all customers but one, excluding customer_id 21. We set AUTOTRACE to TRACEONLY, to enable the statistics and execution plan reports, but to suppress the query output.

```
SQL>  set autotrace traceonly

SQL> alter session set optimizer_goal=rule;

Session altered.

SQL> select * from customer where customer_id <20
   2 or customer_id >20;

22 rows selected.

Execution Plan
----------------------------------------------------------
   0      SELECT STATEMENT Optimizer=RULE
   1    0   CONCATENATION
   2    1     TABLE ACCESS (BY INDEX ROWID) OF 'CUSTOMER'
   3    2       INDEX (RANGE SCAN) OF 'CUSTOMER_ID_NDX'
                (UNIQUE)
   4    1     TABLE ACCESS (BY INDEX ROWID) OF 'CUSTOMER'
   5    4       INDEX (RANGE SCAN) OF 'CUSTOMER_ID_NDX'
                (UNIQUE)

Statistics
----------------------------------------------------------
          0  recursive calls
          0  db block gets
         26  consistent gets
          4  physical reads
```

```
          0  redo size
       1299  bytes sent via SQL*Net to client
        803  bytes received via SQL*Net from client
          5  SQL*Net roundtrips to/from client
          1  sorts (memory)
          0  sorts (disk)
         22  rows processed
SQL>
```

AUTOTRACE has produced the execution plan, which shows the optimizer used (rule) and the two index range scans. The execution statistics reports four physical reads. We shut the instance down to flush the SGA and we try again, this time using the cost based optimizer.

```
SQL> alter session set optimizer_goal=choose;

Session altered.

SQL> select * from customer where customer_id <21
   2 or customer_id > 21;

22 rows selected.

Execution Plan
-----------------------------------------------------------
   0      SELECT STATEMENT Optimizer=CHOOSE (Cost=1 Card=22
                                                 Bytes=462)
   1    0   TABLE ACCESS (FULL) OF 'CUSTOMER' (Cost=1
                                                   Card=22
                                                   Bytes=462)
Statistics
-----------------------------------------------------------
          0  recursive calls
          4  db block gets
         15  consistent gets
          2  physical reads
          0  redo size
       1292  bytes sent via SQL*Net to client
        803  bytes received via SQL*Net from client
          5  SQL*Net roundtrips to/from client
          1  sorts (memory)
          0  sorts (disk)
         22  rows processed
```

The cost-based optimizer opted for a full table scan. The statistics report shows that only two physical reads are needed by Oracle to fetch the 22 rows.

This is a classical case where a full table scan is more efficient than index retrieval. But what happens when we apply the same type of query against a much larger table? In our schema, we have the STOCK table, which holds 600,000 records. If we submit a very similar query, using the REC_SEQ field that we know is indexed, this is what the execution report tells us:

```
SQL> select * from stock where rec_seq < 3 or  rec_seq >
599995;

7 rows selected.


Execution Plan
----------------------------------------------------------
0       SELECT STATEMENT Optimizer=CHOOSE (Cost=8 Card=2
        Bytes=66)
1    0    CONCATENATION
2    1      TABLE ACCESS (BY INDEX ROWID) OF 'STOCK' (Cost=4
                                                      Card=1
                                                      Bytes= 33)

3    2        INDEX (RANGE SCAN) OF 'STOCK_REC_SEQ_NDX' (UNIQUE)
                                              ( Cost=3 Card=1)

4    1      TABLE ACCESS (BY INDEX ROWID) OF 'STOCK' (Cost=4
                                                      Card=1
                                                      Bytes= 33)
5    4        INDEX (RANGE SCAN) OF 'STOCK_REC_SEQ_NDX' (UNIQUE)
                                              (Cost=3 Card=1)


Statistics
----------------------------------------------------------
          0  recursive calls
          0  db block gets
         14  consistent gets
          3  physical reads
          0  redo size
       1279  bytes sent via SQL*Net to client
        686  bytes received via SQL*Net from client
          4  SQL*Net roundtrips to/from client
          1  sorts (memory)
          0  sorts (disk)
          7  rows processed
SQL>
```

The cost-based optimizer this time behaved exactly like the rule-based optimizer. It made Oracle use two index range scans, instead of fetching all blocks containing 600,00 records. The query is of the same type as the preceding one, but the cost-based optimizer chose different execution plans due to the different size of the tables. We can conclude that the cost-based optimizer is smarter than the rule-based optimizer.

The AUTOTRACE facility simplifies SQL performance analysis, but has a major drawback. In order to display statistics and execution plan, SQL*Plus performs the query. Enabling the TRACEONLY parameter only suppresses the query output, but the statement is still processed by Oracle. When the EXPLAIN PLAN command is executed instead of relying on the AUTOTRACE facility, no rows are fetched, but the execution plan is stored in the PLAN_TABLE. If you are unsure whether a statement will produce a full table scan of a large table, use EXPLAIN PLAN. You will know the answer almost immediately. Other developers will complain if the engine slows considerably down because you are playing with AUTOTRACE, performing resource hungry full table scans while optimizing your queries.

When we used the ABS function to exclude the index on REC_SEQ in a preceding example, we actually influenced the optimizer. In a way, we tricked it, forcing Oracle out of its "natural" behavior. Does this mean that it is possible to influence the Oracle optimizers by using the same technique? The answer is yes. Not only can the execution plans of the two optimizers be influenced, but Oracle also provides the means to do so, without using artificial tricks like the one shown in our preceding example. The mechanism that allows programmers to change the behavior of the optimizers is based on a series of *hints*, or keywords, which appear in the SQL statements as comments. An example of a statement containing a hint follows:

```
select  /*+FIRST_ROWS */ customer_name from customer
where customer_id > 16;
```

A few things are worth mentioning. The syntax to enable the hint: The plus sign, after the comment symbol, is mandatory. A hint must follow the SQL Data Manipulation Language (DML) statement. If the comment containing the hint is not placed right after the DML statement, Oracle ignores it.

Oracle allows one only hint per statement block. A statement block is a parent statement or a subquery of a composite statement, a SELECT, UPDATE or DELETE statement, or an element of a compound query; for instance, a compound query comprised of two query elements connected of a UNION includes two statement blocks. Each of the two can be influenced by a hint.

If hints are incorrectly specified or conflicting with each other, they are simply ignored by Oracle. If table aliases are used in the query, hints must refer to the tables by using the same aliases. For instance, to instruct the optimizer to use the Parallel Query Option (PQO) for a table scan, the /*+PARALLEL */ hint can be used. To refer to a specific table in a join, the following syntax must be used:

```
select /*+PARALLEL(cus,6) */ cus.customer_name, con.con-
tact_id from customer cus, contact con
where cus.contact_id = con.contact_id and con.contact_id >
23879;
```

The statement above instructs Oracle to use the PQO with a degree of parallelism of 6 when performing a full table scan of the customer table.

The most commonly used hints, with a brief explanation, follow:

ALL_ROWS	Requests the use of the cost-based optimizer with a goal of best throughput. (That is, the statement will be performed consuming the minimal possible amount of resources.)
FIRST_ROWS	The best response time to retrieve the first rows will be the goal of the optimizer when this hint is used.
RULE	The rule-based optimizer is requested through this hint. The rule based only understands this hint. Hints are ineffective in a rule-based context.
ORDERED	Instructs the optimizer to join the tables in the order they appear in the SQL statement.
INDEX(table_name, [index_name])	Instructs the optimizer to use the specified index to retrieve rows from the table. If no index is specified, use any available index.
FULL(table_name)	Forces the optimizer to perform a full table scan for the specified table.
CACHE	Requests the optimizer to keep the rows fetched through a full table scan in the SGA, to optimize further re-use
STAR	Asks the optimizer to privilege the STAR methodology over other methods of table join.

You can influence the behavior of the cost-based optimizer through hints. What about the rule-based optimizer? Unfortunately, the rule-based optimizer offers very few options. It doesn't recognize hints, so the only way to influence it is by excluding specific indexes from being used in joins, and by carefully choosing the position of the driving table in a join. The common method used to disable an index on a numeric column is by adding 0 to the column in the where clause, as in

```
where customer_id + 0 = :loc_cust_id;
```

To obtain the same effect for alphanumeric columns, you should concatenate a null string to the column, as in

```
where customer_name ||'' = :loc_cust_name;
```

Oracle is flexible enough to allow the two optimizers to be concurrently active. A database parameter, OPTIMIZER_GOAL, can be optionally set to RULE, forcing a rule-based optimization for all queries, or to CHOOSE. In choose mode, Oracle will try to use the cost-based optimizer if it finds statistics in the data dictionary tables; otherwise, it will use rule-based optimization semantics. The optimizer can be chosen for a session, by using the ALTER SESSION SET OPTIMIZER_GOAL syntax. By using hints, the optimizer can be chosen on a per statement basis.

If Oracle finds hints during the parsing of the statement, it automatically switches to the cost-based optimizer, even if either the session or the database defaults to rule-based optimization. This is particularly dangerous when statistics for the database objects is not gathered, that is, the analyze process is not performed on tables and indexes comprising the application. By using a hint, the cost-based optimizer is automatically activated by Oracle. If the optimizer does not find statistics on the tables included in the statement, it assumes that the tables are empty. The net result can be a full table scan on a very large table that the cost-based optimizer mistakenly assumes as empty.

The recommendation is to use the cost-based optimizer for all new projects and to consider switching to the cost-based optimizer for applications that are still using the rule-based optimizer. This process has to be carefully evaluated, and extensive testing must be performed. Applications that have been fine tuned in a rule-based environment and are performing well can experience problems if the cost-based optimizer is enabled without planning. In the long run, only the cost-based optimizer will survive; a migration path from the rule-based environment must be planned in time.

8.4.2 TRACE AND TKPROF

The explain plan command and the autotrace facility of SQL*Plus are very convenient tools for initial sketching of SQL statements. Their advantages are ease of use and client availability. Developers involved on client side of a client-server application are expected to submit tuned SQL. Often they don't even know where the Oracle back-end database resides. They need only to know the SQL*Net Transparent Network Substrate (TNS) identifier to be able to connect. They are not concerned with back-end issues and sometimes they don't even own a user account of the host machine. Yet, by using the standard Oracle client tools such as explain plan and SQL*Plus autotrace, they can perform an initial tuning of the core SQL statements.

The ease of use of the above mentioned tools is associated with a few limitations:

- ❑ Explain and autotrace are useful for analysis of single statements in controlled conditions
- ❑ The statistics produced by these tools are not detailed enough

An application usually submits to the Oracle engine multiple SQL statements. Explain and autotrace are fine for studying the behavior of a single SQL statement, but they cannot be proficiently used for the analysis of multiple statements. Furthermore, the statistics displayed by autotrace do not include CPU time or number of rows processed by each step of the statement.

In order to analyze multiple statements in batch mode, gathering detailed statistics on each, you must use the Oracle SQL trace facility. SQL tracing must not be confused with Oracle Trace, which we encountered in section 8.3.6. To use Oracle Trace, an application must be instrumented, and code must be written to capture events of interest into a file. SQL tracing doesn't require any instrumentation and can be enabled either instance-wise or on a per session basis.

When SQL tracing is enabled, Oracle appends to a file useful statistics on each SQL statement executed during a session. Every session generates one trace file. The simplest way to activate SQL tracing is by issuing an ALTER SESSION command with the SET SQL_TRACE qualifier set to TRUE. Note that this can be done in a client environment. In order to use the tools provided by Oracle to format the trace file into a human readable output, one has to have access to the server where the database resides.

In order for SQL tracing to correctly compute CPU and elapsed time, a database parameter must be set. The parameter is:

```
timed_statistics = true
```

There is a slight system overhead associated to the use of this parameter. While it is useful to enable timed statistics in development environments, you should consider pros and cons of this option for production environments.

Other database parameters affecting the use of SQL tracing are:

USER_DUMP_DEST	It determines the directory where the trace files are created
MAX_DUMP_FILE_SIZE	It determines the maximum length of each trace file

It is also possible to enable SQL tracing by default for all sessions connecting to a database. This is the last resort when it isn't possible to enable tracing for a specific application in any other way. For instance, you don't have access to the source code and you cannot turn tracing on for the specific session. Enabling SQL tracing at a database level considerably slows down the overall performance of the database, and risks filling the disk very quickly where the user dump directory is stored. To enable SQL tracing for all sessions the parameter SQL_TRACE should be set equal to TRUE in the database parameter file.

If you want to avoid the alter session command in the application code, and you can determine the Oracle session Id and serial number of the session you want to trace; then it is possible to enable tracing from a different session.

Let us imagine that you have a third party application that you suspect is sending untuned SQL to an Oracle instance. You don't have access to the source code of the application in question, yet you want to assess the quality of the SQL statements produced by the client. In this case, you would initiate a client connection from the application being monitored, using a username not used by anyone else in the system. From another Oracle session, it would be possible to interrogate the fixed memory table V$SESSION to find Oracle Sid and serial number of the client connection given its username. The SQL query to accomplish that follows:

```
select sid,serial#
from v$session
where username like upper('<USERNAME>'))
```

Once the Oracle Sid and the serial number are known, tracing can be enabled by using the stored procedure set_sql_trace_in_session provided with the built-in package DBMS_SYSTEM. The syntax follows:

```
dbms_system.set_sql_trace_in_session(<session>,<serial>,
true);
```

The next step, after having enabled tracing, is to use the application, in order to execute the SQL statements to produce useful trace files. Tracing can be switched off by logging off, by explicit invocation of the alter session command that sets sql_trace to false, or by using DBMS_SYSTEM. If the third parameter of set_sql_trace_in_session is set to false, tracing is turned off.

The task of identifying the generated trace file is not easy. A few obstacles might be on your way, for instance, locating the trace file. The file system directory where the file must be searched is specified in the fixed table V$PARAMETER. You can query Oracle to find this out:

```
select value from V$PARAMETER where name ='user_dump_dest';
```

Note that 'user_dump_dest' must be typed in lowercase. The directory indicated by user_dump_dest might well contain hundreds of files. Common methods to help identifying the wanted file are:

- ❑ File timestamp examination
- ❑ Use of grep to identify specific portion of SQL statements
- ❑ Use of the operating system process Id if used as file tagging

If you are the only developer using SQL tracing, then you could look for the most recent trace file in user_dump_dest. You should be able to identify your file.

If several developers are using SQL tracing concurrently, you can tag your file with a dummy SQL statement in your application, as in

```
select 'This is Johns trace file' from dual;
```

You can use then tools like grep to search for the trace file containing the string "This is Johns trace file."

Oracle usually makes use of the operating system process Id to build the string that becomes the trace file name. A typical trace filename can be named:

```
ora_<pid>.trc or oracle_<pid>.trc
```

If your application makes its operating system process identifier available to you, you can identify the trace file in user_dump_dest by the process id included in the filename.

In Unix, another potential problem is that the trace file may be protected. By default the file produced by an SQL tracing session belongs to Oracle, the account that "owns" the Oracle software. In many cases, developers cannot read the trace file. An undocumented database parameter, _TRACE_FILES_PUBLIC, can be set to TRUE in the Oracle initialization file to allow all developers to access the trace files. Alternatively, a privileged shell script, executable by all developers, can be used to make the trace file name, passed as parameter, readable to the requesting user.

Having identified the file brings you halfway through the process of interpreting the trace statistics. What follows is an example of a raw trace file, that is, not yet formatted to become human readable:

```
...
...
FETCH #1:c=0,e=0,p=0,cr=16,cu=0,mis=0,r=15,dep=0,og=4,
        tim= 665700
FETCH #1:c=0,e=0,p=0,cr=16,cu=0,mis=0,r=15,dep=0,og=4,
        tim= 665718
FETCH #1:c=0,e=0,p=0,cr=16,cu=0,mis=0,r=15,dep=0,og=4,
        tim= 665735
```

```
FETCH #1:c=0,e=0,p=0,cr=16,cu=0,mis=0,r=15,dep=0,og=4,
        tim= 665752
FETCH #1:c=1,e=1,p=0,cr=16,cu=0,mis=0,r=15,dep=0,og=4,
        tim= 665766
FETCH #1:c=1,e=1,p=0,cr=16,cu=0,mis=0,r=15,dep=0,og=4,
        tim= 665813
STAT #1 id=1 cnt=0 pid=0 pos=0 obj=0 op='CONCATENATION '
STAT #1 id=2 cnt=7471 pid=1 pos=1 obj=0 op='NESTED LOOPS '
STAT #1 id=3 cnt=1 pid=2 pos=1 obj=2515 op='TABLE ACCESS
        FULL COMPANY '
STAT #1 id=4 cnt=7471 pid=2 pos=2 obj=2526 op='TABLE ACCESS
        BY INDEX ROWID STOCK '
STAT #1 id=5 cnt=7471 pid=4 pos=1 obj=2528 op='INDEX RANGE
        SCAN '
STAT #1 id=6 cnt=0 pid=1 pos=2 obj=0 op='NESTED LOOPS '
...
...
```

In order to make sense out of the above hieroglyphics, the tkprof trace file formatter must be used. tkprof resides in the directory that stores the Oracle binaries. In Unix, it resides in $ORACLE_HOME/bin. In MS Windows NT, it resides in <x>:\ORANT\BIN. tkprof accepts a few parameters on the command line. In order to work, it needs at least two parameters: The first is the trace file and the second is the name of a file that will contain the formatted output. An important parameter is "explain," which specifies the connection that will be used to generate execution plans. If the explain parameter is not present, tkprof won't generate any execution plan.

Another useful parameter is sort, which gives the user great control over the production and display of the statistics formatted by tkprof. A typical tkprof invocation command line can be:

```
tkprof ora00256.trc output.txt explain=/
```

In this case, the default sorting options provided by tkprof have been accepted. The sort parameter is a complex parameter, comprised of one or more sort keys, which are in turn a combination of two parts. The first part determines the type of calls to be sorted; the second part indicates the values to be sorted.

The first sort key component can be:

- prs—parse: requires sort on values during parse calls
- exe—execute: sort on values during execute calls
- fch—fetch: sort on values during fetch calls

The second sort key component can be:

- cnt—count: sort on number of calls
- cpu—CPU: sort on CPU consumption
- ela—elapsed: sort on elapsed time
- dsk—disk: sort on disk reads
- qry—query: sort on consistent reads
- cu—current: sort on current reads
- mis—misses: sort on library cache misses
- row—rows: sort on rows processed

By concatenating a first sort key component with a second sort key component, as in:

```
fch + ela = fchela (sort on elapsed time during fetch calls)
```

one can obtain a sort key. There are a few illegal combinations; for instance, row can be appended only to exe or fch, and mis can be concatenated only to prs.

A common sort key is:

```
tkprof ora00256.trc output.txt explain=/ sort=(prsela,
exeela,fchela)
```

The formatted output by tkprof would be sorted by elapsed time.

It is time now to put everything together and use SQL tracing on real queries. The SQL*Plus session which enables SQL tracing follows:

```
SQL> alter session set sql_trace=true;

Session altered.

SQL>select 'SEWO trace file' from dual;
SQL>select b.company_name,a.date_value,a.low,
  2 a.close,a.high,a.volume from
  3 stock a, company b where
  4 a.ticker_id = b.ticker_id
  5 and a.ticker_id = 21
  6 and rec_seq > 550000
  7 /
SQL> 500 rows selected.
SQL> exit
```

Now we have to look for the trace file. We use the Unix command grep to scan all files in user_dump_dest, searching for “SEWO”:

```
$ cd $ORACLE_HOME/rdbms80/trace
$ grep SEWO *.trc
ORA00282.TRC:select 'SEWO trace file' from dual
$
```

We identified our file, ORA00282.TRC. We can now invoke tkprof to format the trace file into an output file:

```
$ tkprof80 ora00263.trc output.txt explain=/

TKPROF: Release 8.0.3.0.0 - Production on Fri Jul 3 10:4:17
        1998

(c) Copyright 1997 Oracle Corporation. All rights reserved.
$
```

Since we used an operating system authenticated account, ops$ebonazzi, we connect to Oracle via a slash (/). Consistently, we also connect with a slash when we want to explain our execution plan (explain=/). Note that we didn't use any sort option, because our trace file contains the statistics for only one statement. The sort option is useful when the trace file includes a long SQL session, with possibly hundreds of statements, and you want to sort them in order to find the most expensive statements first.

We now have a tkprof-formatted output in output.txt. The next step is to edit the file and interpret the statistics:

```
select b.company_name,a.date_value,a.low,
a.close,a.high,a.volume from
stock a, company b where
a.ticker_id = b.ticker_id
and a.ticker_id = 21
and rec_seq > 550000

call     count     cpu    elapsed       disk      query    current      rows
----     -----   -----    -------    -------     ------    -------     -----
Parse        1    0.02       0.19          0          0          0         0
Execute      1    0.00       0.00          0          0          0         0
Fetch       35    3.22      70.32       6042       6609          0       500
----     -----   -----    -------    -------     ------    -------     -----
total       37    3.24      70.51       6042       6609          0       500

Misses in library cache during parse: 1
Optimizer goal: CHOOSE
Parsing user id: 18  (OPS$EBONAZZI)
```

(continued)

```
Rows     Execution Plan
----     ---------------------------------------------------
   0     SELECT STATEMENT   GOAL: CHOOSE
 500      NESTED LOOPS
6000       TABLE ACCESS (BY INDEX ROWID) OF 'STOCK'
6001        INDEX (RANGE SCAN) OF 'STOCK_PK' (UNIQUE)
 500       TABLE ACCESS (BY INDEX ROWID) OF 'COMPANY'
 500        INDEX (UNIQUE SCAN) OF 'COMPANY_TICKER_ID' (UNIQUE)
```

The top part of the output reports the executed SQL statement. The bottom part shows a familiar execution plan, which we already encountered when we introduced explain plan. Note, however, that each execution step has an associated number of rows. These are the rows returned by each step. These statistics, which are very useful for SQL fine-tuning, are available only with tkprof.

The central part of the output represents the "core" of SQL tracing statistics. The tabular report comprises eight columns. The first four are self-explanatory. The fifth column, named disk, represents the number of disk reads required to satisfy the SQL query. The sixth column, named query, represents the number of times a buffer was returned in consistent mode. This means that that data was only for queries, and not modified since the SELECT statement was submitted.

The seventh column, named current, represents the number of times a buffer was retrieved to satisfy INSERT, DELETE, or UPDATE SQL statements. The last column, named rows, represents the number of rows processed by an SQL statement.

Some authors, for example, G. Harrison [1997], propose to group together the query and the current columns, calling the resulting column "logical reads," because the distinction between the two columns appears to be irrelevant while performing SQL tuning.

The statistics normally displayed by tkprof offer many clues about the efficiency of an SQL statement. However, with minimum computations, it is possible to derive a few essential ratios, which summarize the overall efficiency of the statement being analyzed. In addition, computing the ratios can reveal interesting aspects of the statement, which can go unnoticed during the first examination of the output produced by tkprof.

Four ratios are usually computed from the raw statistics displayed by tkprof:

1. Logical reads divided by rows processed—The numbers are total query + total current divided by total rows. In the above example: 6609 + 0 / 500 = 13.218. This ratio gives an indication of how expensive each row is, in terms of blocks retrieved. If one row "costs" more than 10 blocks, there is usually room for improvement.

2. Parse count divided by execute count—In our case, this ratio is not really significant, because we processed only one statement. When one statement is parsed once and executed many times, high values for this ratio may indicate poor cursors' reuse. In Pro*C, for example, the pre-compiler parameters MAXOPENCURSORS and RELEASE_CURSORS should be assessed to make sure they are not used inappropriately. See Chapter 11 for a detailed discussion on the Pro*C pre-compiler parameters.
3. Rows fetched divided fetch count—In the above example: 500 / 35 = 14.29. This ratio gives an indication on how efficiently the Oracle host array capabilities have been used. A low value for this ratio indicates that Oracle host arrays have not been used.
4. Physical disk reads divided by logical reads (total query + total current)—In the above example: 6042 / 6609 = 0.91 or 91%. This ratio indicates how many misses have occurred in the buffer cache. In our case, 91% is definitely too high. We should keep this ratio in the neighborhood of 10%. One way to obtain that is by increasing the size of the buffer cache (if the memory resources of the machine allow for that).

SQL tracing is one of the most powerful tools in the hands of Oracle developers. It is the ultimate tool for SQL analysis and performance tuning, as long as it is used with realistic test data. This is even more important in sites that use cost-based optimization. The statistics produced by SQL tracing/tkprof are distorted if the volume of data stored in the test database differs significantly from the production environment. In Chapter 9 we will discuss how to arrange a proper test environment, to reduce this kind of risk.

The optimization techniques illustrated in this section are the basic techniques that should be common knowledge among Oracle developers. This is not a book on Oracle performance tuning, and we have to stop here. Developers who want to deepen their knowledge of Oracle performance in general can consult the book "Oracle Performance Tuning," by M. Gurry and P. Corrigan, O'Reilly and Associates, 1996. This book covers performance tuning from a perspective closer to a DBA rather than to a developer. For an SQL specific reference, one should look at "Oracle SQL High Performance Tuning" by Guy Harrison, Prentice Hall 1997.

8.5 Testing Strategies

In the waterfall model of SDLC (see Chapter 2), testing is an activity that is (supposedly) conducted towards the end of the project, after the software has been built and before it is deployed to the production environment. One of the major problems associated with the rigid separation between the various phases of the waterfall model is that the time required to accomplish strict test procedures, and to comply with rigorous quality standards, is very long.

Building the test harnesses to satisfactorily test a large and complex software system, especially if it is interfaced with many diverse environments and machines, is extremely complicated and time consuming. Testing a system takes at least the same time as building it, if not more. In order to shorten the project schedule, technique researchers have studied and implemented them to achieve parallelism between the construction and testing phases.

Database-centric projects should determine the ER model very early in the design stage. Once the database design has been "frozen," user interface prototypes can be built to satisfy two goals:

- Allow the human-computer interaction specialists to refine the user interface
- Allow the test team to start building the testing scripts for black-box testing

Horizontal prototypes contain all the high-level functionality of a system, but don't implement the lower-level details. Conversely, a vertical prototype implements most of the high-level and the low-level functionality for a restricted part of the system being built. By carefully studying an optimal combination of the two different types of prototypes, designers can help testers to sketch testing strategies at the beginning of the construction phase. When a system has to be interfaced with other systems, the testing team can start creating test scripts as soon as the interface control documents have been finalized.

Anticipating testing as much as possible in SDLC helps to lower the costs of a project. Beside the economical reason, a more philosophical thought justifies initiating test-related activities very early in the design phase. If system and acceptance testing are discussed with the customers or project stakeholders during the initial analysis, chances are that the real requirements of the system being built will be specified in the test plan.

If test planning and design slip ahead in the SDLC, there is a potential risk to create an ad hoc plan that is closer to the solution, rather than to the problem. That is, the testing strategy could perpetuate assumptions and mistakes made by the designers while defining a model for the solution of the business problem.

To avoid preparing a test plan that reflects the solution rather than the requirements for a system, senior test designers and test team leaders should be involved during the early phase of analysis, instead of being given the software specifications at the end of the design phase.

8.5.1 TEST TECHNIQUES

There are two fundamental categories of testing techniques, which are not in opposition, but rather complement each other. The so-called *white-box* testing techniques try to prove that all independent paths of a module have been utilized, all logical decisions have been taken in both directions, and all loops have been tested using both minimum and maximum allowed values for the controlling variable. White-box testing pertains to the internal functioning of a module.

The *black-box* testing techniques are aimed at proving that input is correctly verified and either accepted or refused, that output is coherently and consistently produced according to the given input and that the overall integrity of information processed by the module is preserved. Black-box testing is used to verify the correct functioning of the software modules at the interface level.

Developers are usually responsible for the creation of white-box test harnesses at a unit level. Tools that facilitate test coverage analysis, like the ones we examined in Section 8.3.4, help developers implement white-box testing. White-box techniques are also useful for integration testing. The latter involves making sure that multiple modules, independently developed by different programmers, are coherent with each other once they are linked together to produce the binary executable file.

All developers should conduct white-box module-level testing during the construction phase. This activity is an inherent part of software building and cannot be easily delegated to components of the test team. To help programmers develop comprehensive white-box test harnesses, tools are available that automatically generate test drivers, which are compiled with the units under test resulting in test bed programs.

The role of an independent test group cannot be underestimated. There is a natural tension between developers, who tend to be defensive in their approach to testing, and testers, whose main task is to uncover defects left by developers. A successful test is a test that uncovers as many defects as possible. Developers tend to test well-known application paths, with numbers that fall in "reasonable" number ranges. Unfortunately, the notion of "reasonable range" is subjective and corresponds to the developer's idea of the application being built. A user perspective can be different and, consequently, the user's idea of range reasonableness could diverge significantly.

Given the different approach taken by developers and testers, it is much more likely for a person who is not emotionally involved with the source code produced to uncover defects. This is why the test group must be independent from the development team.

Usually the test team produces test scripts for black-box and regression testing. Regression testing is a growing battery of tests applied to new releases of a software product to make sure that the modifications introduced to the source code between releases don't change the expected behavior of the system. Why is this battery of tests growing? The answer is that every detected bug should originate a corresponding test script to make sure that that specific bug is not reintroduced in successive releases. In addition, it is likely that new features will be introduced with new releases. Consequently, new test scripts are needed to keep up with the newly introduced features.

Creating test scripts is a complex and demanding task. Testing test scripts is usually excruciatingly difficult. Sometimes, the only way to test software components is by writing programs in third generation languages like "C" or Cobol. This is particularly true for back-end processing, when interfaces to legacy systems and batch processing are a significant part of the system being built. In general, user interface testing is simplified by tools that allow one to capture screen forms in baselines, which are used to compare bit-by-bit the same screen forms captured in successive runs. If the two bitmaps differ, it means that the new release influenced the display to video of some elements. This difference could be due to a bug inadvertently introduced, or to a new feature purposely incorporated in the new release. In the latter case, the test script must be modified not to flag the new feature as a bug.

Most automated regression testing tools allow the tester to specify a *prologue* script, or a script that is triggered before the battery of tests is executed. At the end, an *epilogue* script can be automatically invoked to clean up the testing environment and to generate statistics on the tests run. Usually the prologue script loads the database with baseline data, so that all tests fetch and manipulate the same data over many runs.

Regression testing is an essential activity that continues for the entire lifetime of the application. The longer the lifetime of the system, the more regression testing scripts will be produced. The complexity of the regression-testing environment is also likely to increase. Again, tools play an essential role in ensuring an acceptable quality level for the product being built. A system of low-to-medium complexity cannot be manually tested. The effort required to perform regression testing relying on in-house grown procedures and scripts becomes anti-economical in a matter of days, if compared with the modest financial investment in a third party ad-hoc black-box and regression testing tools.

Black-box and regression testing scripts must be repeatedly applied, modified, and adapted to the changing software environment. They go through a life cycle of their own. This means that version control techniques, promotional groups, and configuration management apply to testing scripts as well as to source code.

What are the fundamental characteristics of testing tools, which can be used as evaluation parameters when evaluating competing products to be chosen for a project? We can identify a few key areas:

- Scalability
- Integration
- User feedback
- Test verification
- Script debugging capabilities

A testing tool must be scalable. This means that it must offer the capability to run the battery of tests emulating a user load measurable in hundreds of sessions, each performing high transaction rates. The testing tool should have a minimal impact on the system being tested, in order not to bias the results by its very presence. The test engine should be run on a dedicated machine, able to drive other systems over the network.

A testing tool should be integrated. The components of the package should be able to cooperate with each other to allow for sharing of common data, synchronize process flows, and to perform logical and coherent sequencing of operations. All test activities concurrently performed by the test system should be coordinated from a single point of control, a sort of test "brain" able to drive all components participating in the testing session. This way, results obtained from one testing session can be forwarded to other testing sessions, becoming input parameters of each successive step in the test battery.

Testing tools must provide user feedback. Testing sessions typically take a long time to be executed. The tester must be informed at any time about what's happening. The testing tool should display interactive progress reports on the script lines executed, the transaction count, and the system response times. System performance parameters, such as CPU utilization, swap space and disk space statistics should also be displayed in real-time during testing sessions.

A testing tool must provide enough information to allow testers to determine exactly what happened during the test sessions. In case of test failure, postmortem analysis should be simplified by accurate logging. Good testing tools should offer error-recovery procedures built in the test scripts, in order to minimize the likelihood of a premature abortion of test sessions due to trivial errors.

Writing test scripts is not easy. A good testing tool should provide a script debugger able to handle breakpoints, to print and modify the content of variables and to support code stepping-through. The market offer of test tools is vast and diverse, able to satisfy different needs and budgets.

8.6 Internationalization Issues

Software companies are increasingly operating in a world market. Foreign sales contribute more and more to the overall revenues of software producers. Even when a language translation of the software being produced is not planned, a few localization issues exist. Date and currency are good examples. English speaking countries use different conventions for dates. In the United States, the common way to represent a date is month-day-year. In most other English speaking countries, the preferred way is day-month-year. Other differences pertain to the date separator: In a few countries the commonly used separator between the three fields comprising the date is a hyphen; in others, a slash. The same applies to currencies. The United States and Australia use the dollar; the United Kingdom uses the pound, represented by a different symbol (£).

While localizing software for Asian languages often requires adjustments to user interfaces and input forms, producing software that is customizable for languages that use the Roman alphabet is relatively easy. Most of the basic techniques required to make localization easy are simply good programming practices, which should be adopted anyhow.

The first rule to be enforced for easily customizable software is the complete separation of strings and messages from the source code. Observing this rule certainly simplifies message translation. Separating messages and strings from the source code is also a good programming practice that should be adopted even if localization is not on the agenda.

Having separate messages prevents "magic" text from appearing in the code and allows working and tested code not to be modified when cosmetic changes are required. The advent of the GUI paradigm introduced the idea of having an application comprised of several components, including a "resource" file. A resource file is separate from the source code but is compiled and linked together with the high-level language code to produce an executable. The right place to store the message strings is in that file. MS Windows provides string tables, designed specifically for storing message strings. The source code remains untouched, to produce a localized version it is sufficient to re-link the application with the localized version of the resource file.

If you are writing code that must support localization, there are a few things you must be aware of, to avoid making and perpetuating costly mistakes, whose magnitude only becomes apparent too late in the SDLC. Your company's investment in software localization is inversely proportional to the care each programmer takes in writing easily customizable code. The less care taken by the programmers, the more expensive becomes the internationalization program.

While coding software that must be localized, one should consider that foreign text is generally longer than English. If an English sentence "just fits" in a string of a predetermined length, in a foreign language the same text will almost certainly exceed the string length. English is very concise; Latin languages are not. This implies that programmers cannot rely on specific string length to position text on the screen. Status bars are particularly affected by the different text length. In English, five characters are sufficient to display messages like "Wait," "Run," and "OK." This is rarely the case in Latin languages. To be conservative, one should double the space required in English for corresponding foreign messages.

Foreign grammar is generally different. This implies that messages cannot be composed or re-used on the fly. In English, adjectives precede the nouns they refer to, as in "a good man." In Latin languages, the opposite is true; the noun precedes its adjective. This makes it very difficult to compose sentences by joining together message patterns. Each error situation should have its own specific message.

Another point to be considered when wording messages that will be translated is that in English every noun referring to a nonperson is neutral. In Latin languages every noun is either of feminine or masculine gender. There is no neutral in Spanish, Portuguese, Italian, and French. To further complicate the matter, the gender can vary in different languages. The word *tariff* is of masculine gender in French (le tarif) and of feminine gender in Italian (la tariffa). Changing from "it" to either "she" or "he" can affect the meaning of a whole sentence.

Modern operating systems are shipped with "country kits," which take care of localization issues at OS level. In MS Windows NT, the same is achieved by accessing the "Regional Settings" applet in the control panel. Programmers writing international software shouldn't rely too much on this feature. They should give the user the possibility to override the generic regional settings that the program inherits from the operating system. Changing the OS regional settings affects all applications running in the same machine. An American accountant temporarily relocated in Spain to conduct an audit in the Spanish branch of an American corporation wants to see dots as decimal separators. He would consider commas, which are commonly used in Europe as decimal separators, very confusing. It would be unfair to force all Spanish colleagues to deal with dots, instead of commas, for the entire duration of the audit by changing the OS country kit. The program must provide enough flexibility to make locals and temporary visitors comfortable by allowing them to use the conventions they grew up with.

Foreign currency is another delicate point to be carefully evaluated when considering localization issues. Database and screen fields that handle money should be adequately sized, keeping in mind that in different economies a dollar can buy hundreds or even thousands units of the local currency. In those countries, a personal computer might cost a few million units of local currency. An inventory-keeping program, designed with the dollar scale in mind, can incur the risk of having database and screen fields not large enough to accommodate the different currency scale of foreign economies. This problem affected well-known personal finance programs, such as Microsoft Money, which couldn't be initially sold worldwide because it used four-byte integers to store monetary amounts.

Complying with the elementary rules listed above significantly simplifies the localization effort. As always, guidelines and recommendations should be made at the beginning of the project, and code walkthroughs should periodically check and enforce programming practices designed to ease and facilitate translation in foreign languages.

Oracle provides facilities and tools to help programmers deal with localization issues. The database server is configurable through the National Language Support (NLS) subsystem. The NLS functions are highly customizable at runtime, so that the language sensitive information elements can be properly translated. There are a few categories of language-dependent functions controlled by the NLS mechanism:

- ❑ Number format
- ❑ Date format
- ❑ Currency format
- ❑ Starting day of the week
- ❑ Sorting

Through the NLS system, Oracle 8 supports 46 languages and 67 territories. The two parameters, NLS_LANGUAGE and NLS_TERRITORY, influence the default of the other NLS parameters. They can be set in the instance initialization file, affecting the default language for the entire instance. Alternatively, they can be enabled on a per session basis, through the use of the ALTER SESSION command. An example follows:

```
SQL> alter session set nls_language=italian;

Session altered.

SQL> select to_char(sysdate,'day dd month YYYY') from dual;

TO_CHAR(SYSDATE,'DAYDDMONTH
---------------------------
martedi    07 luglio     1998

SQL>  alter session set nls_language=french;

Session altered.

SQL>  select to_char(sysdate,'day dd month YYYY') from dual;

TO_CHAR(SYSDATE,'DAYDDMONT
--------------------------
mardi     07 juillet   1998
```

The example shows how to dynamically change the formatting of the date. Note that setting a default language for the session also influences the error messages. When the database "speaks French," referring a table that doesn't exist in the user schema produces the following error message:

```
ORA-00942: table ou vue inexistante
```

The corresponding English message would be:

```
ORA-00942: table or view does not exist
```

Oracle fully supports Unicode version 2.0, the multi-byte format with variable width. Unicode version 2 represents a significant enhancement over Unicode 1.1, which was a two-byte fixed-width format. Oracle is backward compatible with Unicode 1.1, but users are advised to switch to Unicode 2. Unicode allows for support of non-Roman alphabet-based languages like simplified and traditional Chinese.

The Oracle support for foreign languages is not limited to the NLS architecture provided with the database server. Applications built on Oracle technologies such as Oracle Developer can benefit from the Oracle Translation Manager

(OTM), an application built using Oracle Forms. OTM provides a visual interface to translation projects, supporting multiple languages concurrently. A very important feature offered by OTM is its ability to "remember" previous translations. It is possible to produce new versions of the same translation, each introducing a few variations, without re-starting the translation process from scratch every time.

OTM also provides batch loading of foreign messages into the database, supporting multiple languages. OTM can compare two different versions of resource files and determine which strings have been changed and which have been added. Version control of translated text is also available, to help managing and controlling large translation projects that support multiple languages simultaneously.

OTM can be used with the three major components of the Oracle Developer suite:

- Oracle forms
- Oracle reports
- Oracle graphics

Summary

This chapter focused on software engineering fundamentals. IT projects that use Oracle technologies can exploit Oracle specific tools and features to increase the quality of code production, but usually this is not enough. Additional software engineering tools, either third party provided or bundled with the operating system, are essential for the success of a project. The chapter initially examined version control concepts and systems, to focus on internal debuggers, profilers, test coverage analyzers and run-time error detection tools. Open Source tools, as well as commercially available software products, have been briefly introduced, and their usefulness and points of strength highlighted. A large section of the chapter examined Oracle specific tools that facilitate the production of high quality SQL queries, EXPLAIN PLAN, SQL Trace/Tkprof and Oracle Trace. Finally, code localization issues have been discussed in the last section of the chapter, together with Oracle provided features to deal with internationalization of software applications.

Chapter 9

MANAGING MULTIPLE ENVIRONMENTS

In this chapter we will consider the issues related to the management of the environments that facilitate application development, testing, and production deployment. It is common practice to provide a separate development environment, which often resides on a dedicated machine to ensure that developers do not interfere with the testing process. A mission critical application supporting the business of a corporation is likely to have three separate environments: development, test, and production—each with its own dedicated hardware. Lower priority applications often share a single hardware platform between the development and test environment. The establishment of strictly controlled practices to maintain synchronization between the environments represents a challenge for developers.

The Oracle security model plays an important role in maintaining order and providing separation between the environments. We will use Oracle privileges, roles, and synonyms to implement development environments that ensure that programmers do not to interfere with each other, without wasting database resources. We will also examine tools that can produce object creation scripts by reverse engineering.

9.1 Development, Test, Production

Several application environments are required to support the development and testing of a complex database-centric application. This technique is used to avoid interference between developers and testers and to isolate the production environment from indiscriminate and uncontrolled changes.

The number of application environments depends on the size of the project, the number of developers involved, and the nature of the application. Large complex projects usually have three physical separate environments, each with its own computer or cluster. Less critical projects combine the development and test environments in one machine.

Environments can be created within the same Oracle instance by using the Oracle schema structure. Alternatively, a separate Oracle instance can be created for each environment. In practice, many projects combine these themselves by providing one instance for development and one for testing. The instances are then subdivided into several schemas, usually one per developer and one per testing environment.

When many schemas are created, it is important to minimize the space required for each. The arrangement that works best is to have one schema contain all application objects and to use public synonyms to access the application objects from the developer schemas. The following example clarifies the concept.

Let us assume we are building a system called "gamma." The main application schema will be named after the project, so we will name it "gamma." The gamma schema will be the owner of all application objects such as tables, indexes, packages, sequences, and so on. The tables will be loaded with sufficient test data to support development and unit testing of the code modules. Each developer will be assigned a database schema, usually named after the developer's username. Instead of re-creating an entire set of tables and objects per developer, we will use synonyms to refer to all of the application's objects.

Oracle supports two types of synonyms, public and private. A public synonym is accessible to all users, whereas a private synonym is visible only within the schema in which it is created. If you want to create a synonym for the table "customer" stored in the gamma schema, the syntax is:

```
create public synonym customer for gamma.customer;
```

All schemas will be able to access the customer table defined in the gamma schema through this synonym.

To create a public synonym, a schema must be granted the CREATE PUBLIC SYNONYMS privilege. To create a private synonym, the CREATE SYNONYM privilege is needed. Synonyms are invaluable for creating and setting up development environments. Developers must be able to change the structure of database objects, develop codes that access and manipulate them, and test their modules without affecting the environments of other developers. This is reciprocal in the sense that developers do not want to see their code broken by someone else's changes. Developers can be prevented from interfering with each other through the synonym mechanism.

No objects are locally defined in a schema assigned to a developer. The code that accesses the database can still run within the developer's schema by accessing objects' public synonyms that point to the objects owned by the application schema (in our example the "gamma" schema).

Let us imagine that developer ebonazzi is given the task of modifying the customer table. An additional column is required to support financial calculations that will be coded and tested. Coding the table modification and new calculations can take several days, possibly a few weeks. The Gamma customer table must maintain its integrity during this period, to ensure that other developers are not disrupted. This is achieved by defining the table locally in the ebonazzi schema. An example of an SQL*Plus session that accomplishes this is shown below.

```
$ sqlplus /

SQL*Plus: Release 3.1.3.5.1 - Production on Mon Jun 22
          00:29:25 1998

Copyright (c) Oracle Corporation 1979, 1994. All rights re-
served.

Connected to:
Oracle7 Server Release 7.1.5.2.4 - Production Release
With the distributed, parallel query and Parallel Server op-
tions
PL/SQL Release 2.1.5.2.0 - Production

SQL> show user
user is "OPS$EBONAZZI"
```

The schema is ops$ebonazzi. The developer now "describes" the customer table, accessing the customer object as defined in the gamma schema.

```
SQL>desc customer
 Name                            Null?    Type
 ------------------------------- -----    ----
 NAME                                     VARCHAR2(30)
 ADDRESS                                  VARCHAR2(50)
 COMPANY_NAME                             VARCHAR2(40)

SQL>
```

A local copy of the customer table is now defined.

```
SQL> create table customer as select * from gamma.customer;

Table created.

SQL>
```

All rows in the customer table defined in the gamma schema have been copied locally to a new table in the ops$ebonazzi schema. This will be useful for unit testing. The local copy of the table can now be modified.

```
SQL> alter table customer add discount_pct number (6,2);

Table altered.

SQL>
```

The local table is now different from the same table defined in the gamma schema. The new version of the table is visible only in the ops$ebonazzi schema. Oracle will try to resolve object names at a local level. If a name doesn't correspond to an object defined locally, that is, within the user schema, Oracle will search through the publicly defined synonyms. This is why all other developers will see the customer table defined in the gamma schema without their code being affected by the changes made to the table locally defined in ops$ebonazzi.

When the change has been made and all modifications unit tested, the change will be propagated to the table defined in the application schema (gamma, in our example). From that moment on, all developers will have access to the modified table. This ability implies that integration testing must be performed before migrating the change to the central schema where it will be accessed by public synonyms. The integration testing is required to assess the impact of the change on all application modules accessing the modified table.

Sometimes the use of public synonyms is not practical. There can be only one public synonym per database object. This limitation can become a problem if in the same instance two tables called "customer" serve different business purposes. In this case, private synonyms can be used. Each schema would create private synonyms pointing to the objects owned by the application schema. When a table is modified, the local synonym pointing to the table must be dropped before the new table can be created. This is necessary because a synonym name must be distinct from all other objects within a schema to prevent ambiguity.

Maintaining multiple schemas to support the development of environments is definitely a good idea for a development project. As we have seen in the previous example, a table defined in the central application schema can be accessed through a synonym from the developers' schemas. In the same way, views, stored procedures and functions, packages, and snapshots can be indirectly accessed through synonyms. Synonyms can also be created for other synonyms.

Test environments also benefit from similar arrangements. Projects that adhere to high quality standards usually adopt a promotional model for testing which is similar to the one considered in Chapter 8. The common testing categories include integration testing, system testing, regression testing, performance testing, and stress testing.

It is possible to establish a logical hierarchy between the various testing strategies. For instance, it is unlikely that performance testing, carried out prior to module integration testing, would be beneficial. Performance and stress testing should be performed using a stable version of the system. It would be frustrating to see the battery of performance tests fail because an incorrect parameter has been passed to a subroutine. This kind of defect should have been detected well in advance, during integration testing.

Integration testing is usually performed at the beginning of the testing cycle. We are assuming that developers perform unit testing satisfactorily. In an ideal environment the configuration manager performs a formal build of the alpha release using the configuration management tools. The support medium containing the release (CD-ROM, tape, etc.) is loaded on the testing machine, and the software is installed in a specific test environment. For the sake of the example, we will call that environment DTEST. DTEST is an environment dedicated to integration testing.

While operating within the DTEST environment, both software and testers will see one consistent version of the database objects and all the ancillary external programs and processes that constitute the application. DTEST doesn't need a large volume of test data. The main goal is to test the internal coherence and the systems inter-module interfaces so that each table can be loaded with a few tens of rows. Reference tables should be loaded with sufficient data to emulate a production system.

A battery of integration tests is run on the DTEST environment. There are two possible outcomes.

- The software being tested manifests problems. In other words, the test session has uncovered defects and bugs. The testers compile a detailed report on each defect and no further testing is performed until the defects are rectified and DTEST is loaded with a new version of the application.
- All tests are performed without uncovering any defect. The software can then be migrated to CTEST for system testing.

According to the size of the test team and the application, a single schema containing all objects for DTEST may not support the concurrent execution of multiple tests (it is likely that system integration testing will require many more test scripts and runs than stress testing will). Every tester should have a schema with replicated objects—rather than synonyms—when the automated testing tools require fresh baseline data to ensure that each test run starts at a consistent point. If multiple tests are conducted in parallel on a single schema, there is the risk of clashes between concurrent testing sessions.

In our example, the CTEST environment is dedicated to system testing. Here the global functioning of the system is tested, using mainly black-box testing techniques. Again, there are two possible outcomes from the CTEST testing sessions: success or failure. When the system tests are successful, the software is migrated to BTEST, where it undergoes regression testing. When the system tests fail, the release is rejected and developers are informed of the problems encountered. When a new release is built, it goes through the same cycle again, starting with DTEST.

Theoretically, each release containing defect corrections should start the testing cycle from scratch. This ensures that new defects introduced during the defect rectification process are detected. In practice this rule is not always followed. The test managers often decide which tests should be repeated and which tests will be skipped. These decisions are usually based on a compromise between quality and cost.

When the software release reaches the stress testing stage, the database should be loaded with realistic data. The tables used for stress testing should be loaded with a similar volume and diversity of data to the tables in the production system. Untuned SQL queries that perform satisfactorily with small data volumes should be detected by performance testing.

While it is important to have realistic data for stress testing, integration and regression testing can be carried out using a limited subset of data. Using one schema per test environment reduces the space needed by the test platform and allows different testing cycles to be run concurrently. For instance, a maintenance release could undergo regression testing concurrently with the integration testing of a new release. Since different schemas are used for different testing environments, the tests do not interfere with each other.

9.2 Synchronizing the Environments

As soon as the same object is replicated in two different physical locations, there is the potential for inconsistency due to loss of synchronization. The same database table can be modified in one environment or in one schema and inadvertently not modified in other environments. This can easily happen if a new release of the software requires a schema change. Consider the following scenario.

The software is installed, the schema is modified, and the software tested. A few defects are found and the release is demoted to development again. A few days later the test team is given the task of testing a maintenance release that requires the old schema definition. If a back-out script is not run or if the back-out script fails due to inadequate testing the tests can behave erratically due to the modified schema.

To avoid this kind of problem, developers and testers must ensure that all database schemas are consistent and synchronized across the development, test, and production environments. Consistency can exist only on a per release basis, so the database schema should be part of the release bundle. The release installation script should also include the Oracle schema changes.

How can the Oracle schema consistency be maintained across different environments? The safest way to obtain schema consistency is by capturing schema snapshots. This is done by reverse engineering the application schema, the one that defines all objects owned by the application. The Oracle data dictionary tables are the ultimate repositories for all database objects present. It is possible to automatically create a DDL script that can be used to re-create the schema objects. This is achieved by recursively accessing the data dictionary tables to extract the schema object definitions.

The reverse engineering process can be performed on two different environments, say development and testing, and the two resulting DDL scripts compared using diff or any other similar tool. This method highlights any differences between schemas.

Reverse engineering the Oracle data dictionary can be accomplished in several different ways. Tools are available from Oracle and third parties. One of these is the Tool for Oracle Application Developers (TOAD). TOAD offers a specific option to reverse engineer an entire schema. A few parameters are available to customize the DDL script output.

TOAD, which was initially available as a freeware tool, has been purchased by Quest Software in November 1998, becoming a commercial product since that moment. Another Quest Software product, SQL Navigator, offers similar features as those offered by TOAD. Both are impressive tools that assist developers in many Oracle-related SQL production and optimization activities. SQL Navigator also include a facility for object definition reverse engineering similar to that offered by TOAD.

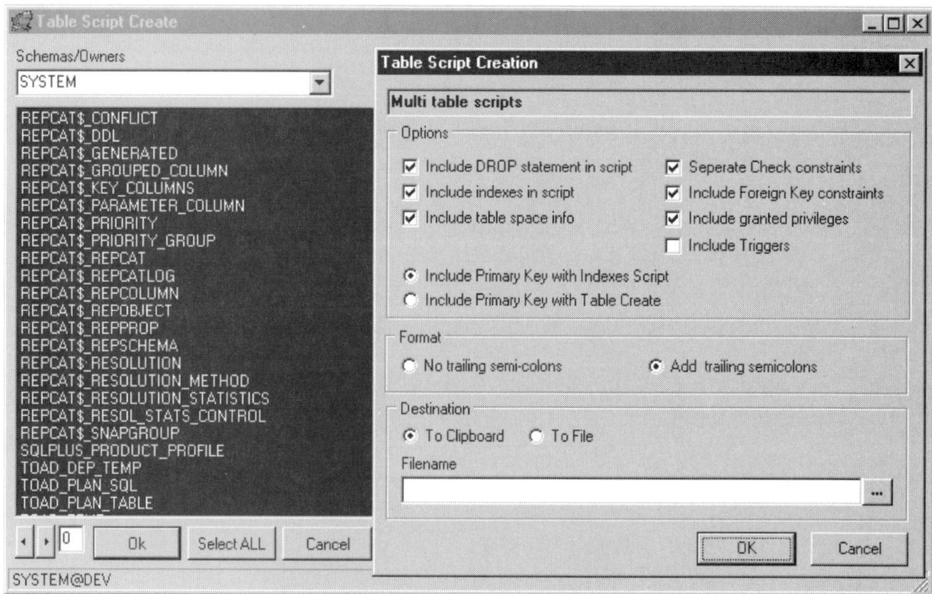

FIGURE 9.1 The data dictionary reverse engineering options in TOAD

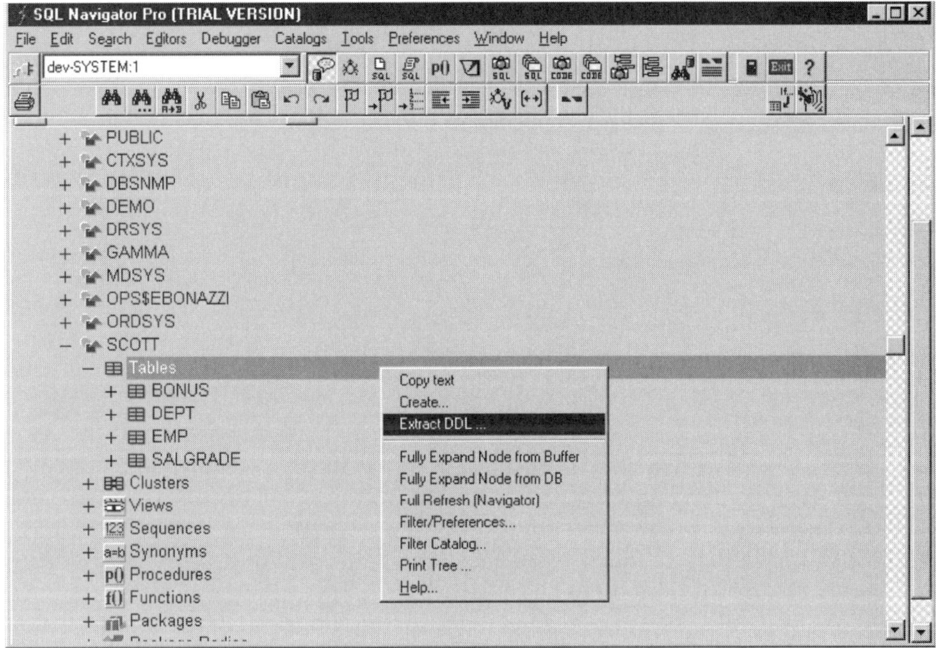

FIGURE 9.2 Schema reverse engineering in SQL Navigator

SQL Navigator offers finer granularity for DDL customization. For instance, it allows target table space insertion in the object creation script without specifying the storage parameters. This is very important, as we will see later in this chapter. TOAD does not have this facility.

When tables and indexes are created using Oracle, the parameters of the *create* command can be used to regulate the initial size of the object and its expected growth. The storage clause of the create command specifies the size of the initial extent, the size of the subsequent extents, and the percentage growth applied to each new extent.

In the following example the customer table is created with a storage clause that specifies an initial extent of one megabyte, a next extent of 512 kilobytes, and an increase of 50%.

```
CREATE TABLE customer
(
  name                VARCHAR2(30),
  address             VARCHAR2(50),
  company_name        VARCHAR2(40)
 )
```

```
PCTFREE    10
PCTUSED    80
INITRANS   1
MAXTRANS   255
TABLESPACE user_data
STORAGE    (
     INITIAL     1M
     NEXT        512K
     PCTINCREASE 50
     MINEXTENTS  1
     MAXEXTENTS  200
  )
```

Specifying a PCTINCREASE parameter greater than zero causes exponential growth of the size of the object. This is undesirable in most cases because the table size grows dramatically after a few extents. Many Oracle sites have adopted the policy of always specifying a zero percent increase for all objects.

The storage parameters are usually the only part of an object definition that vary across different environments. Storage requirements are minimized in a development environment by providing the minimum of test data required for the developers to unit test their modules. The storage parameters of the development database objects will be sized accordingly by specifying small initial and next extents. The same object sizes can be used when the schema is migrated to the testing environment for integration and system testing. These object sizes will probably be inadequate for stress testing or production.

The different storage clause parameters can cause problems when comparing the schemas of two different environments by reverse engineering. If the automatically generated DDL scripts specify storage clauses, it is likely that the diff command will flag many insignificant discrepancies and obscure important differences. SQL Navigator allows users to filter out the storage clause so that only the relevant objection creation parameters will be captured in the generated DDL script.

SQL Navigator allows developers and administrators to reverse engineer the development database schema objects and compare them with reverse engineered production objects, in order to check for consistencies. Another third party tool, Embarcadero DBArtisan, goes one step further: It not only allows for an easy database schema reverse engineering, but provides a visual wizard that can migrate one schema and all associated objects from one database to another.

DBArtisan gives users a great deal of control over reverse-engineering parameters, for instance, allowing for the exclusion of the storage parameters from the DDL script automatically generated.

TOAD and SQLNavigator reverse engineer only the schema objects, allowing the user to run the DDL script automatically generated either by using a separate option of the same tool or by invoking standard Oracle tools like SQL*Plus.

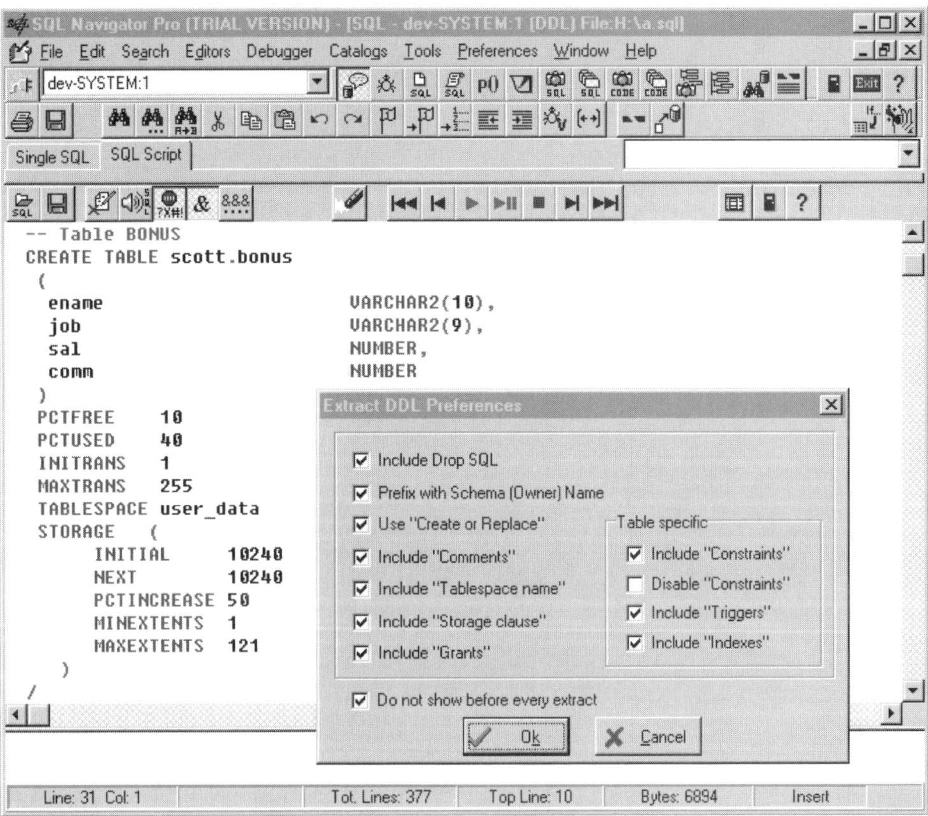

FIGURE 9.3 SQL Navigator allows for exclusion of the storage clause while extracting the DDL script from the Oracle data dictionary

DBArtisan provides a schema migration wizard that allows for an interactive transfer of schema object definitions from a source to a target database. Potential conflicts and object overriding steps are resolved by the user on the fly, as soon as they occur, through an interactive form presented by DBArtisan, which details the problem and requires the user intervention for a resolution.

The window shown in Figure 9.7 provides an example of the migration capabilities of DBArtisan. The wizard found that a role defined in the source database is already defined in the target. It prompts the user to decide whether the role should be overridden or not. The migration wizard always presents the user with similar windows before performing operations that can potentially cause loss of data.

DBArtisan provides more sophisticated options for schema extraction and migration because it is a tool designed more for DBAs than for developers, while

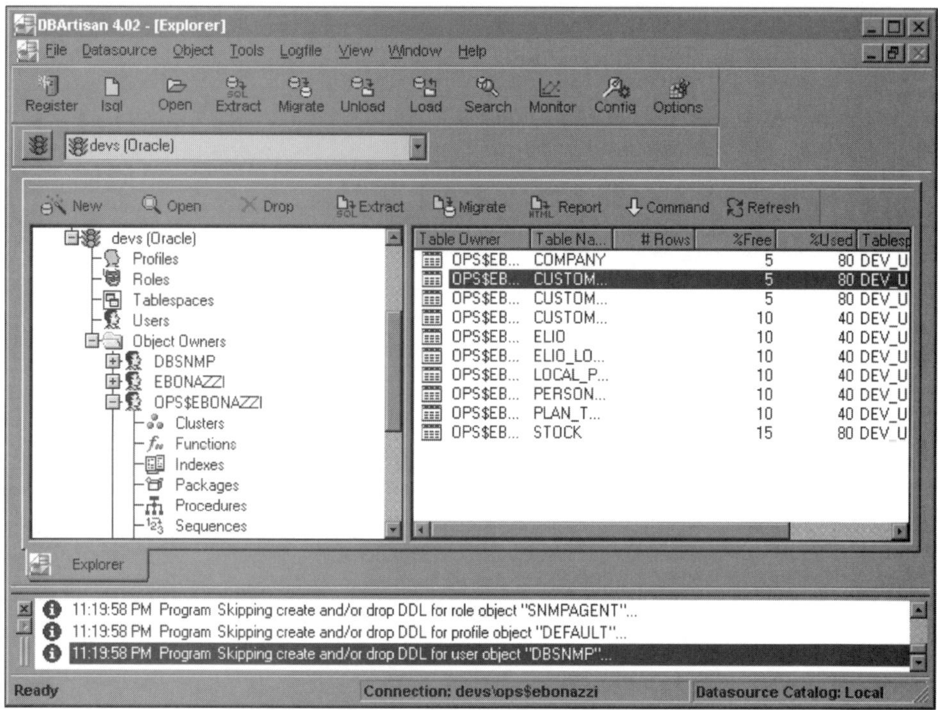

FIGURE 9.4 DBArtisan provides a standard tree control that allows users to navigate through all database schemas and objects

TOAD and SQLNavigator offer features that are useful specifically for developers.

The ultimate tool to support DBAs and configuration managers in ensuring a correct synchronization between databases running in different environments (development, test, and production) has finally been released by Oracle Corporation in mid-1998. The product, called Change Management Pack, is sold as an add-on to the Oracle Enterprise Manager. While the third party tools examined above all offer a reach set of features, including database object reverse engineering, the Change Management Pack (CMP)'s sole purpose is to plan, organize, implement, and deploy database changes.

The CMP is a set of six tools that work together to give an absolute control over the smallest detail of a database change. Each individual application of the CMP group is accessible through an icon or a menu option. The six icons that comprise the CMP are shown in Figure 9.8.

The table below summarizes the functionality provided by the six CMP tools.

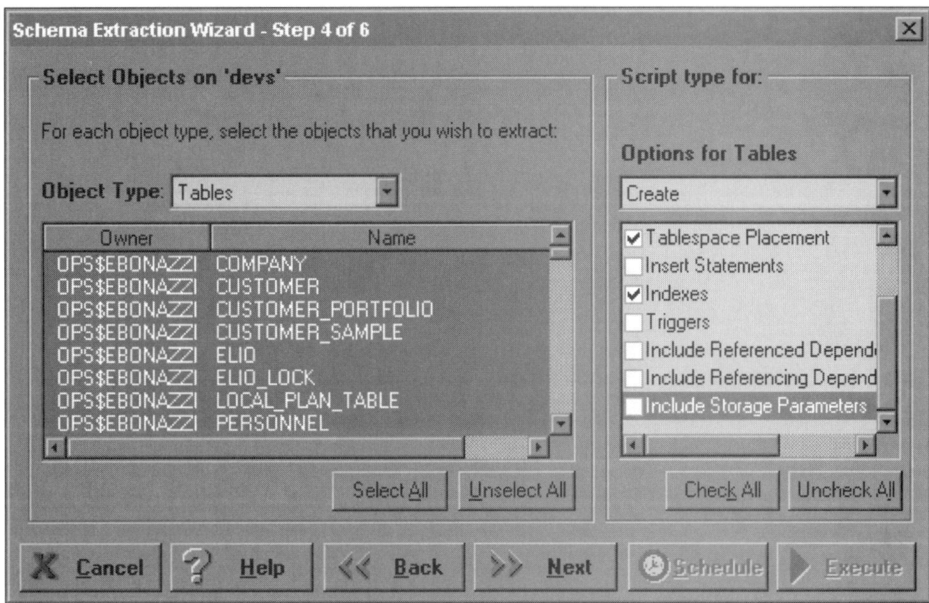

FIGURE 9.5 The reverse-engineering options of DBArtisan are many and fine-grained

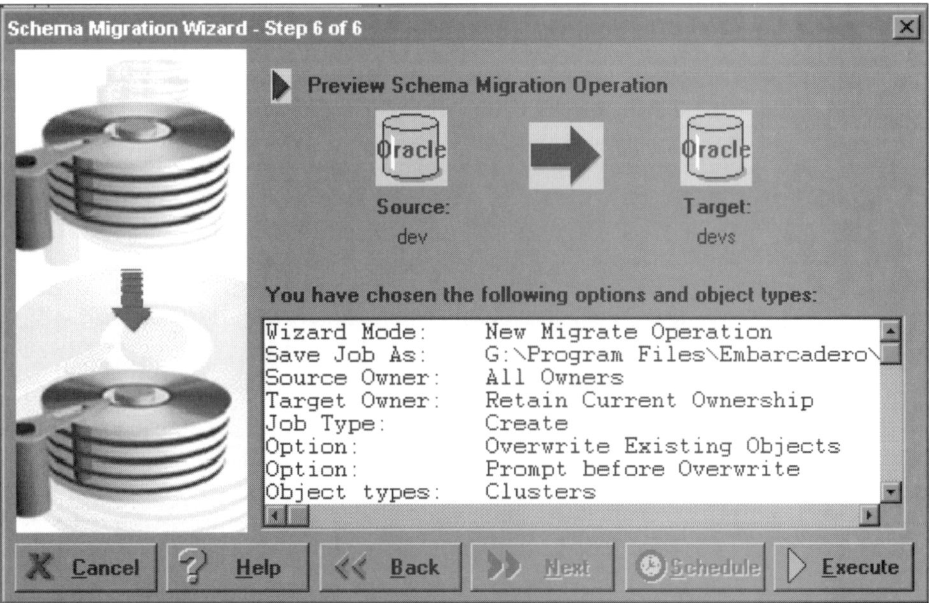

FIGURE 9.6 A six-step wizard drives schema migration from a database source to a database target

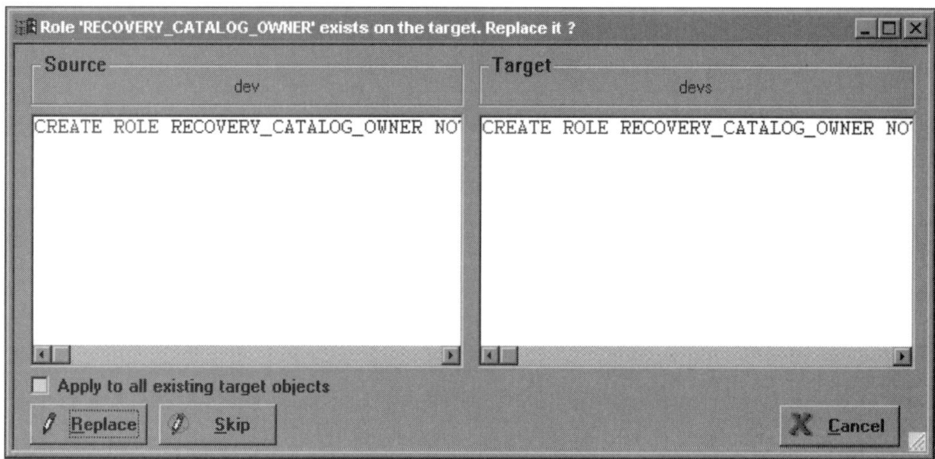

FIGURE 9.7 The migration wizard is asking permission to override an object in the target database

CMP TOOL	PURPOSE
DB Capture	captures one or more definitions from one database
Alter	modifies one or more definitions in one or more databases
DB Diff	compares two sets of definitions from a database or baseline or from two databases, two baselines or a database and a baseline
Plan Manager	organizes all change activities, accessing, and using all other CMP components
Propagate	reproduces one or more definitions from a database in a different schema of the same database or in another database
Quick Change	modifies one definition in one database

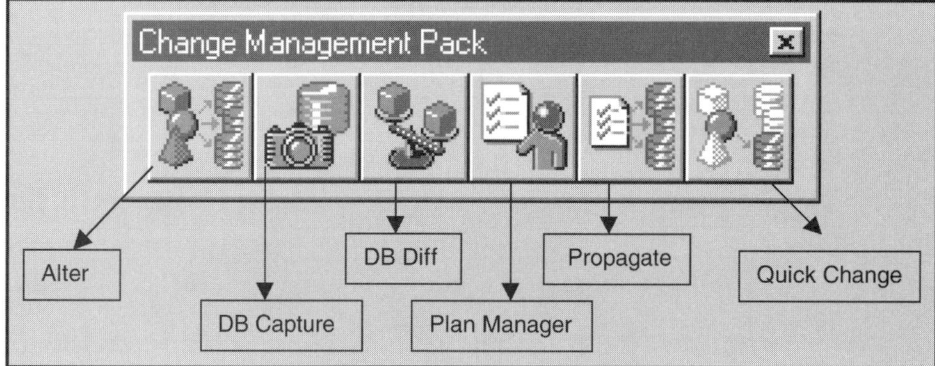

FIGURE 9.8 The CMP group of icons

The Oracle CMP requires users to define a change plan, which is seen as a container of change requests. Two types of change requests that are supported are directives and exemplars.

Directives are a set of changes users specify for an existing and named object definition. CMP tools like Alter or Quick Change help users to compile directives, which are created by visually selecting and highlighting objects in the CMP GUI based tools, and by specifying changes by altering object properties in the object inspector.

Exemplars are complete and stand-alone object definitions that must be reproduced in the target database schemas, either by modifying existing objects to make them identical to the exemplar, or by creating objects from scratch if they don't already exist in the schemas. Exemplars are created by tools such as Propagate or by the DB Diff Synchronization Wizard.

The list of features offered by the six tools is quite impressive. Let us see them in action, beginning with Quick Change, which is the tool most likely to be used extensively by DBAs and configuration managers. The Quick Change Wizard proceeds in six steps, interacting with the user and creating at the end an impact analysis and a change script. After having assessed the impact analysis, a user can decide not to proceed any further, either because the script cannot be

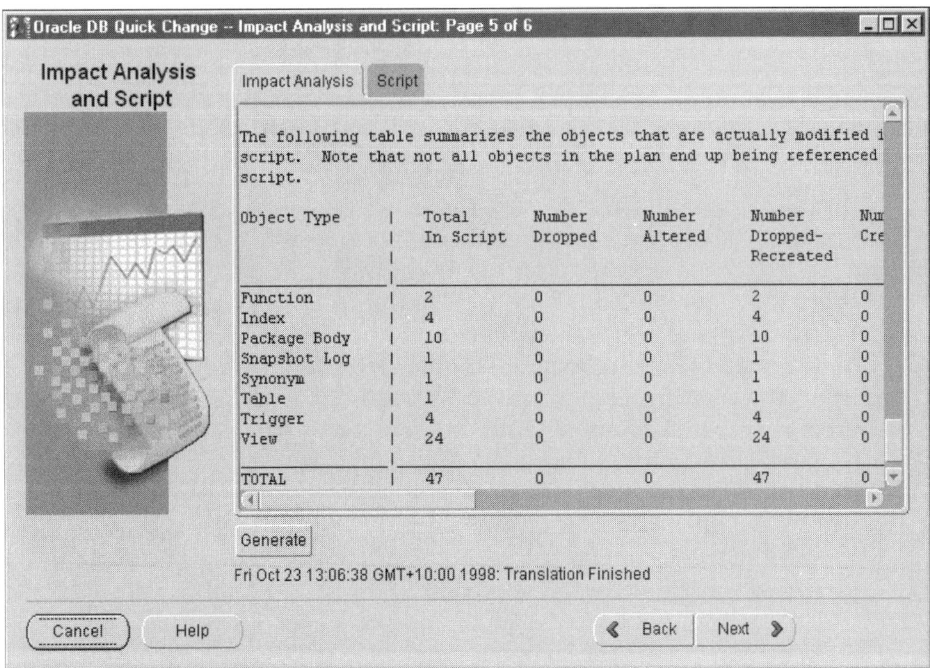

FIGURE 9.9 The Impact Analysis produced by Quick Change

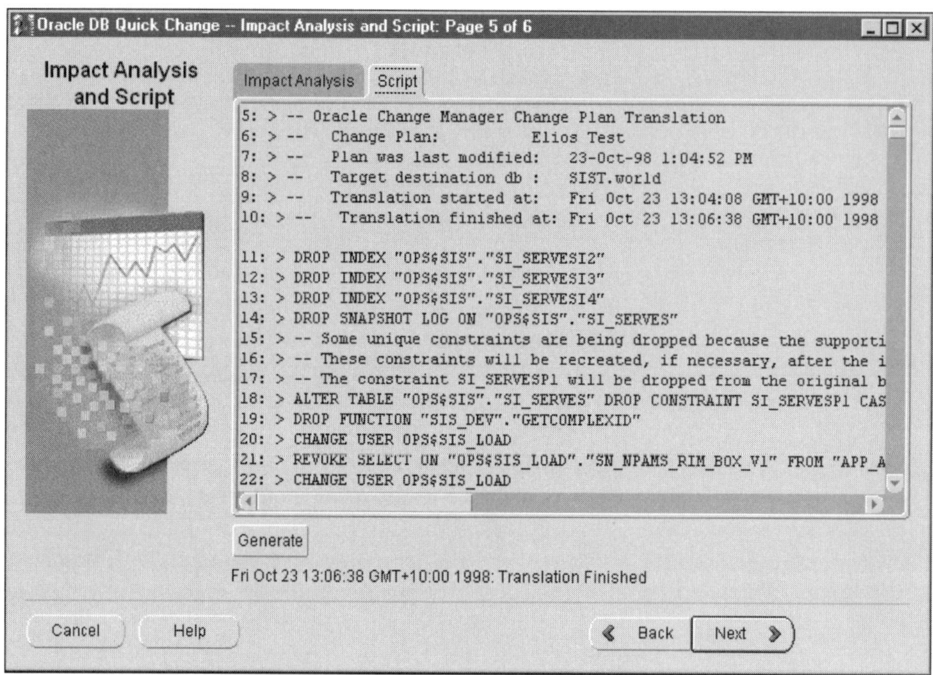

FIGURE 9.10 The change script produced by Quick Change

generated because of problems or because the risk associated to the change is too high. For instance the wizard can determine that to apply the changes, a 9-gigabyte table must be replicated in order to be able to back-out the changes.

DB Diff is another useful tool, impressive for the fine granularity of the options offered to the user. It starts by asking what kind of operation the user wants performed, and whether the two entities being compared are in different databases or in different schemas of the same database or baseline.

DB Diff also allows for fine-grained customization of the types of objects being compared. Users can limit the comparison to specific and selected types of objects. The object type can be a schema type, such as table, index, PL/SQL package, etc. or nonschema type, such as profile, role, tablespaces, etc.

Once the objects have been selected, the DB Diff wizard provides a visual feedback for the comparison process, so the user knows at any point in time the progress and the status of the process.

The results of the comparison can optionally be saved in a HTML file, for an easy access through the company intranet. The DBA can decide to publish the result of the comparison so that senior developers and configuration managers can be involved in the synchronization process. Synchronization decisions can be

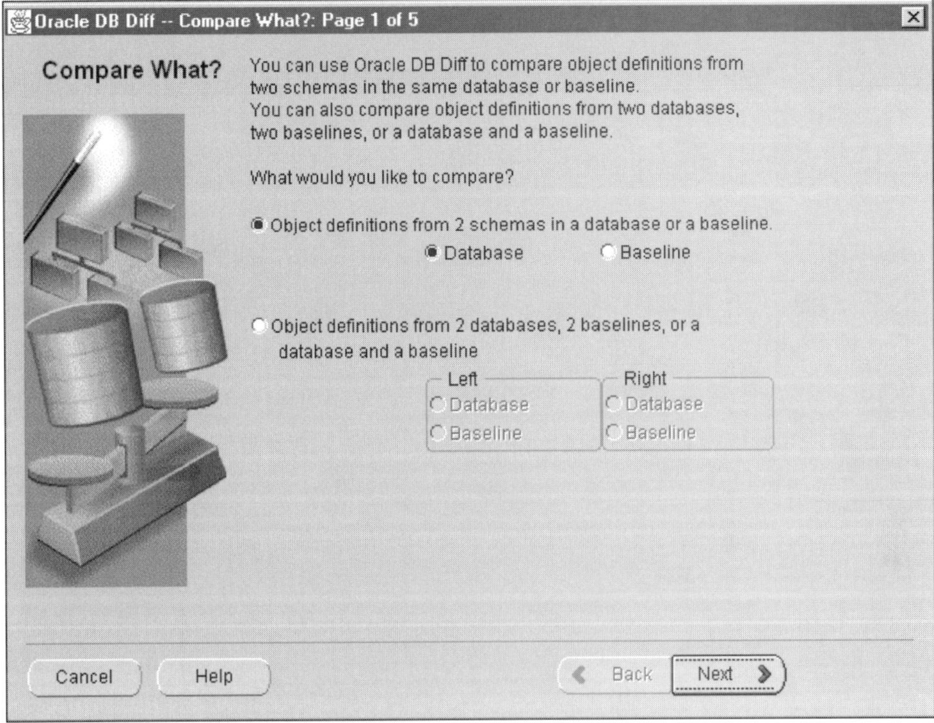

FIGURE 9.11 The first step of the DB Diff Wizard

shared and detailed knowledge of potential problems, if a synchronization script is run, can be disseminated within the development team.

The tool DB Propagate represents the core of the CMP. It allows users to define exemplars and replicate them to one or more target databases.

H also allows for definition of important object attributes during the information gathering process. Users can decide to create an object without specifying physical create attributes, such as storage parameters, or security attributes, such as grants and privileges. Another important option offered by the tool is the ability to disregard constraint names. This is handy where constraints are not explicitly named by the DBA but automatically chosen by Oracle. Once again, the user is in total control of the propagation process, being able to influence the way it is defined and carried out.

DB Propagate shows its nature of enterprise-class tool by allowing users to create Unix Tcl scripts that implement database changes. Tcl is a scripting language supported by SNMP. This means that a DBA can schedule a remote deployment of a change by submitting the Tcl script to the machine hosting the database.

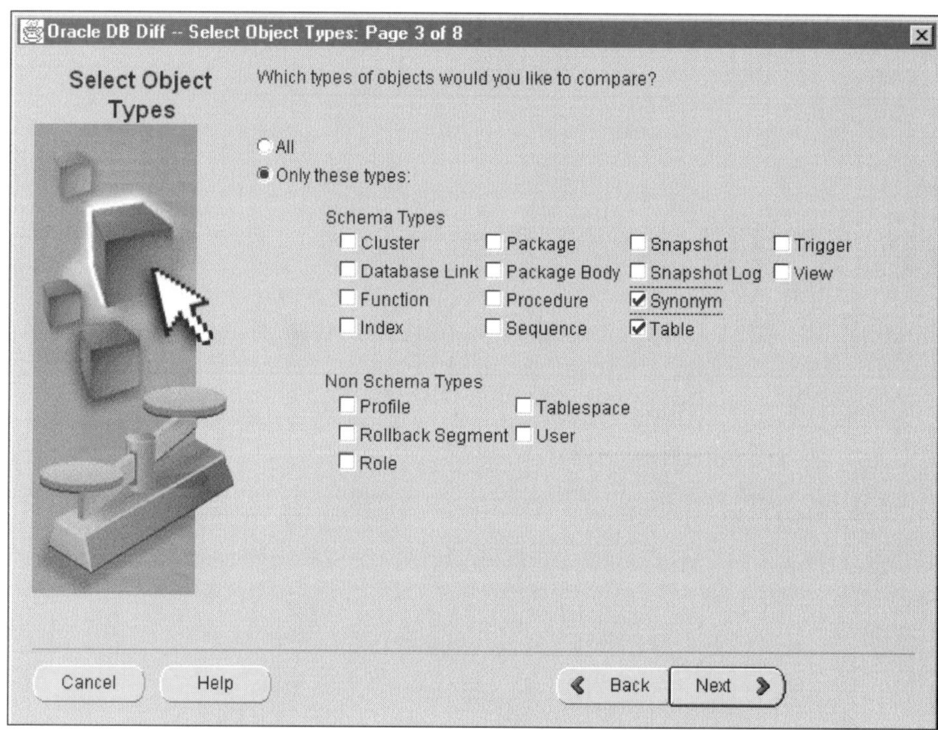

FIGURE 9.12 The options offered to user for object comparison

Plan manager represents the glue between all other components of the CMP. All scripts generated by the CMP components are editable before their execution. Plan Manager generates back-out scripts that can be executed if an error occurs when a change request is deployed to a target database.

The Oracle Change Management Pack is definitely the best available tool for synchronizing databases and schemas across different environments. It is an enterprise-class tool under all aspects, including price. Its licensing policy makes it a little overpriced, because it is not considered a stand-alone tool with a fixed price, but the license fee varies according to the number of users accessing the databases served by the tool, so in large environments its cost can become exorbitant.

If you are budget-constrained, and you cannot afford the CMP or any other third party tool, you can always resort to the last method for reverse engineering database objects, which is free but very labor intensive. This method is based on standard Oracle tools that are bundled with the database server, being always available in all Oracle shops.

The standard Oracle export facility can be used with the help of a scripting language like Perl or awk. Either the entire database or specific schemas can be

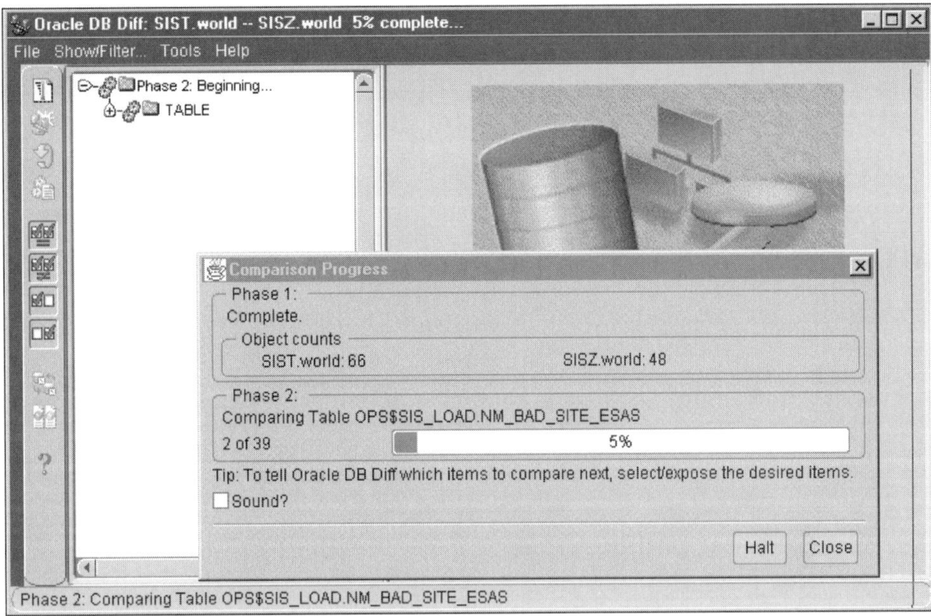

FIGURE 9.13 A visual feedback about the status of the comparison process is provided to the user

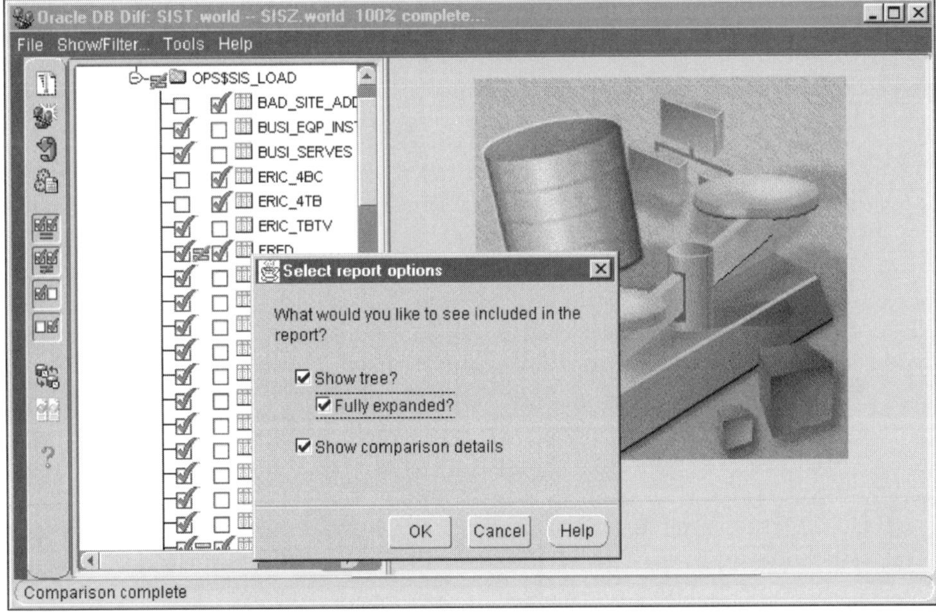

FIGURE 9.14 DB Diff can optionally save the result of its processing in an HTML file

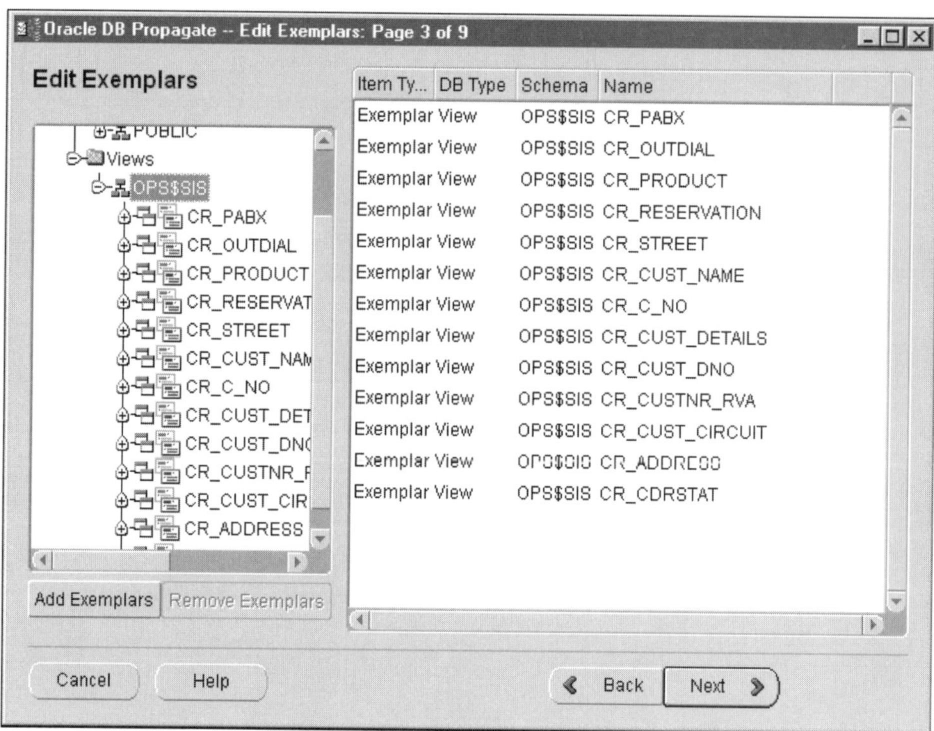

FIGURE 9.15 Propagate allows users to select or define exemplars

exported in an Oracle dump file. If the export parameter *rows* is set to no, only the object definition is exported, and not the data. The dump file can be "imported" in an ASCII file, rather than a database, by using the indexfile parameter. The ASCII file will contain the SQL definition of tables and indexes in standard SQL format. An example of this technique is shown below.

```
exp80 scott/tiger owner=scott rows=n log=d:\allog.txt
file=d:\scott.dmp
```

The exp80 command instructs Oracle to export the objects of the schema owned by scott into the dump file called scott.dmp. In Unix exp80 would be replaced by exp.

The file tables.sql contains the table definitions created by using the indexfile option. Every line included in the *create table* command is prefixed by the comment qualifier REM. While it is easy enough to use an editor to remove all unwanted REMs, the real problem associated with this technique is that the file does not contain the definitions of primary keys. The reason is that Oracle consid-

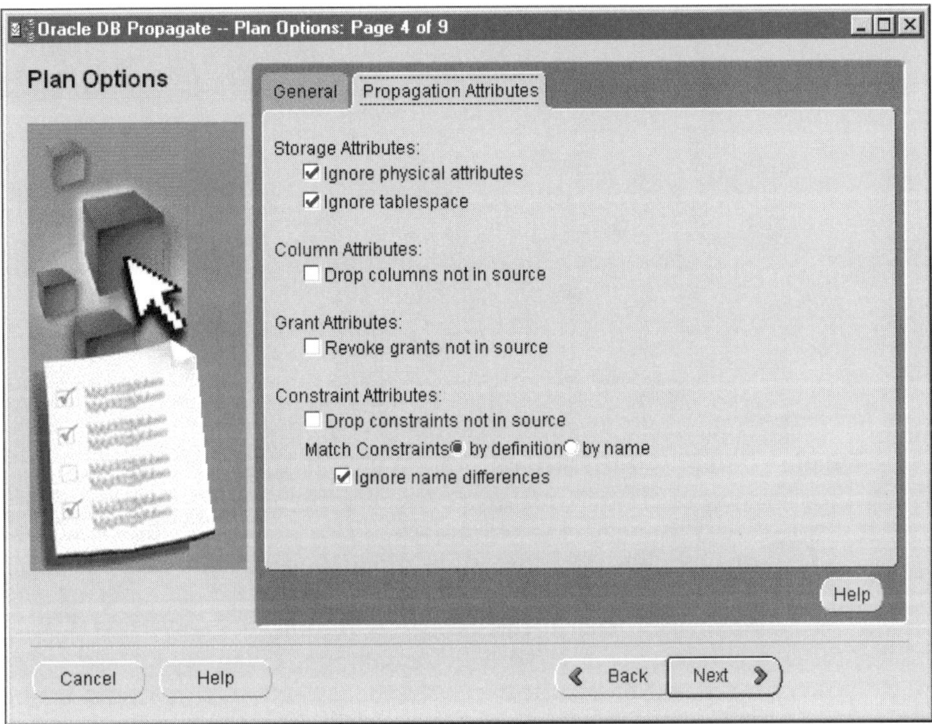

FIGURE 9.16 The user can specify several useful propagation attributes

ers them as constraints rather than indexes. The import facility also records object definitions in the log file using a pseudo-SQL syntax when the show parameter is set to yes (*Y*).

The example below is a log file produced by Oracle when the show parameter is set to yes.

```
Connected to: Oracle8 Enterprise Edition Release 8.0.3.2.2 -
  Production
With the Partitioning and Objects options
PL/SQL Release 8.0.3.2.0 - Production

Export file created by EXPORT:V08.00.03 via conventional
  path
. importing SCOTT's objects into SCOTT
"CREATE TABLE "BONUS" ("ENAME" VARCHAR2(10), "JOB" VAR
  CHAR2(9), "SAL" NUMBER"
", "COMM" NUMBER)  PCTFREE 10 PCTUSED 40 INITRANS 1 MAXTRANS
  255 LOGGING STO"
```

```
"RAGE(INITIAL 10240 NEXT 10240 MINEXTENTS 1 MAXEXTENTS 121
  PCTINCREASE 50 FR"
"EELISTS 1 FREELIST GROUPS 1 BUFFER_POOL DEFAULT) TABLESPACE
"USER_DATA""
"CREATE TABLE "DEPT" ("DEPTNO" NUMBER(2, 0), "DNAME" VAR-
  CHAR2(14), "LOC" VAR"
"CHAR2(13))  PCTFREE 10 PCTUSED 40 INITRANS 1 MAXTRANS 255
  LOGGING STORAGE(I"
"NITIAL 10240 NEXT 10240 MINEXTENTS 1 MAXEXTENTS 121 PCTIN-
  CREASE 50 FREELIST"
"S 1 FREELIST GROUPS 1 BUFFER_POOL DEFAULT) TABLESPACE
"USER_DATA""
```

It is possible to process the log file using either Perl or awk to filter out the double quotes and to reassemble the SQL syntax. It should be noted that it is not possible to prevent the Oracle export utility from placing object storage clauses in the log file. This must be accomplished by filtering the log file.

Although this procedure is a little cumbersome and very labor intensive, it works. The last option is to use Pro*C to reverse engineer the database schemas programmatically. The cost associated with this alternative will probably make buying SQL Navigator a more viable solution. If your site doesn't preclude the use of freeware, consider using TOAD. It is likely that sooner or later the automatic DDL generation will offer an option to exclude the storage clause. Meanwhile, the same effect can be obtained by filtering DDL file to the storage clause parameters.

9.3 The Oracle Security Model

In Section 9.1, we introduced principles that allow developers to avoid replicating the application objects in each developer's schema. This was achieved by defining public or private synonyms for objects defined in the main application schema only. While the concept is valid, an important aspect has been purposely neglected.

If you try to set up an environment by creating synonyms for all application objects, you will incur a security problem when attempting to access the objects from another schema. It is not enough to define a public synonym; the application schema owner must explicitly grant the other schemas adequate privileges for object sharing.

Oracle implements a complex and powerful security system to regulate the access to every object defined in the database. It closely resembles the security subsystem of an operating system such as Unix or OpenVMS. Two classes of

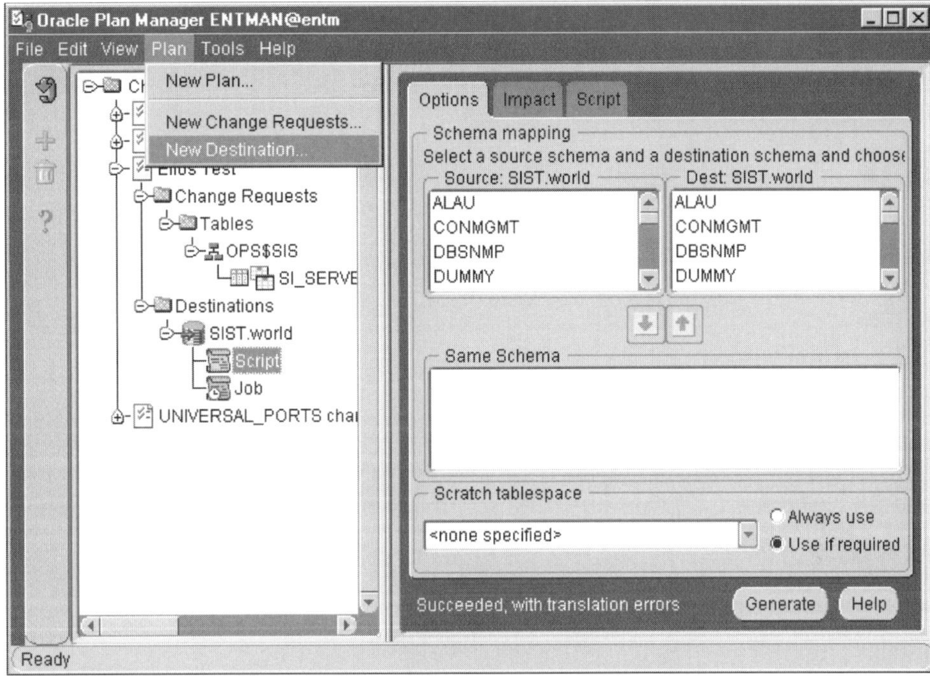

FIGURE 9.17 Plan Manager supervises the activity of all other CMP modules

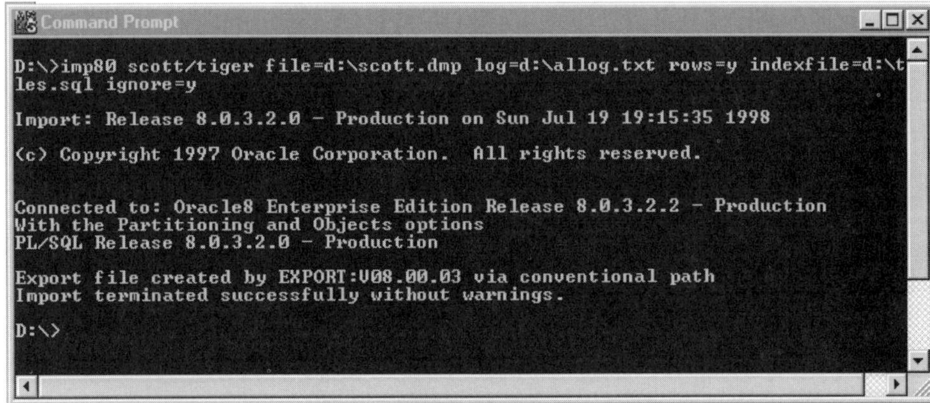

FIGURE 9.18 The import facility used to generate schema objects

privileges exist in Oracle: object level and system level. A system level privilege always overrides an object level privilege.

Object level privileges allow a schema owner to control access to the schema objects from other schemas. Both object level and system level privileges are granted through the GRANT command.

Consider again the example application named "gamma" in section 9.1. The schema named after the application contains all application objects, including a customer table. The application administrator should connect to Oracle using gamma as username and grant the select privilege specifically to the ops$ebonazzi schema. The command is shown below.

```
grant select on customer to ops$ebonazzi;
```

The schema ops$ebonazzi can now select rows from the customer table. This command has to be repeated for each of the schemas requiring to access the customer table in the gamma schema. Oracle provides the following object level privileges.

- ALTER
- EXECUTE
- INDEX
- INSERT
- READ
- REFERENCES
- SELECT
- UPDATE

Many of the privileges are self-explanatory. The *alter* privilege allows the external schema to alter the object definition; *delete* allows the external schema to delete the object, and so forth. The *read* privilege has been introduced with Oracle 8. It allows an external schema to access objects of the BFILE type stored in a file system directory managed by Oracle. The *references* privilege allows an external schema to create a constraint that references a table in the local schema.

System privileges are granted to schemas rather than to objects. That is, a system privilege is not linked to a schema object, but it allows a foreign schema to perform specific operations on objects in all schemas. If the DBA grants the system privilege *select any table* to ops$ebonazzi, that schema can then perform select statements against all tables defined in all schemas, even if the other schemas did not specifically grant the select object level privilege to ops$ebonazzi.

Every Oracle schema is given some system level privileges. The schema used for the connection to an Oracle instance must have the *create session* privilege. A schema must have the *create table* system privilege to create a table. System level privileges regulate all activities and operations allowed in Oracle. They give the DBA a powerful management tool for both security and resource allocation control.

There are a few tens of system level privileges. Many exist in a dual form: single schema level and all schema level. For instance the *create table* privilege allows the grantee to create a table in his or her own schema. The *create any table* privilege allows the grantee to create tables in all schemas.

The system level privileges are characterized by the word "any," as in create *any* index or drop *any* table. They should be used either sparingly or not at all, for schemas owned by developers. These privileges are designed for a super-user such as a DBA or for selected schemas in charge of specific operations such as exporting or backing up the database. Their purpose is not to overcome security related annoyances by providing quick and dirty "solutions" to real problems.

Granting the *select any table* privilege indiscriminately only defeats the purpose of the Oracle security subsystem. The same applies to the other global system level privileges. If a developer cannot select rows from a table owned by another schema once the other schema has granted object level privileges, the DBA should investigate the problem and look for the real cause. The quick and dirty solution of granting the *select any table* privilege on the spot doesn't solve the problem. It simply postpones its real solution and possibly aggravates the situation.

Consider again the gamma application. If the application consists of a few hundred objects, including tables stored procedures and sequences, the *grant* command must be used to grant object level privileges to all developers accessing the application objects from other schemas.

When the team coding the application comprises many developers, granting object level privileges for all objects to all developers soon becomes unmanageable. Luckily, Oracle helps overcome this problem by providing roles, which are collections of privileges. Users can be granted roles instead of privileges. The same role can be granted to multiple users (or schemas). This avoids having to grant the same object level privileges repeatedly to all users. The set of object level privileges is granted only once to a role. All developer schemas are then granted the role, which automatically enables all privileges associated with it.

As usual, an example will clarify the concept. Again we use the gamma schema and customer table. We will create three roles, one that enables a read-only access to the objects, one a little more privileged, which enables read-write access, and a third more privileged role that allows modification of the physical object structures. To create roles, the gamma schema must be granted the *create role* system privilege by the DBA.

```
SQL[gamma]> create role gamma_readers;

Role created.

SQL[gamma]> grant select on customer to gamma_readers;

Grant succeeded.
```

The first role, gamma_readers, has been created with the select object privilege only. This will guarantee a read-only access to the customer object through the gamma_readers role. The next step is to grant the newly created role to the developers who need a read only access to the application schema objects.

```
SQL[gamma]> grant gamma_readers to ops$ebonazzi;

Grant succeeded.
```

We now create a more privileged role, for read-write access.

```
SQL[gamma]> create role gamma_writers;

Role created.

SQL[gamma]> grant select,update,delete,insert on customer

          2 to gamma_writers;

Grant succeeded.
```

We grant this role to the ops$jtaylor schema. The developer J. Taylor needs permission to modify the customer table content.

```
SQL[gamma]> grant gamma_writers to ops$jtaylor;

Grant succeeded.
```

We are now ready to create the most privileged role, the one that allows grantees to modify the structure of the objects.

```
SQL[gamma]> create role gamma_modifiers;

Role created.

SQL[gamma]> grant alter,select,update,delete,insert on
          customer 2 to gamma_modifiers;

Grant succeeded.
```

By selectively granting the roles to database schemas, we can create three categories of users, with appropriate privileges for their needs. This also enforces the security policy of the application.

Roles can be password protected to further enhance security. Roles that potentially can be destructive shouldn't be granted by default to schemas. They should be selectively enabled using the *set role* command, and supplying a password. To create a password protected, role issue the following command.

```
create role gamma_modifiers identified by topsecret;
```

To enable the role for the current session issue the following command.

```
set role gamma_modifiers identified by topsecret;
```

So far we have considered only the customer table. If the gamma schema had hundreds of tables, granting object level privileges to a role for all objects becomes tedious and error prone. Luckily, we can exploit the script generation capabilities of SQL*Plus to accomplish this job. We can use SQL*Plus to create a script that contains all required grant commands by querying the data dictionary tables. An example of the use of this technique is shown below.

```
set feedback off
set heading off
set linesize 132

spool grant_script.sql
select 'grant select,update,delete,insert on
'||table_name||' to

gamma_writers;' from user_tables;

spool off
```

This script generates an SQL script called grant_script.sql that contains the grant command for every local schema table. Using SQL*Plus as a script generator is a very powerful technique. It can be used to accomplish many other administrative tasks. Mastering this technique is highly recommended if you are going to be involved with Oracle technologies. Its application will save you precious time, and the net result will be less error prone scripts.

At the moment of the database creation, Oracle automatically defines the role PUBLIC and grants it to all users by default. The fastest way to share a privilege among all users is to grant the privilege to PUBLIC.

Oracle allows database Administrators to manage security at a column level by using object level privileges granted on columns. Unfortunately, only INSERT, UPDATE, and REFERENCES can be granted at a column level. This means that while it is possible to prevent a user from storing data in a column when inserting a new row or updating an existing row, it is not possible to prevent a user from accessing a column. This can be achieved only by using views that define a subset of columns within a table. Views can also be used to limit access to specific rows, by filtering out the unwanted rows in the views where clause.

The Oracle security system uses profiles to set limits on database resources. If a profile is assigned to a user, he or she cannot exceed the limits associated with that profile. The resources that can be limited through a profile are, among others, CPU consumption per session, number of allowed sessions per user, and CPU consumption per single SQL call. A very useful resource limit is idle time. This limits periods of continuous inactive time during a session, preventing people from staying connected to the database and wasting resources without actually doing anything. After the idle time period has expired, Oracle automatically disconnects the user session, freeing the associated resources.

Profiles are created using the *create profile* command and assigned to users using the *alter user* or *create user* commands. An example is shown below.

```
SQL> create profile DEVELOPER limit
   2 CPU_PER_SESSION UNLIMITED
   3 CPU_PER_CALL 3000
   4 IDLE_TIME 30;

Profile created.

SQL> alter user ops$ebonazzi profile DEVELOPER;

User altered.
```

Profiles are not generally used at Oracle sites, yet they provide the means for good control over database resources. In a development environment, limiting CPU resource consumption for a session can help by stopping processes that mistakenly enter an endless loop before the overall performance of the machine decreases to unacceptable levels.

Oracle 8 introduced a password aging mechanism that makes user password expire after a configurable number of days. When a password expires, it enters the so-called "grace" period, and the user is asked to change the password. The new password security mechanism also locks an Oracle account after a predefined number of failed attempts to connect. All these parameters are set through user profiles. Specifically, the password related limits configurable through the *create profile* command are:

failed_login_attempts Specifies the number of failed login attempts before the account is locked.

password_life_time Specifies the number of days a password can be used for authentication.

password_reuse_time Specifies the number of days a password is prevented from reuse after it has expired.

password_reuse_max Specifies the number of password changes that must occur before the current password can be reused.

password_lock_time Specifies the number of days an account will remain locked after excreding the consecutive failed login attempts.

password_grace_time	Specifies the number of days the system will keep asking the user to change the password before the account is locked.
password_verify_function	Specifies a user-defined PL/SQL function for use as an alternative to the oracle function used for password authentication.

It is likely that Oracle profiles will increase in popularity in the near future. The new password security introduced with Oracle 8 will initially promote their use, opening the way for subsequent wider use of profiles which also include resource limits.

9.4 Application Objects Owner

Once the application is ready for deployment in the production environment, particular care should be taken when determining the layout of directories, naming conventions, privileges, roles, and operating system accounts allowed to run background jobs for reporting and housekeeping.

It is never a good idea to allow all users to connect to the database using one account. Using a single account precludes the use of many features provided by Oracle for pinpointing problems and issues associated with Oracle sessions. It also prevents a security policy from being enforced by the Oracle engine. Allowing all users to connect to Oracle using the schema that owns the application objects is even worse! This allows inadvertent destructive operations to be performed on application objects. Oracle does not allow schema owners to grant privileges to themselves, as the following example shows.

```
SQL> revoke delete on customer from gamma;
revoke delete on customer from gamma
                                 *
ERROR at line 1:
ORA-01749: you may not GRANT/REVOKE privileges to/from your-
self
```

It is not possible to revoke a potentially destructive privilege on objects that are owned by the schema revoking the privilege. The schema that owns the objects is always allowed to alter or drop them without restriction. If the application is interactive users, or if the background processes share the schema that owns the application objects, the risk of inadvertently dropping crucial objects is very high. Furthermore, it is impossible to control the environment and find out what provoked the problem even if the audit trail mechanism has been enabled. If all users share the same account, it becomes impossible to discriminate between sessions to determine the session associated with a user.

The arrangements that work best for applications being deployed in a production environment are as follows:

1. Neither interactive users or background processes are allowed to access the schema that owns all application objects. The only user authorized to connect to the database using the application schema is the application administrator.
2. Include in the installation procedure a script that creates roles that identify the different categories of users and grants object level privileges to those roles. It is useful to identify users who need read-only access, users who need read-write access, and users who need access to alter certain application objects. The different categories of users are assigned appropriate roles according to the required access level.
3. All users connecting to the database should have their own schema. The scope of a user schema over the application objects is determined by the roles assigned to the schema. All application objects are accessed through synonyms.
4. Background and housekeeping processes should also be categorized according to their object access needs like read-only, read-write and alter mode. Appropriate roles granting the required privileges should be created for the housekeeping jobs in the same way as the interactive user processes.

While in a two-tier environment, it is always possible and definitely better to provide a separate schema for each database user, this rule cannot always be followed when a TP monitor is used in a three-tier environment. It is difficult, if not impossible, to force the TP monitor processes to create database connections using different schemas. Most TP monitors allow for connection and transaction monitoring through the use of specific tools provided with the TP monitor software. In this case, application administrators use TP monitor tools rather than Oracle facilities to monitor and control database sessions.

In all other cases each user should connect to the database using his or her own schema. Roles and synonyms should be used to enforce security and to protect crucial application objects from inadvertent alteration or destruction.

The following table summarizes the software engineering practices discussed here and in Chapter 7. Each row in the table describes three different implementations of the most common tasks associated with an Oracle project. For each task the left-most column describes a common poor implementation. The central column describes a better but perfectible implementation, and the right-most column presents an optimal solution.

Software Engineering practices for Oracle projects

FUNCTION	POOR	BETTER	BEST
Code Writing	Embedded SQL appears intermixed with the program main flow. All or most source code files constituting an application contain embedded SQL.	Embedded SQL is isolated in a smaller number of files. The main program flow doesn't contain embedded SQL, but business logic and logical data access are not distinct and coexist in the same function or file.	The program is sub-divided in separate and distinct layers. Embedded SQL is only contained in physical data access functions, coded in separate files, and called by logical data access functions. Business logic interacts only with logical data access functions.
Development environment setup	All developers use only one Oracle schema, accessing the application objects directly.	All developers use their own schemas, replicating all objects.	Each developer is assigned one schema and accesses the application objects via synonyms. Security is enforced through the use of roles.
Testing	Testing is conducted using the development schema.	One separate schema or instance is used for testing.	Several schemas are used in a dedicated instance to conduct testing. Each type of test (integration, system testing, stress testing, etc.) is performed in a dedicated schema. A hierarchical migration path is established and software is promoted to a higher level only when all tests are performed satisfactorily in the lower level.
Production environment setup	Interactive users and background processes connect to the database using the schema that owns all application objects.	Interactive users and housekeeping jobs use different schemas to connect to the database. The schema that owns all application objects is not used by interactive users or background processes.	Interactive users and background processes are grouped in different categories according to their access level to the database. They access all application objects through synonyms and security is enforced through roles, which define database access levels.

9.5 Environment Setup

The application of some common rules and conventions for Oracle database setup can significantly reduce the DBAs learning curve where multiple DBAs maintain multiple database environments for several applications. This is especially important when the same Oracle environment is replicated across different instances. Consider the classical case in which three Oracle instances are used to support an Oracle-based application: development, test, and production. The database naming convention should reflect the environment owning the instance. Using again the "gamma" application, the development instance can be called *gamd,* the testing instance can be called *gamt,* and the production instance can be named *gamp.*

The need for instance consistency with regard to directory layout and datafile location has been addressed by Oracle through the so-called Optimal Flexible Architecture (OFA). The OFA is a set of rules and conventions for database layout and setup that are recommended by Oracle to simplify Oracle database administration across multiple instances and hardware platforms. If a given database layout follows the OFA rules, an Oracle DBA can become acquainted with the database very quickly. The DBA will find the required Oracle files and table spaces in the same location named consistently. The OFA applies mainly to Unix platforms and is a good starting point for ensuring consistency across different instances. Additional rules and conventions should be established and followed at an application level to ensure instance consistency across the development, test, and production environments.

Tablespace fragmentation will be a problem every application will encounter, if preventive measures are not taken to eliminate or at least alleviate its occurrence. Tablespace fragmentation occurs when, within one tablespace, there are extents of free space scattered throughout the extents containing data. Oracle allocates a contiguous chunk of disk space to an object when it is first created. More space must be allocated to host additional data as the object grows. Each chunk of physical disk space is called an extent. If each object created in a tablespace specifies different parameters in the storage clause, Oracle will allocate extents of different size to the objects. During the lifetime of an application, these objects will grow and shrink until the tablespace contains extents of different sizes with free space and data extents intermixed.

The problem associated with this configuration is that Oracle requires contiguous free-space to allocate an extent. The situation therefore arises where, in spite of having enough free space in the tablespace to accommodate a new object extent, the free space cannot be utilized because it is not physically contiguous. A pictorial representation of this situation is shown in Figure 9.19.

Figure 9.19 provides a visual representation of a tablespace that suffers from freespace bubble fragmentation. The three empty extents (shown in white) are surrounded by occupied extents (shown in gray). If the size of a segment exten-

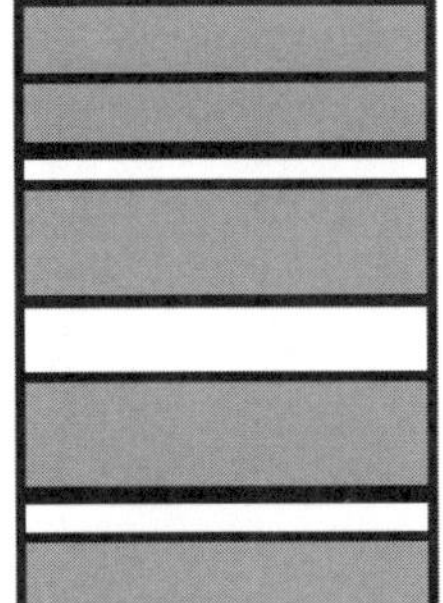

With this extent configuration, it is not possible to join together the free extents to form a larger extent.

FIGURE 9.19 Tablespace fragmentation

sion were greater than the largest free extent but smaller than the sum of all free extents, the segment extension will fail because the free space cannot be coalesced to form a larger empty extent.

To prevent tablespace fragmentation from occurring, one can apply a simple principle. The basic concept is that if one does not want multiple extents of different sizes in the same tablespace, then the only option available is to force all the extents in a single tablespace to be of the same size. This is achieved through automatic inheritance of the tablespace storage parameters when a table or index does not specify a storage clause at creation time. A uniform size in a tablespace provides at least two benefits. It avoids free space bubble fragmentation and it makes the coalescing of free extents in the tablespace superfluous, because the size of each new extent requested by the engine will be always equal to the size of all free extents, already allocated in the tablespace.

When an object is created without specifying the storage clause, it inherits the tablespace default storage parameters. To prevent fragmentation it is necessary to create every table or index in an appropriate tablespace with no storage clause. The tablespace default storage parameters must specify a size for the initial extent that must be equal to the size for the next extent. The size of each object therefore becomes the criterion for its placement in an appropriate tablespace.

With respect again to the gamma application, the database will include the OFA standard tablespaces—RBS, SYSTEM, TEMP, TOOLS, USERS—plus application specific tablespaces organized according to the size of the objects contained in them. The gamma application in the production environment can have three tablespaces for storing tables named:

```
gamma_tables_large  - Initial extent = next extent = 50
  Megabytes
gamma_tables_medium - Initial extent  = next extent = 10
  Megabyte
gamma_tables_small  - Initial extent = next extent = 1
  Megabyte
```

and two tablespaces for storing indexes named:

```
gamma_index_large - Intial extent = next extent = 5
  Megabytes
gamma_index_small - Initial extent = next extent = 512 Kilo-
  bytes
```

The next extent will be of the same size as the initial extent, ensuring that all extents allocated within the same tablespace will have the same size.

What about the gamma development environment? It will have a scaled down version of the three tablespaces hosting tables and the two tablespaces hosting indexes. Instead of having an initial and next extent of 50 MB, the tablespace gamma_tables_large will have the default extent size of 5 MB. The other tablespaces will be sized accordingly.

Adopting an object size based partitioning for tablespaces gives a two-fold advantage. It eliminates the potential for tablespace fragmentation and allows for greater portability of the object creation scripts. Omitting the storage clause from the object creation script and allowing each object to inherit the size of its extents from the tablespace defaults allows the same script to create large objects in the production environment and small objects in the development environment. It now becomes clear why, in Section 9.2, we insisted that a reverse engineering tool must offer the option to exclude the object storage parameters from the DDL script automatically generated.

The same DDL script for creating application objects can be run in the three environments—development, test, and production—generating objects of different size in each environment. There will be only one specific script per environment, the one that creates and sizes the application tablespaces. Reducing the difference between the various Oracle databases to only one tablespace creation script greatly simplifies the administration of multiple instances.

This arrangement makes it easy for an administrator to take snapshots of schema objects and to compare them across different environments. It also contributes to ensure consistency in the areas of object sizing and naming conventions. Consistent naming convention should also be adopted for other database objects, such as database links and operating system directories.

Summary

In this chapter, we focused on managing the environments that are usually needed to support an Oracle based application. From a software engineering point of view, it is advisable to have separate instances to host the different environments that are needed to develop, test, and deploy an application.

Using multiple instances introduces synchronization problems, which can be solved by strict policies for naming convention and systematic checks of schema consistency. Such measures ensure a correct reconciliation between the different schemas supporting the same application.

We analyzed some of the tools available for taking snapshots of the various Oracle schemas for comparison purposes. Specifically, we considered TOAD and SQL Navigator, both available from Quest Software, which offer sophisticated database reverse engineering capabilities, and DBArtisan by Embarcadero Technologies, which offers a more sophisticated schema extraction and migration wizards. They all offer schema reverse engineering as one of the many options available. Oracle Corporation offers an Enterprise Manager add-on called Change Management Pack. This is a tool specifically dedicated to schema management and synchronization. It includes a wealth of options and features that make it the perfect tool for administrators looking after many large Oracle databases. The only drawback is its pricing policy, which makes this great tool a little too expensive.

We also analyzed a testing strategy based on a migration path, which resembles the promotional model for software development version control described in Chapter 8. According to this strategy, a hierarchical migration path is established, based on promotions of software from the lowest to the highest level. Each stage of software testing applies a battery of tests. If the software successfully passes the tests, it is migrated to the next phase or stage. If the software shows problems, it is rejected and goes back to development. Once the software defects have been fixed, the software goes through all testing phases again, starting from the lowest level. This ensures that each change introduced to fix a problem doesn't cause unwanted side effects in other parts of the application.

Finally, we evaluated a strategy that prevents tablespace fragmentation and provides greater portability of database objects across different environments. The basic elements of this strategy are the correct size of the object extents and the placement of the objects in the appropriate tablespace.

Chapter 10

DEVELOPING THE CLIENT

The preceding chapters focused on server issues and problems. Chapter 7, for instance, explained how to correctly structure the application code in distinct layers. Chapter 8 focused more on software engineering techniques to increase performance and quality of code, and Chapter 9 discussed the issues related to the handling of multiple environments. This chapter will focus on the development tools that usually play a crucial role on the client side of client/server applications. When Oracle Pro*C or OCI is used from a PC or a Macintosh to access Oracle databases, the recommendations made in Chapter 7 still apply. On the client side, GUI-based Rapid Application Development (RAD) tools, such as Delphi or Visual Basic, are much more popular than Pro*C or OCI, which are nonvisual and tedious to work with in a GUI-based development.

Client application developers prefer to deal with data-aware visual components, which can be populated with data gathered from Oracle with little effort, sometimes without even using SQL. This chapter will discuss how to choose the client development tools, based on their characteristics and features, with a focus on their realistic performance and scalability, rather than on their capabilities to produce aesthetically appealing graphical user interfaces.

10.1 There Is No Such Thing as the "Best Tool"

On several occasions, colleagues, friends, and technical managers have asked me what was, in my opinion, the "best" development environment to develop client applications. I am afraid I disappointed them because I didn't provide a straight answer. Probably there is no straight answer for such a generic question. Each client RAD tool has its strengths and weaknesses; one could be better at compilation speed and worse with respect to support for Oracle native drivers.

There are different parameters that must be taken into consideration when choosing among the various tools available in the market. Again, choosing the client RAD tool for a project is primarily a business decision rather than a technical decision. One of the parameters is the availability in the market of developers skilled in the tool chosen for the project. When a tool is very popular, as in the case of MS Visual Basic, it is relatively easy to find developers prepared to work at a reasonable rate. Technically speaking, MS Visual Basic cannot compete with sophisticated tools like Forté or Dinasty, which provide a truly object-oriented environment that allows for application partitioning between client and servers. But finding developers skilled in Forté or Dinasty is extremely difficult and rather expensive, while perhaps every technical college teaches Visual Basic.

Another consideration, when choosing a client development environment, is the target platform where the client application must run. If the client population uses only PCs running MS Windows, tools like Inprise Delphi or MS Visual Basic can be included in the competitor list. If the client application must run in a mixed environment, including Apple Macintoshes and Unix workstations, the competition is restricted to a very few players, such as Powersoft Powerbuilder and Oracle Developer, not to mention Forté or Dinasty.

Applications that are critical for the business they support usually require massive investments, which are repaid over a long time. The usual trade-off confronted by financial controllers and technical managers is between the maturity of the chosen technology and its expected lifetime. Nobody wants to venture into the unknown territory of a promising but immature technology. On the other hand, choosing a well-established and mature technology, which appears less risky in the short term, can pose a problem in the long run, if the chosen technology is progressively abandoned by the market before the natural end of the application.

In the mid-80s, the VAX platform was very popular. Products like DEC RdB (now Oracle RdB) and DEC ACMS were the backbones of many successful mission critical applications. At the beginning of the 1990s, the VAX/Alpha platform began its decline, which culminated in the Compaq/DEC merger at the beginning of 1998. Choosing a DEC environment to run a mission-critical application in 1993 would have been a sound decision in the short term, because Unix was still immature and not really suitable to manage large enterprise-class applications. At the end of the 1990s, Unix is the mid-range platform of choice, and OpenVMS has lost its appeal and is slowly disappearing; finding IT professionals capable of maintaining DEC-based applications becomes more and more difficult and expensive. If the expected lifetime of the application, initially conceived in 1993 and operational since 1995, is 10 years, the company using the application should start working towards finding a replacement in 2003. Such an arrangement would leave the application, in its final period, with an obsolete technology of difficult and expensive maintenance. A major breakdown in the last years of the application's lifetime would be extremely expensive, especially when the application-specific expertise achieved by the original designers and developers has gone forever, and the layered software used by the project is not any more adequately supported. Embracing a new technology that looks promising and fashionable, but never really takes off, represents the opposite risk.

Traditional client-server technologies appear, at the end of the nineties, as generally robust and mature, yet on the edge of being phased out by the WEB/Intranet phenomenon. Relying on traditional client-server technologies, such as a two-tier application having Oracle on the back-end being accessed by a front-end written in Visual Basic or Powerbuilder, can be an easy and relatively inexpensive solution on the short term. Towards the end of the application lifetime, that choice could potentially represent a big risk, especially if the expected lifetime of the application is eight or ten years. By that time the traditional client-server paradigm, based on MS Windows front-ends accessing directly back-end databases, could be quite obsolete, leaving the application's maintainers with unsupported or discontinued products during a very delicate phase of the application lifetime.

The traditional client-server model is challenged by two alternative and opposite application development paradigms, the first based on distributed objects and the second based on centralized and powerful servers accessed by thin clients running WEB browsers. Applications based on the first paradigm would be built upon backbones like MS DCOM/ActiveX or OMG CORBA, which take care of the low-level aspects of inter-object communication and remote object instantiation. The appealing advantage offered by this paradigm is a better usage of computing resources in a truly distributed environment, where reusable components are the building blocks of complex applications. Among the drawbacks are a higher total cost of ownership (TCO) due to a much more complex administration and, in the case of MS DCOM/ActiveX, very weak security.

The alternative paradigm proposes centralization as the key to a lower TCO, due to a simplified administration of few and large servers and to the elimination of any deployment overhead. The release by Sun Microsystems of the superservers Enterprise 10,000 (Starfire) machines capable of hosting up to 256 processors and 256 gigabytes of memory is a clear indication of the new wave that sees in the return to mainframe-class servers the solution to the administrative costs brought about by the proliferation of the low-end, Intel-based departmental servers. The "Raw Iron" project, announced at COMDEX 1998 by Oracle Corporation goes in this direction. Oracle 8i, which offers an Oracle-based file system, where files of any kind can be stored under the direct control of the engine, runs under an extremely slim operating system, which provides just the minimal set of primitives necessary for Oracle 8i to run.

The role of Java, clearly not only and not any more a language but a true platform, alternative to desktop operating systems, cannot be underestimated. The Gartner Group predicts that Java will constantly increase its market shares to become the dominant development platform in the first years of the new century. The exponential growth of e-commerce and Internet-based transactions favors browser-based solutions, rather than MS Windows-based applications.

All these trends considered together have one point in common, represented by the progressive decline of the traditional client-server environments. Still, the RAD tools market is characterized by fierce competition, where competitors offer new releases of their products very frequently, incorporating in the tools new and increasingly powerful features. The marketing departments orchestrate massive campaigns to push their customers to upgrade, magnifying the virtues of the newly introduced features.

This chapter will strive to put the various RAD tools in the right perspective, shifting the focus from the over-advertised and often superfluous "advanced" features of each product to the real critical factors for the success of a client-server application.

10.2 The Major Players in the Client-Server Arena

Excluding the niche market represented by the very high-end development tools of the caliber of Forté or Dynasty, the significant competitors in the client-server market are four:

- Oracle Corporation
- Microsoft
- Inprise
- Sybase/Powersoft

Oracle Developer, the enterprise-class RAD product offered by Oracle Corporation, only competes with other vendors when the back-end database is Oracle. Its reliance on PL/SQL makes it heavily dependent on the proprietary environment. The tools offered by the other vendors, on the other hand, can be interchangeably used to interface to different back-end databases.

A common business practice adopted by RAD vendors is to offer their products in different configurations, from the inexpensive entry level, aimed at the academic and hobbyist market, to the so-called Client-Server or Enterprise configuration. The latter is usually shipped with native drivers for the connection to the most common database engines (Oracle, Sybase, Informix) and with sophisticated components such as HTTP, FTP, or socket servers. At an intermediate level, the so-called "Professional" configuration usually includes the Internet components but excludes the native drivers for the database connection. In most cases the professional edition allows for ODBC connections. The cost varies between approximately one hundred dollars for the entry-level edition, to a few hundred dollars for the professional edition to a few thousand dollars for the client-server or enterprise edition.

10.2.1 ORACLE CORPORATION

Oracle Developer, formerly Developer/2000, is the tool that allows developers to create applications that interact with an Oracle database. It doesn't follow the commonly accepted operational standards established by its competitors, such as Visual Basic or Delphi, but relies on its own methods and visual metaphors to provide programmers with a powerful, yet cumbersome, development environment.

Oracle Developer is a multi-platform IDE, which also supports Motif in a Unix or OpenVMS environment. Its unorthodox look-and-feel in an MS Windows-based environment is due partially to specific design decisions, which privileged a consistent interface across different GUIs, and partially to its character-based origins, which forced designers at Oracle Corporation to take an evolutionary rather than revolutionary migration path. Developers skilled in Oracle Forms release 3, strictly character-based, could have switched to Oracle Forms 4.0, the first Oracle Forms release to be implemented in a GUI environment, with minimal retraining. What is currently called Oracle Developer is a package that comprises a set of tools previously available under several names, such as Oracle Forms, Oracle Reports, Oracle Menus, etc.

Another peculiarity of Oracle Developer is the language used, the Oracle proprietary procedural extension to SQL (PL/SQL). While the look-and-feel of Oracle Developer is definitely not in line with mainstream Windows-based RAD tools, the Oracle Developer Windows implementation uses extensively MS Windows-only concepts and technologies, such as OLE and the Multiple Document Interface (MDI). These features are not supported by the various Motif releases of Oracle Developer.

The Project Builder (Figure 10.1) is a sort of command-and-control console that can launch all tools offered by the Oracle Developer package.

The five large icons displayed on the left-hand side are picture buttons that launch, from top to bottom, the Form Builder, the Report Builder, the Graphics Builder, the Procedure Builder, and the Query Builder.

The Form Builder is the tool that will be used extensively to interact with the end-user. Unlike its competitors, which all offer a toolbar displaying controls that can be freely dragged and dropped onto windows, Form Builder reasons in terms of items, blocks, canvasses, and windows.

Items are objects like data values or command buttons, used by the user to interact with the application. They are logically grouped into blocks and visibly arranged in canvasses. Several canvasses are contained in a window.

The first step required to build a form is to define the blocks that will be displayed in the canvasses. The block wizard in Figure 10.2 can assist in this process.

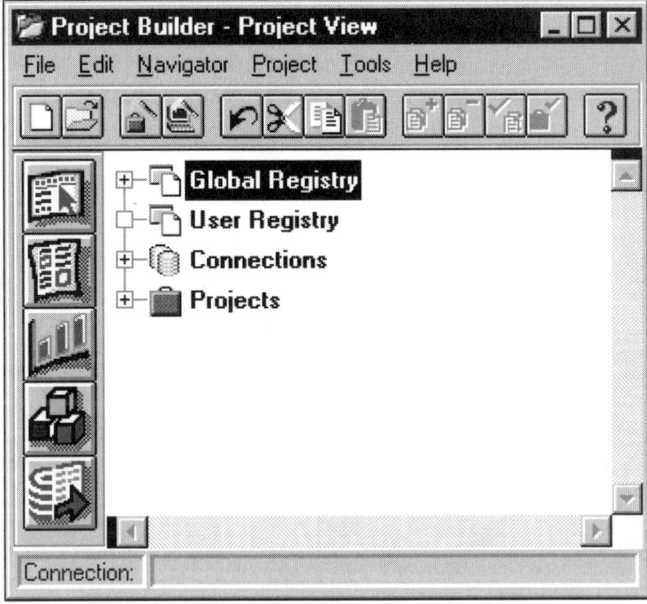

FIGURE 10.1 Oracle Developer Project Builder

The wizard connects to the database and displays the schema objects to the user, who can choose the source table or view an individual column from the list of available columns, automatically generated by the wizard.

When all required blocks are built, the next logical step is to invoke the layout editor to link each block to the canvas that will be used to display the block items to the users. The layout wizard shown in Figure 10.3 can be used to simplify the process.

While the layout wizard quickly links blocks to canvasses, the layout editor allows for fine-grained drawing and placing of all items in the canvas.

Developers who approach Oracle Developer after having worked with other RAD tools that adopt a window-centric discipline usually find the canvas-centric philosophy confusing and cumbersome. Developers trained in Delphi can adapt painlessly to Visual Basic, but must spend a considerable amount of time retraining in Oracle Developer, due to the unorthodox approach taken by the tool to accomplish even elementary tasks.

An important element of the Form Builder is the relation, which is an object that handles the relationship between two associated blocks. The block wizard can implicitly create a relation when the user specifies a master-detail form module. It can also be created explicitly, using the new relation dialog box.

Other significant elements that contribute to the rich set of building blocks offered by Form Builder are List Of Value items (LOV fields) and text editors. A

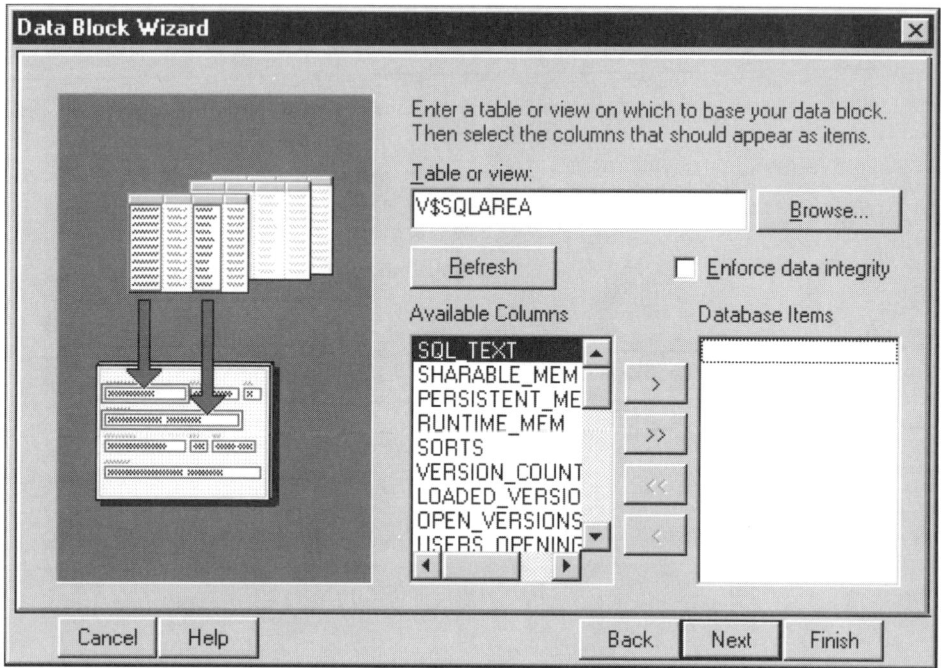

FIGURE 10.2 The Data Block Wizard at work

LOV field presents to the user a predetermined set of values to choose from at run-time. The list can be static, that is, the values are hard-coded at design time, or dynamic, based on the values contained in a database column.

A LOV field is based on a Record Group, which can be created before and independently from the corresponding LOV field, or during the LOV field creation.

In Figure 10.6, the LOV field has been created together with its associated record group, based on an SQL query. It is also possible to create record groups independently, manually entering the list of values at design time. This is accomplished by highlighting the "Record Groups" node of the module tree presented in the object navigator and clicking on the "New" icon (see Figure 10.7).

While the default Forms editor is generally sufficient for basic text items, Oracle Developer users can design their own customized editors, which become objects with properties that can be assigned to text items. Multiple editors can be created, each with different behavior; for instance, one might wrap words reaching the end of the line. Each individual text item displayed in a form can be assigned a different and customized text editor, in addition to the default provided by Form Builder.

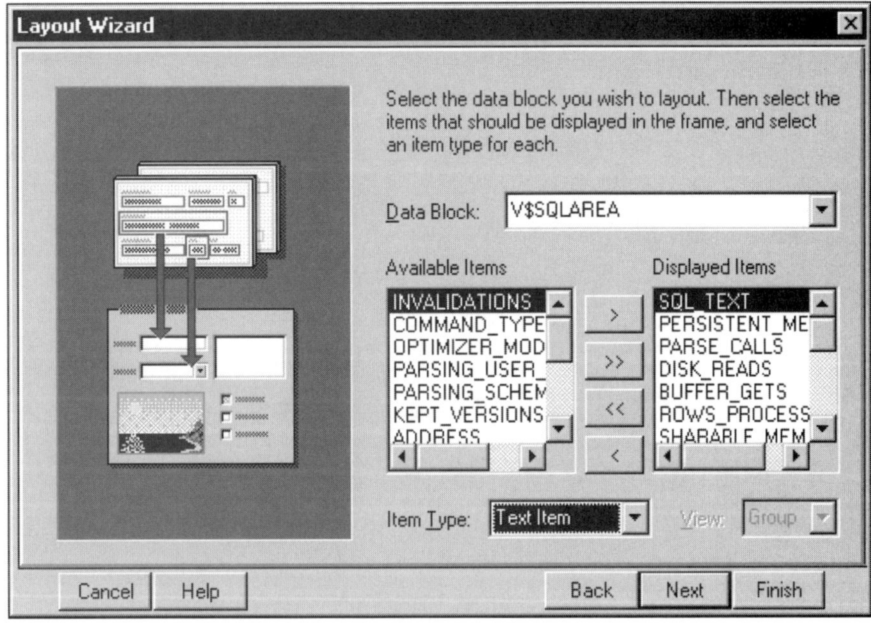

FIGURE 10.3 The Layout Wizard at work

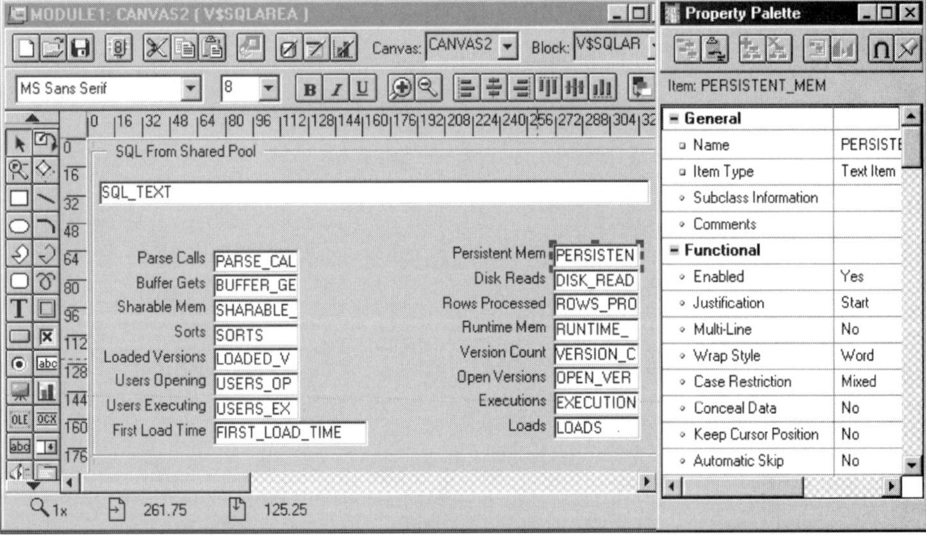

FIGURE 10.4 The layout produced by the Layout Wizard

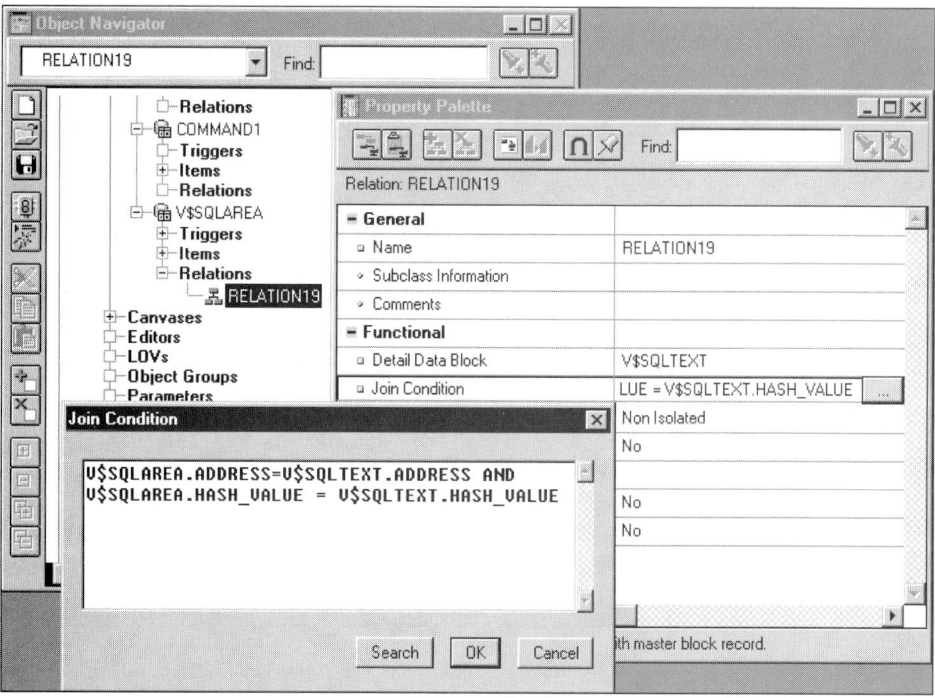

FIGURE 10.5 A relation links the V$SQLAREA and V$SQLTEXT data blocks

The glue that links everything together and gives life to an Oracle Developer application is PL/SQL. PL/SQL anonymous blocks and package subprograms are organized in program units, or triggers, fired by events occurring in forms, blocks, or items. PL/SQL is used to add or amend built-in application functionality in a procedural way, allowing fine-grained control over all items constituting the application developed in Oracle Developer.

Five types of triggers are supported, each recognizable by its prefix. More than one hundred built-in triggers are supported in Oracle Developer. The trigger types are:

TRIGGER TYPE	PURPOSE
PRE-	Fires just before an action is executed.
POST-	Fires just after an action is executed.
WHEN-	Fires in addition to the standard processing associated with the event.
ON-	Fires instead of the standard processing associated with the event.
KEY-	Fires instead of a key standard function.

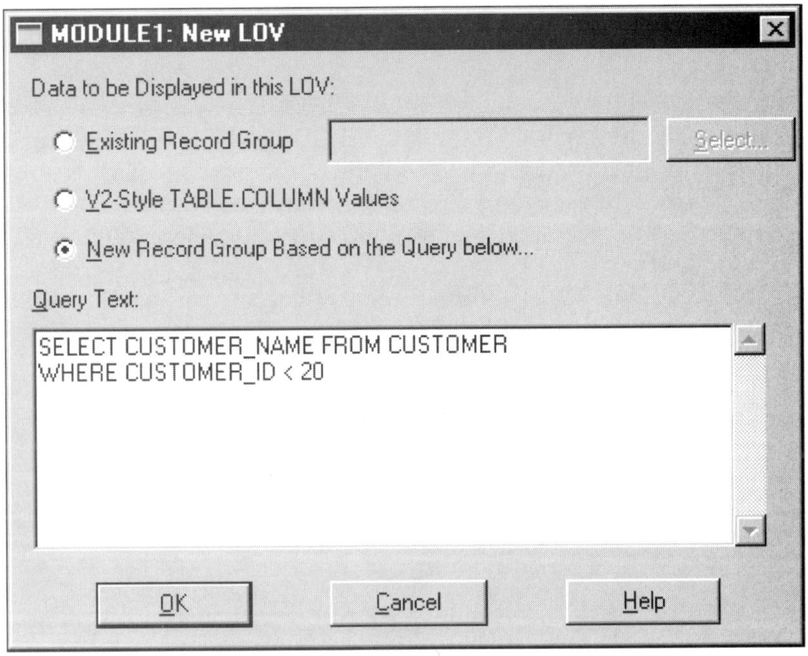

FIGURE 10.6 Creation of a LOV field

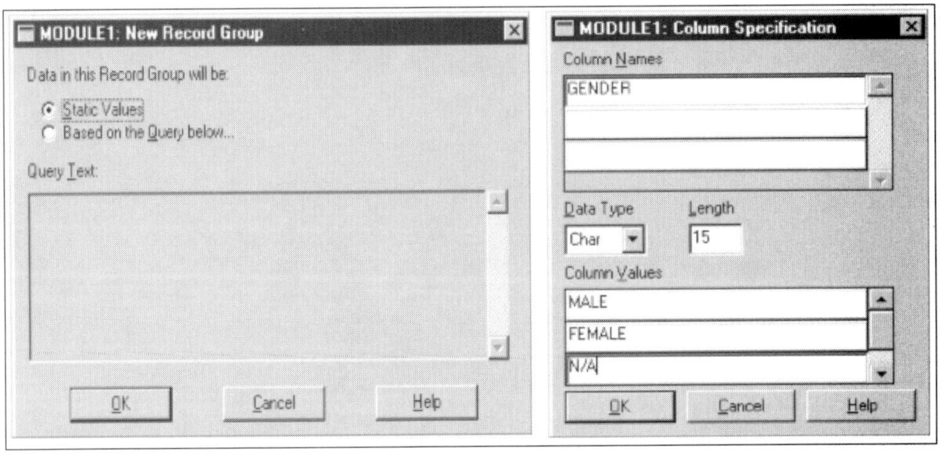

FIGURE 10.7 The record group "gender" specifies a hard-coded list of values

The scope of a trigger is determined by its hierarchical position in the form tree. There are three possible levels in the trigger hierarchy. In Figure 10.8, the object navigator shows the tree representing the entire Forms hierarchy. There is one form-level trigger—ON-CLEAR-DETAILS; two block-level triggers—ON-CHECK-DELETE-MASTER and ON-POPULATE-DETAILS; and an item-level trigger (for the INVALIDATIONS item) in the process of being created.

Another category of triggers is available to Forms programmers: the user-defined (or user-named) triggers, which fire only when called by a built-in, event-actioned trigger.

For writing PL/SQL code, Forms Builder provides a PL/SQL editor, shown in Figure 10.9, which can be explicitly launched by the user, or automatically invoked by double clicking on a trigger.

Writing code is by definition an error-prone activity. To detect software defects mistakenly introduced by developers using PL/SQL, the form can be compiled in "debug mode," which makes Form Builder automatically invoke the PL/SQL debugger when the form is tested. When the debugger is activated, it is

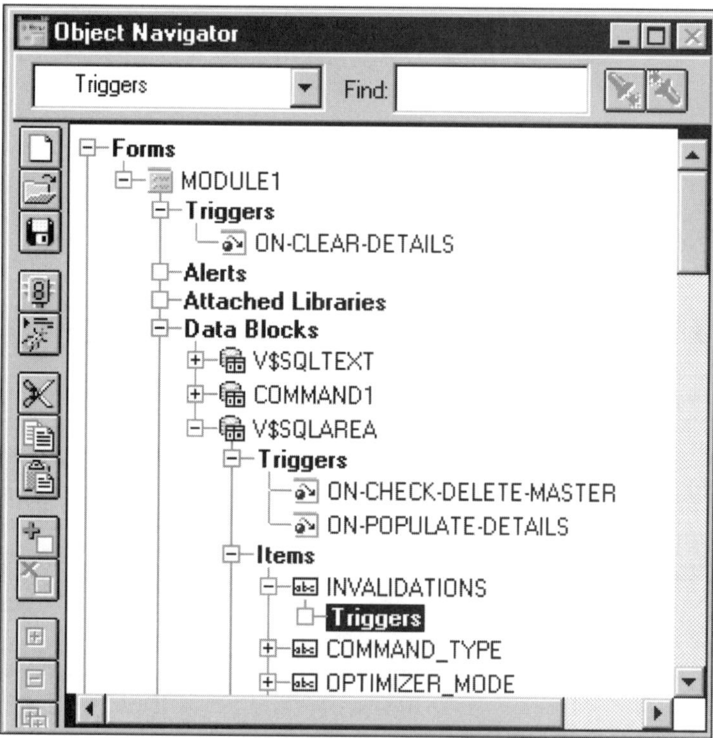

FIGURE 10.8 Object Navigator showing the trigger hierarchy

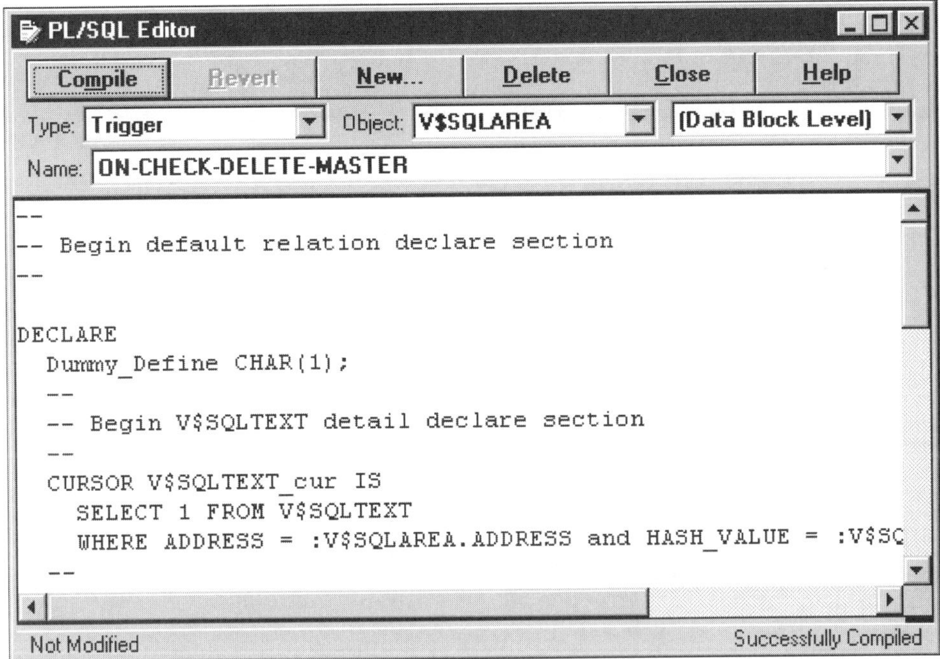

FIGURE 10.9 The PL/SQL editor provided by Oracle Developer

possible for a developer to set execution breakpoints and to step line by line-in-the code fired by the various forms-related events.

Oracle Developer includes a menu builder that allows for easy creation of menus, which can be associated with individual windows or with the main MDI frame in the case of an MDI application. The menu builder (Figure 10.11) is very intuitive and allows for good productivity.

Form Builder provides a PL/SQL debugger, Figure 10.10, useful to debug PL/SQL code stored in Forms triggers and package sub-programs. The scope of this debugger is local to the forms developed on the client, that is, Oracle server triggers and stored procedures are not accessible through the Forms Builder debugger. For this reason, Oracle Developer includes Procedure Builder (Figure 10.12) a tool explicitly designed to reverse engineer, compile, and debug database server and stored procedures from a client workstation. Procedure Builder looks rather essential, or even Spartan, to developers who used tools like Quest SQL Navigator or SFI SQL Programmer. Procedure Builder provides no syntax coloring and the working environment doesn't offer the rich set of functions and facilities provided by the competing tools.

The remaining components included in Oracle Developer, Reports and Graphics, are used to generate written reports from database tables, and graphs

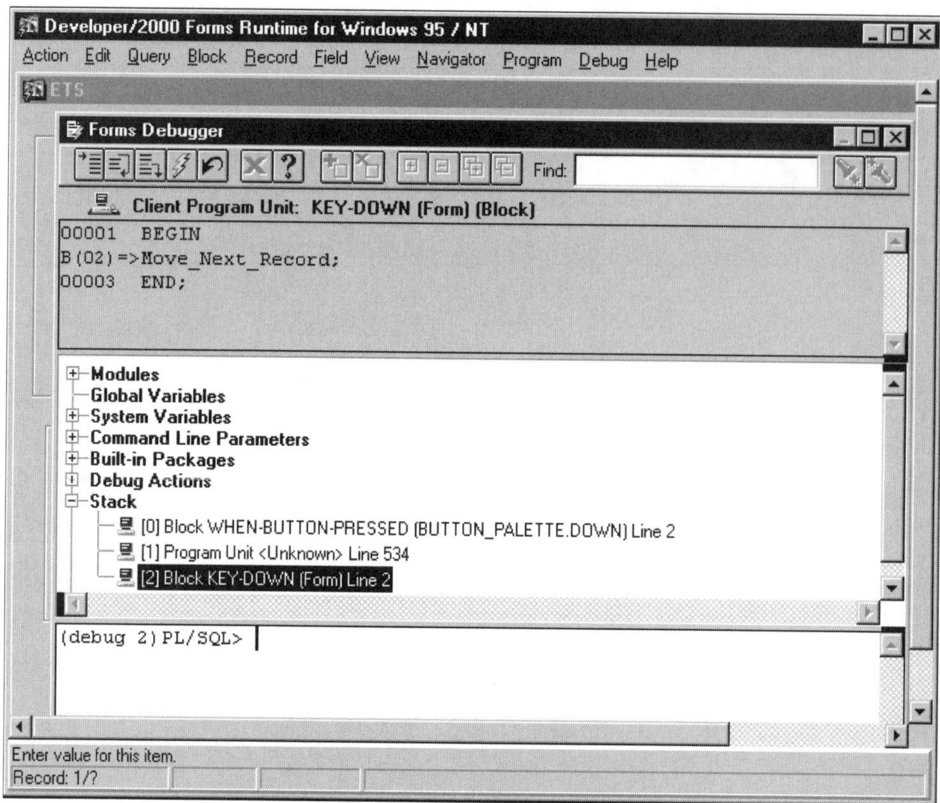

FIGURE 10.10 PL/SQL debugger in action

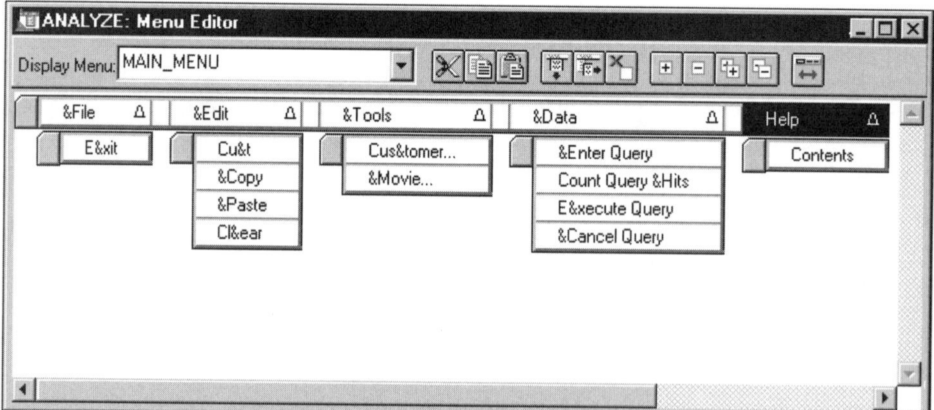

FIGURE 10.11 Menu Builder at work

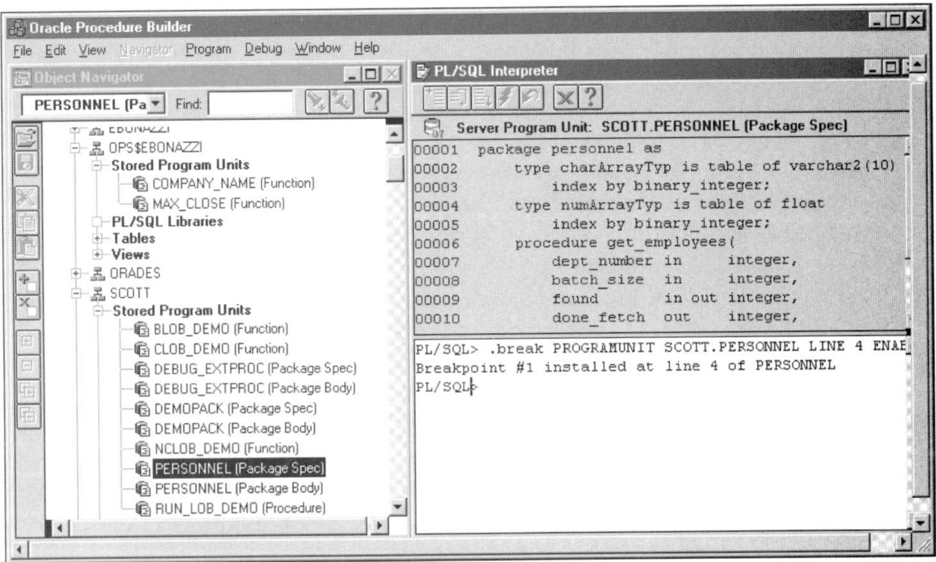

FIGURE 10.12 Procedure Builder at work.

and charts, which can be interactively displayed either in Forms or in written reports. They are reasonably easy to use, thanks to the Report Wizard and the Graph Genie.

Oracle Developer Summary In spite of its rather peculiar look and feel, Oracle Developer can be appealing for sites where large investments have been made in Oracle-based technologies. Server developers, presumably already familiar with PL/SQL, can easily and seamlessly apply their skills in a client environment with no further training.

The Oracle Developer run-time system must be installed from a CD-ROM in a shared disk of a LAN or in the local disk of all workstations running applications written in Oracle Developer. Such an arrangement prevents an easy deployment of an application through the WEB. Consider a tool like TOAD (Tool for Oracle Application Developers), for example. The ZIP file containing the application written in Delphi plus the connectivity layer (a third party library using Oracle OCI) is as large as 1 MB, easily downloadable using a WEB browser or FTP, from *www.toadsoft.com*. It would be extremely impractical to deploy the many megabytes of the Oracle Developer run-time system, plus the Forms executable files, using the same medium. Furthermore, the Oracle Developer run-time system is not royalty free, which further limits the deployment of an application written using this product.

Oracle Developer is essentially an interpreted system, inherently slow if compared to true machine-code executables such as the .EXE files produced by Delphi or Visual Basic. The only advantage offered by Oracle Developer is its multi-platform support, which extends to the major Unix systems, OpenVMS, and Apple Macintoshes.

Perhaps the most compelling reason not to choose Oracle Developer for new projects is the strategic direction taken by Oracle Corporation, which seems to break away from the client/server paradigm in favor of WEB-only solutions. The concurrent release of Oracle 8i and JDeveloper 2.0, together with the "Raw Iron" project and the statements made by Larry Ellison, Oracle's CEO, about the death of the client/server paradigm, clearly indicate that Oracle Corporation will be pushing a Java-centric, CORBA-based solution for accessing WEB-enabled database servers across the enterprise intranets.

This does not mean that Oracle Developer will be de-supported in the near future. It is likely that Oracle Corporation would face a customer rebellion if it did, given the considerable investment made by Oracle customers in this technology. It simply means that the company's focus will be put more on solutions that by their very own nature will be alternative to the client/server paradigm.

One should also consider that Oracle Corporation is the only competitor that doesn't provide middleware components in the proposed architecture for the enterprise. Microsoft customers adopting Visual Studio can achieve scalability using MTS (Microsoft Transaction Server), which provides TP-monitor like services through a very easy-to-use programmatic interface.

Sybase/Powersoft offers an MTS-like product called Jaguar CTS that can handle transactions involving databases running on Unix machines, and, thanks to an interface to IBM-CICS, can extend its connectivity to IBM mainframes.

Inprise/Borland offers perhaps the most complete middleware solution: It includes MIDAS, a product specifically engineered for MS Windows NT servers; Entera, able to ensure middleware connectivity using well proven technologies, such as DCE and message queuing, and linking Microsoft technologies to the more powerful Unix environments; and Visigenic, the most popular CORBA implementation, sold in tens of millions worldwide.

Historically, Oracle Corporation considered TP monitors and middleware software as competitors rather than complementary technologies to its flagship database. It is indicative that Oracle Corporation bought from DEC the Codasyl database, DBMS, the relational database, RdB, the Common Data Dictionary (CDD), DEC Rally, RdB Expert, and other database-related tools. ACMS, the very successful DEC TP monitor, which could have been bought by Oracle for a very convenient price, was left out of the list of products of interest and remained the property of DEC.

Oracle Corporation developed the Multi-Threaded Server (MTS) as a cheap and easy to use alternative to TP monitors, and Oracle8 offers Advanced Queuing (AQ), an optional component that implements application queuing using database tables as queue repositories.

Developing a TP monitor requires a long time and a consistent investment. The sudden popularity of WEB-centric applications, which require middleware software to ensure proper security and scalability, found Oracle Corporation without an adequate middleware offer. By integrating CORBA and Java in the database kernel, Oracle Corporation is able to provide a robust and elegant solution, which uses standard technologies, rather than a proprietary TP system, to fulfil customers' expectations for secure and scalable e-commerce. This strategy implies, yet again, a break away from a traditional client/server approach and the promotion of an alternative Java and WEB-based application development paradigm. While it is possible to use Oracle Developer in conjunction with a TP monitor such as BEA Systems TUXEDO via the Foreign Function Interface (FFI), the Oracle-provided interface, called D2TX, only gives developers a PL/SQL bridge to the low-level TUXEDO APIs. This means that Oracle Developer does not automatically populate data-aware controls such as LOVs, but code must be written to manually populate all Forms controls that receive their values from the database.

Application designers and architects should consider twice the decision of adopting a pure client/server approach for new projects. If client/server still appears as the most viable solution for their application, they should probably look at alternative tools rather than Oracle Developer, which is not likely to play in the future a central role in the Oracle strategy for application development.

10.2.2 MICROSOFT

At one end of the spectrum, Oracle Corporation pushes for nonWindows based IT solutions. At the opposite end, Microsoft built its fortune on the PC-based client/server paradigm, which it has tried to perpetuate for as long as it can. MS Visual Studio, the Microsoft development suite that includes C/C++, Basic, Java, FoxPro, and InterDev, kept improving release after release. Visual Studio 6 is the first release of the suite that can be proficiently used with an Oracle database at the back-end without the support of third party connectivity software.

Visual Basic, the preferred environment for building GUI front-ends, improved considerably with release 5, which first introduced a true compiler, and kept improving with release 6, which introduces OleDB-based data-aware controls and MTS component debugging.

Visual Basic Enterprise is shipped with the richest set of components, leaving behind both Powerbuilder and Delphi. It is arguably the easiest RAD tool to use, but its simplicity implies a programming environment which is less powerful than, say, Delphi. For instance, Visual Basic supports only an apartment-threaded model; pointers are not supported, so linked list and complex data structures are outside the reach of the average Visual Basic programmer.

Unlike Powerbuilder, Visual Basic, as shown in Figure 10.14, supports a two-way editing environment, where controls displayed in the form being built show the code associated with their events in a separate, easily accessible win-

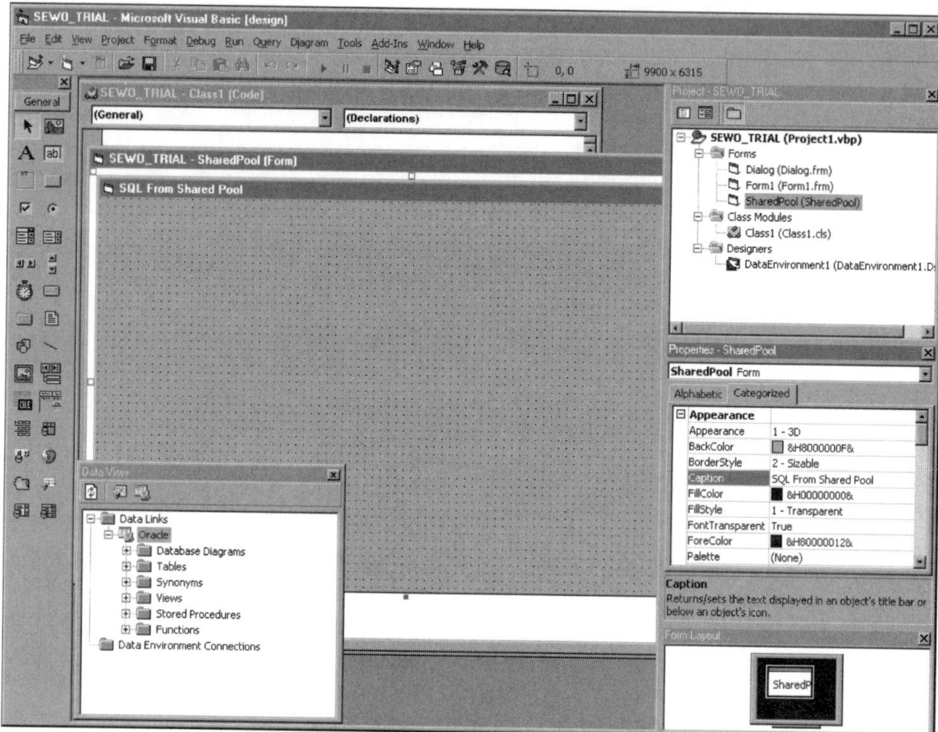

FIGURE 10.13 The Visual Basic IDE

dow. All events belonging to all controls in the active window are accessible at a glance in the same file. This arrangement, first introduced by Delphi release1, greatly simplifies code production and debugging. The object inspector is also a tool that helps to increase developers' productivity by showing the basic properties of the selected objects in an ergonomic way.

Visual Basic Enterprise Edition ships with a few tens of components. Since it is very unlikely to use them all in the same project, to avoid an IDE over-cluttered with many components that wouldn't be used anyway, Visual Basic allows the user to choose the components he or she wants to see displayed in the component toolbar (Figure 10.15).

Visual Basic provides a very advanced debugger, the only one capable of stepping through code residing in remote DCOM components, such as MTS objects.

A Visual Basic debugging session, see Figure 10.16, is easily conducted thanks to the many facilities provided, such as watch windows that display the content of sensitive variables and breakpoints that can be set anywhere in the code.

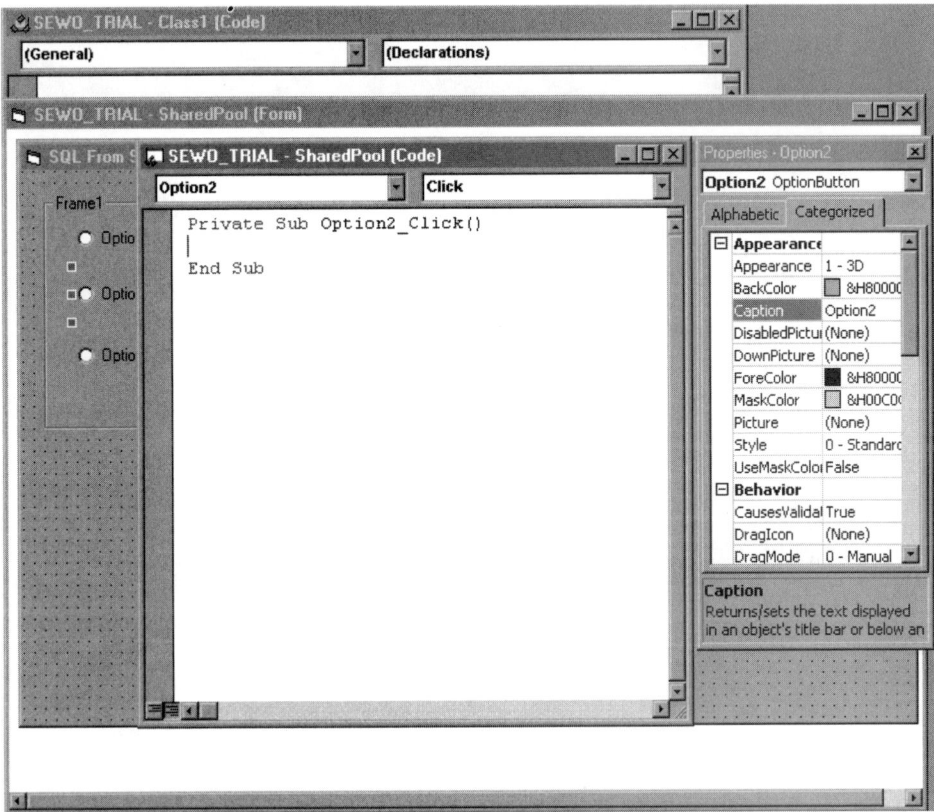

FIGURE 10.14 The two-editing environment in Visual Basic release 6

Stepping through the lines of code is simple and effective, and developers never lose the feeling of being in control of what is happening in the debugging session.

The Visual Basic 6 compiler improved its speed and the speed of the code produced over release 5, but it still doesn't match Delphi for optimization, diagnostics, general options, and speed. The EXE file produced by Visual Basic is not yet a complete stand-alone executable, needing a large DLL to be able to run. In spite of this, the overall performance of a deployed application is more than satisfactory.

The real improvement over all older releases is the new data-access model, or the programmatic interface to interact with back-end databases. Until Visual Basic 6, the only viable interface to external databases was ODBC-based (RDO or DAO). This solution worked well only with MS SQL Server 6.5, which used ODBC as its native interface. ODBC has never been the preferred solution to connect to an Oracle database. Mission-critical applications interfacing with Oracle

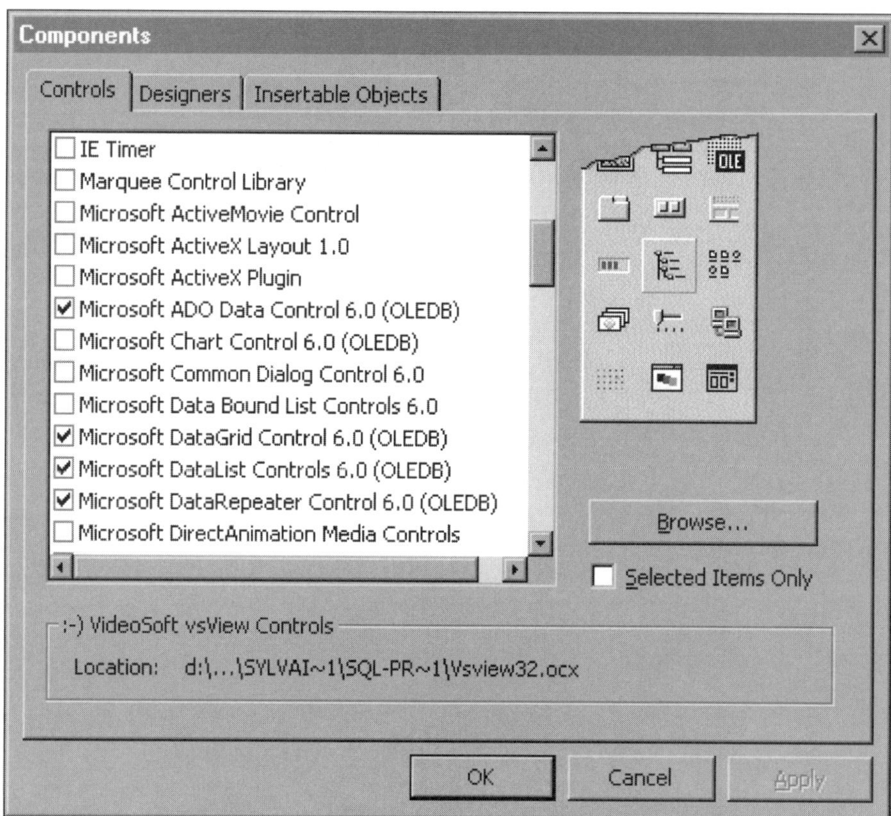

FIGURE 10.15 Visual Basic allows users to choose the components that will be displayed in the component toolbar

directly, in a two-tier configuration, would have been better implemented using third party OCI-based connectivity software, such as SFI SQL Sombrero, or Oracle Objects for OLE.

The new data-access model, ActiveX Data Objects (ADO), is a lean, low-memory footprint layer that seats between either the data-aware controls or the user-written VB code and OleDB. The OleDB service provider for Oracle interfaces directly to OCI, giving a considerable performance improvement over any ODBC-based solutions. The programmatic interface to ADO is simple and intuitive and as easy to use as Oracle Objects for OLE (Figure 10.17).

The improved compiler, the simple-to-use environment, and the new data-access model contribute in making Visual Basic one of the strongest competitors in the client/server arena. Its corporate acceptance is also due to the extreme popularity of the product. Visual Basic is a universally known language, which in

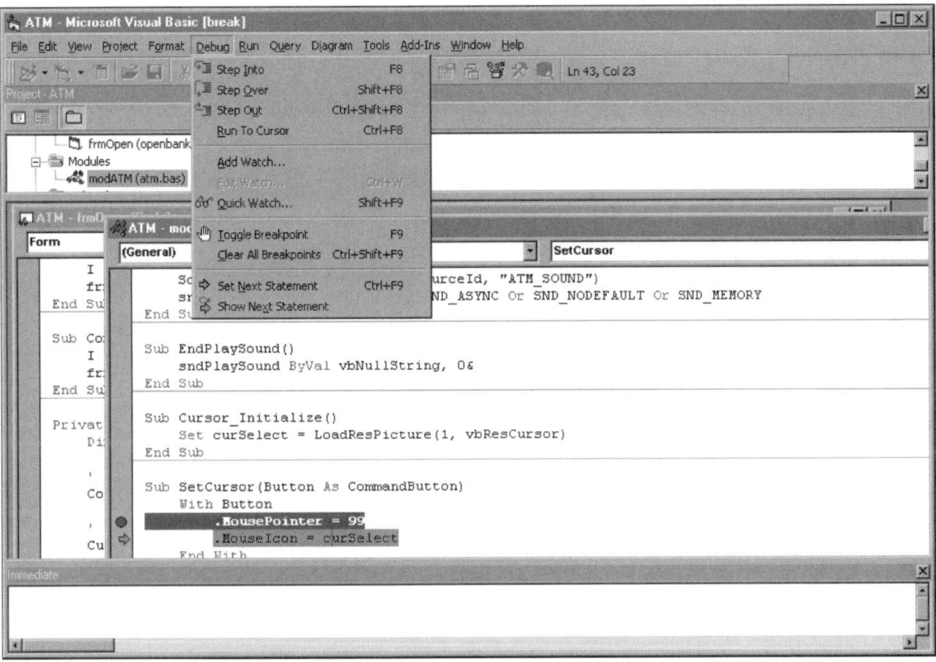

FIGURE 10.16 A Visual Basic debugging session

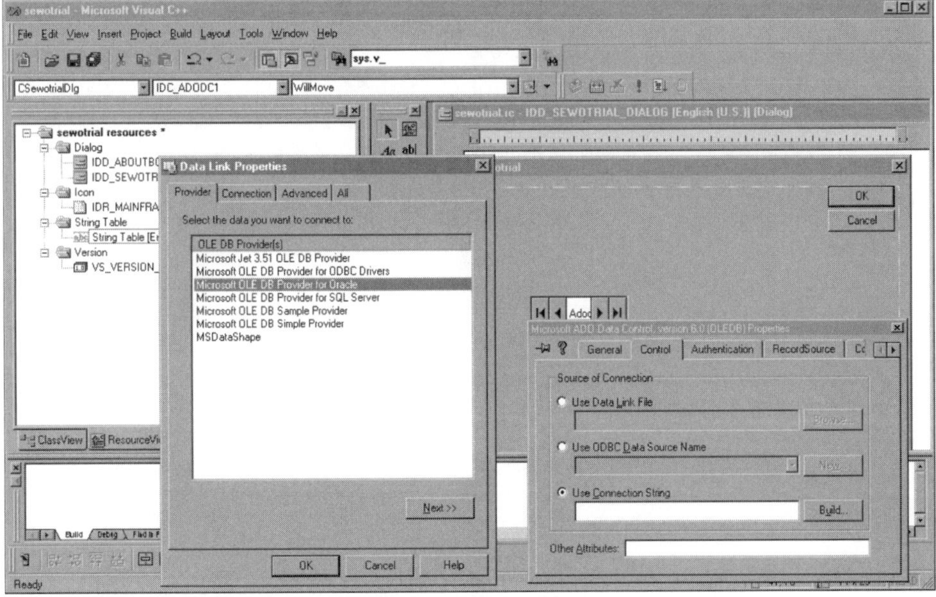

FIGURE 10.17 Using ADO/OleDb from Visual C/C++

business terms translates into easy-to-find and less expensive manpower for project staffing.

Visual Basic has its own drawbacks, though. Its implementation of the object-oriented paradigm is weak, if compared to Delphi, which in release 4 allows for function overloading. Probably the most serious limitations of Visual Basic are its language, its lack of pointers, and the absence of bit-field manipulation operators. While Visual Basic is good enough for most tasks performed by a client application, basically presentation services, the most advanced tasks can be accomplished only in Visual C/C++. This implies having different skills in the development team, which further complicates the administrative burden of conducting an IT project.

Really advanced three-tier applications must often resort to Visual C/C++ to implement the most delicate components, in order to be able to use the free-threading model, which is available only to Microsoft developers who are proficient C++ programmers. In general, transactionally enabled components greatly benefit from a C/C++ implementation built using the Active Template Library (ATL) when they are accessed by hundreds of users.

Visual Basic Summary Visual Basic release 6 is a serious contender in the client/server market. While its adoption for client/server based on Oracle back-end technologies had been problematic in the past, due to the inadequacy of the ODBC data-access model, the recent introduction by Microsoft of the OleDB/ADO data-access model removes an important obstacle to a more generalized acceptance of Visual Basic in projects that use Oracle on the back-end.

Visual Basic release 6, coupled with Microsoft Transaction Server, offers levels of scalability previously reachable only by high-end Unix-based minicomputers. To achieve the top features offered by Microsoft technologies, it is imperative to use a much more difficult environment, such as Visual C/C++. This is probably the most serious disadvantage of Visual Basic. While Object Pascal can be used in Delphi to accomplish virtually any task, the language bundled with VB is not as powerful and shows its limits when confronted with tasks like bit-field manipulation and thread management.

Projects implementing advanced mission-critical applications must use a mixed development environment, where the presentation services can be realized in Visual Basic and complex business logic incorporated in nonvisual data components must sometimes be implemented using Visual C/C++. Inevitably, an environment where two skill sets must coexist implies a heavier administrative burden.

10.2.3 INPRISE/BORLAND.COM

The only technically sound alternative to Visual Studio, in the client/server arena, is represented by Inprise, a company that changed radically its nature, mission, and goals in little more than one year. Formerly known as Borland, Inprise re-defined itself as a provider of enterprise class components for distributed computing; its metamorphosis led to the name change. Inprise offers a family of well-integrated products, glued together by well-designed and robust middleware such as MIDAS and Entera. The two compilers shipped by Inprise (Delphi and C++ Builder) are the technology leaders in their class. Popular third party client/server products that help developers to be more productive while developing Oracle applications use Delphi. Quest Software TOAD and SQL Navigator are good examples.

Delphi pioneered the two-way visual editing environment and set the usability standard for RAD tools when it was first released in 1994. Subsequent releases constantly improved the features offered by the compiler. Delphi 4, released in 1998, supports all major distributed computing protocols and paradigms. While Microsoft tends to lock developers adopting their technologies in a rigid proprietary environment, for instance, by supporting only ActiveX/DCOM, Inprise favors a nonpartisan approach towards standards and protocols, supporting, for example, both CORBA and ActiveX, and both MS ISAPI and Netscape NSAPI. Inprise is serious about distributed computing and middleware. The Visigenic implementation of the CORBA standard is the most widely used, and Inprise is the first company offering a DCE-CORBA bridge. The Entera line of products is based on DCE. After the acquisition of Visigenic, Inprise faced the challenge to unify the two owned families of products, the DCE-based Entera and the CORBA-based Visigenic. Inprise does not support only open systems and large servers; its offer includes MIDAS, a collection of services aimed at delivering distributed application tailored for the MS Windows NT environment.

The king of the Inprise offering is still Delphi, the most popular non-Microsoft development tool.

Figure 10.18 shows a development session in Delphi 4. Note the object inspector on the left side, and both the form (on the right side) and the code that responds to the events fired by the controls contained in the form (at the bottom of the visual environment).

The Delphi IDE is very ergonomic and allows for high productivity. The compiler is incredibly fast, like the executable produced from the Object Pascal code. The integrated debugger is also very effective and well engineered.

For advanced developers the real advantage over Visual Basic is the absolute control over Win32 threads. Delphi applications can support the most advanced threading models, the so-called free-threaded model, while Visual Basic applications support only the apartment-threaded model. Apartment-threaded servers use multiple threads for individual component instances, but a single thread services all requests for an object. Conversely, free-threaded servers support any number of threads that can execute any object's methods at any time. They are the ultimate ingredients for scalability.

Delphi makes extensive use of the Visual Component Library (VCL), an object-oriented wrapper around the Windows APIs. But Object-Pascal is powerful enough to be used without VCL, if the need arises. Delphi can create tiny exe-

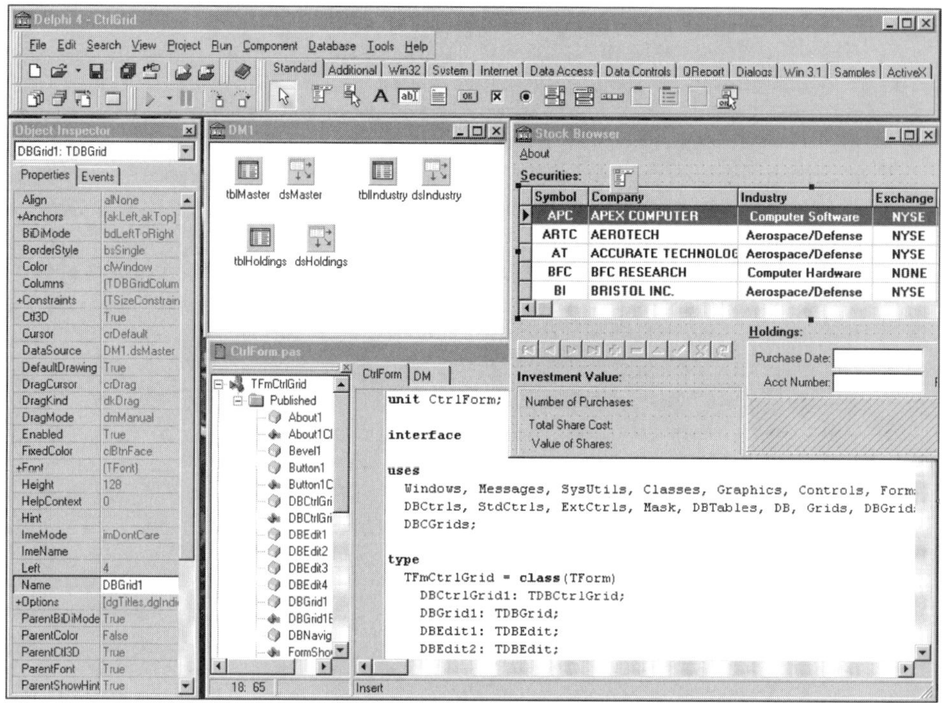

FIGURE 10.18 A typical Delphi session

cutables when Windows APIs are called directly, bypassing the VCL. Unlike Visual Basic, Object Pascal supports pointers, which can be used to implement linked lists and more complex data structures.

Low-level tasks that, in the MS Visual Studio environment, would be beyond Visual Basic capabilities, requiring a Visual C++ implementation, in the Delphi environment can be accomplished in Object Pascal, which allows for much more flexibility.

The VCL is powerful, yet simple to use. It is the secret of Delphi's success, thanks to its easy to remember visual metaphors and real object-oriented capabilities. In Delphi, like in Powerbuilder, it is possible to subclass forms, to create more specialized versions of the same form at different levels of the inheritance chain. This feature, shown in Figure 10.21, is not offered by Visual Basic.

Delphi offers many components, accessible through the component palette, placed on the top right of the IDE (Figure 10.20). The component palette is a tabbed notebook control, where the components are grouped together and easily accessed through the visual tabs.

An important feature offered by Delphi is the Data Module, which allows data components to be grouped together in one centralized unit. All forms display-

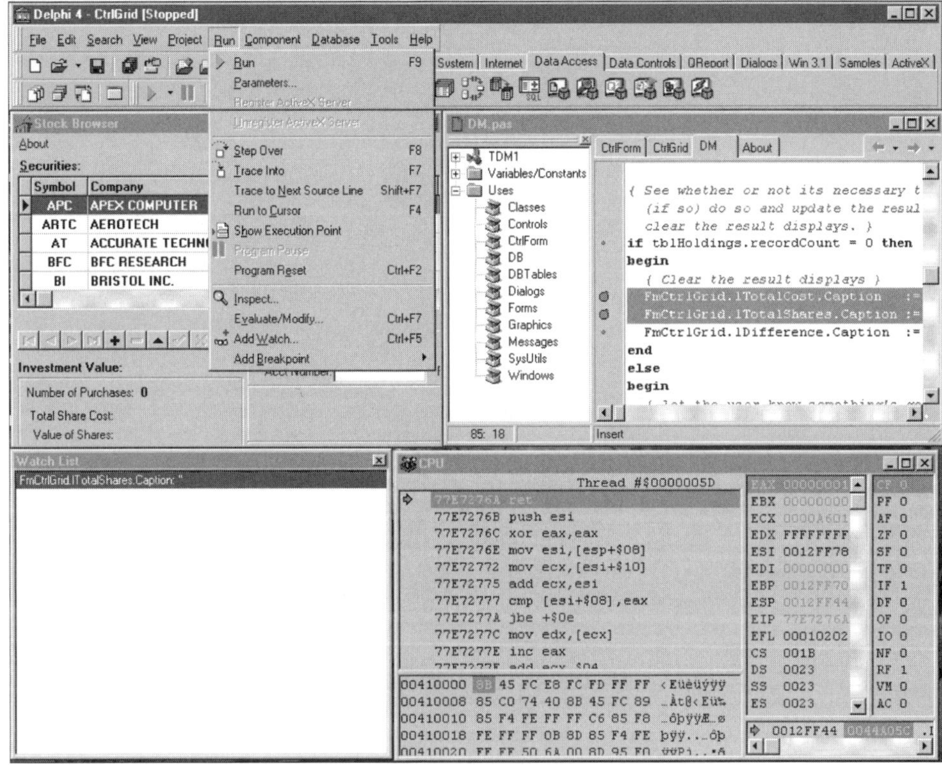

FIGURE 10.19 The Delphi integrated debugger at work

ing data sourced from data modules will be kept synchronized when changes occur. Data modules are convenient objects for business logic implementation. They can also become transactional components capable of handling ACID[1] messages when either Inprise MIDAS or Microsoft MTS is used (Figure 10.23).

The combined power of Delphi and VCL offers the best environment for client/server developers. Unlike Visual Basic, Delphi executables don't need runtime DLLs. If no OCX components are used, an entire application can be shipped with only one EXE file.

Is Delphi immune from any drawback? Unfortunately not. The weakest part of the Delphi architecture is the Borland Database Engine (BDE). The BDE is a database connectivity layer that abstracts the interface to data sources. In the in-

[1]ACID is an acronym widely used in the world of TP monitors. ACID transactions are Atomic, Consistent, Isolated, and Durable. For an explanation of these terms, refer to Chapter 16.

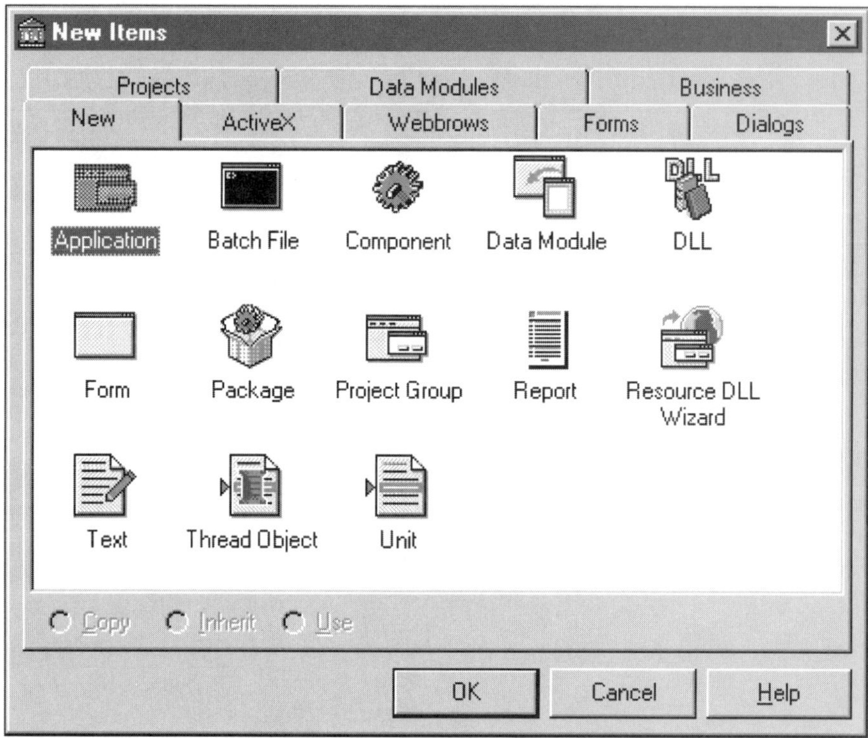

FIGURE 10.20 Available VCL items

tentions of Delphi designers the BDE allows for database independence. Data aware controls are de-coupled from physical data sources, so that developers can theoretically build applications that use Oracle, SQL Server, Sybase, and Informix interchangeably. The concept in itself is plausible; unfortunately, its implementation doesn't fulfil the expectations. The BDE becomes one more layer on top of SQL*Net/Net8 plus Delphi connectivity drivers, slowing down database fetches and update operations. If the BDE is used with Inprise SQLLinks, the response time is just acceptable. But if the BDE is used to interface to an ODBC driver, the response time worsens. While the Delphi Professional edition ships with ODBC drivers, Inprise SQLLinks is only included in the more expensive Client/Server edition.

One more disadvantage of the BDE is its deployment policy, which makes it unsuitable for shipping applications over the WEB.

Using the BDE for an Oracle-based application is justifiable only if either MIDAS or Entera are included in the architecture. This implies using the native SQLLinks drivers, which mitigate the inherent low-speed database access associated with the BDE. Mission-critical applications cannot use ODBC drivers, which

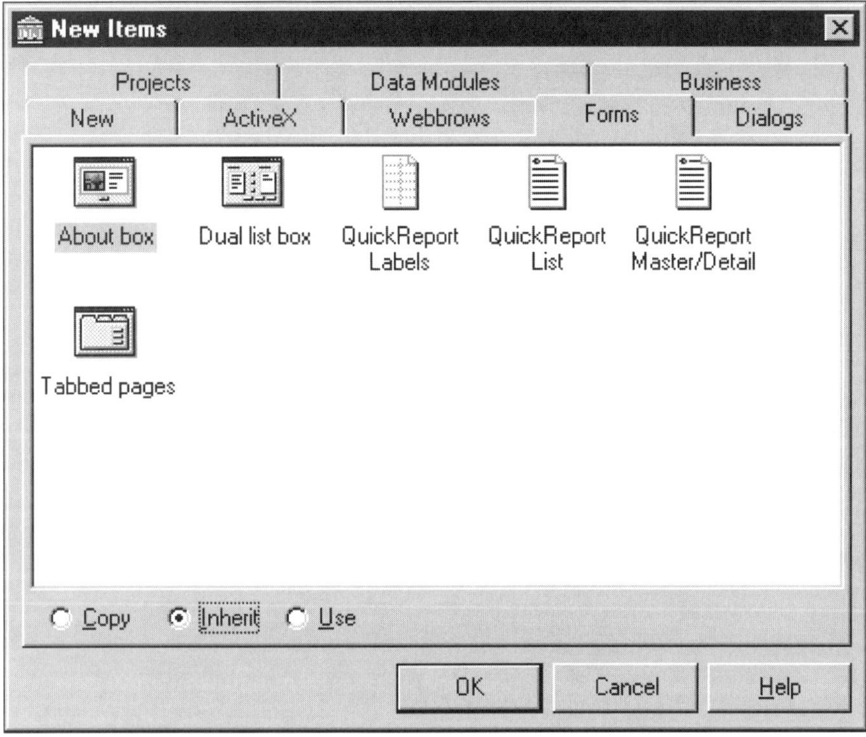

FIGURE 10.21 In Delphi, forms can be subclassed (inherited)

not only worsen the database access speed but also suffer from several compatibility problems (see the Oracle connectivity sections ahead in this chapter).

The database connectivity layer plays a crucial role in ensuring an adequate level of performance and scalability. Microsoft has finally understood the inadequacy of the ODBC model, which is in the phasing-out process, and shipped the OLEDb/ADO database access layer, which gives Visual Basic 6 an edge over the BDE for database connectivity.

Is the less than optimal performance of the Inprise BDE a sufficient reason not to choose Delphi for mission-critical, client/server applications? Luckily,

FIGURE 10.22 The Delphi component palette

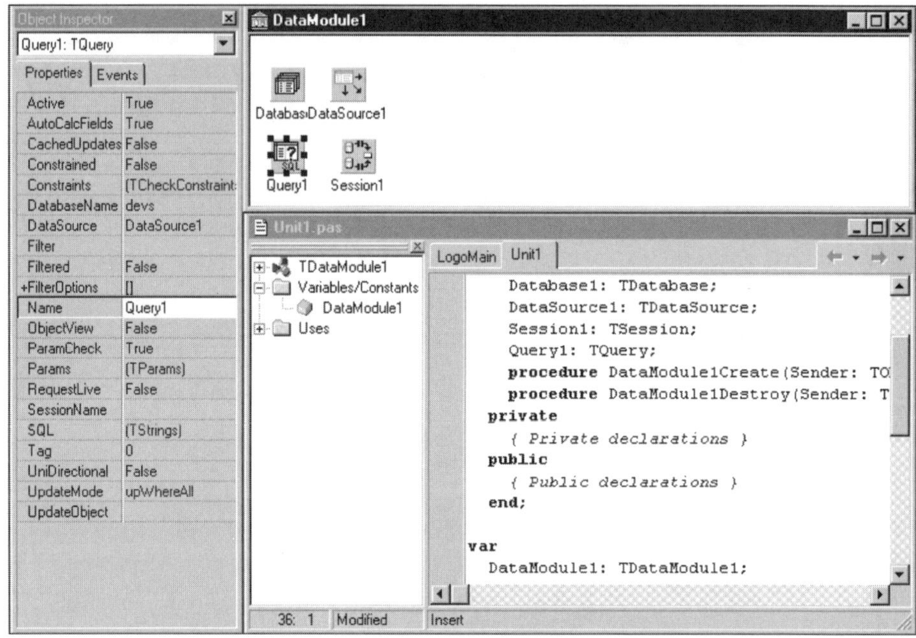

FIGURE 10.23 Delphi Data Modules are used to group data access components

third party libraries, which allow for a complete bypass of the BDE, are available. In Section 10.3.1, a valid alternative to the BDE will be presented.

If strict company policies prevent the adoption of third party libraries from small companies that cannot survive in the long run, and the adoption of Delphi automatically means adopting the BDE, then only a solution based on the low-level native SQLLinks drivers can be satisfactory. Even better, an application developed using Inprise technologies should implement middleware components, an area in which Inprise excels. Using SQLLinks implies the purchase of the client/server edition of Delphi, which appears a little expensive, especially if many developers are involved in the production of code. My personal advice is to resist the temptation of opting for the cheap solution represented by Delphi Professional edition plus ODBC drivers. I have seen several projects commit this mistake, only to be forced later to adopt SQLLinks, after having realized the absolute inadequacy of the ODBC solution. Needless to say, changing mind when the project reaches an advanced phase is much more expensive than adopting the client/server edition at the beginning.

What can be said for Delphi is also valid for C++ Builder, the other Inprise RAD jewel. C++ Builder offers a great compiler and the VCL, which makes building GUI applications in C/C++ almost as easy as in Visual Basic (Figure 10.24).

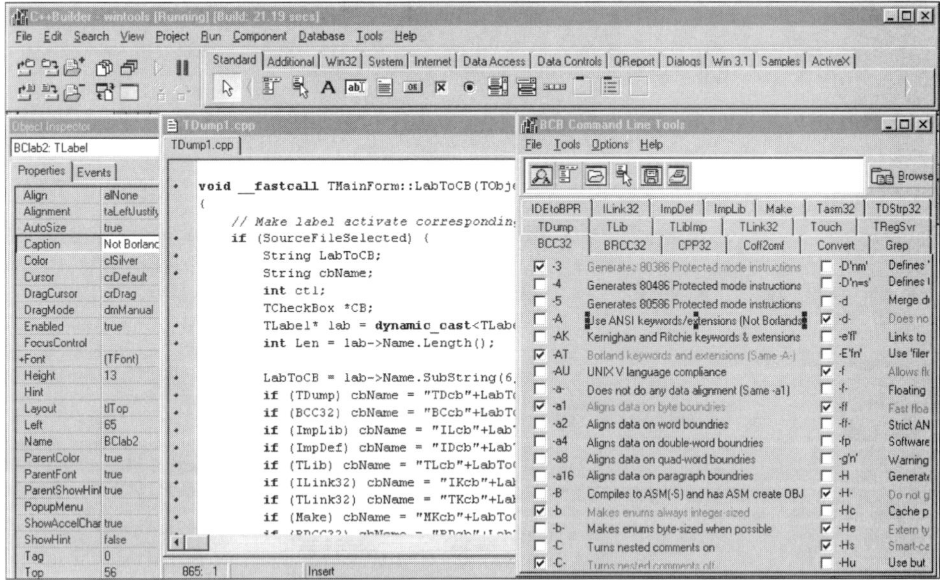

FIGURE 10.24 The VCL-based C++ Builder development environment

While Visual Basic is arguably easier to use than Delphi, the VCL model implemented in C++ Builder gives it an edge over the Microsoft MFC-based environment shipped with Visual C++. C++ Builder shares with Delphi the drawback represented by the BDE. While it is possible to avoid the use of the BDE, for instance, by using direct Oracle OCI calls from the OCIW32.DLL library shipped with SQL*Net/Net8, this solution implies the loss of all data-aware controls. The same can be said for ADO. It is possible to use Microsoft database connectivity from Delphi, but all list boxes, combo boxes, grids, etc. must be manually populated, a process that translates in a big productivity drop. As for Delphi, third party OCI-based libraries are available for C++ Builder as well. Alternatively, when the use of the BDE is unavoidable, a SQLLinks-based solution represents a reasonable compromise, especially if Inprise middleware technologies are also used.

Delphi and C++ Builder Summary Delphi offers the best compiler available for MS Windows client/server applications. C++ Builder is also one of the top compilers, and both Delphi and C++ Builder use the VCL, a very productive environment for building GUI applications. Very successful third party products dedicated to Oracle developers are coded in Delphi, demonstrating that Inprise products are well suited for Oracle based client/server applications.

While both compilers (Delphi and C++ Builder), the components provided and the GUI framework (VCL) are world-class and arguably the best in their category; the Borland Database Engine (BDE) is not extremely fast and of difficult deployment over the WEB. The lack of speed is mitigated if the BDE is used in conjunction with SQLLinks, the Inprise low-level native drivers for the back-end databases, such as Oracle, Sybase and Informix. If Inprise middleware technologies are used, the BDE cannot be avoided. When Delphi or C++ Builder is used in two-tier client/server applications, a better solution is to use third party OCI-based libraries that do not access the BDE.

The Inprise BDE with an Oracle ODBC connection is not suitable for a mission critical application. Such a configuration is suitable only for personal applications built by IT professionals who want to learn how to use Delphi in their spare time.

10.2.4 SYBASE/POWERSOFT

Powersoft, the development tool division of Sybase, offers an impressive set of tools that includes Powerbuilder, a complete C++-based IDE, Power++, a RAD tool for creation and deployment of WEB applications, a RAD Java IDE, PowerJ++, and Jaguar CTS, a transaction-oriented component that combines the features of a TP monitor with an object request broker.

The most popular tool is Powerbuilder, a real veteran in the client/server arena. Powerbuilder set the standard for enterprise-class RAD tools of the first client/server generation, reaching the peak of its success in the mid-1990s. At the beginning of the decade, Powerbuilder was really ahead of its time, offering visually accessible object-oriented features, such as the possibility of inheriting windows definitions, extending the behavior of the ancestor objects while sub-classing. One of the key reasons of Powerbuilder's success was its support for a great variety of databases, most of them accessible via native, low-level drivers. Another critical factor was the availability of the Data Window control, a very intelligent visual component that allows for an easy data gathering and displaying of information stored in remote databases. A few mouse clicks were enough to link a grid component to a database table, for a quick and easy data fetching executed at run-time. The lines of code required to populate a Data Window with data fetched from the server, and to allow users to navigate through the rows displayed in the grid, were significantly fewer than those required by any other tool available during the first client/server generation.

Unfortunately, over the years Powersoft became complacent and fell behind the competition in several key areas. Powerbuilder's approach to application development hasn't changed since its inception; the tool shows its age and its lack of innovation in areas such as the compiler and the editing environment. Nevertheless, Powerbuilder still maintains a significant share in the client/server market and is still successful among thousands of loyal PB developers who push for its adoption in new projects.

Powerbuilder is an MDI application in which code painters represent the children sheets. A code painter is an environment where developers define ap-

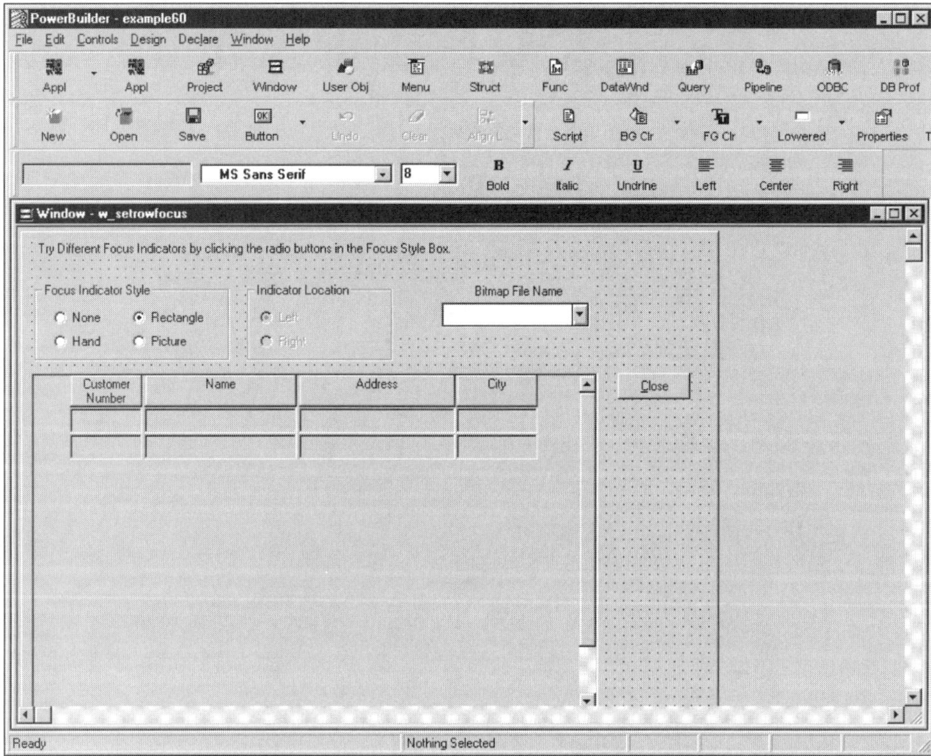

FIGURE 10.25 Powerbuilder 6.0 showing the window painter

pearance and behavior of objects and control. The window painter, for instance, is used to design windows and child objects such as list boxes, combo boxes, radio buttons, etc. (see Figure 10.25). Developers place the various objects on the window visually, by dragging and dropping controls from a toolbar into the window displayed in the window painter (Figure 10.26).

A central component in the Powerbuilder architecture is the proprietary language Powerscript, which can be succinctly defined as a hybrid between "C" and Basic. It offers powerful "C"-like constructs, such as operator post- and pre-increment or decrement (a++, a--, --a, ++a) but, like Basic, lacks support for pointers, severely limiting the possible data structures that can be used natively in Powerscript. Linked lists, for example, cannot be used directly from Powerscript. The latest Powerbuilder release includes an external component that implements linked lists by exposing a set of APIs callable from Powerscript.

All objects defined in Powerbuilder are stored in libraries, characterized by the PBL extension, in an internal format only accessible from Powerbuilder. While it is possible to export the object definitions in ASCII files, the PBL libraries

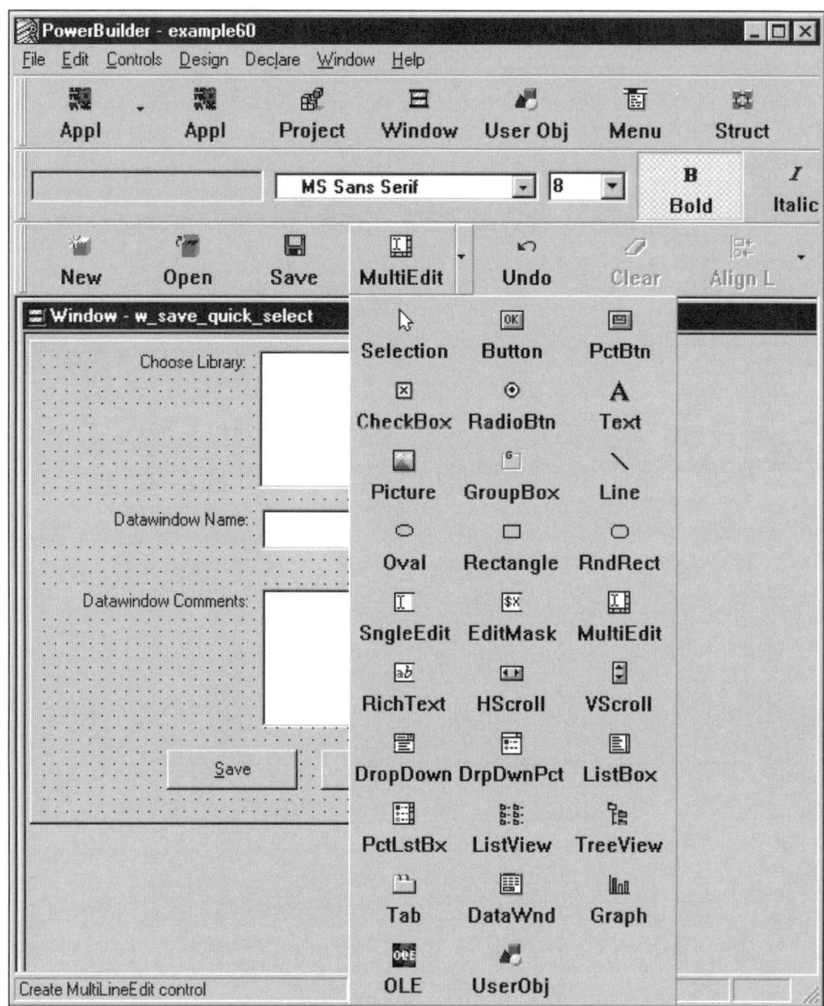

FIGURE 10.26 The window painter and the component toolbar

are needed by Powerbuilder to produce the running executable. It is also possible to convert a PBL library into a DLL-like object, characterized by the PBD extension, which can be used at run-time by a Powerbuilder-generated application.

Powerbuilder doesn't offer a two-way editing environment, where code triggered by events firing from visual controls can be accessed at a glance, as in Delphi or Visual Basic. This is one of the major drawbacks of the Powerbuilder development environment. When a developer opens the window painter and selects a window, which is loaded from a PBL library into the visual environment, in order to see the code he or she must select each control displayed on the window and open the "code painter." No visual indication exists to signal that a specific control has code associated with it. If a window contains many controls, it becomes time consuming and unproductive to select each control to check if code has been written for it. Figure 10.27 shows the Powerbuilder window painter, where the "Retrieve" command button has been selected.

In order to determine whether Powerscript code has been written for the "Retrieve" button, one should click the right-end mouse button while the control is selected. A pop-up menu appears, showing a few available options. The first option, "Script," opens the code painter, enabling an editing session for all events associated with the selected control (Figure 10.28).

Recognizing that the lack of a two-way editing environment can become a problem in large and complex projects that include several hundred windows, Powerbuilder provides a cross-reference tool that produces a well-formatted report detailing all controls appearing in all windows, each with its associated code. The cross-reference tool doesn't provide the same degree of flexibility of a two-way editing environment, but it is useful for code documentation purposes (Figure 10.29).

In a classical two-tier client/server environment, Powerbuilder still performs at its best, thanks to its most powerful feature, the data window object. The

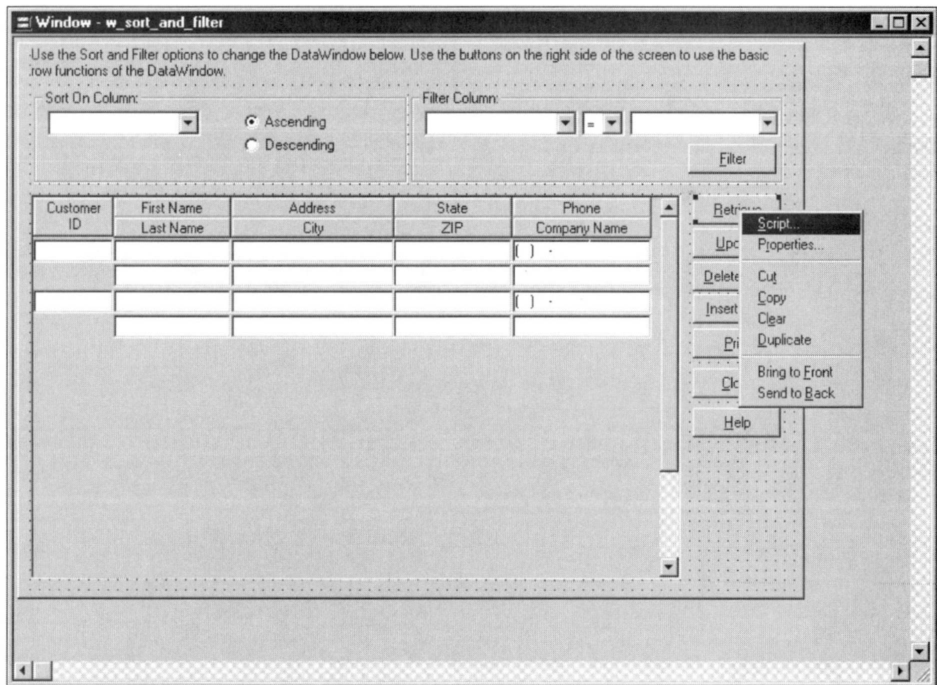

FIGURE 10.27 The "Retrieve" button has been selected in order to see the script associated with it

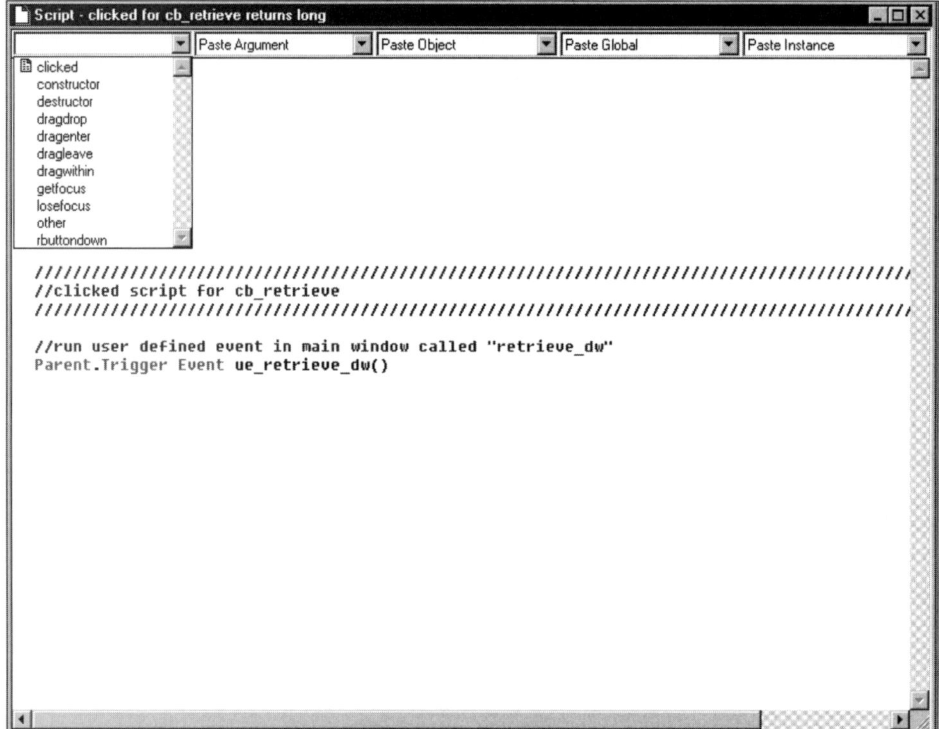

FIGURE 10.28 The code painter opened for the "Retrieve" command button

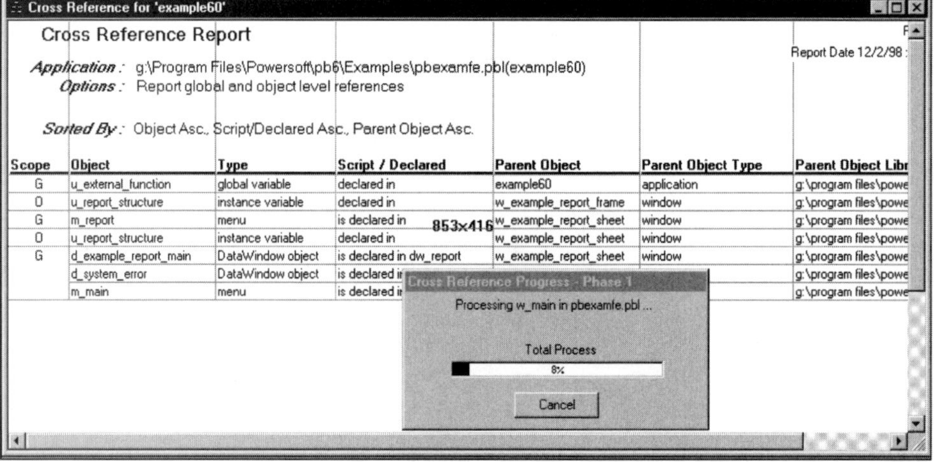

FIGURE 10.29 The cross-reference tool provided by Powerbuilder

data window painter allows users either to edit an existing data window or to create a new one from scratch. The painter assists in creating new data windows by presenting five types of possible data sources and 10 types of data window presentation styles. Developers must choose one data source and one presentation style, as shown in Figure 10.30, to access the data source dialog, which allows defining the source of the data that will be displayed in the data window.

A data window can use an "External" data source, an arbitrary structure of fields interactively defined by developers that becomes a result set. Alternatively, the result set can be obtained by submitting an SQL query or by invoking a stored procedure that returns a result set. All these operations are performed visually by developers through appropriate painters.

The rich set of presentation styles gives developers many options for displaying the fields fetched from the database in the data window canvas.

Developers create data window objects using the data window painter. Data window objects contain only the logic necessary to fetch the required data from the database. In the window painter, a data window control will be dragged on the window being built and associated with the data window object previously built in the data window painter (Figure 10.31).

The data window control exposes a set of events that fire at different stages of the lifetime of the data window, such as before and after retrieving the data

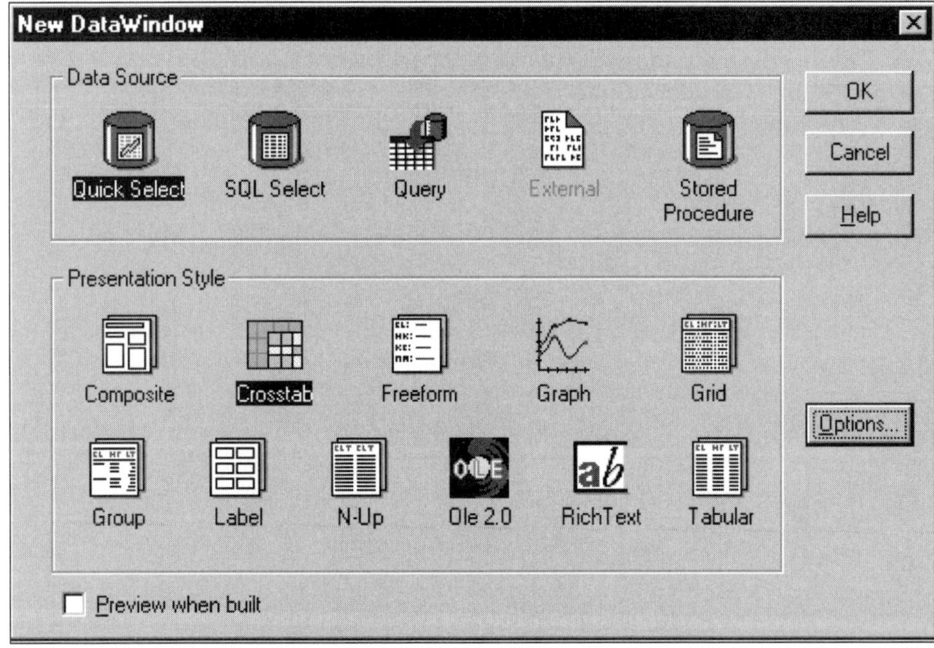

FIGURE 10.30 Data Sources and Presentation Styles for a new Data Window

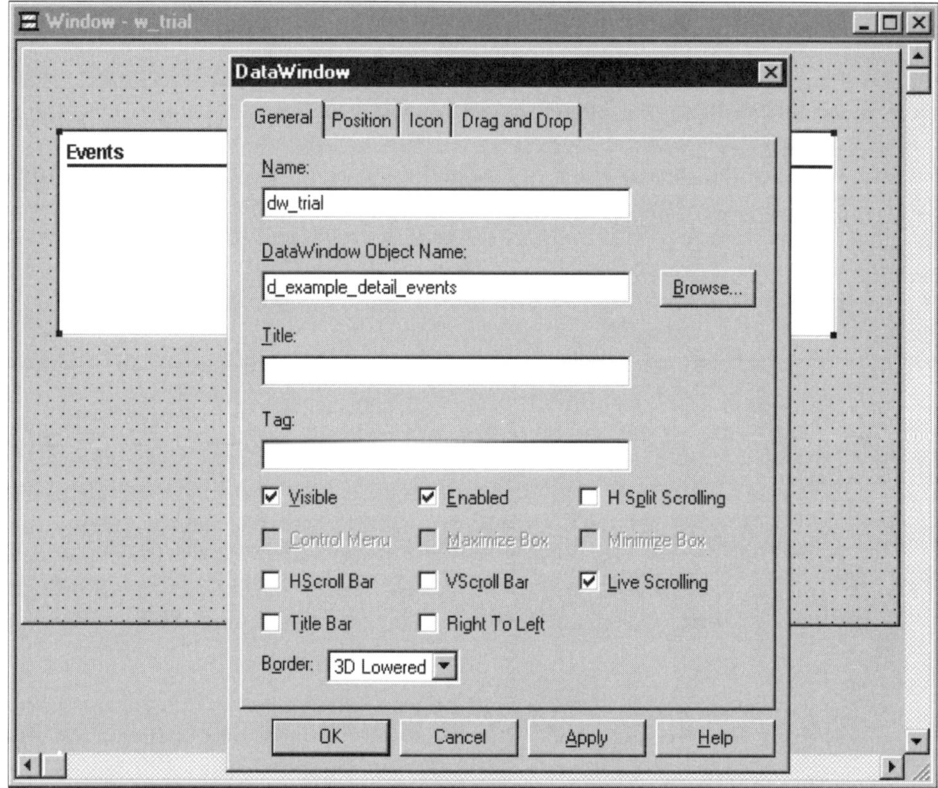

FIGURE 10.31 A Data Window control is associated with its Data Window Object

from the database, gaining and losing focus, being clicked or double-clicked, etc. Powerscript code can be written to respond to the events, ensuring fine-grained control over all aspects of data gathering and displaying.

Powerbuilder releases six ships with a much-improved debugger, a real breakthrough when compared with previous releases. The debug painter, as shown in Figure 10.32, can now start a debugging session that gives developers a great deal of control over the Powerscript code being analyzed. A toolbar groups together icons representing the most commonly used debugging commands, and the screen is divided in four sections, one dedicated to the code currently being debugged and one showing the source history, or a list of all scripts "visited" by the debugger in the current session. The third section displays the content of all variables currently in scope, and the fourth section keeps under control all variables being "watched."

User Objects are important components of the Powerbuilder environment. They are object-oriented objects which are inherited from standard PB ancestors

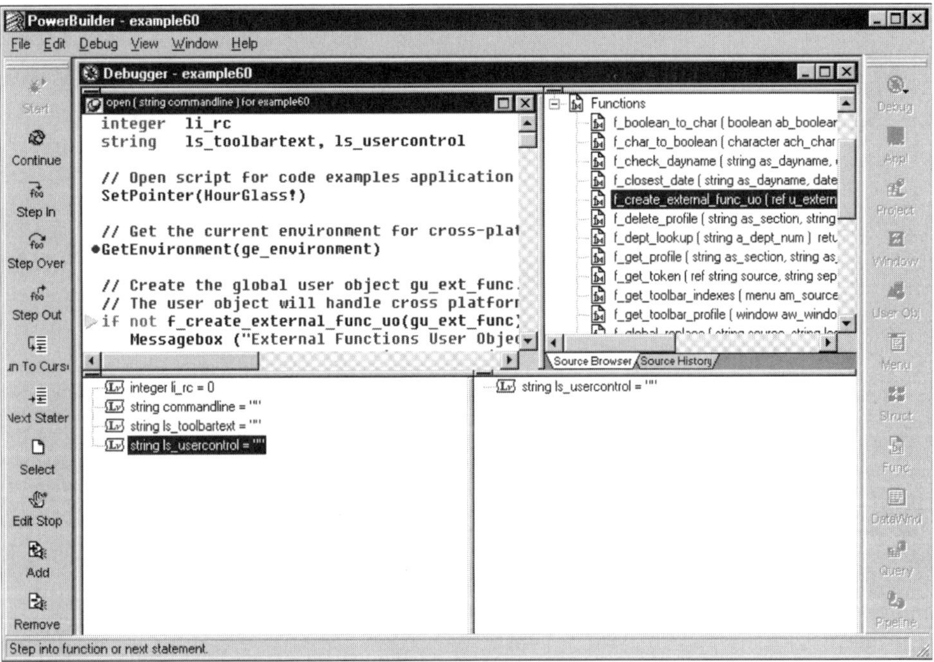

FIGURE 10.32 A debugging session in Powerbuilder

and extended with user-defined attributes and methods implemented in Powerscript.

They are perfectly suitable for business logic implementation, thanks to their ability to group together business-related functions. User Objects (Figure 10.33), can be nonvisual, essentially classes without intrinsic visual components, or visual. The nonvisual User objects can be Custom, Standard, or C++. Custom nonvisual objects are the most generic objects definable in Powerbuilder and support only two events: when they are instantiated (or *constructed*) and when they are destroyed (or *destructed*). Standard nonvisual objects are objects inherited from basic objects already existing in the Powerbuilder environment, such as *Connection* or *Transaction*. It is possible, for example, to customize a connection object by subclassing the standard connection provided by Powerbuilder and adding new functionality through Powerscript code.

It is also possible to subclass standard visual objects, such as command buttons, list boxes, combo boxes, etc., to add user-defined methods to them. In order to use visual controls of the same size in all windows comprising the application, to obtain a consistent look and feel, it is possible to create customized versions of the standard visual controls by subclassing them and setting a predetermined height and width.

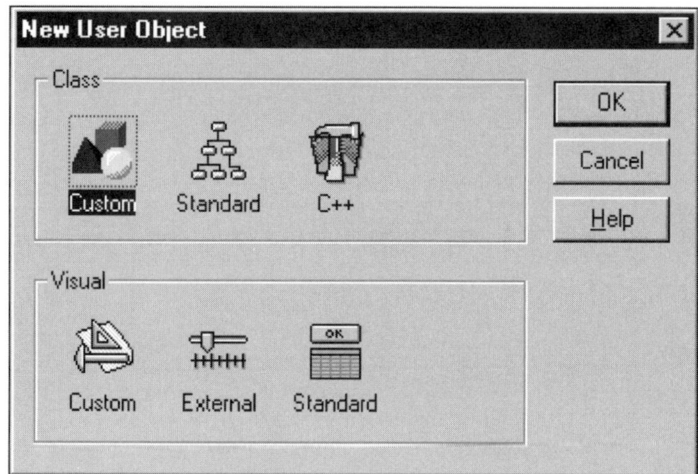

FIGURE 10.33 User Object definition

The major weakness of the Powerbuilder environment is the compiler. Traditionally, Powerbuilder has been an interpreted environment, where the final "executable" was a p-code exe. Powerbuilder release 5 introduced a "compiler," which doesn't directly compile the Powerscript code, but the "C" code produced by a translator. The translator transforms all Powerscript scripts into "C," which is compiled by the Watcom "C" compiler shipped with Powerbuilder. There are several problems with this approach, for instance, its speed, or lack of. Translating and compiling a medium-size Powerbuilder application can take between a half to one hour on a Pentium-class machine. The executable produced is one order of magnitude slower than Delphi or Visual Basic. Even more importantly, sometimes the compilation stops halfway through, and the diagnostics messages are not helpful in understanding what caused the problem. Powerbuilder release 6 did not significantly improve the compiler, which still requires the translation pass.

The old p-code executable is still supported, and its production takes a fraction of the time required to "compile," so during development, it is better to test the application running the p-code executable. The machine code executable should only be produced just before releasing the production version of the application. This works very well in theory, but what if the compilation stops and a machine code executable cannot be produced when the deadline for the release is rapidly approaching?

Many Powerbuilder developers developed the habit of producing a machine code executable every couple of days, "just to make sure that everything still works." Given the time required to do so, this translates in loss of productivity because Powerbuilder "monopolizes" the machine used for the compilation, which cannot be used for other tasks.

Both p-code and machine-code executables require run-time libraries to run. The Powerbuilder "deployment kit" for an application that uses Oracle is approximately as large as 5 MB. While no royalties must be paid for the deployment kit, the overhead required to run a Powerbuilder-created application is very high. It would be problematic to ship a PB application through the WEB, given the several megabytes of DLL that must be downloaded to make the application run.

Powerbuilder Summary In spite of a few major weaknesses, Powerbuilder is still a strong contender in the client/server arena. With release 5, Powerbuilder made its move into a three-tier client/server model, introducing "Distributed Powerbuilder," or the possibility to code middle-tier components in Powerbuilder. The release of Jaguar Component Transaction Server (CTS) further enhances the three-tier capabilities of Powerbuilder release 6, which is available not only for the Windows platform, but also for the most commonly used Unix systems (Sun, HP, IBM).

While in a Windows environment, Powerbuilder appears a little out of date because of its look and feel and the lack of a two-way editing environment, in a Unix environment Powerbuilder has a few rivals. Powersoft can legitimately claim that Powerbuilder for Unix is one of the most productive environments for building motif-based applications.

Powerbuilder suffers from a few major drawbacks that severely limit a larger adoption of it for new projects. The most serious problem is the lack of a real compiler capable of producing true machine code executable from Powerscript code. The p-code executable is extremely slow, usually one order of magnitude slower than Delphi. The machine code executable is a little faster, but still considerably slower than Delphi. Producing a machine code executable is painfully slow and error prone.

The second most limiting drawback is its lack of a two-way editing environment, which forces developers to physically access all controls in a form to check if Powerscript scripts have been written to respond to the events fired by the controls.

If Powersoft does not address these issues quickly and radically, Powerbuilder is destined to lose market shares in favor of more modern tools, such as Visual Basic and Delphi.

10.3 Connecting to Oracle

The software used to connect to Oracle plays a crucial role in determining the overall performance and scalability of a client/server application. All major providers of client RAD tools offer database connectivity software drivers. Their performance and effectiveness vary considerably, and designers and developers must be made aware of the characteristics of each database connectivity solution, to be able to implement the correct design decision.

10.3.1 NATIVE DRIVERS / THIRD PARTY OCI DRIVERS

In a traditional two-tier client/server architecture, the most efficient way to connect to an Oracle database is to use the native SQL*Net/Net8 low-level drivers provided by Oracle. SQL*Net/Net8 client must be installed on each client workstation accessing the database or, alternatively, on a shared disk of a LAN. A client application that uses the Oracle Call Interface from MS Visual C/C++, for instance, only needs to include 2 OCI DLLs, OCI.DLL and OCIW32.DLL. The OCI DLLs in turn call the SQL*Net DLLs, which must be installed and accessible from the local computer. Oracle developers on the client side don't interact with SQL*net directly, but via calls through either Pro*C or OCI. All SQL*Net primitives are internally handled by Pro*C or OCI libraries. No further software layers are needed between the application and Oracle.

RAD tools such as Delphi, Powerbuilder, and Visual Basic can connect to Oracle by using either ODBC or native drivers. The Client/Server or Enterprise editions ship with native drivers, which are obviously faster and more scalable than ODBC. The native Oracle drivers shipped by Powerbuilder are fast and efficient. Inprise provides SQLLinks, a set of native drivers for the major databases, including Oracle. While the Oracle drivers included in SQLLinks are supposedly as fast as the ones provided by Powerbuilder, the Inprise architecture includes one more layer between the data-aware controls and the native SQLLinks drivers, the BDE. While the BDE overhead is not as big as ODBC, the overall response time of a Delphi application that uses the Inprise connectivity layers is noticeably slower than for the same application using a third party OCI library.

Figure 10.34 shows the software layer chain that links a data-aware control displayed on a Delphi form to the data stored in an Oracle database. It is possible to improve the connectivity-related performance of a Delphi or C++ Builder application by using third party libraries that completely bypass the BDE. A popular product, among Delphi developers, is Direct Oracle Access (DOA), by Allround Automations, a company based in The Netherlands. DOA is a set of seven nonvisual and one visual components. The nonvisual components are:

COMPONENT NAME	TYPE	PURPOSE
ToracleSession	Nonvisual	Connects to Oracle and controls transactions
ToracleLogon	Nonvisual	Interactively accepts a connection string for ToracleSession
ToracleQuery	Nonvisual	Executes an SQL statement or PL/SQL block in a session. It is a very low-level component, used instead of data-aware components

COMPONENT NAME	TYPE	PURPOSE
ToraclePackage	Nonvisual	A convenient interface to procedures, functions, variables and constants contained in a server-defined PL/SQL package
ToracleDataset	Nonvisual	It is the source for all data-aware components. It uses ToracleQuery internally.
ToracleEvent	Nonvisual	Allows a client application to react to dbms_alert signals and dbms_pipe messages in a background execution thread.
ToracleProvider	Nonvisual	It allows Delphi and C++ Builder developers to create multi-tiered applications.
ToracleNavigator	Visual	It is used instead of TDBNavigator to support an Oracle-based Query By Example (QBE) mode.

Once installed, the DOA components appear in the Delphi or C++ Builder component toolbar, under the "Data Access" tab.

The DOA components are extremely powerful, providing the most advanced features exposed by Oracle to Delphi or C++ Builder. DOA supports not only features like database alerts or pipes, SQL Trace, Oracle optimizer choosing, and transaction savepoints but also the latest and more advanced features provided by Oracle8, such as password expiration, LOBs, and objects. In addition, the way Delphi and C++ Builder developers interact with the components is in line with Oracle "culture" and look and feel. For instance, query parameters are arbitrary names prefixed by a colon, as Pro*C developers would expect (Figure 10.36).

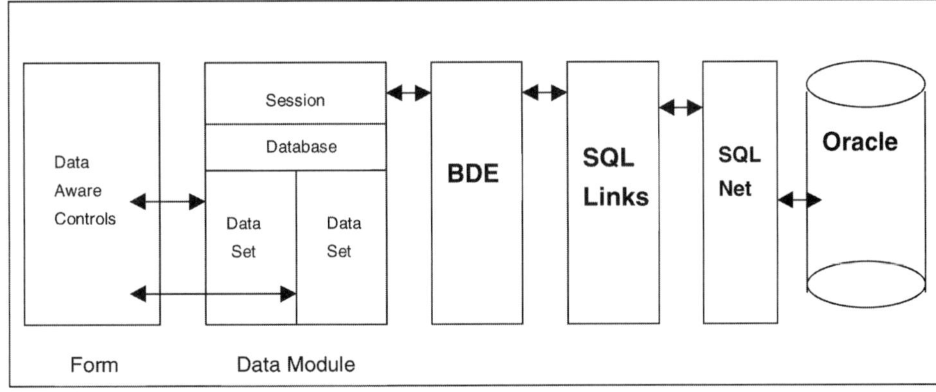

FIGURE 10.34 The BDE-based Inprise architecture

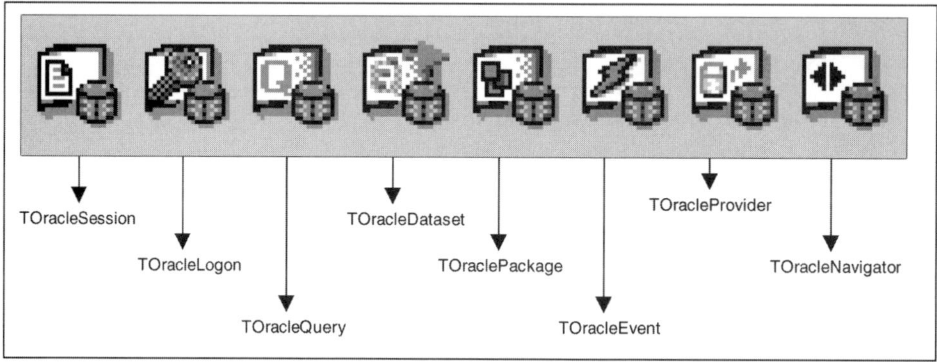

FIGURE 10.35 DOA components as they appear in the component toolbar

Using non-Oracle specific data access models, such as OleDB, forces Oracle developers to use unfamiliar metaphors, for instance, specifying query parameters with question marks, rather than colon-prefixed variable names. The DOA components are an ideal solution for developers with an established expertise in Oracle tools, who want to make a transition to client RAD tools for building client/server applications.

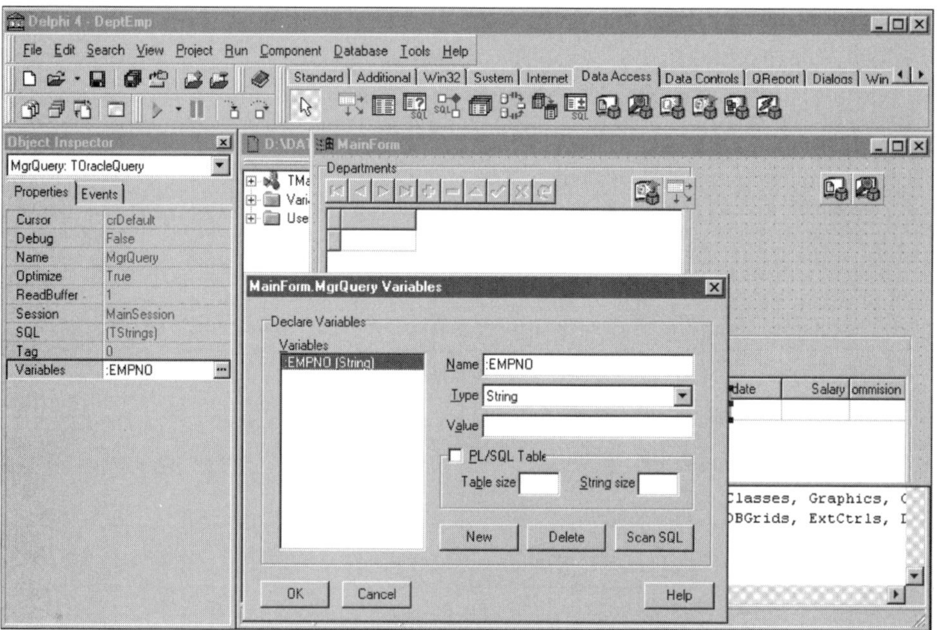

FIGURE 10.36 Bind variable definition (:EMPNO) in a TOracleQuery component

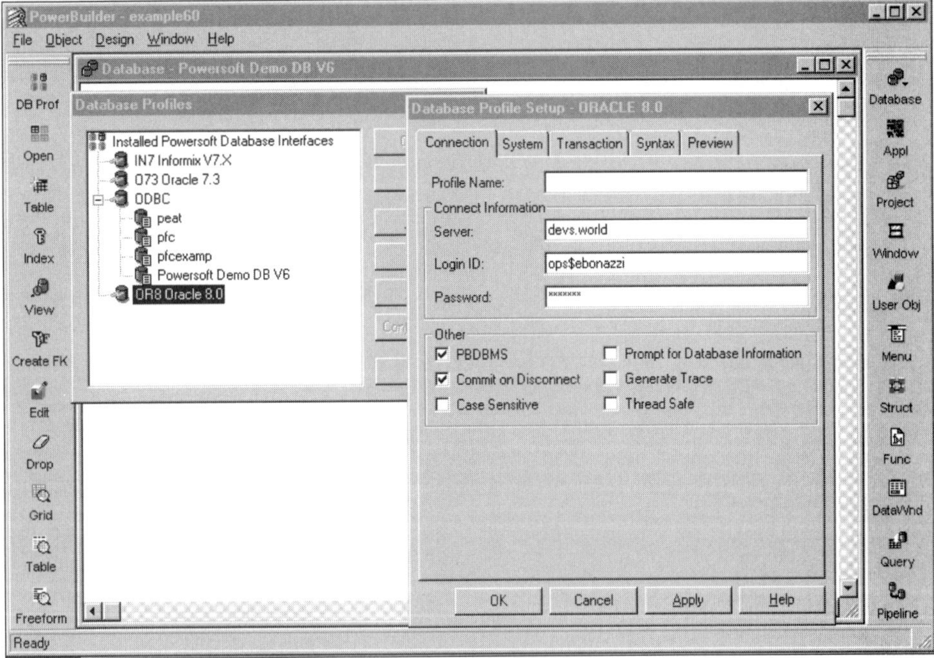

FIGURE 10.37 Oracle8 native drivers in Powerbuilder

The Client/Server edition of Powerbuilder ships with efficient native Oracle drivers. Again, the advice is to resist the temptation to buy the cheaper editions of Powerbuilder, which allow only for ODBC connectivity, to implement large mission-critical applications.

The native drivers provided by Powerbuilder Client/Server have always been one of the strongest features of the product. There is no reason to look elsewhere for good third party libraries for connectivity, as in the case of Delphi or C++ Builder.

10.3.2 MICROSOFT CONNECTIVITY

ODBC has been the dominant database connectivity paradigm endorsed by Microsoft in recent years. ODBC-based database connections have worked well when performed in small LAN environments—for example, several PCs accessing not very large databases implemented in MS SQL Server or Sybase SQL Anywhere. For both SQL Server and SQL Anywhere, ODBC is the native interface, or the fastest way to store and retrieve data. The same cannot be said for Oracle and the other major players in the database market. The ODBC model has been an unsatisfactory solution for remote back-end databases, such as Oracle, Sybase or Informix. Apart from the evident performance penalty associated with ODBC connections, the ODBC model by its very nature unifies the interface to multiple databases using a "lowest common denominator" approach, which penalizes the database engines offering the most advanced features.

The performance penalty is due to the ODBC software, which is a thick layer that seats between the application and the native drivers used by the back-end database to access the information stored in tables. When a PC running a client/server application that connects to Oracle uses ODBC, SQL*Net/Net8 must be installed as well. ODBC doesn't replace the Oracle connectivity software needed to connect to the engine. On the contrary, the ODBC driver needs SQL*Net to be able to connect to Oracle. From an Oracle perspective, the ODBC layer is absolutely superfluous, because it doesn't offer any added value for data gathering from the server to the client.

The "lowest common denominator" approach favors the use of vanilla ANSI SQL, easily portable across different vendors. While this approach works for low-end applications accessed by a limited number of users, it would be very restrictive for high-end, mission-critical applications. Accessing records physically by ROWID, using the power of the Oracle DECODE function and the user-defined functions in SQL statements, is not legal in ODBC. Using the ODBC provided "Passthrough" function, which sends the string containing the SQL statement to the database engine without attempting any interpretation, defeats the purpose of ODBC. An application that makes extensive use of "Passthrough" SQL calls is inherently nonportable, doesn't benefit from the ODBC-provided database independence, yet suffers from the performance penalty associated to the ODBC layer.

The market offers several implementations of the ODBC standard for Oracle. The Microsoft ODBC driver and Oracle ODBC driver are popular choices among client/server developers. Intersolv ODBC drivers are also quite popular. In order to point the ODBC driver to the required database, the ODBC administrator must be used. Microsoft provides the ODBC administrator, while the various ODBC drivers can be provided by third party vendors. The interface that allows users to specify the connection parameters varies between the different ODBC implementations. Figure 10.38 shows an ODBC connection to Oracle defined for the Microsoft ODBC driver for Oracle.

Figure 10.39 shows the definition of the connection parameters for an Oracle-provided ODBC driver.

Microsoft Corporation finally realized that the ODBC model for database access was unsuitable for large, mission-critical applications supporting large user populations. Furthermore, ODBC and RDO, the programmatic interface used by older releases of Visual Basic and Visual C/C++, support only relational databases. The database connectivity software of the new generation, OleDB, is DCOM based and supports nonrelational data sources, such as e-mail systems and spreadsheets, with a single and coherent model. OleDB provides many low-level primitives, which allow advanced developers to create OleDB interfaces for

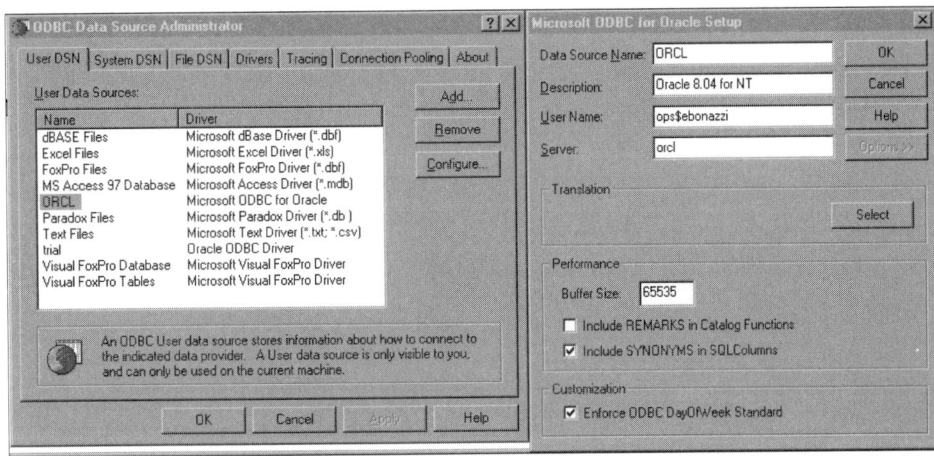

FIGURE 10.38 ODBC connection defined for the Microsoft ODBC driver for Oracle

non-standard data sources, called *OleDB providers*, or to interface to OleDB providers via *OleDB consumers*. Using OleDB directly is tedious and verbose, and in general not necessary for application developers, who do not need this level of complexity just to retrieve or store data from/to data sources. ActiveX Data Objects (ADO) relieves application developers from the low-level complexity associated with OleDB by providing a high-level interface, which is simple but powerful enough to satisfy the needs of most client/server applications.

The Microsoft Data Access Components (MDAC) release 2.0 ship with an OleDB provider for Oracle that guarantees an efficient link to Oracle databases. The initial implementation doesn't provide access to the advanced Oracle8 fea-

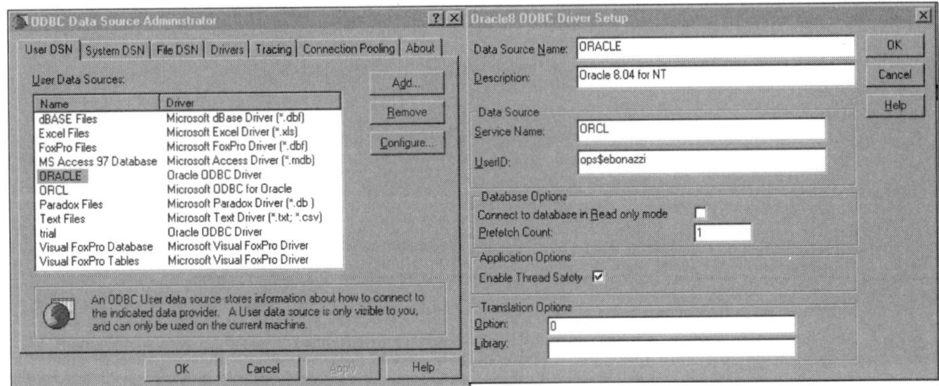

FIGURE 10.39 ODBC connection defined for the Oracle ODBC driver

tures, due to the OCI7 interface used by OleDB for Oracle. ADO 2.0, used in conjunction with OleDB for Oracle, allows for parameterized queries and stored procedures calling, and can be useful in serious client/server applications connected to an Oracle server, which make use of pure relational calls. In addition, OleDB, and consequently ADO, support connection pooling, an essential feature when middleware technologies are used to provide increased performance, scalability, and security of client/server applications.

The ADO object model is simple and effective, exposing methods and attributes required to proficiently use a remote data source. Seven objects comprise the model:

1. Connection
2. Command
3. Parameter
4. Recordset
5. Field
6. Property
7. Error

In addition, four types of collections are needed to operate with the ADO components:

1. Fields
2. Properties
3. Parameters
4. Errors

Figure 10.40 shows a pictorial representation of the ADO model. In its simplest form, ADO requires the definition of only two objects, a Connection and a Recordset. The following Visual Basic example shows a very basic ADO operation that uses a single Connection and a single Recordset.

```
Dim cn As New ADODB.Connection
Dim rs As New ADODB.Recordset

cn.Open "Provider=MSDAORA;Data Source=devs;
            UserID=scott;Password=tiger"
rs.CursorLocation=adUseServer
rs.Open "select table_name from user_tables", cn,
      adOpenForwardOnly,adLockReadOnly
rs.MoveFirst
While rs.EOF <> True
      Debug.Print rs(0).Value
```

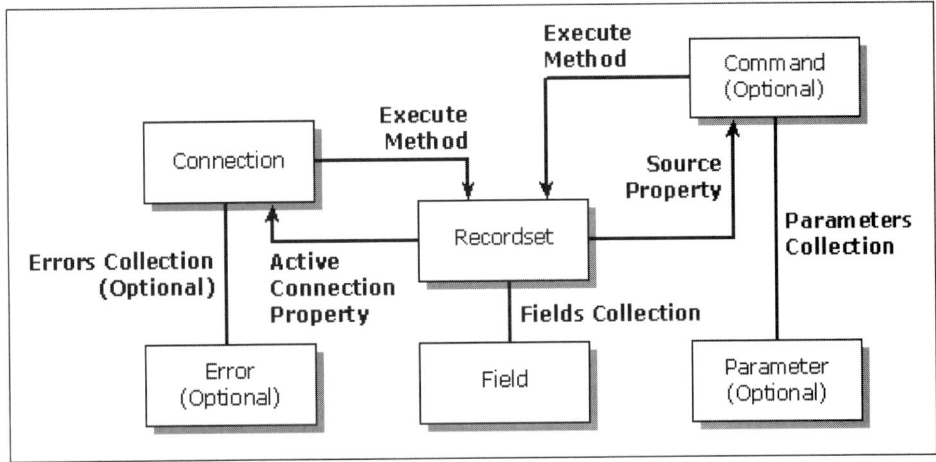

FIGURE 10.40 The ADO model[1]

```
Wend
rs.close
cn.Close
```

Commercial applications must implement robust error-handling capabilities and parameterized queries to avoid excessive parsing of SQL statements in the Shared Pool. This implies using more ADO objects, for example, Error and Command. The following Visual Basic example shows an SQL statement that uses bind variables (parameterized queries, in ADO parlance) and performs error handling.

```
Dim cn As New ADODB.Connection
Dim rs As New ADODB.Recordset
Dim er As New ADODB.Errors
Dim cm As New ADODB.Command

On Error GoTo ADOError

cn.Open "Provider=MSDAORA;Data Source=devs;
            UserID=scott;Password=tiger"
rs.CursorLocation=adUseServer
cm.ActiveConnection=cn
cm.CommandType=adCmdText
```

[1]*Source:* Joyce Chen and Richard Patterson, *ADO and SQL Server Developer's Guide*, Microsoft MSDASDK Documentation [1998].

```
cm.CommandText="select table_name from dba_tables where
                owner=?"
cm.Parameters.Append cm.CreateParameter("owner",adVarChar,
                                        adParamInput,30)
cm(0) = "SCOTT"
Set rs=cm.Execute
rs.MoveFirst
While rs.EOF <> True
      Debug.Print rs(0).Value
Wend

ADOError:
Dim LocErr As Error

Set er = cn.Errors
For Each LocErr In er
      Debug.Print LocErr.SQLState
      Debug.Print LocErr.NativeError
      Debug.Print LocErr.Description
Next
cn.Close
rs.Close
```

The example shown above demonstrates the simplicity of the ADO model. Note, however, the naïve error-handling mechanism offered by Visual Basic. A tool that claims to be object-oriented should offer a proper mechanism for exception handling, rather than a sequential jump to an instruction or label.

Visual Basic release 6 offers ADO-based data-aware controls, allowing for a simple and unified mechanism for data gathering across visual forms and nonvisual business objects, which in general are both used in commercial client/server applications.

In order to use the Microsoft OleDB provider for Oracle at its best, one should read the article by Steve Starck titled "Microsoft OleDB Provider for Oracle: Tips, Tricks, and Traps," available at the following URL address:

```
http://www.microsoft.com/msdn/news/feature/datajul98/ole4orc
l.htm
```

An alternative to OleDB for a low-level connection to Oracle is offered by Sylvain Faust Inc., which ships popular third party Oracle tools such as SQL Programmer. The product is SQL Sombrero, an ActiveX/OLE control that encapsulates Oracle Call Interface version 7 (OCI7) calls. While the programming effort required from developers is unusual in the VB environment, the overall results repay the tediousness of programmatically populating the visual controls displayed in forms with data gathered via low-level OCI calls, with a clear performance advantage.

10.3.3 INPRISE BDE/SQL LINKS

The Inprise-provided data access module implies, as seen in the preceding sections, a performance penalty due to the BDE, if compared to alternative solutions such as the Allround Automations Direct Oracle Access drivers. This doesn't mean that BDE/SQLLinks cannot be used in Delphi-based mission-critical applications. Especially if other components of the Inprise well-articulated middleware offer are used, for example, OLEEnterprise or MIDAS in the MS Windows NT environment, or Entera, in a wider enterprise Unix-based environment, BDE/SQLLinks represent the crucial piece of the Inprise puzzle.

All Delphi or C++ Builder data-aware controls use the BDE seamlessly. The BDE administrator allows for an easy configuration of Oracle data sources.

The BDE Administrator provides a user-friendly interface for configuring parameters and attributes of Oracle connections (Figure 10.41).

Note that database connections and database navigation are not performed directly from Delphi or C++ Builder, but specific, external applications must be launched to accomplish these tasks. Database Explorer, an application that exposes an icon in the Delphi or C++ Builder group, is the Inprise tool for database navigation. Visual Basic appears to be more integrated because it allows developers not to rely on the IDE to perform these tasks.

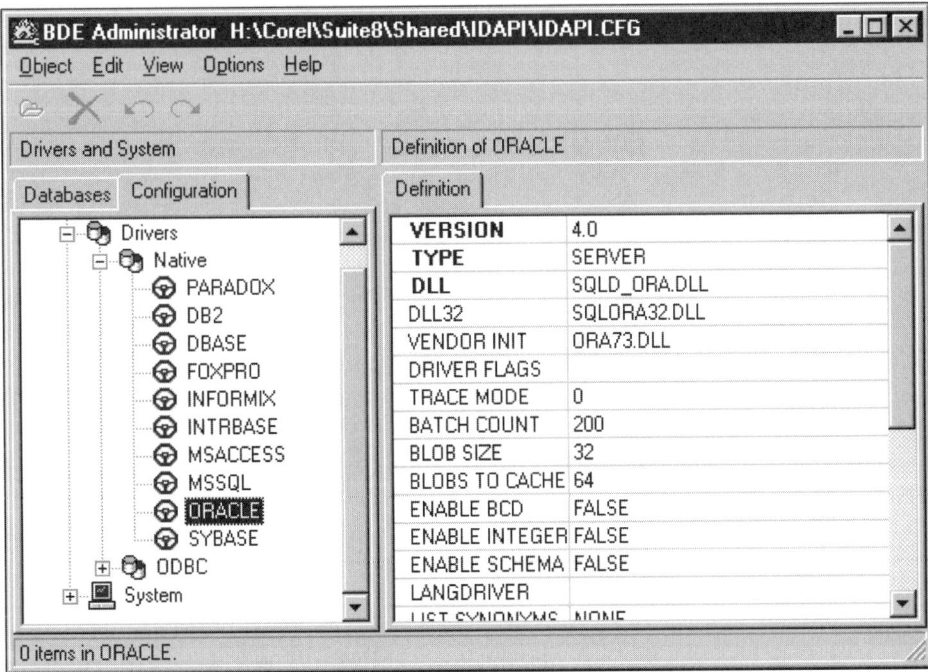

FIGURE 10.41 Oracle data source definition through the BDE

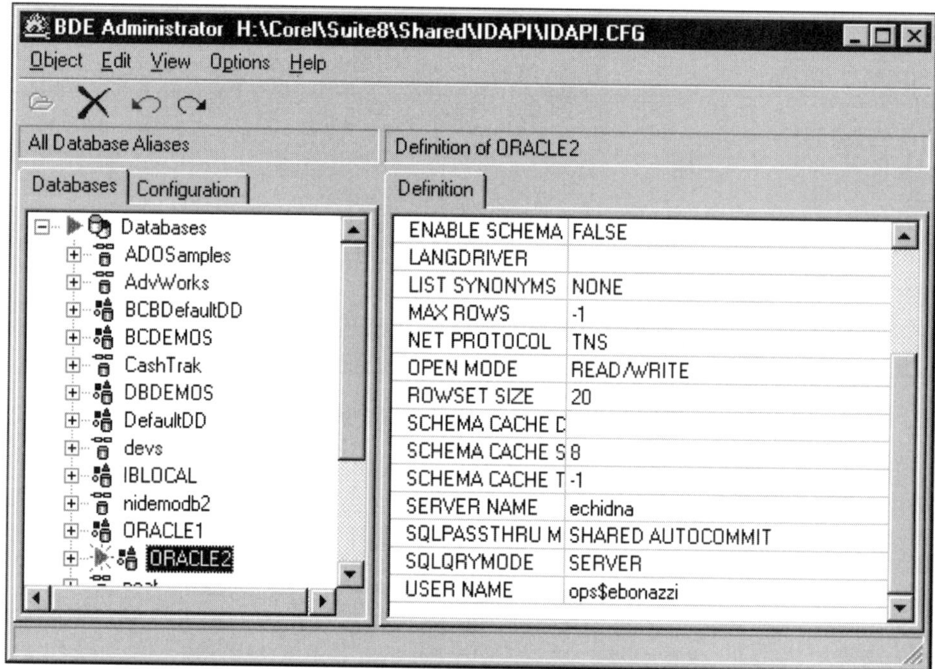

FIGURE 10.42 Oracle connection low-level parameters through the BDE

The BDE exposes a set of 195 API calls, which cover all areas of database interaction, such as cursor and session management, record locking, error handling, and data conversion. Using low-level BDE APIs guarantees efficient database interaction for non-visual data components. Developers who don't need that degree of control over database operations can use Delphi or C++ Builder data-aware controls, which can be populated by invoking standard methods in the TQuery, TTable, or TStoredProc objects. In other words, the most commonly used database operations are exposed through the Visual Component Library (VCL), so that developers can, for instance, iterate through fields in a cursor using high-level Object Pascal or C++ code. If you are familiar with the Microsoft Data Access Components, you can think that BDE calls are like OleDB APIs, while accessing data through the VCL is like using ADO.

10.3.4 ORACLE OBJECTS FOR OLE

Years before Microsoft developed OleDB, Oracle Corporation had been offering Oracle Objects for OLE (OO4O). The object model envisaged by OO4O bears many similarities to OleDB, OO4O definitely predates OleDB. The object hierarchy of OO4O is shown in Figure 10.43.

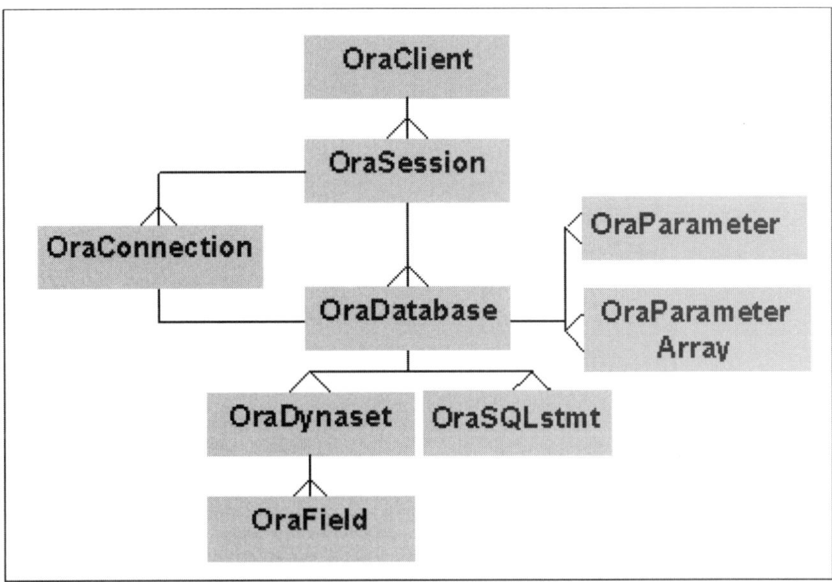

FIGURE 10.43 Oracle Objects for OLE object model

The figure shows the nine objects upon which the OO4O model is based. OO4O exposes two sets of APIs, one to be used from Visual Basic (or Visual Basic for Application) and one to used from Visual C/C++.

The architecture of OO4O is based on three major components. The most important is the *Oracle Objects Server*, which is an OLE "In Process" server that supports a collection of programmable objects for Oracle databases. Since an OLE "In Process" server has no user interface and is not embeddable, the only way to interact with it is either through the *Oracle Data Control* or through the *Oracle Objects for OLE C++ Class Library*. Any application that supports OLE Automation, such as VB or VBA (from Excel or Access), is able to use the Oracle Data Control. The OLE C++ Class Library is more low-level, yet more powerful.

Oracle Objects for OLE interfaces directly to OCI, providing optimal performance for Oracle database access. Before Microsoft released OleDB for Oracle, OO4O was one of the few high-performance alternatives to ODBC for developers using Microsoft RAD tools to access Oracle databases.

The Oracle Data Control exposes few but powerful APIs, very easy to use from Visual Basic. The following example shows a simple Excel macro that populates a spreadsheet getting the data from an Oracle instance. The table accessed by the macro is the CUSTOMER table in the OPS$EBONAZZI schema. The table contains two fields, CUSTOMER_NAME, defined as VARCHAR, and CUSTOMER_ID, defined as NUMBER. The Excel macro fetches the first 30 records returned by Oracle and displays the customer data in the first two columns of the spreadsheet.

```
Sub CustomerData()
  'Declare OO4O variables
  Dim OraSession As Object
  Dim OraDatabase As Object
  Dim CustDynaset As Object

  Dim flds() As Object
  Dim fldcount As Integer

   Set OraSession =
   CreateObject("OracleInProcServer.XOraSession")
     Set OraDatabase = OraSession.OpenDatabase("DEVS",
     "ops$ebonazzi/supersecret", 0&)
   Set CustDynaset = OraDatabase.CreateDynaset("select *
   from customer", 0&)

   Range("A1:B30").Select
   Selection.ClearContents

    'Declare and create an object for each column.
    'This is done to improve efficiency
    fldcount = CustDynaset.Fields.Count
    ReDim flds(0 To fldcount - 1)
    For Colnum = 0 To fldcount - 1
     Set flds(Colnum) = CustDynaset.Fields(Colnum)
    Next

    'Column Headings in the first row
    For Colnum = 0 To CustDynaset.Fields.Count - 1
     ActiveSheet.Cells(1, Colnum + 1) = flds(Colnum).Name
    Next

    'Display the fetched data in the spreadsheet, A1 to B30
    For Rownum = 2 To CustDynaset.RecordCount + 1
     For Colnum = 0 To fldcount - 1
      ActiveSheet.Cells(Rownum, Colnum + 1) = flds
      (Colnum).Value
     Next
     CustDynaset.DbMoveNext
    Next
   ' Move the cursor in A1
   Range("A1:A1").Select
End Sub
```

```
Sub EraseData()
   ' Clear cell content from column A1 to column B30
    Range("A1:B30").Select
    Selection.ClearContents
   ' Move the cursor in A1
    Range("A1:A1").Select
End Sub
```

The two macros CustomerData() and EraseData() can be triggered by two command buttons displayed in an area of the spreadsheet that won't be populated with data gathered from Oracle.

OO4O supports stored procedure calling and bind variables. The next Visual Basic example shows the APIs used to bind a query parameter for a query that will be parsed only once in the shared pool, but executed repeatedly by the client application.

```
Option Explicit
Global OraDatabase As Object

Global Const Connect$ = "OPS$EBONAZZI/SUPERSECRET"
Global Const DatabaseName$ = "DEVS"
Global Const StockQuery$ = "select * from stock where
                        stock_id = :stock_id"
'StockData is an Oracle Data Control dragged in a VB form.
'Refreshing the data control without setting the
'Recordsource creates the underlying Session
'and Database.
StockData.Connect = Connect$
StockData.DatabaseName = DatabaseName$
StockData.Refresh ' Creates Session and Database objects
Set OraDatabase = StockData.Database
' Create the query parameter
OraDatabase.Parameters.Add "stock_id", 0, 1
' Set a value for the parameter
OraDatabase.Parameters("stock_id").Value = 25

StockData.RecordSource = StockQuery$
StockData.Refresh ' Execute the query
```

From the perspective of Visual Basic developers, Oracle Objects for OLE lost part of its appeal once Microsoft released OleDB for Oracle, because all data aware controls in Visual Basic release 6 can be bound to Oracle data source using Microsoft standard components. Given the performance advantage of OO4O, its simplicity and elegance, third party less popular development environments that support OLE automation, such as CA Realizer, can still make good use of it.

10.4 The Software Engineering Focus

Performance and scalability of a client-server application largely depend on the good design of the server components, which include network traffic minimization, adequate resource balancing between client and server, and efficient low-level connectivity.

The development tool used on the client usually plays a minimal role in determining the success of an application. It is much more important, in the overall economy of a mission-critical application, which transport is used to connect to Oracle, rather than which client tool. Inprise Delphi offers the best compiler available, in terms of speed, optimizations and error reporting. If Delphi were used to fetch data from Oracle using an ODBC connection, the Delphi's advantage would be jeopardized by the inefficiency and poor scalability of the ODBC link.

Visual Basic, which offers a less sophisticated compiler, would be a better choice if used with low-level drivers, such as Embarcadero SQL-Sombrero or OleDB for Oracle. The overall application performance would be superior, even if the client code were compiled using an inferior compiler.

The point is that in large, mission-critical applications, the decisive factor is the server, not the client. Scalability and performance are determined by sound design decisions that affect the server implementation. The second most important aspect is the vehicle used to connect to Oracle. The most brilliant tool would underperform if used in conjunction with either ODBC or the MS Jet Engine, which sends only to the engine strings containing literal SQL, instead of SQL statements with select-list items and bind variables. Conversely, an interpreted and inherently slow environment, such as Oracle Developer, would perform better because it uses SQL*Net natively.

The client application program that incorporates the presentation logic is generally irrelevant in determining the overall application performance. Powerbuilder is the tool that produces the slowest code among the RAD tools considered above. If the client-server application that uses Powerbuilder as front-end is well designed and adequately sized, with periodical tuning of both engine parameters and SQL statements, and the client program doesn't include business logic, but strictly presentation services, would it be cost effective switching to Delphi to improve its speed?

Delphi and C++ Builder produce the fastest code, but with all optimizations turned on, in the scenario presented above, they would probably increase the client response time by a negligible 5–10%, which doesn't justify the porting effort.

The importance of the client development tool is even further minimized when the application uses middleware services. The focus shifts to the middle tier, where architects and designers concentrate their efforts to obtain the wanted characteristics of scalability, security, robustness, and performance.

I recently worked in a project that was initially conceived at the beginning of the nineties. The core application is a workflow management system used to manage the activities of the workforce of a major corporation. The application has more than 5,000 registered users and approximately 1,800 connected and active users during peak hours. The back-end is a DCE environment, which uses Transarc Encina as the TP monitor on a high-end 8-processor Unix server, accessed by four smaller Unix machines that off-load the communication traffic between the server and the many clients that are constantly connected.

Being conceived at the beginning of the nineties, one of the application requirements stated that the supported client configuration was an Intel 386 PC equipped with 4 megabytes of RAM. This prerequisite excluded the use of Encina on the client, given its incompatible minimal requirements. Other requirements concerned the "sociability" of the application, or its capability of being used together with other MS Office applications.

The presentation layer was implemented in Visual Basic release 3.0, the client communication layer was implemented using Dynamic Link Libraries written in Borland C++ release 4.0. The application has been ported to MS Windows NT Workstation 4.0, which is currently used by the field workforce, without changing one line of code.

After a successful assessment for year 2000 compliance, the application, considered mission critical for the corporation's business, received the official green light for its usage well beyond the beginning of the new century. The client program is still a 16 bit VB 3.0 p-code executable that requires the VBRUN300.DLL library, plus the other VBX components, but runs without problems in an NT 4.0 environment. Its GUI look and feel shows its age and its pre-Windows 95 conception, yet the workforce doesn't seem to care too much for its esthetic drawbacks.

The real strength of the application is its server implementation, which proficiently uses a complex DCE environment and a robust and scalable TP monitor (Transarc Encina), to support several hundreds of users concurrently connected. The communication layer is another important factor that explains the success of this application. It is extremely lean and light, TCP-based, with little but essential functionality, yet very effective. Each client connects to one of the four COMM computers, and the TP monitor does the real "donkey work" of satisfying client requests across the large SMP computer that hosts the Oracle database. While the client shows its age, a decision has been made not to re-write or port the application to more recent releases of Visual Basic. The back-end will remain unchanged and the next step for the client application will probably be a migration to a WEB browser-based solution.

This example not only shows the importance of the server side in client/server applications, but also demonstrates that large corporations are more interested in using an application for the longest possible time, to recover the initial costs, rather than continuously update the front-end GUI with more fashionable and flamboyant animated gadgets shipped with the latest release of the RAD tool of choice.

Summary

This chapter discussed the development of client/server applications accessing Oracle databases from the perspective of the client. While standard Oracle technologies, such as Pro*C and OCI, can be proficiently used also in a client environment, the industry trend favors the adoption of GUI-based RAD tools for the implementation of the presentation services. A few major contenders were assessed:

- Oracle Developer
- Delphi — C++ Builder
- Visual Basic — Visual C++
- Powerbuilder

The assessment focused on scalability and suitability for mission-critical applications rather than client-only features such as number of components shipped with the product or how ergonomic and easy-to-use is each IDE. To ensure rapid response time when the back-end database is interrogated, the software used for connectivity plays a crucial role. The chapter considered the Oracle connectivity solutions offered by the RAD tool vendors, such as Microsoft OleDB or Inprise SQLLinks, and third party products, such as Allround Automations DAO or Sylvain Faust Inc.'s SQL Sombrero, indicating strengths and weaknesses of each proposed solution.

The final part of the chapter stressed the importance of the server side for overall scalability and performance of client/server applications. Using the most efficient client RAD tool is not enough to ensure performance, if the connectivity to Oracle is not adequate and the server implementation wasn't designed with performance and scalability in mind.

Chapter 11

ORACLE TOOLS: PRO*C/C++

In this chapter we start a review of the most commonly used Oracle tools to interact with the database. Pro*C deserves to be mentioned first because, since the beginning of the Oracle success story, it has been the principal vehicle for storing and retrieving data to/from the database. The following chapters will also consider the Oracle Call Interface (OCI) and PL/SQL.

Pro*C remains the king among the Oracle tools. The emerging serious contender for the crown is probably Java, but the latter has still to demonstrate its ability to keep the promises made since its first appearance, while Pro*C is definitely the most popular data access tool used today, especially in mission critical applications.

The Pro*C manual shipped with Oracle release 8.0x is reasonably thick—more than 700 pages, including the index—and all serious Oracle developers should be familiar with it. This chapter is definitely neither a surrogate of the manual nor a crash course in Pro*C. The purpose of the chapter is to highlight a few crucial points for a correct use of Pro*C in order to achieve performance, scalability, and simplified maintenance of the source code. A few key points introduced in Chapter 7—How to Structure the Server Code—will be further developed in this chapter, which will use many code examples to better illustrate the concepts being discussed.

The initial part of the chapter will focus on the use of Pro*C in a procedural environment. Such topics as error handling, host array processing and integration with PL/SQL will be covered in great detail. The focus will shift further ahead in the chapter, to session contexts, multi-thread programming, and piecewise fetch and insertion of binary large objects (BLOBs). The handling of dynamic SQL will also receive an adequate coverage, together with Oracle OCI interoperability.

The last part of the chapter will consider the new Oracle 8 extensions, introduced to allow developers to handle objects types in Pro*C. In particular, the Oracle Type Translator (OTT), the object cache, and the navigational and associative interfaces for object fetching and manipulation will be discussed and several examples will be provided.

The source code provided has been tested under Sun Solaris 2.6 and MS Windows NT 4.0 (Service Pack 4). To maintain close compatibility between the two environments, all NT examples are console applications. This chapter focuses on Pro*C issues, not on GUI programming. Endowing the Pro*C examples with a graphical vest increases only by an order of magnitude the number of required lines of code, giving no added value to the focus of the discussion, which is Pro*C. Furthermore, given the profound difference between Motif and Windows, the examples would necessarily be very different in the two environments, increasing complexity and decreasing readability. The GUI bigots will have to bear the character-based examples, sacrificing esthetical elegance for simplicity.

11.1 Error Handling in Pro*C

Error handling is a crucial element of a well-structured commercial application. While interacting with Oracle, developers "lose control" of what's happening when an embedded SQL statement is submitted to the engine. Oracle receives the statement and a number of possible outcomes can occur:

- The statement is wrong and the parsing step fails.
- The statement is correct; all rows interested by the DML statement are updated successfully.
- The statement is correct but not all rows included in the selection criterion could be updated.
- The statement is syntactically correct, but no rows satisfy the selection criteria.
- The statement is correct, but the manipulation of the data provokes referential integrity violations.
- Oracle is not able to process any statement due to system-related causes such as running in restricted session mode, being in the shut down phase, or not running at all, or the maximum number of processes allowed to connect to Oracle has been reached.
- The statement is syntactically correct and doesn't cause referential integrity violations, but the data cannot be inserted or updated for space related problems.

The list above is definitely not exhaustive, but it includes the most common causes for SQL statement failures. To programmatically process all errors coming from the interaction with the engine, Oracle provides a few mechanisms:

- SQLCODE
- SQLSTATE
- SQLCA

SQLCODE and SQLSTATE are status variables, that is, the Oracle success status is returned in the form of a code stored in one of the two status variables. SQLCA allows for a more detailed error investigation because it is a structure that contains several fields holding precious information about the most recent interaction with the Oracle engine.

SQLCODE contains only error codes (not warnings) and has been deprecated by the ANSI SQL 92 committee. SQLSTATE is a 5-byte array that contains a 2-byte class code field followed by a 3-byte subclass code. The class code determines the broad area of the error or warning code, while the subclass field stores the specific error or warning code. Examples of class codes are:

CLASS CODE	ERROR OR WARNING CONDITION
00	Successful Completion
01	Warning
22	Data Exception
40	Transaction Rollback

Examples of subclass codes are:

CLASS + SUBCLASS CODE	CONDITION
22012	Division by Zero
22008	Datetime Field Overflow
40002	Integrity Constraint Violation
40003	Statement Completion unknown

SQLSTATE holds much more information than SQLCODE and should be used in its preference if compatibility with databases other than Oracle is a requirement.

In an Oracle native environment the SQLCA structure is the best option. The MODE precompiler option determines the use of the error handling. Setting MODE to ANSI forces a developer to declare either SQLCODE or SQLSTATE. Failing to do so provokes a precompiler error. Declaring an SQLCA structure is optional, and it does not conflict with the ANSI standard status variables. When MODE is set to ORACLE, an SQLCA structure must be defined. If SQLCODE is also defined in the same program Oracle does not make use of it. Since the SQLCA structure is the Oracle preferred way to implement error handling, we focus on this method in the remainder of this section.

The SQLCA structure contains several fields, but most are either reserved for future use or obsolete. The fields that are currently used by Oracle and useful for error handling are:

- sqlcode
- sqlerrm.sqlerrml
- sqlerrm.sqlerrmc
- sqlerrd[2]
- sqlerrd[4]
- sqlwarn[0] to sqlwarn[5]

The sqlcode field stores the Oracle error code, which is a negative number. The only exception to this rule is the "no data found" code, which is either +100 when the precompiler mode is set to ANSI or +1403 when the precompiler mode is set to Oracle.

The embedded structure sqlerrm contains two fields, sqlerrml and sqlerrmc. The first is an integer that specifies the length in bytes of the error text contained in sqlerrmc. The latter can only store up to 70 characters, which is enough for most Oracle error messages.

Sometimes an error message is recursively built by various Oracle software layers, each appending an error string to the error message. In this case, the resulting error message could well exceed 70 characters, and developers have to resort to the sqlglm function to retrieve the entire message. sqlglm accepts three parameters:

```
sqlglm (     char * text_buffer,
             size_t  *buffer_size,
             size_t *message_length);
```

text_buffer is where Oracle stores the blank-padded error message, buffer_size is the length of the text buffer in bytes, and message_length specifies how many characters of the Oracle error message must be stored in the text buffer. The maximum length of an Oracle error message is 512 bytes.

An important field of the SQLCA structure is sqlerr[2], that is, the third position of the sqlerrd array. When an SQL operation affects host arrays, the number of rows successfully processed by the statement is stored in that position of the sqlerrd array. Let us imagine that we are inserting 20 rows in only one SQL operation. If the 17th row provokes a referential integrity violation, the number stored in sqlerrd[2] is 16. This allows the developer to easily identify the row that caused the SQL statement to fail.

The fourth position of the sqlerrd array holds an offset that indicates the character position at which a parse error begins. The parse error refers to the most recently executed SQL statement. Warning messages coming from Oracle are stored in the sqlwarn array. The first cell of the array is set to "W" if a warning occurred. Other useful flags are:

- sqlwarn[1] This flag is set to "W" if a character output variable was truncated in the interaction with Oracle.
- sqlwarn[3] This flag is set to "W" if the number of columns in a query select list does not match the number of host variables provided to the SQL statement.
- sqlwarn[4] This flag is set when every row in a table is processed by an update or delete statement without a where clause.
- sqlwarn[5] This flag is set when the PL/SQL command to create a procedure, a function or a package failed to compile.

Pro*C provides an automated error detection mechanism through the use of the keyword WHENEVER. The syntax is explained below.

```
EXEC SQL WHENEVER <condition> <action>;
```

The WHENEVER keyword provokes the emission of C code by the precompiler that forces the program to check error or warning conditions after the execution of all SQL statements.

The possible conditions managed by WHENEVER are SQLERROR, SQLWARNING, and NOT FOUND. Among the possible actions that a program can take following the occurrence of a condition, Pro*C provides DO, DO BREAK, CONTINUE, DO CONTINUE, GOTO, and STOP.

While the SQLERROR and SQLWARNING conditions can invoke routines or influence the flow of the program, NOT FOUND is useful to exit from loops that, for example, are fetching rows from the database. The statement

```
EXEC SQL WHENEVER SQLERROR goto error_occurred;
```

provokes the emission of "C" code that checks the Oracle success status after each executed statement and in case of error jumps to the error_occurred label.

The following example shows the use of NOT FOUND to exit from an endless loop that fetches rows into a host array:

```
...
EXEC SQL WHENEVER NOT FOUND GOTO end_fetch;
for(; ;)
{
      EXEC SQL FETCH tbl_nam_crsr into :szTableName;
      ...
}
end_fetch:
return(success);
```

It is now time to take a close look at what happens when the precompiler expands the embedded SQL contained in a Pro*C program into "C" calls to the SQLLIB library. We will use a very simple example, a select count that computes the number of all tables owned by the current schema. Initially we won't be using the WHENEVER construct and we will examine the result of the precompilation. Subsequently, we will modify our Pro*C program to insert a couple of WHENEVER statements to observe the impact of those statements on the automatically produced "C" code. The program is shown below.

```
EXEC SQL INCLUDE SQLCA;
#include "Sewo.h"
#include "Example.h"

GLOBAL int nDBSelectTblCount (int * nTblCnt )
{

        EXEC SQL SELECT
            count(*)
        INTO :nTblCnt
        FROM
            USER_TABLES;
        if(sqlca.sqlcode != 0)
            return(1);
        else
            return( 0 );
}
```

The "C" listing produced by the precompilation operated by Pro*C follows.

```
...
#include "Sewo.h"
#include "Example.h"

GLOBAL int nDBSelectTblCount (int * nTblCnt )
{
```

```
   /* EXEC SQL SELECT
      count(*)
   INTO :nTblCnt
   FROM
       USER_TABLES; */
{
   struct sqlexd sqlstm;

   sqlstm.sqlvsn = 10;
   sqlstm.arrsiz = 1;
   sqlstm.sqladtp = &sqladt;
   sqlstm.sqltdsp = &sqltds;
   sqlstm.stmt= "select count(*)into :b0 from USER_TABLES ";
   sqlstm.iters = (unsigned long )1;
   sqlstm.offset = (unsigned long )5;
   sqlstm.selerr = (unsigned short)1;
   sqlstm.cud = sqlcud0;
   sqlstm.sqlest = (unsigned char  *)&sqlca;
   sqlstm.sqlety = (unsigned short)0;
   sqlstm.sqhstv[0] = (         void  *)nTblCnt;
   sqlstm.sqhstl[0] = (unsigned long )4;
   sqlstm.sqhsts[0] = (         long )0;
   sqlstm.sqindv[0] = (         void  *)0;
   sqlstm.sqinds[0] = (         long )0;
   sqlstm.sqharm[0] = (unsigned long )0;
   sqlstm.sqadto[0] = (unsigned short )0;
   sqlstm.sqtdso[0] = (unsigned short )0;
   sqlstm.sqphsv = sqlstm.sqhstv;
   sqlstm.sqphsl = sqlstm.sqhstl;
   sqlstm.sqphss = sqlstm.sqhsts;
   sqlstm.sqpind = sqlstm.sqindv;
   sqlstm.sqpins = sqlstm.sqinds;
   sqlstm.sqparm = sqlstm.sqharm;
   sqlstm.sqparc = sqlstm.sqharc;
   sqlstm.sqpadto = sqlstm.sqadto;
   sqlstm.sqptdso = sqlstm.sqtdso;
   sqlcxt((void **)0, &sqlctx, &sqlstm, &sqlfpn);
}

   if(sqlca.sqlcode != 0)
      return(1);
   else
      return( 0 );
}
```

Pro*C comments out the SQL statement and produces a "C" block, initializing the relevant structure fields of the structures needed by the Oracle SQLLIB to represent the SQL statement. The library call that actually executes the statement is *sqlcxt()*.

The new user program, which makes use of the WHENEVER statement, is shown below.

```
EXEC SQL INCLUDE SQLCA;
#include "Sewo.h"
#include "Example.h"

GLOBAL int nDBSelectTblCount (int * nTblCnt )
{
        EXEC SQL WHENEVER SQLERROR GOTO handle_error;
        EXEC SQL WHENEVER SQLWARNING GOTO handler_warning;

        EXEC SQL SELECT
            count(*)
        INTO :nTblCnt
        FROM
            USER_TABLES;
        handle_error:
            return(1);
        handle_warning:
            return(0);
        return( 0 );
}
```

The program handles potential errors and warnings resulting from the SQL statement using the WHENEVER SQLERROR and the WHENEVER SQLWARNING syntax. In either case, the abnormal situation is resolved by a GOTO statement, which diverts the program flow to a "C" label. Pro*C expands the WHENEVER syntax as shown in the next example.

```
#include "Sewo.h"
#include "Example.h"
GLOBAL int nDBSelectTblCount (int * nTblCnt )
{

        /* EXEC SQL WHENEVER SQLERROR GOTO handle_error; */

        /* EXEC SQL WHENEVER SQLWARNING GOTO handler_warning; */
```

```
        /* EXEC SQL SELECT
            count(*)
        INTO :nTblCnt
        FROM
            USER_TABLES; */
{
        struct sqlexd sqlstm;

        sqlstm.sqlvsn = 10;
        sqlstm.arrsiz = 1;
        sqlstm.sqladtp = &sqladt;
        sqlstm.sqltdsp = &sqltds;
        sqlstm.stmt = "select count(*) into :b0 from USER_TABLES ";
        …
```

Omitted lines

```
        …
        sqlstm.sqpadto = sqlstm.sqadto;
        sqlstm.sqptdso = sqlstm.sqtdso;
        sqlcxt((void **)0, &sqlctx, &sqlstm, &sqlfpn);
        if (sqlca.sqlcode < 0) goto handle_error;
        if (sqlca.sqlwarn[0] == 'W') goto handler_warning;
}

        handle_error:
            return(1);
        handle_warning:
            return(0);
        return( 0 );
}
```

The expansion of the WHENEVER keyword operated by Pro*C is shown in bold in the above listing. After the call to *sqlcxt()* to process the SQL statement, the sqlcode field of the SQLCA structure is checked for negative values if WHENEVER SQLERROR has been used. Negative values are returned by Oracle in sqlcode only if an error has occurred. If the SQL statement was executed by Oracle without problems, the value returned in sqlcode is zero.

If WHENEVER SQLWARNING was used, the precompiler inserts, after the call to *sqlcxt()*, a check on the first position of the sqlwarn array contained in the SQLCA structure. If any warning resulted from the most recently executed SQL statement, the first cell in the sqlwarn array will contain a capital W. This is the mechanism used to realize that Oracle issued a warning while processing an SQL statement.

A useful error handling construct is the one that uses the DO action. The keyword DO in a WHENEVER statement allows a routine to be called following either an error or a warning occurred during the processing of an SQL statement.

Prior to release 2.0 of Pro*C, the routine could not receive any parameter and could not return any value. With Pro*C release 2.0, the routine invoked by DO can receive parameters and return a value. The following example shows a WHENEVER statement that invokes an error handling routine passing the SQL statement (as expanded by the pre-compiler) and the SQLCA structure.

```
EXEC SQL WHENEVER SQLERROR DO sts = ProcessError
(&sqlstm.stmt,&sqlca);
```

If the `ProcessError` routine returns 0 whether the program flow can continue and a value different from 0 if the Pro*C function must return to the caller, the sts variable should initially be set to 0, and consistently checked after each SQL call. The value stored in sts will determine whether the Pro*C function must be stopped and the control given back to the caller function.

11.1.1 BUILDING AN ERROR HANDLER IN PRO*C

In this section we are going to build an error handler as a re-usable component across different Pro*C projects. Instead of relying on the WHENEVER SQLERROR construct, we want a generic plain "C" function that is able to handle and report a subset of most common SQL errors. We also want the error handler to selectively store error occurrences in a database table, to help us compile an ABC category of the most common errors of our application. In other words, we want a complete and robust error handler, usable in potentially all Oracle Pro*C projects.

To implement our error handler, we need two database tables: one that stores all error messages and codes used by the application (we will call it ERROR_MESSAGE); and one that stores all error occurrences that must be logged (its name will be ERROR_LOG). The structure of the two tables is shown below.

Error Message

#	FIELD NAME	DATATYPE	PURPOSE
1	FACILITY	VARCHAR2(15)	The application subsystem that generated the error
2	ERROR_CODE	NUMBER(10)	The numeric code corresponding to an error message
3	ERROR_SEVERITY	VARCHAR2(1)	Fatal, Error, Warning, Informational
4	REPLACE_TEXT	VARCHAR2(1)	The error text must be expanded (Y/N)
5	TEXT	VARCHAR2(200)	The actual text of the error
6	LOG_FLAG	VARCHAR2(1)	The error must be logged (Y/N)
7	TERMINATE_FLAG	VARCHAR2(1)	The application must terminate abruptly following the error (Y/N)

#	FIELD NAME	DATATYPE	PURPOSE
8	MESSAGE_TYPE	VARCHAR2(1)	Server side or client side provoked the error (C/S)
9	USER_MESSAGE	VARCHAR2(200)	For client-side error, the text that must be displayed through the MessageBox Win API
10	MESSAGE_CAPTION	VARCHAR2(20)	The caption of the message box
11	BUTTON_NBR	NUMBER(1)	Number of buttons to be displayed in the message box windows (1 – Ok, 2- YesNo, 3 – YesNoCancel)
12	DEFAULT_BUTTON	NUMBER(1)	The button highlighted by default in the message box
13	ICON_NBR	NUMBER(1)	The icon type to be displayed in the message box (Information, Exclamation, Stop, etc.)

Error Log

#	FIELD NAME	DATATYPE	PURPOSE
1	MESSAGE_DATE	DATE	Timestamp of error logging
2	USERNAME	VARCHAR2(30)	Username of the user who provoked the error
3	MESSAGE_CODE	NUMBER(10)	Error code
4	MESSAGE_DESCR	VARCHAR2(200)	Error message
5	MESSAGE_CONTEXT	VARCHAR2(200)	Further error specification
6	MESSAGE_SEVERITY	VARCHAR2(1)	Fatal, Error, Warning, Informational
7	MESSAGE_TYPE	VARCHAR2(1)	Server side or client side provoked the error (C/S)
8	FILENAME	VARCHAR2(255)	Source code filename of the routine that provoked the error
9	LINE_NBR	NUMBER(5)	Line number in the source code file of the line that provoked the error
10	ASR_JOB_NBR	NUMBER(8)	For batch jobs, the sequence number of the job that provoked the error
11	SERVER_PROCESS_NBR	NUMBER(8)	Process Id of the process that provoked the error
12	WINDOW_NAME	VARCHAR2(40)	For client-side errors, the window active at the moment the error occurred
13	OBJECT_DESCR	VARCHAR2(40)	For client-side errors, the window object with focus at the moment of the error
14	EVENT_DESCR	VARCHAR2(20)	For client-side errors, the MS Windows event that provoked the error
15	SQL_ERROR_CODE_NBR	NUMBER(5)	Oracle error number
16	SQL_ERROR_TEXT	VARCHAR2(70)	Oracle error message (taken from the SQLCA structure
17	SQL_NROWS_NBR	NUMBER(5)	For host array operations, the last row in the batch that could be successfully processed

When an error occurs, the error handler is called and the error code is passed as a parameter. The error handler fetches all error information from the ERROR_MESSAGE table and performs all necessary expansions to format an error record to be stored in the ERROR_LOG table. The error code is used by the error handler to uniquely identify a specific error message. The error code is the primary key of the ERROR_MESSAGE table.

An error message can contain parameters that are substituted with run-time values by the error handler. For example, an error message can be formulated as "Could not find file {FILENAME}". The parameter enclosed between curly brackets would be expanded by the error handler with the specific file name that the application couldn't find and open.

The error record stores the filename and line number of the source code line that causes the error. In order to do that properly, a "C" macro must be used to call the error handler routine. If the error handler were called directly by the application, the filename and line number would always be the same, pointing to the error handling routine instead of the real point in the source code that provoked the error.

The error handler that we are going to build exposes three function calls that are used throughout the application to interact with it. The first function call is the macro that invokes the error handler passing the "C" constants __FILE__ and __LINE__, named *RecordError()*. RecordError() receives three parameters, a pointer to an error structure containing relevant error information, an error code and a string that specifies the context where the error occurred. The third parameter is optional, meaning that an empty string can be passed to the error handler.

The second function call is *nCheckDbError()*, which is used to test the result of all SQL operations. nCheckDbError() receives three parameters, a pointer to the Oracle SQLCA structure, a pointer to the error structure, and an enumerated type that defines what SQL operation the most recently SQL statement submitted to the engine (select, open, fetch, update, etc.).

The third function call formats the parameters of the error message, and receives a variable number of arguments. Its name is *FormatErrorArgs()* and its first parameter is a pointer to the error structure. The following parameter is the number of arguments being passed, and the following arguments are the message parameters to be expanded by the error handler.

An additional function, *vpAllocateErrorStructure()*, is used only once to allocate the error structure. The error handler has been tailored to work with an application that uses the four code layers introduced in Chapter 7. The error structure should be allocated by the control layer and passed back and forth across the various layers. The format of the error structure is shown below.

```
typedef struct error_info
{
      struct sqlca  structSQLCA;
      DBStatusT     nReturnCode;
```

```
        int             nApplMsgNbr;
        char            szApplContMsgText[CONTEXT_MSG_SIZE + 1];
        int             nASRJobNbr;
#ifndef MS_NT
        pid_t           nProcessId;
#else
        DWORD           nProcessId;
#endif
        char            szUserName[UNAME_LEN + 1];
        BOOL            BoolStop;
        char            pszFileName[EH_MAX_FILE_NAME_LEN + 1];
        long            lLineNumber;
        int             nNumberOfArgs;
        char            **ppchMsgArgs;
        struct          error_info *pstructThisError;
}ERROR_DETAILS;
```

The first field is a copy of the Oracle SQLCA structure taken from the most recently executed SQL statement. The second field is an enumerated type that defines a small subset of database errors that we want to handle directly. The third field is the error code that uniquely identifies a message stored in the ERROR_MESSAGE table. The fourth field is a string containing a further error description, usually describing the application context that generated the error.

The fifth field—nASRJobNbr—is used by batch jobs. Consider a Unix shell script that executes a few batch tasks in sequence. The shell script maintains a counter that is incremented every time a new job is launched. Before launching the job, an environment variable—ASRJOBNBR—is set by the shell script and read by the error handler. If an error occurs, it becomes easy to find out exactly which job in the sequence provoked the error.

The sixth field contains the process Id of the process that caused the error. The seventh field—szUserName—stores the username of the process that caused the error. The eighth field is a boolean that indicates whether the application must be abruptly terminated following a fatal error.

The ninth field contains the file name of the source code file that caused the error, and the next field—lLineNumber—stores the line number. In nNumberOfArgs, the error handler stores the number of arguments that must be expanded to replace the message placeholders, and the next field contains a pointer to an array of strings, each containing one parameter for the message expansion.

The last field—pstructThisError—contains the pointer to the error structure itself. This field is set by the error structure initialization routine and checked by the error handler. If the error structure is not correctly initialized, or if it becomes corrupt during normal program processing, the error handler has the means to find out what happened.

It is now time to show how to use the error handler. A very simple program connects to Oracle and computes the number of tables created in the login schema. All error handler functions are used in the example.

The Error Handler in Action

```
#include <stdio.h>
#include <stdlib.h>
#include "Sewo.h"
#include "ErrorHandler.h"
#include "ConnectDb.h"

GLOBAL statusT nDBSelectTblCount(int *, ERROR_DETAILS *);

int main(int argc, char **argv)
{
    ERROR_DETAILS          *pstructError;
    DB_CONNECT_STRUCT      structConnect;
    statusT                sts;
    int                    nTblCount;

    memset(&structConnect,'\0',sizeof(structConnect));

    if( (pstructError=
      (ERROR_DETAILS *) vpAllocateErrorStructure()) == NULL)
    {
        fprintf(stdout,
           "Cannot allocate error structure. Aborting...\n");
        exit (-1);
    }
    strcpy(structConnect.szUsername,argv[1]);
    strcpy(structConnect.szPassword,argv[2]);
    sts = nDBConnectDb(&structConnect,pstructError);
    if (sts != success)
    {
        RecordError(pstructError,60,
            "Main program could not connect to Oracle");
        free(pstructError);
        exit(-1);
    }
    if ( (sts = nDBSelectTblCount(&nTblCount,pstructError))
                      != DB_RTN_STATUS_OK)
    {
        FormatErrorArgs(pstructError,1,argv[1]);
        RecordError(pstructError,2023,"");
```

```
40:         free(pstructError);
41:         exit(-1);
42:     }
43:     printf("The schema %s contains %d tables\n",argv[1],-
        nTblCount);
44:     free(pstructError);
45:     exit(0);
46: }
```

Error Handler Example

- *11* Error handler structure definition
- *18–19* Memory allocation of the error handler structure
- *27* The physical data access function *nDBConnectDb()* is called to connect to Oracle. A pointer to the error structure is passed to the function.
- *30* If the Oracle connection function return status indicates that the connection attempt failed (line 28), the error handler macro is called to log the error. The error message has an error code of 60, and the contextual error string specifies that the connection was attempted from the main program line.
- *31* The error structure memory is de-allocated.
- *35* The physical data access function responsible for computing the number of tables owned by the application schema is called. The error structure, once again, is passed as a parameter.
- *38* If the return status of the physical data access function indicates that an error occurred, an error message parameter is formatted by calling *FormatErrorArgs()*. The original error message was "Could not compute table number for schema {SCHEMA}." The username passed to the program from the command line will replace the word surrounded by curly brackets in the error message.
- *39* The error handler macro is invoked again; this time the error message is 2023, and no further error specification string is passed to the error handler.
- *44* Before exiting the program, the memory allocated to the error structure is freed.

The Oracle Connection Function

```
EXEC SQL INCLUDE SQLCA;
#include "Sewo.h"
#include "ErrorHandler.h"

#include "ConnectDb.h"

statusT nDBConnectDb (DB_CONNECT_STRUCT     *pIn,
                      ERROR_DETAILS         *pstructError)
```

```
 9: {
10:     DB_OPERATION     etDBOper = CONNECT;
11:     char             nopasswd[2];
12:     DBStatusT        sts;
13:
14:     if( (strlen(pIn->szUsername)) > 0)
15:     {    /* If Username has been provided */
16:          EXEC SQL CONNECT :pIn->szUsername
17:          IDENTIFIED BY :pIn->szPassword;
18:     }
19:     else  /* Connection with slash */
20:     {
21:          nopasswd[0]='/';
22:          nopasswd[1]='\0';
23:
24:          EXEC SQL CONNECT :nopasswd;
25:     }
26:     if ( (sts = nCheckDbError (&sqlca,
27:                                  pstructError,
28:                                  etDBOper)) != 0)
29:     {
30:          return (error);
31:     }
32:     if ( pstructError->nReturnCode != DB_RTN_STATUS_OK )
33:          return (error);
34:     return(success);
35: }
```

Oracle Connection Function

10 The DB_OPERATION enumerated type specifies that the operation being attempted is a connection. etDBOper will be passed to the error handler function *nCheckDbError()* as a parameter.

26 After the SQL command CONNECT the error handler function that checks all database-generated errors is called. The Oracle SQLCA structure is passed to the function. If an error occurred, the SQLCA structure is copied into the error structure. The error handler will format the error message accessing information contained in the local SQLCA copy found in the error structure. nCheckDbError() also stores the result of the error check in the error structure, in the nReturnCode field.

32 The nReturnCode field is checked to determine whether the most recently executed SQL operation returned successfully. The return status of the connection function is set accordingly.

Computing the Application Schema Table Count

```
 1: static char SEWO_SelectCountTbl_c[]="$Header$";
 2: EXEC SQL INCLUDE SQLCA;
 3: #include <string.h>
 4: #include <fcntl.h>
 5: #include "Sewo.h"
 6: #include "ErrorHandler.h"
 7:
 8: GLOBAL statusT nDBSelectTblCount(int *nTblCount,
 9:                                  ERROR_DETAILS *pstructError)
10: {
11:    DBStatusT sts;
12:    DB_OPERATION    etDBOper = SELECT;
13:
14:    EXEC SQL SELECT
15:    COUNT(*) INTO :nTblCount
16:    FROM  USER_TABLES;
17:
18:    if ( (sts = nCheckDbError (&sqlca,
19:                               pstructError,
20:                               etDBOper)) != 0)
21:          return (error);
22:    if ( pstructError->nReturnCode == DB_RTN_STATUS_FAIL )
23:          return (error);
24:    return( success );
25: }
```

Application Schema Table Count

12 The enumerated type etDBOper specifies a select operation.

14–16 The SQL statement is submitted to the engine.

18–20 The error handler function nCheckDbError() is called to check the result of the most recently executed SQL statement. The result is stored in the nReturnCode field.

22–24 The nCheckDbError return code is checked to determine whether an Oracle error did occur. The return status of the application schema table count function is set accordingly.

The error handler can be used for both Oracle-related and application-related errors. In the second case, the SQLCA fields will be left blank in the ERROR_LOG table.

The above example has shown how to use the error handler. We are now going to examine the source code of the two core functions that comprise the error handler, nCheckDbError() and nErrorHandler(). As already mentioned, nErrorHandler() is never called directly, but through the *RecordError()* macro.

To fully understand the code in the two core functions, the analysis of the include file with all macro and constant definitions is in order.

Error Handler include file

```
#ifndef ERROR_HANDLER_H
#define ERROR_HANDLER_H         1
static char Sewo_ErrorHandler_h[]="$Header$";
#ifndef MS_NT
#include <unistd.h>
#else
#include <windows.h>
#endif
#include <stdarg.h>
#include “sqlca.h”
#define EH_MAX_FILE_NAME_LEN             255
#define EH_MAX_ERR_MSG_LEN               400
#define EH_MAX_TEXT_TEMPLATE_LEN         255
#define CHECK_DB_ERROR_FAIL              2006
typedef enum
{
        NONE,
        FETCH,
        SELECT,
        INSERT,
        UPDATE,
        OPENCRS,
        CLOSCRS,
        CONNECT,
        LOCK,
        COMMIT,
        ROLLBACK,
        DISCONNECT
}DB_OPERATION;
/* Standard SQL codes returned from the Database */
#define SQL_OK                  0
#define DUP_KEY                 -1
```

```
#define NO_MORE_DATA              1403
#define CHILD_FOUND               -2292
#define PARENT_NOT_FOUND          -2291
#define NULL_VALUES_PRESENT       -1405

#define ERR_HANDLER_ERROR         -1
#define CORRUPT_STRUCT_ERR        2005
#define FETCH_ERR_FAIL            2003
#define INSERT_ROW_FAIL           2004

#define ARGS_MISMATCH             -1

#define CONTEXT_MSG_SIZE          101

#define CORRUPT_STRUCT_ERR_MSG  "Error handler received \
a corrupt structure"
#define FETCH_ERR_FAIL_MSG      "Error message could not \
be fetched from DB"
#define INSERT_ROW_FAIL_MSG     "Error handler could not \
write an error record"


#define RecordError(pstructLocalError,nErrNum,szErrString) {\
   nErrorHandler(__FILE__,__LINE__, \
   pstructLocalError,nErrNum,szErrString) ; }

#ifdef DEBUG

        GLOBAL  void vLocalAssert(char *, unsigned int);

#define         ASSERT(condition)       \
                if(condition)           \
                        NULL;           \
                else                    \
                        vLocalAssert(__FILE__,__LINE__)
#else
#define         ASSERT(condition)       NULL
#endif

/*
** The following values are returned from
** routine nCheckDbError:
*/
```

```
typedef enum
{
 DB_RTN_STATUS_OK,
 DB_RTN_END_OF_SET,
 DB_RTN_REC_NOT_FOUND,
 DB_RTN_DUP_KEY_ERROR,
 DB_RTN_ADDNL_REC_FOUND,
 DB_RTN_WARN_DATA_TRUNC,
 DB_RTN_WARN_INVLD_LIST,
 DB_RTN_CHILD_FOUND_IN_DELETE,
 DB_RTN_PARENT_NOT_FOUND_IN_INS,
 DB_RTN_STATUS_FAIL
}DBStatusT;


/*
** The next two constants are used to
** return 'error'/'no error'
** from a routine which does not require
** a database operation
*/
#define NO_ERROR_FOUND  0
#define ERROR_FOUND     1

#define UNAME_LEN       30

typedef struct sqlca SQLCASTR;

typedef enum
{
        logtofile,
        logtodb
}LOG_LOCATION;


typedef enum
{
 success,
 error
}statusT;

typedef struct error_info
{
```

```
      struct sqlca     structSQLCA;
      DBStatusT        nReturnCode;
      int              nApplMsgNbr;
      char             szApplContMsgText[CONTEXT_MSG_SIZE];
      int              nASRJobNbr;
#ifndef MS_NT
      pid_t            nProcessId;
#else
      DWORD            nProcessId;
#endif
      char             szUserName[UNAME_LEN + 1];
      BOOL             BoolStop;
      char             szFileName[EH_MAX_FILE_NAME_LEN + 1];
      long             lLineNumber;
      int              nNumberOfArgs;
      char             **ppchMsgArgs;
      struct           error_info *pstructThisError;
}ERROR_DETAILS;

typedef struct
{
 ERROR_DETAILS  *pstructErrorDetails;
 char           szMsgTextTemplate[EH_MAX_TEXT_TEMPLATE_LEN+1];
 char           chMsgSeverity;
 char           chMsgType;
 LOG_LOCATION etLogLocation;
}MESSAGE_LOG_ENTRY;


GLOBAL  char LocalErrorFile[EH_MAX_FILE_NAME_LEN+1];
GLOBAL  void *vpAllocateErrorStructure(void);
GLOBAL  DBStatusT nCheckDbError( SQLCASTR *, ERROR_DETAILS *,
                   DB_OPERATION  );
GLOBAL  int nErrorHandler( char *, int , ERROR_DETAILS *,
                int, char * );
GLOBAL  int nStripNulls ( char *, short int );
GLOBAL  int nRemTrailingBlanks( char * , short int );
GLOBAL  BOOL isnumber(char *);
GLOBAL  void vRemLeadingBlanks(char *, short int );
GLOBAL  void vRemCtrlAndBlanks( char *, short int );
GLOBAL  void FormatErrorArgs(ERROR_DETAILS *,...);
GLOBAL  int nInitializeErrorStructure (ERROR_DETAILS *);
#endif
```

Error Handler Constants and Macros

10 The Oracle provided sqlca.h file is included to export the definition of the sqlca structure.

17–31 The enumerated type DB_OPERATION is defined. A DB_OPERATION instance is passed to the *nCheckDbError()* to tell the function what kind of SQL operation the error handler has to check (select, open cursor, connect, etc.).

35–40 A subset of potential Oracle errors is defined. *nCheckDbError()* will return either DB_RTN_STATUS_OK, if no error has been detected, or DB_RTN_STATUS_FAIL if the error detected is not included in the error subset. Otherwise it will return one of the well-known errors in the subset.

51–56 The basic error messages are defined. These messages are recorded in the error log file if the database in not accessible, and the required error message cannot be fetched from Oracle.

59–61 The macro *RecordError* is defined. It invokes *nErrorHandler()* passing the "C" compiler constants __FILE__ and __LINE__.

63–74 An alternative assertion function is defined. The standard *assert()* provided by the compiler generates a textual representation of the condition being tested. That string occupies precious space in the stack. Our alternative *assert()* function avoids this problem.

80–92 The enumerated type DBStatusT is defined. It represents all possible error values returned by nCheckDbError().

108–112 The enumerated LOG_LOCATION is defined, to determine where the error message has to be logged. If Oracle is inaccessible, the error handling code will automatically log the error is the local filesystem.

121–140 Error structure definition.

142–149 The structure MESSAGE_LOG_ENTRY is defined. The structure is passed to the message log writer, which expands the message arguments, records the error and stops the application in case of a fatal error.

After having introduced the include file, we can examine the core functions that give the error handler most of its functionality. nCheckDbError() handles all Oracle-related error checking, returning a meaningful error code to the caller. We want to be able to intercept a few common errors with which the application can deal programmatically. For instance, we are deleting a few rows from a table, which is a parent of another table in a parent-child relationship. We attempt the deletion and the error handler returns *DB_RTN_CHILD_FOUND_IN_DELETE.* We can build our code in a way such that instead of returning an error, a deletion of all children is attempted.

nCheckDbError() returns three different kinds of error code. If no error occurred, it returns DB_RTN_STATUS_OK. If an error occurs that is not included in the ones we want to process programmatically, DB_RTN_STATUS_FAIL is returned. If one error occurs that is included in the subset we want to intercept, that error is returned by nCheckDbError(). The common errors or return statuses that nCheckDbError() is able to recognize are:

CODE RETURNED BY nCheckDbError()	MEANING
DB_RTN_END_OF_SET	A fetch operation returned all rows identified by the where clause
DB_RTN_REC_NOT_FOUND	The select statement didn't find any row
DB_RTN_DUP_KEY_ERROR	An insertion statement attempted to store a duplicate value In the primary key field(s)
DB_RTN_ADDNL_REC_FOUND	A select statement found more than one row
DB_RTN_WARN_DATA_TRUNC	A truncation occurred while fetching rows
DB_RTN_WARN_INVLD_LIST	The number of columns in a query select list does not equal the number of host variables provided
DB_RTN_CHILD_FOUND_IN_DELETE	A deletion operation failed because children rows were found in a child table. Referential integrity prevents rows to be orphaned
DB_RTN_PARENT_NOT_FOUND_IN_INS	An insertion in a child table failed because the corresponding parent row couldn't be found in the parent table

The source code of nCheckDbError() is shown below.

```
GLOBAL DBStatusT nCheckDbError(SQLCASTR      *pstructSQLCA,
                               ERROR_DETAILS *pstructError,
                               DB_OPERATION  etDbAccessType)
{
   if ( (char *) nInitializeErrorStructure( pstructError )
                                              != NULL)
        return ( ERR_HANDLER_ERROR );

    /* Interpret the sqlcode value */
    switch ( pstructSQLCA->sqlcode )
    {
        case SQL_OK:  /* If sqlca reports all OK */
            if ( (etDbAccessType == FETCH ) &&
                 ( pstructSQLCA->sqlerrd[2] > 0))
                          /* Is the true fetch   */
                         /* part of a fetch     */
                         /* statement (not open */
                         /* or close)           */
```

```
                pstructError->nReturnCode = DB_RTN_ADDNL_REC_
                FOUND;
              else
                pstructError->nReturnCode = DB_RTN_STATUS_OK;
              break;
          case DUP_KEY: /* Error storing a duplicate key */
              pstructError->nReturnCode = DB_RTN_DUP_KEY_ERROR;
              break;
          case NO_MORE_DATA: /* Fetch reached the last row */
              if ( etDbAccessType == FETCH )
                pstructError->nReturnCode = DB_RTN_END_OF_SET;
              else
                pstructError->nReturnCode = DB_RTN_REC_NOT_ FOUND;
              break;
          case CHILD_FOUND:
              pstructError->nReturnCode =
                DB_RTN_CHILD_FOUND_IN_DELETE;
              break;
          case PARENT_NOT_FOUND:
              pstructError->nReturnCode =
                DB_RTN_PARENT_NOT_FOUND_IN_INS;
              break;
          case NULL_VALUES_PRESENT:
         /* Warning: there are null values  */
              pstructError->nReturnCode = DB_RTN_STATUS_OK;
              /* This is not a real error, so set the return */
              /* status as everything would be OK            */
              break;
          default:
              pstructError->nReturnCode =
                      DB_RTN_STATUS_FAIL;
              break;
    } /* End switch */
 if (pstructError->nReturnCode == DB_RTN_STATUS_OK )
 {
    if ( pstructSQLCA->sqlwarn[1] == 'W' )
       pstructError->nReturnCode = DB_RTN_WARN_DATA_TRUNC;
    if ( pstructSQLCA->sqlwarn[3] == 'W' )
       pstructError->nReturnCode = DB_RTN_WARN_INVLD_LIST;
 }
 /* Copy the received SQLCA into the SQLCA */
 /* substructure in ERROR_DETAILS */
 memcpy( &pstructError->structSQLCA, pstructSQLCA,
         sizeof( pstructError->structSQLCA) );
```

```
62:
63:  return pstructError->nReturnCode;
64: } /* End function */
```

The nCheckDbError() function

5–6 The received error structure is initialized, that is, all fields set to NULL.

10 The sqlcode field of the error structure is checked to determine the Oracle return status of the most recently executed SQL statement.

12 The SQL_OK (0) return status is evaluated.

13 If the SQL operation is a fetch . . .

14 and sqlerrd[2] is greater than 0, this means that the most recently executed fetch found additional rows in the database.

19 Set the return code to indicate that the most recently executed fetch found additional records.

20 If the SQL operation the error handler is evaluating is not a fetch . . .

21 then the return code is set to OK.

23–25 If the SQLCA struture reports a duplicate key error, an appropriate mnemonic is set as return value of the error handler.

26–31 If SQLCODE reports +1403 (no more data) and the SQL operation was a fetch, the return status of the error handler is set to indicate that the all rows have been fetched. Otherwise, in case of different SQL operations (such as SELECT) NO_MORE_DATA means that the statement didn't retrieve any row.

32–35 If SQLCODE indicates that a deletion failed because children rows were found, the error handler sets an approriate return status.

36–39 If SQLCODE indicates that an insertion failed because a parent row couldn't be found, the error handler sets an approriate return status.

40–45 If SQLCODE reports the presence of null values in the fetched or selected rows, the error handler chooses to neglect the "error" and sets the return status to OK.

46–49 If the error handler couldn't recognize any error message coming from the engine, and the return status is different from 0, it means that something "serious" occurred. The return status is set to error.

51–57 If SQLCODE reports everything OK, but warnings did occur, the return status of the error handler is set to signal to the caller about the presence of the Oracle-generated warnings.

60–61 The received SQLCA structure is entirely copied into the sqlca substructure in the error structure. If an error occurred, the calling function will receive back an error structure carrying all necessary information about the Oracle error. That information will be passed to *RecordError()* to be logged.

63 The status code is pased back to the calling function.

The error logging function is responsible for checking the received error structure, making sure that it is not corrupt, and for trying to fetch the error message from the database to format an error entry to be stored in the ERROR_LOG table. If the error message contains placeholders for run-time provided arguments, they are expanded when the message is logged to the database. Should the database be inaccessible, the message is logged without expansion on the local file system. The source code of the error logging function is shown below.

Error Logging Function (invoked through the *RecordError()* macro)

```
GLOBAL int nErrorHandler ( char *FileName,
                           int LineNumber,
                           ERROR_DETAILS *pstructError,
                           int  nErrorNum,
                           char *szContextString)
{
   ERROR_DETAILS         *structLocalError,*pErrDet;
   MESSAGE_LOG_ENTRY     structMsgLogEntry;
   ERROR_MSG        LocErr;
   ERROR_MSG_IND          LocErrInd;
   statusT                fetchSts;
   int                   nReturnCode, sts;
   char                  *AsrJobNbr=NULL;
#ifndef MS_NT
   struct passwd         *LocPasswd;
   uid_t                 LocUid;
#else
   char             szNTUser[51];
#endif

   /* Initialize the structures defined locally */
   memset(&structMsgLogEntry,'\0',sizeof(structMsgLogEntry));
   memset(&LocErr,'\0',sizeof(LocErr));
   memset(&LocErrInd,’\0’,sizeof(LocErrInd));

   pErrDet = (ERROR_DETAILS *) vpAllocateErrorStructure();
   if (pErrDet == NULL)
      return ( ERR_HANDLER_ERROR );
   /* Get the env variable which determines the job number */
   AsrJobNbr = getenv ("ASR_JOB_NBR");
   strcpy(pstructError->szFileName,FileName);
   pstructError->lLineNumber=LineNumber;
   /* Test to see if the received structure is corrupt */
   if ( pstructError->pstructThisError != pstructError )
   {
```

```
      /* if pstructError is corrupt, then build up the local */
      /* error structure to be logged                        */
     structLocalError=
       (ERROR_DETAILS *) vpAllocateErrorStructure();
     if ( AsrJobNbr)  /* If AsrJobNbr has been set */
     structLocalError->nASRJobNbr = atoi ( AsrJobNbr );
       /* Then record the converted ASRJobNbr to the struct */
     /*Store __FILE__ & __LINE__ to the local error structure */
     nRemTrailingBlanks(structLocalError->szFileName,
                        sizeof(structLocalError->szFileName));
     if( ( strlen(structLocalError->szFileName)) == 0)
     {
          structLocalError->lLineNumber = LineNumber;
          strcpy(structLocalError->szFileName, FileName );
     }
     /* Obtain the pid via the UNIX or NT system call */
#ifdef MS_NT
     structLocalError->nProcessId = GetCurrentProcessId();
     memset(szNTUser,'\0',sizeof(szNTUser));
     GetNTUsername(szNTUser);
     strncpy(structLocalError->szUserName,szNTUser,UNAME_LEN);
#else
     structLocalError->nProcessId = getpid();
     /* Obtain the Username via the Unix system call */
     LocUid = getuid();
     LocPasswd = getpwuid(LocUid);
     strncpy(structLocalError->szUserName,LocPasswd->pw_name,
             sizeof(structLocalError->szUserName));
#endif
     /* Signal that the error structure was currupted */
     structLocalError->nApplMsgNbr = CORRUPT_STRUCT_ERR;
     /* Copy the appropriate error message */
     strcpy(structLocalError->szApplContMsgText,
            CORRUPT_STRUCT_ERR_MSG);
     structMsgLogEntry.pstructErrorDetails = structLocalError;
     sts = nLogMessage( &structMsgLogEntry);
     nReturnCode = ERR_HANDLER_ERROR;
     free(structLocalError);
     free(pErrDet);
     return (nReturnCode);
  }
  if ( AsrJobNbr)  /* If AsrJobNbr has been set */
       pstructError->nASRJobNbr = atoi ( AsrJobNbr );
  /* copy __FILE__ & __LINE__ to the error structure */
```

```
  nRemTrailingBlanks(pstructError->szFileName,
                      sizeof(pstructError->szFileName)-1);
  if( ( strlen(pstructError->szFileName)) == 0)
  {
        pstructError->lLineNumber = LineNumber;
        strcpy(pstructError->szFileName, FileName );
  }
  /* Store Process Id and Username in the structure */
#ifdef MS_NT
  pstructError->nProcessId = GetCurrentProcessId();
  GetNTUsername(szNTUser);
  strncpy(pstructError->szUserName,szNTUser,UNAME_LEN);
#else
  pstructError->nProcessId = getpid();
  LocUid = getuid();
  LocPasswd = getpwuid(LocUid);
  strncpy(pstructError->szUserName,
 LocPasswd->pw_name,
 sizeof(pstructError->szUserName));
#endif
  pstructError->nApplMsgNbr = nErrorNum;
  if( (strlen(szContextString)) > 0)
       strcpy(pstructError->szApplContMsgText,
         szContextString);
  /* Copy the received error structure into
  ** the log msg struct
  */
  structMsgLogEntry.pstructErrorDetails = pstructError;
  /* Prepare the parameter structure to
  ** be passed to nDBFetchErrorMsg
  */
  LocErr.nErrorCode= pstructError->nApplMsgNbr ;
  /* Call nDBFetchErrorMsg to obtain the error details */
  if ( ( fetchSts = nDBFetchErrorMsg ( &LocErr,
                                       &LocErrInd,
                                       pErrDet)) != success)
  {
     /* We could not fetch the error from the DB */
     /* Log to file instead of DB                */
     structMsgLogEntry.chMsgType = 'A';
     structMsgLogEntry.chMsgSeverity = 'W';
     structMsgLogEntry.etLogLocation = logtofile;
     nLogMessage( &structMsgLogEntry);
```

```
     /* Now log the "fetch error" message */
     /* Initialize the local error structure */
     structLocalError =
       (ERROR_DETAILS *) vpAllocateErrorStructure();
     /* re-initialize the log message struct */
     memset(&structMsgLogEntry,'\0',
       sizeof(structMsgLogEntry));
     /* Populate the local error struct with
     ** fetch error details
     */
     strcpy( structLocalError->szFileName, __FILE__ );
     structLocalError->lLineNumber = __LINE__ ;
#ifdef MS_NT
     structLocalError->nProcessId = GetCurrentProcessId();
     GetNTUsername(szNTUser);
     strncpy(structLocalError->szUserName,szNTUser,UNAME_LEN);
#else
     structLocalError->nProcessId = getpid();
     /* Obtain the Username via the Unix system call */
     LocUid = getuid();
     LocPasswd = getpwuid(LocUid);
     strncpy(structLocalError->szUserName,LocPasswd->pw_name,
     sizeof(structLocalError->szUserName));
#endif
     strcpy( structLocalError->szApplContMsgText,
             FETCH_ERR_FAIL_MSG);
     structLocalError->nApplMsgNbr = FETCH_ERR_FAIL;
     structMsgLogEntry.pstructErrorDetails = structLocalError;
     structMsgLogEntry.chMsgSeverity = 'W';
     structMsgLogEntry.chMsgType = 'A';
     strcpy(structMsgLogEntry.szMsgTextTemplate,
     "Error Handler could not write the previous error on the ");
     strcat(structMsgLogEntry.szMsgTextTemplate,
      "DB. It is likely that the process could not access the DB");
     nLogMessage( &structMsgLogEntry);
     free(structLocalError);
     pstructError->BoolStop = TRUE;
  }
  else
  {
    /* We could fetch from the DB all the error details */
    strcpy( structMsgLogEntry.szMsgTextTemplate,
            LocErr.szText);
```

```
166:     structMsgLogEntry.chMsgSeverity =
167:        LocErr.chErrorSeverity[0];
168:     structMsgLogEntry.chMsgType =
169:        LocErr.chMessageType[0];
170:     if ( LocErr.chLogFlag[0] == 'Y' )
171:     /* If the error is to be logged */
172:     {
173:        structMsgLogEntry.etLogLocation=1;
174:        if ( (sts = nLogMessage( &structMsgLogEntry))
175:                                 == NO_ERROR_FOUND)
176:             pstructError->BoolStop=FALSE;
177:        else
178:             pstructError->BoolStop = TRUE;
179:     }
180:     else /* Do not log the error */
181:        pstructError->BoolStop = FALSE;
182:     if (LocErr.chTerminateFlag[0]=='Y')
183:     {
184:        free(pErrDet);
185:        exit(1);
186:     }
187:   }
188:   free(pErrDet);
189:   return (NO_ERROR_FOUND);
190: }
```

Error Logging Function

34–76 The received error structure is examined to make sure that it hasn't been improperly initialized or corrupted. If the structure doesn't appear to be reliable, a second error structure is allocated and initialized, and an error message is logged to the local file system. The error handler then returns control to the calling function.

77–111 The error structure fields are populated with relevant information.

113–115 An attempt to fetch the error massage from the database is made.

117–160 If the error message cannot be fetched from the database, an alternative error structure is allocated, initialized, and populated, and an error is logged to the local file system.

164–181 The error message has been fetched from the ERROR_MESSAGE table, and the error handler checks if the error has to be logged.

182–185 If the error occurred is considered to be fatal, exit from the application after having freed the memory allocated to the error structure.

We examined only the core functionality provided by the error handler; in the chapter subdirectory of the companion CD you will find all needed files. They are:

FILENAME	CONTENT
Sewo.h	Project wide constants, Pro*C macros to copy strings in and out of VARCHARs
ErrorHandler.h	Structure and constant definitions for Errorhandler.c
ErrorHandler.c	The error handler core functions
FetchErrorMsg.h	Structure definition and function prototype for FetchErrorMsg.pc
FetchErrorMsg.pc	Physical data access function for getting an error message from the ERROR_MESSAGE table
InsertErrorRow.h	Structure definition and function prototype for InsertErrorRow.pc
InsertErrorRow.pc	Physical data access function for storing an error message into the ERROR_LOG table
sqlca.h	SQLCA structure definition (provided by Oracle)

11.1.2 THE ORACLE COMMUNICATION AREA (ORACA)

The SQLCA structure stores only information about errors and warnings occurred during the processing of an SQL statement. Developers interested in monitoring the efficiency of SQL statements submitted to the engine can enable the use of the Oracle Communication Area (ORACA) by Pro*C. The ORACA contains useful diagnostic and statistical information about the most recently executed SQL statement. The ORACA must be specifically enabled, either by invoking the precompiler with an appropriate command line option (oraca=yes) or by including an EXEC ORACLE statement in the source code (EXEC ORACLE OPTION (ORACA=YES)).

There is a significant overhead associated with the use of the ORACA. This means that it should be enabled only during development and turned off when the code is production ready. In "C" this is easily accomplished through the use of the "#ifdef DEBUG" compiler directive. The significant fields included in the ORACA structure are shown below.

#	FIELD NAME		CONTENT
1	oracchf	long	Check cursor cache consistency (if > 0)
2	oradbgf	long	Enable DEBUG mode checking (if > 0)
3	orahchf	long	Enable heap consistency check (if > 0)
4	orastxtf	long	SQL statement enabling flag
5	orastxt	struct	Stores the SQL text of the most recently executed statement
6	orasfnmc	struct	Stores the file name of the source file containing the statement
7	orasnlr	long	Line number in the source file containing the SQL statement

(continued)

#	FIELD NAME		CONTENT
8	orahoc	long	Highest number of open cursors requested
9	oramoc	long	Max number of cursors required
10	oracoc	long	Current number of open cursors
11	oranor	long	Number of cursor re-assignment
12	oranpr	long	Number of parse operations
13	oranex	long	Number of executes

The first four fields in the ORACA structure are "input" fields, that is, they are set by the developer to force the desired debugging and diagnostics level. For example, assigning a value greater than 0 to the orahchf field requests a consistency check of the heap memory.

To enable statistical collecting for the cursor cache, you must set the oracchf field to a value different from 0. The real advantage of using the ORACA facility is given by its ability to provide cursors statistics. Its main disadvantage is that the statistics are computed only after either a COMMIT or a ROLLBACK. If you are submitting several or many queries (that do not require to be committed), the ORACA cursor fields are not populated. This means that arguably the best use of the ORACA facility is at the end of a user session, invoked once to provide a summary of the session cursor management, rather than after each statement.

In order to show a possible use of the ORACA facility, we are going to build a function, called *PerformORACAAnalysis()*, which receives a pointer to the ORACA structure as a parameter, and appends all cursor statistics to a file. The include file is very simple:

```
#ifndef INC_ORACA_H
#define INC_ORACA_H     1
#include "Sewo.h"
#include "oraca.h"

GLOBAL int PerformORACAAnalysis(struct oraca *);
#endif
```

The function simply receives a pointer to the ORACA structure and logs all cursor statistics in a file.

```
include <stdio.h>
#include <time.h>
#include <stdlib.h>
#include "ORACAAnalysis.h"
```

```
char szOracaAnalysisFile[]="ORACA.LOG";
GLOBAL int PerformORACAAnalysis(struct oraca * structOraca)
{
      FILE *fp;

      if ((fp = fopen(szOracaAnalysisFile,"at")) == NULL)
            return(1);

fprintf(fp,"==========================================\n");
      fprintf(fp,"SQL: %s\n",structOraca->orastxt.orastxtc);
      fprintf(fp,"Filename: %s\n",structOraca->orasfnm.
              orasfnmc);
      fprintf(fp,"SQL at line: %ld\n",structOraca->oraslnr);
      fprintf(fp,"Max value of MAXOPENCURSOR: %ld\n",
              structOraca->orahoc);
      fprintf(fp,"Maximum open cursors: %ld\n",structOraca-
              >oramoc);
      fprintf(fp,"Number of cursor cache re-assignements:
              %ld\n",structOraca->oranor);
      fprintf(fp,"Number of parses: %ld\n",structOraca-
              >oranpr);
      fprintf(fp,"Number of executions: %ld\n",structOraca-
              >oranex);
      fflush(fp);
      return(0);
}
```

Developers who want to use the ORACA facility have two options. They either call *PerformORACAAnalysis()* after each SQL statement or they call it only once, at the end of every logical unit of work performed against the Oracle database, which could group together several to many SQL statements. Opting for the first strategy gives a finer granularity but requires one COMMIT per SQL statement. The second strategy relieves the burden from the engine but gives only a summary of the cursor management statistics.

The following is the function that computes the number of tables owned by the login schema, previously used in the error handler example, revised to include a call to *PerformORACAAnalysis()*. The "C" pre-processor directive "#ifdef DEBUG" is used to avoid calling the ORACA analysis (and the corresponding COMMIT) when the code is compiled for production.

```
EXEC SQL INCLUDE SQLCA;
EXEC SQL INCLUDE ORACA;
#ifdef DEBUG
```

```
EXEC ORACLE OPTION (ORACA=YES);
#endif
#include <string.h>
#include <fcntl.h>
#include "Sewo.h"
#include "ErrorHandler.h"
#include "ORACAAnalysis.h"

GLOBAL statusT nDBSelectTblCount(int *nTblCount,
                                 ERROR_DETAILS *pstructError)
{
      DBStatusT   sts;
      DB_OPERATION    etDBOper = SELECT;
#ifdef DEBUG
      oraca.oradbgf = 1;
      oraca.oracchf = 1;
      oraca.orastxtf = 3;
#endif
        EXEC SQL SELECT
      COUNT(*) INTO :nTblCount
        FROM  USER_TABLES;
        if ( (sts = nCheckDbError (&sqlca,
                                   pstructError,
                                   etDBOper)) != 0)
                          return (error);
        if ( pstructError->nReturnCode == DB_RTN_STATUS_FAIL
)
                          return (error);
#ifdef DEBUG
      EXEC SQL COMMIT WORK;
      PerformORACAAnalysis(&oraca);
#endif
        return( success );
}
```

The ORACA facility is one of the first mechanisms provided by Oracle to tune SQL statements, introduced well before SQL trace and tkprof. While Oracle trace offers the advantage of not requiring any specific instrumentation, it cannot provide detailed information about cursor management and re-use of a single statement.

If the "parse count over executes ratio," computed from the statistical output of tkprof, is high, and the SQL statement in question is not dynamic, this might be an indication that cursors are poorly re-used on the client side. The

ORACA facility can then be used to further investigate the cause of excessive parsing of the SQL statement.

11.2 Host Array Processing

One of the features that really influences the overall performance of an application, especially if it is networked, is the capability of transferring as much data as possible in the fewest network roundtrips possible. In Oracle this is accomplished by using host arrays. That is, multiple rows are inserted, retrieved or updated in one pass.

Using the Oracle host array capability is very easy, as it doesn't require any arcane or difficult technique. It is in fact sufficient to define arrays, populate every cell with data, and pass them to Oracle. The precompiler works out the dimension of the array and inserts into the required tables a number of rows that equals the dimension of the array. Accordingly, in case of a query, the program passes to Oracle an empty array, which gets populated with the content of as many rows as the dimension of the array, if the where clause selects a large enough number of rows.

If in one SQL operation involving host arrays the host variables are dimensioned using different sizes, Oracle will use the smallest array received from the program as the global size for all variables. For instance, if three host arrays are defined as

```
char  customer_name[10][31];
char  company_name[8][41];
int   age[5];
```

and they are used together in an SQL statement, as in

```
EXEC SQL OPEN example_cursor AS
SELECT customer_name,company_name,age from cust
WHERE area_code = :loc_area;

...
...
EXEC SQL FETCH example_cursor INTO
:customer_name,
:company_name,
:age;
...
```

Oracle will fetch up to a maximum of five rows from the database because the driving dimension is the one defining the age integer variable.

It is possible to control the number of rows fetched into a cursor by using the FOR keyword. FOR requires a host variable specifying the limit for the fetch operation, as in

```
int limit = 4;
...
...
FOR :limit
EXEC SQL FETCH example_cursor INTO
:customer_name,
:company_name,
:age;
...
```

In this case the number of rows fetched by Oracle would equal the limit of 4. FOR can be used with EXECUTE, FETCH, INSERT, UPDATE, DELETE, and OPEN. While in most cases the use of FOR is of a limited usefulness, the inclusion of the OPEN command in the list can become really handy. Consider the following scenario.

An Oracle table is used as a queue. A few processes store entries in the table, and a background process de-queues the table by fetching the records and dispatching them to other systems. The single de-queuing process becomes a bottleneck, and the designers of the application decide to set up parallel de-queuing, by doubling the number of background processes.

In order for the two processes not to interfere with each other, a pessimistic locking strategy is to be adopted. That is, one process will fetch and lock a configurable number of rows, say 10, and will apply the required business logic to dispatch the information found in the queue to the external systems. While processing each record, a flag will be set in the queue, stating that one background process is currently "owing" the row.

The second background process fetches the same amount of rows, using the flag as selection criterion. It will fetch all rows that have not yet been sent and that are not currently being processed by the other background process.

The two processes are both using a pessimistic locking strategy, which means that the first process that locks is best served, and the other waits until the first process either commits or rolls back the transaction.

If the queue has a backlog of a few hundred entries, say 1500, then the first process would open the cursor, locking 1500 rows and forcing the second process to wait. Then it would fetch only 10 rows from the 1500 locked, starting the de-queuing task. The second process would do the same, locking 1490 rows to fetch only 10.

The time required to open such a large cursor is considerable. And most of the time spent opening the cursor would be wasted, because the process would only de-queue 10 rows.

In this case the FOR keyword comes to help. The application designers can limit the opening of the cursor, and consequently, the time required to do so, by using the following construct:

```
int limit = 10;
EXEC SQL DECLARE background_task CURSOR FOR
SELECT transaction_id, source_system.
      destination_system, customer, ...etc
FROM OUT_QUEUE
WHERE SENT FLAG = 'NOT SENT' or SENT_FLAG != 'PROCESSING'
FOR UPDATE;
EXEC SQL
FOR :limit
OPEN background_task cursor;
```

Limiting the opening of the cursor to 10 rows does the trick and reduces the amount of time the second process has to wait until the lock is released. The number of rows fetched now equals the number of rows locked during the cursor open operation. This is possible only if the select statement doesn't use a GROUP BY or an ORDER BY clause.

Given their performance advantage, host arrays should be always used in preference to singleton operations.

The support offered by Pro*C to host arrays has increased in functionality in recent years. The first breakthrough in the Oracle precompiler technology was represented by the introduction of Pro*C release 2.0. The major advancement occurred in the area of the parsing technology built in the precompiler. Pro*c incorporated a full "C" language preprocessor, which made possible the support for host variable structures. In addition, the DECLARE section, which was mandatory in previous releases of the precompiler, was no longer required.

Prior to Pro*C release 2, all variables passed to and used by an SQL statement had to be made visible to Oracle through the DECLARE section. It wasn't possible to group together host variables in a structure. Each variable had to be individually declared. This arrangement had a negative impact on the code layering practice.[1] In fact, the logical data access function was generally coded to pass a structure to the physical data access function, containing all fields to be populated by Oracle. The physical data access function, in case of an insert operation, was used to receive the structure and copy all structure elements into locally declared host variables. In case of a select operation, all locally declared host variables had to be copied one by one into the structure received by the logical data access function.

That coding practice was tedious, error-prone, and detrimental for the overall performance of the database operations. With Pro*C release 2.0, it was finally possible to pass a structure containing all fields to be populated to an SQL statement. The structure could be defined in the logical data access function and passed directly to a physical data access function without requiring the tedious copy-in/copy-out passage.

In addition, Pro*C release 2 made possible the use of a second structure, containing indicator variables, mapped in a one-to-one relationship with the main structure, for handling NULL values fetched from database columns. The following example shows the features introduced by Pro*C release 2.

```
typedef  struct
{
      char  TickerId[10][9];
      char  date_value[10][15];
      float High[10];
      float Low[10];
      float Close[10];
      long  Volume[10];
}STOCK;

typedef struct
{
      short TickerIdInd[10];
      short date_valueInd[10];
      short HighInd[10];
      short LowInd[10];
      short CloseInd[10];
      short VolumeInd[10];
}STOCK_IND;

/*Logical data access function, inserting a few stocks into the
STOCK table */
```

[1] See Chapter 7 for a detailed explanation about code layering techniques.

```
int nLDInsertStocks(void)
{
      STOCK         structLocStock;
      STOCK_IND     structLocStockInd;
      int           sts;

      memset(&structLocStock,'\0',sizeof(structLocStock));
      memset(&structLocStockInd, '\0',sizeof(structLocStockInd));

      /* Populate the structure fields with stock values */
      strcpy(structLocStock.TickerId[0],"IBM");
      strcpy(structLocStock.date_value[0],"19980712123407");
      structLocStock.High[0]=146.89;
      … /* all structure is populated */
      …
      structLocStockInd.VolumeInd[8] = -1; /* We set a NULL */
                                           /* value here   */
      … /* the indicator structure is populated… */
      …
      sts = nDBInsertStocks(&structLocStock,& structLocStockInd);
      /* The physical data access function is called to insert */
      /* the stock records in the stock table. The reference   */
      /* to the two structures is passed to the function       */
}

/* Physical data access function. It resides in a file */
/* characterized by the .PC extension                 */
int nDBInsertStocks(STOCK * pstructStock,
                    STOCK_IND * pstructStockInd;
{
      EXEC SQL INSERT INTO STOCK
      (TICKER_ID,
       DATE_VALUE,
       LOW,
       HIGH,
       CLOSE,
       VOLUME)
       VALUES(:pstructStock INDICATOR :pstructStockInd);
      if (sqlca.sqlcode == 0)
            return (SUCCESS);
      else
            return(ERROR);
}
```

The improvement over previous releases of Pro*C was considerable, yet a few limitations were still there. In particular:

- Array of structures were not supported.
- The indicator structure had to contain all fields declared in the main structure.

The indicator variable structure must contain all fields to match the fields defined in the main structure. Even if one column is defined in the database as not null and theoretically wouldn't require an indicator variable, the indicator structure with Pro*C release 2 must still contain its entry.

Other important features introduced with Pro*C release 2 are the support for the optimizer hints, which we encountered in Chapter 8, and the support for the DO action of the WHENEVER call, able to receive parameters and return a value (see earlier sections of this chapter). Pro*C version 2.1 introduced a limited support for the "C++" language and cursor variables, which allow a "C" program to fetch a result set returned by a PL/SQL stored procedure. Pro*C version 2.2 introduced support for multi-threaded applications, whether or not the host operating system implements threads.

A second important breakthrough in the Oracle precompiler technology came along with the release of Oracle 8 (June 1997). The Pro*C precompiler release number was increased and brought in line with the database server release (8.0). Pro*C 8.0, in the area of host arrays, finally introduces the long awaited support for array of structures. In addition, the ancillary structure used to store the indicator variables of a host array operation can contain a subset of the fields present in the main structure.

The support for array of structures suffers from a few important limitations. Array of structures cannot be used under the following circumstances:

- Inside embedded PL/SQL blocks.
- In the WHERE or FROM clauses.
- In the SET clause of an UPDATE statement.
- When using dynamic SQL method 4.[2]

Array of structures cannot contain nested structures, and the "C" declaration of the structure must have a structure tag. The following declaration is illegal:

```
struct               /* illegal: tag undefined! */
{
      char surname[31];
      struct address; /* illegal: nested structure */
```

[2]Dynamic SQL in Pro*C will be the topic of a section further ahead in this chapter.

```
      char nicknames[4][21]; /* illegal: 2-dimension array
*/
}employee[30];
```

The following declaration fixes the previously introduced defects:

```
struct person
{
      char surname[31];
      char address[51];
      char nickname[21];
}employee[30];
```

Pro*C release 8 allows an array of structures used to store indicator variables to have fewer fields than the corresponding main structure. Pro*C maps an indicator variable to the corresponding field using positional semantics. For instance, given the following array of structures:

```
struct person
{
      char          first_name[31];
      char          surname[51];
      int           age;
      short int     sex;
      char          nickname[31];
      char          birth_date[11];
}friends[20];
```

and the following indicator structure:

```
struct person_ind
{
      short         first_name_ind;
      short         surname_ind;
      short         age_ind;
}friends_ind[20];
```

Oracle will use the three fields in the indicator structure to indicate whether the first three fields of the main structure contain nulls or truncated values. The remaining three fields in the main structure should be declared in the database as NOT NULL, because they don't have any associated indicator variable. If while fetching those fields Oracle finds a null value, the SQL operation will return the error:

```
ORA-01405: fetched column value is NULL.
```

The array size of the indicator array of structures cannot be smaller than the corresponding main structure. This means that in our example we cannot set the dimension of the *friends_ind* array of structures to a value less than 20, which is the dimension of the *friends* array of structure.

11.3 Pro*C and PL/SQL

Since the first appearance of Oracle PL/SQL (in one of the latest releases of Oracle 6), Pro*C has been able to take advantage of the server-side procedural processing offered by PL/SQL. As soon as we enter the PL/SQL territory compatibility becomes an issue. If you are supporting an application that must use the services provided by heterogeneous databases and your code must be compatible with databases other than Oracle, then skip this section. PL/SQL is strictly Oracle proprietary and presumes a strong commitment to Oracle technologies by its users.

On the other hand, if your application is not likely to be ported to other environments, and you can freely rely on Oracle technologies, consider using PL./SQL extensively, especially in a client server environment. The potential performance gain provided by the server-side processing makes PL/SQL the natural choice for data-intensive client applications that use Oracle SQL*Net/Net8 as the main vehicle for database access.

Pro*C supports embedded PL/SQL blocks. One PL/SQL block, no matter how many SQL statements it contains, is considered as one SQL operation by the precompiler. The entire content of a PL/SQL block is transferred to the server, where it is compiled and executed. The results are then sent back to the client program through the network. If a complex set of business logic rules require three tables to be queried and the results assessed in order to determine, say, the interest rate to be applied to a financial operation, coding that set of rules in an anonymous PL/SQL block can provide a significant performance advantage.

Consider what happens when a Pro*C program using embedded SQL queries a table, fetching the results from a cursor. The memory for the cursor is allocated; then the SQL statement is parsed, and the bind variables are associated to the statement placeholders. The DML statement is executed and the query is ready to retrieve the rows selected by the WHERE clause. If host arrays are not used—or even if they are used, but the number of rows retrieved is large, and the fetching requires more calls—the number of network roundtrips increases steadily. Since the business logic to be applied requires three tables to be queried, the process above described must be repeated three times.

Consider now the same situation, this time replacing the three embedded SQL calls with one anonymous PL/SQL block. One or perhaps two network roundtrips are sufficient to send the PL/SQL block to the server. The three cursors are allocated, opened, and fetched on the server side. No network traffic is involved.

The variable containing the final result of the complex computation, the interest rate to be applied to the financial operation, is sent back to client program with a single network roundtrip once all computations are done. The network saving obtained through the use of this technique is considerable. If the number of users accessing this application is large, say, in the order of one or two thousand, using PL/SQL makes a significant difference.

Using an anonymous PL/SQL block is easy. The PL/SQL code must be enclosed within the EXEC SQL EXECUTE and END-EXEC keywords.

```
int age;
long int employee_code = 2431;

/*----<PL/SQL Block----------------------
EXEC SQL EXECUTE
BEGIN
      SELECT emp_age into :age
      WHERE emp_code = : employee_code;
END;
END-EXEC;
/*----<PL/SQL Block>----------------------
printf("The age of the employee code 2431 is %d\n", age);
```

The Pro*C fragment shown above demonstrates that host variables can be freely intermixed with PL/SQL code. Unfortunately, there are a few limitations; for instance, C structures cannot be used directly, and host arrays must be mapped to PL/SQL tables. These limitations make PL/SQL anonymous blocks very useful for applying complex business logic that return a limited amount of information, but are not suitable for returning large result sets. When compiling Pro*C programs that contain PL/SQL blocks, you must use the SQLCHECK command line option to change the default value of *syntax* to either *semantics* or *full*. This forces the Oracle server to parse the PL/SQL block. Using the SQLCHECK option also requires the USERID option to be set, in order to provide an account login that will be used by the precompiler to connect to Oracle.

If you must retrieve a large result set from the database, say, an invoice consisting of a header (one record), several to many line items (multiple records) and a footer (one record), then using embedded SQL and host arrays is better than relying on a PL/SQL block. Fetching multiple rows into a host array will keep networks roundtrips to a minimum, but the network traffic needed to send the rows from the Oracle server to the client program cannot be avoided.

Oracle server release 7.2 introduced the feature that allows a result set to be returned by a stored procedure. If you have a database server that is accessed by diverse software components written in different languages for both client and server environments, it makes sense to centralize the data retrieval operations and to offer a consistent interface to the data to all software components.

Consider the following scenario:

> A database server is accessed by a few client applications written in Powerbuilder and Delphi. Several cleaning-up housekeeping tasks run on the server and are executed once a day, typically after midnight. A complex data change auditing system, implemented using database triggers, captures all data modifications occurred during the day and keeps an external database synchronized through an uploading process that runs overnight.
>
> The housekeeping tasks and the synchronization process are coded in Pro*C. All software components comprising the complex system share the need to retrieve the same data, such as all invoices entered into the system in one working day. The client tools will access the invoice data to display the invoice form on the PCs used by clerical personnel dealing with customers. The housekeeping tasks will access the invoice data to check its consistency. The synchronization process will access all newly entered invoices to send them to the external remote database.

Using a PL/SQL package that defines three procedures for retrieving an invoice (get_invoice_header, get_invoice_line_items, and get_invoice_footer) and calling the same package from all software components streamlines your code and makes code management easier.

In order to retrieve result sets from stored procedures, specific precompiler syntax must be used. A *cursor variable* must be defined, which is a handle (a pointer) for a cursor memory area. The real cursor must be defined and opened from the server side, using PL/SQL code. To declare a cursor variable in the Pro*C program the type specification SQL_CURSOR must be used. It is also mandatory to allocate memory to the cursor variable using the EXEC SQL ALLOCATE syntax, as in the following example.

```
...
SQL_CURSOR  inv_line_items;
float fUnitPrice,
fLineSubtotal;
```

```
VARCHAR     szDescription;
int         nInvoiceNumber,
nLineNumber
nQuantity,
nInvNum;
...
EXEC SQL ALLOCATE :inv_line_items;
/* An anonymous PL/SQL block will cause the cursor
** to be opened on the server side... */
EXEC SQL EXECUTE
BEGIN
      invoice.get_invoice_line_items_oc(:inv_line_items,
                                         :nInvoiceNumber);

END;
END-EXEC;
EXEC SQL WHENEVER NOT FOUND DO break;
for(; ; )
{
      EXEC SQL FETCH :inv_line_items INTO
      : nInvNum, :nLineNumber, :szDescription,
      :fUnitPrice, :nQuantity, :fLineSubtotal;
      printf(# %2d %s %10.2f %d %12.2f\n",
      nLineNumber, szDescription, fUnitPrice,
      nQuantity, fLineSubtotal);
}
...
```

Fetching data through calls to stored procedures provides a decisive advantage if security affecting the environment where your application runs is an issue. If your client application uses an SQL*Net/Net8 connection and the interaction with Oracle implies that the user has the privilege to read and write the tables accessed, then nothing will stop a saboteur from accessing the database using alternative means. As usual, an example better illustrates the concept.

> A client application is written in Delphi. The user types in username, password, and connection string at the moment of the initial login. If the same user installs SQL*Plus on the client PC—if it is not already installed—and uses the same login parameters, then it is possible for him or her to insert and potentially delete data with no control whatsoever. All data consistency checks built

in the application would be completely bypassed. Only the database-enforced constraints would still work under these circumstances.

If, on the other hand, all data is fetched through stored procedures, the user who logs in from the client side needs to be granted only an execute privilege on all stored procedures used by the application. The application administrator can safely revoke from all users the privileges to select, insert, update, and delete data from/to the application tables. The stored procedures will still work, but the users will be prevented from accessing the tables stored in the application schema directly.

To show how to use cursor variables, we are going to implement a small application that reads an invoice from the database, given the invoice number. As already mentioned, an invoice is stored in the database using three tables. The table structure for each table follows.

INVOICE_HEADER

FIELD NAME	DATATYPE	CONTENT
INV_NUMBER	NUMBER(10)	Invoice number for our company
INV_DATE	DATE	Date appearing on the invoice
SUPPLIER_CODE	NUMBER(7)	Supplier that sent the invoice
RECV_DATE	DATE	Date invoice actually received
SUPPLIER_INV_NBR	NUMBER(12)	Invoice number according to the supplier numbering scheme
INIT_PERIOD	DATE	Initial date covered by this invoice
END_PERIOD	DATE	End date covered by this invoice

INVOICE_LINE_ITEM

FIELD NAME	DATATYPE	CONTENT
INV_NUMBER	NUMBER(10)	Invoice number to link each line item to the parent table
INV_LINE_NUMBER	NUMBER(4)	Line number on the invoice matrix
ITEM_DESCR	VARCHAR2(200)	Description of the item being invoiced
UNIT_PRICE	NUMBER(12,2)	Price for a single item unit
QUANTITY	NUMBER(10)	Total items being invoiced
LINE_SUBTOTAL	NUMBER(12,2)	Total price for all items in this line

INVOICE_FOOTER

FIELD NAME	DATATYPE	CONTENT
INV_NUMBER	NUMBER(10)	Invoice number to link each line item to the parent table
INVOICE_TOTAL	NUMBER(12,2)	Total being invoiced
COMMISSION	NUMBER(12,2)	Commission to be paid to the salesman
VARIOUS_FEE	NUMBER(12,2)	Miscellaneous fees to be paid
SALES_TAX	NUMBER(12,2)	Government sales tax

The header and the footer of the invoice are stored in one record each. Each line item is stored in a separate record, so we need a cursor to fetch a batch of line items. This will be implemented as a cursor variable, so that the result set returned by the stored procedure can be a data source for different client software components, such as Delphi, Powerbuilder, Pro*C, etc.

The PL/SQL package that implements the retrieval of our invoice is shown below. A word of warning: The PL/SQL code is by no means complete and bulletproof. In particular no checks are done to verify that the SQL operations completed successfully, and no exceptions are thrown. Only the minimal functionality to make the example work is implemented.

```
CREATE OR REPLACE PACKAGE INVOICE AS
TYPE LineItemsTyp IS REF CURSOR RETURN INVOICE_LINE_ITEM%ROWTYPE;
PROCEDURE  get_invoice_header( INV_NUM    IN NUMBER,
                               INV_DATE   OUT VARCHAR2,
                               SUPPLIER_CODE    OUT NUMBER,
                               RECV_DATE        OUT VARCHAR2,
                               SUPPLIER_INV_NBR OUT NUMBER,
                               INIT_PERIOD      OUT VARCHAR2,
                               END_PERIOD       OUT VARCHAR2,
                               PAYMENT_TERMS    OUT NUMBER);
PROCEDURE      get_invoice_line_items_oc(
                    line_items_curs IN OUT LineItemsTyp,
                                  INV_NUM       IN NUMBER);
PROCEDURE   get_invoice_footer(INV_NUM         IN   NUMBER,
                               INVOICE_TOTAL   OUT  NUMBER,
                               COMMISSION      OUT  NUMBER,
                               VARIOUS_FEE     OUT  NUMBER,
                               SALES_TAX       OUT  NUMBER);
END INVOICE;
/
CREATE OR REPLACE PACKAGE BODY  INVOICE AS
 PROCEDURE  get_invoice_header(INV_NUM          IN  NUMBER,
                               INV_DATE         OUT VARCHAR2,
                               SUPPLIER_CODE    OUT NUMBER,
```

```
                              RECV_DATE         OUT VARCHAR2,
                              SUPPLIER_INV_NBR  OUT NUMBER,
                              INIT_PERIOD       OUT VARCHAR2,
                              END_PERIOD        OUT VARCHAR2,
                              PAYMENT_TERMS     OUT NUMBER) IS
  CURSOR inv_head (inv_num IN NUMBER) IS
  SELECT TO_CHAR(INV_DATE,'MM-DD-CCYY'), SUPPLIER_CODE,
         TO_CHAR(RECV_DATE,'MM-DD-CCYY'), SUPPLIER_INV_NBR,
         TO_CHAR(INIT_PERIOD,'MM-DD-CCYY'),
         TO_CHAR(END_PERIOD,'MM-DD-CCYY'),
         PAYMENT_TERMS
  FROM INVOICE_HEADER
  WHERE INV_NUMBER = inv_num;
 BEGIN
   OPEN inv_head(INV_NUM);
   FETCH inv_head INTO INV_DATE,SUPPLIER_CODE,RECV_DATE,
        SUPPLIER_INV_NBR,
        INIT_PERIOD,END_PERIOD,PAYMENT_TERMS;
   CLOSE inv_head;
 END;
 PROCEDURE   get_invoice_footer(INV_NUM          IN   NUMBER,
                              INVOICE_TOTAL     OUT  NUMBER,
                              COMMISSION        OUT  NUMBER,
                              VARIOUS_FEE       OUT  NUMBER,
                              SALES_TAX         OUT  NUMBER) IS
 CURSOR inv_foot(inv_num IN NUMBER) IS
 SELECT INVOICE_TOTAL,COMMISSION,VARIOUS_FEE,SALES_TAX
 FROM INVOICE_FOOTER
 WHERE INV_NUMBER = inv_num;
 BEGIN
   OPEN inv_foot (INV_NUM);
   FETCH inv_foot  INTO INVOICE_TOTAL,COMMISSION,
                   VARIOUS_FEE,SALES_TAX;
   CLOSE inv_foot;
 END;
 PROCEDURE get_invoice_line_items_oc (
                  line_items_curs   IN OUT LineItemsTyp,
                  INV_NUM           IN NUMBER) IS
 BEGIN
 OPEN line_items_curs FOR
        SELECT *
        FROM INVOICE_LINE_ITEM
        WHERE INV_NUMBER = INV_NUM
        ORDER BY INV_LINE_NUMBER;
END;
END;
/
```

The Invoice Package

1–2 Package and cursor variable declaration. The keyword REF characterizes the cursor as a cursor variable. The return type is an invoice_line_item record.

3–20 The stored procedures that constitute the package are declared together with their parameter list. At line 12, the cursor variable is first referenced. The *get_invoice_line_items_oc* stored procedure receives the cursor variable as an IN OUT parameter.

21–59 The package body is defined. The two stored procedures to retrieve the invoice header and footer are defined. They will simply fill in the received parameters with values fetched from the invoice database tables.

60–62 The *get_invoice_line_items_oc* stored procedure is defined. It will receive the invoice number of the required invoice as the IN parameter.

64 The cursor, received as IN OUT parameter, is opened.

65–68 The SQL query that retrieves the rows is associated with the defined cursor.

The PL/SQL code needed to implement a cursor variable did not present a high degree of complexity. The client Pro*C code that accesses a cursor variable is no more complex. Two new Pro*C syntax elements are needed to accomplish the goal. The first is the SQL_CURSOR datatype, which flags to the precompiler that the code will be using a cursor variable. The second is the EXEC SQL ALLOCATE statement, which explicitly allocates memory for the cursor through a call to the SQLLIB library. The Pro*C program that fetches the invoice data is shown below.

```
#include <stdlib.h>
#include <stdio.h>
#include <windows.h>

EXEC SQL INCLUDE SQLCA;

int FetchInvoice(int);
int Connect(char *, char *);

main(int argc, char **argv)
{
 int   sts;
 if ( (sts = Connect(argv[1],argv[2]))!= 0)
 {
        fprintf(stdout,"Could not connect, aborting...\n");
        exit(-1);
```

```
  }
  if ( (sts = FetchInvoice(atoi(argv[3]))) != 0)
  {
        fprintf(stdout,"Could not fetch invoice data\n");
        exit(-1);
  }
  exit(0);
}

int FetchInvoice(int nInvNumber)
{
  sql_cursor   inv_items;
  int          inv_num;
  int          inv_line_num;
  char         szItemDescr[201];
  float        fUnitPrice;
  long         lQuantity;
  float        fLineSubtotal;
  char         szInvDate[11];
  int          nSupplierCode;
  char         szRecvDate[11];
  int          nSupplInvNum;
  char         szInitPeriod[11];
  char         szEndPeriod[11];
  int          nPaymentTerms;
  float        fInvoiceTotal;
  float        fCommission;
  float        fVariousFee;
  float        fSalesTax;

  memset(szItemDescr,'\0',sizeof(szItemDescr));
  EXEC SQL ALLOCATE :inv_items;

  EXEC SQL WHENEVER SQLERROR DO exit(-1);

  EXEC SQL EXECUTE
  BEGIN
        invoice.get_invoice_header(:nInvNumber,:szInvDate,
                                   :nSupplierCode,:szRecvDate,
                                   :nSupplInvNum,:szInitPeriod,
                                   :szEndPeriod,:nPaymentTerms);
  END;
  END-EXEC;
  szInvDate[10]='\0';
```

```
  szRecvDate[10]='\0';
  szInitPeriod[10]='\0';
  szEndPeriod[10]='\0';

  printf("Inv.Num.:%d %s SupplierCode: %d payment terms %d days\n",
              nInvNumber,szInvDate,nSupplierCode,nPaymentTerms);

  EXEC SQL EXECUTE
  BEGIN
        invoice.get_invoice_line_items_oc(:inv_items,:nInvNumber);
  END;
  END-EXEC;

  EXEC SQL WHENEVER NOT FOUND DO break;
  for(;;)
  {
        EXEC SQL FETCH :inv_items INTO :inv_num,:inv_line_num,
                    :szItemDescr,:fUnitPrice,
                    :lQuantity,:fLineSubtotal;
        szItemDescr[200]='\0';
        printf("Line num. %d %s  price: %f quantity: %ld\n",
              inv_line_num,szItemDescr,fUnitPrice,lQuantity);
  }
  EXEC SQL WHENEVER NOT FOUND CONTINUE;
  EXEC SQL EXECUTE
  BEGIN
        invoice.get_invoice_footer(:nInvNumber,:fInvoiceTotal,
                          :fCommission, :fVariousFee,
                          :fSalesTax);
  END;
  END-EXEC;
        printf("Invoice Total: %f Sales tax: %d %\n",
              fInvoiceTotal,fSalesTax);
  EXEC SQL CLOSE :inv_items;
return 0;
}
int Connect(char * szUsername, char * szPassword)
{
  EXEC SQL CONNECT :szUsername IDENTIFIED BY :szPassword;
  if (sqlca.sqlcode != 0)
        return -1;
  else
        return (0);
}
```

The Pro*C client

26 The *FetchInvoice()* function is defined. FetchInvoice() will call the three stored procedures contained in the invoice package to fetch all required invoice data.

28 InvItems is defined as SQL_CURSOR.

29–45 All invoice elements are defined. Their values will be set by the stored procedures.

48 The inv_items cursor is allocated through the call to SQLLIB.

52–58 An anonymous PL/SQL block is used to execute the *get_invoice_header()* stored procedure. The stored procedure receives all invoice header elements as parameters.

68–72 A cursor variable is a cursor that is under the control of the server, that is, it must be opened from the server side. This is accomplished through the call made by an anonymous PL/SQL block to the stored procedure that opens the cursor using PL/SQL syntax on the server side.

74 The WHENEVER NOT FOUND construct allows for exiting the endless loop once all rows have been fetched.

75–83 An endless loop repeatedly fetches all rows from the cursor variable. The relevant invoice line items are printed.

84–91 The PL/SQL block executes the stored procedure that fetches the invoice footer elements.

92–93 The invoice footer elements are printed.

94 The EXEC SQL CLOSE command instructs the server to close the cursor variable.

The cursor variable mechanism allows for great flexibility, because the result set returned by a stored procedure can be a data source usable by most Rapid Application Development (RAD) tools. Client development environments such as Powerbuilder and Delphi, as well as Pro*C can retrieve their data using cursor variables.

Cursor variables can be used with host arrays to fetch batches of rows from the server. This minimizes network roundtrips and can significantly increase the overall application performance. Another way to retrieve multiple rows in one lot from a PL/SQL stored procedure is by mapping Pro*C arrays into PL/SQL tables, which are the PL/SQL objects that most closely resemble arrays. The major advantage offered by PL/SQL tables is that they don't have to be dimensioned prior to their use. They can grow without limits, which means that the ultimate limits are the server memory resources.

It is possible for a Pro*C client to interact with a server-side stored procedure that repeatedly fetches rows and stores the result in PL/SQL tables. The client will then use "C" arrays to retrieve the rows stored in the PL/SQL tables. In order for such retrieval to take place, a few parameters passed back and forth from the client program and the server package act as a sort of "protocol" between the client and the server. The client "tells" the server how many rows are expected per batch and if the cursor must be closed. The server returns the number of rows fetched and an indicator that tells the client if other rows must still be fetched or all rows identified by the where clause have been fetched already.

The invoice package must be reworked to support this technique. The amended package follows.

The Invoice Package Revisited

```
CREATE OR REPLACE PACKAGE INVOICE AS
TYPE   ItemDescrArray IS TABLE OF VARCHAR2(200)
       INDEX BY BINARY_INTEGER;
TYPE   IntegerTable IS TABLE OF NUMBER
       INDEX BY BINARY_INTEGER;
TYPE   FloatTable IS TABLE OF FLOAT
       INDEX BY BINARY_INTEGER;

PROCEDURE    get_invoice_header(INV_NUM     IN NUMBER,
                                INV_DATE    OUT VARCHAR2,
                                SUPPLIER_CODE      OUT NUMBER,
                                RECV_DATE   OUT VARCHAR2,
                                SUPPLIER_INV_NBR OUT NUMBER,
                                INIT_PERIOD OUT VARCHAR2,
                                END_PERIOD  OUT VARCHAR2,
                                PAYMENT_TERMS      OUT NUMBER);

PROCEDURE    get_invoice_line_items(INV_NUM IN  NUMBER,
                          ARRAY_DIM   IN     NUMBER,
                          COUNT_ITEMS        IN OUT NUMBER,
                          CURS_CLOSE  IN     NUMBER,
                          FETCH_END   OUT    NUMBER,
                          LINE_NUMS   OUT    IntegerTable,
                          DESCRIPTION OUT    ItemDescrArray,
                          PRICE       OUT    FloatTable,
                          HOW_MANY    OUT    IntegerTable,
                          LINE_TOTAL  OUT    FloatTable);

PROCEDURE   get_invoice_footer(INV_NUM            IN    NUMBER,
                               INVOICE_TOTAL      OUT   NUMBER,
                               COMMISSION         OUT   NUMBER,
                               VARIOUS_FEE        OUT   NUMBER,
                               SALES_TAX          OUT   NUMBER);
```

```
END INVOICE;
/
CREATE OR REPLACE PACKAGE BODY  INVOICE AS
 CURSOR LineItems (INV_NUM IN NUMBER) IS
 SELECT INV_LINE_NUMBER,ITEM_DESCR,UNIT_PRICE,QUANTITY,
        LINE_SUBTOTAL
 FROM   INVOICE_LINE_ITEM WHERE INV_NUMBER = INV_NUM;
 PROCEDURE   get_invoice_header( INV_NUM          IN   NUMBER,
                            INV_DATE            OUT VARCHAR2,
                            SUPPLIER_CODE       OUT NUMBER,
                            RECV_DATE           OUT VARCHAR2,
                            SUPPLIER_INV_NBR    OUT NUMBER,
                            INIT_PERIOD    OUT VARCHAR2,
                            END_PERIOD     OUT VARCHAR2,
                            PAYMENT_TERMS OUT NUMBER) IS
 CURSOR inv_head (inv_num IN NUMBER) IS
 SELECT TO_CHAR(INV_DATE,'MM-DD-CCYY'), SUPPLIER_CODE,
        TO_CHAR(RECV_DATE,'MM-DD-CCYY'), SUPPLIER_INV_NBR,
        TO_CHAR(INIT_PERIOD,'MM-DD-CCYY'),
        TO_CHAR(END_PERIOD,'MM-DD-CCYY'),
        PAYMENT_TERMS
 FROM INVOICE_HEADER
 WHERE INV_NUMBER = inv_num;
BEGIN
 OPEN inv_head(INV_NUM);
 FETCH inv_head INTO INV_DATE,SUPPLIER_CODE,
       RECV_DATE,SUPPLIER_INV_NBR,
       INIT_PERIOD,END_PERIOD,PAYMENT_TERMS;
 CLOSE inv_head;
END;
PROCEDURE   get_invoice_footer( INV_NUM        IN   NUMBER,
                            INVOICE_TOTAL OUT  NUMBER,
                            COMMISSION    OUT  NUMBER,
                            VARIOUS_FEE   OUT  NUMBER,
                            SALES_TAX     OUT  NUMBER) IS
 CURSOR inv_foot(inv_num IN NUMBER) IS
 SELECT INVOICE_TOTAL,COMMISSION,VARIOUS_FEE,SALES_TAX
 FROM INVOICE_FOOTER
 WHERE INV_NUMBER = inv_num;
BEGIN
 OPEN inv_foot (INV_NUM);
 FETCH inv_foot  INTO INVOICE_TOTAL,COMMISSION,
       VARIOUS_FEE,SALES_TAX;
 CLOSE inv_foot;
```

```
78: END;
79: PROCEDURE  get_invoice_line_items( INV_NUM   IN NUMBER,
80:                                ARRAY_DIM     IN       NUMBER,
81:                                COUNT_ITEMS   IN OUT NUMBER,
82:                                CURS_CLOSE    IN       NUMBER,
83:                                FETCH_END     OUT      NUMBER,
84:                                LINE_NUMS     OUT      IntegerTable,
85:                                DESCRIPTION   OUT      ItemDescrArray,
86:                                PRICE         OUT      FloatTable,
87:                                HOW_MANY      OUT      IntegerTable,
88:                                LINE_TOTAL    OUT      FloatTable) IS
89: BEGIN
90: IF CURS_CLOSE = 1 THEN
91:    IF LineItems%ISOPEN THEN
92:       CLOSE LineItems;
93:       RETURN;
94:    END IF;
95: ELSE
96:    IF NOT LineItems%ISOPEN THEN
97:       OPEN LineItems(INV_NUM);
98:    END IF;
99: END IF;
100: COUNT_ITEMS := 0;
101: FETCH_END :=0;
102: FOR ii IN 1..ARRAY_DIM LOOP
103:   FETCH LineItems INTO LINE_NUMS(ii), DESCRIPTION(ii),PRICE(ii),
104:                  HOW_MANY(ii), LINE_TOTAL(ii);
105:    IF LineItems%NOTFOUND THEN
106:         CLOSE LineItems;
107:         FETCH_END := 1;
108:         EXIT;
109:    ELSE
110:         COUNT_ITEMS:= COUNT_ITEMS +1;
111:      END IF;
112: END LOOP;
113: END get_invoice_line_items;
114: END;
115: /
```

The New Invoice Package

2–7 Three PL/SQL types are created. They are PL/SQL tables created to map the "C" host arrays that will be passed to the *get_invoice_line_items()* stored procedure. The user defined types map an array of floats, an array of integers, and an array of strings, each 200 characters long.

9–78 This part of the package is identical to the previous release.

79–88 *get_invoice_line_items()* is defined. INV_NUM is the parameter carrying the invoice number of the invoice to be fetched. ARRAY_DIM is the dimension of the "C" host array, and the number of line items expected by the client in one batch. COUNT_ITEMS is defined as an IN OUT parameter, and will carry back to the client the number of rows fetched by the server–side cursor. CURS_CLOSE is a flag that when set to 1 forces the server to close the cursor and terminate the fetch. The remaining parameters are all of the user-defined types, and will carry the invoice items fetched back to the client.

90–93 If the client requested to close the cursor and to abandon any further fetching, the cursor is closed and the stored procedure returns.

96–98 If the cursor is not open, proceed to the opening of the cursor.

100–101 The two variables storing the total number of rows fetched and the flag that indicates to the client that the server has finished fetching all rows identified by the invoice number are initialized to 0.

102 The loop starts. The natural end of the loop is when the array dimension is reached.

103–104 One row is fetched into the ith position of the PL/SQL table.

105–111 If the most recently executed fetch did not find any row, the cursor is closed and the FETCH_END flag is set to 1. This will signal the client that the server fetched all requested rows and closed the cursor. Otherwise, the COUNT_ITEMS variable, which store the total number of rows fetched, is incremented by one.

112 The loop that fetches the invoice line items is closed.

113 The stored procedure is completed.

We are done with the server. The Pro*C client must also be modified to be able to take advantage of the array fetching operated by the server-side stored procedure.

The Pro*C Client Revisited

```
#include <stdlib.h>
#include <stdio.h>
#include <windows.h>

EXEC SQL INCLUDE SQLCA;

int FetchInvoice(int);
int Connect(char *, char *);

```

```
main(int argc, char **argv)
{
 int   sts;
 if ( (sts = Connect(argv[1],argv[2]))!= 0)
 {
        fprintf(stdout,"Could not connect, aborting...\n");
        exit(-1);
 }
 if ( (sts = FetchInvoice(atoi(argv[3]))) != 0)
 {
        fprintf(stdout,"Could not fetch invoice data\n");
        exit(-1);
 }
 exit(0);
}

int FetchInvoice(int nInvNumber)
{
 typedef char ItemDescr[201];


 EXEC SQL TYPE ItemDescr IS VARCHAR2(201) REFERENCE;


 int          inv_line_num[5];
 ItemDescr    ItemDescrArr[5];
 float        fUnitPrice[5];
 long         lQuantity[5];
 float        fLineSubtotal[5];
 char         szInvDate[11];
 int          nSupplierCode;
 char         szRecvDate[11];
 int          nSupplInvNum;
 char         szInitPeriod[11];
 char         szEndPeriod[11];
 int          nPaymentTerms;
 float        fInvoiceTotal;
 float        fCommission;
 float        fVariousFee;
 float        fSalesTax;
 int         nArrayDim;
 int          nCountItems;
 int          nCursorClose=0;
 int          nFetchEnd;
```

```
int          ii;


memset(&ItemDescrArr,'\0',sizeof(ItemDescrArr));


EXEC SQL WHENEVER SQLERROR DO exit(-1);

EXEC SQL EXECUTE
BEGIN
      invoice.get_invoice_header(:nInvNumber,:szInvDate,
                                 :nSupplierCode,:szRecvDate,
                                 :nSupplInvNum,:szInitPeriod,
                                 :szEndPeriod,:nPaymentTerms);
END;
END-EXEC;
szInvDate[10]='\0';
szRecvDate[10]='\0';
szInitPeriod[10]='\0';
szEndPeriod[10]='\0';

printf("Inv.Num.:%d %s SupplierCode: %d payment terms %d days\n",
          nInvNumber,szInvDate,nSupplierCode,nPaymentTerms);
nFetchEnd=0;
nCountItems=0;
nArrayDim = 5;
for(;;)
{
      EXEC SQL EXECUTE
      BEGIN
            invoice.get_invoice_line_items(
            :nInvNumber,:nArrayDim,:nCountItems,:nCursorClose,
            :nFetchEnd,:inv_line_num,:ItemDescrArr,:fUnitPrice,
            :lQuantity,:fLineSubtotal);
      END;
      END-EXEC;
      for(ii=0;ii<nCountItems;ii++)
      {
            printf("Line num. %d %s  price: %f quantity: %ld\n",
                   inv_line_num[ii],ItemDescrArr[ii],
                   fUnitPrice[ii],lQuantity[ii]);
      }
      if (nFetchEnd)
```

```
 97:                 break;
 98:     }
 99:
100:
101:     EXEC SQL EXECUTE
102:     BEGIN
103:           invoice.get_invoice_footer(:nInvNumber,:fInvoiceTotal,
104:                                      :fCommission, :fVariousFee,
105:                                      :fSalesTax);
106:     END;
107:     END-EXEC;
108:           printf("Invoice Total: %f Sales tax: %d %\n",
109:                  fInvoiceTotal,fSalesTax);
110:     return 0;
111: }
112:
113: int Connect(char * szUsername, char * szPassword)
114: {
115:     EXEC SQL CONNECT :szUsername IDENTIFIED BY :szPassword;
116:     if (sqlca.sqlcode != 0)
117:           return -1;
118:     else
119:           return (0);
120: }
```

The New Pro*C Client Fetches Server-Side Host Arrays

26 Definition of the FetchInvoice() function. The received parameter stores the invoice number of the invoice being fetched.

28 The ItemDescr user type is defined. It is a string that can contain up to 200 characters.

31 Datatype equivalencing[3] is used to map the ItemDescr string to an Oracle VARCHAR2 with a length of 201 characters. The REFERENCE keyword indicates that ItemDescr is a pointer.

34–54 Variables and host arrays required to fetch all invoice elements are defined. Line 35 specifies an array of pointers to strings.

57 The array of pointers is initialized to NULL.

60–76 The header of the invoice is fetched. There is no difference between this version and the previous version, which used cursor variables.

---

[3]Datatype equivalencing allows developers to override the default mapping operated by Pro*C between Oracle external datatypes and host language datatypes. See the Oracle Pro*C manual for further explanation.

77–79 The three variables needed as a "protocol" between the client and the server are initialized. Since the client uses a host array size of five positions, nArrayDim is initialized to 5. nCursorClose is initialized to 0 while it is defined. A value of 1 assigned to nCursorClose would force the server to close the cursor interrupting the fetch.

80 An endless loop will force all invoice line items to be fetched. The exit condition from the loop will be the test against the nFetchEnd variable, which is set to 1 by the server when the last row has been fetched.

82–88 The *get_invoice_line_items()* stored procedure is called, passing the required invoice number (nInvNumber), "protocol" variables (nArrayDim, nCountItems, nCursorClose, and nFetchEnd) and host arrays (inv_line_num, ItemDescrArr, fUnitPrice, lQuantity and fLineSubtotal).

90–95 The result of the fetch is printed.

96–97 If the server indicates that no more rows have to be fetched, the endless loop is terminated. Otherwise *get_invoice_line_items()* is called again, until all rows identified by the where clause are fetched. The server automatically closes the cursor when the most recently executed fetch returns an error.

101–111 The invoice footer is fetched and printed. No difference with the previous version.

By mapping "C" host arrays into PL/SQL tables and forcing the stored procedure on the server to fetch multiple rows in one batch, we achieved a better use of network resources. Unfortunately, this technique requires a programmatic interface, such as Pro*C, while cursor variables can be used by RAD tools such as Delphi and Powerbuilder.

We are now in a position to summarize our findings on the interaction between Pro*C and embedded SQL or PL/SQL.

In a two-tier environment, the required security level should drive the choice of the technique to be used. If security is important, embedded SQL shouldn't be used. Anonymous PL/SQL blocks, stored procedures, and server-side host array fetching should be considered instead. If security is not an issue, a mixture of embedded SQL and anonymous PL/SQL blocks can be used. In this case embedded SQL would be the choice for fetching multiple rows that must be transferred to the client. PL/SQL blocks can be used to execute on the server complex business logic with a relatively low number of results that must be received by the client through network roundtrips.

In a three-tier environment security is generally managed by middleware. The clients are not connected to the database through SQL*Net/Net8, but they dialogue with application components or services using the means provided by the middleware used (usually TCP/IP sockets). Furthermore, the middle tier runs on the server and business logic and data are managed on the server-side.

TECHNIQUE	PROS	CONS
Embedded SQL	Well known technique Host arrays can be used	Many network roundtrips Weak security
Anonymous PL/SQL blocks	Network traffic minimized Access to server-side packages The short variant of cursor definition (FOR..LOOP) can be used Improved security over embedded SQL	Host arrays must be mapped to PL/SQL tables Complex "C" language types such as arrays and structures are not natively supported
Cursor Variables	Flexibility and versatility Usable by client RAD tools Good security	Cursor must be opened from the server side
Server-side host array fetching	Combines the best of cursor variable features with support for host array processing and client control of the dimension of the host array	Requires a programmatic interface Client visual RAD tools cannot use this technique

When a client requests data from the database, the middle tier retrieves the data and formats a message or a workspace that is sent to client. In this case, embedded SQL can be freely used by the code comprising the middle tier. Middleware components in general, and TP monitors in particular, all provide some form of connection pooling, to lessen the amount of processes connected to Oracle.

The middleware-controlled servers usually connect to the database using either Oracle or operating system authentication. Since SQL processing occurs on the server side, stored procedures and anonymous PL/SQL blocks don't provide a significant performance advantage over embedded SQL. The opposite is indeed true; embedded SQL is slightly faster than PL/SQL when the program with embedded SQL runs on the server and connects directly to Oracle (no SQL*Net required). This makes sense, because PL/SQL is p-code executed within the Oracle engine, while a Pro*C executable is in machine-readable format. The same Pro*C program, run remotely over an SQL*Net/Net8 connection, is slower than an identical program coded in PL/SQL because of the network roundtrips needed to fetch the data. If SQL*Net/Net8 is used to connect to a database residing on the same computer where the Pro*C process runs, performance is roughly equivalent to PL/SQL.

There are two schools of thought with regard to the use of PL/SQL. One sees favorably the use of PL/SQL to implement business logic in both two-tier and three-tier environments. The other advocates the use of PL/SQL only in a two-tier environment. In a three-tier environment, the use of PL/SQL is discouraged, mainly for scalability reasons. If business logic is enforced programmatically in the middle tier and not in Oracle, the engine is not overloaded with heavy PL/SQL processing and can serve a higher number of connected TP processes, each serving in turn multiple clients, thanks to connection pooling techniques.

Such a configuration can achieve scalability by increasing the number of front-end server processes by adding more machines dedicated to the support of the middle tier. The assumption here is that one Oracle instance is capable of being accessed by more processes if it acts as a passive data repository rather than running hundreds or even thousands of stored procedures and anonymous PL/SQL blocks concurrently, in order to satisfy the queries of several hundreds of connected users.

Figure 11.1 shows an initial configuration of an application that uses a TP monitor and server agents that perform connection pooling to serve multiple clients.

Scalability can be achieved by splitting the application server into a database server, which hosts only the back-end database, and by plugging in to the configuration two additional computers dedicated to running the middle-tier processes. This configuration offers the advantage that no code change is required to the application when it scales from the initial one-only server configu-

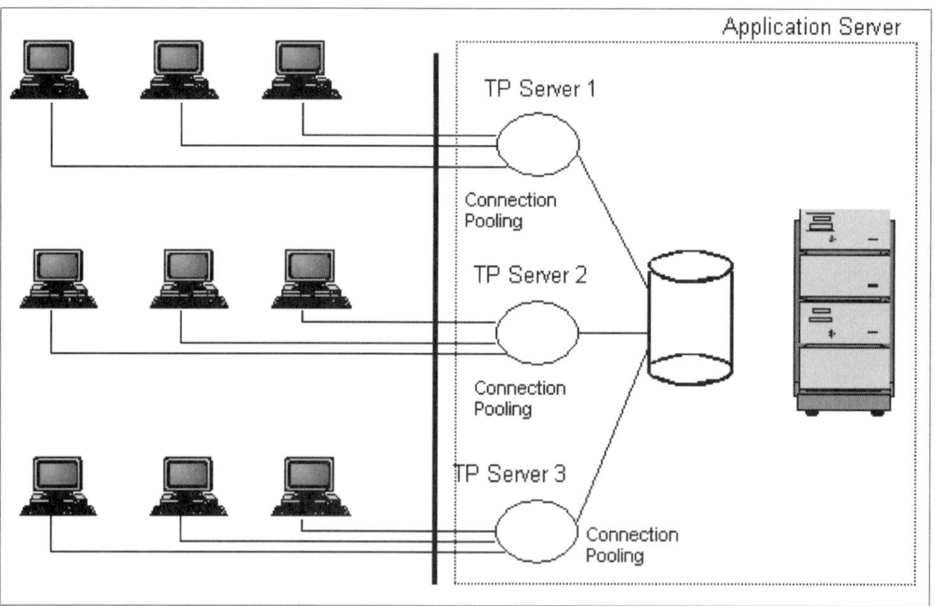

FIGURE 11.1 Single Server TP Monitor configuration

ration to the more advanced three server based structure. Figure 11.2 shows the scaled-up configuration.

The supporters of the use of PL/SQL in the middle tier argue that scalability can be achieved anyway through the Oracle Parallel Server. As discussed in Chapter 4, this is not always possible, if the nature of the application doesn't allow for proper partitioning, which translates into a good *scaleup* factor.

Several factors must be considered when deciding the environment or language to be used to implement the business logic of an application. If portability to other database environments is not a requirement and PL/SQL can be used, the next factor to be considered is the application environment. A two-tier environment is a good candidate for business logic implemented using PL/SQL. In a three-tier environment this is debatable, and the decisive factor is the overall number of concurrent users accessing the application and the potential for future scalability required by the application designers. If the number of concurrent users exceeds the capabilities of a single computer, forcing the designers to adopt a complex hardware architecture, it is probably more flexible to code the business logic in either Pro*C or OCI rather than in PL/SQL.

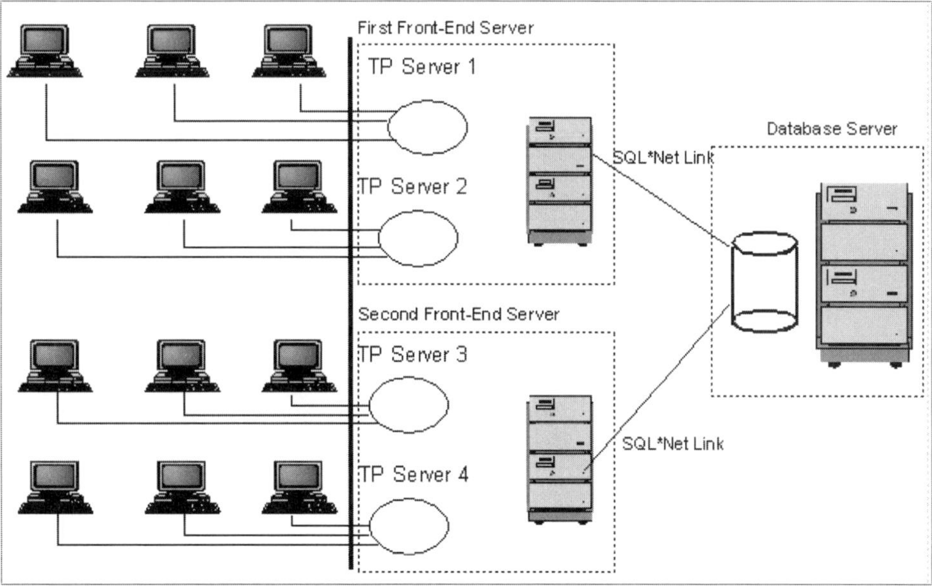

FIGURE 11.2 The addition of two computers dedicated to middle-tier processing makes it possible to scale-up the application.

11.4 Support for C++

With the release of Pro*C 2.1 Oracle Corporation introduced a limited support for C++. The support is limited because the precompiler preprocessor recognizes only C syntax, thanks to a complete C parser built in to the precompiler.

The introduction of the C parser represented a real breakthrough in the precompiler technology, allowing Pro*C programs to use constants defined through the *#define* directive. Furthermore, the EXEC SQL DECLARE section, previously used to make C variables visible to Oracle, was no longer needed, and complex native C structures and pointers to structures were finally usable directly in Pro*C programs as Oracle host variables.

Unfortunately, to be able to support C++ code, the C parser must be disabled, or at least partially disabled. This means that the DECLARE section must be used when the Pro*C precompiler is used against C++ code. Furthermore, the SQLLIB library is implemented in C and all its functions must be declared as *extern* when called from a C++ program. This is taken care of by Pro*C when it emits code compatible with C++. Setting the CODE option to CPP on the command line at the moment of the precompiler invocation enables this emission.

The support for C++, for the above reasons, is far less than optimal. If an application coded in C++ accesses relational tables, it is more efficient for it to interact with Oracle through a physical data access layer coded in plain "C". In other words, if the attributes of an object are decomposed into relational tables to give them persistence, and recomposed from relational tables the next time the object is instantiated, some of the benefits of object-orientation are intrinsically lost. In this context, resorting to "C" to obtain a performance boost is not the real compromise on "OO" purity.

The application can still maintain its object-oriented nature even if the value of the class attributes is fetched from the database using the old but performant "C" language. To illustrate how to call physical data access functions written in "C" from a business logic layer coded in C++, we are going to re-edit the C++ program introduced in Chapter 7, Section 7.3, Using Composition in OO. That example showed how to use pure "OO" techniques to de-couple physical data access functions from business logic. In this context we are going one step further, implementing the routines responsible for the Oracle interaction in "C" instead of C++.

In the example in Chapter 7, the C++ physical data access method received the attributes to be filled with Oracle data as a list of parameters. The precompiler was able to detect the size of each parameter thanks to a local DECLARE section that specified datatype and dimension of each attribute. In our new example, we want to avoid defining a local DECLARE section so that we can pass the received parameters straight to Oracle, bypassing the copy-in/copy-out passage.

If the class constructor passes to the "C" function several pointers to strings, the precompiler is not able to determine the size of each. The code still compiles, but the precompiler assumes a size of 4 bytes for each parameter, which is the size of the pointer to a string (in most operating systems). When the program runs, there are two scenarios. Either the program crashes signaling a memory access violation, or the printed attributes are truncated after the fourth character.

To allow the precompiler to work properly, all class attributes must be stored in a structure, and the pointer to the structure must be passed to the external "C" data access function. The C++ accessor functions hide the change in the implementation to the users of the customer class services, and the "C" function has the means to determine the size of the class attributes. The reworked example is shown below.

Class Attribute Structure Definition

```
 1: #ifndef FETCH_CUST_H
 2: #define FETCH_CUST_H 1
 3: typedef struct
 4: {
 5:     char    szCustName[31];
 6:     char    szCustAddress[51];
 7:     char    szCustTel[16];
 8:     char    szCustFax[16];
 9: }CUSTOMER_DATA;
10:
11: #endif
```

New Attribute Structure

5–8 The attributes of the customer class are now defined within the customer_data structure.

The Customer Class Definition

```
#ifndef CUSTOMER_H
#define CUSTOMER_H 1
#include "FetchCust.h"

class customer
{
   public:
    customer(int nCustCode);
    char * get_cust_name(void);
    char * get_cust_address(void);
    char * get_cust_telephone(void);
    char * get_cust_fax_number(void);
    int    get_status(void);
   protected:
    CUSTOMER_DATA customer_data;
    int      nStatus;
```

```
17:    private:
18:      int            nCustCode;
19: };
20:
21: #endif
```

The Customer Class

7 The class constructor takes the customer code as the input parameter.
12 A new method is defined, to report the status of the database operation. Together with the introduction of the customer_data structure, this is the only significant difference over the same example presented in Chapter 7.

The Customer Class Implementation

```
#include <stdlib.h>
#include <iostream.h>
#include "customer.h"
#include "FetchCust.h"

const int SUCCESS = 0;

extern "C"
{
 int OraConnect(char *, char *);
 int FetchCust(int,CUSTOMER_DATA *);
}

char * customer::get_cust_name(void)
{
    return customer_data.szCustName;
}

char * customer::get_cust_telephone(void)
{
    return customer_data.szCustTel;
}

char * customer::get_cust_fax_number(void)
{
    return customer_data.szCustFax;
}

char * customer::get_cust_address(void)
```

```
{
     return customer_data.szCustAddress;
}

int    customer::get_status(void)
{
 return nStatus;
}

customer::customer(int nCode)
{
 nCustCode = nCode;
 nStatus = SUCCESS;
 nStatus = FetchCust(nCode,&customer_data);
}


int main( int argc, char **argv)
{
 int nSts;
 char * szName;

 //argv[1] is the username, argv[2] the password,
 //argv[3] the customer code
 if ( (nSts = OraConnect(argv[1],argv[2])) != 0)
 {
       abort();
 }
 customer cust(atoi(argv[3]));
 if (cust.get_status() == SUCCESS)
 {
       szName = cust.get_cust_name();
       cout << "Fetched user: "
       << (char *) szName << endl << endl;
       return 0;
 }
 else
 {
       cout << "Could not find required customer "
       << endl << endl;
       return -1;
 }
}
```

A C++ Implementation

7–11 The two "C" functions called by this application are declared as *extern* C.

13–36 The accessor functions are defined, to expose the internal attributes of the class. They access the class attributes in the customer_data structure.

38–44 Class constructor. It initializes two class attributes and calls the "C" function FecthCust to get the customer data from Oracle.

47 The main program starts.

54–57 The program operates the database attachment through the "C" function OraConnect.

58 The customer object is instantiated. The class constructor takes the input value and calls the "C" function FetchCust to get the attribute values from Oracle.

59 The get_status method informs the caller about the return status of the database operation. If the object has been successfully instantiated with all its attributes, the customer name is printed, otherwise an error message informs the user that something abnormal occurred.

The Data Access Layer

```
#include "FetchCust.h"
EXEC SQL INCLUDE SQLCA;

int OraConnect(char * szUsername, char * szPassword)
{
 EXEC SQL CONNECT :szUsername IDENTIFIED BY :szPassword;
       if (sqlca.sqlcode != 0)
             return -1;
       else
             return (0);
}


int FetchCust(     int nCode, CUSTOMER_DATA  * cust_data)
{

 EXEC SQL SELECT
 NAME,
 ADDRESS,
 TELEPHONE,
 TELEFAX
 INTO :cust_data
 FROM CUSTOMER_SAMPLE
```

```
24:   WHERE CUST_CODE = :nCode;
25:
26:   if (sqlca.sqlcode != 0)
27:               return -1;
28:         else
29:               return (0);
30: }
31:
```

A "C" Physical Data Access Layer

4–11 A basic Oracle connection routine.

14–31 The FetchCust function takes two parameters and fetches the data from Oracle into them directly, that is, no declare section is needed. This is because the file is a "C" file, and the precompiler can be invoked with the parse=full option. The precompiler works out the dimension of all structure members, and passes to Oracle the exact number of bytes allocated to each member.

If you compare this version of the example with the one in Figure 7.10, you will notice that this version is much more compact because it avoids the copy-in/copy-out steps necessary when a declare section is used. If an application instantiates one customer object per minute, the time wasted by the several memory copy operations is negligible. On the other hand, if an application instantiates 20 or 30 customer objects per second, the time spent copying bytes across different sections of the computer memory becomes significant. A profiler can accurately measure the real impact, as we pointed out in Chapter 8. Alternatively, Oracle Trace can be used to achieve the same result (Chapter 13).

11.5 Precompiler Options

The Pro*C precompiler shipped with Oracle 8.0x offers 40 command-line options that allow the developer to influence code generation, ANSI compliance, Pro*C specific structure usage (ORACA) and Oracle version compatibility modes. Serious Oracle developers should familiarize themselves with most of the command-line options. From a performance and scalability point of view, three precompiler options are very important, to the extent that their setting becomes crucial for the support of most demanding applications. These options are listed in the table below.

PRO*C OPTION	DEFAULT	DESCRIPTION
MAXOPENCURSORS	10	Max number of concurrently open cursors that Pro*C tries to keep open
RELEASE_CURSOR	NO	Instructs Oracle either to release or not to release the cursor after the SQL statement has been executed
HOLD_CURSOR	NO	Instructs Oracle to mark a cursor as re-usable after the SQL statement has been executed

The maximum number of cursors that an Oracle session can maintain open is determined by an instance-wide parameter called OPEN_CURSORS. Its default value is usually set to 50. If the MAXOPENCURSORS Pro*C parameter is set to a value higher than OPEN_CURSORS, Oracle will try to maintain open as many cursors as specified by the instance parameter, irrespective of the value reported by MAXOPENCURSORS. If MAXOPENCURSORS is set to a value less than OPEN_CURSORS, and all cursor cache entries are active, Oracle will allocate a new entry in the cursor cache, exceeding the MAXOPENCURSORS value.

The HOLD_CURSOR and RELEASE_CURSOR settings cooperate to influence the behavior of Oracle with regard to cursor management. The two parameters can be set on-line, using the EXEC ORACLE OPTION construct. The following table illustrates how the concurrent setting of these two parameters influences the Oracle cursor management.

The obvious strategy is to force Oracle to release the links to the cursor cache for statements that are executed infrequently, and to keep the links for the

HOLD_CURSOR	RELEASE_CURSOR	EFFECT
NO	NO	Oracle executes the statement and marks the link to the cursor cache as re-usable. The link is not removed immediately.
YES	NO	Oracle executes the statement and maintains the cursor link to the cursor cache. Subsequent executions of the same statement won't cause a re-parse of the cursor.
NO	YES	Oracle executes the statement and after the cursor has been closed, it removes the link to the cursor cache. Any subsequent execution of the same statement will cause a cursor re-parse.
YES	YES	Oracle executes the statement and after the cursor has been closed, it removes the link to the cursor cache. Any subsequent execution of the same statement will cause a cursor re-parse.

statements repeatedly executed. This is accomplished by constantly setting HOLD_CURSOR to YES and by setting RELEASE_CURSOR to either YES just before an infrequently executed SQL statement or NO just before a repeatedly executed statement. This is possible because the scope of the EXEC ORACLE OPTION directive is positional. In other words, an EXEC ORACLE OPTION (HOLD_CURSOR=YES) stays in effect until another EXEC ORACLE OPTION is set further ahead in the code.

The default value for MAXOPENCURSORS is 10, which is insufficient in most cases. A value of 50 is a good starting point. To fine tune the optimal number for MAXOPENCURSORS and OPEN_CURSORS, you can temporarily enable the ORACA structure to collect cursor statistics. See section 11.1.2 for details about the ORACA use.

11.6 Dynamic SQL in Pro*C

Static SQL, which makes use of bind variables, is the preferred option to achieve performance and scalability in OLTP applications. There are occasions, though, when dynamic SQL is unavoidable, for instance, to implement administrative database tasks such as creating new users, dropping and creating tables and indexes, and granting and revoking privileges. Applications in the realm of Decision Support Systems (DSS) oftentimes offer visual query builders to simplify the interaction with the database by people whose skills are more managerial than technical.

A visual query builder inevitably favors user friendliness at the expense of efficiency. This is particularly true when the SQL statements produced by the query builder don't use parameterized queries, that is, they hard code the where clause values in quotes rather than create colon prefixed variables for the where clause. In a DSS context it doesn't really matter if a single query is not optimized, because it is likely that it will run only once. Even if that inefficient query is submitted regularly, it doesn't do a lot of damage because it runs against a database purposely set to support a few users performing ad-hoc and expensive queries. In these contexts, dynamic SQL can be proficiently used to the benefit of users and administrators.

Pro*C offers four different methods to submit dynamic SQL to the Oracle engine. Methods 1 and 2 are used for SQL statements that are not queries; method 3 allows developers to build dynamic queries that contain a number of output variables and input bind variables known at compile time. Method 4 allows developers to code complex select queries that contain bind variables and output items unknown at compile time.

Before we delve into complex dynamic SQL concepts a discussion on how Oracle processes SQL statements is in order. It is a common belief that cursors are used only with queries that fetch multiple rows. This is because the embedded SQL keyword CURSOR is used only when a select statement fetches one or more rows from a database table into a previously opened cursor.

In reality, Oracle opens a cursor for every SQL statement it processes. That is, a cursor is a memory area, sometimes called *context area*, allocated by the SQL engine where an SQL statement and all information about it are stored. Parsing a statement means associating a specific SQL statement with a context area. A cursor can be left open and associated with different statements by parsing different statements into the same context area. When the cursor is closed, the context area is freed and the cursor structure discarded.

In several other occasions, we stated that parsing is an expensive operation. For this reason, if a statement uses bind variables and is repeatedly executed, it makes sense to open a cursor, parse the statement, and leave the cursor open and dedicated to the statement. Not all client tools give developers total control over cursor handling. Pro*C allows developers to influence the way cursors are managed through the HOLD_CURSOR and RELEASE_CURSOR options. The Oracle Call Interface, discussed in Chapter 12, provides even greater control over cursor management.

Dynamic SQL methods 2, 3, and 4 allow developers to open a cursor and parse a statement into the cursor multiple time. This is necessary only when the wording of the new SQL statement is different from the statement already executed in the context area. If the statement is the same, and only the bind variables contain different values between the calls, parsing can also be skipped. This arrangement gives the best performance, minimizing both cursor allocation and statement parsing. Dynamic SQL method 1 allocates a cursor, parses the statement, and executes it in one pass. Method 1 is the only one that doesn't allow for cursor control. It should be used only under absolute certainty that the SQL statement processed will be executed only once.

Methods 1 and 2 are easy to code and don't require a thorough understanding of all dynamic SQL concepts. Method 3 is a little more complex and requires more processing steps, but it is still manageable and can be well understood by developers who must maintain the code once the product is running in a production environment. Dynamic SQL method 4 is complex, cumbersome, and requires a deep knowledge of dynamic SQL concepts, including SQL internal datatype conversion and coercion. The amount of processing steps and the code associated with them are considerable, and its maintenance accordingly difficult.

In other words dynamic SQL method 4 is to be avoided. If an application cannot avoid giving its users the freedom to submit dynamic queries to the Oracle engine, the Oracle Call Interface (OCI) should be considered, instead of Pro*C.

The table below illustrates the processing steps required by each method. Note how the complexity increases with the increasing of the method number.

PRO*C METHOD	STEPS REQUIRED
1	EXEC SQL IMMEDIATE :stmt_string
2	EXEC SQL PREPARE stmt_name FROM :stmt_string EXEC SQL EXECUTE stmt USING host_variables_list
3	EXEC SQL PREPARE stmt_name FROM stmt_string EXEC SQL DECLARE cursor_name CURSOR FOR stmt_name EXEC SQL OPEN cursor_name USING host_variables_list EXEC SQL FETCH cursor_name INTO host_variables_list EXEC SQL CLOSE cursor_name
4	EXEC SQL PREPARE stmt_name FROM stmt_string EXEC SQL DECLARE cursor_name CURSOR FOR stmt_name EXEC SQL DESCRIBE BIND VARIABLES FOR stmt_name EXEC SQL OPEN cursor_name USING DESCRIPTOR bind_descriptor_name EXEC SQL DESCRIBE SELECT LIST FOR stmt_name INTO select_descriptor_name EXEC SQL FETCH cursor_name USING DESCRIPTOR select_descriptor_name EXEC SQL CLOSE cursor_name

Method 1 is useful for SQL statements that don't contain host variables and are executed only once. Perfect candidates for method 1 are Data Definition Language (DDL) statements, that is, statements that manipulate database objects, like DROP TABLE, CREATE TABLE, CREATE INDEX, etc. With method 1, an SQL statement is parsed and immediately executed. Re-submitting the statement causes a second parse.

```
/* A Dynamic SQL Method 1 example */
char  dyn_stmt[201];
...
...
strcpy(dyn_stmt,"CREATE TABLE TRIAL ( first_field VARCHAR2(30),\
       second_field NUMBER(10))';

EXEC SQL EXECUTE IMMEDIATE :dyn_stmt;
```

Method 2 is a little more sophisticated because it allows developers to use host variables and to reuse the opened cursor without reparsing. This is accomplished in two steps. The first step allocates and names a cursor, and the second step, which can be repeated many times, executes the statement, each time associating different host variables with the cursor. Method 2 doesn't support SQL queries, that is, the SELECT keyword cannot be used.

The following example shows method 2 in action. An interactive application repeatedly asks the user to input the customer code of customers to be removed from the customer table. The cursor that has the associated delete statement is *prepared* only once, but *executed* as many times as the user requests. The bind variable carrying the customer code is refreshed each time with a different code.

```
int   cust_code;
char  dyn_stmt[101];
char  line[81];

strcpy(dyn_stmt,"DELETE FROM customer where \
CUST_ID = :cust_code");
EXEC SQL PREPARE STMT FROM :dyn_stmt;
for (;;)
{
      printf("Enter customer code \
      (customer will be deleted)\n");
      printf("Enter 0 to finish\n");
      gets(line);
      cust_code = atoi(line);
      if (cust_code == 0)
            break;
      EXEC SQL EXECUTE STMT USING :cust_code;
}
EXEC SQL COMMIT WORK;
```

If the dynamic SQL statement to be submitted to the engine is a query, either method 3 or method 4 must be used. If the select list items and the bind variables are known at compile time, method 3 can be used. Method 3 requires more steps than method 2 because a query is involved, which requires fetching data into the select items. The example below shows dynamic SQL method 3 in action. A customer is fetched from the database customer table. The customer Id is defined as a bind variable, originating a parameterized query.

```
char  szDynStmt[101];
char  szName[31];
char szAddress[51];
int   cust_id;

strcpy(szDynStmt,"Select name, address from customer\
       where cust_id = :v1");
```

```
EXEC SQL PREPARE STMT FROM :szDynStmt;
EXEC SQL DECLARE CUR1 CURSOR FOR STMT;
EXEC SQL OPEN CUR1 USING :cust_id;
EXEC SQL WHENEVER NOT FOUND DO break;
for (;;)
{
      EXEC SQL FETCH CUR1 INTO :szName, :szAddress;
      printf("Customer name: %s\n",szName);
      printf("Customer address: %s\n",szAddress);
}
printf("SQL statement processed %d rows.\n",
       sqlca.sqlerrd[2]);
EXEC SQL CLOSE CUR1;
```

Since all the query elements are known at compile time, including the output items—szName and szAddress—and the input bind variables—cust_id—the program declares them and allocates the memory necessary for each. Note that the overhead due to the SQL statement being dynamic is minimal. The only additional step required is the one defined by the PREPARE keyword. Static SQL requires declaring a cursor, opening it, fetching rows into it, and closing it once finished with it, which is equivalent to what is required with dynamic SQL method 3.

When the elements of an SQL query are unknown at compile time, dynamic SQL method 4 must be used. The complexity associated with method 4 is due to the absolute lack of information about select-list items and bind variables at compile time. In the method 3 example presented above, we could define the select-list variables *szName* and *szAddress* because we knew their datatypes and size. The same applies to *cust_id*, the bind variable. When all this information is not known at compile time, a Pro*C program using dynamic SQL method 4 must find out the name, the datatype, and the size of all variables participating in a query at run-time.

To this purpose, method 4 requires the developer to define a structure called *sqlda*, SQL Descriptor Area. The elements of the structure store information about name, size, and datatype of each select-list item or bind variable participating in the query. Since a select query can contain one or one hundred variables, most of the SQLDA structure elements are pointers to arrays. A specific SQLLIB function is called to initialize the SQLDA structure, dimensioning the arrays to a required size. This function changed its name in Pro*C 8. It was previously called *sqlald()*; the new name is *SQLSQLDAAlloc()*. The SQLDA structure, as defined in *sqlda.h*, is shown below.

```
struct SQLDA
{
long    N; /* Descriptor size in number of entries          */
```

```
char   **V; /* Ptr to Arr of addresses of main variables    */
long    *L; /* Ptr to Arr of lengths of buffers             */
short   *T; /* Ptr to Arr of types of buffers               */
short  **I; /* Ptr to Arr of addresses of indicator vars    */
long     F; /* Number of variables found by DESCRIBE        */
char   **S; /* Ptr to Arr of variable name pointers         */
short   *M; /* Ptr to Arr of max lengths of var. names      */
short   *C; /* Ptr to Arr of current lengths of var. names  */
char   **X; /* Ptr to Arr of ind. var. name pointers        */
short   *Y; /* Ptr to Arr of max lengths of ind. var. names */
short   *Z; /* Ptr to Arr of cur lengths of ind. var. names */
};
```

If an SQL statement contains both select-list items and bind variables, the number of which is unknown at compile time, two SQLDA structures must be used: one for the select-list items, or the statement output variables; and one for the bind variables, or the statement input variables. If either the select-list items or the bind variables are known at compile time, their corresponding method 3 statements can be used. For instance, if the select-list items are known at compile time the following syntax will be used:

```
EXEC SQL FETCH <cursor_name> INTO <select_item_list>
```

instead of

```
EXEC SQL FETCH <cursor_name> USING DESCRIPTOR
<select_descriptor_name>
```

Similarly, in case all bind variables are known at compile time, the following method 3 syntax can be used:

```
EXEC SQL OPEN <cursor_name> USING <bind_variable_list>
```

instead of:

```
EXEC SQL OPEN <cursor_name> USING DESCRIPTOR
<bind_descriptor_name>
```

Defining, allocating, and using the SQLDA structures is not enough when dealing with method 4. Another tedious and error-prone task is mapping the host variable datatypes with Oracle datatypes. This is particularly true for Oracle numbers and dates, because if they are not coerced into host variable compatible datatypes the program will receive the Oracle internal format. Dates are stored in

Oracle as seven bytes objects and the internal Oracle format for numbers is not compatible with the host program number formats.

Using dynamic SQL method 4 with a query, the bind variables and select-list items of which are not known at compile time, requires 18 well defined steps. They are summarized in the table below.

STEP #	ACTION	PURPOSE
1	Declare a string to hold the SQL statement	The string will be used by the PREPARE method 4 call to parse the statement.
2	Declare SQLDA for select-list items and bind variables	Two pointers to the SQLDA structure will be used in the program.
3	Reserve space for the SQLDA structures	Either *sqlald()* or *SQLSQLDAAlloc()* is used to allocate memory for the SQLDAs.
4	Use an arbitrary number to set the maximum number of select-list items and bind variables	The N SQLDA structure field is set to the same number used by sqlald() to allocate memory for the two SQLDAs.
5	Copy the SQL statement in the host string	The host string containing the statement will be used by the other calls in the program.
6	PREPARE the query from the host string	The SQL statement contained in the host string is parsed and given a name.
7	DECLARE a cursor FOR the query	A cursor is defined and a select statement associated to it.
8	DESCRIBE the bind variables INTO the bind descriptor	The bind variable SQLDA is filled with information about each bind variable. This is possible because the statement has been already parsed.
9	Reset the number of placeholders in the SQLDA structure to the number found by DESCRIBE	The field N of the bind variable SQLDA is set to the number actually found by DESCRIBE.
10	Reserve space for the bind variables and assign values to them	The SQLDA structure now contains all information required to properly size the bind variables contained in the SQL statement.
11	OPEN the cursor USING the bind descriptor	The cursor needs to know all bind variables to execute the statement using the where clause. The bind descriptor provides all necessary information.
12	DESCRIBE the select list INTO the select descriptor	The server has opened the cursor. The client program can now interrogate the cursor to find out about the select-list items.

(*cont.*)

STEP #	ACTION	PURPOSE
13	Reset the number of select-list items in the SQLDA structure to the number found by DESCRIBE	The field N of the select-list SQLDA is set to the number actually found by DESCRIBE.
14	Define length, precision and scale for each select-list item. Allocate memory for all select-list items	The select-list SQLDA fields are manipulated to coerce dataype conversion and memory is allocated to accommodate the size of all select-list items.
15	FETCH a row from the database INTO the data buffers pointed to by the select descriptors	The select-list descriptor receives data from the database. The client program can access the select-list values contained in the select-list SQLDA.
16	Process the select-list items	Business logic is applied to the data retrieved.
17	Release all memory allocated to select-list items, bind variables, indicator variables and descriptors	When all rows have been fetched from the database, the memory allocated to all items participating in the query must be released.
18	CLOSE the cursor	Before exiting the program, it is good practice to close the cursor. The cursor can be reutilized by other queries in the same program. In this case, the cursor can be left open for subsequent reuse.

A developer dealing with method 4 needs to know all details about Oracle internal datatypes and must decide how to coerce them into C-compatible datatypes. The amount of details and knowledge required by a developer to use method 4 makes it unsuitable for most applications. Furthermore, the resulting Pro*C code becomes so complex and convoluted that its maintenance is problematic.

Processing dynamic SQL statements in Oracle OCI represents a better solution. In OCI, dynamic SQL can be processed much more easily using fewer lines of code. This doesn't mean giving up Pro*C completely in favor of OCI. It is still possible to use Pro*C for all but dynamic SQL processing and only code the dynamic SQL routines in OCI. With the release of Oracle 8, OCI has become a crucial component for the development of Oracle applications. It is likely that more and more Oracle shops will adopt it as the principal tool to develop complex and performant applications.

On the other hand, the huge amount of Pro*C code written for the Oracle 6 and 7 environments that need to be ported to Oracle 8 in order to exploit the newly introduced features indicates that Pro*C will maintain a relevant position among the Oracle development tools. The best solution is arguably to integrate the two worlds, intermixing Pro*C code with OCI calls when OCI provides either more elegant solutions or features not accessible directly from Pro*C. The next section will discuss how to interface Pro*C to OCI.

11.7 Interfacing Pro*C to OCI

Oracle OCI release 8 represents a major upgrade from the previous release, to the extent that OCI 8 and OCI 7 can be considered two different products. The two sets of APIs are completely different, as well as the underlying philosophy and the approach to SQL statement processing of the two releases. The big difference between the two versions is reflected in the way Pro*C interfaces to OCI.

11.7.1 INTERFACING PRO*C TO OCI RELEASE 7

OCI release 7 relies on three descriptors to work. They are the Host Data Area (HDA), the Logon Data Area (LDA), and the Cursor Data Area (CDA). The HDA is used only by an OCI program during a connection to Oracle. The OCI 7 call *orlon()*, which performs the connection to Oracle, links an LDA to an HDA. From that moment onwards, an OCI program needs only the LDA and CDA structures to work. The *oopen()* call, which creates a cursor, links a CDA to an LDA. The CDA descriptor is passed to all OCI calls that manipulate the cursor, such as *oparse()*, which parses an SQL statement into the cursor, or *obndra()*, which associates a program variable with a where clause placeholder in the SQL statement.

When OCI APIs are called from a Pro*C program, the connection to Oracle must occur using the Pro*C statement EXEC SQL CONNECT. The Host Data Area is maintained by SQLLIB and doesn't need to be passed to the OCI environment. The only descriptor needed by an OCI environment to work is the LDA. A Pro*C program that interfaces to OCI calls must define an LDA descriptor and link it to the connection descriptor before passing it as a parameter to OCI calls. This is accomplished by the *sqllda()* function, which is called by Pro*C after a successful connection to Oracle. sqllda() fills in all descriptor fields of the LDA descriptor, linking that specific LDA to the connection environment opened by Pro*C. An example of this technique is shown below. The Pro*C program connects to Oracle, defines the LDA descriptor, and calls an OCI function that computes the number of tables defined in the default schema.

```
EXEC SQL INCLUDE SQLCA;
#include "oci.h"
#include <stdlib.h>
#include <stdio.h>
#include <string.h>
```

```

int Connect(char *, char *);
int nExecuteOciCall(Lda_Def * , int * );

int main(int argc, char **argv)
{
 int    sts;
 int    nTableCount=0;
 Lda_Def lda;

 if ( (sts = Connect(argv[1],argv[2]))!= 0)
 {
        fprintf(stdout,"Could not connect, aborting...\n");
        exit(-1);
 }
 sqllda(&lda);
 if ( (sts = nExecuteOciCall(&lda,&nTableCount)) != 0)
 {
        fprintf(stdout,"Could not compute table count\n");
        exit(-1);
 }
 printf("The schema contains %d tables\n",nTableCount);

}

int Connect(char * szUsername, char * szPassword)
{
 EXEC SQL CONNECT :szUsername IDENTIFIED BY :szPassword;
 if (sqlca.sqlcode != 0)
        return -1;
 else
        return (0);
}

int nExecuteOciCall(Lda_Def * LocLda, int * nTableNumber)
{
 Cda_Def             LocCda;
 char                szSqlStmt[101];
 int                 nTableCount;

 strcpy(szSqlStmt,"Select count(*) from user_tables");

 if (oopen(&LocCda,LocLda, (text *) 0, -1, -1, (text *) 0, -1))
        return 1;
```

```
50:
51:   if (oparse(&LocCda, (text *) szSqlStmt,-1,0,2))
52:         return 1;
53:
54:   if (odefin(&LocCda,1,(ub1 *) &nTableCount,(int) sizeof(int),3,-1,
55:         (sb2 *) 0, (text *) 0,-1,-1,(ub2 *) 0, (ub2 *) 0))
56:         return 1;
57:   if (oexfet(&LocCda,1,0,0))
58:         return 1;
59:   *nTableNumber = nTableCount;
60:   oclose(&LocCda);
61:   return 0;
62: }
```

Interfacing Pro*C to Oracle OCI release 7

2	The OCI include file defines the required descriptor required for Pro*C —OCI interoperability.
15	The LDA descriptor if defined
21	The LDA descriptor is filled with the Pro*C connection context.
40–62	The nExecuteOciCall() function is implemented using OCI release 7 APIs.

11.7.2 INTERFACING PRO*C TO OCI RELEASE 8

OCI release 8 introduces the notion of opaque handles and descriptors that store information about the various OCI contexts. The most important handle is the environment handle, the allocation of which is mandatory in all OCI applications. Other commonly used handles are the error handle, the service context handle and the statement handle.

The service context handle contains three subhandles that represent the operational context for the OCI calls to an Oracle server. They are the server handle, which identifies a data source, a user session handle, which defines the user's security domain, and the transaction handle, which defines the transactional context where the SQL statements are executed.

The OCI 8 environment is more complex than its release 7 counterpart, but it achieves the goal of reduced network roundtrips and increased overall performance. To interface Pro*C code to OCI release 8 APIs, one should proceed by connecting to the database using the familiar EXEC SQL CONNECT statement. This establishes an SQLLIB connection context, which can be mapped to an OCI opaque handle by calling *SQLEnvGet()*. The latter is defined in *sql2oci.h*, which must be included in the Pro*C program.

The OCI function receives the environment handle from Pro*C and allocates the required additional handles against it. This allows the OCI function to prepare and execute an SQL statement. The example presented for OCI release 7 is shown below, reworked for OCI release 8.

```
EXEC SQL INCLUDE SQLCA;
#include "sql2oci.h"
#include <stdlib.h>
#include <stdio.h>
#include <string.h>

int Connect(char *, char *);
int nExecuteOciCall(OCIEnv * , int * );

int main(int argc, char **argv)
{
 int          sts;
 int          nTableCount=0;
 OCIEnv       *EnvH;

 if ( (sts = Connect(argv[1],argv[2]))!= 0)
 {
       fprintf(stdout,"Could not connect, aborting...\n");
       exit(-1);
 }
 if ( (sts = SQLEnvGet(SQL_SINGLE_RCTX,&EnvH)) != OCI_SUCCESS)
 {
       fprintf(stdout,"Could not obtain OCI environment\n");
       exit(-1);
 }

 if ( (sts = nExecuteOciCall(EnvH,&nTableCount)) != 0)
 {
       fprintf(stdout,"Could not compute table count\n");
       exit(-1);
 }
 printf("The schema contains %d tables\n",nTableCount);

}

int Connect(char * szUsername, char * szPassword)
{
 EXEC SQL CONNECT :szUsername IDENTIFIED BY :szPassword;
 if (sqlca.sqlcode != 0)
       return -1;
 else
```

```
        return (0);
}

int nExecuteOciCall(OCIEnv * EnvH, int * nTableNumber)
{
 OCIDefine    *DefH= (OCIDefine *) 0;
 OCIStmt      *StmtH;
 OCIError     *LErrH;
 OCISvcCtx    *SvcH;
 char         szSqlStmt[101];
 int          nTableCount;
 int          sts;

 strcpy(szSqlStmt,"Select count(*) from user_tables");
 if ( (sts = OCIHandleAlloc( (dvoid *) EnvH, (dvoid **) &StmtH,
                      OCI_HTYPE_STMT, (size_t) 0,
                      (dvoid **) 0)) != OCI_SUCCESS)
 {
       return 1;
 }
 if ( (sts = SQLSvcCtxGet(SQL_SINGLE_RCTX, (text *) 0,
                   (ub4) 0, &SvcH)) != OCI_SUCCESS)
 {
       return 1;
 }
 if ( (sts = OCIHandleAlloc((dvoid *) EnvH, (dvoid **) &LErrH,
                     (ub4) OCI_HTYPE_ERROR, (ub4) 0,
                     (dvoid **) 0)) != OCI_SUCCESS)
 {
       return 1;
 }
 if ( (sts = OCIStmtPrepare(StmtH,LErrH,(text* ) szSqlStmt,
                     (ub4) strlen((char *) szSqlStmt),
                     (ub4) OCI_NTV_SYNTAX,
                     (ub4) OCI_DEFAULT)) != OCI_SUCCESS)
 {
       return 1;
 }
 if ( (sts = OCIDefineByPos(StmtH,&DefH,LErrH,1,
                     (dvoid *) &nTableCount,
                     (sword) sizeof(sword), SQLT_INT,
                     (dvoid *) 0, (ub2 *) 0, (ub2 *) 0,
                     OCI_DEFAULT)) != OCI_SUCCESS)
 {
```

```
 86:         return 1;
 87:   }
 88:   sts = OCIStmtExecute(SvcH,StmtH,LErrH, (ub4) 1, (ub4) 0,
 89:                    (CONST OCISnapshot *) NULL,
 90:                    (OCISnapshot *) NULL, OCI_DEFAULT);
 91:   if (sts == OCI_SUCCESS)
 92:   {
 93:         *nTableNumber = nTableCount;
 94:         return 0;
 95:   }
 96:   else if ( sts == OCI_NO_DATA)
 97:   {
 98:         *nTableNumber = 0;
 99:         return 0;
100:   }
101:   else
102:         return 1;
103: }
```

Interfacing Pro*C to Oracle OCI release 8

2 sql2oci.h is included. It contains the definitions of the functions used to interface Pro*C to OCI release 8.

14 A pointer to an OCI environment handle is defined.

21–25 The environment handle is mapped to an SQLLIB connection context through a call to SQLEnvGet(). This handle will be passed to the OCI function.

27–31 The OCI function is called, passing the pointer to the environment handle as a parameter. The other parameter is a pointer to an integer, which will receive the number of tables defined in the default schema.

47–50 Four OCI handles will be used by the OCI function being defined. They are a define handle, an error handle, a statement handle, and a server context handle.

56–87 The required handles are allocated by calling the respective allocation functions.

88–90 The SQL statement that computes the number of tables defined in the default schema is submitted to the database engine.

91–103 The result of the statement is evaluated and interpreted. The function then returns to the caller. Note that the memory de-allocation of the OCI handles is not shown in the code, yet should be performed if the program doesn't detach from the database yet continues processing.

Chapter 12 will cover Oracle OCI in details. To understand why it is better to use OCI rather than Pro*C to process dynamic SQL, go straight to Chapter 12. The material presented in this section gives a preliminary knowledge that you will find useful when OCI specific calls must be used from a Pro*C-based environment.

The typical case is an application that uses static SQL in most cases, but must also support dynamic SQL. All static SQL can be coded using Pro*C while the dynamic SQL routines can be implemented in OCI, using the bridging mechanism discussed in this section.

11.8 Developing Multi-Threaded Applications

Pro*C release 2.2 introduced for the first time support for lightweight processes or threads when the operating system used by the Oracle system supports this feature. All commonly used operating systems support threads, including MS Windows NT, the major Unix flavors such as Sun Solaris, HP/UX, IBM AIX, and DEC Unix. Threads are also supported by OpenVMS, which implements them directly in the kernel starting from release 7.1.

The programming paradigm based on the use of threads introduces a few benefits that are particularly useful for database-centric applications. Most importantly, the use of threads increases the overall throughput of an application allowing for overlapping operations. Threads avoid most of kernel synchronization overhead and minimize the need for global data. Threads should be used extensively in new applications, and Oracle developers should become familiar with them and possibly master them in order to build better applications able to exploit the increased throughput.

The thread support provided by Pro*C allows for building sophisticated applications where threads can share cursor resources. One thread can open a cursor, fetch the first batch of rows from it, and then terminate, letting another thread fetch a second batch of rows. The cursor can then be closed by a third thread.

In order to support threads, Pro*C implements session contexts, which are connections to the Oracle database that can be used interchangeably by threads. One session context can be shared among multiple threads, provided that some form of synchronization is implemented to prevent two threads from concurrently accessing the same session context.

Designers can also opt for the one thread-one session context model, where each thread uses a dedicated connection to the database. While this technique is useful in few and very specific cases, it suffers from several drawbacks that limit its usefulness and definitely make it unsuitable for most applications. First of all, the proliferation of threads must be strictly controlled; otherwise, one user can saturate all available database connections by misusing the application. Furthermore, connecting to Oracle is an expensive operation that takes some time. If one application connects multiple times by spawning multiple threads, the initial startup time will be longer and will be perceived by the user.

In most cases, it is more convenient to implement a process-level connection pooling mechanism, by defining one or a few session contexts and forcing all threads to share them. Synchronization must be provided in this case, usually through the use of mutexes, condition variables, or semaphores in Unix/OpenVMS and mutexes, critical sections, and semaphores in MS Windows NT.

Specific Pro*C syntax is needed to support threads. The command line option THREADS must be set to YES if driving the Pro*C precompilation from the command line or from a make file. Alternatively, in the NT GUI world, the visual interface to Pro*C provides a check box that must be ticked.

The embedded SQL statement EXEC SQL ENABLE THREADS must be the first executable SQL statement in the multi-threaded program. When the command-line option and the embedded statement enabling threads are set, the precompiler expects to find one or more context allocations. In other words, it ex-

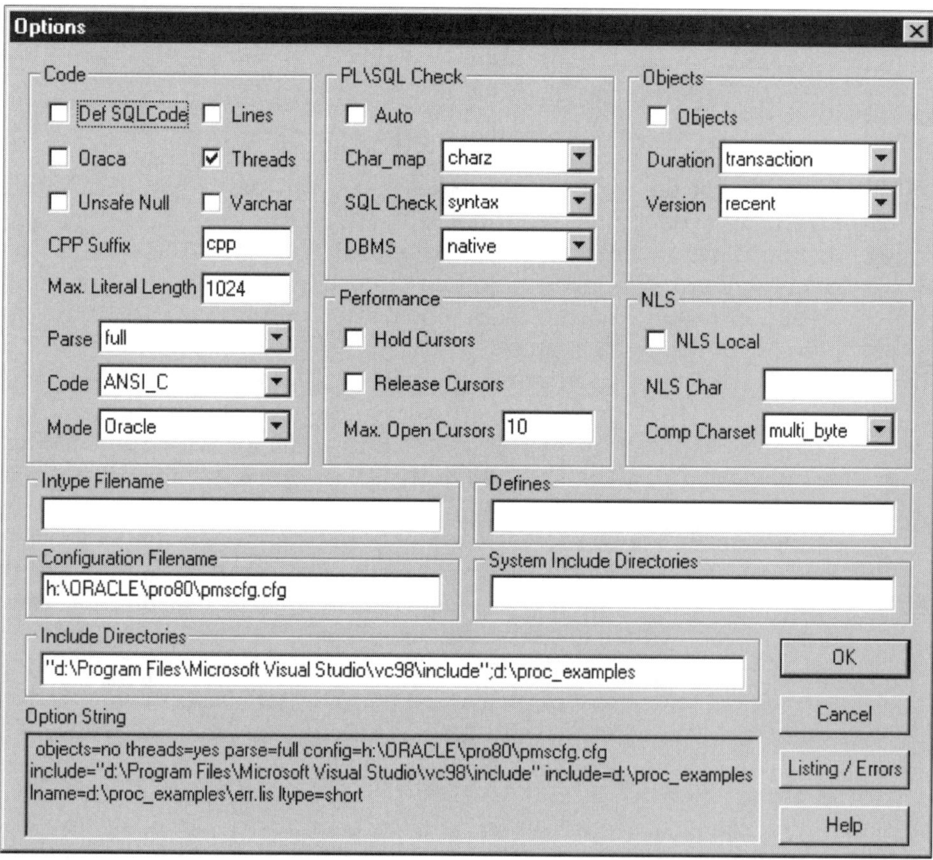

FIGURE 11.3 When precompiling a multi-threaded program in the NT environment, the "Threads" check-box must be ticked.

pects to find the embedded SQL statements EXEC SQL ALLOCATE CONTEXT and EXEC SQL CONTEXT USE. If the precompiler doesn't encounter these embedded statements, the precompilation fails with PCC error 2390, or "No EXEC SQL CONTEXT USE statement encountered."

Each runtime session context must be allocated, used, and freed. The Pro*C support for threads ensures that the SQLLIB functions are thread-safe, but developers should exercise particular care when dealing with SQL components that are not under a direct SQLLIB control. A typical example is the use of the SQLCA structure. If only one global SQLCA is used throughout the entire program and more than one session context is defined, two threads can access its fields without synchronization, causing disastrous consequences. Declaring one local SQLCA per session context prevents this problem from occurring.

The following example uses Solaris threads. Three database routines are executed by three threads, which use a mutex to synchronize their access to the only connection available. The connection context is passed to the threads as a parameter. This avoids defining the connection context as a global variable. An even more elegant solution would be defining a structure containing the connection context plus the two mutexes used by the application threads for synchronization. This way, the mutexes can also be defined locally in *main()* and not globally; the structure can be passed to the threads, thus increasing information hiding and modularity.

```
EXEC SQL INCLUDE SQLCA;
#include <stdio.h>
#include <thread.h>
#include <synch.h>

#define NO_MORE_ROWS 1403

static mutex_t db_mutex = DEFAULTMUTEX;
static mutex_t scr_mutex= DEFAULTMUTEX;

void *table_func(void *);
void *index_func(void *);
void *colmn_func(void *);

int main (int argc, char **argv)
{
  sql_context          main_ctx;
  char                 szLine[81];
  thread_t             t1,t2,t3;
  int                  ii,
                       jj;

```

```

  EXEC SQL ENABLE THREADS;

  EXEC SQL CONTEXT ALLOCATE :main_ctx;

  EXEC SQL CONTEXT USE :main_ctx;
  EXEC SQL CONNECT :argv[1] IDENTIFIED BY :argv[2];
  if (sqlca.sqlcode != 0)
  {
         exit(1);
  }
  mutex_lock(&db_mutex);
  thr_create(NULL,0,table_func,(void *) main_ctx,THR_DETACHED,&t1);
  thr_create(NULL,0,index_func,(void *) main_ctx,THR_DETACHED,&t2);
  thr_create(NULL,0,colmn_func,(void *) main_ctx,THR_DETACHED,&t3);
  fprintf(stdout,"Press enter to see the threads in action...\n");
  fgets(szLine,80,stdin);
  mutex_unlock(&db_mutex);
 thr_exit(0);
}

void * table_func(void * ctx)
{
  char   szTableName[10][31];
  int    limit=10;
  int    ii,
         kk=1;
  int    nFetched,
         nRows,
         rows_done;
  memset(szTableName,'\0',sizeof(szTableName));
  mutex_lock(&db_mutex);
  EXEC SQL CONTEXT USE :ctx;
  EXEC SQL DECLARE tbl_cur CURSOR FOR
          SELECT TABLE_NAME FROM USER_TABLES;
  EXEC SQL OPEN tbl_cur;
  for(rows_done=0;;)
  {
         EXEC SQL FOR :limit FETCH tbl_cur INTO :szTableName;
         nFetched = sqlca.sqlerrd[2] - rows_done;
         rows_done += nFetched;
         if(sqlca.sqlerrd[2] == 0)
                break;
         mutex_lock(&scr_mutex) ;
```

```
        for(ii=0; ii< nFetched; ii++,kk++)
                fprintf(stdout,"Table %d name: %s\n",
                        kk,szTableName[ii]);
        fprintf(stdout,"----------------------\n");
        mutex_unlock(&scr_mutex) ;
        if(sqlca.sqlcode == NO_MORE_ROWS)
                break;
    }
    EXEC SQL CLOSE tbl_cur;
    mutex_unlock(&db_mutex);
    thr_exit(0);
}

void * index_func(void * ctx)
{
        char    szIndexName[10][31];
        int     limit=10;
        int     nFetched,
                rows_done;
    int     ii,
                kk=1;
        memset(szIndexName,'\0',sizeof(szIndexName));
    mutex_lock(&db_mutex);
    EXEC SQL CONTEXT USE :ctx;
    EXEC SQL DECLARE ndx_cur CURSOR FOR
            SELECT INDEX_NAME FROM USER_INDEXES;
    EXEC SQL OPEN ndx_cur;
    for(rows_done=0;;)
    {
        EXEC SQL FOR :limit FETCH ndx_cur INTO :szIndexName;
        nFetched = sqlca.sqlerrd[2] - rows_done;
        rows_done += nFetched;
        if(sqlca.sqlerrd[2] == 0)
                        break;
        mutex_lock(&scr_mutex) ;
        for(ii=0; ii< nFetched; ii++,kk++)
                        fprintf(stdout,"Index %d name: %s\n",
                                kk,szIndexName[ii]);
        fprintf(stdout,"-------------------\n");
        mutex_unlock(&scr_mutex) ;
        if(sqlca.sqlcode == NO_MORE_ROWS)
                break;
    }
    EXEC SQL CLOSE ndx_cur;
```

```
111:   mutex_unlock(&db_mutex);
112:   thr_exit(0);
113: }
114: void *colmn_func(void * ctx)
115: {
116:           char    szTabColName[10][31];
117:           int     limit=10;
118:           int     nFetched,
119:             rows_done;
120:   int      ii,
121:             kk;
122:           memset(szTabColName,'\0',sizeof(szTabColName));
123:   mutex_lock(&db_mutex);
124:   EXEC SQL CONTEXT USE :ctx;
125:   EXEC SQL DECLARE tbc_cur CURSOR FOR
126:             SELECT COLUMN_NAME FROM USER_TAB_COLUMNS;
127:   EXEC SQL OPEN tbc_cur;
128:   for(rows_done=0;;)
129:   {
130:           EXEC SQL FOR :limit FETCH tbc_cur INTO :szTabColName;
131:           nFetched = sqlca.sqlerrd[2] - rows_done;
132:           rows_done += nFetched;
133:           if(sqlca.sqlerrd[2] == 0)
134:                           break;
135:           mutex_lock(&scr_mutex) ;
136:           for(ii=0; ii< nFetched; ii++,kk++)
137:                 fprintf(stdout,"Column %d name: %s\n",
138:                        kk,szTabColName[ii]);
139:           fprintf(stdout,"------------\n");
140:           mutex_unlock(&scr_mutex) ;
141:           if(sqlca.sqlcode == NO_MORE_ROWS)
142:                 break;
143:   }
144:   EXEC SQL CLOSE tbc_cur;
145:   mutex_unlock(&db_mutex);
146:   thr_exit(0);
147: }
```

Sun Threads

3 The Sun thread definition file is included.

8–9 Two mutexes are defined, to synchronize the access to the database and to the standard output.

11–13	Definition of the three routines, which will be executed by the spawned threads.
17	The Pro*C connection context is defined.
24	Embedded SQL statement that informs the SQLLIB that threads will be used in the program.
26	Connection context allocation.
28–29	Connection to Oracle linked to the defined connection context.
34	Thread 0 (the program mainline) accesses the DB mutex to prevent the threads spawned in the next statements from executing.
35–37	Three threads are created, each executing a different SQL statement. In order to run, they must wait until thread 0 release the synchronization mutex.
44–78	The *table_func()* function displays all tables defined in the default schema. It queries the data dictionary table USER_TABLES to gather the required information. Before accessing the database using the connection context received as a parameter, it tries to get control over the DB mutex. This represents the synchronization mechanism used to share the connection context between the three threads.
80–113	The *index_func()* function displays all indexes defined in the default schema. It queries the data dictionary table USER_INDEXES to gather the required information.
114–147	The *column_func()* function displays all columns defined in the default schema. It queries the data dictionary table USER_TAB_COLUMNS to gather the required information.

The following program is a port to an NT environment of the previous example. NT threads and mutexes are used, but the structure of the program is unchanged. As in the previous example, the three threads are spawned but prevented to run by the main thread until the user presses the *enter* key. At that point, the three threads compete for access to the mutex that guarantees exclusive access to the connection context established by *main()*.

```
EXEC SQL INCLUDE SQLCA;
#include <windows.h>
#include <stdio.h>
#include <stdlib.h>
#include <process.h>

#define NO_MORE_ROWS 1403
HANDLE db_mutex;
HANDLE scr_mutex;

DWORD WINAPI table_func(LPVOID);
```

```
DWORD WINAPI index_func(LPVOID);
DWORD WINAPI colmn_func(LPVOID);

int main (int argc, char **argv)
{
  sql_context         main_ctx;
  char                szLine[81];
  HANDLE              t1,t2,t3;
  DWORD               t1_id,t2_id,t3_id;
  DWORD               dwThreadResult;

  EXEC SQL ENABLE THREADS;

  EXEC SQL CONTEXT ALLOCATE :main_ctx;

  EXEC SQL CONTEXT USE :main_ctx;
  EXEC SQL CONNECT :argv[1] IDENTIFIED BY :argv[2];
  if (sqlca.sqlcode != 0)
  {
          exit(1);
  }
  db_mutex = CreateMutex(NULL,FALSE,NULL);
  scr_mutex = CreateMutex(NULL,FALSE,NULL);
  /* if( (dwThreadResult =
          WaitForSingleObject(db_mutex,INFINITE)) != WAIT_OBJECT_0)
  {
          printf("Could not obtain mutex. Aborting...\n");
          exit(-1);
  } */
  t1 = CreateThread(
                        NULL,
                        0,
                        table_func,
                        main_ctx,
                        0,
                        &t1_id);
  if ( t1 == NULL)
  {
          printf("Could not create thread. Aborting...\n");
          exit(-1);
  }
  t2 = CreateThread(
                        NULL,
                        0,
```

```
                           index_func,
                           main_ctx,
                           0,
                           &t2_id);
  if ( t2 == NULL)
  {
        printf("Could not create thread. Aborting...\n");
        exit(-1);
  }
  t3 = CreateThread(
                           NULL,
                           0,
                           colmn_func,
                           main_ctx,
                           0,
                           &t3_id);
  if ( t3 == NULL)
  {
        printf("Could not create thread. Aborting...\n");
        exit(-1);
  }
  fprintf(stdout,"Press enter to see the threads in action...\n");
  fgets(szLine,80,stdin);
  /* if (! ReleaseMutex(db_mutex))
  {
        printf("Could not release mutex. Aborting...\n");
        exit(-1);
  } */
 exit(0);
}

DWORD WINAPI table_func(LPVOID ctx)
{
  char   szTableName[10][31];
  int    limit=10;
  int    ii,
         kk=1;
  DWORD   dwThreadResult,
         dwScrMutex;
  int    nFetched,
         rows_done;
  memset(szTableName,'\0',sizeof(szTableName));
  if( (dwThreadResult =
         WaitForSingleObject(db_mutex,INFINITE)) != WAIT_OBJECT_0)
```

```
  {
        printf("Could not obtain mutex. Aborting...\n");
        exit(-1);
  }
  EXEC SQL CONTEXT USE :ctx;
  EXEC SQL DECLARE tbl_cur CURSOR FOR
         SELECT TABLE_NAME FROM USER_TABLES;
  EXEC SQL OPEN tbl_cur;
  for(rows_done=0;;)
  {
        EXEC SQL FOR :limit FETCH tbl_cur INTO :szTableName;
        nFetched = sqlca.sqlerrd[2] - rows_done;
        rows_done += nFetched;
        if(sqlca.sqlerrd[2] == 0)
              break;
        if( (dwScrMutex =
        WaitForSingleObject(scr_mutex,INFINITE)) != WAIT_OBJECT_0)
        {
              printf("Could not obtain mutex. Aborting...\n");
              exit(-1);
        }

        for(ii=0; ii< nFetched; ii++,kk++)
              fprintf(stdout,"Table %d name: %s\n",
                    kk,szTableName[ii]);
        fprintf(stdout,"----------------------\n");
        ReleaseMutex(scr_mutex);
        if(sqlca.sqlcode == NO_MORE_ROWS)
              break;
  }
  EXEC SQL CLOSE tbl_cur;
  ReleaseMutex(db_mutex);
  return(0);
}

DWORD WINAPI index_func(LPVOID ctx)
{
        char    szIndexName[10][31];
        int     limit=10;
        int     nFetched,
        rows_done;
  DWORD dwThreadResult,
        dwScrMutex;
```

```
    int     ii,
            kk=1;
           memset(szIndexName,'\0',sizeof(szIndexName));

    if( (dwThreadResult =
            WaitForSingleObject(db_mutex,INFINITE)) != WAIT_OBJECT_0)
    {
            printf("Could not obtain mutex. Aborting...\n");
            exit(-1);
    }

    EXEC SQL CONTEXT USE :ctx;
    EXEC SQL DECLARE ndx_cur CURSOR FOR
              SELECT INDEX_NAME FROM USER_INDEXES;
    EXEC SQL OPEN ndx_cur;
    for(rows_done=0;;)
    {
            EXEC SQL FOR :limit FETCH ndx_cur INTO :szIndexName;
            nFetched = sqlca.sqlerrd[2] - rows_done;
            rows_done += nFetched;
            if(sqlca.sqlerrd[2] == 0)
                                break;
            if( (dwScrMutex =
          WaitForSingleObject(scr_mutex,INFINITE)) != WAIT_OBJECT_0)
            {
                    printf("Could not obtain mutex. Aborting...\n");
                    exit(-1);
            }
            for(ii=0; ii< nFetched; ii++,kk++)
                                fprintf(stdout,"Index %d name: %s\n",
                                          kk,szIndexName[ii]);
            fprintf(stdout,"----------------------\n");
            ReleaseMutex(scr_mutex) ;
            if(sqlca.sqlcode == NO_MORE_ROWS)
                    break;
    }
    EXEC SQL CLOSE ndx_cur;
    ReleaseMutex(db_mutex);
    return(0);
  }

  DWORD WINAPI colmn_func(LPVOID ctx)
  {
```

```
        char    szTabColName[10][31];
        int     limit=10;
        int     nFetched,
        rows_done;
int     ii,
        kk=1;
DWORD   dwThreadResult,
        dwScrMutex;

        memset(szTabColName,'\0',sizeof(szTabColName));

if( (dwThreadResult =
    WaitForSingleObject(db_mutex,INFINITE)) != WAIT_OBJECT_0)
{
        printf("Could not obtain mutex. Aborting...\n");
        exit(-1);
}

EXEC SQL CONTEXT USE :ctx;
EXEC SQL DECLARE tbc_cur CURSOR FOR
         SELECT COLUMN_NAME FROM USER_TAB_COLUMNS;
EXEC SQL OPEN tbc_cur;
for(rows_done=0;;)
{
        EXEC SQL FOR :limit FETCH tbc_cur INTO :szTabColName;
        nFetched = sqlca.sqlerrd[2] - rows_done;
        rows_done += nFetched;
        if(sqlca.sqlerrd[2] == 0)
                        break;

        if( (dwScrMutex =
        WaitForSingleObject(scr_mutex,INFINITE)) != WAIT_OBJECT_0)
        {
                printf("Could not obtain mutex. Aborting...\n");
                exit(-1);
        }

        for(ii=0; ii< nFetched; ii++,kk++)
                fprintf(stdout,"Column %d name: %s\n",
                        kk,szTabColName[ii]);
        fprintf(stdout,"----------------------\n");
        ReleaseMutex(scr_mutex) ;
        if(sqlca.sqlcode == NO_MORE_ROWS)
```

```
                break;
    }
    EXEC SQL CLOSE tbc_cur;
    ReleaseMutex(db_mutex);
    return(0);
}
```

NT Threads

The example program is virtually identical to the previous one, except for NT specific thread and mutex allocation and use. For a detailed explanation of the program logic, see the comments to the previous example.

11.9 Handling LOB Types in Pro*C

The support for unstructured data in older releases of Oracle has been unsatisfactory. The two datatypes used to store unstructured data in an Oracle database until release 8, LONG and LONG RAW, have historically been suffering from major drawbacks and limitations. Just to name a few, LONG columns cannot be indexed and only one LONG is allowed per table. SQL expressions cannot refer to LONG columns, and LONG columns cannot be used to order and group queries, cannot have constraints or be referenced in constraints, and cannot participate in replicated databases.

To overcome all these limitations, Oracle 8 introduces a completely new family of datatypes designed to handle and store unstructured data. The family comprises four datatypes called Large Objects (LOB):

- BLOB for binary data
- CLOB for single-byte text
- NLOB for multi-byte text
- BFILE for unstructured data contained in external files

LOBs are not physically stored together with the other structured datatypes in the same row. A row contains one or more *LOB locators*, which are pointers to a separate segment containing the LOB (or LOBs). Gone is the restriction on only one LONG per table, and this approach also speeds up full table scans of structured data stored together with LOBs in the same table.

This sounds like good news for Oracle developers, who can finally count on a much better support for multimedia and WEB-based applications. Unfortunately, Oracle Corporation provides LOB native support only through PL/SQL and OCI. Pro*C has been left out. To manipulate LOBs in Pro*C there are two options:

- Include *oci.h* in the Pro*C program and use the OCI functions to manipulate LOBs.
- Use PL/SQL from Pro*C to manipulate LOBs.

We will consider the first technique in Chapter 12, while discussing the Oracle Call Interface, and the second technique in Chapter 13, which is dedicated to PL/SQL.

11.10 The Object-Relational Paradigm

Oracle Corporation finally delivered the long awaited object support with the release 8 of the flagship database. Oracle was the first commercially available relational database at the end of the 1970s. All Oracle tools, attitude, and mentality have been built upon the relational model. This model has been universally adopted because of its advantages over the hierarchical/network model.

At the beginning of the relational era, critics of the relational model pointed their finger to the perceived poor performance delivered by the relational databases available in that period. The lack of performance or, even more, the perceived lack of performance that affected the first wave of relational databases, was gradually overcome by improvements in the optimizer and new indexing methods. By mid-1980s, nobody questioned the relational model, which had definitely supplanted the hierarchical model.

Today the object-oriented paradigm represents a real mind set shift and is in sharp contrast with a relational approach. The latter is based on decomposition while the first is based on encapsulation. In a relational world, an invoice is split into a table containing invoice header information, a second table containing the line items, and possibly a third table containing the invoice footer. Primary and foreign keys govern the underlying relationship between related entities. The code that accesses and manipulates the data is kept separate and distinct from the data itself. It can reside in the database (stored procedures, stored functions, packages), in 4GL environments (Oracle Forms), or 3GL environments (Pro*C, OCI).

In an object-oriented world, the invoice object contains both data and code needed to access the data within the same entity. The data elements are called *attributes* and the code elements are called *methods*. An object-oriented database gives persistence to the objects that are instantiated by the OO language used. The state of the object is saved for later retrieval by the object-oriented application. The object is saved in its entirety and retrieved without performing and mapping between the database representation of the datatypes and the language implementation of the datatypes used. To use a common sentence among the object-oriented database developers, there is no *impedance mismatch* between database and language.

Object-oriented languages have been around for almost two decades, but only relatively recently have they reached a wide acceptance in commercial environments. The market offers object-oriented databases, which suffer from the same drawbacks that plagued their relational counterpart at the beginning of the relational era: performance (or the lack of). As for the relational databases at the beginning of the 1980s, it is more a perceived lack of performance rather than a real one, but most large mission-critical applications in major organizations still use relational engines rather than object-oriented databases.

The Oracle support for objects follows the hybrid object-relational approach. This means that support for objects is built on top of an underlying relational structure. The database maintains its strongly relational nature together with its speed and robustness, but developers can define abstract data types encapsulating in one object attributes and methods (PL/SQL and Java procedures). The main advantage of this approach is in its evolutionary nature that eases the transition to object orientation without requiring burning all bridges with the relational world. Designers and developers can gradually get acquainted with object-oriented tools and a way of thinking while delivering working applications that use techniques taken from the two worlds (object and relational).

The real disadvantage associated with an object-relational approach is that the mapping code required by an object-oriented language to fetch and use the "objects" stored in the database represents a large overhead. Conservative estimates consider the percentage of mapping code to be up to thirty percent of all code required by the application. This disadvantage is compounded in its negative impact by the data dependence of the mapping code, which means that for every small change in the physical structure of the object, the mapping code has to be modified accordingly. This defeats the core principle of object-orientation, which advocates a model where data hiding plays an essential role, together with encapsulation, to achieve loose coupling and strong cohesion of the modules comprising an application.

Object-oriented designers usually spend a lot of time and energy in defining the *interfaces* to the classes comprising the application. They are not concerned with implementation details internal to the classes until very late in the development stage. As long as the interface that a class exposes to the world doesn't change, the way methods are implemented within a class can vary during the development stage without causing code rework to the other classes. This is due to the high level of information hiding intrinsically provided by the object-oriented model.

When one more layer is introduced, as in the case of the hybrid object-relational model, changing the internal implementation of class methods often provokes major modifications to the way data is fetched from the database and manipulated. This means reworking the substantial portion of mapping code that is implemented to overcome the impedance mismatch between the relational structure of the data storage mechanism and the object-oriented nature of the application accessing the data.

Unfortunately, the list of the Oracle object support weaknesses is not finished. In order to support client side object manipulation, Oracle Corporation has introduced new functionality in tools like Pro*C, OCI, and PL/SQL, the use of which is extremely complex and often cumbersome. Oracle support for objects is also fragmented and inconsistent. The keyword "object" is used to mean and define different things in similar contexts. Objects have different "personalities"; they can be *object tables, row objects,* and *column objects.* Abstract datatypes are also called objects, which adds even more confusion. Let us take a close look at the syntax used to define Oracle objects.

The basic unit in any object definition is the object type.

```
CREATE TYPE person_t AS OBJECT
(
      first_name  VARCHAR2(20),
      last_name   VARCHAR2(30),
      address     VARCHAR2(50),
      home_tel    VARCHAR2(15),
      mobile_tel  VARCHAR2(15),
      office_tel  VARCHAR2(15),
      birth_date  DATE
);
```

An object table is a table created using the following syntax.

```
CREATE TABLE person OF person_t;
```

In this case *person* is called a row object because it occupies an entire row of an object table. The following example defines a column object and includes an object into a relational table.

```
CREATE TABLE personnel
(
      employee    person,
      hire_date   date,
      emp_code    number(7)
);
```

The confusing aspect is in the lack of distinction between the type definition, which describes only elements and behavior, and the physical materialization of it into an entity that occupies memory and/or disk space and has associated methods. In other words, the two concepts of class and object, which are kept separate and distinct in all OO languages, tend to coincide in the Oracle 8 world, where the abstract types are referred to as objects as well as their instantiations. The word "object" appears in the object type definition (`CREATE TYPE <type_name> AS OBJECT`). The word object also appears consistently in the Oracle documentation when referring to instantiations of object types.

Moreover, a few annoying limitations related to the "purest" form of object definable in Oracle 8—the object tables—reveal once again the "experimental" nature of object support in the release 8.0x of the engine. The most important among these limitations is that object tables cannot be partitioned, precluding their use in Very Large Databases (VLDBs).

Using object tables also brings about the *dangling ref* problem. Oracle gives every row object a unique identifier, called an object identifier. An object identifier allows the corresponding row object to be referred to from other objects or from relational tables. An Oracle provided datatype called REF represents such references. Accessing an object through its REF is called de-referencing the REF.

The main issue related to REFs is that Oracle doesn't automatically invalidate the REF when the object pointed to by the REF either doesn't exist any more, or is not in scope, perhaps because it has changed its privileges. A REF that doesn't reference any more an object is called a *dangling REF*. This represents a further burden for developers, who have to make sure that each object still exists when navigating through objects. An Oracle extension to SQL, IS [NOT] DANGLING, provides developers the means to identify dangling REFs in the database.

It doesn't make much sense comparing two objects in their entirety to determine a ranking between the two; it is usually one or more attributes of the object that are compared. In C++, this is accomplished by overloading the equality operator. Oracle 8 does not support operator overloading but offers two special PL/SQL methods that are used for object ranking. These methods are MAP and ORDER, and are mutually exclusive, which means that object types may have only one of the two methods defined.

The MAP method returns a number that is used by Oracle to rank the instances of a specific object type. The ORDER method receives an instance of the same object type and compares its relevant attributes with the current instance. It returns a negative integer if the current instance is less than the one received as a parameter, 0 if the two instances are equal, and a positive integer if the current instance is greater than the one received as a parameter. What follows is an example of a MAP method, applied to the object type *person_t*.

```
CREATE OR REPLACE TYPE person_t AS OBJECT
(
      first_name  VARCHAR2(20),
      last_name   VARCHAR2(30),
      address     VARCHAR2(50),
      home_tel    VARCHAR2(15),
```

```
        mobile_tel  VARCHAR2(15),
        office_tel  VARCHAR2(15),
        birth_date  DATE,
        MAP MEMBER FUNCTION
        age RETURN NUMBER,
        PRAGMA RESTRICT_REFERENCES (
        age, WNDS, WNPS, RNDS, RNPS)
);
CREATE OR REPLACE TYPE BODY person_t AS
MAP MEMBER FUNCTION age RETURN NUMBER IS
      BEGIN
            return TO_NUMBER(BIRTH_DATE);
      END;
END;
```

A tedious limitation imposed upon MAP methods is the one related to the *purity level* that a MAP method must have. Purity level is defined as the extent to which a method is free of side effects. Side effects are references to database tables or packaged variables. The *pragma* statement contained in the object definition specifies four constants for the age method. The meaning of the mnemonics used in the statement is shown in the table below.

CONSTANT	MEANING	EXPLANATION
WNDS	Writes No Database State	No database tables are modified.
WNPS	Writes No Package State	No packaged variables are modified.
RNDS	Reads No Database State	No database queries are performed.
RNPS	Reads No Package State	No packaged variables are referenced.

Map member functions must adhere to the most restrictive purity level. This means that they cannot even read database tables or packaged variables. If we wanted to change our previously defined map method to return the number of days elapsed since the birth date of each person, we could not use SYSDATE in our computation, as shown in the following example.

```
SQL> edit
CREATE OR REPLACE TYPE BODY person_t AS
MAP MEMBER FUNCTION age RETURN NUMBER IS
BEGIN
return SYSDATE - BIRTH_DATE;
```

```
  5  END;
  6* END;
SQL> /
Warning: Type Body created with compilation errors.
SQL> show errors
Errors for TYPE BODY PERSON_T:
LINE/
COL    ERROR
----  -------------------------------------------------------------
0/0    PL/SQL: Compilation unit analysis terminated
2/12   PLS-00452:Subprogram 'AGE' violates its associated pragma
```

The implementation of the Oracle function SYSDATE must access either a database table or a packaged variable. This lowers the purity level of the map method to a degree that is unacceptable by Oracle. The same limitation affecting the required purity level also applies to ORDER methods.

Another major limitation that affects the object implementation in Oracle 8.0x is the inability to modify object types once they have been included in tables. If you want to modify the person_t object type after having created an object table based on person_t, Oracle complains with the following error message:

```
SQL> /
CREATE OR REPLACE TYPE person_t AS OBJECT
*
ERROR at line 1:
ORA-02303: cannot drop or replace a type with type or table
dependents
```

This limitation totally defeats the concept of encapsulation, upon which the entire object-oriented model is based.

The object-relational hybrid model tries to conciliate two paradigms that have nothing in common, privileging the relational model when a conflict between the two models arises. The bottom line of the object-relational model is that the SQL-92 specification cannot in any way be sacrificed while extending the model to include support for objects. The resulting object implementation is unsatisfactory for the following reasons:

- Inheritance, one of the most important OO features, is not supported.
- Because of lack of inheritance, polymorphism is not supported. PL/SQL supports only function overloading.

- The few object-oriented features, which are offered by the object-relational model, suffer from several limitations and are implemented through artifices that are perceived as unnatural by object-oriented developers.
- Object manipulation and client cache navigation (see next sections) are supported only in C, which is not an object-oriented language.

Nevertheless, considering that this is only the first step by Oracle Corporation into the world of objects, a few positive features can be identified:

- Support for Abstract Data Types (ADT)
- Support for VARRAYS and nested tables (Collections)
- Support for object cache to minimize network roundtrips

The above mentioned features can be proficiently used by applications based upon a relational model. The remaining sections of this chapter will illustrate how to proficiently use Oracle object-oriented extensions from an application context based on the relational paradigm.

11.11 Oracle Type Translator (OTT)

The Oracle Type Translator (OTT) is a utility provided by Oracle that maps object definitions stored in the database to "C" structures. While developers can manually accomplish this task, its error-prone nature and repetitiveness make it a perfect candidate for an automated tool.

OTT needs a configuration file that specifies the types that must be mapped into "C" structures and other information. OTT calls this file an INTYPE file; it must be manually edited in Unix/OpenVMS systems and can be built visually in MS Windows-based systems, thanks to the INTYPE file assistant tool. Other mandatory parameters that must be passed to the OTT command line are the connection string to the schema where the types are defined and the target language used to generate the "C" structures. The latter can be only K&R "C" or ANSI "C".

OTT produces at least two files: the include file containing the structures mapping the object type, and an OUTTYPE file that contains information useful for the Pro*C precompiler. In fact, the OUTTYPE file must be passed to Pro*C when the object extensions are used in the code.

When OTT is used to map objects into "C" structures for the Oracle Call Interface, one more output file must be produced. It is a "C" file containing initialization code for the object types being used by the OCI program. This step is not necessary when Pro*C is used instead of OCI, because the SQLLIB takes care of all required initialization.

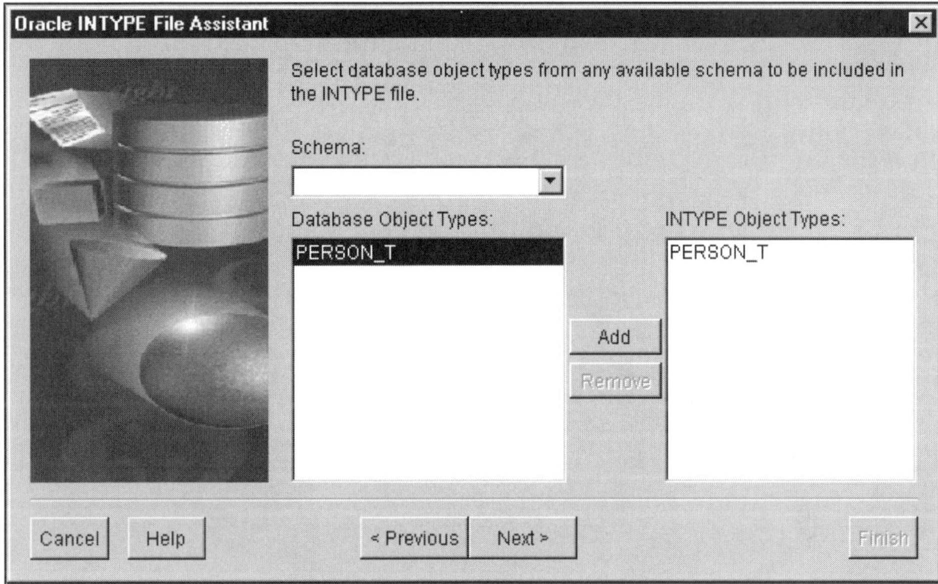

FIGURE 11.4 Oracle provides the INTYPE file assistant to visually create the INTYPE file for MS Windows systems.

The following example shows how to use OTT. The default schema contains an object type called person_t defined as follows:

```
SQL> desc person_t
 Name                            Null?    Type
 ------------------------------- -------- ----
 FIRST_NAME                               VARCHAR2(20)
 LAST_NAME                                VARCHAR2(30)
 ADDRESS                                  VARCHAR2(50)
 HOME_TEL                                 VARCHAR2(15)
 MOBILE_TEL                               VARCHAR2(15)
 OFFICE_TEL                               VARCHAR2(15)
 BIRTH_DATE                               DATE

METHOD
------
 ORDER MEMBER FUNCTION AGE RETURNS NUMBER
 Argument Name            Type                In/Out Default?
 ------------------------ ------------------ --------------
 A                        PERSON_T            IN
```

We want to map person_t into a corresponding "C" structure that will be used in a Pro*C program. The first step is the creation of the INTYPE file. It will be defined as:

```
Filename in_person.typ. Content:
      CASE = LOWER
      TYPE "PERSON_T"
            HFILE = "person.h"
```

OTT can now be invoked with the following command line arguments:

```
OTT INTYPE=in_person.typ CODE=C OUTTYPE=out_person.typ
```

Two files are produced by OTT. The first is *person.h,* which contains the "C" representation of the person_t object type.

```
Filename: person.h

      #ifndef PERSON_ORACLE
      # define PERSON_ORACLE

      #ifndef OCI_ORACLE
      # include <oci.h>
      #endif

      typedef OCIRef PERSON_T_ref;

      struct PERSON_T
      {
         OCIString * first_name;
         OCIString * last_name;
         OCIString * address;
         OCIString * home_tel;
         OCIString * mobile_tel;
         OCIString * office_tel;
         OCIDate birth_date;
      };
      typedef struct PERSON_T PERSON_T;

      struct PERSON_T_ind
      {
         OCIInd _atomic;
         OCIInd first_name;
         OCIInd last_name;
```

```
    OCIInd address;
    OCIInd home_tel;
    OCIInd mobile_tel;
    OCIInd office_tel;
    OCIInd birth_date;
};
typedef struct PERSON_T_ind PERSON_T_ind;

#endif
```

The second file is out_person_typ, which contains definitions that will be meaningful for the precompiler when the "C" program containing embedded object calls will be precompiled.

```
Filename: out_person.typ

      CASE = LOWER

      TYPE OPS$EBONAZZI.PERSON_T AS PERSON_T
        VERSION = "$8.0"
        HFILE = person.h
```

It is worth noting that OCI initialization types are also used in a Pro*C environment. Code is automatically generated by OTT to include the file "oci.h". With Oracle 8, the Oracle Call Interface, once rarely used by Oracle developers, gained momentum and arguably became the best supported development environment for database-centric applications based on Oracle technologies.

OTT shouldn't be invoked directly by developers, but rather embedded in the makefile that builds the entire application. OTT doesn't override the files it produces if nothing has changed since last invocation time. OTT is provided with built-in logic that prevents unnecessary regeneration of identical files in order to avoid triggering automatic recompilation of up-to-date files.

11.12 The Object Navigational and Associative Interfaces

Programmatic object support is provided by Oracle through two interfaces. They are not mutually exclusive, on the contrary, they can be used together. As we will see, in most cases the navigational interface needs an associative call in its processing.

The associative interface has a more relational *personality* because it uses standard SQL statements to fetch objects stored in the database. It is more versatile than its navigational counterpart, because it can be used to access *column objects*. The latter are objects that are included in relational tables, coexisting with standard SQL datatypes in the same row. The navigational interface works only with pure objects, also called *row objects*. This is because only row objects have REFs, and the navigational interface identifies the objects to be copied into the object cache using their REF.

The two interfaces share one embedded SQL statement, ALLOCATE, used to allocate space for a specific object in the object cache when using the associative interface, to allocate space for an object REF when using the navigational interface. The two data fetch mechanisms used by the interfaces are otherwise very different. The associative interface uses the standard SQL SELECT, INSERT, and UPDATE statements to manipulate objects in the object cache. The navigational interface uses its own specific syntax to accomplish the same goal.

A common trait of the two interfaces is that they manipulate a *transient* copy of persistent objects that are transferred into the object cache. Once the objects have been modified in the object cache, both interfaces require the developer to make the changes permanent by synchronizing the transient copy of the objects with their permanent counterpart in the database. The support for objects and the interaction of the host program with the object cache introduce a set of new terms and concepts that developers who want to use the object extension cannot ignore. What follows is a list of the new terms commonly used when using Oracle objects.

TERM	DEFINITION
Pinning	Dereferencing an object allowing a program to access it in the object cache
Unpinning	Communicating to the object cache that an object is no longer used
Refreshing	Replacing the current version of object in the object cache with the corresponding object stored in the database
Dereferencing	Using the object REF to create a version of it in the object cache
Freeing	Removing an object from the object cache de-allocating the memory used
Marking	Informing the object cache that the current object has been updated and is in need of being updated on the server
Unmarking	Informing the object cache that the object no longer needs to be updated on the server
Flushing	Making the changes to an object in the object cache permanent by updating the server

As already pointed out, the associative interface is much closer to the relational model than the navigational interface is. In fact, it uses the very well-known SQL command SELECT to fetch either objects or relational tables containing column objects into the object cache. By issuing the standard INSERT,

UPDATE, and DELETE commands, the transient copy of the object stored in the object cache is checkpointed to the database.

The deviation from standard SQL is minimal. Two new embedded SQL commands have been introduced to support the associative interface, ALLOCATE and FREE. They allocate memory in the object cache for an object and release memory from the cache, respectively. To fetch an object from the database to the object cache, the INTO clause of the embedded SQL command SELECT support an object as operand. An example follows:

```
customer    *cust;

EXEC SQL ALLOCATE :cust;

EXEC SQL SELECT INTO :cust FROM
CUSTOMER WHERE customer_id = :cust_id;
```

In the above example, *customer* is a "C" structure generated by the OTT. The ALLOCATE command reserves space for the customer object in the object cache. The object is empty until successful SELECT fills it with information fetched from the database. The program can then manipulate the transient copy of the customer object. To make the changes permanent the following command is issued:

```
EXEC SQL INSERT INTO CUSTOMER VALUES (:cust);
```

Standard SQL transactional commands, such as COMMIT and ROLLBACK must be used to complete the transaction.

The navigational interface, in contrast, doesn't use standard SQL commands at all. The syntax used is characterized by the EXEC SQL OBJECT prefix. The table below summarizes the object navigational new keywords.

KEYWORD	USE
OBJECT CREATE	Creates a referenceable object in the object cache
OBJECT DEREF	Pins the object identified by its REF in the object cache
OBJECT RELEASE	Unpins the object in the object cache
OBJECT DELETE	Marks the object(s) as deleted in the object cache
OBJECT FLUSH	Synchronizes the object cache with the database
OBJECT UPDATE	Marks the object(s) as updated in the object cache

Two additional commands are used with both navigational and associative interfaces to convert object elements into "C" types and vice versa. They are OBJECT GET and OBJECT SET. The two interfaces can be used interchangeably throughout a Pro*C program. It often happens that an associative select of object

REFs is required in a navigational context to fetch from the database the REFs of objects to be pinned in the object cache via navigational commands.

The table below shows a typical sequence of navigational commands used to allocate an object in the object cache, fetch data from the database into it, change the state of its attributes, and checkpoint the object back into the permanent storage. For the sake of the example, a hypothetical invoice object is used, called invoice. It is assumed the OTT generated a "C" structure mapping the invoice object elements into it, an invoice_ref, and an auxiliary invoice_ind structure to hold the invoice indicator variables.

STEP	PURPOSE

`invoice *inv;`
`invoice_ref *inv_ref;`
`invoice_ind *inv_ind;`
`int inv_id;`
	The three structures: inv, inv_ref, and inv_ind are OTT generated. The program defines pointers to them. inv_id is a host variable used to store the invoice Id of the required invoice.

`EXEC SQL ALLOCATE :inv_ref;`	ALLOCATE is used to reserve space for the invoice REF in the object cache.
`EXEC SQL` `CREATE OBJECT ;inv;`	CREATE is used to reserve space in the object cache for an invoice object.

`EXEC SQL SELECT`
`REF(i) INTO :inv_ref`
`FROM INVOICE i`
`WHERE INV_ID = :inv_id;`
	The associative interface is used to fetch the REF of the wanted invoice from the database using a standard SQL SELECT command.

`EXEC SQL OBJECT DEREF` `:inv_ref INTO :inv:inv_ind;`	The transient copy of the invoice object in the object cache is populated with database sourced data.
`EXEC SQL OBJECT SET` `:inv->pay_date TO :pay_date;`	The pay_date attribute of the invoice object is changed in the object cache. OBJECT SET converts C datatypes into object attributes.
`EXEC SQL OBJECT` `UPDATE :inv;`	The inv object is marked as updated in the object cache. Oracle returns an error if one tries to flush an object that has not been previously updated.
`EXEC SQL OBJECT FLUSH :inv;`	The change is propagated to the database.
`EXEC SQL OBJECT CACHE` `FREE ALL;`	The object cache is emptied.
`EXEC SQL COMMIT WORK;`	The transaction is completed.

The syntax that supports object manipulation is a little cryptic and definitely not standard. Seasoned Pro*C programmers must learn a totally new set of commands and must deal with a new approach, getting acquainted with new tricks of the trade that have very little in common with the established SQL standard.

Oracle Corporation claims that the object cache gives a performance advantage over the SQL interface when lots of objects must be individually accessed for complex changes. In other words, when complex business logic is to be applied to a large number of objects, the navigational interface is most performant. When a simple change must be applied to many rows or objects in the database, SQL is still more performant, being executed entirely within the Oracle kernel. Increasing the salaries of all employees by 5% represents a typical example. Nothing can beat SQL for such a task, given the relational foundations of the Oracle engine.

To confirm the Oracle claims, we will code a simple application in two versions, one that uses the standard relational commands to fetch and manipulate a large collection of records from the database. The same business logic will be reworked to make use of the object cache. To measure the time spent by the two applications, we will use the DBUG package, introduced in chapter 8.

The STOCK table will be used by the relational application. A STOCK_T type, containing the same fields as STOCK, will be defined in a different schema. The STOCK object table will be created from STOCK_T. The STOCK table structure is shown below.

```
SQL> desc stock
 Name                            Null?    Type
 ------------------------------- -------- ------
 TICKER_ID                       NOT NULL NUMBER
 DATE_VALUE                      NOT NULL DATE
 LOW                                      NUMBER
 HIGH                                     NUMBER
 CLOSE                                    NUMBER
 VOLUME                                   NUMBER
 REC_SEQ                         NOT NULL NUMBER
```

The STOCK object table is populated with the same data as its relational counterpart. In the OPS$EBONAZZI schema, the STOCK table contains 600,000 rows. In the EBONAZZI schema, the STOCK object tables contains the same number of rows, this time as row objects. The STOCK table has been artificially populated with random values. It emulates the historical trend of 100 stocks for 6000 stockmarket days. Selecting from STOCK using the DATE_VALUE field to limit the selection criterion to 1 day will always return 100 rows. Selecting from STOCK using TICKER_ID to limit the selection criterion to 1 stock Id will always return 6000 rows.

The two applications will select one stock market day worth of stocks (100 rows) and will modify the values of the high, low, close, and volume columns, updating the database. The same will be done for 1 stock. The entire stock trend (6000 rows) will be fetched from the database and all numeric values will be randomly changed in the client memory, updating the stock table. This operation should take long enough to expose the more performant application. The object-relational based application will fetch initially 100 and subsequently 6000 objects into the object cache. The OBJECT SET and OBJECT GET commands will be used to change the values of all object attributes. All objects will be flushed back to the database at the end. The test will be conducted on a Sun Ultra 5 workstation, equipped with 128 megabytes of RAM, running the Oracle Enterprise Server release 8.05.

The two programs are too large to be presented in this chapter. You can find them in the companion CD, in the *chap11/benchmark* directory. The makefile contains both targets; StockSQL builds the relational version while StockObj builds the object-relational version.

The result confirmed Oracle's claim. Pinning all fetched objects in the object cache, applying all the changes, and flushing all objects back to the database work significantly faster than using the standard relational approach.

The timestamp printed by the DBUG package would be expressed in Oracle as 'YYMMDD HH24MISS", plus the hundredths of seconds. The program ran on October 17th, 1998 at 10:50 PM. It took 2 min 44 sec to complete. One minute and 30 sec were spent updating 6000 rows (the *UpdateStockHistory()* function).

The following picture shows the output from the object-relational application.

The program using the object-relational interface took 2 min 17 sec, 27 sec fewer than its relational competitor. This confirms Oracle Corporation's claim about the greater speed of the object-relational interface when lots of small objects are fetched into the object cache. A careful analysis of the result reveals other

```
Terminal
Window  Edit  Options                                   Help
$ StockSql ops\$ebonazzi alpha64
981017 225014.58: |   INFO: Connecting to Oracle...
981017 225014.58: |   >OraConnect
981017 225014.91: |   <OraConnect
981017 225014.91: |   INFO: Connected to Oracle as ops$ebonazzi
981017 225014.91: |   >FetchStockMarketDay
981017 225014.98: |   <FetchStockMarketDay
981017 225014.98: |   INFO: Computing Coefficients...
981017 225014.98: |   INFO: Finished computing. Updating DB...
981017 225014.98: |   >UpdateStockMarketDay
981017 225015.07: |   <UpdateStockMarketDay
981017 225015.08: |   INFO: Fetching Stock history...
981017 225015.08: |   >FetchStockHistory
981017 225128.85: |   <FetchStockHistory
981017 225128.85: |   INFO: Starting applying changes to fetched data...
981017 225128.87: |   INFO: Finished computing. Updating DB...
981017 225128.87: |   >UpdateStockHistory
981017 225258.49: |   <UpdateStockHistory
981017 225258.59: <main
$
```

FIGURE 11.5 The output from the application that uses a relational approach

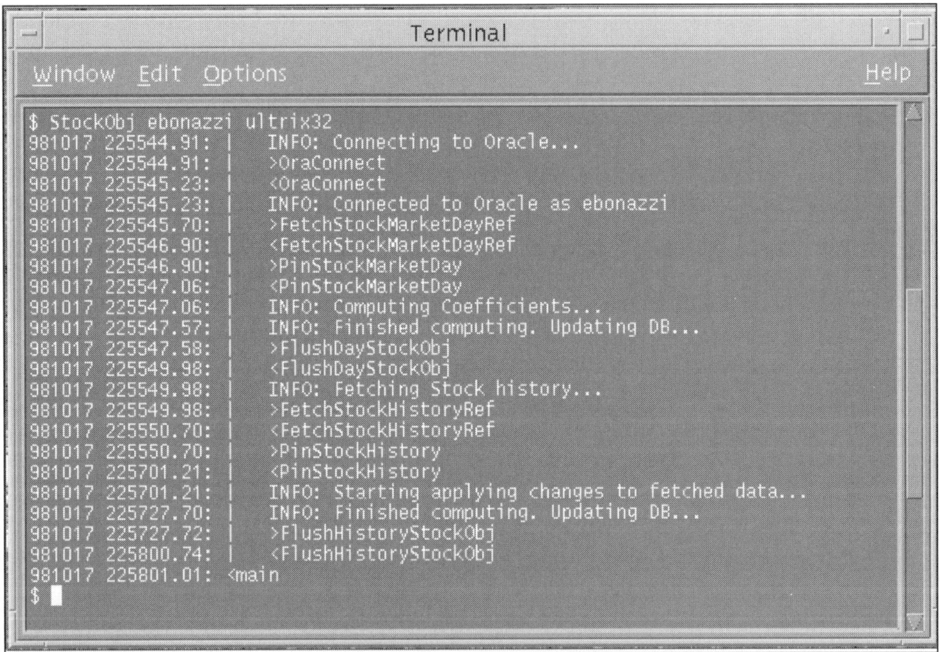

FIGURE 11.6 The output from the application that uses an object-relational approach

very interesting aspects. The program that uses the object-relational interface was able to flush 6000 objects back to the database in only 33 sec, an astonishing speed when compared to the relational interface. But if writing the objects back to the database gave the object-relational program an advantage of almost 1 min, why is the final difference between the two only 27 sec?

The program using the object-relational paradigm must perform one operation more than its relational counterpart. It must use the associative interface to fetch the REFs of the wanted objects. Looking at the DBUG output, we can conclude that this is not the real reason, because to perform the REF fetching takes only approximately 1 sec.

Apart from flushing 6000 objects to the database, the second lengthiest operation is updating the objects in memory. The program that uses the relational interface takes .02 sec to update the array of 6000 cells, because it accesses the memory locations directly. Updating the objects in the object cache takes an incredibly long time, approximately 26 sec. This is due to the OBJECT GET and OBJECT SET commands used for accessing the attributes of the objects. Datatype conversion is also implicitly performed by the two commands, which further increases the overhead associated with the use of objects.

Our very simple benchmark taught us two important lessons about the object-relational interface. First, accessing an object in the database through its

REF is very fast. Second, accessing the attributes of the objects in the object cache through an OBJECT GET command and modifying their value through an OBJECT SET command are very slow.

Summary

This very long chapter discussed one of the most important interfaces that Oracle Corporation offers to developers who want to access data residing in an Oracle database from a 3GL environment, Pro*C. Even when a client-server application uses a RAD client front-end such as VisualBasic or Delphi, it is likely that back-end operations such as housekeeping tasks, batch reporting, interfacing to legacy systems, are carried out by Pro*C programs.

We focused initially on Pro*C error handling and reporting, considering advantages and drawbacks of the Oracle-provided error-handling mechanisms. Host-array processing was an important topic discussed in Section 11.2. Host arrays are responsible for dramatic performance improvements and should be used extensively. Interfacing Pro*C with PL/SQL was discussed in Section 11.3. PL/SQL blocks can be processed in Pro*C the same as SQL statements, exploiting the processing power of the back-end server without incurring in network roundtrips.

Section 11.4 examined the support of Pro*C for C++, highlighting its deficiencies and proposing alternative solutions. The precompiler options have been considered in section 11.5, which focused on cursor re-use and management using options such as HOLD_CURSOR, RELEASE_CURSOR and MAXOPENCURSOR.

Dynamic SQL was extensively covered by Section 11.6, which showed how to use the various Pro*C dynamic SQL methods (1 to 3). We introduced Dynamic SQL method 4 to highlight its poor and difficult implementation, which makes the OCI a better solution for processing SQL statements that are truly dynamic (both select-list items and bind variables unknown at compile time).

To allow a Pro*C program to use the OCI for specific tasks, the interfacing between Pro*C and OCI has been discussed in Section 11.7, which has shown how to interface Pro*C with OCI release 7 and with OCI release 8. The topic of Multi-threaded processing was covered in Section 11.8, which proposed an implementation using Solaris threads and an implementation using Windows NT threads.

The final topics that conclude the chapter are all related to the object-relational paradigm. The Oracle type Translator (OTT) and the object navigational and associative interfaces were analyzed, and a simple and instructive benchmark showed how efficient accessing objects through their REFs is, but how inefficient it is to read and write object attributes.

Chapter 12

BEYOND PRO*C: THE ORACLE CALL INTERFACE

In this chapter we will analyze the Oracle Call Interface (OCI). Once considered an "esoteric" interface to Oracle used by a small minority of developers for really low-level tasks, the OCI has gained new focus and momentum with the release of Oracle 8. Several of the new features of Oracle 8 are supported only through either the OCI or PL/SQL. The very same interface has been totally revised by Oracle Corporation, to an extent that the OCI8 can be considered a new product when compared to the OCI7. Oracle Corporation went even further, by adopting the OCI as the interface by Oracle own 3GL-based products and the database. Previously, the interface internally used by Oracle was the User Program Interface (UPI), which has never been disclosed to the public. It is likely that all low-level features once offered by the UPI will be ported to the OCI. Serious Oracle developers should have an exposure to the OCI, at least to understand when it should be used in preference to Pro*C.

Initially we will consider the OCI7 calls, which will ease us into the OCI world. Further ahead in the chapter we will cover OCI8 specific topics, such as schema metadata reverse engineering, large object manipulation, and dynamic SQL processing.

12.1 OCI Release 7

For someone with a background in Pro*C and other Oracle tools, approaching the OCI for the first time is a very instructive experience. The Oracle internal SQL processing, which can only partially be understood while using more high-level interfaces, becomes suddenly clear as soon as one deals with the OCI. In this section, we will approach the OCI release 7 elementary calls with the purpose of learning the basic OCI philosophy. Further ahead in the chapter we will make the transition to the OCI release 8, which is characterized by an increased complexity associated to an increased number of features.

12.1.1 OCI DATA STRUCTURES

Every OCI program needs to define a few mandatory data structures that are used to store host, logon, and cursor parameters throughout the lifetime of the connection to the database server. The table below summarizes the required data structures.

STRUCTURE NAME	DESCRIPTION	REQUIRED NUMBER
hda	Host data area	One per concurrent connection
lda	Logon data area	One per concurrent connection
cda	Cursor data area	One or more, up to one per SQL statement processed in the program

Each concurrent connection to Oracle requires an lda/hda pair. The host data area and the logon data area are passed as parameters to the OCI call that establishes the connection to the database.

The OCI data structures are defined in a few .h files that must be included in all "C" programs that use OCI calls. The include files are `oratypes.h`, `ocidfn.h` and either `ociapr.h` when using an ANSI compiler or `ocikpr.h` when using a Kernigan & Ritchie compiler.

The hda structure must be defined as a 256-byte array of unsigned char when using 32-bit operating systems and a 512-byte array of unsigned char when using 64-bit operating systems. Standardizing on a 512-byte array makes your code more portable, given that in a 32-bit environment, the hda array can be larger than the required 256 cells.

The lda and cda data structures are defined in `ocidfn.h` as `Lda_Def` and `Cda_Def`, respectively. The hda must be declared as either global or static and must be filled with binary zeroes before being passed as a parameter to the OCI logon call. The lda and cda structures can be locally defined. The following code fragment shows a typical OCI initialization section of an OCI program.

```
#include "ociapr.h"   /* this also includes oratypes.h */
                      /* and ocidfn.h                  */

ub1   hda[512];   /* hda definition */

int main(int argc, char **argv)
{
      Lda_Def      locLda;
      Cda_Def      cursor1;
      Cda_Def      cursor2;
      text         *ConnStr="SYSTEM/MANAGER";
      . . .
      . . .
      memset(&hda[0],'\0',sizeof(hda));
      if(olog(&locLda[0],&hda[0],ConnStr,-1,
            (text *) 0, -1, (text *) 0, -1, OCI_LM_DEF))
      {
            ProcessError(&lda[0]);
            exit(FAILURE);
      }
      etc,
      etc. . .
```

OCI programs use the hda structure only once, at the moment of the connection to Oracle. Every cursor defined in the OCI program will be associated to the Oracle connection using the lda. In the above example, the connection to Oracle is established using the *olog()* call, which takes both hda and lda as parameters.

12.1.2 IN OCI RELEASE 7 EVERYTHING IS A CURSOR!

In order to process SQL statements or PL/SQL blocks, one must define a cursor, which is a memory area that holds all information required by Oracle to accept, parse, and execute SQL statements. At the beginning, this seems a little counter-intuitive, or even confusing, because according to the SQL ANSI standard, a cursor is a memory area that receives multiple rows fetched by a query with a WHERE clause that identifies more than one record.

According to the terminology adopted by the OCI, the cda provides a mapping between a cursor defined in a user program and the parsed representation of the SQL statement in the server. In order to process SQL Data Definition Language (DDL) statements, which have nothing in common with queries and fetching of multiple rows, a cursor must be defined and opened, and the DDL statement associated with it must be executed. The same applies to Data Manipulation Language (DML) statements.

Every OCI program must follow a few sequential steps when interacting with Oracle. They are summarized in the Table 12.1 below.

Not all steps listed in the table below are mandatory. If the SQL statement to be executed is a DDL statement that doesn't have any associated bind variable, only steps 2, 3, and 7 are needed. This can be further reduced to two steps only, opening the cursor and parsing the statement if the OCI nondeferred parsing mode is used.

In order to avoid unnecessary network roundtrips, the OCI allows developers to defer the parsing of the statement until it is actually transmitted to the server. When this feature is enabled, the statement is partially parsed locally by the *oparse()* OCI call. Only basic parsing can be performed, that is, statement syntax checking. If the statement contains references to nonexistent database objects, the local parsing will not be able to detect the error. To actually force Oracle to parse and execute the statement, it's necessary to call *oexec()* after having called *oparse()*. This reduces multiple calls to one, postponed to the very last moment, and minimizes network traffic.

When deferred parsing is not used, a call to the OCI *oparse()* function parses and executes the statement at once if the statement is not a query and doesn't contain bind variables.

Other steps listed in Table 12.1 can be avoided depending on the nature of the statement. If all output variables of a query are known at compile time, there is no need to call *odescr()* to describe them. Similarly, if the statement contains no bind variables, the call to either *obndra()* or *obindps()* can be avoided.

Table 12.1 OCI/Oracle Interaction Sequence

STEP #	DATA STRUCTURE	OCI CALL	PURPOSE
1	hda, lda	olog()	Lda and hda are linked in a connection to Oracle.
2	lda, cda	oopen()	A cursor is associated with its logon data area.
3	cda	oparse()	An SQL statement is parsed into its cursor.
4	cda	obndra(), obindps()	SQL statement bind variables are associated with their cursor.
5	cda	odescr()	Identification is made of all output variables in queries where they are unknown at compile time.
6	cda	odefin() odefinps()	Select output variables are associated with their cursor.
7	cda	oexn()	The statement is executed.
8	lda	ocom(),orol()	The transaction is either committed or rolled back.
9	cda	oclose()	The cursor is closed.

12.1.3 ERROR HANDLING IN THE OCI

Throughout the various chapters of the book, we have reiterated that adequate error handling is crucial for quality and robustness of a commercial application. This is even more important when dealing with such a low-level interface as the OCI. The error handling capabilities offered by the OCI are summarized below.

OCI ERROR MANAGEMENT	MEANING	SUGGESTED ACTION
OCI call return code	All OCI functions return 0 if no error occurred.	Check the return status of all OCI routines.
Cursor structure return code field	If an error occurred, the Oracle error number appears in the *rc* field of the cursor structure.	For each unsuccessful return status, evaluate the error code in the cursor data area structure.
oerhms() OCI call	The Oracle error code can be expanded into a message by this OCI call.	Oerhms() can be used to format a human-readable error message.

There are a few exceptions to the rule that all OCI functions return a status code. One is the oerhms() call, which returns the length of the error message. Another important routine that doesn't return a status code is *sqllda().* sqllda() is usually called by a Pro*C program that calls the OCI functions.

All most commonly used OCI calls return a value different from 0 if an error occurred. It is good programming practice to test the return value of all OCI functions in order to take appropriate action in case of error.

With the OCI notions introduced so far, we are now able to write our first complete program. We will submit two SQL statements to the engine: the first, a DDL statement that drops a table; the second, a query that selects all tables owned by the owner passed as a parameter to the query. The second query will use the DBA_TABLES data dictionary views, so the schema owner used for the connection should have the appropriate privileges to select from DBA_TABLES.

```
#include <stdio.h>
#include <stdlib.h>
#ifdef MS_NT
#include <memory.h>
#endif
#include <string.h>
#include "ociapr.h"  /* this also includes oratypes.h  */
                      /* and ocidfn.h                  */
#define NO_DATA_FOUND 1403
#define STRING_TYPE  5
#define TABLE_DOES_NOT_EXIST 942
```

```
#define NON_DEFERRED_MODE 0
#define DEFERRED_MODE 1

ub1     hda[512];    /* hda definition */

char * GetOraMsg(Lda_Def *,int );

int main(int argc, char **argv)
{
 Lda_Def    locLda;
 Cda_Def    cursor1;
 Cda_Def    cursor2;
 text       *ConnStr=(text *) "SYSTEM/MANAGER";
 text       *stmt1=(text *)   "drop table example_table";
 text       *stmt2=(text *)   "select table_name from dba_tables"
                              "where owner=:TBL_OWN";
 char       szTblName[10][31];
 char       szOwner[31];
 int        ii,
            nRowsDone,
            nn;

 memset(&hda[0],'\0',sizeof(hda));
 memset(szTblName,'\0',sizeof(szTblName));
 memset(szOwner,'\0',sizeof(szOwner));

 strcpy(szOwner,argv[1]);
 if(olog(&locLda,&hda[0],ConnStr,-1,
        (text *) 0, -1, (text *) 0, -1, OCI_LM_DEF))
 {
        fprintf(stdout,"Could not login to Oracle\n");
        fprintf(stdout,"Aborting...\n");
        exit(1);
 }

 if (oopen(&cursor1,&locLda,(text *) 0,-1,-1,(text *) 0,-1))
 {
        fprintf(stdout,"%s\n",
               GetOraMsg(&locLda,cursor1.rc));
        exit(1);
 }
 if (oopen(&cursor2,&locLda,(text *) 0,-1,-1,(text *) 0,-1))
 {
        fprintf(stdout,"%s\n",
```

```
                GetOraMsg(&locLda,cursor2.rc));
        exit(1);
    }
    if (oparse(&cursor1,(text *) stmt1,-1,NON_DEFERRED_MODE,2))
    {
        if(cursor1.rc == TABLE_DOES_NOT_EXIST)
           fprintf(stdout,"Table already dropped\n");
        else
        {
                fprintf(stdout,"%s\n",
                  GetOraMsg(&locLda,cursor2.rc));
                exit(1);
        }
    }
    if (oclose(&cursor1))
    {
        fprintf(stdout,"%s\n",
                GetOraMsg(&locLda,cursor2.rc));
        exit(1);
    }

    if (oparse(&cursor2,(text *) stmt2,-1,DEFERRED_MODE,2))
    {
        fprintf(stdout,"%s\n",
                GetOraMsg(&locLda,cursor2.rc));
        exit(1);
    }

    if (odefin(&cursor2,1,(ub1 *) szTblName, 31, STRING_TYPE,-1,
            (sb2 *) 0,(text *) 0,-1,-1,(ub2 *) 0,(ub2 *) 0))
    {
        fprintf(stdout,"%s\n",
                GetOraMsg(&locLda,cursor2.rc));
        exit(1);
    }
    if(obndrv(&cursor2,(text *) ":TBL_OWN",-1,(ub1 *) szOwner,
        sizeof(szOwner), STRING_TYPE,-1, (sb2 *) 0,
        (text *) 0,-1,-1))
    {
        fprintf(stdout,"%s\n",
                GetOraMsg(&locLda,cursor2.rc));
        exit(1);
    }
    if (oexec(&cursor2))
```

```
{
        fprintf(stdout,"%s\n",
                GetOraMsg(&locLda,cursor2.rc));
        exit(1);
}
for (nRowsDone = 0 ; ;)
{
        memset(szTblName,'\0',sizeof(szTblName));

        if (ofen(&cursor2,10))
        {
                if ( (cursor2.rc == NO_DATA_FOUND) &&
                        (cursor2.rpc ==0))
                {
                        fprintf(stdout,"No tables found\n");
                        break;
                }
                if (cursor2.rc != NO_DATA_FOUND)
                {
                        fprintf(stdout,"%s\n",
                                GetOraMsg(&locLda,cursor2.rc));
                        exit(1);
                }
        }
        nn = cursor2.rpc - nRowsDone;
        nRowsDone += nn;
        for ( ii = 0; ii < nn; ii++)
            fprintf(stdout,"Table: %s\n",szTblName[ii]);
        if (cursor2.rc == NO_DATA_FOUND) break;
}/* End endless for */
if (oclose(&cursor2))
{
        fprintf(stdout,"%s\n",
                GetOraMsg(&locLda,cursor2.rc));
        exit(1);
}

if (ocom(&locLda))
{
        fprintf(stdout,"%s\n",
                GetOraMsg(&locLda,cursor2.rc));
        exit(1);
}
ologof(&locLda);
```

```
144: }
145:
146: char * GetOraMsg(Lda_Def * LocLda,int nOraErr)
147: {
148:          static char    szOraErr[71];
149:          oerhms(LocLda,(sb2) nOraErr,(text *) szOraErr,
150:                 (int) sizeof(szOraErr));
151:          szOraErr[70]='\0';
152:          return(szOraErr);
153:
154: }
```

OCI Release 7 at Work

1–7 .h files inclusion. ociapr.h automatically includes the two other required files.

15 The host data area is defined as a global.

21 The logon data area is locally defined.

22–23 Two cursor data areas are defined, one for each SQL statement processed.

24–26 A connection string and two strings containing the SQL statements to be submitted to the engine are defined.

28 szTblName is a host array that will contain all table names fetched from the database.

38 szOwner is the query parameter (bind variable) that is passed to the program via the command line.

39 A connection to the database server is attempted by calling *olog().*

47–58 The two cursors required by the program are allocated.

59–69 The first SQL statement is already complete; no further preparation is required. It can be parsed and executed in one pass. Note that to accomplish this, the nondeferred parsing mode flag is set (last but one parameter in the *oparse()* call).

70–75 The cursor can be closed because it is no longer needed.

77–82 The second statement contains one bind variable and one output variable. It requires further preparation before being submitted to the engine. The statement is parsed using the deferred mode.

84–90 The statement output variable is linked to the cursor by calling *odefin().* The second parameter passed to *odefin()* specifies the position of the output variable in the statement.

91–98 The query parameter is bound to the statement calling *obndrv().*

99–104 The statement is executed (the cursor is opened).

105–129 The rows are fetched in lots of 10 for each call to *ofen().*

130–135 The second cursor is closed after use.

137–142 The transaction is committed using *ocom()*. This passage is not necessary but shown to illustrate the use of *ocom()*. The next statement, *ologof()*, automatically performs a commit during disconnection.

146–154 The GetOraMsg function receives a pointer to the LDA and an Oracle error code. It expands the error code into a meaningful message by calling *oerhms()* and returns it to the caller.

The example shown above reflects the most commonly used OCI calls. We defined two cursors, one for each statement, but we could have reused the same cursor to process two different statements. The point is that the OCI allows for total control over cursor allocation, use, reuse, and de-allocation. The absolute limit is fixed by the instance-wide OPEN_CURSORS parameters and, possibly, by memory limitation on the client side. Apart from this, developers enjoy maximum freedom and control when dealing with OCI cursor management.

There are a few issues that developers must be aware of when venturing for the first time in the OCI territory. It is possible to turn on the automatic commit facility through the OCI call *ocon()*. The reverse is accomplished by invoking *ocof()*. The *ologof()* OCI call that logs a connection out from Oracle performs an implicit commit. If an OCI program terminates abruptly, all pending connections are automatically rolled back. Committing is an expensive operation that takes time and absorbs precious Oracle resources on the server. It is not a good idea to enable automatic committing for all statements. Strive to identify precisely the boundaries of each business transaction in your application, and commit sparingly at the end of each logical atomic transaction.

The example shown above should work with all Oracle 7 server releases and Oracle 8. The two OCI calls used to bind the input variable and to define the output variable in the second SQL statement (*obndrv()* and *odefin()*) are supported in Oracle 7.0x to Oracle8. They are considered obsolescent, which means that they have been superseded by new OCI calls that perform the same task, usually more efficiently, but they are still supported.

Being obsolescent is the first step towards retirement. Usually an obsolescent routine becomes obsolete (that is, no longer supported) in the interval of one or two major releases. Oracle 7.3 introduced two OCI calls to perform variable binding and defining, *obindps()* and *odefinps()*, which made *obndrv()*, *obndrn()*, and *obndra()* obsolescent. Using the two new calls would limit the compatibility of an OCI application to Oracle 7.3 and greater. The new calls perform the same task of the calls being replaced; in addition, they allow for an easier and cleaner piecewise insertion and extraction of LONG and LONG RAW datatypes when used in conjunction with an Oracle 7.3 engine.

All OCI calls used in the above example are now obsolescent. The OCI release 8 introduced major changes and improvements and all OCI routines are new and called with new names, characterized by an OCI prefix. For several of the new OCI8 calls, it is possible to find a one-to-one correspondence with an OCI7 call. A few OCI8 routines do not have any OCI7 counterpart. It is possible to compile and link programs that use OCI7 calls against OCI8 libraries. It is also possible to mix OCI7 and OCI8 calls in the same programs, with a few limitations. The connection to the Oracle server must occur using OCI8 semantics, and an OCI7 lda can be obtained using *OCISvcCtxToLda()*. Only one service context can be in OCI7 mode if multiple service contexts share the same server handle.

The OCI release 8 introduced a major breakthrough in performance and network traffic minimization. Many of the operations that previously required accessing the server have been moved to the client, allowing developers to operate data conversion and schema metadata manipulation locally, with no network roundtrips involved. In addition, the OCI8 supports the new calls required for object manipulation and object cache access. The net result has been increasing the number of OCI calls from less than 30 in OCI7 to a several hundred in the OCI8.

It is definitely worthwhile switching to the OCI8 for new projects, primarily because all OCI7 routines are now obsolescent. A new application will have a shorter lifetime if written using OCI7 calls. If you are to maintain a legacy application that makes use of OCI7 calls, consider using both OCI7 and OCI8 calls in the same program. If you are constrained to use the OCI7 because of strict company policies, consider the following OCI7 performance related issues.

- ❑ Use deferred parsing
- ❑ Use host arrays
- ❑ Avoid using odescr()

The second last parameter of the *oparse()* call is called *defflg* (deferred flag). If the program has been linked in deferred mode, a value for defflg different from 0 will cause deferred parsing of the statement. For all statements that cannot be executed when parsed, deferred parsing should be used to avoid one unnecessary network roundtrip.

If a statement is either a query or a DML statement using bind variables, it cannot be executed by the parse step because more OCI calls must be used to complete the statement preparation. If deferred parsing is used, the statement is associated with its cursor and minimal syntax checking performed. The bind variables can then be associated with the cursor, as well as the output variables in case of a query.

This completes all steps required to prepare a statement for its execution. The statement can now be submitted to the server for parsing and execution, using one network roundtrip only. If nondeferred parsing is used, the parse step is performed on the server side. The only advantage offered by this option is that statement syntax and semantics can be thoroughly checked. In case of failure of *oparse()*, the program can avoid calling the other OCI routines related to the same statement. Assuming that in most cases statement parsing is successful, it is convenient to always use deferred parsing.

In several preceding chapters, the benefits associated with the use of host arrays have been highlighted. The same applies to the OCI, which offers calls capable of performing array operations. For historical reasons, all array enabled OCI calls have their scalar counterpart. OCI calls that are not array enabled have been included in very old releases of Oracle, when host arrays were not supported, and have survived the introduction of host arrays. What follows is a list of array enabled OCI calls with their scalar counterpart.

SCALAR FUNCTION	ARRAY ENABLED FUNCTION	PURPOSE
obndrn() obndrv()	obndra()	Variable binding: obndra() can be used to bind an array of bind variables.
oexec()	oexn()	Statement execution: oexn() can be used to execute a statement that has associated host arrays.
ofetch()	ofen()	Rows fetching: ofen() can be used to fetch rows into a host array.

The array enabled OCI calls should always be used in preference to their scalar counterparts to increase performance by minimizing network traffic.

When deferred parsing is enabled, an SQL statement can be parsed and executed in only one network roundtrip. Unfortunately, this is not true when the OCI *odescr()* call is used, because odescr() cannot be deferred. When an SQL statement is built dynamically at run-time, the number and the datatype of its output and bind variables is not known at compile time. The OCI7 provides the odescr() call to produce a list of all output variables of a select statement. Unfortunately, a similar routine is not provided for all bind variables contained in an SQL statement. This must be done by developers using "C". The OCI8 provides the *OCIStmtGetBindInfo()* call that relieves developers from the burden of coding "C" routines to scan the SQL statements looking for bind variables.

The *odescr()* OCI call should be used only when processing dynamic SQL to limit a severe impact on the overall performance of the application.

12.2 The OCI Release 8

The introduction to the market of Oracle8 brought about major changes in the Oracle Call Interface. The most evident are probably the disappearance of cursors and the introduction of handles, which are opaque pointers to OCI data structures that hold all necessary information for the interaction with the Oracle server. They are opaque because the information contained in them is not directly accessible by developers, but encapsulated and available only through accessor functions. Handles have attributes whose value can be modified by calling *OCIAttrSet()* and read by calling *OCIAttrGet()*. Consider the session handle, for example. It must be passed to the OCI call *OCISessionBegin()* to establish a session. The session handle has two parameters, OCI_ATTR_USERNAME and OCI_ATTR_PASSWORD that must be set before calling OCISessionBegin(). This is done by invoking OCIAtrrSet() twice, as in the following example.

```
. . .
. . .
OCISession   *SesH;
OCISvcCtx    *SvcH;
OCIError     *ErrH;
char         *szUsername="OPS$EBONAZZI";
char         *szPassword="supersecret";
. . .
. . .
OCIAttrSet((dvoid *) SesH, (ub4) OCI_HTYPE_SESSION,
    (dvoid *) szUsername, (ub4) strlen((char *)szUsername),
    (ub4) OCI_ATTR_USERNAME, ErrH);
OCIAttrSet((dvoid *) SesH, (ub4) OCI_HTYPE_SESSION,
            (dvoid *) szPassword,
            (ub4) strlen((char *)szPassword),
(ub4) OCI_ATTR_PASSWORD, ErrH);
. . .
. . .
sts = OCISessionBegin(SvcH,ErrH,SesH,OCI_CRED_RDBMS,
                        (ub4) OCI_DEFAULT);
```

In exactly the same way, *OCIAttrGet()* can be used to read parameters stored in opaque handles after an OCI call that populates the handle parameters.

The OCI8 introduced several handles to give developers a high degree of control over all aspects of application interaction with a database server (or servers). They are in a hierarchical relationship, where a parent handle can have one or more children, as in the case of the Service Context handle. The hierarchically most important handle is the Environment handle, which requires a specific OCI call for initialization *(OCIEnvInit())*. All other handles are initialized using the *OCIHandleAlloc()* call. The following table lists the OCI8 handles.

HANDLE	PARENT	PURPOSE
Environment		It defines a context where all other OCI functions are invoked. Memory resources are associated with it.
Error	Environment	It maintains information about errors and warnings occurred during OCI calls. *OCIErrorGet()* is used to extract error information in human readable.
Service Context	Environment	It determines the operational context of all OCI calls made to a server. Its three principal components have been decoupled into three separate handles: Server handle, which represents a data source; User session handle, which defines users' privileges and access levels; and Transaction handle, which defines the database transaction context where all database calls operate.
Statement	Environment	It identifies a statement context. Together with the bind and define handles, it encapsulates all information required to manage SQL statements or PL/SQL blocks.
Describe	Environment	It maintains schema metadata and PL/SQL object information. It is populated by *OCIDescribeAny()*.
Security	Environment	It is used by the Oracle Security Server.
Complex Object Retrieval (COR)	Environment	It maintains information required to navigate through objects, enabling complex and efficient object fetching.
Server Context	Service Context	It represents a physical connection to a data source.
User Session	Service Context	It represents the User's security domain.
Transaction	Service Context	It identifies transaction-oriented information such as session state, savepoints, etc.
Bind	Statement	It stores all information related to one bind variable, meaningful within the context of a statement handle.
Define	Statement	It stores all information related to one output variable of a SELECT statement, meaningful within the context of a statement handle.

Allocating all required handles takes many lines of startup code, especially when compared to either the OCI7 or Pro*C 8. This will become evident in our first OCI8 example, which is a reworked edition of the previous example used to illustrate the OCI release 7. The OCI8 example requires approximately 260 lines of code to do what the OCI7 did in 154. This example uses the software layering techniques illustrated in Chapter 7.

Instead of declaring all required handles either globally or locally in the main function, as per the sample code shown in the OCI8 Oracle manual, the example groups them together in a structure, and passes a pointer to that structure to all ancillary routines. This technique minimizes the number of parameters required to be passed between the various modules comprising the application.

The main "C" function acts as the control layer, which invokes a separate routine called *ProcessBusinessLogic()*. The latter mimics the business logic layer and in turn calls two routines that perform the task of interacting with the database. For the sake of simplicity, the logical data access layer function that fetches all tables belonging to the schema passed as a query parameter prints them to the standard output. In real life applications, it is the business logic that manages the data fetched from the database. Usually this is accomplished by passing to the logical data access layer routines a pointer to the root node of a linked list, as shown in Chapter 7. Alternatively, if the number of rows retrieved from the database is known in advance, an array of structures can be used.

The focus, here, is the OCI release 8, so the example has been kept as simple as possible, avoiding creation and traversing of a linked list or array processing.

OCI Release 8 example - the include file

```
 1: #ifndef OCI_EXAMPLE_2
 2: #define OCI_EXAMPLE_2
 3:
 4: #define GLOBAL extern
 5: #define LOCAL static
 6:
 7: #define SUCCESS 0
 8: #define ERROR 1
 9:
10: typedef struct
11: {
12:         OCIEnv          *EnvH;
13:         OCIServer       *SrvH;
14:         OCISession      *SesH;
15:         OCIStmt         *StmtH_1;
16:         OCIStmt         *StmtH_2;
17:         OCIError        *ErrH;
18:         OCISvcCtx       *SvcH;
19: }ALL_OCI_HANDLES;
20:
21: GLOBAL int ProcessBusinessLogic(char *);
22: GLOBAL int LDDropTable(ALL_OCI_HANDLES *, char *);
23: GLOBAL int LDGetTableNames(ALL_OCI_HANDLES *, char *);
24: GLOBAL int DBInitialize(ALL_OCI_HANDLES *);
25: GLOBAL int DBConnect(ALL_OCI_HANDLES *, char *, char *);
26: GLOBAL int DBCleanUp(ALL_OCI_HANDLES *);
27: #endif
```

OCI8 Example. Handle structure and function forward declarations

10–19 All required OCI handles are grouped together in a structure. A pointer to this structure will be passed to the functions in all different layers.

The structure defines one environment handle, one server, and one session handle, two statement handles, one error handle and, last but not least, one service context handle.

21 These functions, characterized by the LD prefix, emulate a logical data access layer.

24–26 The three functions forward declared here emulate the physical data access layer.

OCI Release 8 Example. It Uses Code Layering Techniques.

```
#include <stdio.h>
#include <stdlib.h>
#ifdef MS_NT
#include <memory.h>
#endif
#include <string.h>
#include "oci.h"  /* new oci include file */
#include "OCIExample2.h"


int main(int argc, char **argv)
{
  int    sts;

  fprintf(stdout,"OCI Release 8 example\n");
  fprintf(stdout,"Control logic\n");

  if( (sts = ProcessBusinessLogic(argv[1])) != SUCCESS )
  {
          fprintf(stdout,"Business function failed\n");
          fprintf(stdout,"Check log files...\n");
          exit(1);
  }
  else
   fprintf(stdout,"Control logic cleaning up and exiting...\n");
  exit(0);
}





GLOBAL int ProcessBusinessLogic(char * szOwner)
{
  ALL_OCI_HANDLES     OCIHandles;
```

```
  char          szUsername[31]={"SYSTEM"};
  char          szPassword[31]={"MANAGER"};
  char          *stmt1=(char *)     "drop table example_table";
  int           sts;

  if( (sts = DBInitialize(&OCIHandles)) != SUCCESS)
  {
        fprintf(stdout,"Could not initialize OCI environment\n");
        return(ERROR);
  }
  if( (sts = DBConnect(&OCIHandles,szUsername,szPassword)) !=
                                        SUCCESS)
  {
              fprintf(stdout,"Could not connect to Oracle\n");
              return(ERROR);
 }
  if( (sts = LDDropTable(&OCIHandles,stmt1)) != SUCCESS)
  {
        fprintf(stdout,"Could not drop example_table\n");

 }
  if( (sts = LDGetTableNames(&OCIHandles,szOwner)) != SUCCESS)
  {
        fprintf(stdout,"Could not fetch table names\n");
              return(ERROR);
  }
  if( (sts = DBCleanUp(&OCIHandles)) != SUCCESS)
 {

        fprintf(stdout,"Could not de-allocate OCI handles\n");
        return(ERROR);
 }

  return(SUCCESS);
}

GLOBAL int DBInitialize(ALL_OCI_HANDLES *H)
{
  int    sts;

  memset(H,'\0',sizeof(ALL_OCI_HANDLES));

  sts = OCIInitialize((ub4) OCI_DEFAULT, (dvoid *)0,
                     (dvoid * (*)(dvoid *, size_t)) 0,
```

```
                    (dvoid * (*)(dvoid *, dvoid *, size_t))0,
                    (void (*)(dvoid *, dvoid *)) 0 );
 sts = OCIEnvInit( (OCIEnv **) &H->EnvH, OCI_DEFAULT,
                              (size_t) 0,(dvoid **) 0 );

 sts = OCIHandleAlloc( (dvoid *) H->EnvH, (dvoid **) &H->ErrH,
                    OCI_HTYPE_ERROR, (size_t) 0, (dvoid **) 0);
 if ( sts != SUCCESS)
        return(ERROR);

 /* server contexts */
 sts = OCIHandleAlloc( (dvoid *) H->EnvH, (dvoid **) &H->SrvH,
                    OCI_HTYPE_SERVER, (size_t) 0, (dvoid **) 0);

if ( sts != SUCCESS)
      return(ERROR);

 sts = OCIHandleAlloc( (dvoid *) H->EnvH, (dvoid **) &H->SvcH,
                    OCI_HTYPE_SVCCTX, (size_t) 0, (dvoid **) 0);
if ( sts != SUCCESS)
        return(ERROR);

 sts = OCIServerAttach( H->SrvH, H->ErrH, (text *)"dev8",
                      strlen("dev8"), 0);
if ( sts != SUCCESS)
        return(ERROR);

 /* set attribute server context in the service context */
 sts = OCIAttrSet( (dvoid *) H->SvcH, OCI_HTYPE_SVCCTX,
                (dvoid *) H->SrvH, (ub4) 0, OCI_ATTR_SERVER,
                (OCIError *) H->ErrH);
if ( sts != SUCCESS)
        return(ERROR);

 sts = OCIHandleAlloc((dvoid *) H->EnvH, (dvoid **) &H->SesH,
                     (ub4) OCI_HTYPE_SESSION, (size_t) 0,
                     (dvoid **) 0);
if ( sts != SUCCESS)
         return(ERROR);

 sts = OCIHandleAlloc( (dvoid *) H->EnvH, (dvoid **) &H->StmtH_1,
               (ub4) OCI_HTYPE_STMT, (size_t) 0, (dvoid **) 0);
if ( sts != SUCCESS)
        return(ERROR);
```

```

  sts = OCIHandleAlloc( (dvoid *) H->EnvH, (dvoid **) &H->StmtH_2,
                  (ub4) OCI_HTYPE_STMT, (size_t) 0, (dvoid **) 0);


 if ( sts != SUCCESS)
         return(ERROR);

  return(SUCCESS);
}

GLOBAL int DBConnect(ALL_OCI_HANDLES *H, char *szUsername,
                  char *szPassword)
{
  int    sts;

  sts = OCIAttrSet((dvoid *) H->SesH, (ub4) OCI_HTYPE_SESSION,
                       (dvoid *) szUsername,
                       (ub4) strlen((char *) szUsername),
                       (ub4) OCI_ATTR_USERNAME, H->ErrH);
 if ( sts != SUCCESS)
         return(ERROR);

  sts = OCIAttrSet((dvoid *) H->SesH, (ub4) OCI_HTYPE_SESSION,
                       (dvoid *) szPassword,
                       (ub4) strlen((char *) szPassword),
                       (ub4) OCI_ATTR_PASSWORD, H->ErrH);
 if ( sts != SUCCESS)
         return(ERROR);

  sts = OCISessionBegin (H->SvcH, H->ErrH, H->SesH, OCI_CRED_RDBMS,
                           (ub4) OCI_DEFAULT);

  sts = OCIAttrSet((dvoid *) H->SvcH, (ub4) OCI_HTYPE_SVCCTX,
                       (dvoid *) H->SesH,
                       (ub4) 0, (ub4) OCI_ATTR_SESSION, H->ErrH);

 if ( sts != SUCCESS)
         return(ERROR);
  return(SUCCESS);
}

GLOBAL int LDDropTable(ALL_OCI_HANDLES *H, char * szStmt)
{
```

```
  int    sts;
  text     Error[512];
  sb4      ErrorCode;

  sts = OCIStmtPrepare(H->StmtH_1, H->ErrH,(text *) szStmt,
                       (ub4) strlen((char *) szStmt),
                       (ub4) OCI_NTV_SYNTAX, (ub4) OCI_DEFAULT);
 if ( sts != SUCCESS)
         return(ERROR);

  sts = OCIStmtExecute(H->SvcH, H->StmtH_1, H->ErrH, (ub4) 1,
                       (ub4) 0,(CONST OCISnapshot *) NULL,
                       (OCISnapshot *) NULL, OCI_DEFAULT);
  if ( sts == OCI_ERROR)
  {
         OCIErrorGet(H->ErrH, (ub4) 1, (text *) NULL,
                      &ErrorCode,Error, (ub4) sizeof(Error),
                      OCI_HTYPE_ERROR);
         fprintf(stdout,"Error: %s\n",Error);
         return(ERROR);
  }
  return(SUCCESS);
}

GLOBAL int LDGetTableNames(ALL_OCI_HANDLES *H, char * szOwner)
{
  int     sts;
  int    ii;
  int    nTblCount=1;
  char    *szStmt="select table_name from dba_tables "
                 "where owner=:TBL_OWN";
  char   szTblNames[10][31];
  int    done = 0;
  static  OCIDefine *Def = (OCIDefine *) 0;
  static  OCIBind   *Bnd = (OCIBind *) 0;

 sts = OCIStmtPrepare(H->StmtH_2, H->ErrH, (text *) szStmt,
                         (ub4) strlen((char *) szStmt),
                         (ub4) OCI_NTV_SYNTAX, (ub4) OCI_DEFAULT);
 if ( sts != SUCCESS)
         return(ERROR);

  sts = OCIDefineByPos(H->StmtH_2, &Def, H->ErrH, 1,
                       (dvoid *) szTblNames, 31, SQLT_STR,
                       (dvoid *) 0, (ub2 *) 0, (ub2 *) 0, OCI_DEFAULT);
```

```
 if ( sts != SUCCESS)
         return(ERROR);

  sts = OCIBindByName(H->StmtH_2,&Bnd,H->ErrH, (text *) ":TBL_OWN",
                  -1, (dvoid *) szOwner, strlen(szOwner)+1, SQLT_STR,
                       (dvoid *) 0, (ub2 *) 0, (ub2 *) 0, (ub4) 0,
                       (ub4 *) 0, OCI_DEFAULT);
 if ( sts != SUCCESS)
         return(ERROR);

  sts = OCIStmtExecute(H->SvcH,H->StmtH_2,H->ErrH,(ub4) 0, (ub4) 0,
                      (CONST OCISnapshot *) NULL,
                      (OCISnapshot *) NULL, OCI_DEFAULT);
  while(1)
  {
         memset(szTblNames,'\0',sizeof(szTblNames));
         sts = OCIStmtFetch(H->StmtH_2, H->ErrH, (ub4) 10,
                            (ub4) OCI_FETCH_NEXT,
                            (ub4) OCI_DEFAULT);

         for(ii=0;ii<10;ii++,nTblCount++)
         {
                 if( (strlen(szTblNames[ii])) > 0)
                         fprintf(stdout,"Table %d: %s\n",nTblCount,
                                 szTblNames[ii]);
                 else
                 {
                         done = 1;
                         break;
                 }
         }
         if (done)
                 break;
  }
  return(SUCCESS);
}

GLOBAL int DBCleanUp(ALL_OCI_HANDLES *H)
{

  (void) OCIHandleFree((dvoid *) H->EnvH, (ub4) OCI_HTYPE_ENV);
  (void) OCIHandleFree((dvoid *) H->SrvH, (ub4) OCI_HTYPE_SERVER);
  (void) OCIHandleFree((dvoid *) H->SesH, (ub4) OCI_HTYPE_SESSION);
  (void) OCIHandleFree((dvoid *) H->StmtH_1, (ub4) OCI_HTYPE_STMT);
  (void) OCIHandleFree((dvoid *) H->StmtH_2, (ub4) OCI_HTYPE_STMT);
```

```
258:    (void) OCIHandleFree((dvoid *) H->ErrH, (ub4) OCI_HTYPE_ERROR);
259:    (void) OCIHandleFree((dvoid *) H->SvcH, (ub4) OCI_HTYPE_SVCCTX);
260:    return(SUCCESS);
261: }
```

OCI Release 8 Program Example

11–27 The "C" main function acts as the control layer. It simply performs housekeeping startup tasks and invokes the business logic layer. Upon completion of the business logic modules, the control layer performs the necessary cleanup and shuts down the application.

33 This is the business logic layer. It supervises all data gathering operations and error handling. Upon detection of unrecoverable errors, it returns to the control layer, signaling that an error occurred.

35 The structure containing all OCI handles is instantiated.

41–45 The initialization routine is called. This routine is responsible for allocating all required OCI handles and descriptors.

46–51 The function that performs database attachment is called. Username and password are passed as parameters, together with the pointer to the structure containing all allocated OCI handles.

52–56 The first SQL statement is processed. The logical data access function is called passing a pointer to the structure containing all OCI handles and the statement string.

57–61 The second SQL statement is processed by *LDGetTableNames().* As for the previous SQL statement, the pointer to the structure holding all OCI handles is passed to the function, together with the command line parameter that specifies the schema owner.

62–67 The allocated OCI handles are freed by *DBCleanUp().*

72–133 This routine initializes the OCI environment and allocates all required OCI handles, attaching the application to the database server.

135 This routine performs the connection to Oracle.

140–143 The *OCIAttrSet()* call is used to set the username parameter of the session handle to the username string received as parameter to the function.

147–150 The *OCIAttrSet()* call is used to set the password parameter of the session handle to the password string received as parameter to the function.

154–155 An Oracle session is started. The session handle now contains both username and password, and the standard Oracle security system is used (OCI_CRED_RDBMS). The user credentials are verified by the back-end database.

157–159 The authentication context attribute of the service context is set.

166 This function executes the DDL statement that drops a table called example_table.

172–174 The statement is prepared by associating the statement string with the statement handle. The *OCIStmtPrepare()* function accepts an error handle, which can be queried to find out the cause of an error when the return status of the OCI routine indicates that an error occurred.

178–180 The statement is executed. Note that no further processing is required, because the statement doesn't contain bind variables or select-list items.

181–188 If the statement execution fails, the error handle is queried to find out the cause of the error.

192 This function executes the second statement, a select query that contains one output item and one bind variable.

197 The statement string contains the bind variable :TBL_OWN.

199 szTblNames is a host array that will hold the table name fetched from the database table DBA_TABLES.

201–202 One define and one bind handles are defined.

204–206 The select statement is prepared. The string containing the statement is associated with the statement handle.

210–212 The select-list item is defined by calling *OCIDefineByPos()*. This call associates the host variable szTblNames to the statement handle, setting its datatype to STRING.

216–219 The :TBL_OWN bind variable is associated with the statement handle, setting its datatype to STRING. The variable has been identified by its name. An alternative way to associate a bind variable with the statement handle is by its position in the statement. In this case the OCI function *OCIBindByPos()* must be used.

223–225 The statement is executed. Note that the fourth parameter has been set to 0, thus forcing the select statement to open the cursor without fetching rows in the same network roundtrip. A better solution would be to set the fourth parameter to 10, so in only one network roundtrip the statement is executed and the first lot of rows returned.

226–246 An endless loop is started. At each iteration 10 rows are fetched into the select-list item through the *OCIStmtFetch()* call. The loop terminates where all rows have been fetched.

250–261 This routine takes care of memory de-allocation of all OCI handles allocated by the program.

12.3 The OCI Advantage

With release 8 the Oracle Call Interface has been reengineered with a strong focus on performance. Its design shows that the Oracle engineers strove to minimize network roundtrips and increase the overall performance and response time of

OCI-based applications. There are several specific areas where using the OCI is advantageous in terms of increased response time and easier and cleaner code than Pro*C.

The following is a list of common operations that the OCI tends to handle better than Pro*C.

OPERATION	OCI FUNCTIONS
Schema metadata querying and database object reverse engineering	Describe handle and *OCIDescribeAny()*
Dynamic SQL processing	Implicit DESCRIBE for select output variables and *OCIStmtGetBindInfo()* for bind variables.
Large object fetching and manipulation	OCI offers 23 calls for LOB and BFILE handling. Pro*C doesn't support LOB processing at all.
DML commands with RETURNING clause	In only one network roundtrip, it is possible to insert host arrays and reread back the values just inserted.
Advanced Queuing	*OCIAQenq()* and *OCIAQDeq()* are the interface to Oracle Advance Queuing. Pro*C doesn't support AQ natively.
Object navigation and datatype conversion	The OCI offers 34 functions for complex object navigation and 94 functions for datatype conversion. In addition, it provides a specific handle (the COR handle) and several useful attributes to facilitate object manipulation.

12.3.1 SCHEMA METADATA QUERYING AND REVERSE ENGINEERING

Applications that need to query the schema metadata have historically been tedious to code and heavy on the network because of the large number of network roundtrips associated with the recursive description of the schema objects. For instance, displaying the structure of all tables owned by the login schema in a tree control that unfolds and cascadingly shows indexes and fields associated with the parent tables is a daunting task if performed using either Pro*C or the OCI7. The approach taken by the OCI8 is very different and definitely more effective.

The OCI8 provides a Describe handle that stores useful parameter and attributes available to developer after *OCIDescribeAny()* has been called to populate the Describe handle with metadata information. It is not new syntax that does the same as before, only with different names. Within the Describe handle information is organized in the form of a hierarchical tree, where at the top one can find the parent object, and in the lower levels, the objects related to their parent. OCIDescribeAny() cannot be used to describe an object that is not a top-level object. For instance, in order to obtain information about a column, OCIDescribeAny() must be called to describe the table containing the wanted column.

The Describe handle resides in the client cache. This means that after the initial network roundtrip necessary to populate the handle, all subsequent calls to *OCIParamGet()* to query about attributes and parameters belonging to the object of interest are resolved locally, without accessing the Oracle instance any further.

The Describe handle provides a large list of parameters, including lists that can be recursively accessed by program code. In this case, one parameter holds the number of items contained in the list. For example, if OCIDescribeAny() is used to describe a table, the `OCI_ATTR_NUM_COLS` parameter stores the number of columns contained in the table. Using *OCIAttrGet()* it is possible to query the Describe handle to get the value stored in `OCI_ATTR_NUM_COLS`, as in the example shown below.

```
OCIAttrGet(<Parameter Handle>, OCI_DTYPE_PARAM, &nColNum, 0,
            OCI_ATTR_NUM_COLS, <Error Handle>);
```

The *nColNum* variable is passed by reference to the OCI function. Upon successful completion of the call, nColNum will contain the number of columns belonging to the table of interest. It is therefore possible to begin a loop that will fetch all required column parameters. The following example shows this technique.

```
static OCISvcCtx        *SvcH;  /* Service Context handle */
static OCIError         *ErrH;  /* Error handle           */
static OCIDescribe      *DscH;  /* Describe handle        */
. . .
/* Handle allocation, Environment Creation, etc...
. . .
ub2   DataType[100];
text szTblName[] ="CUSTOMER";
ub4 nTblNameLen = strlen(szTblName);
OCIParam *ParmH;        /* parameter handle */
OCIParam *ColListH;     /* handle to a list of table columns
*/
OCIParam *ColH;         /* column handle */
/* obtain the describe handle for the table */
if (OCIDescribeAny(SvcH, ErrH, szTblName, nTblNameLen,
      OCI_OTYPE_NAME, 0,OCI_PTYPE_TABLE, &DscH))
      return (ERROR);
/* obtain the parameter handle */
if (OCIAttrGet(dschp, OCI_HTYPE_DESCRIBE,
      &ParmH, 0, OCI_ATTR_PARAM,ErrH))
      return (ERROR);
/* Fetch the number of columns in the table */
if (OCIAttrGet(ParmH, OCI_DTYPE_PARAM, &nColNum, 0,
      OCI_ATTR_NUM_COLS, ErrH))
```

```
        return (ERROR);
/* obtain the handle to the column list of the table */
if (OCIAttrGet(ParmH, OCI_DTYPE_PARAM, &ColListH, 0,
        OCI_ATTR_LIST_COLUMNS, ErrH)==OCI_NO_DATA)
        return (ERROR);
/* Loop through the column list and retrieve
the data-type for each column. Also, recursively describe
column types. */
for (ii = 1; ii <= nColNum; ii++)
{
        /* Fetch parameter for iith column */
        if (OCIParamGet(ColListH, OCI_DTYPE_PARAM,
              ErrH, &ColH, ii))
        return (ERROR);
        /* grab datatype for iith column */
        if (OCIAttrGet(ColH, OCI_DTYPE_PARAM,
              &DataType[ii-1], 0,OCI_ATTR_DATA_TYPE, ErrH))
        return (ERROR);
}
```

OCIDescribeAny() can be used to gather information about PL/SQL objects such as stored procedures, stored functions, and packages. It allows developers to also gather information about Oracle8 objects. Information about PL/SQL elements and object types is still stored in the Describe handle, but in different parameters. The positive aspect of the new schema metadata query system is in its consistent interface—OCIDescribeAny()—to obtain disparate information about totally different database objects.

Thanks to OCIDescribeAny() Oracle developers are now able to efficiently retrieve database object information useful in applications that require schema reverse engineering. This gives the OCI8 an edge over Pro*C.

12.3.2 DYNAMIC SQL PROCESSING

Dynamic SQL is another task that is performed much more elegantly in the OCI than in Pro*C. This is especially true when the SQL statement is truly dynamic, that is, both select output variables and where clause bind variables are unknown at compile time. In other words, the OCI can be efficiently used to replace Pro*C dynamic SQL method 4. To understand why, one should consider the standard OCI steps for SQL statement preparation and binding. Figure 12.1 illustrates the OCI steps required to process SQL statements.

The first consideration after having looked at the figure is that in the OCI, the treatment of static SQL doesn't differ much from its dynamic counterpart. An SQL statement built dynamically needs only one more step but requires the same number of network roundtrips. The reason is that when the OCI8 executes the

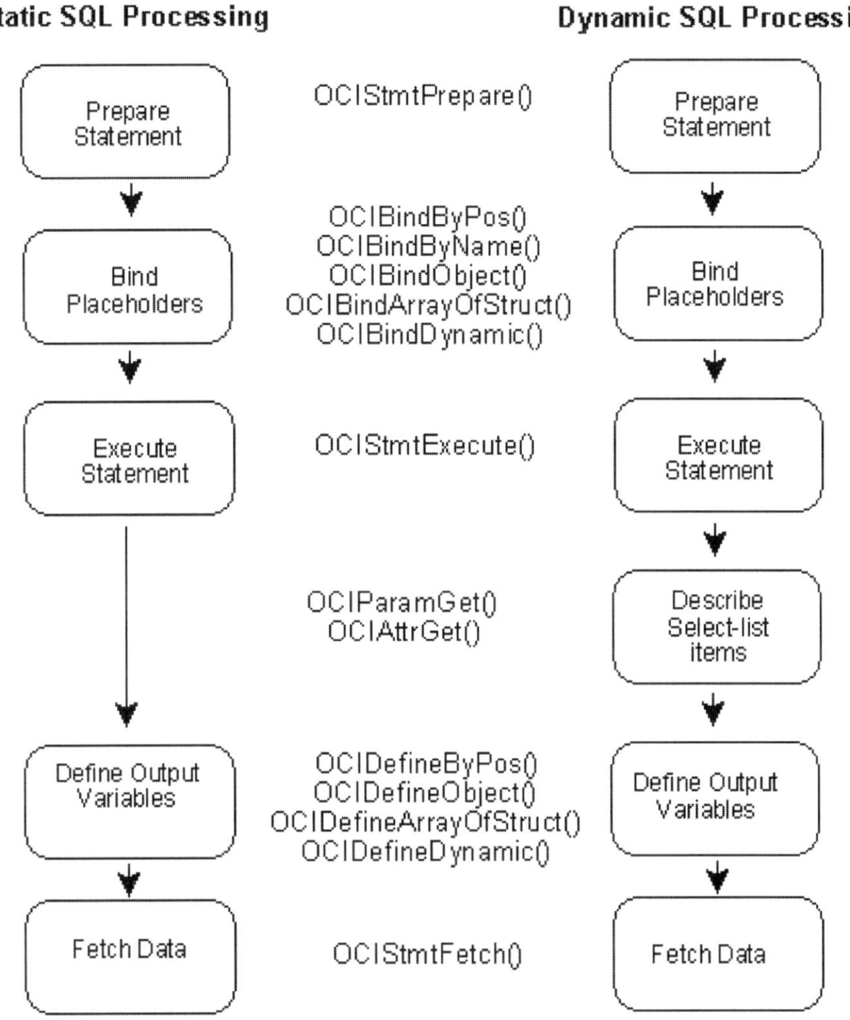

FIGURE 12.1 OCI Steps for SQL Processing

statement, the select-list becomes available in the statement handle. One network roundtrip is enough to execute the statement and gather all information from the server about the select-list item. This represents a considerable improvement over the OCI7, which provided the *odescr()* call. odescr() performed one network roundtrip per 16 select-list items to describe, in addition to the network roundtrip performed by either *oexec()* or *oexen()* to execute the statement.

Performance is not the only advantage offered by the OCI over Pro*C. The additional amount of code required to support dynamic SQL is minimal, and the syntax used and coding style are very much in line with the other OCI statements. Dynamic SQL method 4 in Pro*C seems an aberration, totally inconsistent with the rest of the same Pro*C program that processes static SQL. Maintaining dynamic SQL processing in Pro*C is much more onerous than in the OCI, which does the same job more cleanly and with fewer lines of code.

12.3.3 LARGE OBJECT MANAGEMENT

Another area where the OCI manifests a clear superiority is in the handling of large binary objects, introduced with Oracle8 to overcome most of the limitations imposed by the Oracle7 LONG and LONG RAW datatypes. The OCI8 still supports piecewise fetches and insertions of VARCHAR2, LONG, and LONG RAW datatypes, offering an additional method based on callback routines to handle piecewise operations dynamically. But the OCI8 also supports LOB buffering for internal LOB values (BFILE types are not supported in the first releases of Oracle8). When LOB buffering is enabled through the *OCIEnableBuffering()* call, LOBs are buffered in the client cache reducing the number of network roundtrips necessary to perform LOB insertions and updates. The following table shows the OCI LOB functions that support LOB buffering.

OCI FUNCTION	PURPOSE
OCIDisableBuffering()	Disables LOB buffering for the LOB locator specified as a parameter
OCIEnableBuffering()	Enables LOB buffering for the LOB locator specified as a parameter
OCILobFlushBuffer()	Flushes the LOB buffer writing changes made to the LOB identified by the input parameter to the database
OCILobRead()	Reads a portion of a LOB into the LOB buffer
OCILobWrite()	Writes data from a LOB buffer to the database

Pro*C does not support LOB operations natively. It is possible to call PL/SQL blocks or procedures/packages that use the Oracle provided DBMS_LOB package to manipulate LOBs from Pro*C, but this technique has the disadvantage that no local LOB cache is provided and therefore requires many more network roundtrips than the corresponding OCI processing. The OCI8 is a better alternative, which offers more performance and control over LOB operations. In mission critical context the OCI is currently the only reasonable option for LOB management.

12.3.4 DML STATEMENTS WITH A RETURNING CLAUSE

Using the RETURNING clause with a DML statement allows developers to combine two SQL statements into one, effectively saving a server round-trip. This is allowed by new syntax introduced by Oracle8. By adding an extra clause to the traditional UPDATE, INSERT, and DELETE statements, a query is added to the DML statement and executed in one network roundtrip. In the OCI, the values are returned to the application through the use of OUT bind variables, as in the following example.

```
UPDATE CUSTOMER SET ID = ID + :inAddId,
       ADDRESS = :inAddress,
       WHERE NAME = :inName
RETURNING ID, NAME, ADDRESS, TELEPHONE INTO
            :outId, :outAddress, :outTelephone;
```

Note that with DML statements, the WHERE clause can identify multiple rows. This means that the statement can affect multiple rows in the table. Furthermore, a DML statement can be executed multiple times in a single *OCIExecute()* statement. For this reason an OCI application that uses the RETURNING clause is not in a position to determine in advance how much data will be returned at runtime. As a result, the variables corresponding to the RETURNING...INTO placeholders must be bound in OCI_DATA_AT_EXEC mode.

In addition, the application must define its own dynamic data handling callback routines (rather than using the OCI_DATA_AT_EXEC polling mechanism). Even if developers know for sure that only one row will be fetched by the RETURNING clause, they are still required to bind the OUT variables in OCI_DATA_AT_EXEC mode and use callback functions.

The out variables must be bound using either *OCIBindByName()* or *OCIBindByPos()*, and *OCIBindDynamic()* must be called for each OUT variable, to associate a callback function with the OUT variables.

The callback functions must provide storage to accommodate the returned data. In addition, they must contain error-handling logic able to deal with situations where the statement fails after an initial partial success. For instance, a where clause can select 12 rows, and the statement can fail after having received 5 rows. The database server would still send the five rows back to the caller, which must be prepared to receive them before returning an error.

The RETURNING clause is extremely useful when inserting LOBs into the database. Normally, an application must insert an empty LOB locator into the database, and then SELECT it back out again to be able to manipulate it. Using the RETURNING clause, an OCI application can combine these two steps into a single, more efficient statement.

Again, the OCI implementation of this important feature promotes the adoption of the OCI in applications that strive to get the maximum performance possible out of an Oracle engine. Similar functionality is not offered in Pro*C.

12.3.5 ADVANCED QUEUING

Oracle8 Enterprise edition introduces message queuing, a new feature that used to be offered only by middleware products such as BEA Systems Message/Q or IBM MQ Series. Traditional client-server applications are based on a request/response paradigm, which implies strict sequentiality in the dialogue between the client and the server. In other words, the client submits a request to the server and blocks until the response arrives. While the request/response paradigm is effective for most applications, a growing number of business domains require a different handling of the interactions between systems and users of the systems. It is not only possible, but also useful to de-couple the request for services from the supply of the requested services.

An application can queue messages that are read by the recipient at its convenience, rather than straightaway. The same application can read the answer to the messages at a later time, without forcing the interactive user to wait to regain control of the computer until the server has completed its processing cycle. Workflow management has traditionally been the preferred environment for message queuing, but other business domains are now showing a strong interest in this relatively new paradigm.

Oracle8 provides sophisticated message queuing, which allows for the implementation of several variations of the message-based application paradigm. The simplest form is represented by the "one producer—one consumer" model, where one producer may enqueue different messages into one queue. Each message will be dequeued and processed once by one of the consumers. A message can be given an expiration time. If the message is not retrieved before the expiration time, Oracle can flag the message as expired and therefore unavailable for retrieval by the consumer. More sophisticated models are characterized by the "Many producers—One Consumer" or "Many Producers—Many Consumers of Discrete Messages" variations of the same paradigm, and are all supported by Oracle Advanced Queuing.

Message queuing provides the necessary infrastructure for the implementation of an even newer application paradigm, called "Publish and Subscribe". This paradigm is also know under the name of "push technology," and is characterized by the de-coupling of the producers of messages and the consumers of the same messages. The consumers subscribe to queues of interest and receive all the messages "published" by the producers. The two roles are interchangeable and consumers can unsubscribe from queues at any time. The basic principle is that the producer doesn't need to know the recipients of its messages. The message queuing system makes sure that each consumer will receive the one message only once.

Oracle8 supports the "Publish and Subscribe" paradigm, opening the door to a great variety of client-server application models. As in the case of LOB management, there are only two native interfaces to Oracle Advanced queuing, one for PL/SQL and one for the OCI. Pro*C is not supported natively, leaving Pro*C developers with the dilemma of choosing the most appropriate interface. Once again, I believe that the OCI is the way to go, because of its performance advantage. The OCI8 interface to Oracle Advanced Queuing is implemented through 2 OCI functions and 4 descriptors, as shown in the table below.

OCI FUNCTION	PURPOSE
OCIAQEnq()	Enqueues messages to the message queue specified as a parameter
OCIAQDeq()	Dequeues messages from the message queue specified as a parameter
OCI DESCRIPTOR	**PURPOSE**
OCIAQMsgProperties	Allows developers to specify message characteristics such as priority, delay, expiration time, recipient list, etc.
OCIAQEnqOptions	Allows developers to specify enqueuing options such as transactional behavior and sequence deviation
OCIAQDeqOptions	Allows developers to specify dequeuing options such as transactional behavior, dequeue mode, consumer name, etc.
OCIAQAgent	The purpose of the Agent descriptor is to identify a producer or a consumer of a message and the protocol used to transfer messages to and from the queues.

The OCI AQ descriptors are standard descriptors that are accessed through the usual OCI calls to allocate descriptors (*OCIDescriptorAlloc()*), to fetch data out of them (*OCIAttrGet()*), and to insert data into them (*OCIAttrSet()*). The two OCI calls to enqueue and dequeue messages take a service context handler and an error handler as parameters, together with other queue and message-oriented parameters.

12.3.6 OBJECT NAVIGATION

The OCI provides a fine-grained support for object manipulation. Pro*C, in contrast, supports objects in a coarse-grained way. An example is given by the pair OBEJCT SET – OBJECT GET commands offered by Pro*C to convert "C" datatypes into object elements and vice versa. Developers are not completely in control of what occurs during datatype conversion. The OCI provides two calls per supported datatype, one to convert from an object element to a "C" datatype and one to do the reverse.

Most of the interaction with Oracle, which occurs when fetching and storing objects, is hidden in the SQLLIB, which provides a high-level interface for Pro*C developers. The OCI8 implementation, on the contrary, exposes most of the low-level details that give OCI developers greater control over the database operations required to manipulate object-relational elements. Pro*C can be used proficiently in a strongly relational context that occasionally makes use of Oracle8 objects. The OCI should be used instead if the application being built uses the object-relational model extensively.

12.3.7 THE BEST OF THE TWO WORLDS

The previous sections (12.3.1 to 12.3.6) highlighted several areas where the OCI performs better than Pro*C. If one takes into account only performance, the OCI would be the winner in most cases. But the judgement on the interface of choice is generally based on, for instance, maintainability of the code, availability of skills on the market, company background, and several other factors. It is easier (and, consequently, less expensive) to hire Pro*C programmers than OCI programmers. The amount of lines of code required to process plain vanilla SQL statements is less when using Pro*C, where no handles have to be allocated and no accessor functions have to be extensively used to access data in the opaque OCI structures. This translates to easier and less expensive maintainability of the application throughout its lifetime.

The solution is using both Pro*C and the OCI. Section 11.7 covered in detail how to interface Pro*C and the OCI. Pro*C should be used to process standard SQL statements or PL/SQL blocks, while the OCI should be used to access more sophisticated features offered by the Oracle server, such as Advanced Queuing or the object extensions. Dynamic SQL is another domain where the OCI offers an edge over Pro*C. Pro*C and the OCI can cooperate very well to offer developers the best of the two worlds.

12.4 The OCI: Best Companion for C++

The support offered by Pro*C to C++ can be summarized in one sentence: "too little, too late." It was first introduced in late 1995, with Pro*C release 2.2, years after C++ had become one of the most popular languages in the industry, especially in the territory where Oracle was the database server of choice—the Unix world. As already pointed out in the chapter dedicated to Pro*C, the "C" preprocessor must be disabled when using the precompiler to process C++ programs. This implies the use of a DECLARE section that causes redundant and error-prone code. Efficiency is also penalized, because the content of C++ variables must be copied into host variables declared within the DECLARE section, and then recopied back to C++ variables after the SQL statements have been executed and the host variables populated with database-sourced data.

A popular alternative to Pro*C, adopted by many projects based on C++ as the language of choice, is a class or a set of classes that encapsulate OCI semantics. The C++ wrapper classes usually offer a consistent and object-oriented-like interface that hides OCI implementation details. A C++ programmer can access Oracle data without compromising on OO purity, writing code that follows OO rules and semantics thanks to the wrapper class to the OCI.

Both commercial and freeware classes are available on the market. DBTools.h++ by Rogue Wave Software is probably the most popular commercially available solution, while OTL, written by Sergei Kuchin, is one of the most popular freeware alternatives. One of the most elegantly implemented OCI wrapper set of classes is available in the article "The Oracle Call Interface and C++," in Dr. Dobb's Journal in November 1995. The implementation suggested in that article is not complete, but the ideas discussed by the two authors (Jeremy Woo-Sam and Tony Murphy) are a very good starting point for developers who decide to build a customized version of their own.

If you are considering building a C++ library to interface to Oracle through the OCI, visit the Dr. Dobb's Journal WEB page and fetch both the article and the source code (www.ddj.com). The Dr. Dobb's article is a little old and covers only the OCI release 7. Nevertheless, the programming concepts proposed in the article are still valid for an OCI8 implementation. The OCI Template Library (OTL) release 2 has been implemented using the new OCI8 calls and is definitely one of the best options for developers who want to access Oracle data from a C++ program. The source code is freely downloadable from the following WEB address:

```
http://home.sprynet.com/sprynet/skuchin/otl_1pg.htm
```

The only obstacle to a wider adoption of the OTL is its status of free product. Many large corporations have strict policies that forbid the adoption of free software for large and mission critical applications.

Summary

The chapter discussed the Oracle Call Interface (OCI). Initially we examined the OCI calls and primitives offered by Oracle release 7, to get acquainted with an interface that is quite different from Pro*C, Pro*Cobol, and PL/SQL. The underlying OCI philosophy remains the same with OCI release 8, but the number of calls increased by an order of magnitude. The introduction of handles, or opaque structures that hold all necessary information for the interaction with the database server, added even more complexity to the programming model of the OCI.

Yes, the OCI is not simple. It requires a steeper learning curve than Pro*C and in most cases, more lines of code are needed to accomplish with the OCI what in Pro*C is simpler and shorter. Nevertheless, serious Oracle developers should become familiar with it because it outperforms Pro*C in areas like dynamic SQL processing, database object reverse-engineering, and object-relational processing.

Large object manipulation and Oracle Advanced Queuing do not offer a Pro*C interface, leaving developers with the option of using either PL/SQL or the OCI. The latter is the option of choice when performance is a crucial ingredient of an application being built.

The last topic covered in this chapter is the OCI used in conjunction with C++. The support offered by Pro*C to C++ is far from optimal, so a number of alternatives, either commercial or freeware, has grown in the market. One of the best implementations, the OCI Template Library (OTL), is available as freeware. Companies that cannot use free software can consider DBTools.h++, by Rogue Wave Software, for accessing an Oracle database from C++ code.

Chapter 13

ORACLE TRACE

In this chapter we will examine one of the latest additions to the family of the Oracle tools, Oracle Trace, which is the Oracle re-edition of an old tool well-known to OpenVMS users, DEC Trace. The latter was bought by Oracle Corporation from DEC together with RdB, Rally, Common Data Dictionary, and a few other tools.

Oracle Trace, as the name indicates, allows Oracle applications to be traced so that statistical information about their use can be gathered. To make this possible, the applications being monitored must be instrumented, that is, specific API calls must be used in the code to enable tracing.

After a brief overview of the Oracle Trace utility, the chapter will examine the added value that designers can expect from this utility, how to use it proficiently, and how to control the data gathering mechanism from the Oracle Enterprise Manager.

13.1 Oracle Trace Components

Oracle Trace is a complex product that requires the cooperation of several software modules and a client/server configuration. On the server side, Oracle Intelligent Agent must be running, together with the Oracle Trace Collection Services, which are components that perform data collection into files.

Additionally, the applications being traced must be instrumented. The Oracle database server and SQL*Net/Net8 are internally instrumented, allowing developers to gather application behavior data even when the custom-written application being traced is not instrumented. This allows for a generic data gathering of limited usefulness, because the events being monitored cannot be related to specific sections of the application being traced. For a more precise and exhaustive analysis, the application code should be instrumented with API calls to the Oracle Trace facility.

On the client side, the Oracle Enterprise Manager (OEM) console drives most of the Oracle Trace operations. The OEM Diagnostics Pack (formerly, Performance Pack), which includes the Oracle Trace component, must also be installed. While most Oracle Trace operations can be performed on the server side using command line utilities, creating the product definition file, which defines the set of application events that must be traced, can be done only through the client GUI.

13.1.1 SERVER SIDE COMPONENTS

After Oracle Trace has been installed on the server side, the $ORACLE_HOME/bin directory contains four Oracle Trace executables, used to perform the administrative tasks required to manage Oracle Trace collections.

UTILITY	PURPOSE
otrccol	Command-line interface used to start and stop collections
otrccref	Creates three Oracle Trace administrative files necessary for the facility to work
otrcfmt	Uploads collection data to Oracle tables from files stored in the file system
otrcrep	Produces formatted reports directly from the OS files

Oracle Trace collections can be managed either through the OEM console or directly on the server, using the *otrccol* program. Once the instrumented application has run on the server, the data collected during the session is available in a file, in an internal format that is not published by Oracle Corporation. Users of the Oracle Trace facility have two options: either they format the collected data invoking *otrcrep*, which produces formatted text output that can be redirected to a file; or they use *otrcfmt*, which uploads the collected data to Oracle tables, which can be accessed by reporting tools allowing for greater flexibility while conducting the analysis on the collected data.

To work properly, Oracle Trace requires the presence of several files that describe the active collections and list the events that must be sampled in the collections files. Specifically, the following is a list of the required files:

FILE	PURPOSE
facility.dat (process.dat)	Lists all processes available to participate in collections (In release prior to Oracle8 the file was called process.dat.)
collect.dat	Lists currently active collections

(*cont.*)

FILE	PURPOSE
regid.dat	Lists Registration Ids associated with collection processes
<product>.fdf	Product Definition File—describes the instrumented data that can be collected during the running of an application
<product>.phd	Product Hierarchy Definition file—contains all relationships between events as defined in the collection files
<collection_name>.cdf	Collection Definition File—describes the event set of a collection
<collection_name>.dat	Output of Oracle Trace file—contains all information gathered during the running of the instrumented application

The Oracle Trace Collection Services control files are regid.dat, facility.dat, and collect.dat. If they don't exist they can be recreated at any time by using the otrccrf utility. They should be placed in $ORACLE_HOME/otrace/admin in Unix and in <DISK>:\ORANT\OTRACEXX\ADMIN in Windows NT. XX stands for the major release of Oracle.

At the beginning of a collection cycle, the three collection services control files should be recreated to ensure a fresh start. When Oracle Trace is used against a 7.3 instance, one more step is required, creating the TRACESVR user and compiling two Oracle-provided packages, DBMS_ORACLE_TRACE_AGENT and DBMS_ORACLE_TRACE_USER. This is accomplished by running the otrcsvr.sql script, located in $ORACLE_HOME/rdbms/admin, after having logged in as SYS.

13.1.2 CLIENT SIDE COMPONENTS

Oracle Trace requires a large part of the administrative tasks to be done on a client workstation running MS Windows (9x or NT). The Oracle OEM and the Diagnostics Pack must be installed, and all remote services where instrumented applications are to run must have been "discovered" by OEM. In other words, Oracle Intelligent Agent must be installed and running in all nodes, and the remote services must have been accessed at least once by the workstation where the OEM is installed.

Two major tasks are performed through the Oracle Trace client GUI: 1) the creation of the Product Definition files; and 2) the creation and submission of Oracle Trace collections.

A product definition file defines a single set of events that must be collected by an Oracle Trace session. Each product definition file is identified by the .FDF extension. It is not possible to start an Oracle Trace collection without at least one product definition file.

Designers can decide to sample every aspect of a large application, instrumenting each function and database interaction. They may have two goals in mind, measuring both performance and throughput. Running the application instrumented in such way risks producing a huge collection file, difficult to manage and to store in the database for analysis. Furthermore, too much information is equivalent to no information at all, given the implicit difficulty to summarize into few meaningful indicators large collections of data.

For this reason, it is possible to create product definitions that include selected sets of events that focus on specific and limited areas of the application being sampled. Multiple product definitions can be created for one application, and selectively run by different collection sessions, each targeted at the analysis of distinct aspects of the application's behavior.

To create a product definition, the Oracle Trace GUI must be run in admin mode. In MS Windows, one should create a shortcut that launches the GUI executable (EPC.EXE) with the "/A" option on the command line. This will enable the two options "EDIT" and "CREATE" on the product menu. Through those options, it is possible to access the production definition form (Figure 13.1).

The items displayed in the "General" tabbed page are crucial for the identification of the collection by the Oracle Trace server software. They are passed as parameters to most API calls that instrument the application being traced. The second page accessible from the form allows Oracle Trace users to define items, which can be optionally associated to events (Figure 13.2). While Oracle Trace

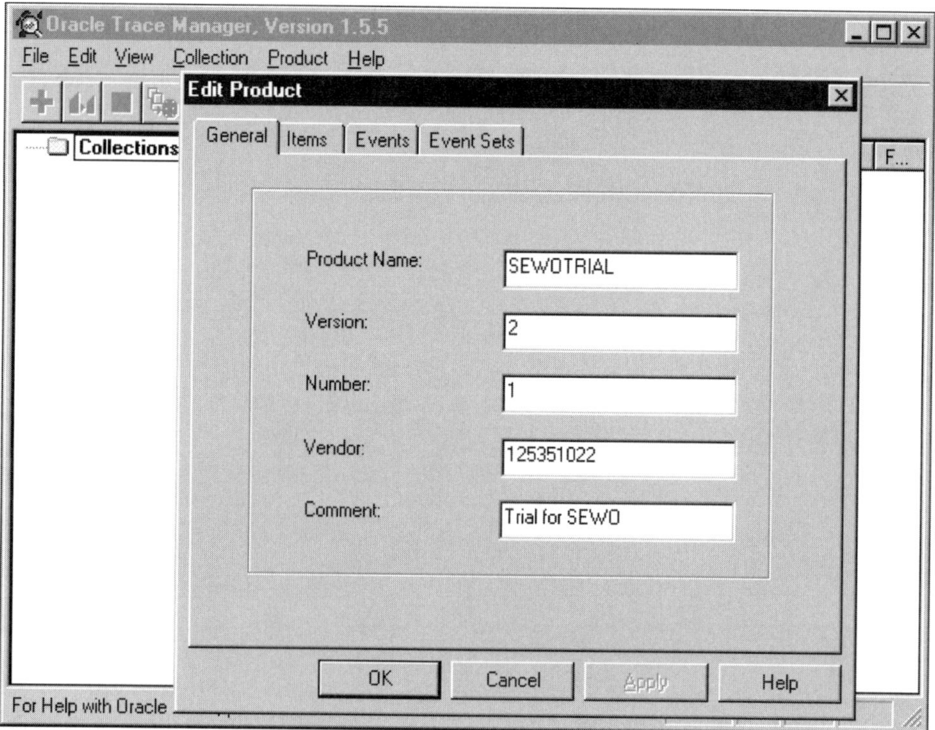

FIGURE 13.1 The product definition form

provides a set of predefined items, users of the product can freely extend the set of items to suit their needs.

The main function of a product definition file is to list the events that an Oracle Trace collection must sample when the application runs (Figure 13.3). This is done through the two remaining pages accessible from the "Create Product" form. Clicking on the "Events" tab allows the user to define the events being sampled, one by one. Clicking on the "Event Sets" tab opens the page that allows users to group together the events defined in the previous step into an event set (Figure 13.4). The events that are included in the event set will be saved in the product definition file (.FDF extension).

The second important task that can be accomplished using the Oracle Trace client GUI is the definition of an Oracle trace collection. A "wizard" drives the user through the process. The significant steps are the selection of the event sets, the restriction of collected data by user name or wait events, and the scheduling of the collection.

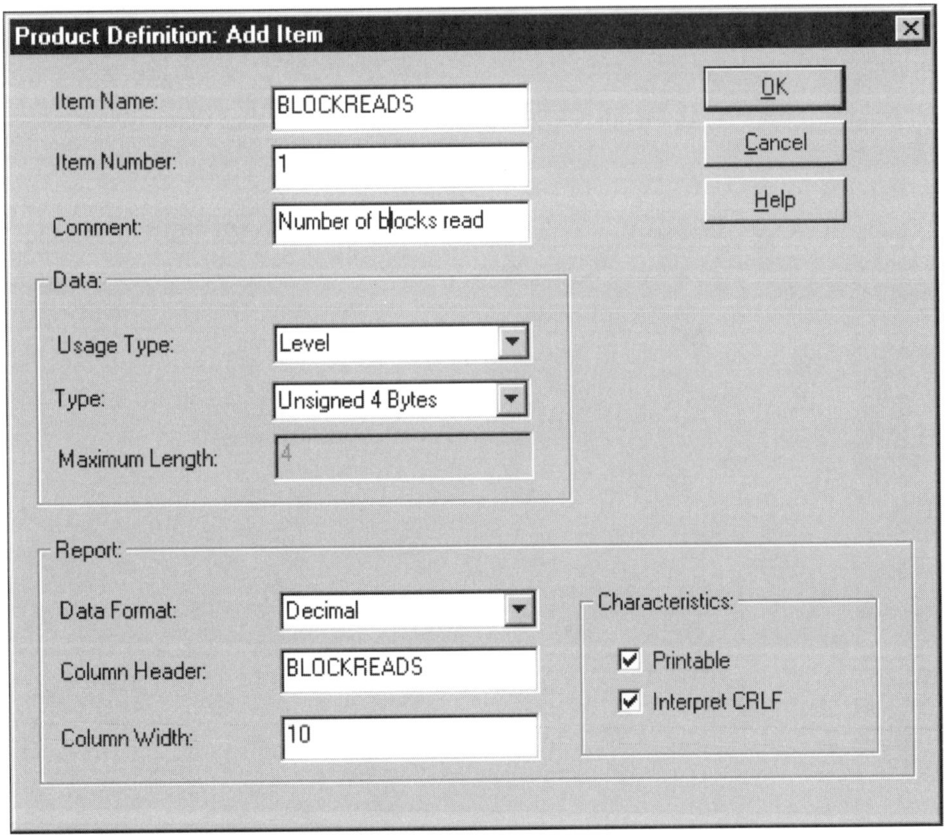

FIGURE 13.2 Adding an item to a product definition

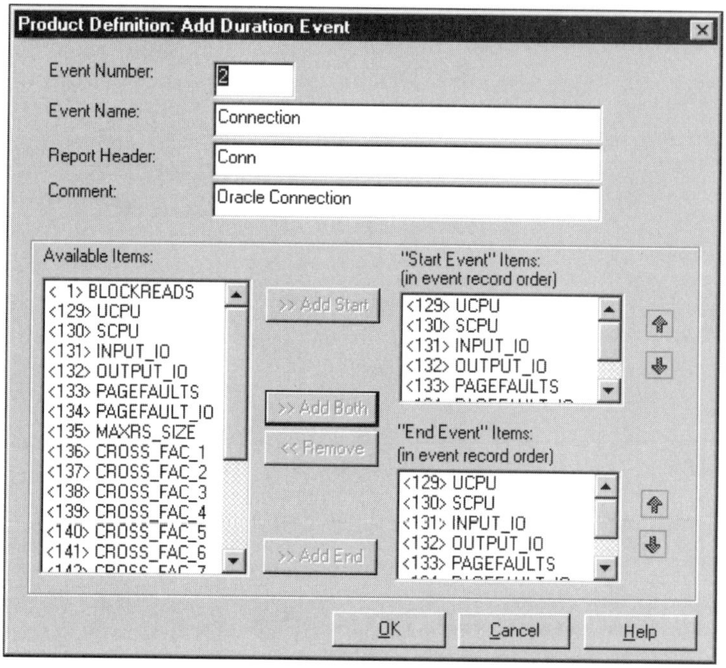

FIGURE 13.3 Adding an event in Oracle trace

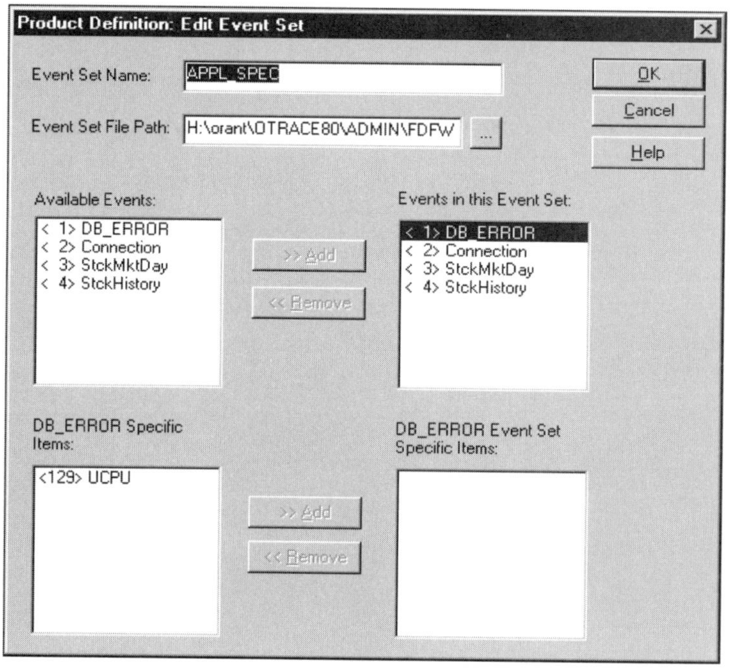

FIGURE 13.4 Multiple events are grouped together in an event set

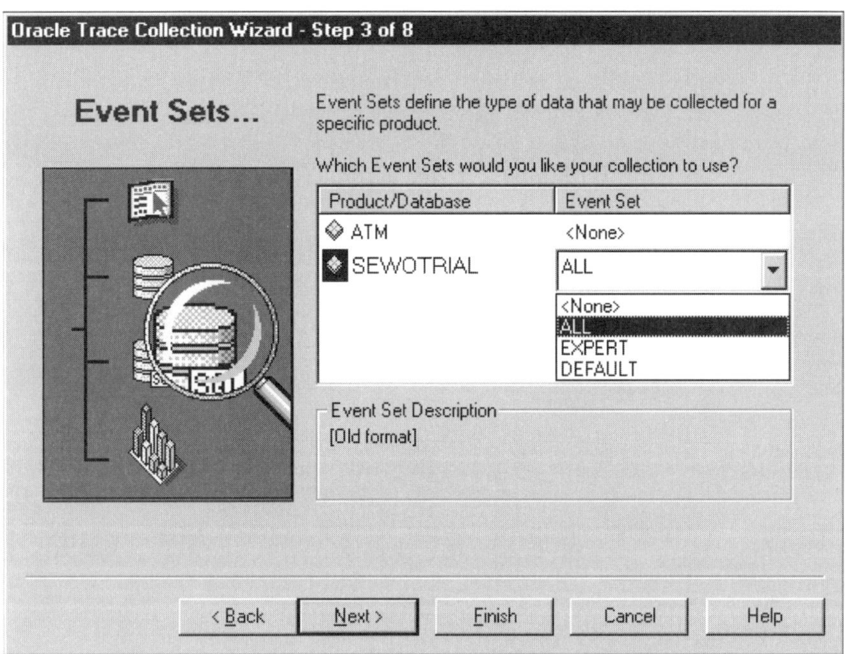

FIGURE 13.5 Selection of the event set for the required collection

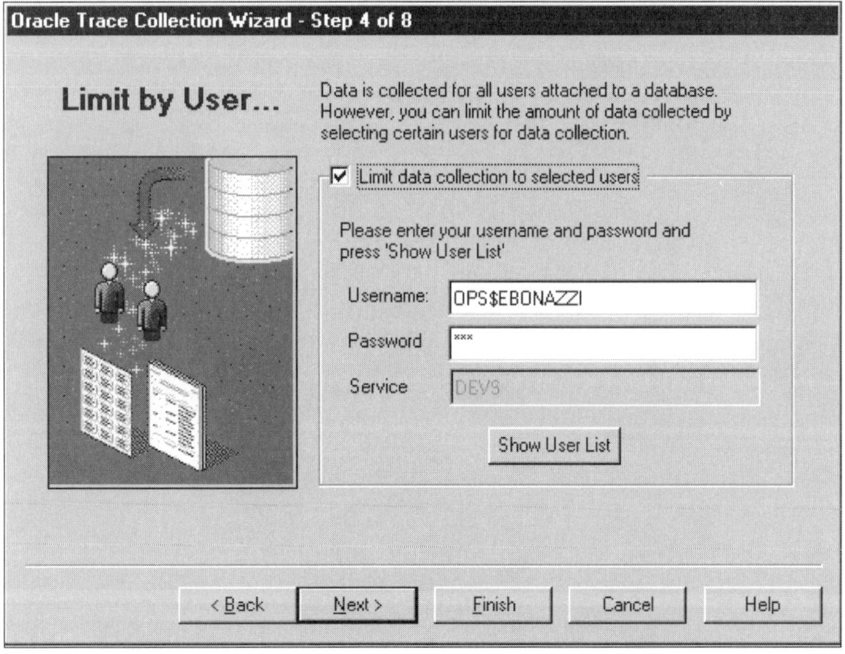

FIGURE 13.6 Restricting the collected data to a single user

It is possible to restrict the collection data by user name(Figure 13.6). This feature is useful to limit the volume of the collection file and to control the collected information. It is possible to limit the collected data to only one user, or a set of users, through one form of the Oracle Trace Collection definition wizard.

If the target database is an Oracle server release 8.04 or greater, it is possible to restrict the number of wait events for which trace data is collected. By default, Oracle Trace collects all wait event data, which could lead to a significant overhead and a fast growing collection file. Since not all wait events are really important for a tuning exercise, it is possible to filter out those events the importance of which is negligible. This is done through a form presented by the collection creation wizard (Figure 13.7).

The last task presented by the collection creation wizard is the scheduling of the collection runs. Several options are presented to the user, who can choose between a once-off run starting either immediately or deferred to a later time, or multiple runs scheduled in the future (Figure 13.8). The Oracle Intelligent Agent will be responsible for submitting all collection runs defined in this step. The ad-

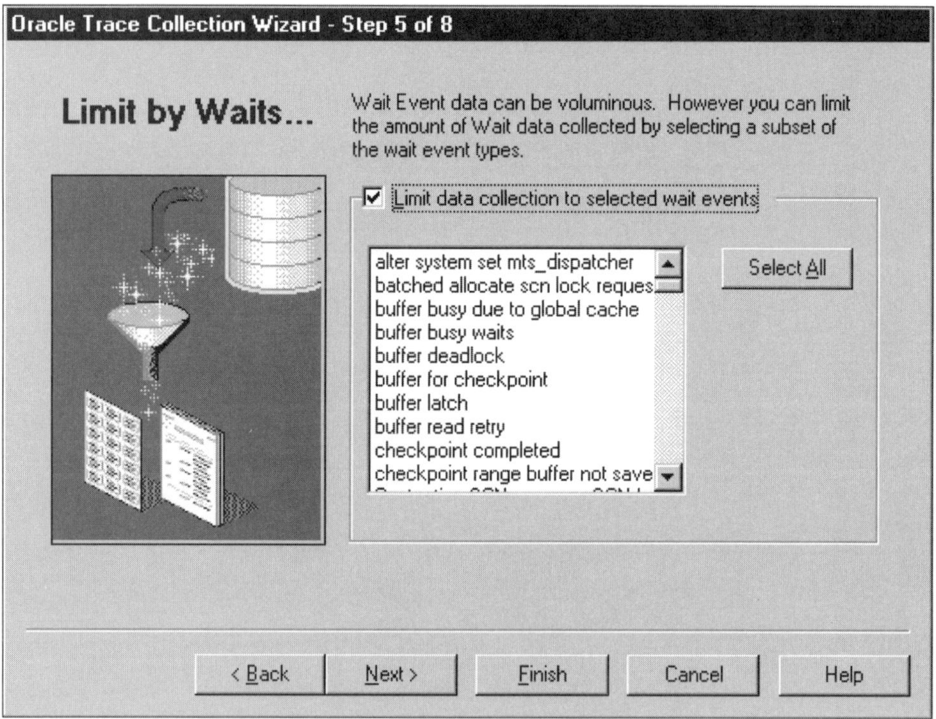

FIGURE 13.7 Filtering out unwanted wait events

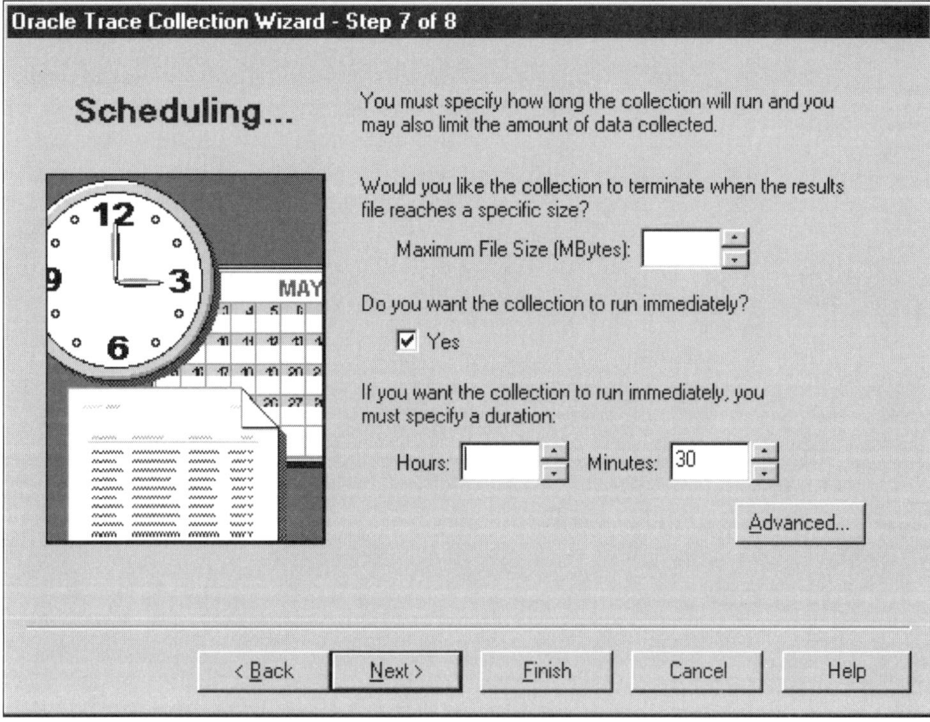

FIGURE 13.8 Oracle Trace Collection Scheduler

vanced scheduling option applet allows users to define collection runs in a similar way to the definition of Unix cron jobs.

13.2 Using Oracle Trace—Deciding What to Sample

Using Oracle Trace can be beneficial in different stages of an application software lifecycle. When the application is still in the development phase, instrumenting the code and conducting detailed analysis on the trace output can help capacity planners to finalize the hardware configuration, extrapolating the results obtained on the development machine. Different data collection sessions, more focused on performance, can help designers and developers pinpoint bottlenecks and potential problems that went undetected in the previous stages of the project.

Collecting Oracle Trace statistics once the application has been delivered can help the maintainers of the application to better understand the user population. By defining an appropriate event set, a collection session can be used to categorize the application functionality with the goal of ranking the most accessed options and to isolate those functions that are even rarely or never used.

One of the problems affecting development teams of large organizations that deploy applications used nationwide is the lack of interaction and feedback between the users and the developers. This is even more exacerbated when the application is so large that the development team is spread across different locations, often geographically distant from each other. Tracing an application can help to reduce the gap between users and developers, for instance, by making the latter aware of the crucial functionality regularly accessed by the user population. This also helps reduce the "gold plating" syndrome, focusing developers on the really important aspects of the application being delivered.

Conducting an Oracle Trace session can be seen as taking the radiography of an application, which exposes the way it is used in real life. After having decided that an application should use Oracle Trace, the next step should be to identify and categorize the important events to be sampled. Oracle Trace understands two different types of events:

- Point Events
- Duration Events

Point events are instantaneous occurrences of events, the life of which do not span over time. An example is recording an option chosen by a user interacting with the application.

Duration events are characterized by having a beginning and an end, such as a complex select query. Designers might be interested in knowing how long the query took to return the rows and what resources it used. In this case, the code can be instrumented with two calls to Oracle Trace, one before submitting the query, marking the beginning of the duration event, and one after the query has completed, marking the end of the event.

Items are another important concept in Oracle Trace. They are defined as information units associated with events. The GUI interface to Oracle trace, accessible from the OEM console, allows developers to create product definitions, which are associations of items with events. Oracle Trace identifies three types:

- Product-specific items
- Resource Items
- Cross-product Items

Product specific items can be defined, as shown above, when a product definition file is created through the Oracle Trace GUI that runs on a client workstation. Oracle Trace provides the following resource items:

ITEM	PURPOSE
UCPU	CPU time in user mode
SCPU	CPU time in kernel mode
INPUT_IO	Number of times file system performed input
OUTPUT_IO	Number of times file system performed output
PAGEFAULTS	Total number of page faults
PAGEFAULT_IO	Number of hard page fault
MAXRS_SIZE	Maximum resident set size used[1]

[1]Oracle Trace was born as DEC Trace, which used to run under OpenVMS. This value was originally the working set size used by the application. In a Unix environment, the working set has been renamed "resident set".

Linking the resource items to the user-defined events allows for statistics gathering on resource consumption per event.

A very important feature offered by Oracle Trace is the possibility to relate events across applications. The Oracle server and SQL*Net/Net80 are Oracle Trace instrumented. When a user application submits to an Oracle shadow process the request to execute an SQL statement, the resource time taken by SQL execution is accounted to the Oracle process, not to the user process. Oracle Trace users rely on cross-product items to be able to correlate inter-application events. API calls are provided to set and get the values for the cross-product items across different processes.

An example helps to clarify the concept. Let us imagine we are instrumenting an application function called "account_balance". At the beginning of the function, an Oracle Trace API sets the beginning of a duration event; then a few SQL statements are performed to compute the account balance, and the API call that sets the end of the duration is called, before returning to the caller.

If the resource items were associated with the account_balance event when the collection was defined, this information will be enough to compute the resources used by the system to perform the account_balance function. The collection file will contain resource data for the account_balance function, specifically instrumented by application developers, and resource data for each of the SQL statements performed by the function, because the Oracle server is instrumented by default. If the same SQL statements were submitted by different functions of the same applications, it would be impossible to discriminate between the SQL statements performed by account_balance and the SQL statements performed by the other functions.

If the account_balance function sets the cross-product item before submitting the SQL statements to the engine using the appropriate APIs, the resource data pertaining to the SQL statements will be "marked" in the collection file as "owned" by the account_balance function, providing in this way the required association between the user-defined function and the SQL statements executed by the Oracle server on its behalf.

Deciding the granularity of the events being sampled is the most demanding task for designers and developers who want to instrument applications using Oracle Trace. The trade-off is between a limited set of events available—only 127 events can be defined—and the detail of the required statistics. Another element to be considered is the size of the collection file, which can grow at an extremely fast pace if too many events are collected at once.

It is not a good idea to define a few, very coarse-grained events that include a large set of functions or SQL statements. The resulting statistics, obtained by the corresponding Oracle Trace collection, can be difficult to interpret. In addition, the overhead associated with running the application can be significant, and the volume of data accumulated in the collection file extremely large.

A wiser strategy is to define a reasonably large number of application events. Ideally, all functions and associated with SQL statements should be logically grouped together in events. Several product definition files should be produced for the same application, at least one per major functional area of the application being sampled. With this arrangement, it is much easier to selectively enable tracing for specific and restricted parts of the application, aiming for more accurate and meaningful data to be collected.

13.3 Oracle Trace APIs

Building a precise plan that identifies what to trace and why is the first step for a successful use of the product. Events and event sets should be designed prior to disseminating the application's source code with Oracle Trace APIs.

In this chapter, only the most important and commonly used API calls will be examined, in order to illustrate a correct use of Oracle Trace. A detailed explanation of the complete set of APIs is available on the "Oracle Trace Developer's Guide" manual, shipped with the Oracle Enterprise Manager.

The most important data structure used by an Oracle Trace instrumented program is the Event Flag Array, which is populated by the *epc_init()* call. epc_init() initializes the Oracle Trace facility and must be called prior to all other Oracle Trace calls. The Event Flag Array is an array of 128 4-byte integers used to communicate to the application the events to be traced, included in the current product definition. Consider the following example:

An application defines 10 events in total, numbered event 1 to event 10. A product definition specifies that only events 2, 5, and 7 must be traced. The initial call to epc_init() passes a pointer to the Event Flag Array to Oracle Trace. The array is populated, taking the value for each position from the product definition file. If the array is called EvenFlag[], then the array positions 2, 5, and 7 will contain 1, and the other positions will contain 0. Before recording point or duration events, the application code should test the value contained in the corresponding array position. An example is shown below.

```
if (EventFlag[2])
{
  epc_start_event(API_VERSION,VENDOR,FACILITY_NUMBER,2,
                  &Transaction_handle,0,NULL,0,0,0,0);
  status = ComputeAverage(&avg_struct);/*This is a call to */
        /* a business function which contains SQL calls */
  epc_end_event(API_VERSION,VENDOR,FACILITY_NUMBER,2,
                  &Transaction_handle,0,NULL,0,0,0,0);
}
```

While the code presented above works, its readability can be improved by using hash-defined constants, instead of numbers, to refer to the events. The constants should be consistent with the event names defined in the product definition file. The "Create Product" form displayed by the Oracle Trace GUI allows users to associate an event name to an event number. For instance, event number 3 identifies a point event named "DB_ERROR". This event should be traced when an unexpected database-related error occurs. The instrumented application should contain the line

```
#define DB_ERROR 3
```

in either an include file or at the beginning of the "C" code. Using the user-defined constant improves the readability of the subsequent calls:

```
if(EventFlag[DB_ERROR])
{
      epc_event(API_VERSION,VENDOR,FACILITY_NUMBER,DB_ERROR,
                  0,0,0,0,0);
}
```

If the event name is kept consistent in "C" code and product definition file, designers can easily reconcile the Oracle Trace calls with the events they defined while creating the product definition.

The first three parameters of most Oracle Trace APIs are Version, Vendor, and Product Number. These parameters are set when the product definition is created. Version is the Oracle Trace API version, either 1 for Oracle Trace shipped with Oracle 7.3 or 2 for Oracle Trace shipped with the database server version 8. Vendor is a string that uniquely identifies the company instrumenting the application. Oracle Corporation recommends using a string containing the IP address of the company, omitting the dot separators. For example, if the IP address of a company is 125.35.10.22 the corresponding vendor string should be "125351022".

The third parameter, product number, must be unique within the vendor organization. It allows Oracle Trace to uniquely identify a collection. The same vendor usually defines several collections, possibly for the same application. The combination of the vendor string with the product number can be seen as the "primary key" that allows Oracle Trace to correctly identify the required collection.

Instrumenting an application is easy, as the number of API calls is limited. Apart from the initialization routine, which must be called at the beginning of the application to enable all subsequent Oracle Trace calls, the collection of events is performed through three API calls, and when cross-product items are used, another set of three API calls does the job. Two additional APIs allow for multithreaded collections. The following table lists the Oracle Trace API calls.

INITIALIZATION ROUTINE	PURPOSE
epc_init()	Registers an executing program with Oracle Trace
Event Collecting	
epc_start_event()	Starts a duration event
epc_end_event()	Ends a duration event
epc_event()	Executes a point event
Cross-product Items	
epc_set_cf_items()	In a client/server environment, this call sets all values for the cross-product items used by the current product
epc_cf_value()	Sets values for cross-product items within the same process
epc_get_cf_items()	In a client/server environment, this call retrieves all cross-product items set by a client process
Multi-threading	
epc_context()	Starts or resumes a thread context
epc_delete_context()	Terminates trace collection for a thread

Developers requested to instrument an application should follow the steps shown below.

1. Obtain from the designers who defined the product definitions for the application a list containing all events to be traced. Each event should be clearly identified as either of duration type or of point type.
2. All event numbers should be converted into "C" constants, corresponding to the event names used in the product definitions.
3. A call to *epc_init()* should be inserted at the beginning of the application code.

4. The code constituting a traceable event should be wrapped within an Oracle Trace API call, starting with an "if" test that checks the event flag array to determine if the event is to be traced.
5. In case cross-product items are used, before collecting an event an appropriate API call should be issued to inform Oracle Trace to synchronize the subsequent events with the required item.

13.4 Formatting and Analyzing Oracle Trace Data

Instrumenting application code, creating product definitions, determining collections, and scheduling collection runs are only the preliminary and preparatory steps that contribute to the final goal, the analysis of trace data.

Once the collection session terminates, all collected raw data is accumulated in a .CDF file, the format of which is not published by Oracle Corporation. Designers interested in analyzing trace data have two options:

- ❑ Use the otrcrep utility to produce reports directly from the .CDF file
- ❑ Format the collected data into Oracle tables, which can be accessed and analyzed using standard tools (SQL*Plus, Oracle Developer Reports, third party report writers, etc.)

The first option produces voluminous reports that are difficult to interpret. It should be seen as a "quick and dirty" interim solution to provide a very rough analysis, only able to pinpoint major performance problems. The second option is much more effective because it allows for cross-referencing of data, producing a more precise and fine-grained analysis, aimed at an effective fine-tuning of the application.

To read the trace data from the .CDF file into Oracle, the Trace Formatter GUI client can be used. Its icon appears in the toolbar provided by the Diagnostics Pack. The Format Collection dialog box allows users to specify the trace collection file and the target database where the collected data is to be uploaded. Alternatively, the command line interface *otrcfmt* can be invoked, supplying trace collection file and database connection string as parameters.

Irrespective of the method chosen, the Oracle schema identified by the connection string will host the tables containing trace data. To ensure uniqueness of the table names used to store trace data, Oracle Trace uses a complex formula, which produces long and meaningless table names. The formula is:

```
V_VENDOR#_F_PRODUCT#_E_EVENT#_PROD_VER
```

Applied to the Oracle8 Server execution event, the resulting table name is V_192216243_F_5_E_9_8_0. The same table, obtaining tracing an Oracle 7 database, would be V_192216243_F_5_E_9_7_3.

Oracle Corporation recommends that you define synonyms, using meaningful names, to point to the automatically created trace tables. The *sample* subdirectory, located under the *otrace/admin* tree, contains a few SQL*Plus scripts useful for performing basic formatting of the raw trace data. The *otrcsyn.sql* script creates synonyms for all Oracle Server and SQL*Net instrumented events. Oracle Trace users should use the Oracle provided scripts as an example for creating synonyms for the user defined events.

One of the provided scripts, *otrcfunc.sql*, defines the *elapsed()* PL/SQL function, useful for computing the elapsed time of duration events in seconds. Oracle Trace stores time data in nanoseconds.

otrcdtl.sql creates a summary table that contains summary data for all SQL statements. The tables produced by the formatting utilities do not have any index created by default. This can lead to inefficient report extractions, so Oracle Corporation recommends creating supporting indexes for the fields used as keys to access and correlate trace data. A list of trace fields that should be indexed for fast report generation is provided in the Oracle Trace Developer's manual.

When cross-product items are used to correlate user defined events with Oracle Server events, ad-hoc queries should be designed and run against the trace tables to provide a more precise picture of potential application bottlenecks and performance problems. If the focus of the trace collection is on capacity planning or profiling, rather than on performance, different queries can be submitted to obtain the required information. The point is that Oracle Trace provides only raw data. Interpreting that data to extract useful hints on how the application performs is entirely up to the users of the product.

Summary

This chapter explored Oracle Trace, one of the most recent additions to the rich set of tools that Oracle Corporation provides to developers who use Oracle technologies.

Oracle Trace is not an "easy" tool. It requires a careful coordination between the server utilities, included in the Oracle Trace package, and the client GUI tools, which drive important aspects of trace data gathering, such as product and collection definition and scheduling of the collection runs. Oracle Trace requires developers to instrument their code using a reduced set of APIs, which has been illustrated in the chapter.

A few hints have been given to developers and designers who want to use Oracle Trace to profile their applications. One of the most important decisions is one that affects the granularity of the user-defined events. A too fine-grained set of events risks exhausting the available event numbers (only 127). A too coarse-grained set of events risks producing statistics of difficult interpretation and huge collection files.

The last part of the chapter focused on trace data formatting into Oracle tables for detailed analysis, using the Oracle provided SQL scripts. The trace tables created automatically by the format utility need a little work by Oracle Trace users to become really effective in producing the required statistics. Synonyms and indexes should be created to speed up report generation and to simplify statistics reading. A PL/SQL function should be created to compute the event elapsed time in seconds. This is accomplished by running a set of SQL scripts provided by the package and illustrated in the last section of the chapter.

Chapter 14

PROCEDURAL SQL

This chapter analyzes the Oracle proprietary extension to the ANSI SQL standard, called PL/SQL, which stands for procedural SQL. PL/SQL brings procedural constructs like IF-THEN-ELSE or LOOP .. ENDLOOP into the SQL world, dramatically enhancing SQL's possibilities as a true database-centric language. A great deal of the computational power offered by the Oracle engine is based upon PL/SQL, which is offered in several different facets. Database triggers and stored procedures must be coded in PL/SQL. Oracle provides several standard PL/SQL packages that facilitate database administration and enhance or implement key database features, such as an Oracle driven cron-like facility for job scheduling, communication with external programs through Oracle pipes or alert mechanisms, session and transaction control, etc.

PL/SQL is without doubt one of the major components of the Oracle architecture. Unless Oracle is used as a totally passive data repository that only provides data upon requests performed through standard SQL, chances are that PL/SQL will be used. Consequently, serious Oracle developers must be intimately confident with it.

The approach taken by this chapter is consistent with the rest of the book. This chapter is neither a crash course in PL/SQL nor a surrogate of the syntax used by PL/SQL. The chapter will discuss how to proficiently use PL/SQL to improve scalability and performance of mission critical applications based on Oracle technologies. To accomplish this goal, we will cover several key PL/SQL topics, such as correct implementation of business logic in PL/SQL constructs, triggers, and stored procedures, as well as how PL/SQL can be used to increase speed and features of standard SQL queries. The most useful Oracle standard packages will be analyzed, with a specific focus on packages that help development of applications rather than database administration.

Another important topic in this chapter will be the interface between PL/SQL and 3GL procedures written in "C" and available as shared libraries to the Oracle environment. The procedures are called 3GL callout or external procedures, and represent a powerful extension to the Oracle architecture.

The chapter will finish by showing how to protect PL/SQL code from potential competitors using the wrapper facility, and by considering a few third party tools that can greatly enhance developers' productivity while coding in PL/SQL.

14.1 Oracle Extension to ANSI SQL

PL/SQL is an Oracle proprietary extension to ANSI SQL. This very fact limits the portability of PL/SQL. Applications that must achieve database independence have two options: 1) They simply do not use proprietary extensions to SQL, such as Oracle PL/SQL or Microsoft Transact/SQL. 2) They abstract the code layer that uses proprietary procedural extensions in libraries and maintain one library per supported database.

If the application being built is really database-centric, the second option is more likely to be adopted. It is difficult to achieve good performance, scalability and an acceptable degree of code maintainability without using proprietary procedural extensions. Conversely, if the application accesses the back-end database sporadically, and database vendor independence is part of the requirements, the first option presents a few advantages.

Chapter 11, in Section 11.3, which discusses integration of Pro*C and PL/SQL, analyzed the position of a school of thought that advises against the adoption of PL/SQL in three-tier applications. This approach is justified in terms of scalability gains that can be obtained by storing the business logic in the middle tier, rather than in stored procedures or packages. The basic assumption, here, is that one Oracle instance can serve many more users if it is used as a passive repository of data, rather than as an active enforcer of business rules coded in PL/SQL. If the business logic is offloaded in 3GL compiled programs, scalability can be achieved by multiplying the computers running the middle tier processes, without changing the application code (see Figures 11.1 and 11.2).

Even if in a three-tier application all business rules are enforced in the middle tier (and definitely this is a good practice), a certain amount of PL/SQL is usually unavoidable, at least in two key areas:

- when triggers are used to enforce referential integrity.
- when PL/SQL is used as a "query helper" to minimize logical reads or to overcome SQL limitations.

Section 5.4.2 demonstrated how it is impossible to implement referential integrity using foreign keys when a core table references many ancillary tables. To perform properly, each foreign key requires the support of an index. It isn't uncommon having a core table contain 20 or 30 fields of foreign keys to an equal number of tables. Creating 20 or 30 indexes to support each foreign key would be impractical because of the overhead associated with the insertion of a single row in the core table.

The proposed solution to this problem was to categorize the foreign keys in order of importance, using foreign keys and indexes for the most important fields (the "A" category). For the second most important category of fields (the "B" category), referential integrity was to be maintained through database triggers. For the "C" category of fields, referential integrity was to be postponed and offloaded to batch procedures that would reconcile all parent-child relationships in a second moment.

The proposed solution implies the use of PL/SQL, at least for the "B" category of fields, the integrity of which is to be ensured by triggers coded in PL/SQL. PL/SQL can also be efficiently used to implement the batch procedures responsible for checking and enforcing referential integrity for the "C" category of fields. This can be cleverly accomplished through the DBMS_JOB package, which offers a completely Oracle driven cron-like facility.

PL/SQL can also be used as a "query helper". PL/SQL user-defined functions can be used in SQL commands exactly like built-in functions, such as NVL or LPAD. Expensive subqueries can be elegantly avoided by using a user-defined function instead. Furthermore, user-defined functions can be used in outer joins to overcome some of the limitations imposed by the Oracle implementation (see Section 14.4).

14.2 Business Logic and PL/SQL

Perhaps the most difficult challenge for designers and developers who decide to use PL/SQL to implement business logic in database-centric applications is the granularity of the business objects. A business object can suffer from an excessive fine-grained implementation, which translates too many and too small PL/SQL procedures that call each other to provide the required functionality. A business object can also suffer from an excessive coarse-grained implementation, which translates too few extremely large PL/SQL monoliths that cause problems because they are rarely called but occupy a large portion of the Oracle-shared pool.

A common mistake made by designers and developers is the lack of identification and separation of presentation logic from business logic. The client should perform initial field validation, involving the server only when a consistency check requires a database lookup. Small and static reference tables should be cached on the client side, to offload as much field validation from the server to the client as possible. A single check made locally by five hundred clients goes unnoticed in the economy of a complex transaction. If the same operation is implemented on the server side, it must be performed five hundred times, possibly concurrently, with the potential of becoming a bottleneck.

Another common mistake is to implement business logic in PL/SQL code that is not self-contained and generic enough to be shared by multiple clients. In other words, if a stored procedure or package, in order to perform its task, requires knowledge that only one specific client can provide, its re-use is severely limited. The same business rule might be enforced by several different instances of the client, or by different clients implemented in different languages or environments.

If the interface to the stored procedure or package is well-defined and consistent, and all input parameters coherent with the basic knowledge required by the business object to perform its task, all clients, irrespective of their language or environment, can use the same PL/SQL code. A client shouldn't send information to a stored procedure about the position or the name of an input field of an electronic form. These implementation details should be completely hidden to the server, which must be isolated from changes that affect only the client. Conversely, a client doesn't need to know about tables and joins occurring on the server, when a specific PL/SQL object provides a requested service. As long as the interface between client and server doesn't change, the database structure can be completely redesigned, without modifying the client calls to the PL/SQL objects.

A software design technique particularly suitable for the implementation of business logic in PL/SQL is the one called "Software Contracts". A software contract specifies the behavior of a software entity and its associated routines and subroutines, outlining the responsibilities of both the user of the software entity and the software entity itself.

If the responsibilities stated in the software contract are not completely met, either the caller or the callee are in breach of the contract, which is an indication of a software defect. Each contract is defined by three essential elements, which are enough to completely specify the software contract:

- ❑ Pre-conditions
- ❑ Post-conditions
- ❑ Invariants

Pre-conditions represent the responsibilities of the consumer of the service provided by the software entity. The pre-conditions must by met before requiring the services of the software entity (in this specific case, the stored procedure or package coded in PL/SQL).

Post-conditions represent the responsibilities that the software entity must fulfil while providing the requested service. Invariants are conditions imposed upon both consumer and provider of the service, and define responsibilities common to the software entity and its client.

To illustrate the use of software contracts, we will consider a function that computes the bonus to be given to a salesperson who has reached a specific target, expressed as a percentage of increase of his or her sales of the current year over the preceding year. The function will receive three parameters, salesperson's Id, percent increase of sales that triggers the concession of the bonus, and the bonus to be given, expressed in terms of a percentage of the current salesperson's salary. The function will return the bonus to be given to the salesperson rounded to the closest dollar. For example, calling the *compute_bonus()* function with the following parameters

```
bonus_amount = compute_bonus(22378,12.7,3.5)
```

means that we want the function to compute the bonus for employee of Id 22378, and that the bonus will be 3.5% of the current salary. The bonus will be given only if the salesperson increased his or her current year sales by at least 12.7% over the preceding year.

We can restate the above in terms of a software contract between the caller (our program) and the callee (the *compute_bonus()* function). The pre-conditions are:

1. The salesperson Id must be a valid Id corresponding to a salesperson present in the database and currently working for the company.
2. The sales percent increase threshold that triggers the bonus if reached must be a floating-point number greater than 0.
3. The percent of the salesperson's salary that represents the bonus must be a floating-point number greater than 0.

Pre-condition number 1 specifies that it is the responsibility of the caller to validate the data that identifies a salesperson. Pre-conditions 2 and 3 specify that it is the responsibility of the caller to make sure that the two floating-point numbers passed to the routine are greater than 0. The post-condition is that the result of the function must be a positive integer. If the salesperson did not reach the target, the bonus will be 0, which is an acceptable value.

In this specific software contract, the invariants are the salesperson Id, the sales percent increase, and the percent of salary corresponding to the bonus. Neither the caller nor the callee, for the entire duration of the contract, can modify the invariants. If the two parts participating in the contract fulfil their respective obligations the contract will be honored, and the software will be defect-free.

The invariants play an important part in the software contract, and usually they are not easily visible. Neglecting to specify the state of invariants can lead to ambiguity and "shadow areas" that ultimately cause software defects. When PL/SQL is used to implement business logic, particular care must be used when declaring the parameter modes of functions and procedures. A parameter can be declared as IN, OUT, and IN OUT. A parameter declared as IN is considered as a constant and cannot be modified by the called function or procedure. An OUT parameter can be set by the subroutine (within certain limits), and an IN OUT parameter will pass its value to the subroutine, which can modify it during its computational processing.

Older releases of Oracle reset the IN parameters at the function exit point (most definitely a bug). In our case, this would mean for the callee to be in breach of the contract, because an invariant has been modified.

Another useful technique that assists while writing PL/SQL code that implements business logic is subdividing complex functions into service layers. Each routine should perform one and only one assignment, coherent with the elementary business task that it implements. Complex functionality should be broken down in simpler and atomically self-contained modules, which can be reused by other modules residing in different layers.

We can apply this technique designing a PL/SQL procedure that performs a financial transfer from a source account to a target account, both belonging to the same customer. The procedure receives four parameters:

```
perform_transfer(CUST_ID,ACCT_ID_FROM,ACCT_ID_TO,AMOUNT)
```

PARAMETER #	PARAMETER NAME	PURPOSE
1	CUST_ID	Uniquely identifies a customer owning the accounts
2	ACCT_ID_FROM	Account number of the source account
3	ACCT_ID_TO	Account number of the target account
4	AMOUNT	Amount of money to be transferred

The following example in pseudo-code represents a poor implementation of our procedure.

```
CREATE OR REPLACE PROCEDURE PERFORM_TRANSFER (CUST_ID IN INTEGER,
                                              ACCT_ID_FROM IN INTEGER,
                                              ACCT_ID_TO IN INTEGER,
                                              AMOUNT IN NUMBER) IS
Define the cust_auth cursor for fetching customer authorization data
Define the balance_curs cursor for fetching account related data
```

```
BEGIN
        /* Get customer data to verify that the customer in question
           is authorized to withdraw data from the source account */
        fetch authorization_pattern from ACCCOUNT
               WHERE CUSTOMER = CUST_ID
               into cust_auth;
        If cust_auth.authorization_pattern = insufficient
               Raise exception
        End if
        /* Get source account balance. We cannot allow the customer
           to withdraw more than he or she owns in the source account */
        Fetch balance from ACCOUNT
               WHERE account = ACCT_ID_FROM
               into balance_curs;
        IF balance_curs.balance < AMOUNT
                Raise exception
        End if
        /* We can finally perform our transfer */
        /* The withdrawal first… */
        UPDATE ACCOUNT SET
        BALANCE = BALANCE - AMOUNT
        WHERE ACCOUNT = ACCT_ID_FROM;
        /* Credit the amount to the target account */
        UPDATE ACCOUNT SET
        BALANCE = BALANCE + AMOUNT
        WHERE ACCOUNT = ACCT_ID_TO;
        COMMIT;

        EXCEPTION
               WHEN OTHERS
               ROLLBACK;
END;
```

The implementation shown above is very naïve. The example is oversimplified because only the balance of the two accounts is modified, and no record is kept of the transaction occurred. Nevertheless, the problem of this implementation is not its oversimplicity, but the way the procedure is structured. Transferring funds from an account to another can be broken down in four distinct operations:

1. Check the customer authorization.
2. Check the balance of the source account.
3. Debit the source account of the requested amount.
4. Credit the target account of the requested amount.

It is likely that all four operations will be performed in several different parts of our client program. Checking if a customer is authorized to withdraw funds from an account is a very common operation, which will be requested by many other procedures, for instance, when a simple withdrawal is requested from an ATM. The same can be said for checking the balance of the account before authorizing a withdrawal. What follows is a better implementation, which follows the service layering approach.

```
CREATE OR REPLACE PROCEDURE PERFORM_TRANSFER (CUST_ID IN INTEGER,
                                              ACCT_ID_FROM IN INTEGER,
                                              ACCT_ID_TO IN INTEGER,
                                              AMOUNT IN NUMBER) IS
status INTEGER;
BEGIN
       status = check_cust_authorization(CUST_ID, ACCT_ID_FROM)
       IF (status)
              RAISE EXCEPTION
       END IF
       Status = check_cust_account(ACCT_ID_FROM, AMOUNT)
       IF (status)
              RAISE EXCEPTION
       END IF
       status = withdraw_from_account(ACCT_ID_FROM, AMOUNT)
       IF (status)
              RAISE EXCEPTION
       END IF
       status = deposit_to_account(ACCT_ID_TO, AMOUNT)
       IF (status)
              RAISE EXCEPTION
       END IF
END;
```

With this new implementation our procedure uses the services provided by four smaller and simpler units of work.

The PERFORM_TRANSFER procedure implements a well-defined and self-contained business operation, easily identifiable by both IT professionals and business analysts. This operation can be further subdivided in building blocks that can be easily reused by other high-level business functions belonging to the same hierarchical level of PERFORM_TRANSFER. The latter can be included as a building block of a more complex operation, defined at a higher hierarchical level, for example, a PERFORM_ATM_TRANSACTION that allows a customer to perform several operations at once from an ATM.

Implementing business logic through service layering builds a "Chinese box"-like system, where bigger boxes contain smaller boxes. The ultimate atomic unit is the simplest possible service that cannot be broken down any further. At the opposite extreme, a very complex operation is a collection of simpler operations performed sequentially.

14.3 Database Triggers

Triggers define an action to be fired by the database engine whenever a table is the subject of an SQL statement that modifies its state. In other words, only DML statements (INSERT, UPDATE, and DELETE) can fire triggers. In Oracle, every SQL statement goes through four different phases during its execution:

1. Before the statement is executed
2. After the statement is executed
3. Before a single row is modified
4. After a single row is modified

Three DML operations and four statement execution stages yield a total of 12 possible triggers of the same type per table. Oracle release 7.1 lifted the limitation of one trigger per execution stage, so in recent releases of the database server, it is possible to define several triggers, all firing during the same execution stage.

The first issue, here, has to do with database housekeeping and administration, which in this case affects not only the DBA, but developers as well. If a sensible naming convention is not enforced, the only way to recognize when the database fires the triggers is by reverse engineering their definition from the data dictionary, which is often impractical.

A naming convention used in many Oracle shops is to name the trigger after the table, with a three-letter suffix separated by an underscore. The suffix identifies the trigger type, according to the following convention:

	LETTERS	MEANING
First letter	B or A	Before or After
Second letter	D, U or I	Delete, Update or Insert
Third letter	R or S	Row or Statement

According to this convention, an after insert trigger the fires after the statement has been executed against the CUSTOMER table will be named

```
CUSTOMER_AIS
```

Similarly, a trigger that fires before an SQL DELETE statement affects each row of the EMPLOYEE table will be named

```
EMPLOYEE_BDR
```

Unfortunately, triggers offer more complex challenges to designers and developers than the simple one already resolved. Every serious SQL developer has incurred in some way or another the infamous ORA-04091 error, which spells: "table <xxx> is mutating, trigger/function may not see it." The meaning of this error is not as obscure as it seems the first time one looks at it. This error condition affects only row-level triggers, and the error message informs the user that PL/SQL code executed by the defined trigger is accessing the same table that fired the trigger. Oracle is not in a position to guarantee a consistent view of the table in question, because the table is *mutating*.

A row-level trigger cannot fire PL/SQL code that accesses the table to which the trigger is attached. Sometimes this restriction appears too strong, but the good news is that a solution exists. The mutating table problem affects only row-level triggers, not statement-level triggers. The trick is to move away the code that self-references the table being modified from the row-level phase to the after-statement phase. One DML statement can interest several or many rows when the WHERE clause selects multiple entries, or when the WHERE clause is not included at all in the statement. A mechanism to save each row state must be implemented in order for the after statement trigger to access and check each row interested by the DML modification.

For row-level triggers, Oracle offers the before image of the row in the :OLD structure and the modified image of the row in the :NEW structure. For example, if the CUSTOMER table contains three fields, NAME, ADDRESS, and TELEPHONE, a row level trigger can refer to the values that were stored in the table prior to the modification as :OLD.NAME, :OLD.ADDRESS, and :OLD.TELEPHONE. Similarly, the row-level trigger can refer to :NEW.NAME, etc., to retrieve the new value after the modification took place.

The row-level trigger and the after statement trigger must communicate, if the checks operated by the row-level trigger have to be deferred and performed by the statement-level trigger. This is possible thanks to a supporting PL/SQL package that defines tables that store the before and after image of each record modified by the SQL statement.

The package is initialized by a before statement trigger, accessed by the row-level trigger that copies the :OLD and :NEW structures into the PL/SQL tables, and used by the after statement trigger that can perform its own checks accessing the before and after image data structures populated by the row-level trigger.

As usual, an example better clarifies the concept. Suppose we have a table that stores information about all dealers selling the products of our company. We want to keep the dealers that are most successful in selling our products and we want to revoke the dealership contract from the dealers that are not performing. Since a few sales is better than no sales at all, our database implements the rule that if the dealer being revoked is the last remaining dealer in the area, then the dealership contract should be kept. In other words, we want the revoking operation to fail. At the same time, when a dealer ceases to represent our company in one area, all remaining dealers in the same area will receive a communication containing an encouragement to do better in order not to share the same fate as the dealer who lost our contract.

One deletion from the dealer table can affect more than one dealer, so our complex business logic cannot be triggered by an after delete statement, which wouldn't know how many dealers have been revoked by the single delete statement. The same business logic cannot entirely reside in a row-level trigger, because we need to access the same table that fired the trigger to identify the remaining dealers in the area without incurring a mutating table error.

To implement our complex business logic without causing a mutating table error we are going to code a PL/SQL package which comprises three procedures, a few package-level tables and a package-level variable, a counter that is initialized by a before statement trigger and incremented by each row-level trigger. The counter will tell the after statement trigger how many rows have been deleted by the SQL statement. In our package, we are going to use the DBMS_SQL extension introduced by Oracle8, because they offer a more concise syntax. The same concepts can be applied in an Oracle7 environment, after having adapted the PL/SQL syntax.

```
CREATE OR REPLACE PACKAGE DEL_DEALER AS
PROCEDURE PKG_INITIALIZE;
PROCEDURE ADD_ENTRY(DEALER_ID IN NUMBER,
                    AREA IN VARCHAR2);
PROCEDURE CHECK_AREA_SEND_MSG;
END DEL_DEALER;
/
CREATE OR REPLACE PACKAGE BODY DEL_DEALER IS
LOC_DEALER_CODE      DBMS_SQL.number_table;
AREA_CODE            DBMS_SQL.varchar2_table;
ROWS_PROCESSED       NUMBER:=0;

PROCEDURE ADD_ENTRY (DEALER_ID IN NUMBER,
                     AREA IN VARCHAR2) IS
BEGIN
-- This procedure adds two entries to the PL/SQL
-- tables. It will be called by a row-level trigger
-- that will pass the values stored in the :OLD
-- struture.
       ROWS_PROCESSED       := ROWS_PROCESSED+1;
```

```
        LOC_DEALER_CODE(ROWS_PROCESSED):= DEALER_ID;
        AREA_CODE(ROWS_PROCESSED) := AREA;
END;

PROCEDURE PKG_INITIALIZE IS
BEGIN
-- This procedure initializes the package variable
-- the maintains the table row counter. If the package
-- has been called previously, the tables populated with
-- old data are erased.
        IF ROWS_PROCESSED > 0 THEN
                LOC_DEALER_CODE.delete;
                AREA_CODE.delete;
        END IF;
        ROWS_PROCESSED := 0;
END;

PROCEDURE CHECK_AREA_SEND_MSG IS
NO_DEALERS_IN_AREA EXCEPTION;
DEAL_CODE     NUMBER;
NUM_DEALERS   NUMBER;
CURSOR IN_AREA_DEALERS (AREA_C VARCHAR2) IS
SELECT DEALER_CODE FROM
        DEALER WHERE AREA = AREA_C;
BEGIN
-- This procedure accesses the DEALER table as part
-- of its processing to apply the business logic implemented
-- by the designers of the application. Note that it accesses
-- the same table that fired the trigger which called the
-- package. This procedure must be called by an after
-- statement trigger, otherwise it will cause a mutating table
-- error.

       FOR II IN 1..ROWS_PROCESSED LOOP
       -- For all dealers deleted by the statement
             SELECT COUNT(*) INTO NUM_DEALERS FROM DEALER
             WHERE AREA = AREA_CODE(II);
             -- verify that at least one dealer survives in the
             -- area
               IF NUM_DEALERS = 0 THEN
                     -- else raise an error
                     RAISE NO_DEALERS_IN_AREA;
             END IF;
             OPEN IN_AREA_DEALERS (AREA_CODE(II));
```

```
                LOOP
                -- Fetch the dealer code of all remaining dealers
                -- in the area
                       FETCH IN_AREA_DEALERS INTO
                               DEAL_CODE;
                       EXIT WHEN IN_AREA_DEALERS%NOTFOUND;
                       -- Insert their code in a table that holds
                       -- all letters that will be sent by a batch
                       -- procedure executed once a day.
                       INSERT INTO LETTER_TO_BE_SENT (DEALER_CODE,
                                                       MESSAGE_TYPE)
                               VALUES(DEAL_CODE,'Encouragment');
                END LOOP;
                CLOSE IN_AREA_DEALERS;
        END LOOP;
EXCEPTION
        WHEN NO_DEALERS_IN_AREA THEN
         DBMS_OUTPUT.PUT_LINE('No other dealers in the area...');
END;
END DEL_DEALER;
```

The PL/SQL procedures are encapsulated in a package. This is a good idea, because they can be easily tested without actually firing a trigger. In addition, until release 7.3 of the database server, the triggers were compiled each time they were called. It was a well-known trick of trade shared by senior Oracle designers that minimizing the size of the trigger instructions in older Oracle releases to a few essential lines helped avoid forcing the engine to compile complex business logic every time a trigger was fired.

The recent releases of Oracle overcome this limitation; nevertheless, it is still useful to offload complex business logic from triggers to packages, to facilitate debugging. The following three triggers implement the enforcement of the business logic in the database.

```
CREATE OR REPLACE TRIGGER DEALER_BDS
BEFORE DELETE ON DEALER
BEGIN
        DEL_DEALER.PKG_INITIALIZE;
END;

CREATE OR REPLACE TRIGGER DEALER_ADR
AFTER DELETE ON DEALER FOR EACH ROW
BEGIN
        DEL_DEALER.ADD_ENTRY(:OLD.DEALER_CODE, :OLD.AREA);
END;
```

```
CREATE OR REPLACE TRIGGER DEALER_ADS
AFTER DELETE ON DEALER
BEGIN
      DEL_DEALER. CHECK_AREA_SEND_MSG;
END;
```

When the mutating table error was introduced above, we said that it affects only row-level triggers. This is not completely true, because if a foreign key is defined with the ON DELETE CASCADE option and one deletion in the parent table provokes one or multiple cascading deletions in the child table, the child table is still mutating when the after statement trigger fires.

To avoid a mutating table error in this case, the parent table should implement a before delete trigger that sets a globally visible flag in the package that implements the business logic applied when a deletion occurs. All procedures in the package can check that flag to verify if they can access the table being deleted. If the flag signals that a cascading deletion is in process, they should refrain from processing, simply returning to the caller. The global flag will be reset by an after statement trigger implemented in the parent table.

Triggers are a very powerful tool that must be used carefully. Their power can backfire on developers who don't consider the consequences of triggers, either implicitly defined through referential integrity (ON DELETE CASCADE) or explicitly coded and fired by SQL statements.

PL/SQL code associated with triggers executes synchronously. This means that the control is not returned to the caller until all procedures fired by the triggers have been completed. If deleting one customer fires the deletion of all orders made by that customer, which in turns cascadingly deletes the order lines associated to all orders, a few hundreds or a few thousands of rows can be deleted in one request. If a form displayed by a client application running under MS Windows interactively requested the initial deletion of the customer, the user could be watching an hourglass for a few minutes before regaining control of the application. This is usually unacceptable and rarely desirable.

Furthermore, even if from a purely relational point of view it makes sense to cascadingly remove parent and children rows at once, the accounting department wants to see the orders submitted by a customer that ceases to be our company's customer for the entire duration of the fiscal year. Thus, relational purity must compromise with business practices. In this case a field that acts as a flag signaling a logical deletion, rather than a true, physical deletion would be the solution.

When an interactive application is allowed to delete entries from the database, and this operation can potentially interest multiple rows, it is a good idea to postpone the physical deletion to ad-hoc housekeeping tasks that run in batch mode during off-peak hours. Oracle provides a cron-like facility, implemented through a package named DBMS_JOB, which comes in handy in these situations.

14.4 PL/SQL as a Query Helper

In a few instances, we considered the opinion of some three-tier architecture designers who prefer to encapsulate the application business logic into the middle tier, avoiding proprietary procedural SQL code that runs under the control of the database kernel. We conceded that this can be a good idea when scalability is of primary importance for the application being built. We also have to remember that scalability implies having tuned SQL statements sent to the database engine. It would be useless offloading all business logic to the middle tier using tools like Pro*C when SQL processing is not optimized.

Increasing the number of computers that run middle tier processes wouldn't be beneficial either. The bottom line is that SQL plays a fundamental role in determining the overall performance of an application. SQL is the ultimate bottleneck. If your statements aren't tuned, pumping more hardware into the physical architecture that runs your application won't help.

If PL/SQL is properly used, it can provide a significant performance increase, under several circumstances. Even if the application business logic is not enforced through PL/SQL running in the first tier, PL/SQL code can still be proficiently used to obtain performance gains.

One of the most powerful features of PL/SQL, introduced with Oracle release 7.1, is the ability to incorporate PL/SQL functions into SQL statements. The functions are user defined, yet they become part of the standard set of functions used by the SQL engine, exactly like TRIM or LPAD. There are obviously a few restrictions, but not to an extent that limits their usefulness. First of all, the user defined functions must all return SQL datatypes, not PL/SQL datatypes such as BOOLEAN or tables. In addition, all function parameters must be declared as IN parameters. The most severe limitation is that they cannot perform any database update. This is reasonable, because nobody wants mutating table errors triggered by PL/SQL functions called by SQL statements.

The real power of user defined functions is in their ability to appear anywhere in select queries and DML statements in general. For instance, they can be used as conditions in a WHERE clause, or in a SET clause of an UPDATE statement. Even complex clauses such as GROUP BY and HAVING can use PL/SQL functions. This means that they can be used to help SQL to perform better. Consider once again the STOCK table used in Chapter 11 to benchmark relational database operations against object-relational operations. STOCK is a relatively large table (600,000 rows), containing historical stockmarket data. The company related data is stored in the COMPANY table, and the linking field between COMPANY and STOCK is TICKER_ID. If one wants to compute the occurrences of all stock observations given their company name, this is the SQL statement that would do the job:

```
select c.company_name, count(*) from company c, stock s
where c.ticker_id = s.ticker_id
group by c.company_name;
```

The most expensive part of the above SQL statement is the join between the two tables. There is a way to reduce the impact of this query on the engine. If one creates the following PL/SQL function:

```
create or replace function company_name (tick_id IN NUMBER)
RETURN VARCHAR2 IS
c_name company.company_name%TYPE;
BEGIN
      select company_name into c_name
      from company where ticker_id = tick_id;
      RETURN c_name;
END company_name;
```

The query could be reworked in this way:

```
select company_name(ticker_id), count(*)
from stock
group by ticker_id;
```

avoiding the table join. Is the new query performing better than the first one? The answer is given by TKPROF (see Chapter 8 if you don't remember what TKPROF is). The following is the TKPROF formatted output for the first statement:

```
select a.company_name, count(*)
from company a, stock b
where a.TICKER_ID = b.TICKER_ID
group by a.company_name

call     count      cpu    elapsed     disk    query   current    rows
-------  -----   ------    -------    -----   ------   -------    ----
Parse        1     0.07       0.07       29      203         1       0
Execute      1     0.00       0.00        0        0         0       0
Fetch        8    12.10      13.58     7811     8018         0
-------   ----    -----      -----     ----    -----    ------    ----
total       10    12.17      13.65     7840     8221         1     100

Misses in library cache during parse: 1
```

```
Optimizer goal: CHOOSE
Parsing user id: 22   (OPS$EBONAZZI)

Rows      Execution Plan
----      ----------------------------------------
0 SELECT STATEMENTGOAL:   CHOOSE
600000  SORT  (GROUP BY NOSORT)
600000   NESTED LOOPS
100    TABLE ACCESS (BY INDEX ROWID) OF 'COMPANY'
101     INDEX (FULL SCAN) OF 'COMPANY_PK' (UNIQUE
```

The next TKPROF formatted output shows what the SQL engine did when the PL/SQL function was used. There are actually two statements to be considered, because TKPROF considers the PL/SQL function as a separate statement.

```
select company_name (ticker_id), count(*)
from stock
group by ticker_id
call     count       cpu    elapsed      disk     query    current     rows
-------  -----    ------    -------     -----    ------    -------     ----
Parse        1      0.10       0.10        45       243          1        0
Execute      1      0.00       0.00         0         0          0        0
Fetch        8     10.84      11.60      5131      5138          0      100
-------  -----    ------    -------     -----    ------    -------     ----
total       10     10.94      11.70      5176      5381          1      100

Misses in library cache during parse: 1
Optimizer goal: CHOOSE
Parsing user id: 22   (OPS$EBONAZZI)
 Rows     Execution Plan
------    ----------------------------------------
     0    SELECT STATEMENTGOAL: CHOOSE
600000     SORT (GROUP BY NOSORT)
600001      INDEX   GOAL: ANALYZED (FULL SCAN) OF 'STOCK_NDX100'
                (NON-UNIQUE)
****************************************************************
SELECT COMPANY_NAME
FROM
  COMPANY WHERE TICKER_ID = :b1
```

```
call     count       cpu    elapsed       disk      query    current        rows
------- ------  -------- ---------- ---------- ---------- ----------  ----------
Parse        1      0.00       0.00          0          0          0           0
Execute    100      0.02       0.02          0          0          0          99
Fetch      100      0.01       0.01          3        200          0         100
------- ------  -------- ---------- ---------- ---------- ----------  ----------
total      201      0.03       0.03          3        200          0         199
Misses in library cache during parse: 1
Optimizer goal: CHOOSE
Parsing user id: 22  (OPS$EBONAZZI)(recursive depth: 1)
 Rows     Execution Plan
------    -------------------------------------------
  0       SELECT STATEMENTGOAL: CHOOSE
100        TABLE ACCESS (BY INDEX ROWID) OF 'COMPANY'
100         INDEX (UNIQUE SCAN) OF 'COMPANY_TICKER_ID' (UNIQUE
```

The TKPROF output shows that the second statement, the one that uses the user defined PL/SQL function, outperformed the statement containing "pure" SQL. The number of disk reads decreases significantly when the PL/SQL function is used.

User defined functions not only improve SQL performance, but can make possible operations that wouldn't otherwise be possible using standard SQL. A classical example is an OUTER JOIN performed against a subquery, which is not a legal construct in Oracle SQL. Using again the STOCK and COMPANY tables, we want to select all companies and the maximum close value ever reached by their stock. We want to list all companies, even if they don't have any entry in the STOCK table. Ideally, the SQL statement required for such query would be:

```
select c.company_name,s.close from
company c, stock s
where s.ticker_id(+) = c.ticker_id AND
s.close(+) = (select max(close) from stock s where
           c.ticker_id = s.ticker_id);
```

If you try and submit the above statement to Oracle, it would complain with an ORA-01799 error message, "a column may not be outer-joined to a subquery." A PL/SQL function provides the required workaround.

```
CREATE OR REPLACE FUNCTION MAX_CLOSE(TICK_ID IN NUMBER)
RETURN NUMBER IS
      HIGHEST_CLOSE NUMBER;
BEGIN
      SELECT MAX(CLOSE) INTO HIGHEST_CLOSE
```

```
        FROM STOCK WHERE TICKER_ID = TICK_ID;
        RETURN (HIGHEST_CLOSE);
END MAX_CLOSE;
```

The initial query, which provoked the error ORA-01799, can be resubmitted as:

```
select c.company_name,s.close from
company c, stock s
where s.ticker_id(+) = c.ticker_id AND
s.close(+) = MAX_CLOSE(c.ticker_id);
```

This time Oracle will not complain.

Not only can stored functions be used to increase standard SQL command capabilities, but PL/SQL packages can as well. Coding several related user defined functions in a package, from a software engineering point of view, is definitely a good idea. Introducing PL/SQL packages brings about additional restrictions and things that developers must be aware of, to avoid potential mistakes and hours of frustration spent asking themselves why things are not working as expected.

All packages are created in two stages. First the formal definition of all variables, procedures, and functions, together with their parameters, is submitted to the engine for compilation. If the first step is successful, the package body, which contains the implementation of what is defined in the package, can also be submitted and compiled.

Oracle sees only the formal definition of the package, not the details of the package implementation. The consequence is that Oracle is not in a position to determine whether each function contained in the package really complies with the restriction imposed upon the user defined PL/SQL function that will be used in SQL statements. In other words, Oracle cannot determine whether a function is refraining from modify a database table by looking only at the formal definition of the package.

The only way to inform Oracle about the expected behavior of functions and procedures contained in a package is by setting the *purity level* of the package. We have already encountered this concept in Chapter 11, examining MAP and ORDER methods that can be set to objects to allow Oracle to rank object instances (Section 11.10).

Purity level is defined as the extent to which a function or a procedure is free of side effects. Side effects are references to database tables or packaged variables. A specific PL/SQL construct can be used to set purity levels, the RESTRICT_REFERENCES pragma.

The basic requirement of a PL/SQL function that will be used in an SQL statement is that it doesn't update database objects. In purity level terms, it must complain to the WNDS restriction (Write No Database State). In the formal definition of the package, the following line must appear, to expose the purity level of the MAX_CLOSE function:

```
PRAGMA restrict_references (MAX_CLOSE, WNDS);
```

While specifying a WNDS restriction is mandatory for all PL/SQL functions used in SQL statements, there is something more that should be done to help the cost-based optimizer to find the best possible execution plan for the SQL statements.

This is especially true when the Oracle Parallel Query Option (PQO) is used. If a function that will be used as part of an SQL statement also asserts WNPS (Write No Package State) and RNPS (Read No Package State), the SQL statement that calls that function can be run in parallel.

This makes sense. We encountered the Oracle PQO in Chapter 4 and we know that when a query or a DML statement is run in parallel, the task is subdivided and multiple processors run each part of the query. If a function included in the query saves its state into package variables, there is no synchronization mechanism that can guarantee that the variables in question won't be accessed and modified by other processors running sibling parts of the same query. A close parallel can be drawn with threads. In this case they would all access the same resource in absence of a mutex to regulate priorities and rights of access in an orderly manner.

To avoid the sibling parts of the same query, carried out by multiple processors, to interfere with each other, the optimizer would simply run the query serially. For this reason it is important to specify the highest possible purity level for package functions that are likely to be called by SQL statements.

14.5 Packages

Stored procedures and stored functions are currently supported by most relational databases. Oracle extended this feature by implementing PL/SQL packages, which are collections of PL/SQL objects grouped together and delimited by appropriate syntax (the BEGIN..END pair). They are different from stored procedures or unnamed PL/SQL blocks because they are highly structured, allowing for multiple procedures, functions, cursors, and variables to leave in them. PL/SQL is not an object-oriented language, yet it provides several object-oriented features that are really useful, such as procedure/function overloading and powerful de-coupling between the definition and the implementation of procedures and functions.

A package can be subdivided in two components, the package definition and the package body. The definition can be submitted to the engine for compilation independently from the package body, which provides the implementation for the procedures and functions specified in the package definition. A second package, say package B, can refer to procedures and functions defined in the first package, package A, and still compile successfully even if the package body of the package A has not yet been coded. The focus here, as in object-oriented environments, is on the interface, which must precede the implementation. As long as the interface to procedures and functions doesn't change, their implementation is hidden from the definition and can be accomplished in a second moment.

Another important feature offered by packages (and PL/SQL blocks) is procedure/function overloading. A procedure name can be multiply defined as long as its parameters differ, that is, the signature of the procedure/function must be different to let the PL/SQL compiler uniquely identify the procedure or function to call. While this is definitely useful, it suffers from a few limitations that PL/SQL developers must know. First, the datatypes comprising the signature of the procedure or function must belong to different datatype families to be considered different. This means that FLOAT, INTEGER, and REAL, which are numbers, are all considered part of the same family, and, therefore, an overloaded procedure that only differs because one parameter is declared as REAL in one procedure and as FLOAT in the overloaded procedure would generate a PLS-00307 error. ('too many declarations of <func/proc_name> match this call'). The same applies to datatypes like CHAR, VARCHAR2 and LONG, which are all considered subtypes of the character type.

Second, developers familiar with C++ might be tempted to overload functions that return different types. Unfortunately, this also doesn't work. Oracle is not able to determine the return type of a function at the moment of the function call. The return type of a function cannot uniquely sign a function. The only way to overload a function is by defining parameters that differ in their datatypes.

Packages, rather than stored procedures or stored functions, should always be preferred when PL/SQL is chosen either for implementing business logic, or simply in acting as SQL helper, as we considered above. Oracle extends the functionality provided by the engine through the use of several packages, which are shipped in all Oracle installations. Developers and designers should be familiar with standard Oracle-supplied packages. They offer powerful and useful capabilities, which will be examined in the next section.

14.6 Supplied Packages

Every standard Oracle installation includes vendor supplied PL/SQL packages that extend the engine capabilities in several key areas, such as dynamic SQL availability to PL/SQL, programmatic manipulation of user session parameters, batch scheduling capabilities, programmatic transaction, and locking control, etc. Applications can use several supplied packages together, compounding their power to implement truly sophisticated features, once reserved only to complex and expensive transaction monitors. An example can be given by two sessions that communicate with each other through an Oracle pipe (using the DBMS_PIPE package). The first session can send messages to the second session outside its transaction domain. That is, the first session can actually change database state without being forced to perform a commit. The second session can store the received message in a queue, using the services provided by DBMS_AQ. Message de-queuing can be, in turn, performed by a stored procedure or a package implemented as a batch task, utilizing the services provided by DBMS_JOB.

14.6.1 DBMS_SQL

The DBMS_SQL supplied package was first introduced with Oracle 7.1 to overcome one of the major limitations imposed upon PL/SQL programmers by the previous releases of PL/SQL: the inability of programmatically submit DDL statements to the engine. Until the release 7.1 of Oracle, it was impossible to create a table or an index from a PL/SQL program. DBMS_SQL offers access to dynamic SQL from within PL/SQL programs; it is a powerful package, but its power is associated with a fair degree of complexity.

To be able to dynamically build and process an SQL statement, developers must follow the steps we examined when we introduced OCI release 7 (Chapter 12, Section 12.1.2). As in OCI7, the fundamental data structure required for processing a statement is the cursor, which must be allocated and opened before associating an SQL statement with it. In PL/SQL, cursor allocation happens a little differently from OCI. OCI allows for direct manipulation of the Cursor Data Area, which is "C" structure, while PL/SQL only offers a handle to a cursor, defined as an integer. The variable defined to hold the cursor handle is populated at the moment of the opening of the cursor, which occurs when the DBMS_SQL.OPEN_CURSOR method is called. The cursor handle will be passed as a parameter to all subsequent DBMS_SQL invoked methods.

The next step is to parse the SQL statement, that is, check SQL syntax and statement semantics, associating it with the cursor. The DBMS_SQL.PARSE method takes care of this step.

After the statement has been successfully parsed, the input variables can be bound to the cursor by calling DBMS_SQL.BIND_VARIABLE. In case of an SQL query, the select-list items can be defined by calling DBMS_SQL.DEFINE_COLUMN.

The statement is now ready to be executed. This happens by invoking the DBMS_SQL method EXECUTE. The latter is implemented as a function, which returns the number of rows processed by the nonquery statements. In case of a query, the return function is to be ignored. In case of DML or DDL statements, the cursor can now be closed or utilized for other statements, because we are done with the dynamic SQL process. If the statement dynamically built is a query, two more steps are required. The rows identified by the where clause must be fetched, and the column values stored in the cursor must be retrieved from the cursor into local variables. The first method is either DBMS_SQL.FETCH_ROWS or DBMS_SQL.EXECUTE_AND_FETCH, if the execute and fetch steps are combined in one statement.

The second method is COLUMN_VALUE, which receives the cursor handle as first parameter, followed by the relative position of the column in the SQL statement and by the local variable that will receive the value retrieved from the cursor. In case of an OUT parameter of an anonymous PL/SQL block, the correct method is VARIABLE_VALUE, which identifies the variable, the value of which is to be retrieved not by its position in the statement but by its variable name.

Oracle Corporation offers the EXECUTE_AND_FETCH method, implemented as a function that returns the number of rows fetched, with the purpose of minimizing the network roundtrips required to process both EXECUTE and FETCH in two distinct steps.

The community of PL/SQL developers has welcomed the introduction of DBMS_SQL for its power and elegance. Something, though, had been left out from the package at the moment of its first release, the possibility of handling host arrays. This hole has been closed by Oracle8, which is shipped with a modified version of DBMS_SQL that allows for host array manipulation. Select-list items can be arrays, defined through the DEFINE_ARRAY method. Bind variables can be arrays, in this case, the method offered by the package to bind them to the cursor is BIND_ARRAY.

The package defines one array type per datatype family. Host arrays that are defined or bound to cursors must belong to the types defined by the DBMS_SQL package, which is a little restrictive. For instance, if you defined a type that is an array of integers using the following syntax:

```
type IntegerTable is table of integer index by binary_integer;
```

and you try to use it as a select-list item, the DEFINE_ARRAY method will fail to compile, because it is expecting the package-defined type Number_Table.

A list of the predefined array types follows.

- Number_Table
- Varchar2_Table
- Date_Table
- Blob_Table
- Clob_Table
- Bfile_Table

In Chapter 11, while examining the interfacing of Pro*C and PL/SQL (Section 11.3), we used a cursor variable that was opened on the server side and subsequently filled with data fetched by a server side procedure stored in a package. The example showed how to interface Pro*C defined cursor variables with PL/SQL call, but the server-side processing was a little inefficient. The cursor was in fact filled by repeatedly calling a single row fetch, copying the fetched values to the host arrays received from Pro*C. The revised DBMS_SQL package allows us to rework the example presented in Chapter 11, improving the server side processing by using host arrays. The reworked example is shown below.

```
PROCEDURE     get_invoice_line_items(
                            INVC_NUM        IN      NUMBER,
                            ARRAY_DIM       IN      NUMBER,
                            COUNT_ITEMS     IN OUT  NUMBER,
                            CURS_CLOSE      IN      NUMBER,
                            FETCH_END       OUT     NUMBER,
                            LINE_NUMS       OUT     dbms_sql.Number_Table,
                            DESCRIPTION     OUT     dbms_sql.Varchar2_Table,
                            PRICE           OUT     dbms_sql.Number_Table,
                            HOW_MANY        OUT     dbms_sql.Number_Table,
                            LINE_TOTAL      OUT     dbms_sql.Number_table) IS
loc_curs   number;
indx       number:=1;
loc_stmt   varchar2(300);
num_rows   number;
BEGIN

IF CURS_CLOSE = 1 THEN
    IF dbms_sql.is_open(loc_curs) THEN
          dbms_sql.close_cursor( loc_curs);
          RETURN;
    END IF;
ELSE
    IF NOT dbms_sql.is_open(loc_curs) THEN
      loc_curs:= dbms_sql.open_cursor;
      loc_stmt:='SELECT INV_LINE_NUMBER,ITEM_DESCR,UNIT_PRICE, QUANTITY,'
      || 'LINE_SUBTOTAL FROM INVOICE_LINE_ITEM WHERE INV_NUMBER =
          :INV_NUM';
      dbms_sql.parse(loc_curs,loc_stmt,dbms_sql.native);
      dbms_sql.bind_variable(loc_curs,'INV_NUM',INVC_NUM);
      dbms_sql.define_array(loc_curs,1,LINE_NUMS,ARRAY_DIM,indx);
      dbms_sql.define_array(loc_curs,2,DESCRIPTION,ARRAY_DIM,indx);
      dbms_sql.define_array(loc_curs,3,PRICE,ARRAY_DIM,indx);
      dbms_sql.define_array(loc_curs,4,HOW_MANY,ARRAY_DIM,indx);
      dbms_sql.define_array(loc_curs,5,LINE_TOTAL,ARRAY_DIM,indx);
      num_rows := dbms_sql.execute(loc_curs);
   END IF;
END IF;
```

```
COUNT_ITEMS := dbms_sql.fetch_rows(loc_curs);
IF COUNT_ITEMS < 10 THEN
    FETCH_END :=1;
END IF;
RETURN;
END get_invoice_line_items;
```

The keywords in bold mark the DBMS_SQL methods used to dynamically process SQL statements.

14.6.2 DBMS_JOB

The DBMS_JOB package allows for submission of PL/SQL tasks to a batch queue maintained by Oracle. The tasks are run at user-specified intervals, or once off. This package is used internally by Oracle to manage basic replication (the Oracle snapshots). To be able to de-queue the jobs from the batch queue, at least one background process, controlled by the instance, is required. Background processes dedicated to run the PL/SQL procedures queued on the batch queue are identifiable by the name 'SNPx', where x can be from 0 to 9 or from A to Z.

This arrangement allows for a maximum of 36 SNP processes dedicated to either replication or de-queuing of PL/SQL jobs. Two database initialization parameters control the creation of the SNP processed and the wake-up interval, which determines the time granularity of the batch subsystem. The first parameter is JOB_QUEUE_PROCESSES, which defaults to 0 and can accept a maximum value of 36. The second parameter is JOB_QUEUE_INTERVAL, which is expressed in number of seconds. The valid range for this parameter is between 1 and 3600; the default is 60. This means that DBAs can force an instance to check the batch queue from a minimum interval of 1 sec up to a maximum interval of 1 hr.

Designers and developers should carefully evaluate the granularity of the wake-up intervals. If the wake-up interval is very short, the SNP subsystem will wake up too often, most of the times for nothing, wasting precious system resources. On the other hand, if the job interval specified at a job level uses a time granularity of seconds, but the instance wake-up interval is set in minutes, the batch queue will accumulate several or many PL/SQL jobs that cannot be run until the next wake-up. When the SNP processes finally start de-queuing the batch queue, all pending jobs will be triggered at the same time.

Since each job is executed by one SNP process, if too many jobs have accumulated in the batch queue, it could happen that not enough SNP processes are available for de-queuing. Oracle implements a job execution re-try policy that will attempt to execute again the job that failed. Oracle will try to execute the failed job several times, doubling the interval time at each attempt. However, if a job fails to be executed after 16 attempts, Oracle will flag that job as broken. In the worst case scenario, too many jobs accumulated in the batch queue of an instance with an inadequate wake-up time will provoke an increasing backlog that will cause most of the jobs to be flagged as broken.

The default value of 1 min for JOB_QUEUE_INTERVAL is generally a good starting point, which avoids wasting OS resources but is capable of a prompt de-queuing of the batch queue. The Oracle manual that illustrates the DBMS_JOB package is not the Application Developer Manual, as for most of the Oracle supplied packages, but the Administrator's Guide. This implies that this package is intended to be a tool for database administration, rather than for development.

The current implementation of DBMS_JOB suffers from a few drawbacks, mainly in the security area. There is only one batch queue per database, and each user is either authorized to use DBMS_JOB without restrictions, through the execute privilege on the package, or is not authorized at all. There is no way to prevent a single authorized user from bogging down the entire batch subsystem by submitting hundreds of PL/SQL jobs.

Furthermore, when a user submits a job to the job queue, Oracle identifies that user as the owner of the job. Only a job's owner can alter the job, force the job to run, or remove the job from the queue. The DBA is not in control, and this can lead to dangerous situations, especially in mission critical environments.

DBMS_JOB is an ideal tool for periodic administrative tasks, such as analyzing tables and indexes to populate the data dictionary tables with statistics used by the cost-based optimizer, or application-specific jobs that reconcile parent and child tables when referential integrity cannot be enforced via foreign key constraints. Occasionally, DBMS_JOB can also be used to carry out application-specific tasks, provided that the application designers take adequate precautions to prevent the potential problems described above.

Personally, I used DBMS_JOB on one occasion, to off-load a print job that used to take too long to be executed from the client. That specific job was rarely requested (at most once a day), but the operator was forced to do something else while his PC was busy computing an incredibly complex report for approximately half an hour. If either the printer or the PC had problems halfway through the production of the report, the job had to be re-launched.

I modified the client to submit the request for the complex report to a database table. A PL/SQL package was created to perform all complex calculations and store the results in a table defined ad hoc to match the fields required by the report. Upon completion of the report, the same package signaled that the report was ready by setting a flag in the table used to submit the report in batch. The same table was accessed by the user who requested the batch job to check on the status of the job. The complex report running asynchronously on the server-side, allowed the client PC to be used for normal operations.

The package containing the offloaded reporting logic was a job submitted through the DBMS_JOB package launched every 5 min by the batch subsystem. A second procedure of the package, scheduled to run weekly, cleaned up the table containing the report results.

To avoid potential security problems due to a misuse of the database queue, one user was created to manage all batch jobs. The execute privilege on the DBMS_JOB package was given to that user and revoked from all other users of the database. Only the DBA and the application administrator knew the password to access the user authorized to submit batch jobs.

A heavily accessed Oracle instance that also participates in distributed transactions, where the SNP background processes are internally used by Oracle, shouldn't be burdened with an application driven use of the batch queue. If the nature of the application you are building requires an intensive use of the features offered by the DBMS_JOB package, consider the use of 3GL procedures that are periodically run by operating system driven mechanisms, such as cron jobs in Unix, batch jobs in OpenVMS, and services in Windows NT.

The DBMS_JOB package exposes 10 methods for job submission and management. The table below summarizes the DBMS_JOB methods.

METHOD	PURPOSE
SUBMIT	Submits a job to the batch queue and receives a Job Id generated by DBMS_JOB, which uses the SYS.JOBSEQ sequence
ISUBMIT	Submits a job to the batch queue providing a user defined Job Id
CHANGE	Modifies one or more attributes of an already queued job
BROKEN	Flags a job on the queue as broken, thus preventing its execution by DBMS_JOB
INTERVAL	Changes the required interval for which a job is scheduled to run
NEXT_DATE	Modifies the time of the next execution of the job
REMOVE	Removes a specific job from the batch queue
RUN	Triggers an immediate run of the job specified as a parameter
USER_EXPORT	Returns the a string containing a PL/SQL block or a call to a stored procedure that is invoked when the job is run by DBMS_JOB
WHAT	Modifies the PL/SQL procedure that a job is going to run

The use of the package is straightforward, apart from the identification of the next interval at which a specific job must run. When a job must be scheduled every 30 min or every hour, the next interval is easily set as SYSDATE + 1/48 and SYSDATE + 1/24 respectively. But when the required scheduled time becomes more complex, a combination of SQL date functions must be used, as in:

```
'NEXT_DAY (ADD_MONTHS (TRUNC(SYSDATE,''Q''),3),''TUESDAY'') + 11/24'
```

to specify the first Tuesday of each quarter at 11 AM.

14.6.3 DBMS_SESSION

The DBMS_SESSION package provides a programmatic interface to session related parameters, the ones that can be altered by issuing an SQL ALTER SESSION command.

A few methods of the DBMS_SESSION package are well-known and often used, such as SET_SQL_TRACE to enable SQL tracing as in

```
DBMS_SESSION.set_sql_trace(TRUE);
```

or IS_ROLE_ENABLED to check if a specific role has been enabled for the current session.

Other methods, a little more obscure and less often used, are useful as well. Methods such as CLOSE_DATABASE_LINK, for instance, can be used when a PL/SQL program accesses information from different instances via database links. An instance initialization parameter, OPEN_LINKS, sets the maximum number of connections to remote instances that a session is allowed to maintain open. The default for OPEN_LINK is 4, but every open connection is expensive in terms of utilized resources, so open connections should be kept to a minimum.

A program that needs to interrogate multiple remote instances is exposed to the risk of exhausting the maximum number of open connections. Since OPEN_LINKS is an instance-wide parameter, it wouldn't be a good idea to increase it only to allow that specific PL/SQL program to run. The best option is to close the database link that connects the current session to remote databases when the required information has been gathered. If the program used a database link named "NorthSales" for a remote query, as in:

```
select customer_name, total_order from
customer_order@NorthSales
Where area='Alaska';
```

Calling the CLOSE_DATABASE_LINK method explicitly closes the database link:

```
DBMS_SESSION.CLOSE_DATABASE_LINK('NORTHSALES');
```

Additional database links can be subsequently opened and then closed by the PL/SQL procedure without hitting the instance-wide parameter that limits the database link kept open concurrently.

Another useful method offered by DBMS_SESSION is RESET_PACKAGE, which de-instantiates all packages created by the current session. It is a good idea to call RESET_PACKAGE before closing the session, especially if PL/SQL tables were used. PL/SQL tables, together with all other PL/SQL objects, are instantiated in the SGA, occupying precious memory. There is no method available to de-allocate a table, and assigning an empty PL/SQL table to the one already created and filled with data doesn't really solve the problem. RESET_PACKAGE wipes out completely all structures instantiated during the session, including tables.

14.6.4 DBMS_SHARED_POOL

The DBMS_SHARED_POOL package allows for controlling the PL/SQL objects in the shared pool. The shared pool is a portion of the Oracle System Global Area (SGA) that contains the dictionary cache, some session information, and, mainly, the library cache, which holds information about all shared PL/SQL statements and objects. The shared pool is an entity finite in size, which means that when new statements and objects cannot be accommodated in it because of lack of space, aged statements and objects are discarded to reclaim the space needed for the new entries. The LRU algorithm (Least Recently Used) used to obtain the space will discard the statements and objects that are less often used.

DBMS_SHARED_POOL allows developers to override the default LRU algorithm, forcing specific objects never to be discarded. Forcing a package or a stored procedure to remain in the shared pool is called "pinning". The same package allows for unpinning the PL/SQL objects that were previously pinned in the shared pool. The table below summarizes the package methods supported by DBMS_SHARED_POOL.

METHOD	PURPOSE
sizes	Identifies all objects in the shared pool that are larger than the size specified as a parameter
keep	Pins the object specified as a parameter in the shared pool
unkeep	Unpins the object specified as a parameter from the shared pool
aborted_request_threshold	Limits the size of allocations allowed to flush the shared pool if the LRU algorithm cannot satisfy the request size from the free lists

The sizes method displays a list that includes all objects that exceed an arbitrary size passed as a parameter. For instance:

```
SqlPlus> set serveroutput on size 2500
SqlPlus> execute sys.dbms_shared_pool.sizes(2500);
```

The above statement, submitted from an Sql*Plus session, displays all objects currently stored in the shared pool that are larger than 2500 kilobytes. The keep method is defined as

```
procedure keep(name varchar2, flag char DEFAULT 'P');
```

by default, keep takes one parameter, a string containing the package or the procedure name to be pinned in the shared pool. The default behavior can be overridden by providing the second optional parameter. Developers are allowed to pin cursors, providing the address and the hash value of the cursor instead of the procedure name, and specifying 'C" as the second parameter of the keep method. An example follows.

```
SQL> select substr(SQL_TEXT,1,50),ADDRESS,HASH_VALUE from v$sqlarea
  2  where PARSING_USER_ID <> 0;

SUBSTR(SQL_TEXT,1,50)
                                                  ADDRESS  HASH_VALUE
-------------------------------------------------- -------- ----------
SELECT DECODE('A','A','1','2') FROM DUAL           02880E60  1.949E+09
SELECT USER FROM DUAL                              028A4A74  3.441E+09
begin DBMS_APPLICATION_INFO.SET_MODULE(:1,NULL); e 02884D60  583813323
...
omitted lines
...                                                0287EA74  758387529
select table_name from dba_tables
SQL>
SQL> execute sys.dbms_shared_pool.keep('0287EA74,758387529','C');
PL/SQL procedure successfully completed.
```

In the example above, we wanted to pin the cursor corresponding to the SQL statement "select table_name from dba_tables". We identified the statement entry in the V$SQLAREA table, selecting its address and hash value. The keep procedure could then be called, passing a concatenation of the address plus the hash value as the first parameter, and the "C" mnemonic as the second parameter.

14.6.5 DBMS_OUTPUT

The DBMS_OUTPUT package has for a long time been the only way to understand what was occurring inside a package or a stored procedure during its processing. Its main purpose is to display lines of text to the screen and to accept lines from the standard output. It does not provide any formatting feature; everything is displayed as a string of text.

While Oracle Forms, until release 4.5, provided a full-featured PL/SQL debugger, it understood only PL/SQL release 1 syntax. In sites where Oracle Forms was not used, and therefore not purchased, DBMS_OUTPUT was the only form to "debug" PL/SQL code. Fortunately, the situation recently improved a great deal, because Oracle Forms 5, included with Oracle Developer, understands and debugs the most recent PL/SQL constructs. Furthermore, Oracle now ships with the DBMS_DEBUG package, which allows for the creation of sophisticated

PL/SQL debuggers. Section 14.9 examines third party tools that offer powerful debugging capabilities to PL/SQL developers.

The DBMS_OUTPUT package must be enabled, either through the ENABLE method provided by the package or by a specific command implemented in SQL*Plus or SVRMGR, "SET SERVEROUTPUT ON". PUT_LINE is probably the most popular method of the entire package, used to display a single line of text to the standard output.

The default buffer size of 2000 bytes is generally insufficient, causing the package to raise a buffer overflow exception. It is a good idea to specify a larger buffer size when the package is first enabled. This is done in two ways, either by setting SERVEROUTPUT with the SIZE option from SQL*Plus, or by invoking the ENABLE method, specifying a larger buffer size as a parameter (DBMS_OUTPUT.ENABLE(1000000)).

14.7 External Procedures

Oracle Forms developers enjoyed the privileged position of being able to access 3GL procedures running on the server side, integrating them with PL/SQL code fired by Oracle Forms triggers. This feature was initially implemented through user exits and subsequently refined through the Foreign Function Interface, implemented in the FFI package, available with Oracle Forms 4.0. Oracle8 introduces external procedures, giving developers access to procedures written in "C" from any language or tool capable of interfacing to shared libraries or dynamic link libraries. There are, however, a few restrictions and a few preconditions that must be met before external procedures can be used.

External procedures cannot be invoked by sessions connected to the database via the multi-threaded server option. The most likely outcome of a shared session that tries to access an external procedure would be an ORA-28576 error, "lost RPC connection to external procedure agent," possibly followed by a few ORA-00600 errors, signaling internal error codes. External procedures can be coded only in "C", and only on operating systems that support dynamic invocation of routines stored in shared libraries. The most commonly used operating systems fall in this category, including Windows NT, Sun Solaris, HP/UX, etc., so this is not really a restriction.

A specific Net8 listener must be started to listen for external procedure invocation, so the DBA has to enable an entry in the Net8 configuration files to instruct the network subsystem to start the EXTPROC listener. Developers can check for the presence of the EXTPROC listener on the system by using the listener control utility. Figure 14.1 illustrates this technique.

The EXTPROC listener spawns an agent per session to handle the calls to external procedures. The good news is that only one process is needed for an en-

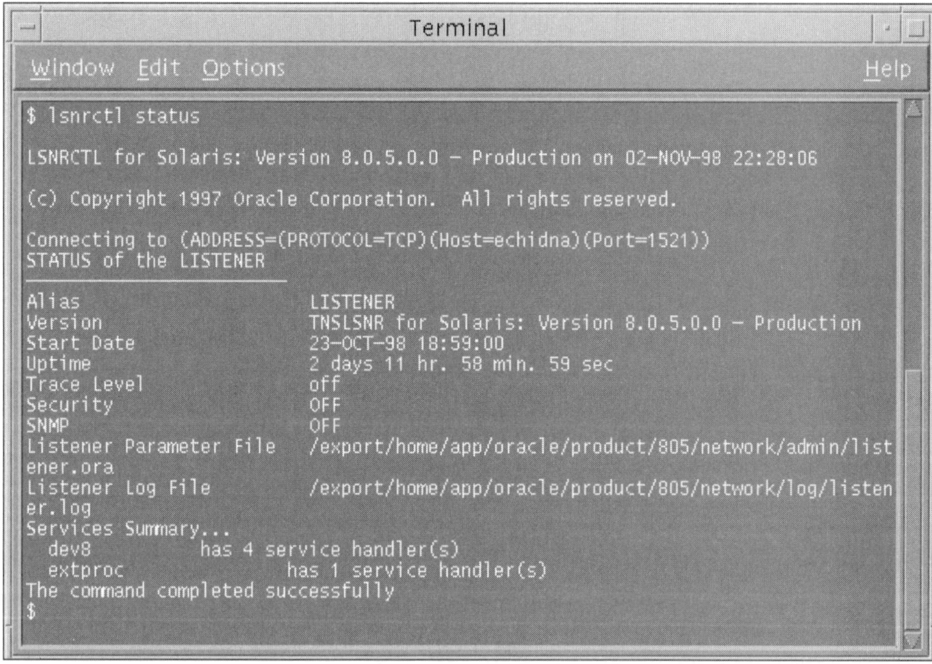

FIGURE 14.1 lsnrctl displays the external procedure listener (extproc)

tire session, so the Oracle session that invokes an external procedure only incurs in the overhead of the process creation once. All subsequent external procedure invocations will find the external procedure agent already alive and waiting for work to do.

The bad news is that each session needs a process that handles external procedure calls. The number of processes that a specific hardware architecture is able to support is one of the limiting factors for the scalability of an application. We have considered in preceding chapters how to offload the Oracle "shadow" processes from the machine hosting the instance to multiple front-end computers in an attempt to spread the number of user processes among several cooperating computers. External procedures must run on the same machine hosting the Oracle instance. Database links cannot be used for external procedure invocation.

This restriction alone prevents a wider use of external procedures in applications accessed by a large numbers of users. The typical OLTP system, with hundreds or even thousands of terminals that access a central database, perhaps using middleware technologies to accomplish that, cannot afford an uncontrollable proliferation of external procedure agents to satisfy external procedure requests made by application code. This doesn't mean that external procedures are a useless feature. If adequately controlled, external procedures can find their place even in applications providing services to hundreds or thousands of concurrently connected users.

A few application domains can greatly benefit from a correct implementation of external procedures: for example, all applications that require interfacing to real-time systems such as laboratory equipment or Programmable Logic Controllers (PLC) in industrial environments; or when really complex calculus algorithms must be applied to data stored in database tables that require intensive computation, such as differential equations, numerical integration or Fast Fourier algorithms. Financial applications often require complex statistical analysis, which is not handled very well by PL/SQL, given its nature of pseudo-interpreted language.

On the other hand, the scalability of an application would be severely impacted if external procedures were used to support predicate clauses of the most often used SQL statements.

In order to be able to call an external procedure, it is necessary to define a PL/SQL wrapper. PL/SQL statements will call the external procedures through the PL/SQL proxy defined in *alias libraries*. The syntax used to this purpose is as follows:

```
CREATE LIBRARY EXT_UTILS AS '/usr/oracle/ext_utils/utils.so';
```

The CREATE ANY LIBRARY privilege must be granted to the developer who creates the libraries. The action of creating a PL/SQL wrapper for an external procedure is called "registering an external procedure." This is accomplished through the use of new PL/SQL syntax, the EXTERNAL clause, as in the following example:

```
CREATE FUNCTION compute_mcd( x BINARY INTEGER, y BINARY INTEGER)
RETURN BINARY INTEGER AS EXTERNAL
LIBRARY EXT_UTILS
NAME "ComputeMcd"
LANGUAGE C;
```

The above example shows the simplest way to call an external procedure. In most cases, however, the external procedure business is much more complicated, for instance, when null values or indicator variables must be handled.

PL/SQL datatypes don't have a one-to-one correspondence with "C" datatypes, and "C" doesn't have the concept of nullity. In order to make PL/SQL and "C" communicate efficiently, a PARAMETER clause can be named, to further specify the formal parameter list provided at the beginning of the function definition. The PARAMETER clause accepts a few qualifying properties, such as:

PARAMETER PROPERTY	USE
INDICATOR	The parameter flagged with this attribute signals if another parameter is NULL.
LENGTH	PL/SQL doesn't internally use null terminated strings. Length allows developers to tell "C" functions how long are the strings passed.
MAXLEN	MAXLEN doesn't apply to IN parameters, but has the same function as LENGTH for IN OUT, OUT, and RETURN parameters.
CHARSETID	When using NLS nondefault character sets, CHARSETID and CHARSET FORM identify the character set data being passed.

We can now rework our previous PL/SQL wrapper for the compute_mcd function as follows:

```
CREATE FUNCTION compute_mcd( x BINARY INTEGER, y BINARY INTEGER)
RETURN BINARY INTEGER AS EXTERNAL
LIBRARY EXT_UTILS
NAME "ComputeMcd"
LANGUAGE C
PARAMETERS (
x, x INDICATOR, y, y INDICATOR, RETURN INDICATOR, RETURN);
```

The "C" function that matches the PL/SQL definition is:

```
int * ComputeMcd(int x, short x_ind, int y, short y_ind,
                 short * ret_ind);
```

When pointers to parameters, rather than the value of the parameters, must be passed to an external function, the PARAMETERS clause can be used to modify the passing convention of the formal parameters. For example, consider the following function:

```
CREATE FUNCTION compute_months_between(
            final_month IN BINARY INTEGER,
            begin_month IN BINARY INTEGER)
AS EXTERNAL
Etc, etc,
PARAMETERS (
final_month BY REF, begin_month BY REF);
```

The two formally specified parameters are further qualified by the PARAMETERS clause, which indicates to PL/SQL that they have to be passed to the external procedure by reference.

There is a restriction on the number of parameters that can be passed to an external procedure. Theoretically, the maximum number of parameters is 128, but each float or double passed by value counts for two parameters. This limit is at the same time too high and too low. It is too high because it allows developers to code monster "C" functions that take more than 100 parameters, which from a software engineering point of view is not advisable. It is too low because 128 parameters are not enough to pass, for example, historical data to an external statistical function that analyzes historical trends. Unfortunately, only scalar variables can be passed to external functions; PL/SQL tables are not allowed. Luckily, external procedures can access the database and fetch data stored in tables. An external procedure can open a new session to the database, originating a new transaction that has nothing in common with the original session that called the external procedure. The advantage of this method is that the new session can change the state of the database, being allowed to commit changed data. The disadvantage is that one more process is required, further increasing the overhead associated with the use of external procedures.

When external procedures must access database data in read-only mode, a better method is provided by the external procedure facility. The PARAMETER clause can specify a CONTEXT structure to be passed to the external "C" routine. The CONTEXT structure corresponds to an OCI structure called *OCIExtProcContext*. When an external routine receives the context structure, it may allocate memory under Oracle control, raise PL/SQL exceptions, and manipulate OCI handles for callback calls to the server, all within the context of the process spawned by the EXTPROC agent.

Let us imagine the following scenario. We want to offload to an external procedure the computation of a regression analysis of two variables, say income and age, which are sampled in the database, one observation per row. We want to limit the analysis on a per area basis, so we have to pass one parameter to the external function that will be used to extract from the database income and age data only for the specified area. The external function must return the regression analysis parameters, that is, slope, regression coefficient, and correlation coefficient. The PL/SQL wrapper for such a function follows:

```
CREATE FUNCTION INCOME_AGE_REGRESSION (
      AREA_CODE    IN   BINARY INTEGER,
      SLOPE        OUT FLOAT,
      REGR_COEFF   OUT FLOAT,
      CORR_COEFF   OUT FLOAT)
RETURN BINARY INTEGER AS EXTERNAL
      NAME "IncomeAgeRegression"
      LIBRARY Regression
      WITH CONTEXT
      PARAMETERS (
```

```
CONTEXT,
AREA_CODE, SLOPE BY REF, REGR_COEFF BY REF,
CORR_COEFF BY REF);
```

The "C" function implementing the regression analysis will be defined as:

```
int IncomeAgeRegression(OCIExtProcContext *ExtContext,
                        int AreaCode, float *Slope,
                        float * RegrCoeff, float *CorrCoeff)
```

The context structure allows the external procedure to hook into the OCI environment and to submit callback calls to the database. The OCI function used to accomplish that is *OCIExtProcGetEnv()*. The "C" function must define an OCI environment handle, a service context handle, and an error handle, as in the following example:

```
OCIEnv**EnvH;
OCISvcCtx    **SvcH;
OCIError     **ErrH;
...
sts = OCIExtProcEnvGet(ext_context,&EnvH,&SvcH,&ErrH);
...
```

Once the basic OCI handles have been properly initialized, our function can access the database and fetch the income and age data, using the received parameter area_code in the where clause of the SQL statement to limit the regression analysis only to the required areas.

There are a few limitations that must be taken into account when opting for callback calls rather than dedicated sessions to access the Oracle database from an external function. OCI calls such as *OCISessionBegin()*, *OCITransCommit()*, *OCIServerAttach()*, and *OCIEnvInit()* cannot be invoked from external procedures that use callbacks. Basically, all OCI handles or calls that allow one to change the state of the database are not allowed. External procedures should comply with the WNDS purity level, that is, "Write No Database State."

When the WITH CONTEXT clause is used in the PL/SQL wrapper to external functions, it is possible for the process spawned by the EXTPROC agent to allocate memory that will be freed by Oracle when control is returned back to PL/SQL. Furthermore, it is possible to raise exceptions that will be treated like Oracle internally generated expressions, or to raise user-defined exceptions with associated user-defined messages. The OCI functions that provide the developers with the above mentioned services are:

OCI FUNCTION	PURPOSE
OCIExtProcAllocCallMemory()	Allocates an amount of memory specified as a parameter for the duration of the procedure call
OCIExtProcRaiseExcp()	Raise a predefined exception that must correspond to a valid Oracle exception number in the range 1..32767
OCIExtProcRaiseExcpWithMsg()	Raises a user-defined exception with an associated exception message

The three OCI service functions receive the context structure *OCIExtProcContext* as their first parameter.

There are several things that can go wrong when coding an external procedure. For instance, mapping between PL/SQL datatypes and "C" datatypes is a difficult task, especially when the PARAMETERS clause modifies the formal parameter definition. The EXTPROC listener can be listening using a protocol that is not supported by the local installation. The external procedure agent can crash for memory related problems. Oracle provides a package that can be used for external procedure debugging. The basic requirement is a debugger capable of attaching to a running process.

The package that helps debug external procedures is called DEBUG_EXTPROC. It isn't installed by default by Oracle with the standard packages, but is available in the demo directory of the plsql area, in Windows NT plsql<xx>, where xx stands for the Oracle major release.

To use the provided debugging facilities the STARTUP_EXTPROC_AGENT method of the DEBUG_EXTPROC package must be invoked from a SQL*Plus session. This will start the external procedure agent. Using the operating system provided means, developers should identify the process Id of the agent. The debugger should be launched from a second session, attaching to the process Id found during the previous step. A breakpoint to the *pextproc* procedure should be set, to block the execution of the external agent invoked by PL/SQL. From the SQL*Plus session, the external procedure should be invoked from PL/SQL. The debugger should stop at *pextproc()*, giving developers the chance to set a breakpoint into the user defined function being debugged.

If you can step into your code from the debugging session attached to the process spawned by the EXTPROC agent, you are doing well. The next very delicate moment will be passing the return value and the IN OUT or OUT parameters back to PL/SQL. If at the moment of launching the STARTUP_EXTPROC_AGENT procedure you received the following error message from Oracle:

```
ORA-28575: unable to open RPC connection to external
procedure agent
```

it means that your listener is not working properly. Try using tnsping and the extproc listener name as defined in tnsnames.ora.

If you can step through your code, but PL/SQL reports the Oracle error:

```
ORA-28576: lost RPC connection to external procedure agent
```

the cause is most likely a parameter incorrectly set, either an incorrect datatype mapping or a parameter passed by reference instead of value or vice versa. This error is also reported by oracle if the agent crashed for any other reason, such as memory access violation.

External procedures are definitely an advanced feature, which requires careful design and implementation. They can kill the scalability of an application if not properly used, but offer a powerful solution in the hands of competent designers and developers for real-time system interfacing and computationally intensive tasks.

14.8 Hiding PL/SQL Code

In order to avoid exposing your PL/SQL code to either potential competitors or other developers who could misuse your packages relying too much on undocumented features, Oracle provides a utility that transforms PL/SQL code contained in clear ASCII files into object code. This object code representation is difficult to reverse-engineer and guarantees an adequate protection of PL/SQL code, but it is still portable across the various Oracle supported platforms. This saves developers from keeping up-to-date versions of object-code for all platforms supported by their applications.

Processing a PL/SQL ASCII file to convert it into an illegible object-code format is called *wrapping*. The Oracle provided utility that performs the conversion is called WRAP under Unix and WRAPxx under Windows NT, where xx stands for the Oracle release. It is definitely a good idea to wrap your PL/SQL before releasing a production version.

While this is true for stored procedures and package bodies, it is probably better not to wrap the package definitions, especially if the application is not shipped with a detailed manual that clearly documents package method parameters and types. If the package definition is left unwrapped, maintenance programmers can always reverse-engineer it in case of doubt about the datatype of a specific parameter. This is especially true when the maintenance programmers are not working in-house, but in the customer site that does not provide all required facilities to track-down source code or documentation written months or even years before.

The WRAP utility takes one mandatory and one optional parameter. The mandatory parameter is INAME, followed by an equal sign and the name of the input file to be wrapped. The optional parameter is ONAME, followed by an equal sign and the name of the output file containing object code. In absence of the optional parameter, the object code file will be called with the same name of the input file and PLB as the extension (**PL**/SQL **B**inary). An example follows.

```
wrap iname=trigger_pkg oname=trigger_pkg.obj
```

The above example uses the optional parameter ONAME to override the default name of trigger_pkg.plb that would be given by default by WRAP. The input file is supposed to have a .sql extension. Many Oracle sites use a different convention for the extension of the ASCII files containing PL/SQL code, like .pls or .plq. In this case the INAME file must specify the extension, as in

```
wrap iname=trigger_pkg.pls oname=trigger_pkg.plb
```

14.9 Third Party Tools

Since its first appearance, PL/SQL has been positively judged by the community of Oracle developers for its powerful features and seamless integration with the database server. Most PL/SQL developers, however, would have agreed in identifying that the lack of support for debugging is the only real weak point of PL/SQL, at least until release 7.3. Oracle 7.3.4 and 8.x now offer an adequate support, in terms of primitives available to allow PL/SQL and OCI programmers to hook into the internal debugging engine. Two software companies have been quick in incorporating advanced debugging capabilities in their products: Sylvain Faust International (SFI) and Quest Software.

The two competing products are SQL-Programmer by SFI and SQL Navigator by Quest. The purpose of this section is to bring to the attention of designers and developers the existence of such products, and not to provide a technical judgement for selecting the better of the two tools. They are both great tools that offer a pleasant working environment for PL/SQL programmers, allowing for reverse engineering on the fly of all database objects, powerful editing environments that include color syntax, and SQL statement tuning.

Developers, who used to rely on DBMS_OUTPUT to disseminate PUT_LINE statements in key points of their code to check the value of the variables used, or to make sure that the application flow was correct, will hardly believe that they finally can use the same environment and facilities so far reserved to Borland Delphi or MS Visual Studio users.

It is possible to step line by line through PL/SQL code, setting breakpoints and evaluating and modifying variables on the fly. SQL-Programmer (Figure 14.2) uses the same visual metaphors as MS Visual Studio. The following is an example of the SQL-Programmer taskbar used in a debugging session:

The icons represent, from left to right: show the next executable statement; step into the function; step over the function; step out of the current function; execute the lines of code until the position of the caret; show the watch window; show stack window; compile with debugging information.

MS Visual Studio users will feel at home in such an environment. No learning curve is required. The GUI concepts that drive the debugging sessions are so intuitive that even non-MS Visual Studio users will become acquainted very quickly with the debugging environment. This is true for both products, even if SQL Navigator, shown in Figure 14.3, uses slightly different icons for the same meaning.

SFI SQL-Programmer supports Oracle, Sybase, and MS SQLServer. Quest's SQL Navigator supports only Oracle. The SQL Navigator features for SQL tuning are a little more sophisticated than those for SQL-Programmer, which have to accommodate and mediate between different needs according to the different supported engines.

Both tools offer close integration with version control systems such as MS Visual Source Safe and PVCS. The PL/SQL code can be either reverse-engineered on the fly from the database or obtained through the version control system. A very nice feature offered by SQL Navigator is the automatic creation of a wrapper stored procedure used to call a package being debugged. The wrapper allows the

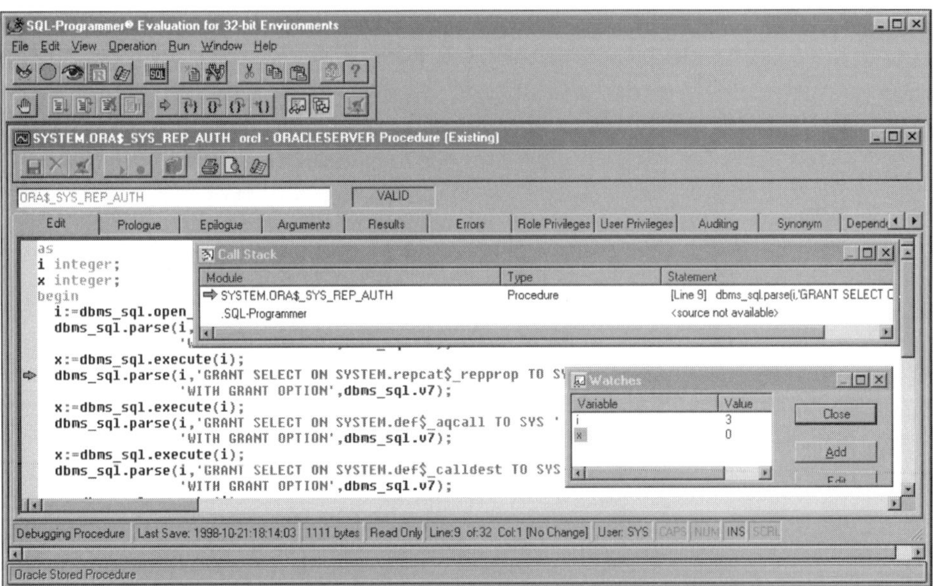

FIGURE 14.2 Sql-Programmer at work—A typical debugging session

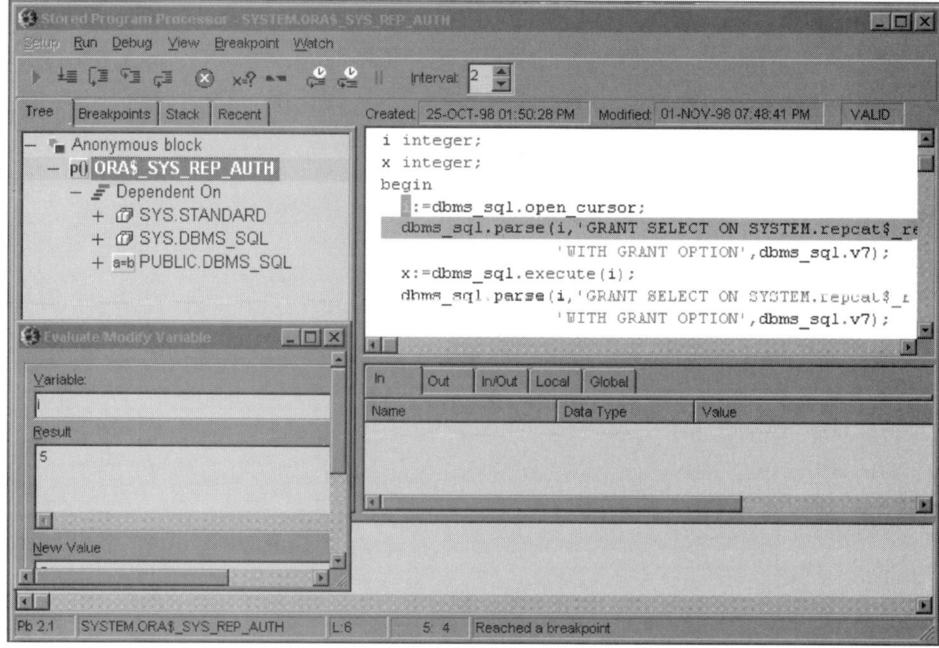

FIGURE 14.3 SQL Navigator at work—A typical debugging session

user to provide values for the parameters of the package and the debugging session can begin.

SQL-Programmer implements prologue and epilogue windows where developers can define scripts and objects that will be run or defined before and after the stored procedure or package have been executed. This feature is particularly useful during regression testing, when baseline data must be loaded before the test is conducted, and discarded upon completion of the battery of tests.

Developers with appropriate privileges can reverse-engineer both PL/SQL code and database object definitions (Figure 14.4 and 14.5). All happens by pointing, clicking, and double-clicking. Magically, the editor shows the code or the SQL statement that defines an object. They can both be executed straight away, again by pointing and clicking. Gone are the days where every single task had to be painfully carried out by manually creating extraction scripts run through SQL*Plus, spooling the output to file to be manipulated in a separate session. Both tools offer all database objects visible in a treelike visual metaphor, which is very effective in highlighting the hierarchical relationship that links the various database objects.

The efficiency of an SQL statement can be tuned using the SQL tuning options offered by both packages. In this field SQL Navigator offers more sophisti-

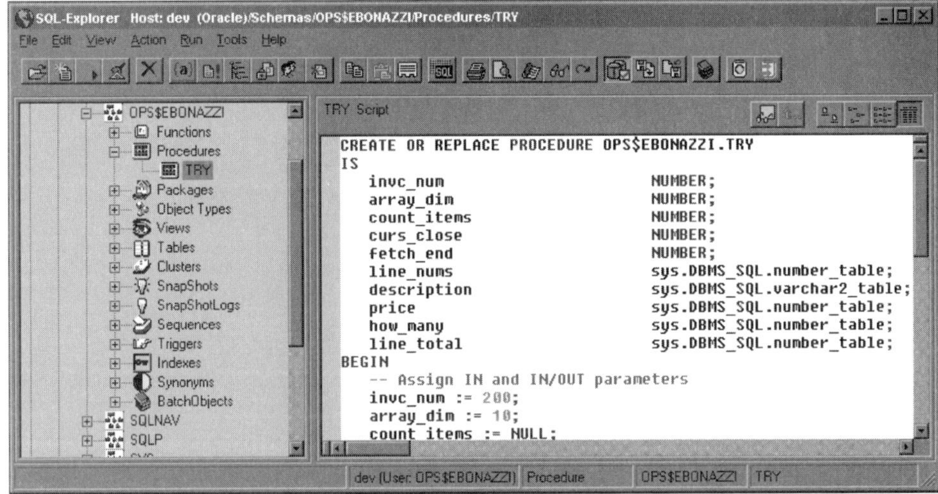

FIGURE 14.4 SQL-Programmer allows for database object browsing and object reverse-engineering on the fly into the default editor

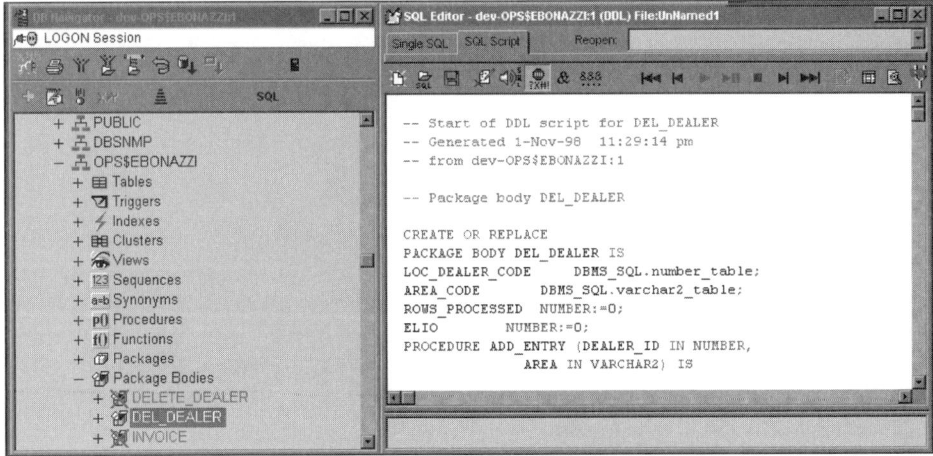

FIGURE 14.5 The powerful SQL Navigator DB browser uses the tree control to display the database object hierarchy

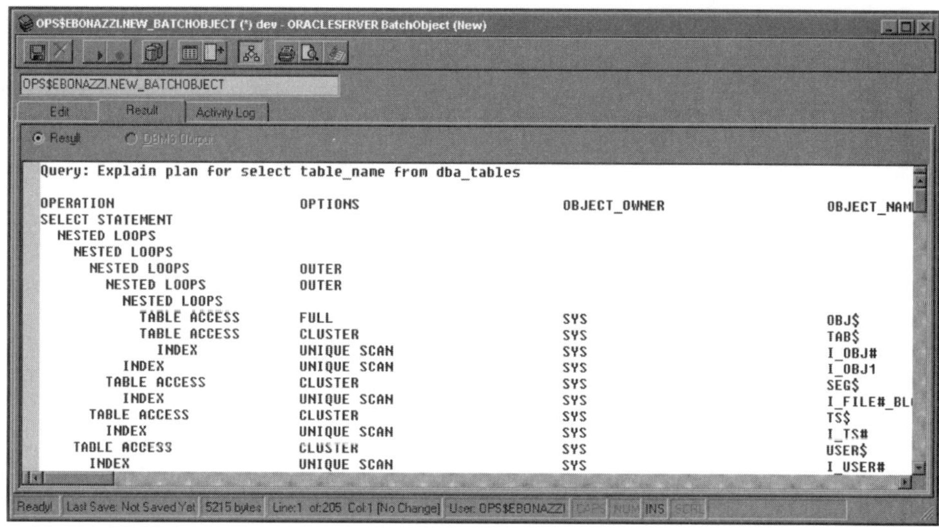

FIGURE 14.6 SQL-Programmer displays the Oracle output from explain plan

cated analysis than its competitor, but we should remember that SQL Navigator supports only Oracle, while SQL-Programmer must provide a good compromise among all supported back-end engines. SQL-Programmer executes the explain plan for the statement (see Chapter 8 if you don't remember what explain plan is) and displays the Oracle text without further manipulation (Figure 14.6).

SQL Navigator uses SQL Tuner, a product add-on that must be purchased, to conduct SQL analysis. The features provided justify the additional price. It offers different scenarios where the same statement is run with several combinations of SQL hints, so that the most efficient plan generated by the Oracle optimizer can be chosen, as shown in Figure 14.7. The statement can be executed, and the statistics sampled by SQL Navigator can be displayed in a window easily accessible through the pointer (Figure 14.8).

Here a carefully designed visual interface is coupled with a very sophisticated SQL analysis, providing the users with a first class combination. There are no excuses any more for submitting poor SQL statements to an Oracle engine. Tuning SQL statements has become easier than ever, thanks to the productivity gains obtained through the use of tools like SQL Navigator.

Figure 14.9 shows the scenario analysis made possible by SQL Tuner, an add-on to SQL Navigator that requires an additional license.

Both SQL-Programmer and SQL Navigator cost a few hundred dollars per single developer license. The productivity gain that can be obtained through their use sets the break-even point for these tools to a period of time measurable in days, if not in hours.

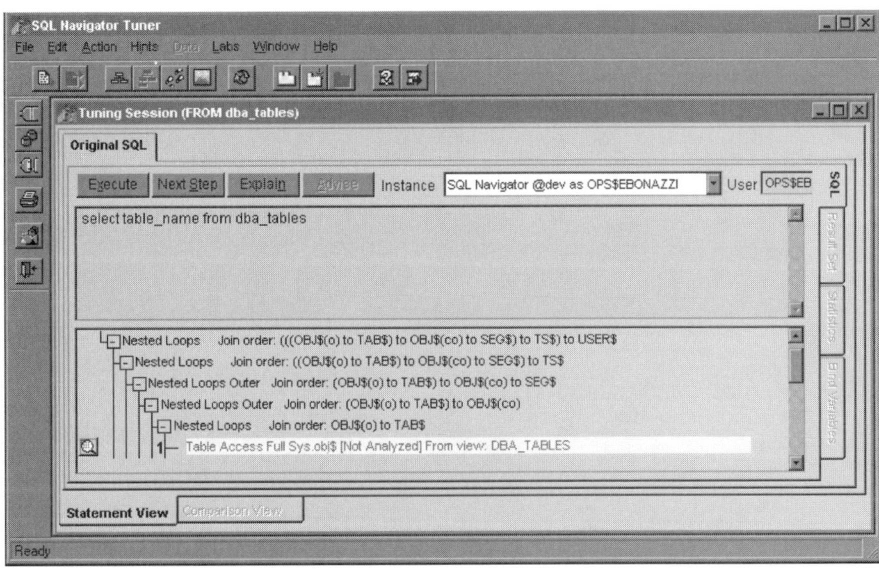

FIGURE 14.7 SQL Navigator displays a sophisticated explain plan

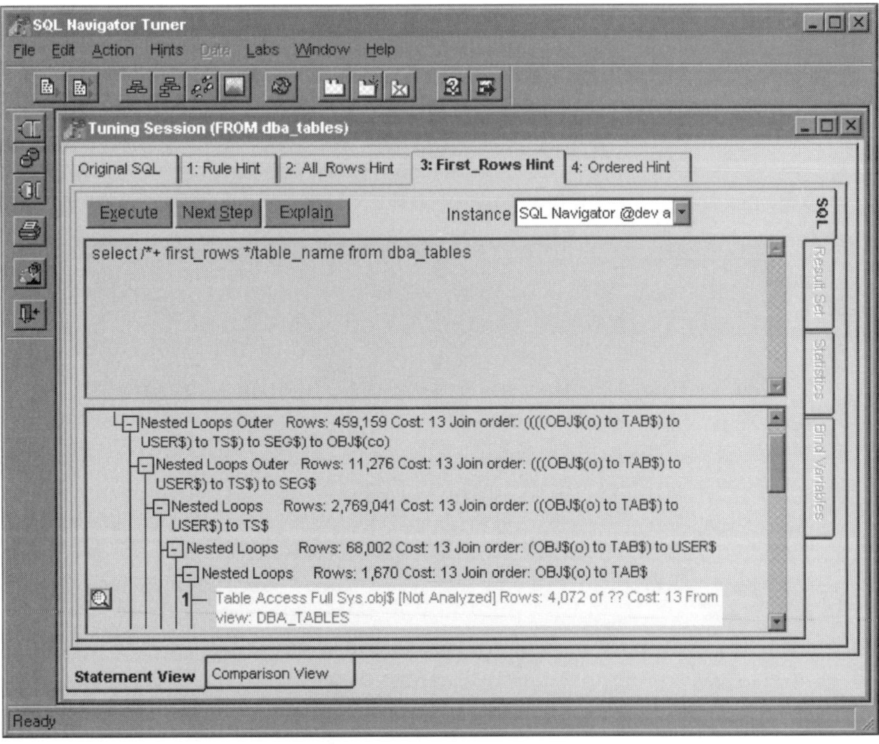

FIGURE 14.8 After a statement is executed, the statistics are available to the user

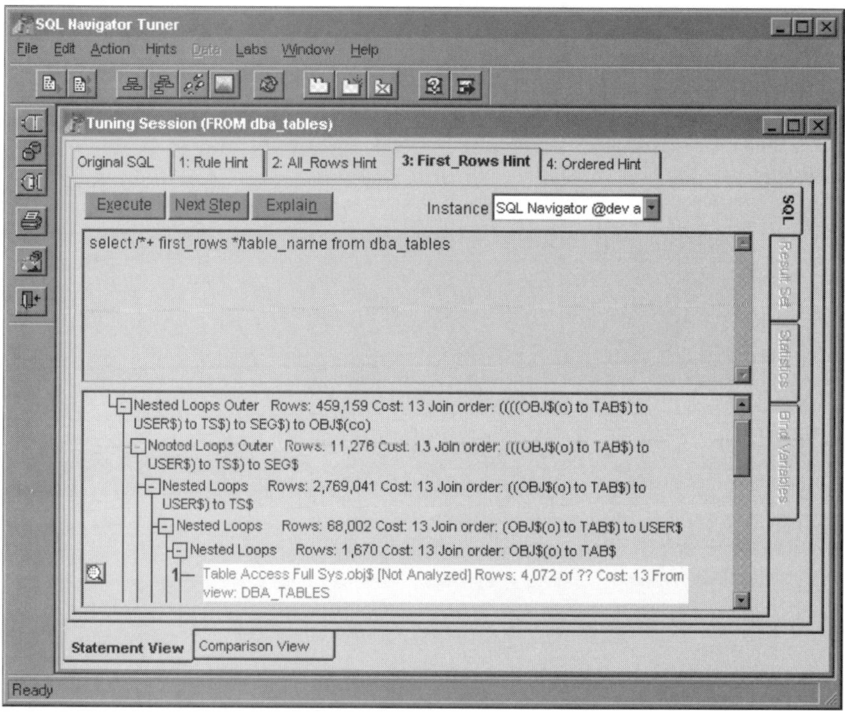

FIGURE 14.9 The original SQL statement is still accessible, but several scenarios have been generated by SQL Tuner to identify the most efficient combination

Summary

This chapter covered the Oracle proprietary extension to SQL, named PL/SQL, or procedural SQL, that represents one of the most powerful tools for handling data stored in Oracle databases.

We examined how PL/SQL can be proficiently used to implement business logic in the database. We also discovered that PL/SQL can be used to speed up SQL queries, by virtue of user-defined functions that act as SQL query helpers. A few advanced features of PL/SQL have been explored, such as triggers that avoid the mutating table error and external procedures.

The chapter illustrated a few Oracle supplied packages that can greatly improve the productivity of PL/SQL developers. Finally, we learned how to protect our PL/SQL code from indiscreet eyes, and we examined a couple of third party tools that allow for easy reverse-engineering of database objects and for line by line debugging of PL/SQL code.

Chapter 15

GETTING DATA IN/OUT OF ORACLE

This chapter deals with unorthodox ways to store data into Oracle tables or retrieve data from them. Several chapters of this book described the canonical tools commonly used to interact with Oracle, such as SQL statements embedded in Pro*C, Pro*Cobol, and other high-level languages, or PL/SQL, an ideal environment for server side processing, particularly suited for enforcing business logic on data stored by application programs. This chapter will focus instead on less popular means and techniques that can be used to interact with Oracle instances.

The Oracle architecture has been traditionally very database-centric, so much so that Oracle 8i implements complete file system capabilities within the database. Sometimes, however, database activity occurring within the realm of the Oracle kernel must be coordinated with external processes. Oracle 8.x offers an elegant solution through the implementation of external procedures, discussed in section 14.7. Unfortunately, external procedures are available only in Oracle8, while many Oracle7 applications still exist, being not only maintained, but in many cases enhanced. It is possible to coordinate the activity of external processes also from Oracle7, using techniques based on database pipes and alerts, discussed further ahead in this chapter.

One of the most powerful new features, which appeared in Oracle 8.0x and is further enhanced in Oracle 8i, is Advanced Queuing (AQ). AQ has been briefly introduced in Chapter 12 in the discussion the Oracle Call Interface. This chapter will examine Oracle AQ more in detail and provide a few code examples to illustrate its use.

Finally, every modern computing environment must deal with Perl, the wonderful creation of Larry Wall, one of the most influential figures in the open source movement. The elegant simplicity and powerful features of Perl can be proficiently used to process data stored in Oracle databases, thanks to a bridge that allows Perl to seamlessly speak to Oracle.

15.1 Communicating with the External World

When an external process needs to interact with Oracle, several simple methods can be used by application developers to access data stored in Oracle tables. A background process can be run periodically to scan specific tables used as queues, look for work, perform the tasks specified by the data found in the tables acting as queues, commit the transaction, and exit. The triggering mechanism for the job can be a batch queue in OpenVMS, a Cron job in Unix, or an NT service. Alternatively, complex schedulers can be used, for instance, CA-Unicenter.

Whatever the means used, the concept is that Oracle is the passive instance, while the control is firmly on the side of the external process, which drives Oracle according to its needs. Sometimes the opposite must occur, that is, an Oracle controlled procedure must coordinate the activity of an external process, which is waiting for "orders" coming from Oracle. A PL/SQL stored procedure, for instance, would like to access data acquired from a computer controlled device, or signal to an external process that an Oracle internal event has occurred, for example, new data has been inserted in a table. The external process would then be supposed to refresh its data, rereading the table that has been modified. This type of Oracle-triggered and Oracle-controlled processing is made possible by mechanisms provided through the use of two built-in packages DBMS_ALERT and DBMS_PIPE.

15.1.1 ORACLE PIPES AND ALERTS

Oracle provides two ways to interact with processes running externally to the engine. They share a few similarities. For instance, they both can send a message to the external process, but the main difference is that alert signaling, implemented through the DBMS_ALERT package, is delivered only upon successful transaction. That is, in case of transaction rollback, the processes that registered their interest in being notified by the Oracle kernel at the occurring of well-known events are not alerted.

In contrast, a message sent using the DBMS_PIPE package would reach the other end of the pipe irrespective of the outcome of the current transaction. This characteristic makes database pipes useful to capture "transient" data that would disappear in case of transaction failure. Consider an exception handler written by a novice PL/SQL programmer, which stores in a table the content of the fields being changed by a transaction. For the programmer, it would be useful to capture the data that made the transaction fail for post-mortem analysis. The fundamental flow with this approach is that the exception handler runs in the same transaction context of the transaction that fails. This means that in case of error, not only is the data changed by the procedure discarded, but the post-mortem data stored by the exception handler is also rolled back. An elegant solution to this problem is to implement an error writer in a separate session. The exception handler of the main procedure can send the data to be stored in the post-mortem table to the error writer through database pipes, before rolling back the transaction. The session running the specialized error writer would commit the messages, ensuring persistence to the data useful for post-mortem analysis.

The DBMS_ALERT package is normally used in conjunction with database triggers to signal the occurrence of specific events to external processes interested in being notified when the events happen. A typical example is a stock market analysis package that displays stock trends in real time. The graph displaying the trend must be refreshed each time the stock value is changed. The client application would register its desire to be notified when the stock table is modified by issuing a *dbms_alert.register()* call. If the well-known event were called "stock_change", the client code would look like:

```
EXEC SQL EXECUTE
BEGIN
      dbms_alert.register('stock_change');
END;
END-EXEC;
do
{
      sts = DisplayStockGraph();
      EXEC SQL EXECUTE
      BEGIN
          dbms_alert.waitone('stock_change', :message, :status);
      END;
      END-EXEC;
}
while(status == 0);
EXEC SQL EXECUTE
BEGIN
      dbms_alert.remove('stock_change');
END;
END-EXEC;
```

The stock table implements a trigger defined as follows:

```
CREATE TRIGGER stock_change_trg AFTER INSERT OR UPDATE OR DELETE ON stock
BEGIN
      dbms_alert.signal('stock_change', TICKER_ID);
END;
```

The trigger defined at a statement level obtains the requested synchronization between the client plotting on the screen and the refreshing of the stock data performed by the server. The following table lists procedures and functions provided by the DBMS_ALERT package.

PACKAGE MODULE	PARAMETERS	PURPOSE
REGISTER	name IN VARCHAR2	Registers a specific session as interested in being notified upon occurring of an event
REMOVE	name IN VARCHAR2	Removes the session from the registration list
REMOVEALL		Removes all alerts registered by one session from the registration list
SET_DEFAULTS	sensitivity IN NUMBER	Set the expiry time for polling loops
SIGNAL	name IN VARCHAR2 message IN VARCHAR2	Signals all interested sessions that an event has occurred
WAITANY	name OUT VARCHAR2 message OUT VARCHAR2 status OUT INTEGER timeout IN NUMBER	Waits for a signal for any of the alerts registered with the DBMS_ALERT package Note that the alert name is an OUT parameter, returned by the procedure to the calling function
WAITONE	name IN VARCHAR2 message OUT VARCHAR2 status OUT INTEGER timeout IN NUMBER	Waits for a specific alert to be signaled by the Oracle kernel. The alert name is an IN parameter, passed by the calling function to the DBMS_ALERT package

The DBMS_ALERT package doesn't require a polling loop to periodically check for the signaling of events. There are, however, two exceptions to this rule. Polling is required when the Oracle parallel server is used, in order to check on a regular basis for alerts generated by any of the shared instances, or when the WAITANY procedure is called by the client. If a session signals an event, but doesn't commit within one second of the signal, Oracle internally uses a polling mechanism to prevent the uncommitted alert from delivering other signals queued in the registration list.

In general polling, loops, and scalability are the worst enemies. Polling requires a lot of CPU cycles, and if many client processes are concurrently polling to get any signal that can be generated by internal database events, the application can saturate the CPU capabilities with only a few connected users. The recommendation is to use the WAITONE procedure, which doesn't require polling. If multiple alerts can be generated by an application, it is better to implement multiple specialized application servers, each responding to one specific alert, rather than one generic application server responding to all possible signals generated by the database.

The DBMS_PIPE package allows two or more sessions to exchange data through the Oracle SGA. The useful characteristic of database pipes is that they are implemented asynchronously, that is, they don't rely on transaction brackets to initiate or terminate their activity. Database pipes can be defined as public or private. All Oracle users connected to the instance can write to and read from public pipes, provided that they have the execute privilege on the DBMS_PIPE and they know the name of the pipes they require to use. Access to private pipes is restricted to:

- sessions running under the same userid as the creator of the pipe
- stored subprograms executing in the same userid privilege domain as the pipe creator
- users connected as `SYSDBA` or `INTERNAL`

Using the DBMS_PIPE package is straightforward. All messages sent through pipes must be prepared (or packed) using the PACK_MESSAGE procedure, overloaded to receive VARCHAR2, DATE, and NUMBER objects. The SEND_MESSAGE message function is used to put packed messages to a pipe. Similarly, on the other end, the message can be read by a call to RECEIVE_MESSAGE and retrieved into a readable format by calling UNPACK_MESSAGE.

A useful function provided by the package allows developers to find out about the datatype of the next message stored in the pipe. A program reading from pipes can be flexible and unpack messages without a prior knowledge of the format of the message being read. Another useful service function provided by the package is UNIQUE_SESSION_NAME, which returns a name guaranteed to be unique in the context of the session. A pipe can be named after the name returned by the function, thus minimizing the likelihood of receiving an Oracle error caused by a duplicate name of a public pipe.

The following table lists all modules provided by the DBMS_PIPE package.

PACKAGE MODULE	PARAMETERS	PURPOSE
CREATE_PIPE	pipename IN VARCHAR2, maxpipesize IN INTEGER, private IN BOOLEAN	Creates either a public or a private pipe. Public pipes don't need to be created by a call to CREATE_PIPE. Pipes explicitly created must be explicitly destroyed
NEXT_ITEM_TYPE	Returns item_type INTEGER	Returns the dataype of the next item in the message buffer

(*cont.*)

PACKAGE MODULE	PARAMETERS	PURPOSE
PACK_MESSAGE	item IN (VARCHAR2, NUMBER or DATE)	Packs data items into a message buffer
PURGE	pipename IN VARCHAR2	Empties a pipe from all data buffers
RECEIVE_MESSAGE	pipename IN VARCHAR2, timeout IN INTEGER	Receives a message from the specified pipe, storing its content into a message buffer
REMOVE_PIPE	pipename IN VARCHAR2	Removes the specified pipe from the shared memory (Oracle SGA)
RESET_BUFFER	N/A	Empties the message buffers
SEND_MESSAGE	pipename IN VARCHAR2, timeout IN INTEGER, maxpipesize IN INTEGER	Sends the contents of the local message buffer to the specified pipe. The call will return after the timeout has expired, if nothing can be read from the pipe
UNIQUE_SESSION_ NAME	Returns VARCHAR2	Obtains from Oracle a unique name in the context of the session—Useful to uniquely name pipes
UNPACK_MESSAGE	item OUT (VARCHAR2, NUMBER or DATE)	Unpacks the next item from the local message buffer, filled by a call to RE-CEIVE_MESSAGE

Applications can use message passing techniques based on both DBMS_ALERT and DBMS_PIPE. An application server can register its interest in being alerted by a signal when data is available in a pipe. This technique is used by PLEX, a freely available application development environment based on Oracle message passing, discussed in the next section. Oracle alerts and pipes are useful features, supported and available by Oracle7 and Oracle8.0x-8i. In an Oracle8 environment, though, more specialized, sophisticated and robust features are introduced to further enhance communication between the Oracle kernel and external processes. External procedures, which run under the control of Oracle and are spawned through the Net8 listener and Oracle Advanced Queuing are to be preferred to alerts and pipes for interprocess communication and synchronization. In particular, Oracle AQ offers the most sophisticated capabilities, such as call-back functions triggered by the arrival of messages on predefined queues. The publish-and-subscribe communication paradigm can also be easily implemented using the advanced capability of AQ.

Oracle7 is still very popular and unlikely to disappear in the near future. Large corporations still use MS Windows release 3.1, several years after the introduction of Windows 95. It is difficult to find a compelling economic convenience to upgrade to Oracle8 noncritical, support applications that use small or medium size databases, contributing in spite of their relative criticality to the overall success of a company. These applications will die natural deaths, running an Oracle7 instance until that day. In these environments, where small fixes or enhancements are part of the application maintenance, DBMS_ALERT and DBMS_PIPE can still play a relevant part when application servers implement signal or message-driven processing.

15.1.2 AN EXTERNAL PROCEDURE ANCESTOR: PLEX

PLEX (**PL**/SQL **EX**tender), a freeware tool written by two Oracle consultants, is not supported or endorsed by Oracle Corporation. The rule "use at your own risk" is applicable in this case, but given the simplicity of the package and its limited number of lines of code, definitely manageable by developers with average skills in PL/SQL and "C", the risks involved in using PLEX are really limited. A couple of hours spent analyzing the source code of the package should be enough to allow developers to either fix small bugs (if there are any left…) or enhance and customize specific features offered by PLEX. PLEX is offered in a TAR format, showing its Unix origins. I successfully ported and used PLEX in OpenVMS environments. PLEX is fundamentally based on Oracle built-in features, rather than on operating system features, so its port to Oracle-supported OSs should be relatively easy. PLEX is available on the WEB for downloading at the following address: http://www.oracle.com/st/products/features/plsqlutilities.html

PLEX helps developers implement application servers based on database pipes and alerts by generating "C" code (stub files) with embedded SQL. Developers need only to create a skeleton PL/SQL procedure/function, specifying the datatype of input and output parameters and return value. The body of the PL/SQL routine must be empty. PLEX uses the PL/SQL skeleton to create a "real" PL/SQL procedure/function and two Pro*C files that implement all required ancillary functions for parameter passing between the application server and PL/SQL.

Developers can edit one of the two generated files and add application logic in the appropriate spot indicated by a comment (/* USER CODE HERE */). The two generated files can then be compiled and linked together with two other PLEX provided files, plex.pc and heap.pc, to produce an executable image.

The application server generated by PLEX runs as a daemon, waiting for input from Oracle pipes used by the PLEX-generated PL/SQL function, and responding to the same pipes, sending the computed values.

Application server development is extremely facilitated by PLEX, which takes care of all plumbing between Oracle and external processes. PLEX installation is straightforward, provided that:

- The DBMS_ALERT and DBMS_PIPE are available in the database.
- The Oracle account under which PLEX is installed (usually plex) is explicitly given the execute privilege on the two packages.

PLEX is an "old" facility, shipped when the current release of Oracle was 7.1. The make file included with PLEX assumes the presence in the system of a Pro*C make file, named proc.mk and located in $ORACLE_HOME/proc/demo/. More recent releases of Oracle7 and Oracle8 no longer use that directory structure, the Oracle Programmer2000 modules are now installed in a directory tree starting from $ORACLE_HOME/precomp. For this reason, the plex.mk file distributed with PLEX no longer works straight after its installation. It must be modified to include the new Pro*C make file. Alternatively, a brand new make file, customized for PLEX, can be built, specifying the correct targets and including the relevant .pc files of the PLEX distribution.

To install PLEX in a Unix environment, one should connect to the Oracle account (the operating system account of the owner of the Oracle software) and change directory to $ORACLE_HOME. Copy plex.tar in that directory and type

```
tar xvf plex.tar
```

This operation must be performed from $ORACLE_HOME. Choosing other directory trees will cause the installation to fail.

The tar extraction will create a directory tree under $ORACLE_HOME/plex. The next step is to run the plexinst script, located in $ORACLE_HOME/plex/install. The plexinst script invokes plex.mk after having created the database objects. The default plex.mk expects the Pro*C make file in the old directory structure. If the PLEX installation occurs in an Oracle 7.3 or 8.x environment, before invoking plexinst, one should change the directory to $ORACLE_HOME/plex/lib and modify plex.mk to include the Pro*C make file from the right directory; otherwise, plexinst will partially fail. The plexinst script must be invoked with a few command parameters. They are:

1. The Oracle system account and password separated by a slash
2. The password for the account under which the PLEX objects are installed (by default named plex)
3. The default tablespace for the plex schema
4. The temporary tablespace for the plex schema

For example:

```
plexinst system/manager plexpwd users temp
```

The plexinst script must be installed from $ORACLE_HOME/plex/install, and would fail otherwise because it uses relative directory positioning, assuming that it starts from the install subdirectory. Assuming a successful installation, using PLEX from a developer perspective becomes straightforward. Let us imagine we want to access from PL/SQL the Unix system called *gettimeofday()*, which returns seconds and microseconds from January 1, 1970. In Oracle the smallest time unit, available from the V$TIMER dynamic table, is measured in hundredths of seconds, not microseconds. We decide to implement an application server that makes gettimeofday() available through a PL/SQL function.

To accomplish this, we create a new directory, called microseconds, accessible from an account set up for Oracle development. Assuming a Unix environment, we make sure that the directory $ORACLE_HOME/plex/bin is included in the PATH environment variable. In the microseconds directory, we create an SQL script (micro.sql) that defines the PL/SQL stub for our function, as follows:

```
create or replace function microseconds (seconds OUT NUMBER,
                                         microseconds OUT NUMBER)
return NUMBER
AS
BEGIN
      NULL;
END;
/
grant execute on microseconds to plex
/
```

We run the script under the canonical scott/tiger account to create the function and to grant the execute privilege on it to plex.

```
sqlplus scott/tiger @micro.sql
```

Now, the PLEX magic. We invoke the *makesrc* script, which resides in $ORACLE_HOME/plex/bin, passing the Oracle account and password, the PL/SQL procedure/function name and the name, of the application server. For example:

```
makesrc scott/tiger microseconds microseconds_server
```

The script creates the Pro*C stubs and rearranges the PL/SQL function to make it compatible with the PLEX environment. Let us see how our definition of the PL/SQL stub has been changed by makesrc:

```
sqlplus scott/tiger
SQL*Plus: Release 8.1.4.0.0 - Beta on Sun Jan 31 00:06:42 1999

(c) Copyright 1998 Oracle Corporation.  All rights reserved.

Connected to:
Oracle8i Enterprise Edition Release 8.1.4.0.0 - Beta
With the Partitioning and Objects options
```

```
PL/SQL Release 8.1.4.0.0 - Production

SQL> select TEXT from user_source where NAME='MICROSECONDS' order
by line;
TEXT
-------------------------------------------------------------------
function microseconds (seconds OUT NUMBER,
                       microseconds OUT NUMBER)
return NUMBER
AS
—## PLEX GENERATED CODE
       return_value NUMBER;
begin
       plex_server.build_header( 'SCOTT_MICROSECONDS' );
       plex_server.send_receive( 'SCOTT_MICROSECONDS' );
       dbms_pipe.unpack_message( SECONDS );
       dbms_pipe.unpack_message( MICROSECONDS );
       dbms_pipe.unpack_message( return_value );
       return return_value;
end;

14 rows selected.
```

We can now edit the stub file, microseconds.pc, produced by makesrc. The source code added during the editing session is shown in bold.

```
/* Standard include files...
*/#include "plex.h"
/* USER DEFINED INCLUDE FILES MAY BE PLACED HERE */
/***************************************************/
#include <sys/time.h>
/***************************************************/
/*
Common C Data structure used in this implementation
*/
typedef struct tag_SCOTT_MICROSECONDS
{
/* Error code/msg section */
      long                 error_code;
      short                error_code_i;
      char *               error_msg;
      short                error_msg_i;
/* In/Out parameters */
      /* SECONDS was a PL/SQL NUMBER and is OUT */
      double               SECONDS;
```

```
        short                SECONDS_i;
        /* MICROSECONDS was a PL/SQL NUMBER and is OUT */
        double               MICROSECONDS;
        short                MICROSECONDS_i;
/* Return Value section */
        double               return_value;
        short                return_value_i;
}
         SCOTT_MICROSECONDS_plist;
/*
Generated on 28-August   -1998 22:57
Generic initialization code
DO NOT ALTER THIS CODE IN ANY FASHION
*/
static void init( plist )
SCOTT_MICROSECONDS_plist * plist;
{
        plist->error_code_i = -1;
        plist->error_msg_i = -1;
        plist->return_value_i = -1;
}
/*
Generated on 28-August   -1998 22:57
Generic clean up code
DO NOT ALTER THIS CODE IN ANY FASHION
*/
static void done( plist )
SCOTT_MICROSECONDS_plist * plist;
{
        pipe_put_number( (double)plist->error_code,
                         (short)plist->error_code_i);
                   "
        pipe_put_string( plist->error_msg,plist->error_msg_i );
        if (plist->error_code_i || plist->error_code > -20000)
        {
                pipe_put_number((double)plist->SECONDS,
                                plist->SECONDS_i);
                         "
                pipe_put_number((double)plist->MICROSECONDS,
                                plist->MICROSECONDS_i);
                pipe_put_number((double)plist->return_value,
                                plist->return_value_i);
        }
}
/*
```

```
Main body, only visible subroutine in this source
all other functions/procedures are STATIC
DO NOT ALTER THIS CODE IN ANY FASHION
*/
static void user_code();
void SCOTT_MICROSECONDS()
{
SCOTT_MICROSECONDS_plist  plist;
      init(&plist);
      user code( &plist );
      done(&plist);
}
/*
User defined code may appear after this comment
CHANGING ANYTHING ABOVE THIS LINE MAY CAUSE UNEXPECTED
BEHAVIOR FROM THE MAKESRC UTILITY
SOURCE CODE MAY NOT BE PRESERVED IF YOU CHANGE ANY
CODE ABOVE THIS LINE
*/
static void user_code( plist )
SCOTT_MICROSECONDS_plist * plist;
{
/* USER CODE HERE */
      struct timeval tm;
      int     sts;
      if ( sts = gettimeofday(&tm))
      {
             raise_application_error(-20100,"Unix system call
             failed");
             return;
      }
      plist->SECONDS = (double) tm.tv_sec;
      plist->MICROSECONDS = (double) tm.tv_usec;
      plist->return_value = 0;
      plist->return_value_i = 0;}
```

We are done with the customization. The application server must be compiled and linked. In addition to microseconds.pc, the makesrc script produces another file, eplkup.pc, which implements a lookup table that converts a subroutine name into a function entry point. Four files must be precompiled, compiled, and linked together to form a running application server. From $ORACLE_HOME/plex/lib, plex.pc and heap.pc must be included in our make file, linking the two static files from the $ORACLE_HOME/plex/lib directory with the two files dynamically created by makesrc (microseconds.pc and eplkup.pc). Assuming a successful compilation and linking, we can now start our application server with the following command:

```
plex scott/tiger microseconds_server &
```

From SQL*Plus, we can invoke the microseconds function, displaying the results of the two OUT variables, containing seconds and microseconds as returned by the application server. Application servers can obviously be much more complex than our simple example. The point is that the infrastructure for interprocess communication between Oracle and external processes is completely provided by PLEX, which relieves developers from dealing with low-level, error-prone, and repeatable tasks, allowing them to focus on more compelling business problems.

I have tested PLEX in different environments (from Oracle 7.1.3 to Oracle 8.1.4, Unix, and OpenVMS), without encountering any major problem. If free software is not forbidden in your environment, PLEX is one of those "tools of the trade" that can become vary handy under several circumstances.

15.2 Oracle Advanced Queuing

The basic principles of Oracle Advanced Queuing have been introduced in section 12.3.5, in the chapter dedicated to the Oracle Call Interface. Here the discussion about Oracle AQ goes into more detail, covering the most important characteristics and features offered by AQ and providing a few real life examples.

The terminology used by Oracle AQ differs in part from similar terminology used by other queuing environments, such as IBM MQ Series (see Chapter 16). Oracle AQ offers features unique among message-oriented middleware systems, mainly because of the nature of its appendix to a relational engine, which provides very advanced storage capabilities, unmatched by other message queuing systems.

The following table lists the basic terms used in an AQ environment.

QUEUING ENTITY	PURPOSE
Message	The smallest unit of information that can be managed by AQ. It consists of two parts, control information and payload, or user data.
Queue	Repository for messages. There can be two types of queue, normal queues and exception queues, which store messages that cannot be processed for any reason.

(cont.)

QUEUING ENTITY	PURPOSE
Queue Table	Physical location where logical queues store their messages. More queues can be stored in one queue table. Each queue table contains a default exception queue.
Agent	A queue user. Agents can be producers (i.e., they queue messages) or consumers (they dequeue messages). Agents are identified by name, address and protocol.
Queue Monitor	Background process that provides mechanisms for time-based operations such as message expiration, propagation, retry, etc. A parameter in init.ora specifies queue monitor creation and characteristics.

The queuing model offered by AQ allows for great sophistication, giving designers many flexible options for the implementation of message-based applications. The very fact that messages are stored in Oracle tables opens the door to a great deal of possibilities, such as using standard SQL commands and techniques (not to mention Oracle tools such as import/export) and accessing messages stored by applications that use queuing as the major means for communication. When messages are retained in the queue and not discarded after consumption or expiration, message history and event journals can be built using standard SQL queries.

Apart from an intrinsic flexibility due to the way queuing is implemented in Oracle, AQ provides a rich set of advanced capabilities, some of which are not even found in MOM products like BEA Systems Message/Q or IBM MQ Series. The table below summarizes the advanced features offered by Oracle AQ.

AQ FEATURE	COMMENT
Correlation Identifier	Correlation identifiers are part of the control information stored with the message. They can be used to selectively dequeue specific messages.
Message Grouping	When multiple messages belong to one group, they must be stored and retrieved in one atomic transaction. Complex messages can thus be segmented into simple messages, which must be stored and retrieved in one block.
Message Priority and Ordering	Messages can be assigned priority, sort orders, and sequence deviation, to position them relatively to other messages. Complex dequeuing policies can be implemented through this feature.
Propagation	Through standard Oracle database links, it is possible to propagate messages to remote instances.
Time Specification	Messages can be made available only after a certain time or can be defined in a way such that if they are not consumed within a certain interval they expire, that is, they are not available any longer for consumption.

(cont.)

AQ FEATURE	COMMENT
Subscribers and Recipients Lists	Single messages can be defined to be consumed by multiple recipients. A recipient can be an agent or another queue. This feature allows for fan-out parallelism of messages.
Transaction Scope	Enqueuing or dequeuing requests can be bracketed in a transaction that includes multiple steps. Alternatively, it is possible to make the single enqueuing or dequeuing a transaction in itself, guaranteeing an immediate visibility of the message queued to other transactions.
Blocked Dequeuing and Event-Based Dispatching	Polling can be avoided by specifying an interval of time that a dequeuing request is allowed to wait. Alternatively, dequeuing can be triggered by the arrival of a message in a queue (OCI only).
Consumption and Retention	Applications can browse a queue accessing messages that remain in the queue for further consumption. Messages can be retained in the queue even after having been consumed by consumer agents.
Exception Handling	Messages that cannot be consumed according to the specifying constraints (e.g., expiration intervals) are automatically moved to exception queues.

It is possible to administratively define default subscribers for a specific queue. These subscribers are implicit recipients of messages stored in the queue. But Oracle AQ goes even further in ensuring flexibility. It is in fact possible to override programmatically the default subscriber list, and to store a message in a queue for a specific target that is not part of the list of the default subscribers. By using the DBMS_AQADM package appropriately, an administrator can implement complex configurations, supporting fanning-out of messages, where one queue has multiple queues as recipients of the message, or funneling-in of messages, where multiple queues route their message to a single queue. By using message propagation, fanning-out and funneling-in policies can be implemented across distributed databases, potentially propagating thousands of messages to hundreds of nodes with little administrative effort.

Basic queuing capabilities have been offered with Oracle release 8.0x. Oracle 8i further increases the features of AQ, allowing for publish-and-subscribe implementation, asynchronous notification, nonpersistent queues, propagation of messages having LOB-based payloads, rule-based subscribers, and listen capabilities, such as waiting for messages arriving on multiple queues. Given its rich set of sophisticated and powerful features, Oracle AQ is not a "poor man" implementation of a queue-based, message-oriented communication model. On the contrary, AQ can compete head to head with MOM specific products, such as IBM MQ Series (see Chapter 16 for a comparison between AQ and MQ Series).

15.2.1 USING ORACLE AQ

Oracle AQ offers two types of interfaces, administrative and operational. The administrative interface is implemented through a PL/SQL package, DBMS_AQADM. It allows one to create queue tables and queues, to alter and drop them, to manage subscribers, to grant and revoke system privileges, and to schedule propagation policies. Operational interfaces are provided in PL/SQL (DBMS_AQ) and Oracle OCI. A few advanced features are available only through the OCI operational interface, such as registering a callback function for notification when a message is available on a queue.

The first step required to use AQ is to create a queue. In order to do that, a queue table must be defined. If the object option is available, a queue table can be based on a user-defined type. Alternatively, a queue table can be defined as RAW, which will be implemented as a LOB with a maximum size of 32 kilobytes. If the object option hasn't been purchased, Oracle AQ can still be used, but all queue tables must be defined as RAW. AQ is available only with the enterprise edition of Oracle8. The following script creates a queue that uses an object-based queue table.

```
CREATE type Message_t as object
  (Subject      VARCHAR2(30),
   Text         VARCHAR2(80));
/
-- Create a object type queue table and queue:
EXECUTE dbms_aqadm.create_queue_table (
   Queue_table        => 'SEWO_1_TAB',
   Queue_payload_type => 'Message_t');
EXECUTE dbms_aqadm.create_queue (
   Queue_name         =>  'SEWO_1_QUEUE',
   Queue_table        => 'SEWO_1_TAB');
```

In the script, no schema was specified for the queue being created, so the default schema is the owner of the queue. It is now possible to see the created queue by accessing the USER_QUEUES data dictionary view.

```
SQL> select name,substr(queue_table,1,15) QUEUE_TABLE,
substr(queue_type,1,15) QUEUE_TYPE from user_queues;

NAME                             QUEUE_TABLE      QUEUE_TYPE
------------------------------   ---------------  ---------------
AQ$_SEWO_1_TAB_E                 SEWO_1_TAB       EXCEPTION_QUEUE
SEWO_1_QUEUE                     SEWO_1_TAB       NORMAL_QUEUE
```

The create_queue procedure provided by the DBMS_AQADM package automatically creates an exception queue, which is named by the package

AQ$_<queue name>_E. Note, however, that both normal queue and exception queue share the same queue table.

Once created, a queue must be started before being able to accept and store messages. A queue can be started for enqueuing or dequeuing only, using the DBMS_AQADM.START_QUEUE procedure, which accepts the queue name as the first parameter and two boolean values, which specify whether enqueuing and dequeuing are enabled (TRUE) or disabled (FALSE).

```
execute sys.dbms_aqadm.start_queue('SEWO_1_QUEUE',TRUE,TRUE);
```

Some of the characteristics of a queue or a queue table may be changed once they have already been created by invoking the ALTER_QUEUE and ALTER_QUEUE_TABLE, respectively. A particular type of queue, available with the Oracle AQ package, is the nonpersistent queue. A nonpersistent queue doesn't require the creation of a queue table because AQ uses a system-created queue table to store nonpersistent messages, named AQ$_MEM_SC or AQ$_MEM_MC, defined in the same schema as the nonpersistent queue. The SC and MC suffixes indicate a single-consumer queue and a multi-consumer queue respectively. Oracle AQ provides a specific procedure to create a nonpersistent queue, CREATE_NP_QUEUE.

Once a queue has been created and started, inserting messages into it is an easy task. The PL/SQL AQ operational interface, implemented through the DBMS_AQ package, can be used from PL/SQL, Pro*C, and Oracle Objects for OLE (OO4O). Alternatively, the Oracle OCI provides AQ primitives that not only enable queuing/dequeuing of messages, but also allow for the implementation of the Publish-and-Subscribe communication model in OCI-based user-written programs. For a detailed explanation of the communication models, see Chapter 16, Section 16.3.1 (Middleware Paradigms). The following example uses PL/SQL to queue one message to the queue named SEWO_1_QUEUE.

```
DECLARE
enqueue_options dbms_aq.enqueue_options_t;
message_properties dbms_aq.message_properties_t;
message_handle RAW(16);
message Message_t;
BEGIN
message := Message_t('FIRST MESSAGE',
'Software Engineering With oracle. First AQ example.');
dbms_aq.enqueue('SEWO_1_QUEUE',
  enqueue_options,
  message_properties,
  message,
  message_handle);
COMMIT;
END;
/
```

A few things are worth mentioning in the above examples. The ENQUEUE procedure doesn't provide any default; each parameter must be explicitly passed to the procedure. The enqueue options and the message properties, on the other hand, are DBMS_AQ package-provided data structures that are initialized with default values for each field. If developers are happy with those default values, nothing more is required for the enqueuing procedure to work.

Using the OCI to queue a message is definitely more verbose, but not more difficult, than using PL/SQL. The following example stores the same message in the same queue, using OCI calls to accomplish this task. In addition, the OCI examples also dequeues the message, consuming it from the queue immediately after it has been queued.

```
#ifndef SL_ORACLE
#include <sl.h>
#endif
#ifndef OCI_ORACLE
#include <oci.h>
#endif
struct message
{
OCIString *subject;
OCIString *data;
};
typedef struct message message;
struct null_message
{
OCIInd null_adt;
OCIInd null_subject;
OCIInd null_data;
};
typedef struct null_message null_message;
int main()
{
      OCIEnv  *envhp;
      OCIServer     *srvhp;
      OCIError      *errhp;
      OCISvcCtx     *svchp;
      dvoid   *tmp;
      OCIType *mesg_tdo = (OCIType *) 0;
      message msg;
      null_message nmsg;
      message *mesg = &msg;
      null_message *nmesg = &nmsg;
```

```
message *deqmesg = (message *)0;
null_message *ndeqmesg = (null_message *)0;
OCIInitialize((ub4) OCI_OBJECT, (dvoid *)0,
              (dvoid * (*)()) 0,
              (dvoid * (*)()) 0, (void (*)()) 0 );
OCIHandleAlloc( (dvoid *) NULL, (dvoid **) &envhp,
              (ub4) OCI_HTYPE_ENV,52, (dvoid **) &tmp);
OCIEnvInit( &envhp, (ub4) OCI_DEFAULT,
              21, (dvoid **) &tmp );
OCIHandleAlloc( (dvoid *) envhp, (dvoid **) &errhp,
              (ub4)OCI_HTYPE_ERROR,52, (dvoid **) &tmp);
OCIHandleAlloc( (dvoid *) envhp, (dvoid **) &srvhp, (ub4)
              OCI_HTYPE_SERVER,52, (dvoid **) &tmp);
OCIServerAttach( srvhp, errhp, (text *) 0,
              (sb4) 0, (ub4) OCI_DEFAULT);
OCIHandleAlloc( (dvoid *) envhp, (dvoid **) &svchp,
              (ub4) OCI_HTYPE_SVCCTX,52,
              (dvoid **) &tmp);
OCIAttrSet( (dvoid *) svchp, (ub4) OCI_HTYPE_SVCCTX,
              (dvoid *)srvhp, (ub4) 0,
              (ub4) OCI_ATTR_SERVER, (OCIError *) errhp);
OCILogon(envhp, errhp, &svchp, "OPS$EBONAZZI",
              strlen("OPS$EBONAZZI"), "SEWO",
              strlen("SEWO"), 0, 0);
/* Obtain TDO of Message_t */
OCITypeByName(envhp, errhp, svchp,
              (CONST text *)"OPS$EBONAZZI",
              strlen("OPS$EBONAZZI"),(
              CONST text *)"MESSAGE_T",
              strlen("MESSAGE_T"),
              (text *)0, 0,
              OCI_DURATION_SESSION,
              OCI_TYPEGET_ALL, &mesg_tdo);
/* Prepare the message payload */
mesg->subject = (OCIString *)0;
mesg->data = (OCIString *)0;
OCIStringAssignText(envhp, errhp,
                     (CONST text *)"FIRST MESSAGE",
                     strlen("FIRST MESSAGE"),
                     &mesg->subject);
OCIStringAssignText(envhp, errhp,
                     (CONST text *)
                     "Software Engineering With oracle."
                     "First AQ example.",
```

```
                            51,
                            &mesg->data);
        nmesg->null_adt = nmesg->null_subject = OCI_IND_NOTNULL;
        nmesg->null_data = OCI_IND_NOTNULL;

        /* Enqueue into the SEWO_1_QUEUE */
        OCIAQEnq(svchp, errhp, (CONST text *)"SEWO_1_QUEUE", 0, 0,
                 mesg_tdo, (dvoid **)&mesg,
                 (dvoid **)&nmesg, 0, 0);
        OCITransCommit(svchp, errhp, (ub4) 0);

        /********************************/
        /* Dequeue from the SEWO_1_QUEUE */
        /********************************/

        OCIAQDeq(svchp, errhp, (CONST text *)"SEWO_1_QUEUE", 0, 0,
                 mesg_tdo, (dvoid **)&deqmesg,
                (dvoid **)&ndeqmesg, 0, 0);
        printf("De-queued message.\n");
        printf("Subject: %s\n",
                OCIStringPtr(envhp, deqmesg->subject));
        printf("Text: %s\n",
                 OCIStringPtr(envhp, deqmesg->data));
        OCITransCommit(svchp, errhp, (ub4) 0);
}
```

According to our discussion in Chapter 12, Section 12.3.7 (The Best of the Two Worlds), and given the verbosity of OCI code, using Pro*C with embedded PL/SQL to perform simple tasks such as queuing and dequeuing a message is a better solution. The performance loss incurred in switching to Pro*C/PL/SQL is minimal, but the gain in reduced number of lines of code is substantial. A compromise between absolute optimal performance and reduced number of lines of code (and consequently, reduced likelihood of software defects), is represented by the use of a mixed environment, where the connection to Oracle occurs from Pro*C. An OCI environment is also defined in the Pro*C context, and a call to *SQLEnvGet()* is made to obtain the OCI opaque environment handle.

Unfortunately, this technique cannot be used to access the most advanced OCI features such as Publish-and-Subscribe calls, and more general, event-triggered callback routines. To enable event handling, an OCI-based program must initialize the OCI process by calling *OCIInitialize()*, which must precede all other subsequent OCI calls. When the initialization mode specified through OCI-Initialize() is set to OCI_EVENTS, a dedicated listening thread is begun to handle event notifications for the client process. This implies that Publish-and-Subscribe calls are supported only in multi-threaded environments.

The OCI program must also allocate a subscription handle. This is accomplished by the *OCIHandleAlloc()* call, when a handle type of OCI_HTYPE_SUBSCR is allocated. Once the handle obtained, several of its attributes must be set by using *OCIAttrSet()* to set the subscription handle attributes for:

OCI HANDLE	PURPOSE
OCI_ATTR_SUBSCR_NAME	subscription name
OCI_ATTR_SUBSCR_NAMESPACE	subscription namespace
OCI_ATTR_SUBSCR_CALLBACK	notification callback
OCI_ATTR_SUBSCR_CTX	callback context
OCI_ATTR_SUBSCR_PAYLOAD	payload buffer for posting

All these attributes, except OCI_ATTR_SUBSCR_PAYLOAD, must be set before registering a subscription. OCI_ATTR_SUBSCR_PAYLOAD is required before posting to a subscription.

The next step required to set up a Publish-and-Subscribe environment is to define the callback function that will be used with the subscription handle. The callback function, which must return a value of OCI_CONTINUE, follows the specifications shown below.

```
typedef ub4 (*OCISubscriptionNotify)
             ( dvoid *context,
             OCISubscription *subscription_hp,
             dvoid *pay,
             ub4 *pay_length,
             dvoid *description
             ub4 mode );
```

The following table lists each parameter, together with an explanation.

CALLBACK PARAMETER	MEANING
context	The user-defined context specified when the callback was registered
subscription_hp	The pointer to the subscription handle specified when the callback was registered
pay	The payload for this notification. For an Oracle 8.1 release, only ub1 * (a sequence of bytes) is allowed (no object types)
pay_length	The length of the payload for this notification
description	The namespace-specific descriptor. Namespace-specific parameters can be extracted from this descriptor. The structure of this descriptor is opaque to the user and its type is dependent on the namespace
mode	Call-specific mode. The only valid value in Oracle 8.1 is OCI_DEFAULTS

Setting up our Publish-and-Subscribe environment is not yet finished. The *OCISubscriptionRegister()* call must be invoked, to register with the subscription (or subscriptions). A single call to OCISubscriptionRegister() can be used to register interest in being notified when several events occur. The OCI functions introduced with Oracle8i to support the Publish-and-Subscribe communication paradigm are listed below.

OCI FUNCTION	PURPOSE
OCISubscriptionDisable	Disables a subscription
OCISubscriptionEnable	Enables a subscription
OCISubscriptionPost	Posts a subscription
OCISubscriptionRegister	Registers a subscription
OCISubscriptionUnRegister	Unregisters a subscription

An application component can register its interest in being notified when specific events occur, calling *OCISubscriptionRegister()*. The same component can provoke the occurring of an event by calling *OCISubscriptionPost()*, which will cause all other components participating in the application to be alerted, if they subscribed their interest in that event.

It should be noted that Publish-and-Subscribe can be used without queuing. Subscriptions can be notified by calling OCISubscriptionPost(). The same OCI API, OCISubscriptionRegister(), can be used either to register with events that will be triggered only by a call to the post routine, or to register with events that will be triggered by the arrival of a message in a queue.

An additional new feature introduced by Oracle8i is the ability to set up a listening function, which listens for notifications of events on behalf of one or multiple agents. The listen call is implemented in both PL/SQL and OCI environments, DBMS_AQ.LISTEN and OCIAQListen respectively, and is a blocking call that returns when an event occurring in one or multiple queues interests one or more agents registered with the listener.

Oracle AQ and the recently introduced Publish-and-Subscribe APIs provide designers and architects with an extremely rich set of opportunities for the implementation of really sophisticated message-oriented applications. The following table illustrates potential uses of queues and events, in order of increasing complexity.

APPLICATION SET UP	APIs USED	ACHIEVEMENT
One single-consumer queue defined. Two agents, one consumer and one producer.	OCIAQEnq(), OCIAQDeq() Alternatively DBMS_AQ.ENQUEUE and DBMS_AQ.DEQUEUE	First level of disconnected/deferred communication.

(*cont.*)

APPLICATION SET UP	APIS USED	ACHIEVEMENT
One multi-consumer queue defined. Subscribers and recipients are predefined.	OCIAQEnq(), OCIAQDeq() Alternatively DBMS_AQ.ENQUEUE and DBMS_AQ.DEQUEUE	Recipients selectively fetch messages from the queues. Each queue has a dedicated dequeuing process.
One multi-consumer queue defined. Message-specific recipient lists override pre-defined subscribers and recipients.	OCIAQEnq(), OCIAQDeq() Alternatively DBMS_AQ.ENQUEUE and DBMS_AQ.DEQUEUE	Recipients can use queues for which they were not originally registered.
Multiple multi-consumer queues are defined. Listening is enabled to notify multiple agents at once.	OCIAQEnq(), OCIAQListen() Or DBMS_AQ.ENQUEUE, DBMS_AQ.LISTEN	Dequeuing agents are served collectively by one process that listens on multiple queues. One process only is required to serve the dequeuing from multiple queues.
Multiple queues are defined. Callback routines are triggered when messages arrive to the queues.	OCIAQEnq(), DBMS_AQ.ENQUEUE, OCISubcriptionRegister()	Achieved de-coupling between producers and consumers. They don't have to know about each other. Furthermore, a blocking call for dequeuing is not any more required.
Multiple processes register their interest in being notified when specific events occur. The events are originated by processes posting notifications to the subscribers.	OCISubscriptionPost(), OCISubcriptionRegister()	Application components use Oracle services to exchange messages without requiring storage mechanisms such as tables or queues. They don't even need to be connected to Oracle once they have registered their interest in being notified of the occurrence of specific events.

First introduced with Oracle 8.0x, and subsequently refined with Oracle8i, the disconnected/deferred communication paradigm has become an essential part of the Oracle architecture. Oracle AQ has reached maturity and robustness in the space of a few minor releases, to the extent that it can be used extensively in mission-critical applications. With the advent of Internet technologies, the disconnected/deferred communication paradigm is becoming increasingly important, and Oracle Corporation, recognizing its importance, has decided to incorporate disconnected/deferred functionality in its flagship database. It is likely that Advanced Queuing will become much more widely used, especially in WEB-enabled applications.

15.3 Perl—OraPerl/PerlDBI

Perl, **P**ractical **E**xtraction and **R**eporting **L**anguage, developed by Larry Wall, and freely available from the WEB, is one of the most successful tools of the recent history of Computer Science. Conceived with the purpose of running in a Unix environment, Perl has been ported to virtually all commercially available operating systems, including MS Windows NT. One of the reasons for its success is the perfect integration with the Common Gateway Interface (CGI), used during the first wave of internet computing to dynamically produce HTML formatted pages with data gathered from storage mechanisms residing in the back-end. Perl was identified as the perfect tool to return data found from either files or real databases, wrapped with HTML tags, back to the WEB browser of the user originating the call. While the CGI-Perl pair suffers from extremely limited scalability, it has been, and still is, the typical "quick-and-dirty" solution, an inexpensive "patch" to provide WEB enabled publishing of information through the HTTP protocol.

Soon after the appearance of Perl on the IT scene, almost spontaneously Perl extensions were born, to give Perl programs access to the most popular relational engines. The most successful attempt to extend Perl to integrate it with Oracle was OraPerl, a stable and widely used too that allows for a high degree of interaction with Oracle. The problem with this approach was that each interface to a different relational back-end engine had been implemented slightly differently, forcing developers to produce specialized Perl source code for each supported database. To overcome this problem, a new project was started, to specify and build a common interface, sharable among all relational engines, which uses specific modules plugged behind the common library of calls to interface to each different relational engine. The project shipped DBI, which stands for **D**ata**B**ase **I**nterface, providing a common API between applications and relational engines. In order to work, the DBI needs the corresponding DBD (**D**ata**B**ase **D**river) module, which implements each DBI call within the context of the target relational engine.

If OraPerl is used to connect to an Oracle instance, opening a cursor and fetching data before closing the cursor, the following calls will appear in the source code:

```
$lda = &ora_login($system_id, $name, $password)
$csr = &ora_open($lda, $stmt [, $cache])
&ora_bind($csr, $var, ...)
&ora_fetch($csr [, $trunc])
&ora_close($csr)
```

Each call is not only characterized by the ora prefix, but also works in an Oracle context solely. A DBI/DBD-based solution is much more flexible, because the same set of DBI calls would work against different relational engines, provided that the right DBD module is chosen at run-time. The following example uses the DBI interface to connect to an Oracle database, using the canonical scott/tiger account, initially performing a singleton select and then opening a cursor, fetching all rows from the EMP table where EMPNO is greater than 7800.

```
!/usr/local/bin/perl
use DBI;

# connect to the database

$dbh = DBI->connect("dbi:Oracle:ORCL", scott, tiger,
{
        PrintError=> 0,
        AutoCommit => 0
});
# Get one row
@row_ary = $dbh->selectrow_array("select * from emp where rownum = 1");

print "@row_ary\n\n"

# Open a cursor and fetch multiple rows
# the question mark represents a positional bind variable

  my $sth = $dbh->prepare(q
        {
        select * from emp where empno > ?
        }
        ) || die $dbh->errstr;
# Bind the question mark to a value and execute the query
  $sth->execute(7800) || die $dbh->errstr;

# fetch the rows
  while (@row = $sth->fetchrow_array)
  {     print "@row\n";
  }
```

Note that the database calls are now "engine agnostics", very generic and reusable across different database platforms.

Perl offers interesting and extremely powerful capabilities, such as associative arrays, very useful when used to access data stored in Oracle tables.

Summary

This chapter discussed noncanonical means of extraction/insertion of data from/into Oracle databases. Initially, database pipes and alerts have been examined, and their functionality explored, identifying practical and common problems and application situations where pipes and alerts can be proficiently used. A freely available package, PLEX, which is based upon pipes and alerts, has been introduced to demonstrate a sophisticated use of such functionality.

Oracle8 introduced Advanced Queuing, which allows for the implementation of the disconnected/deferred communication paradigm. Oracle8i enhanced several of the AQ features, which have been discussed in the section dedicated to Oracle AQ. The same section examined the Publish-and-Subscribe communication paradigm, made available for the first time by Oracle8i.

Finally, the discussion focused on the interaction between Perl and Oracle, examining two interfaces widely used and freely available from the WEB.

Chapter 16

COMMUNICATING WITH THE SERVER

This chapter will discuss popular solutions for Oracle database connectivity, starting with Oracle SQL*Net/Net8, still the most common means used to access data stored in Oracle databases, and continuing with other, less popular but nevertheless important connectivity alternatives. SQL*Net/Net8 is not always the only or the best networking solution. Sometimes middleware-based implementations are more in line with business requirements, or corporate policy prevents an SQL*Net/Net8 adoption.

16.1 SQL*Net/Net8: The Main Road To Connect to an Oracle Server

SQL*Net/Net8 has historically been the preferred vehicle for client connectivity to Oracle instances running on remote servers. Net8 is a mature, robust, and secure product, which represents a natural evolution from SQL*Net 2.4. In order to keep pace with the Oracle server increased scalability, Net8 has been enhanced to allow a greater number of user connections. In particular, three features have been implemented in the Oracle networking architecture to increase the number of concurrent connections:

- Connection Manager's Connection Concentration
- Connection Pooling
- Listener Load Balancing

The Oracle Connection Manager, a software layer that must be configured and enabled on the server, makes use of multiplexing techniques to combine the network traffic from several or many clients onto a single physical network connection to the server.

Connection pooling allows a limited number of physical, transport-level connections to be shared among a greater number of logical network connections. This occurs by temporarily releasing idle transport connections while maintaining their network sessions. The release of the single transport connection can happen only if it has been idle long enough to reach a preconfigured time-out, all the transport connections in the pool are busy, and an additional network session requests a transport connection.

The main difference between connection concentration operated by the connection manager and connection pooling is that with the latter, an idle client that loses a transport connection can incur the risk of waiting for a different transport connection to become available when it resumes its activity. With connection concentration, a client connection is maintained continuously. Connection pooling is therefore adequate for applications where most of the user time is spent looking at the screen to analyze and interpret the output of a query that returns the expected results. Connection concentration is more suitable where the data flow between clients and the servers is continuous, such as in process control and batch uploading.

Listener load balancing can occur either on the client side, where one listener is chosen randomly from a list of listeners all connecting to the same data source, or on the server side, where active listeners can take their routing decisions based on the current load on each instance dispatcher.

The three features described above are supported only when the Multi-Threaded Server (MTS) option is enabled. MTS concepts and architecture have been discussed in Section 4.4—Design for Scalability. The current direction taken by Oracle Corporation towards database connectivity represents a push to always implement the MTS option on all massively accessed databases, enabling a few selected connections to be dedicated instead of shared. Dedicated connections can be enabled by setting an appropriate parameter in the tnsnames.ora file—(connect_data=(server=dedicated))—and should be used to perform all administrative tasks on the database, and whenever SQL tracing is enabled to capture statement statistics using TKPROF. If SQL tracing is turned on while using a shared connection, the statistics for a single SQL statement can be scattered across several trace files, making its interpretation very hard, if not impossible. Additionally, a dedicated server connection is required if the connected client issues calls to external procedures.

If an MTS configuration cannot be enabled, there is still something that can be done to improve connectivity for a large user population. An adequate number of dedicated server processes can be prespawned by the listener,[1] so that each

[1] This feature is not supported under MS Windows NT.

new connection request can be served immediately without incurring the overhead of a process creation. Furthermore, it is possible to increase the queue size for the Net8 listeners, to allow a greater number of connections to be put on hold while the listener is creating a connection. The requests are served by the listener on a FIFO basis. If multiple connection requests hit the listener concurrently, they are queued until the listener becomes available. If the number of concurrent requests exceeds the queue size, Net8 will refuse to serve the exceeding connections, which will receive an ORA-12541 error, "No Listener". The queue size default can be increased while defining the listener parameters in the listener.ora file.

The latest releases of SQL*Net and Net8 provide an API called SQL*Net OPEN or Net8 OPEN, which allows developers to use the SQL*Net/Net8 infrastructure in networked applications. The API provides very basic services, just enough to allow for simple communication. The only possible "customization" left to developers is to set the blocking or nonblocking mode of the connection. While Net8 OPEN cannot be used for complex networked applications, it is useful for simple tasks to be performed in environments where SQL*Net/Net8 is already deployed and part of the corporate network infrastructure. The API consists of five calls, as shown in the following table.

NET8 OPEN CALL	PARAMETERS	PURPOSE
TNSOPEN	`void **HandlePtr, const char *Name`	Initializes the Net8 OPEN API per-connection handle
TNSCLOSE	`void **HandlePtr`	Shuts down the connection
TNSSEND	`void *HandlePtr, const void *Data, size_t *Length`	Sends data to the Net8 connection handle
TNSRECV	`void *HandlePtr, const void *Data, size_t *Length`	Receives data from the Net8 connection handle
TNSCONTROL	`void * HandlePtr, int *Command`	Sets the connection to blocking or nonblocking mode

It should be noted that the TNSOPEN() call is a misnomer, because it only initializes the environment and returns a connection handle, but it doesn't establish a connection. This is done by TNSSEND() or TNSRECV(), which must follow a TNSOPEN() call in the program flow.

A client/server application that uses the Net8 OPEN API must follow the Net8 model, where a service is executed by a listener when a client requests a connection. The server program will be given a TNS name, and an appropriate entry will be set in the listener configuration file. For example, if a server program that has been coded using the Net8 OPEN APIs resides in an executable called, say, *FirstExample*, the following entry will appear in listener.ora:

```
FirstExample=
(DESCRIPTION=
(ADDRESS=(PROTOCOL=tcp)(HOST=echidna)(PORT=1521)
)
(CONNECT_DATA=(service_name=FirstExample)))
```

Accordingly, the local naming configuration file, e.g. tnsnames.ora, will set an entry as follows:

```
FirstExample=
(DESCRIPTION=
(ADDRESS=(PROTOCOL=tcp)(HOST=echidna)(PORT=1521)
)
(CONNECT_DATA-(SID= FirstExample)))
```

In order for Net8 to locate the FirstExample executable image, it should be put in the same directory as the other Oracle executables, for example, in $ORACLE_HOME/bin.

16.2 When SQL*Net Is Not To Be Used

In a corporate environment, where preexisting policies must be followed and disparate software and hardware platforms must coexist and strict control must be centrally enforced, there are circumstances under which SQL*Net/Net8, in spite of its scalability and robustness, cannot be used. For example, IT policies enforced by a company can dictate that all distributed applications must be implemented using DCE RPC. While the Advanced Networking Option, an optional component of the SQL*Net/Net8 architecture, can delegate sign-on security to DCE and enable the use of Oracle tools transparently in DCE environments, sometimes this is not enough to convince IT technical managers to allow the use of SQL*Net/Net8.

Another common obstacle to the adoption of SQL*Net/Net8 is represented by political decisions that strive to avoid imposing Oracle technologies in environments where Oracle is not the preferred architecture, yet some level of integration must be provided. The use of a "neutral" plumbing technology between Oracle and a different database, perhaps based on RPC calls, can be endorsed to avoid conflicts where a team without any previous exposure to the Oracle architecture is requested to exchange data with an Oracle database interactively. Instead of imposing an SQL*Net/Net8-based solution, which would imply a retraining of the IT personnel not familiar with Oracle, instituting an RPC-based solution can ensure a smooth integration, it being a sort of *lingua franca* between the two different worlds.

16.2.1 SQL*NET ALTERNATIVES

Middleware products generally use a proprietary network layer to implement communication services between clients and servers. Transarc Encina, a TP monitor that is built on top of the DCE infrastructure, represents a notable exception to this rule. In both cases, however, the Oracle proprietary networking environment is not used in conjunction with middleware products. When neither middleware software nor SQL*Net/Net8 is used, popular alternatives are RPC (or RPC-based) solutions or straight TCP/IP sockets.

16.2.1.1 Remote Procedure Call The basic idea behind RPC is to allow clients to execute procedures on other networked computers—thus remote procedures—while hiding as much as possible from developers the complexity of network programming, making a remote procedure call look similar to a local procedure invocation. The pioneer of this technology has been Sun Microsystems, which released the first RPC standard (ONC RPC). The other, more widely adopted RPC standard, is OSF/DCE RPC, which appeared later but conquered a broader support from the industry.

An essential component of an RPC-based architecture is the protocol compiler, which accepts C-like syntax and generates client and server stubs, plus data representation filters, which are used to implement data marshalling for the messages being transferred.

A common scenario occurring in environments where data residing in a remote Oracle database is fetched by a local application that doesn't use the Oracle proprietary network layer can be described as follows:

- The client program issues a remote call passing a pointer to a structure used to represent a row in an Oracle table.
- A daemon running on the server receives the call and triggers a procedure that connects directly to Oracle, fetches the wanted data, formats it into the received structure, and returns control to the caller.
- The client, which was blocked during the execution of the remote procedure, regains control and continue its processing, including the data just fetched from Oracle in its computations.

Client programs can use RPC directly, implementing RPC and data marshalling calls in the source code. Alternatively, they can use RPC-based high-level development environments, where robust and complex RPC services are already implemented and available in the form of APIs. A popular RPC-based environment is Entera, a product by Inprise, which provides RPC-based middleware services, suitable for implementation of three-tier applications.

16.2.1.2 Straight Sockets There are situations where one would really like to use SQL*Net/Net8, but the platform is not supported by Oracle. This often happens with embedded systems and Programmable Logic Controllers (PLC) that supervise, for instance, laboratory equipment, medical devices, or industrial machinery. These devices are usually optimized for data acquisition, but do not offer good storage capabilities. In these cases, when a TCP/IP implementation is available, a socket server can be implemented on the machine where the Oracle instance resides, able to connect to the database and store into an Oracle table the data sampled by the external devices and transmitted through TCP/IP sockets.

The Oracle performance monitoring tool that will be presented further ahead in this book uses this technique to achieve maximum openness and independence from Oracle proprietary or third party protocols. The server daemon uses the OCI interface and connects to the Oracle instance being monitored either directly or via SQL*Net, if available. The Java client connects to the server daemon via sockets, requesting instance statistics and displaying sampled data in a WEB browser. A workstation running the BE OS[2] can be used to monitor one or more Oracle instances even if Oracle doesn't include the BE operating system among the supported platforms.

16.3 Middleware and ACID Messages

Very large applications occasionally challenge even the more advanced scalability and security features built in the Oracle RDBMS and SQL*Net/Net8. Highly transactional OLTP applications, such as financial systems including Automatic Teller Machines (ATM) and airline ticketing systems, are based upon a huge number of small transactions, each as large as a few hundred bytes, consistently and continuously updating a large back-end database. It is not uncommon to support 20 or 30 thousand devices concurrently connected to the back-end system. Such large number of concurrent connections requires the implementation of solutions based on middleware software, such as TP monitors or Message-Oriented Middleware (MOM) products. The industry standard TPC-C benchmark, frequently released by software and hardware vendors, makes a consistent use of TP monitors to achieve the best possible cost per transaction, together with the best throughput.

TP monitors not only increase by an order of magnitude the number of concurrent connections, but also allow for a much improved security, by de-coupling presentation logic from data gathering and business logic. Client applications

---

[2]In 1990, Jean-Louis Gassée, former president of Apple's product division, formed Be, Inc. to build a personal computer based on new assumptions, using cutting edge software design concepts not crippled by compatibility issues with old operating systems and architectures. The result is a revolutionary operating system that supports PowerPC and Intel chips and redefines usability standards for personal computers and workstations. BE OS release 4 is the current version at the moment of this writing.

don't connect directly to the back-end database but to TP services that control operating system access and database connections in a strictly secure manner.

Alternatively, when MOM products are used, client applications communicate to servers using queues, where messages in both senses of communication can be assessed and verified before business logic is applied to their content. In both cases, security can be enforced in the middle tier (or tiers), greatly enhancing the capability of defense against intruders and impersonators.

16.3.1 MIDDLEWARE PARADIGMS

While the classical two-tier client-server configuration is based on a synchronous, request/response model, a more complex configuration, which relies on middleware technologies, can incorporate several cooperating communication paradigms in one application. There is no unanimously accepted classification that clearly states characteristics and boundaries of communication paradigms. Nevertheless, analyzing the features available in commercially released middleware products such as BEA Systems TUXEDO and Transarc Encina, we can identify at least four major communication models

1. Request/Response
2. Conversation based
3. Queue based
4. Event based

The request/response model is still the backbone upon which most interactive applications rely to exchange data between server(s) and clients. According to this communication paradigm, there are two parts involved in the software contract. One is the client, which usually originates the request, and the other is the server, which usually responds to the client's request by providing the requested services. This type of communication is fundamentally synchronous, meaning that the client, after having submitted a request, blocks until the response arrives. If the network is overloaded, or if Oracle is busy serving hundreds of clients, the user of the application can experience a frustrating delay between the submission of the request and the arrival of the response.

If the client is GUI based, the user will most probably see an hourglass or a watch instead of a mouse pointer for a while, until the form is filled with data gathered from the server. Nothing else can be done with the application but wait. In its purest form, the request/response model is *stateless*. The client submits a request, and the server responds and cleans up all memory structures associated with the routine that did the job. No state is maintained through calls, and each new invocation of a service by a client is treated as an atomic, self-contained and independent unit of work. This model is effective in most circumstances and is linearly scalable, meaning that it is sufficient to increase the number of servers to accommodate a larger user base originating a higher volume of transactions.

Sometimes, business requirements dictate different arrangements, where the interactions between client and server must maintain state information throughout the lifetime of the communication. While the basic paradigm is still of the request/response type, the further complication of maintaining state information between calls is significant enough to originate a separate paradigm, called conversation-based communication.

In a stateless request/response environment, different servers can respond to the same request submitted in different moments by a client. Most middleware products provide dynamic load balancing; that is, several server processes are pre-spawned and waiting for requests by the clients. The same request originated from client A can be responded to by server X at 11:25 AM and by server Y at 11:26 AM, depending on how busy the servers are at each moment. In other words, it is the TP monitor that determines which server process is the best choice to carry on the task of responding to a client, based on the load on the system.

With a conversation-based communication, the client interacts with the same server process for the entire duration of the communication. The server process becomes "dedicated" to the client that originated the conversation. The transaction flow is bi-directional, meaning that client and server can potentially exchange several or many messages, originating a complex dialogue that requires state information to be kept across the entire duration of the conversation.

The scalability of such a model is severely limited, because one server process can be "monopolized" by a client for a few minutes. During this time, no other client can utilize the services provided by the server process. If not enough conversational servers have been pre-spawned at application start-up, additional clients requesting the same service will be put in queue, until one conversational server becomes available; this can take several minutes. Even if the number of servers can be dynamically increased by the TP monitor to satisfy an exceptional volume of conversational requests, the time required to spawn a process, and the resource consumption associated with it, would adversely impact the overall application performance.

For these reasons, designers and architects of middleware based applications tend to minimize the use of conversation-based paradigms. While the classical request/response model and its major variation, the conversation-based communication model, are essentially synchronous, the queue-based model introduces an asynchronous communication flow between clients and servers.

Many business practices follow a queue-based approach. Consider the processing of orders placed by the company's salespersons in the "IN" box of the order-processing department. A common arrangement is to have several employees check each order for completeness and consistency, and to pass the successfully checked orders to other employees of the same department, for further processing. Every morning the employees of the order-processing department will find a pile of orders accumulated by the salespersons during the business hours of the preceding day. An inconsistent order is put in a specific box, where it joins other inconsistent orders, forming the "pile" of rejected orders. Other employees will process the rejected orders, contacting the customers in order to sort out all discrepancies.

The important aspect of the workflow above presented is that the single order is not processed *immediately* (as soon as the customer through the salesperson issues it). There is a *lag time* between the moment the order is taken by the salesperson and the moment the order is processed by the appropriate department. The order is created and *queued* and its processing postponed to a later moment. Somewhere along the order processing chain, somebody will *de-queue* the order for its assessment.

Application queues are the IT equivalent of the plastic boxes where the order forms are accumulated in piles. Appending a message to a queue is a question of a few milliseconds. The application that queues the message regains control of the processing flow in almost no time, and is free to go on with other tasks. The processing of the message occurs at a later time, and if one de-queuing process cannot keep up with the workload originated by the number of messages accumulated in the queue, other de-queuing processes can be spawned, to parallelize the de-queuing of the messages. Needless to say, this model offers excellent scalability.

The fourth communication paradigm examined in this section is the event-based model. This model is used when business events, which have the characteristics of being *unsolicited*, must be captured by the application, which must react to the event occurred either by modifying its behavior or by applying specific business logic. A classical example of such an occurrence is the unsolicited event that is triggered by the price of a stock that falls below a predetermined value in a stock market application. This event can happen at any time, and the application must react quickly when the event occurs, but the application is not waiting for the event to happen.

An application that wants to be alerted when a specific event occurs registers its interest with the application supervisor, usually a TP monitor. In most cases, the application provides the supervisor with the address of a callback function that will be called upon the occurrence of the unsolicited event.

In its simplest incarnation, the event-based model involves a single program being notified about the occurrence of an event. Sometimes business requirements are more complex and require a more sophisticated event-based implementation. Two common extensions to the basic model are the ability for the server to alert a predetermined set of clients when the triggering events occur, and the ability to post brokered events to programs interested in being notified upon the occurrence of the events.

The main advantage of the latter model is the complete de-coupling of the originator of the brokered message from the clients that will be alerted. In other words, the application that detects the triggering event and signals the occurrence of the event to the clients interested doesn't need to know the addressees of the alerting message. This is the major difference from the other forms of event-based communication.

When a single program wants to be notified if a specific event occurs, it registers the callback function with the application supervisor. The application supervisor uniquely identifies the client by the means of a client identifier, which represents the address for the notification. When a set of clients must be notified of the occurrence of an event, the program that detects the triggering event broadcasts the alerting message to a set of clients identified by a collective name. This can be a computer name if all clients running on that machine must be notified, or a group name that includes clients based on a business criterion (for example the Accountancy Department, AcctDept).

When brokered events are used, all clients interested in being notified when a specific event occurs *subscribe* to the event. The application program that either detects or triggers the well-known event simply "posts" the occurrence of the event to the application supervisor. It doesn't know how many or which clients will receive the notification. Only the ones that subscribed to the event will be notified. Note that it is possible for a client to subscribe to an event and to unsubscribe at a later stage, if they are not interested any more in the event for which they initially subscribed. The subscriber population, for any given event, is not fixed, but can vary constantly. Only the subscribers that are in the list at the moment of the dispatching of the posted event will be notified.

This form of event-based communication is also called "Publish-and-Subscribe" or "Push Technology" and is most indicated where a single business event triggers multiple events, or interests multiple business agents who must promptly react to unsolicited events. When the application logic is distributed across different computers participating in networks of complex topology, it is important to ensure transactional integrity for each unit of work.

It is important to ensure database consistency at any one time, even if the message that changes the final state of the database is handled by several or many distinct software modules. The classical example is the debit transaction, which must have a corresponding credit counterpart. If an application successfully debits an account but the transaction fails before crediting the target account, the money involved in the operation "vanishes in the ether," leaving the database in an inconsistent state. Conversely, if the crediting half of the transaction succeeds, but the debiting half fails, the money involved in the operation "materializes from the ether," with the net effect of leaving an inconsistent database and an unhappy IT department that must justify financial losses to the board of management of the bank.

To be considered secure, transactions must comply with requirements that are summarized in the ACID acronym, which stands for:

- Atomic—The transaction will complete successfully either in all the nodes participating in the distributed database or in none.

- ❑ Consistent—The transaction will always produce the same results if applied more than once (that is, must be consistently reproducible).
- ❑ Isolated—The view of the data across the entire distributed database at the moment of the transaction must be protected from changes until the transaction has completed across all the nodes.
- ❑ Durable—Once committed, the data updated or appended through the transaction becomes secure.

While ACID messages are relatively easy to implement using a request/response or a conversational paradigm, the effort required from TP monitor vendors and application developers who want to extend the ACID characteristics to messages participating in message queues or "publish and subscribe" paradigms is by far more demanding.

16.3.2 BEA SYSTEMS TUXEDO

The history of TUXEDO goes back to 1983, when the Bell Laboratories Division of AT&T began a project called UNITS (Unix Transaction System). Initially, UNITS was intended as an internal project, supporting Unix-based operations such as LMOS, one of the first successful AT&T projects to start the "down-sizing" wave of the IT industry. The UNITS research group produced DUX (Database for Unix), and TUX (Transactions for Unix), never to be sold commercially. Ideas and concepts from DUX and TUX were subsequently merged into a transaction-enabled client-server framework, initially distributed with the AT&T 3B24000 computer. One of the principal architects of the 3B2 coined the name "TUXEDO", stating that the new framework was "TUX **E**xtended for **D**istributed **O**perations." Since 1989 TUXEDO, has been sold commercially under the name of "The TUXEDO System." By the end of the 1990s, most TPC benchmarks were conducted by database vendors using TUXEDO as a TP monitor, a clear indicator of its recognized leadership in the transaction oriented middleware market for mid-range systems. The TUXEDO system not only supports all middleware paradigms, but it also implements interesting variations and extensions. In order to understand and appreciate the implementation of middleware concepts and ACID properties in TUXEDO, we have to familiarize ourselves with the TUXEDO terminology.

ATMI	Application-to-Transaction Monitor Interface: The TUXEDO communications application programming interface
FML	Field Manipulation Language: An interface for maintaining buffers with field/value pairs

Service	Application routine that performs operations on behalf of requesting clients
Server	Software module that groups services together, accepting requests from clients and returning replies
TMIB	TUXEDO Management Information Base: A collection of application objects definitions available in the form of a centrally located application repository
Transaction Bracketing	The act of delimiting the boundaries of a transaction
Transaction Infection	The passing of transaction properties from one module to another
Transaction Initiator	The application module that begins a transaction
Transaction Terminator	The application module that concludes a transaction
Transaction Coordinator	The role played by the module that supervises the executions of the commitment algorithm
Two-phase Commit, Presumed Abort (2PC-PA)	Algorithm used by TUXEDO to ensure the atomicity of a transaction occurring under TUXEDO's control
Typed Buffer	A memory area allocated by TUXEDO that has as associated data type and a subtype
VIEW	A specific typed buffer that is similar to a "C" structure or a COBOL record
XA	The X/Open Transaction Manager to Resource Manager interface

For the purpose of being interoperable with DCE, TUXEDO offers an RPC-based interface, called TxRPC, which won't be discussed in this section. We will focus on the ATMI interface instead, as it is the most popular way to implement an application built using the TUXEDO infrastructure. Before delving into the ATMI support for middleware paradigms, we present an overview of the TUXEDO architecture.

One of the simplest definitions of the TUXEDO System is that it is a *Service Request Broker*. The TUXEDO infrastructure provides the means for routing, dispatching, managing, and monitoring of service requests, event posting and receiving and queue enqueuing and dequeuing submitted by applications using TUXEDO services.

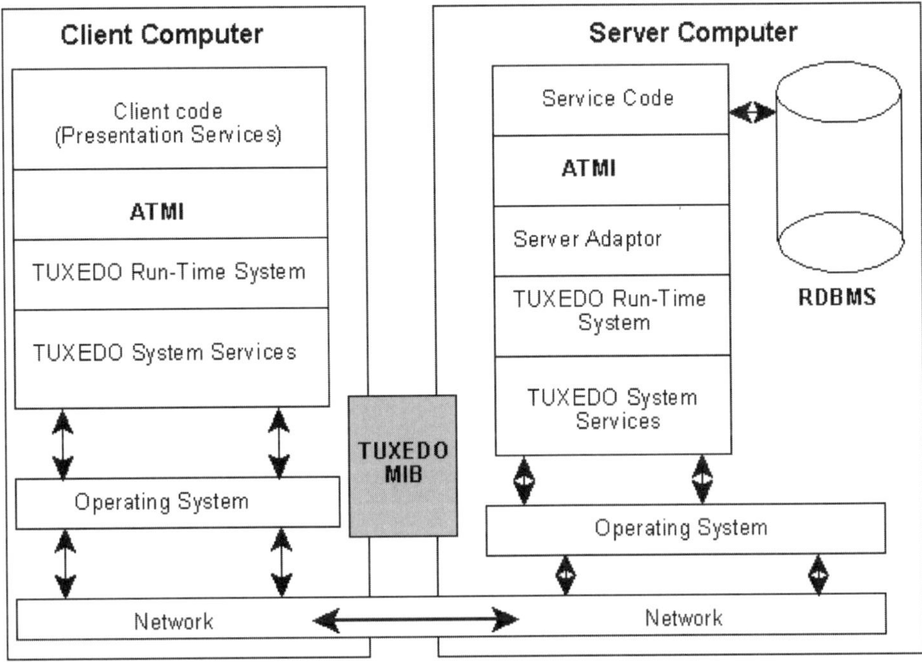

FIGURE 16.1 The TUXEDO System Architecture (*Source*: Adapted from "The TUXEDO System" *Andrade* et al, Addison Wesley, 1996.)

Developers using TUXEDO don't deal directly with low-level networking protocols or data marshaling and unmarshaling routines. They are free to concentrate on application issues, being relieved from the burden of protocol implementation, network programming, and data conversion between computers of different architectures.

Through the ATMI, the TUXEDO System exposes a set of simple but powerful APIs, easily understood and used by developers who must implement three-tier applications. TUXEDO is also highly configurable, providing a set of APIs for application administration and tuning, which allows for real-time adjustment and reallocation of resources while the application is running, without disrupting the normal functionality visible to the users who interact with the system.

16.3.2.1 The TUXEDO MIB In the TUXEDO architecture the TMIB plays a crucial role. The TMIB stores a classification of all distributed objects participating in an application. The TMIB is composed by classes carrying a set of attributes that describe the properties of all managed objects, under the control of the TUXEDO system. Accessor functions (a set of get and set methods) are provided to administrators for attribute querying and modifying. The TMIB can be seen as a virtual database that ensures several types of transparency, greatly simplifying client/server programming by de-coupling client from server logic and by hiding information that is not to be shared across different objects, to avoid introducing unnecessary dependencies among software modules. The TMIB provides:

- *Location Transparency*—Objects participating in a TUXEDO application never refer to each other using fixed or predetermined locations. A service advertises its presence and ability to process requests through the TMIB. Clients requesting its services know only the service name. TUXEDO administrators can decide to move heavily accessed services to different hardware without modifying client code to achieve that.
- *Network Transparency*—TUXEDO clients are able to run from workstations using different network protocols such as Novell IPX or TCP/IP. TUXEDO servers can be implemented in heterogeneous environments, using Unix systems connected to IBM mainframes via SNA L.U.62. ASCII to EBCDIC conversion and byte ordering conversion between little-endian and big-endian machines[3] are taken care of by TUXEDO; developers don't have to worry about network protocols and data conversion. They simply use a consistent set of APIs across all developed modules.
- *Implementation Transparency*—Clients requesting services don't know the implementation details of the servers offering the services. Implementation can change on the server side without modifying the client code, as long as the interface (or the software contract) between the client and the server doesn't change.
- *Administration Transparency*—Business logic and application functioning are totally de-coupled from system administration. Key aspects of an application can be dynamically changed not only without modifying the source code, but in many cases while the application is up and running. While load balancing is automatically performed by TUXEDO, administrators monitoring an application can decide to re-locate heavily accessed modules to under-utilized servers. Using TMIB API calls, it is possible to change the configuration of TUXEDO objects on the fly, modifying the physical structure of the services offered by the system while preserving its logical configuration. The best example of administration transparency is data-dependent

[3] Little-endian machines store two-byte integers with the least significant byte first, followed by the most significant byte. Big-endian machines store the most significant byte first, followed by the least significant byte. Most Unix machines are big-endian, while most PC-based architectures follow a little-endian convention. When a stream of bytes is transferred over the network from, say, a little-endian machine to a big-endian machine, the data must be converted (i.e., the bytes must be swapped).

routing. This feature makes it possible to dispatch requests to specific servers according to the content of selected fields in the message being sent from the client.

16.3.2.2 TUXEDO Servers and Services A typical TUXEDO application comprises client modules that request services from server modules. A TUXEDO server is a collection of services. Each service is a routine that performs an atomic unit of work. A service can carry out its entire task in absolute isolation and return the result to the client. Alternatively, it can use other services to complete its task. Let us consider the following example. A client module displays selected departments from the DEPT table of the SCOTT schema, for instance, the ones located in New York. A service is available to accomplish this task, named *"GetSelectedDepts"*. This service is included in the *"Department"* server, which groups together all department-related services. The client module invokes an ATMI function, say TPCALL, passing through the service name, an input buffer, its length, an output buffer, and its length and a flag field. The input buffer stores the parameter for the request "New York" to fetch only those departments located in New York. The output buffer is empty and will be filled by the "GetSelectedDepts" service. The client calls are shown in the example below.

```
1: FBFR *inBuff;
2: FBFR *outBuff;
3: long outLen;
4: char *szInDept="NEW YORK";
5: inBuff = (FBFR *)tpalloc("FML",NULL,1024);
6: outBuff = (FBFR *) tpalloc("FML",NULL,2048);
7: Fadd(inBuff,DEPT_LOC,szInDept,(FLDLEN)0);
8: sts = tpcall("GetSelectedDepts", inBuff,0,
9:              &outBuff, &outLen,TPNOFLAGS);
```

At line 8, tpcall() invokes the GetSelectedDepts service. The client source is compiled and linked against the TUXEDO system, which provides libraries that resolve all TUXEDO symbols, such as tpalloc() and tpcall(). When the client program is executed, the tpcall() routine instructs the TUXEDO system to "find" the GetSelectedDepts service, which will presumably be available somewhere on the network. The TUXEDO system will look at the TMIB to locate and invoke the service, passing the required buffers to it. Since the service name resolution is performed at run-time each time a service is invoked from a client, the physical location of the service can vary while the application is running, provided that the TMIB advertises the new location. A TUXEDO administrator who wants to relocate the GetSelectedDepts from computer A to computer B will make sure that the server which includes GetSelectedDepts runs on computer B before decommissioning the service from computer A. For a short period of time, the service will be running on both computers to avoid having a client call failing because the service cannot be found anywhere.

The TUXEDO system performs a few significant operations when it resolves the service name. When the service name is found by scanning the TMIB, TUXEDO checks if data-dependent routing applies to the service in question. Let us imagine that in our implementation there are two servers offering the GetSelectedDepts service: the first resides in computer A, servicing all New York Department calls; the second resides in computer B, servicing all other requests. Using TMIB API calls, the TUXEDO administrator has instructed the TUXEDO system to perform data-dependent routing when the GetSelectedDepts is invoked, considering the content of the DEPT_LOC field in the buffer passed to the service. TUXEDO then evaluates the content of the field and dispatches the call to the service running on computer A if "New York" has been set in the input buffer. Alternatively, the server running on computer B serves the client-originated request.

After having evaluated data-dependent routing logic, TUXEDO performs dynamic load balancing, dispatching the request to the server that appears to be less busy at the moment of the service name resolution. The UBBCONFIG file, which is the initialization file read by the TUXEDO System at startup, sets a maximum number of servers and services that TUXEDO is allowed to spawn to serve requests originated by clients. The default values determined at startup can be overridden at run-time by TUXEDO administrators, who can intervene to fix application bottlenecks by allowing more servers to be spawned, possibly dedicating more resources to the running application.

Another benefit implicitly provided by the TUXEDO architecture is connection pooling. Only the servers need to be connected to the database; the clients submitting requests are not physically connected to the database serving the requests. When TUXEDO is used together with Oracle, the clients are not connected to the database via SQL*Net/Net8. TUXEDO provides the protocol independent network layer used for data gathering by the clients. The servers can be connected to Oracle either directly or via SQL*Net, performing all database operations and passing the data fetched from Oracle tables to the requesting clients through TUXEDO buffers. Connection pooling allows many clients to efficiently share one physical connection to Oracle, expanding *de facto* the potential user population by an order of magnitude for highly interactive OLTP applications.

16.3.2.3 Data Conversion The TUXEDO System hides data conversion and data marshaling from developers. This is achieved through the Field Manipulation Language (FML), a set of APIs dedicated to message composing, formatting and retrieving. Most ATMI routines send and receive messages, or typed buffers, which carry requests for data on the way in, and data gathered from the resource managers on the back-end, typically databases, on the way out. These messages are buffers containing fields that cannot be directly accessed by application code. To store and retrieve values from the buffers used by ATMI calls, the FML APIs must be used. If we consider the example shown above, specifically lines 5-7, we can see that an ATMI routine (tpalloc()) is used to allocate two buffers and one FML routine (Fadd()) is used to populate one buffer with a value previously stored in the szInDept variable.

```
5: inBuff = (FBFR *)tpalloc("FML",NULL,1024);
6: outBuff = (FBFR *) tpalloc("FML",NULL,2048);
7: Fadd(inBuff,DEPT_LOC,szInDept,(FLDLEN)0);
```

Fadd() adds a new field value to a fielded buffer. More APIs are provided to retrieve a value from a fielded buffer, such as Fget(), or to change a value stored in a fielded buffer, such as Fchg(). Note that adding a value twice for the same field doesn't return an error, but stores a second occurrence of the same field. This characteristic makes it possible to store multiple rows in one fielded buffer. Needless to say, FML APIs are provided to find the number of occurrences of each field stored in the buffer, so that the receiving routine can loop through the fields fetching all values contained in the buffer.

FML provides a significant contribution for achieving data independence. It ensures that a message will be read at destination no matter what byte-storing convention applies to the sending and receiving computers. Furthermore, when a message is shared across several modules, the number of fields contained in the message can vary without forcing a recompilation of the source code of all modules using the buffer. Consider a message containing customer data that is initialized by a client and then passed to service A to be populated with information fetched from the application database. To accomplish this, other services are invoked from service A, say services B and C.

According to the initial design, the application doesn't make use of the customer's date of birth, so the message passed from the client to all services needed to populate the buffer doesn't contain any reference to a date of birth field. Subsequently, business rules change, and the customer's date of birth becomes necessary to compute the risk coefficient associated with the customer, which was initially arbitrarily assigned by a manager. The client application displays the risk coefficient, which must now be derived from an equation that includes a field that is not part of the message.

The client dialogs with service A, passing a TUXEDO buffer to it. Service A invokes service B, which in the revised edition fetches the date of birth from the database, appending a new field to the message being passed to service C, which now computes the risk coefficient. The message is passed back to service A and then back to the client. To introduce the new business rule to the system, the client software doesn't need to be modified or recompiled, as it already displayed the risk coefficient. Service A doesn't need to be modified or recompiled, as it doesn't know about the date of birth. Only services B and C must be changed to deal with the new field. Accessing data through APIs rather than directly allows for greater flexibility, as the message can be extended without causing a recompilation of all modules accessing it.

While FML is the preferred method to build, transfer and receive messages, TUXEDO also supports VIEW typed buffers, which are "C" structures or COBOL records that can be used as an alternative to FML. Buffers suffer from a few restrictions, for instance, a VIEW cannot be nested in a parent VIEW, and a VIEW cannot contain arrays of structures or pointers. The purpose of these restrictions is to guarantee that a conversion between VIEWS and FML records and back will always be possible. VIEWS are TUXEDO built-in typed buffers, and they provide a simpler and less verbose mechanism for message handling in TUXEDO applications.

The low-level TUXEDO primitives all use FML buffers, but application programmers can define and use VIEWS, which are kind of superimposed on FML buffers. Viewc, the VIEW compiler, takes an ASCII file that describes the VIEW names and their fields as its input, and produces a compiled version of the VIEW buffers plus a "C" header file or a COBOL copybook for inclusion in the application's source code. An FML API, Fvftos(), is used to convert an FML buffer into a "C" structure. Fvftos() takes three parameters: a pointer to an FML buffer, a pointer to the "C" structure defined in the header file produced by the VIEW compiler, and a pointer to a string containing the VIEW name. The Fvstof() API provides the interface for the opposite conversion, from a "C" structure to an FML typed buffer. The advantage of using VIEWs is that an entire buffer is converted by one call into a structure directly accessible by application code, and one call only is needed to reconvert back the data into the received FML buffer when the routine has finished its task. Less code is needed to access all fields in the buffer, and fewer function calls result in performance increase, especially for large buffers containing tens or hundreds of fields. The disadvantage associated with the use of VIEWs is reduced flexibility and a forced recompilation of all modules using the "C" structures or the COBOL copybooks if new fields must be added to the typed buffers used by the application.

16.3.2.4 The TUXEDO Architecture While the TUXEDO System is sold as a single unit (with a few add-ons), it can be subdivided into a few major components. They are:

1. TUXEDO System/T. The core component that provides the backbone of the entire system, and which supports the request/response and conversational communication paradigms, transaction handling and application administration.
2. TUXEDO /WS. Allowing for off-loading of core system capabilities to intelligent devices that participate in distributed applications, these devices can be personal computers, Unix/VMS workstations, or less sophisticated machines such as ATM or cash registers.

3. TUXEDO /Q. This component provides asynchronous message queuing, and store-and-forward capabilities to the system.
4. TUXEDO TxRPC. This component provides DCE interoperability and Remote Procedure Calls, according to the DCE and X/Open standards.

A typical application built upon the TUXEDO infrastructure will have the System/T component running on a few selected large servers (or at least one), a few clients running on the same computers, which carry out housekeeping and administrative tasks. A considerable number of clients running on computers that are physically separate from the main servers, each running the /WS configuration, will allow the application users to access the services provided by the system. It is likely that sophisticated applications will concurrently use several communication paradigms, such as request/response, store-and-forward, and publish-and-subscribe. The /Q (pronounce "slash queue") subsystem provides TUXEDO with an advanced message queuing implementation.

A client program can run on the server where the System/T is installed, or alternatively on a remote workstation where the /WS component provides the TUXEDO infrastructure.

A program designed to work in conjunction with TUXEDO must "join" the TUXEDO system, typically by issuing the ATMI call *tpinit()*. Each client is given a client identifier, used internally by TUXEDO to uniquely identify all programs participating in an application. Optionally, a client can be identified by providing a symbolic name, very useful for administrative purposes. The logical name can be used by TUXEDO administrators to pinpoint performance problems and to find out who is using system resources and how, possibly, to allocate or relocate more servers to increase the application's throughput.

16.3.2.5 TUXEDO Support for Middleware Paradigms TUXEDO supports the middleware paradigms illustrated in Section 16.3.1. It actually offers a few interesting extensions, such as an asynchronous request/response model, unsolicited message handling, and brokered event shipping to clients.

The "donkey work" in applications that use the services provided by a TP monitor is usually performed through a request/response model, where a client requests data from a server and blocks until all expected data is received. This is typical in applications used by operators who dialog with customers over a telephone line. The customer provides a unique identifier, say, the customer number or the social security number, and the operator inputs the number on a form. After a few seconds all customer-related details appear on the screen, and the operator can continue the conversation with the customer's having an exact idea of the customer financial or general situation. The TUXEDO ATMI offers 2 APIs to deal with this communication model.

ATMI CALL	PARAMETERS	PURPOSE
tpcall()	char * service_name, char * request_buffer, long request_buffer_length, char ** reply_buffer, long * reply_buffer_length, long TUXEDO_flags	Called by the client, invokes a TUXEDO service passing an input buffer and receiving an output buffer
tpreturn()	int return_value, long return_code, char * reply_buffer, long reply_buffer_length, long TUXEDO_flags	Called by the service, returns control to the calling client passing back an output buffer

Figure 16.2 illustrates how a client program interacts with a TUXEDO service using the synchronous request/response communication paradigm. Note that while the client calls tpcall() passing one request and one reply buffer, the service receives a structure of type TPSCVINFO, which wraps useful information around the user-provided request buffer.

The TPSCVINFO structure contains the client identifier, the service name, a flag field that can contains several options, a pointer to the input buffer, and a pointer to the long integer that holds the length in bytes of the input buffer. The output buffer is not passed to the remote service. The buffer containing the formatted data fetched by the service is returned to the TUXEDO system by the ser-

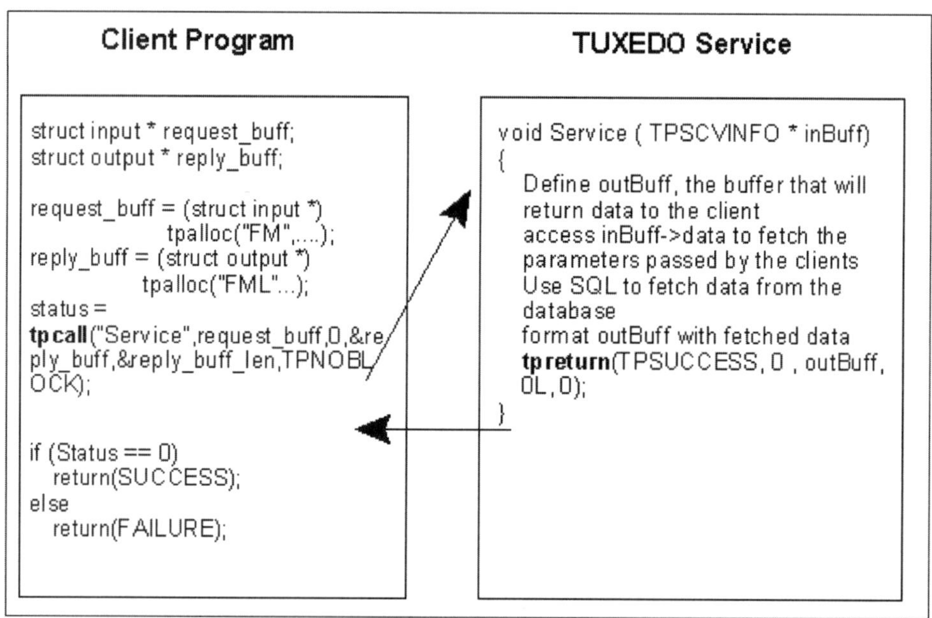

FIGURE 16.2 Request/Response model in TUXEDO

vice through the tpreturn() call. It is the TUXEDO infrastructure that will return the output buffer to the tpcall() routine.

TUXEDO also offers an asynchronous request/response model. As soon as the request is sent to the server, the control is given back to the application, which can continue processing while the requested service is activated on the back-end. The client can either block while waiting for the response from the server, or repeatedly check if a response is available, getting the control back each time and being able to process other requests in parallel.

The following APIs implement the asynchronous request/response model.

ATMI CALL	PARAMETERS	PURPOSE
tpacall()	char * service_name, char * request_buffer, long request_buffer_length, long TUXEDO_flags	calls a TUXEDO service asynchronously.
tpgetrply()	int * call_descriptor, char ** reply_buffer, long * reply_buffer_length, long TUXEDO_flags	gets either a specific reply from the TUXEDO queue, or any available reply if the TPGETANY flag is set.
tpcancel()	int call_descriptor	informs the TUXEDO system that the client is not interested any more in getting a reply.
tpforward()	char * TPSCVINFO, char *data, long data_length, long flags	forwards a client originated request to a different service.

tpacall() returns an integer, the *call descriptor*, which allows the client application to uniquely identify each asynchronous call. The call descriptor is used as a parameter to tpgetrply(), to specify what response the client is waiting for. tpgetrply() can be used in blocking mode, where the application waits until the required response is delivered, or in nonblocking mode, where the control is re-gained by the application if the required response is not yet available. The mode is controlled by the fourth parameter, TUXEDO_flags, which can be set to TPNOBLOCK, to specify a nonblocking mode, or TPNOTIME, to specify a blocking mode which is also immune from *blocking timeouts*. In TUXEDO, two types of time-out can occur. Configurable blocking timeouts make sure that an application doesn't wait indefinitely for something that never occurs. The control is given back to the client application when the time-out expires. The TPNOTIME flag overrides the standard behavior, and should be used carefully.

The second type is the so-called *transaction time-out*. Transaction timeouts occur even if the TPNOTIME flag is set. Transactions are by definition very resource-intensive, for instance, holding database locks until the ACID message has been check-pointed in a safe storage device. The time a transaction stays alive and active should be minimized as much as possible. If a transaction doesn't complete within a reasonably short interval of time, it should be aborted, to avoid dangerous deadlock situations.

A different flag, TPGETANY, is also allowed to appear in a tpgetrply() call. This flag allows for a sophisticated use of the asynchronous request/response model. TPGETANY forces tpgetrply() to ignore the call descriptor passed as the first parameter and return ANY reply available on the TUXEDO queue. TPGETANY can be optionally combined with the TPNOBLOCK flag to force a nonblocking behavior of tpgetrply(). The TPGETANY flag allows developers to use a very powerful technique, called *fan-out parallelism*, where a client submits several or many requests in rapid succession, processing the responses as soon as they are available, in a nonsequential manner.

TUXEDO also allows for a few variations on the request/response theme. For instance, a client calling tpacall() with the TPNOREPLY flag specifies that it is not waiting for any reply. Sending the message to the server can then become a triggering event for a server process. Alternatively, another ATMI call, tpforward() allows for pipelined parallelism, where a TUXEDO service initially called by a client "forwards" the request to a different, possibly more specialized service. A service can then act as a front-end dispatcher, rerouting the service requests coming from the clients according to specific business logic. This technique can be seen as a more sophisticated, application-specific form of data dependent routing. Note that the tpforward() first parameter is the TPSCVINFO structure, which contains all references to the client that originated the request. When the service that received the forwarded request issues a tpreturn() call, the TUXEDO system knows through the TPSCVINFO structure where to route the reply.

It has been said that the request/response model is essentially stateless. That is, no state is maintained between client and server calls. A service does its job in one round, fetches the required information, formats the data buffer to be sent to the client, and returns. All reference data, initialized variables, and results from the processing done while performing its task are lost when the service returns. TUXEDO automatically cleans up the buffers allocated through the tpalloc() ATMI call once the service has completed. The stateless nature of the request/response paradigm guarantees its extreme scalability. On a few occasions, however, this form of communication is not the most appropriate. There are instances where state information must be maintained during a prolonged conversation between a client and a service. A classical case is when a user of an application must be guaranteed that other users do not change the records displayed on his or her monitor. To achieve that assurance, a pessimistic locking strategy can be used. A conversational communication is established between the client and the service, which locks the requested rows on behalf of the client, preventing other users from changing them for the duration of the conversation. When the user has finished with the locked rows, the service releases the locks and gracefully terminates the conversation. The TUXEDO ATMI provides a few APIs to support this paradigm.

The call tpconnect() is used by the conversation originator to establish the conversation with the service. tpconnect() returns a call descriptor that is used by

ATMI CALL	PARAMETERS	PURPOSE
tpconnect()	char * TPSCVINFO, char *data, long data_length, long flags	initiates a dialog with a conversational service
tpsend()	int call_descriptor, char *data, long data_length, long flags, long * event	sends data to the conversation partner
tprecv()	int call_descriptor, char **data, long *data_len, long flags, long *event	receives data from the conversation partner
tpreturn()	int return_value, long return_code, char * reply_buffer, long reply_buffer_length, long TUXEDO_flags	gracefully ends a conversation from the service
tpdiscon()	int call_descriptor	Abruptly terminates a conversation and can only be issued by the originator

the subsequent conversation ATMI calls, such as *tpsend()* and *tprecv()*. Similarities exist between *tpsend()* / *tpacall()* and *tprecv()* / *tpgetrply()*. However, the conversational calls hold one more parameter, the return event. During a conversation, either the client or the service can encounter an error or be forced to exit due to an abnormal situation, such as a network failure. The return event signals such occurrence, making the surviving part aware that the partner is not in a condition to continue the conversation. The following picture represents a typical conversation between a TUXEDO client and a conversational service.

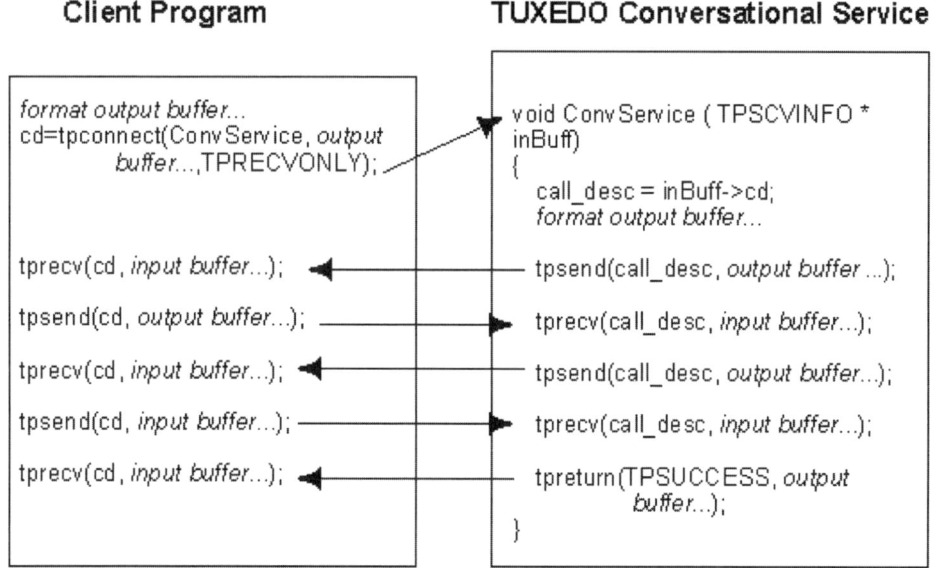

FIGURE 16.3 TUXEDO conversational paradigm

While the TUXEDO administrative subsystem allows application administrators to control the number of conversational services that can be activated concurrently at run-time, as well as how many conversational services of each type must be spawned at start-up, conversational communications are inherently non-scalable and should be avoided at all cost. TUXEDO also supports a time-independent communication paradigm based on application queues. This essentially asynchronous model is made available in TUXEDO through 2 ATMI APIs and a data structure (TPQCTL), called the *queue control structure*.

ATMI CALL	PARAMETERS	PURPOSE
tpenqueue()	char *queue_space, char *queue_name, TPQCTL *queue_control, char *data, long data_length, long TUXEDO_flags	stores a message on the queue named by queue_name in the space queue_space (a collection of queues, one of which must be queue_name)
tpdequeue()	char *queue_space, char *queue_name, TPQCTL *queue_control, char **data, long *data_length, long TUXEDO_flags	dequeues a message for processing from the queue named by queue_name in the space queue_space

The behavior of each queue is determined by the parameters set in the TPQCTL structure. TUXEDO queues are sophisticated objects that offer advanced features, such as the capability for the message to be enqueued with a birth time, a correlation identifier, an associated reply queue, an associated failure queue, a priority, etc. The format of the TPQCTL structure follows:

```
#define TMQNAMELEN      15
#define TMMSGIDLEN      32
#define TMCORRIDLEN     32
struct tpqctl_t         /* control parameters to queue primitives */
{
long flags;             /* indicates which of the values are set */
long deq_time;          /* absolute/relative  time for dequeuing */
long priority;          /* enqueue priority */
long diagnostic;        /* indicates reason for failure */
char msgid[TMMSGIDLEN]; /* id of message before which to queue */
char corrid[TMCORRIDLEN];/* correlation id used to identify message */
char replyqueue[TMQNAMELEN+1]; /* queue name for reply message */
char failurequeue[TMQNAMELEN+1];/* queue name for failure message */
CLIENTID cltid;          /* client identifier for originating client */
```

```
long urcode;            /* application user-return code */
long appkey;            /* application authentication client key */
};
typedef struct tpqctl_t TPQCTL;
```

Usually, only selected fields of the TPQCTL structure are used by a program that enqueues a message. The *flags* field accepts predefined mnemonics that can be ORed to create a complex flag mask. For instance, the following code fragment defines both a correlation identifier and a reply queue for the message being sent.

```
TPQCTLstructQueueControl;
(void) strcpy(structQueueControl.replyqueue,"QUE_REPLY");
(void) strcpy(structQueueControl.corrid,"678.Z");
structQueueControl.flags = TPQREPLYQ | TPQCORRID;
```

TUXEDO application queues offer several methods for sending and receiving messages, each useful for fulfilling different business needs. Messages can be given birth times, in either absolute or relative terms. The default ordering method for time-stamped messages forces TUXEDO to de-queue first the ones with the earliest time. Messages can also be assigned priorities, to influence the ordering criterion for de-queuing. It is also possible to place a message in front of a previously sent message, specifying in the TPQCTL structure the identification of the message that has less priority. TUXEDO will place the most recently sent message in front, skipping the queue.

One of the most advanced features of TUXEDO allows developers to mix the request/response model with application queues. This is possible thanks to the TUXEDO forwarding agent. A client application can try, for example, to submit a synchronous request via tpcall(). If down either the service is or a time out occurs, the client can submit the same request to an application queue, specifying a reply queue in the TPQCTL structure. The queue name specified in the TPQCTL structure corresponds to the service name of the requested service. The TUXEDO forwarding agent understands that the specified queue name is a service and not a queue, and calls tpcall() on behalf of the client. The reply buffer obtained from the service is then queued by the forwarding agent on the reply queue specified in the TPQCTL structure.

TUXEDO supports one more major client-server paradigm, the event-based communication model. In its simplest incarnation, this model allows a client to register a callback function with the TUXEDO system, which is called when the service notifies the client in an unsolicited manner that an event has happened. Natural extensions to this basic model include the possibility for a service to notify multiple clients and the possibility for clients to register their interest in being notified about specific events, relieving the notifying service from keeping track of all interested clients. In the latter model, the service simply communicates to the TUXEDO system that an event has occurred. It is the TUXEDO system that keeps a list of all interested parties, notifying them when the event has occurred. In this model the service is completely de-coupled from the clients receiving its notification. The following table lists all ATMI primitives that support the event-based communication paradigm.

ATMI CALL	PARAMETERS	PURPOSE
tpsetunsol()	function * C_function	registers a callback function with the TUXEDO system
tpnotify()	CLIENTID *clientid, char *data, long data_length , long TUXEDO_flags	removes an event subscription or a set of event subscriptions from the TUXEDO System Event Broker's list of active subscriptions
tpbroadcast()	char *loc_machine_id, char *username, char *client_name, char *data, long data_length, long TUXEDO_flags	allows a client or server to send unsolicited messages to registered clients within the system
tpchkunsol()	void	triggers checking for unsolicited messages
tppost()	char *eventname, char *data, long data_length, long TUXEDO_flags	Posts an event, sending any accompanying data
tpsubscribe()	char *eventexpr, char *filter, TPEVCTL *ctl, long TUXEDO_flags	subscribes to an event or set of events named by eventexpr
tpunsubscribe()	long subscription, long TUXEDO_flags	removes an event subscription or a set of event subscriptions from the TUXEDO System Event Broker's list of active subscriptions

A client application that wants to be notified when an event occurs calls tpsetunsol() , passing the pointer to a function that handles the receiving of the notification. This function must receive three parameters:

```
void my_handler(char *data, long data_length, long TUXEDO_flags);
```

The parameters are passed from the TUXEDO system to the callback function. In this way, either a service routine or a client program can notify a third party when an interesting event has occurred, passing a typed buffer as a parameter. TUXEDO provides two means to trigger the registered callback function. By using tpnotify(), clients or services trigger the callback function of a single client, specifying the client identifier as the first parameter of the ATMI call. With tpbroadcast(), the event can be propagated to several or many client/services simultaneously. The first three parameters of tpbroadcast() are the local machine identifier, the user name, and the client name. Passing a null value for any of these parameters is like passing a wildcard. The three remaining parameters of tpbroadcast() are the usual typed buffer, its length, and a flag mask. Both tpnotify() and tpbroadcast() specify the recipient of the notification in their parameters. This implies that the originator of the notification must have some knowledge of its recipients, that is, their client identifiers or their machine identifiers.

By using tppost(), a notification originator simply "tells" the TUXEDO system that an event of interest has occurred. It doesn't know how many clients or services subscribed their interest in the event. It doesn't know their client identifiers or the machine on which they run. The first parameter of tppost() is the event name. Software components interested in being notified about the occurrence of an event signal their interest to the TUXEDO system by calling tpsubscribe(), which takes an event name or a set of events as its first parameter. To be able to identify more than one event in one parameter, a UNIX regular expression is accepted by tpsubscribe(). When a software component is not interested any more in being notified, it calls tpunsubscribe(), which removes the reference of the component from the subscriber list internally maintained by TUXEDO.

The support for four communication paradigms offered by TUXEDO allows for great flexibility. A service can, for example, notify all clients about its imminent unavailability using the event-based paradigm. The clients can reroute their calls to other services or queue their requests using application queues. The ability to use different communication paradigms within the same application substantially improves sophistication and reliability.

16.3.2.6 TUXEDO Transactions and Oracle The ATMI library offers several APIs that give a fine-grained control over transaction management. When TUXEDO is used together with Oracle, designers can choose between a configuration where Oracle manages its own transactions and a configuration where TUXEDO acts as a transaction coordinator, using its own two-phase commit/presumed abort algorithm to guarantee the ACID properties of the transactions under its control.

Oracle Corporation and most other leading database vendors offer a publicly available interface to their database systems, the XA library, which allows transaction managers to interact with the database instances, acting as resource managers, so that the two software components can coordinate their efforts in managing transactions. The XA primitives are never used directly by TUXEDO or Oracle developers. TUXEDO internally uses the XA primitives to communicate with Oracle, exchanging information about the status and progress of transactions that are under its control.

When TUXEDO is used as a transaction coordinator, developers use the ATMI transaction primitives, and Oracle can be used with other transactionally aware software components, such as databases from other vendors or message-oriented middleware software, for example, IBM MQ Series. The transaction boundaries can span over multiple, heterogeneous databases using multi-vendor middleware software. Alternatively, if Oracle is the only resource manager used by the application, and a sophisticated transaction management is not needed, TUXEDO developers can choose to use not the ATMI transaction primitives but the standard Oracle SQL transaction-oriented verbs (COMMIT WORK, ROLLBACK, SET TRANSACTION, etc) instead. Oracle-managed transactions are faster because they don't incur the performance penalty associated with the use of XA. On the other end, an Oracle-managed transaction cannot span the single service, a significant drawback that can considerably penalize the overall design of the application. The following table lists the transaction oriented ATMI calls.

ATMI CALL	PARAMETERS	PURPOSE
tpbegin()	unsigned long timeout, long TUXEDO_flags	begins a transaction
tpcommit()	long TUXEDO_flags	ends a transaction successfully
tpabort()	long TUXEDO_flags	aborts a transaction, undoing all changes made by the participating services
tpgetlev()	void	returns 0 if the calling service is not part of a transaction, 1 otherwise
tpsuspend()	TPTRANID *transaction_id, long TUXEDO_flags	suspends the transaction active in the caller's process
tpresume()	TPTRANID *transaction_id, long TUXEDO_flags	resumes work on behalf of a previously suspended transaction
tpscmt()	long TUXEDO_flags	controls the returning behavior of tpcommit()

The following example explains the difference between an Oracle-managed transaction and a TUXEDO/XA-managed transaction. A client wants to update customer data residing in a remote resource manager. The service called by the client is "CustomerUpdate". When the transaction is under the direct control of Oracle, the application is coded as follows.

```
Client program:
      tpcall("CustomerUpdate",...data..., ...flags...);
Service:
      CustomerUpdate(TPSCVINFO * inputBuffer)
      {
            ...extract data from input buffer...
            EXEC SQL UPDATE CUSTOMER table based on data;
            EXEC SQL COMMIT WORK;
            tpreturn(TPSUCCESS,...output buffer...);
      }
```

When the transaction occurs under the control of TUXEDO, the application code is as follows.

```
 Client Program:
       tpbegin(30,0);
       ret_code=tpcall("CustomerUpdate",...data..., ...flags...);
       if (ret_code == ERROR)
             tpabort(0);
       else
             tpcommit(0);
Service:
       CustomerUpdate(TPSCVINFO * inputBuffer)
       {
             ...extract data from input buffer...
             EXEC SQL UPDATE CUSTOMER table based on data;
             tpreturn(TPSUCCESS,...output buffer...);
       }
```

When the ATMI transaction-oriented calls are used, a transaction can include several services in one atomic unit of work. Not only do all the services invoked between the tpbegin() and tpcommit() calls become transaction participants, but also the services that are called from other services. TUXEDO introduces the intriguing concept of "transaction infection" to mean that a service, called from another service that is bracketed within a transaction, automatically becomes part of the same transaction. A service can use the ATMI call tpgetlev() to find out if it is currently part of a transaction. In addition, a service can optionally refuse to become part of a transaction by calling tpsuspend(), resuming the transaction (tpresume()) just before returning to the caller.

16.3.2.7 TUXEDO Tips and Tricks. TUXEDO is a sophisticated and complex software product. Designers and developers approaching TUXEDO for the first time are usually overwhelmed by the amount of notions they must rapidly absorb in order to become proficient with the product. The TUXEDO manuals, like the Oracle manuals, are designed to illustrate the concepts being explained in a very "condensed" way, concentrating many notions to a few lines of code. The following is an example taken directly from a TUXEDO manual (BEA TUXEDO Programmer's Guide), which illustrates how to write service routines.

```
#include <stdio.h>          /* UNIX */
#include <atmi.h>           /* TUXEDO */
#include <sqlcode.h>        /* TUXEDO */
#include "bank.flds.h"      /* bankdb fields */
```

```
#include "aud.h"              /* BANKING view defines */
EXEC SQL begin declare section;
static long branch_id;        /* branch id */
static float bal;             /* balance */
EXEC SQL end declare section;
/*
 * Service to find sum of the account balances at a SITE
 */
void
#ifdef __STDC__
ABAL(TPSVCINFO *transb)
#else
ABAL(transb)
TPSVCINFO *transb;
#endif
{
    struct aud *transv;                   /* view of decoded message */
    /* Set pointer to TPSVCINFO data buffer  */
    transv = (struct aud *)transb->data;
    set the consistency level of the transaction
    /* Get branch id from message, do query */
    EXEC SQL declare acur cursor for
        select SUM(BALANCE) from ACCOUNT;
    EXEC SQL open acur;                /* open */
    EXEC SQL fetch acur into :bal;     /* fetch */
    if (SQLCODE != SQL_OK) {           /* nothing found */
        (void)strcpy (transv->ermsg,"abal failed in sql aggregation");
        EXEC SQL close acur;
        tpreturn(TPFAIL, 0, transb->data, sizeof(struct aud), 0);
    }
    EXEC SQL close acur;
    transv->balance = bal;
    tpreturn (TPSUCCESS, 0, transb->data, sizeof(struct aud), 0);
}
```

The above example mixes together business logic, logical, and physical data access logic. Maintaining such a program becomes costly and problematic when changes are required by the business. The concepts explained in Chapter 7, How to Structure the Server Code, also apply to TUXEDO services.

One of the major mistakes that should be avoided at all costs is putting the business logic in the client, rather than in the server. Designing a TP monitor-based, multiple-tier application requires a different mindset that has little in common with the traditional two-tier client/server model. The real challenge is to properly separate business logic from data validation and business logic from application control. Users interact with the application through menu options and command buttons. The client drives the application flow, but the server should provide all the logic necessary to check the validity of the user-provided information and to present the data to the user. The client can perform simple data validation, while complex data validation, that is, data validation that requires database access, should be performed at the back-end.

The distinction between application flow control and business logic is not always simple and clear-cut. A typical example is provided by the menu options that should be either grayed out or unavailable under certain circumstances, usually dictated by business logic. Should the client be aware of the business logic that governs the availability of the menu options, or should the server instruct the client about the menu options that must be available or unavailable at all time?

If too much business logic is concentrated on the client, the application loses the great flexibility offered by the TUXEDO administration facilities, which can instantiate new services according to the system or application load, or change on-the-fly data dependent routing routines in the TUXEDO MIB to divert the application flow to less busy computers.

On the other end, calling server side services to perform simple data validation on user-entered data generates unnecessary network traffic. In this case, it would be better to use the client local intelligence to perform simple user input validation. Finding the balance between client and server business and validation logic is one of the most critical tasks confronted by multiple-tier application designers and architects.

TUXEDO has built-in mechanisms to capture performance information and to generate statistics useful for service benchmarking. Unfortunately, TUXEDO's timings start and end with the service call. In general, users complain about poor responsiveness from their own perspective, which is the end-to-end response time, normally influenced by several factors, such as network traffic, system load, etc. Implementing custom-written performance monitoring code is often the only solution for end-to-end response time capturing. To give users a precise feedback about the system's responsiveness, the time required for a transaction to complete can be optionally recorded in the application status bar. The client application can start the clock ticking immediately after the user has hit the enter key (or clicked the "Submit" button) and display the final time recorded when the last line on the screen has been painted. If the application is not adequately responsive, the application maintenance engineers can compare the end-to-end response time recorded by the users with the TUXEDO-generated statistics, pinpointing potential problems occurring outside the TUXEDO realm.

16.3.3 IBM MQ SERIES

IBM MQ Series is the leader product in the Message Oriented Middleware (MOM) market. It is increasingly used in conjunction with Oracle-based applications in corporate environments, where midrange Unix systems must be integrated with legacy applications residing on mainframes or IBM midrange systems such as AS400. MQ Series is not the only available solution for Oracle-to-mainframe integration. Oracle Corporation offers the Open Gateway Technology, which provides advanced and sophisticated capabilities, such as the ability to join an Oracle table to a DB2 table, or the ability to perform distributed updates and to use PL/SQL statements against non-Oracle databases. While the Oracle Open Gateways are definitely suitable for applications that need a real-time update of all heterogeneous systems participating in a distributed transaction, MQ Series allows for time-independent delivery of application messages. That is, sending and receiving of messages are completely de-coupled, so that the applications exchanging messages can continue to work independently from each other, even when the network is unavailable or one application is down for maintenance.

Chapter 15 explored the recently introduced Oracle features, including Advanced Queuing. Why would a company that invested in Oracle technologies buy a product like MQ Series instead of using Oracle AQ? There are a few key features provided by MQ Series that make it not completely overlapping with Oracle AQ. First of all, Oracle AQ requires an up and running Oracle engine to be able to queue the received messages. The Oracle engine becomes *the single point of failure* for both application and queuing system. This is rarely desirable, especially if the Oracle Parallel Server is not used. It is not realistic to expect a single Oracle engine to be up and running 365 days per year. If messages can arrive at any time, and it is important not to lose any of them, it is better to checkpoint the messages in a queue external to Oracle and to have a background process that updates the Oracle database with the content of the messages consumed from the queue. An MQ Series queue can act as a buffer, queuing messages irrespective of the availability of the Oracle instance, increasing the overall reliability of the system.

In addition, MQ Series opens the doors to the IBM legacy systems, ensuring information synchronization between open systems, desktop systems, and mainframes without requiring a constant connection. The "all-or-nothing" approach typical of the two-phase commit protocol prevents a transaction from succeeding if only one of the participants is momentarily unavailable. Many business models don't require such a high degree of availability, and are to de-couple and fragment their operations in smaller units that can act independently from each other. Consider a downsized application that was previously running on a mainframe and has been ported to an open system. It is likely that the mainframe still wants the consolidated data, reconciled periodically, to be centrally available. The open system performs its tasks and only at predetermined intervals synchronizes with the mainframes, sending consolidated data. This business model is perfectly suitable for MOM products such as MQ series.

MQ Series support for hardware platforms is not limited only to the IBM systems. All major Unix flavors (HP/UX, IBM AIX, Sun Solaris) and MS Windows NT are supported platforms for MQ Series Server, and many more operating systems (including Linux and OpenVMS) are supported for the MQ Series client configuration.

One of the features introduced with MQ Series release 5 allows for coordination of database updates with message activities. A unit of work can include the message consumed from the queue and the insertion of its data into Oracle tables. Failing to commit the transaction reinstates the message in the queue, ready to be later consumed in a second attempt to complete the transaction, by the same or another process.

MQ Series is available in two different configurations, client and server. A client configuration doesn't install any queue manager on the local computer, but only provides MQ Interface (MQI) support. This means that applications running on client machines can use MQI API calls but always connect to remote queues, managed on computers where MQ Series server is installed. A server-to-server configuration offers several advantages over a client-to-server configuration. Communication between MQ clients and servers is established using MQI channels, which are bidirectional and half-duplex, allowing only for synchronous communication.

In contrast, server-to-server communication occurs using message channels, which are unidirectional, asynchronous, and time-independent. Usually, to connect to servers, two message channels are defined, one for each direction of the communication. Support for several operating systems (Linux for instance) is provided only for a client configuration of MQ Series. A client configuration is more appropriate when the local machine is not powerful enough to run a full queue manager with acceptable performance, or when MQ-related administration efforts must be kept to a minimum. The major drawback of a client configuration is its dependence on the availability of the network in order to be able to queue messages on the queue residing on the remote machine. In a server-to-server configuration, if the network link is momentarily unavailable, the application can still queue messages that are buffered locally, until the connection is reestablished and the messages are sent to the application partner, transparently to application users and administrators.

The MQI APIs are identical for both MQ Series client and server. However, different libraries must be linked together with the application object files to produce different executables for each environment.

16.3.3.1 MQ Series Objects In order to understand and evaluate the features provided by a product like MQ Series, it is necessary to introduce a few concepts and the terminology commonly used by MQ Series users. The two central objects of MQ Series are the *queue*, defined as a named object on which applications can put messages and from which applications can get messages, and the *message*, defined as a string of bytes that has a meaning in the context of the application that uses it. In order for applications to be able to store and retrieve messages, a queue must exist.

A queue is created by MQ Series administrative tools and is owned by a queue manager, which is also created via administrative tools. A single queue manager can own (and manage) several or many queues, but each queue must have a name that is unique in the domain of the queue manager.

The two most important attributes of a message are persistence and priority. They are defined in the message descriptor. Each message comprises a message descriptor and application data. The message descriptor contains control information, interpreted by the MQ Series system, which uses it to find out how to deal with the message.

Nonpersistent messages don't survive the restarting of the queue. Persistent messages can be recovered and survive queue restarting and machine crashes. The priority of a message determines the order in which it is retrieved from a queue, and, optionally, can trigger events and start de-queuing processes. Triggering is an MQ Series facility that can start application processes when specific predetermined conditions on a queue are met; for instance, a message with an associated high priority is delivered to the queue.

Messages can be as large as 100 MB (MQ Series release 5). While it is possible to send such large messages, it is rarely practical. MQ Series allows large messages to be split into smaller messages, and then retrieved from the queue in a group. It is possible to hide the split messages from the receiving queue until all have arrived, allowing the receiving process to fetch all of them in an atomic unit of work.

QUEUE TYPE	PURPOSE
Message	This is the most commonly used queue. Application messages are stored to and retrieved from message queues.
Event	This is used to receive event messages. Applications can be instrumented for sending event messages, mainly to monitor performance and channel-related activity.
Initiation	Used to receive trigger messages, at least one initiation queue must be defined for each queue manager supporting triggering.
Transmission	This is used to temporarily store messages that are destined for remote queue managers. At least one transmission queue must be defined for each remote queue manager to which the local queue manager must send messages.
Reply-to	Request messages are required to specify the queue to which the reply must be sent. They are called reply-to queues.
Dead-letter	This is used to collect the messages that could not be routed to their correct destination. If a dead-letter queue is not defined, when a message cannot be delivered the queue stops. Each queue manager should have an associated dead-letter queue.
Command	This is owned by the queue manager and receive administrative commands sent by authorized applications to MQ Series. Command servers defined as part of each queue manager process command messages.
System Default	This is a template queue used by MQ Series to clone specific types of queues. By modifying a System Default Queue, it is possible to change default definitions for all queues of the same type that will be created by MQ Series.

MQ Series uses several different types of queues, some of which have special purposes, like triggering processes or logging MQ Series events. The table on page 600 lists the main queue types commonly used in MQ Series applications.

It is possible to manage and administer MQ Series objects using commands that allow one to:

- ❑ Create and delete queue managers
- ❑ Create and delete queue
- ❑ Start and stop communication channels
- ❑ Grant to and revoke from MQ Series objects security privileges

There are two types of command, one human-readable (MQSC) and one machine-readable (Programmable Command Format or PCF). A character-based command-line interface (mqsc) is provided to administrators for interacting with MQ Series. Alternatively, PCF commands can be used from a system-management application that programmatically administers MQ Series objects. Another option is to use command queues, which accept commands that are processed by command servers associated with queue managers.

It is possible to administer MQ Series objects owned by remote queue managers. In order to do so, channels dedicated to sending commands must be defined, for both senses of the communication. It is also possible to access MQ Series queues using indirection; that is, a queue can be defined as an alias queue, which points to a real queue. This feature allows client programs to access the same queue using different names. Administrators can change the attributes of the queue pointed to by the aliases without requiring any application change.

MQ Series allows for the definition of templates or *model queues*, which are used when application programs ask for *dynamic queue* creation. Dynamic queues are created dynamically by the queue manager (and not statically using the administrative tools), when specific attributes are set by the client program at the moment of the opening of the queue. In order to create a dynamic queue, a model queue must be passed as a parameter, to instruct MQ Series to create the required queue cloning the model queue.

A dynamic queue can be temporary or permanent. A temporary queue can only be used to store nonpersistent messages, as it doesn't survive a restart of the queue manager. A permanent queue is not deleted when it is closed by the application (unless the application explicitly requests the destruction of the queue) and is able to store both persistent and nonpersistent messages. In order to support the new communication paradigms, such as publish-and-subscribe, MQ Series supports distribution lists, which allow applications to send a message to many recipients with a single call.

16.3.3.2 MQ Series and Oracle MQ Series can optionally operate database coordination, using a two-phase commit protocol implemented through the XA library, the same way as in TUXEDO. The MQI library provides three APIs that can be used by MQ Series programs to force database coordination by the queue manager.

- ❑ MQBEGIN
- ❑ MQCMIT
- ❑ MQBACK

Full recovery is guaranteed if the queue manager loses contact with a resource manager during the commit protocol. This means that the message is reinstated on the queue, ready to be consumed by the same or another application process.

In order to enable database coordination by the queue manager, MQ Series administrators must create an XA switch load file for Oracle. An XA switch load file is a shared library that is dynamically loaded by MQ Series processes, enabling the queue manager and the Oracle instance to speak to each other.

In addition, the resource manager parameters must be defined in the MQ Series initialization file, in a specific stanza called XAResourceManager. The following is an example of switch load file to enable database coordination of an Oracle instance by a queue manager under the control of MQ Series.

```
#include <cmcq.h>
#include <xa.h>

extern struct xa_switch_t xaOracleSW;

struct xa_switch_t * MQENTRY MQStart(void)
{
      return (&xaOracleSW);
}
```

Under Unix, the switch load file must be compiled and then linked against the clntsh library, to create a shared library. The file qm.ini, which is queue manager specific and found in the directory created by MQ Series at the moment of the definition of the queue, must be edited and a XAResourceManager stanza must be added, to tell the queue manager about the Oracle instance it must coordinate.

XAOPENSTRING PARAMETER	MEANING
+Acc=P//IP/<username>/<password>	*Mandatory:* Specifies user access information. To use an OPS$ account use P//. Otherwise, give Oracle account and password, as in P/scott/tiger.
+SesTm=<SessionTimeLimit>	*Mandatory:* Specifies the maximum amount of time, in seconds, that a transaction can remain inactive before it is automatically destroyed.

(*cont.*)

XAOPENSTRING PARAMETER	MEANING
+DB=Database Name	*Optional:* Specifies the database name if the Oracle precompilers use the AT clause in their SQL statements.
+GPwd=P/<groupPassword>	*Optional:* Specifies the server group security password, used when more than one user connects to the same Oracle account.
+LogDir=<log directory>	*Optional:* Specifies a directory where XA trace files are stored when problems occur.
+MaxCur= <maximum open cursors>	*Optional:* Specifies the maximum number of cursors that can be concurrently open.
+SqlNet=<connection string>	*Optional:* The SQL*Net connection string is used when the Oracle instance and the MQ Series queue manager reside on different machines.

The XAResourceManager stanza must contain three entries, Name, SwitchFIle, and XAOpenString. Name specifies the resource manager name and can be the Oracle SID. SwitchFile specifies the absolute path of the switch load file. XAOpenString comprises a few mandatory and a few optional parameters.

The following example shows an XAResourceManager stanza that defines an Oracle instance accessible through the classical scott/tiger account, storing the log information in /export/home/oralog, allowing for an inactive transaction time of 20 sec and an SQL*Net connection string that uses the TNS name SEWO_DB.

```
XAReourceManager:
Name = SEWO
SwitchFile = /usr/lib/oraswit
XAOpenString = Oracle_XA+Acc=P/scott/tiger+
               SesTm=20+ LogDir = /export/home/oralog+
               SqlNet=SEWO_DB
```

Enabling queue manager controlled transactions increases reliability and robustness of MQ Series applications. Note, however, that careful planning is required in order to avoid the standstill situation that occurs when a message cannot be atomically consumed from the queue and stored into an Oracle instance. A background process that de-queues the messages stored in an MQ Series queue can consume the message and attempt an insertion into Oracle. If the insertion fails, say, because of a duplicate primary key, the message won't be discarded from the queue when the transaction fails. If the process de-queues messages in a loop following a FIFO policy, then the same message will make the application consistently crash, preventing the processing of all other messages queued after the one which cannot be inserted into Oracle. One way to avoid such a situation is to insert the de-queued messages in temporary tables without constraints, enabling a background process that stores the data accumulated in the temporary tables into the required tables that define referential integrity.

16.3.3.3 MQI Interface From an application perspective, MQ Series is simple to use. The APIs available through the MQI interface are few, yet powerful. Most MQI calls are available in any MQ Series supported platform, with the exception of database coordination, which is not supported on the IBM MVS/ESA and AS400 architectures. The basic flow of an MQ Series program comprises the following steps:

- Connect to a queue manager
- Open a queue
- Optionally start an atomic unit of work (database coordination)
- Get/Put messages
- Optionally end an atomic unit of work
- Close the queue
- Disconnect from the queue manager

The following table lists all MQ Series MQI APIs.

CALL NAME	DESCRIPTION
MQCONN	connects to a queue manager
MQCONNX	connects to a queue manager specifying additional options
MQOPEN	opens a queue
MQPUT	puts a message on an open queue
MQGET	gets a message from a queue
MQPUT1	puts only one message on a queue, opening the queue, putting the message and closing the queue in one call
MQCLOSE	closes an open queue
MQDISC	disconnects from a queue manager
MQBEGIN	starts an atomic unit of work
MQCMIT	commits changes concluding an atomic unit of work
MQBACK	aborts the changes made during an atomic unit of work
MQINQ	inquires about MQ Series object attributes
MQSET	sets MQ Series object attributes

MQI calls are all void functions; that is, each function doesn't return a value indicating the completion status of the call. Each function takes two parameters, *CompletionCode* and *ReasonCode*, passed by reference, which report the outcome of the called MQI function. CompletionCode and ReasonCode are known collectively as *return codes*, as they are used together by application programs to deal with potential abnormal situations or MQ Series returned errors. A completion code can be MQCC_OK, MQCC_WARNING, or MQCC_FAILED. MQI defines many reason codes, covering most error circumstances, such as security violations, attempts to open inexistent queues, attempts to perform get operations not allowed for the specific queue, etc.

The typical way to check the return code of an MQI function is to first determine whether the CompletionCode was successful. In this case, the ReasonCode is always set to MQRC_NONE. If the CompletionCode is either MQCC_WARNING or MQCC_FAILED, then either a cascading "if" statement or a switch statement is performed by the program, testing for few or several expected error conditions. This is particularly useful when the error is recoverable, either by application logic present in the program or by direct intervention of the user.

MQI also uses a set of predefined data structures that store the various options of the calls. For instance, the MQI call MQCONNX accepts a structure of type MQCNO as its second parameter. One field defined in the MQCNO structure, Options, can be set with values that influence the way MQ Series will handle the connection to the specified queue manager. The most important MQI data structures are:

MQI DATA STRUCTURE	DESCRIPTION	PURPOSE
MQCNO	Connect Options	used by MQCONNX to specify extended connection options
MQGMO	Get Message Options	specifies how to read a message from the queue
MQMD	Message Descriptor	contains the control information that accompanies application data
MQOD	Object Descriptor	used to specify an MQ Series object by name
MQOR	Object Record	specifies a single queue name and queue manager name. An array of structures allows for the opening of distribution lists.
MQPMO	Put Message Options	specifies how to queue a single message
MQPMR	Put Message Record	specifies various message properties for a single message. An array of structures allows defining different values for each destination queue when the same message is sent to multiple recipients.
MQRMH	Message Reference Header	defines the format of a reference message. User exits read the structure to be instructed on how to read the message.

In MQ Series, a message can be read in a destructive manner; that is, the message is consumed permanently from the queue. Alternatively, an application can browse messages in a queue looking for a specific message, without consuming the messages scanned while searching. The MQI data structures are used to instruct the MQ Series system how to perform the various operations requested through the APIs. To specify that a get message call should wait until a message is available on the queue, instead of returning immediately, an application program should be structured as follows:

```
...
...
MQGMO getMessageOptions;
...
...
getMessageOptions.Options = MQGMO_WAIT;
getMessageOptions.WaitInterval = 20000;
MQGET(HCon,HObj,&MsgDescr,&getMessageOptions,
      BuffLength,MsgBuffer,&MsgLength,
      &CompletionCode,&ReasonCode);
...
...
```

An interesting feature of MQ Series, introduced with release 5, is the ability to send a message by reference. The message is a logical pointer to external data, such as files, graphic images, blobs, etc. MQ Series will transmit the referenced data in an assured manner, storing it in the destination site. The remote application will interpret the message reference header while invoking a user exit that deals with the incoming message.

The control information associated with each message is made available to application programs through the message descriptor structure. Attributes such as message priority, message lifetime, correlation identifier, etc. are included in the message descriptor structure, passed as a parameter to MQPUT or MQGET. The following example shows how to use the basic MQI APIs to connect to a queue manager, open a queue, put a simple message on the queue, close the queue, and disconnect from the queue manager, going through all steps required by an MQ Series application. The program accepts two command line parameters, queue name and queue manager name, which must be provided.

```
#include <stdio.h>
#include <stdlib.h>
#include <string.h>
#include <cmqc.h> /* includes for MQI */

int main(int argc, char **argv)
```

```
{
   /* MQI structures  */
   MQOD     od = {MQOD_DEFAULT};   /* Object Descriptor    */
   MQMD     md = {MQMD_DEFAULT};   /* Message Descriptor   */
   MQPMO   pmo = {MQPMO_DEFAULT}; /* put message options */

   /* MQI Data Types */
   MQHCONN  Hcon;         /* connection handle              */
   MQHOBJ   Hobj;         /* object handle                  */
   MQLONG   O_options;    /* MQOPEN options                 */
   MQLONG   C_options;    /* MQCLOSE options                */
   MQLONG   CompCode;     /* completion code                */
   MQLONG   OpenCode;     /* MQOPEN completion code         */
   MQLONG   Reason;       /* reason code                    */
   MQLONG   CReason;      /* reason code for MQCONN         */
   MQLONG   buflen;       /* buffer length                  */

   /* Application data */
   char     buffer[100];  /* message buffer                 */
   char     QMName[50];   /* queue manager name             */

   if (argc < 3)
   {
      printf("Usage: mqexample "
       "<queue name> <queue manager name>\n");
      exit(-1);
   }
   strcpy(QMName, argv[2]);
   /* Connect to queue manager  */
   MQCONN(QMName,       /* queue manager      */
          &Hcon,        /* connection handle  */
          &CompCode,    /* completion code    */
          &CReason);    /* reason code        */

   /* Deal with errors */
   if (CompCode == MQCC_FAILED)
   {
     printf("MQCONN Erorr. Reason Code %ld\n", CReason);
     exit( (int) CReason );
   }
   strncpy(od.ObjectName, argv[1], (size_t)MQ_Q_NAME_LENGTH);
   /* Open the target message queue for output */
   O_options = MQOO_OUTPUT; /* Request opening queue */
                           /* for output */
```

```
/* Open the queue */
MQOPEN(Hcon,            /* connection handle            */
       &od,             /* object descriptor for queue  */
       O_options,       /* open options                 */
       &Hobj,           /* object handle                */
       &OpenCode,       /* MQOPEN completion code       */
       &Reason);        /* reason code                  */
/* Deal with errors */
if (Reason != MQRC_NONE)
{
  printf("MQOPEN failed. Reason Code %ld\n", Reason);
}
if (OpenCode == MQCC_FAILED)
{
  printf("Cannot open queue for output\n");
  exit ( (int) Reason);
}
memcpy(md.Format,     /* character string format      */
       MQFMT_STRING, (size_t)MQ_FORMAT_LENGTH);
strcpy(buffer,"This is a trial message to test MQPUT");
buflen = strlen(buffer);
memcpy(md.MsgId,   /* reset MessageId to get a new one */
       MQMI_NONE, sizeof(md.MsgId) );
/* reset CorrelationId to get a new one */
memcpy(md.CorrelId, MQCI_NONE, sizeof(md.CorrelId) );

/* Put a message on the queue */
MQPUT(Hcon,                /* connection handle      */
      Hobj,                /* object handle          */
      &md,                 /* message descriptor     */
      &pmo,                /* default options        */
      buflen,              /* buffer length          */
      buffer,              /* message buffer         */
      &CompCode,           /* completion code        */
      &Reason);            /* reason code            */
/* Deal with errors */
if (Reason != MQRC_NONE)
{
  printf("MQPUT failed. Reason Code %ld\n", Reason);
  exit ( (int) Reason);
}
/* Close the queue */
C_options = 0;                    /* no close options   */
MQCLOSE(Hcon,                     /* connection handle  */
        &Hobj,                    /* object handle      */
```

```
            C_options,
            &CompCode,                    /* completion code      */
            &Reason);                     /* reason code          */
   /* report reason, if any      */
   if (Reason != MQRC_NONE)
   {
     printf("MQCLOSE ended with reason code %ld\n", Reason);
     exit ( (int) Reason);
   }
   /* Disconnect from the queue manager */
   MQDISC(&Hcon,                         /* connection handle  */
          &CompCode,                     /* completion code    */
          &Reason);                      /* reason code        */
   /* Deal with errors  */
   if (Reason != MQRC_NONE)
   {
     printf("MQDISC failed. Reason Code %ld\n", Reason);
     exit ( (int) Reason);
   }
   return(0);
}
```

16.3.3.4 MQ Series Summary MQ Series provides the basic infrastructure for building time-independent, message-based distributed applications. It is the market leader in its category (Message-oriented Middleware or MOM), well supported by third party applications, particularly suited to ease administration (BMC Patrol Suite for MQ Series, Candle MQ Series Command Center, Tivoli Module for MQ Series) and to improve security (Candle MQSecure).

Used with the appropriate settings, MQ Series guarantees message delivery in atomic units of work, implementing a single-phase commit protocol controlled by the queue manager. Optionally, a resource manager such as Oracle can be elected to participate in a transaction controlled by MQ Series, which implements a two-phase commit protocol using the X/Open XA library to coordinate the resource manager activity.

Not only is a single message guaranteed to be delivered to the target queue, but its consumption by the remote application can be transactionally enabled, preventing its disappearance from the queue if the de-queuing application fails to checkpoint its content in the resource manager.

Applications can demand messages to be acknowledged by the consuming application, specifying reply-to queues in the control information that accompanies each message. Publish-and-subscribe policies can be implemented in MQ Series, as well as distribution lists that deliver a single message to multiple recipients in one call.

MQ Series is not significantly more sophisticated than Oracle AQ and it is definitely more expensive, on a head-to-head comparison. But Oracle AQ requires that all clients submitting messages to the queues have SQL*Net locally installed and, more importantly, that Oracle instance implementing the queues always be up and running; otherwise message queuing fails. The only way to guarantee a 24-hour, 7-day message delivery for Oracle-based queues is to implement a parallel server, which requires a cluster architecture, significantly more expensive than an MQ Series license.

In sites that implement single Oracle instances, which can receive messages from remote applications on a 24-hour, 7-day basis, MQ Series can be proficiently used to de-couple message delivery from message content check-pointing into Oracle.

Summary

This chapter focused on middleware products and technologies commonly used in conjunction with Oracle databases. The Oracle proprietary networking software, SQL*Net/Net8, ensures robustness and great scalability for application remotely accessing Oracle instances. Under certain circumstances, however, the use of a TP monitor or message-oriented middleware system is more appropriate. Additionally, the use of SQL*Net/Net8 can be precluded by corporate policies or other reasons, and even if an Oracle proprietary networking solution would be appropriate for the application being implemented, designers and architects must use third party solutions to ensure connectivity to an Oracle database. Sometimes the use of SQL*Net/Net8 is not prevented by corporate policies, but by the software/hardware platform used, which is not supported by Oracle. Two popular networking solutions adopted when SQL*Net/Net8 cannot be used are Remote Procedure Call (RPC) implementations, either coded from the ground up or provided in form of API by software vendors, and TCP/IP sockets, used wherever a TCP/IP implementation is available.

The chapter discussed in detail two products that are becoming increasingly popular in sites where Oracle technologies provide database services, BEA Systems TUXEDO and IBM MQ Series. The first is a TP monitor, one of the oldest to appear in the Unix arena, very mature and robust. The latter is a message-oriented middleware system, used to queue messages that are subsequently dequeued by a remote application. Time independence is the basis for the queue-based communication paradigm supported by MQ Series, particularly suitable for specific business environments such as workflow management.

Chapter 17

CLIENT DEVELOPMENT TOOLS: PUTTING THEM INTO PRACTICE

This chapter presents one software tool developed in four versions, using each of the four development environments analyzed in chapter 10. The application built in this chapter is an Oracle shared pool browser, which is useful to tune SQL statements that have been submitted to the engine. The tool gives developers the ability to display an execution plan for selected statements "on the fly", if the user conducting the analysis has adequate privileges to do so. A set of useful statistics is also displayed by the tool, to assist developers in determining the most "expensive" statements, the ones that should be optimized.

The shared pool browser has been chosen because it is useful, but its implementation is not overwhelmingly complex. It does require, however, a few advanced features from the development tools used to build it, which test their general suitability for building advanced Oracle-based applications. The four client development environments used to build the shared pool browser are:

- Powersoft Powerbuilder release 6.0
- Microsoft Visual Basic release 6.0
- Borland.com Delphi release 4.0
- Oracle Developer release 2.1

The purpose of this chapter is not to perform a classical comparison/benchmark of the most commonly used client-side development tools but instead to identify each tool's basic characteristics and points of strength, the ones which make one tool more suitable than others for specific tasks.

The point made in chapter 10 was that there is no such thing as the "absolute best" tool, which can be implemented in all environments to satisfy all potential requirements of all applications. This chapter will further demonstrate (1) that each tool has its own unique characteristics that can be adequately exploited under particular circumstances, and (2) that each tool has areas of excellence and areas where it doesn't perform as well as the competitors.

17.1 ShrPool, An Oracle Shared Pool Browser

All successfully parsed SQL statements submitted to an Oracle engine are stored in the shared pool, an area of the SGA specifically dedicated to SQL caching. Oracle exposes the memory structures containing the SQL statements through a few V$ views, which can be queried by users who have the SELECT privileges on those views. The shared pool browser presented here uses two V$ views to accomplish its task, V$SQLAREA and V$SQLTEXT.

V$SQLAREA contains most of the statement-level useful statistics and the first one thousand characters of the SQL statement itself. If an SQL statement is longer than 1000 characters, it can be entirely retrieved by accessing the V$SQLTEXT view, which breaks the statement down in "pieces", each as long as 64 bytes. Each statement is uniquely identified by a combination of its address and its hash value.

The columns below appear in both V$SQLTEXT and V$SQLAREA, making therefore possible a join between the two views. A description of each field contained in the two V$ views follows.

V$SQLAREA

VIEW COLUMN	DATATYPE	DESCRIPTION
SQL_TEXT	VARCHAR2(1000)	the first 80 characters of the SQL text for the current cursor
SHARABLE_MEM	NUMBER	the sum of all sharable memory, in bytes, of all the child cursors under this parent
PERSISTENT_MEM	NUMBER	the sum of all persistent memory, in bytes, of all the child cursors under this parent
RUNTIME_MEM	NUMBER	the sum of all the ephemeral frame sizes of all the children
SORTS	NUMBER	the sum of the number of sorts done for all the children
VERSION_COUNT	NUMBER	the number of children present in the cache under this parent
LOADED_VERSIONS	NUMBER	the number of children present in the cache AND with context heap (KGL heap 6) loaded

(cont.)

V$SQLAREA *(continued)*

VIEW COLUMN	DATATYPE	DESCRIPTION
OPEN_VERSIONS	NUMBER	the number of child cursors currently open under this current parent
USERS_OPENING	NUMBER	the number of users that have any of the child cursors open
EXECUTIONS	NUMBER	the total number of executions, totalled over all the children
USERS_EXECUTING	NUMBER	the total number of users executing the statement over all children
LOADS	NUMBER	the number of times the object was loaded or reloaded
FIRST_LOAD_TIME	VARCHAR2(19)	the time stamp of the parent creation time
INVALIDATIONS	NUMBER	the total number of invalidations over all the children
PARSE_CALLS	NUMBER	the sum of all parse calls to all the child cursors under this parent
DISK_READS	NUMBER	the sum of the number of disk reads over all child cursors
BUFFER_GETS	NUMBER	the sum of buffer gets over all child cursors
ROWS_PROCESSED	NUMBER	the total number of rows processed on behalf of this SQL statement
COMMAND_TYPE	NUMBER	the Oracle command type definition
OPTIMIZER_MODE	VARCHAR2(10)	mode under which the SQL statement is executed
PARSING_USER_ID	NUMBER	the user ID of the user that has parsed the very first cursor under this parent
PARSING_SCHEMA_ID	NUMBER	the schema ID that was used to parse this child cursor
KEPT_VERSIONS	NUMBER	the number of child cursors marked to be kept using the DBMS_SHARED_POOL package
ADDRESS	RAW(4)	the address of the handle to the parent for this cursor
HASH_VALUE	NUMBER	the hash value of the parent statement in the library cache
MODULE	VARCHAR2(64)	contains the name of the module that was executing at the time that the SQL statement was first parsed as set by calling DBMS_APPLICATION_INFO.SET_MODULE
MODULE_HASH	NUMBER	the hash value of the module named in the MODULE column
ACTION	VARCHAR2(64)	contains the name of the action that was executing at the time that the SQL statement was first parsed as set by calling DBMS_APPLICATION_INFO.SET_ACTION
ACTION_HASH	NUMBER	the hash value of the action named in the ACTION column
SERIALIZABLE_ABORTS	NUMBER	the number of times the transaction fails to serialize, producing ORA-8177 errors, totalled over all the children

V$SQLTEXT

VIEW COLUMN	DATATYPE	DESCRIPTION
ADDRESS	RAW(4)	used with HASH_VALUE to identify uniquely a cached cursor
HASH_VALUE	NUMBER	used with ADDRESS to identify uniquely a cached cursor
PIECE	NUMBER	Number used to order the pieces of SQL text
SQL_TEXT	VARCHAR2(64)	column containing one piece of the SQL text
COMMAND_TYPE	NUMBER	code for the type of SQL statement (SELECT, INSERT, etc.)

Not all columns defined in V$SQLAREA will be used by our tool. Only a subset that includes the principal statement statistics will be extracted from the view and effectively used by *ShrPool*, our shared pool browser.

The first window that will be presented to the users, after a connection to Oracle has been established, will allow them to operate a selection of the analyzed statements from the shared pool based on filters and order criteria. Figure 17.1 shows an example of the window requesting SQL statement selection criteria.

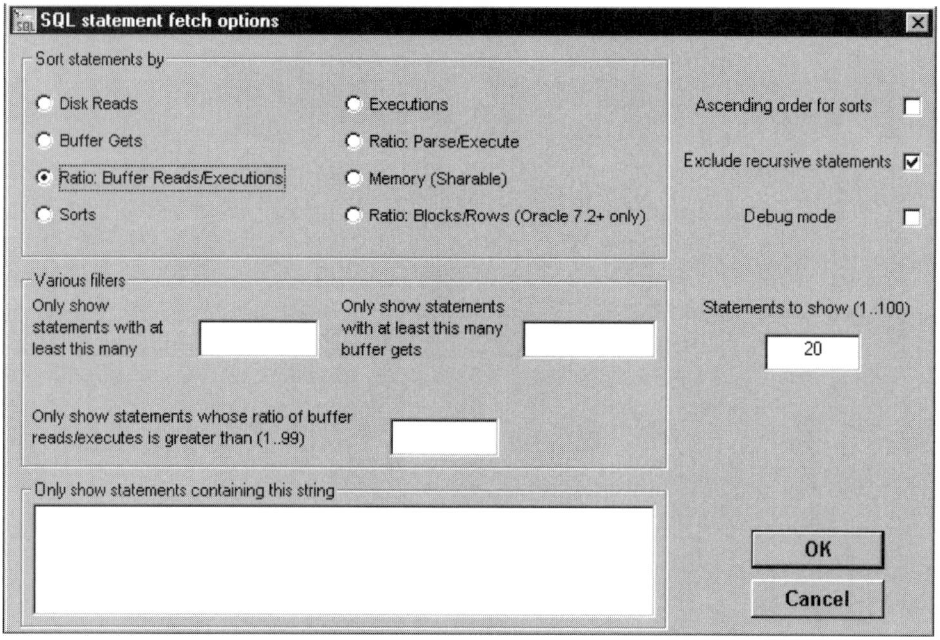

FIGURE 17.1 The SQL Statement Fetch Option Window

The SQL statement used by ShrPool to fetch the required SQL statements from the shared pool will be built dynamically, after the user has filled in the form. A user can influence the sort order for the fetched statements, and can exclude statements that do not match predefined selection criteria, for instance, that have not been executed for at least a specific number of times. The bottom part of the window allows users to specify the inclusion of statements based on parts of the statement itself. ShrPool will take the filter string, prefix it, and suffix it with a percent sign (%), generating a "like" where clause for the SQL_TEXT column. If a user specifies "USER_TABLES" as filter string, the dynamically generated SQL statement will contain the construct "where SQL_TEXT like %USER_TABLES%."

After the users have completed the form and clicked on the "OK" button, behind the scenes, ShrPool will build the statement required to fetch the necessary SQL statements from the shared pool, and will submit the dynamically built statement to the engine. It will then fetch all rows containing SQL statements and statistics, and will display them on the window shown in Figure 17.2.

This window allows users to select a single statement from the ones presented, and to specify whether they want an execution plan. If the statement cannot be explained in the current schema, it is also possible to specify username and password for a second connection to Oracle, which will try to explain the plan for the selected statement using a different schema.

If an execution plan was requested, and Oracle was able to explain the statement, the next form presented to the user will be the one shown in Figure 17.3.

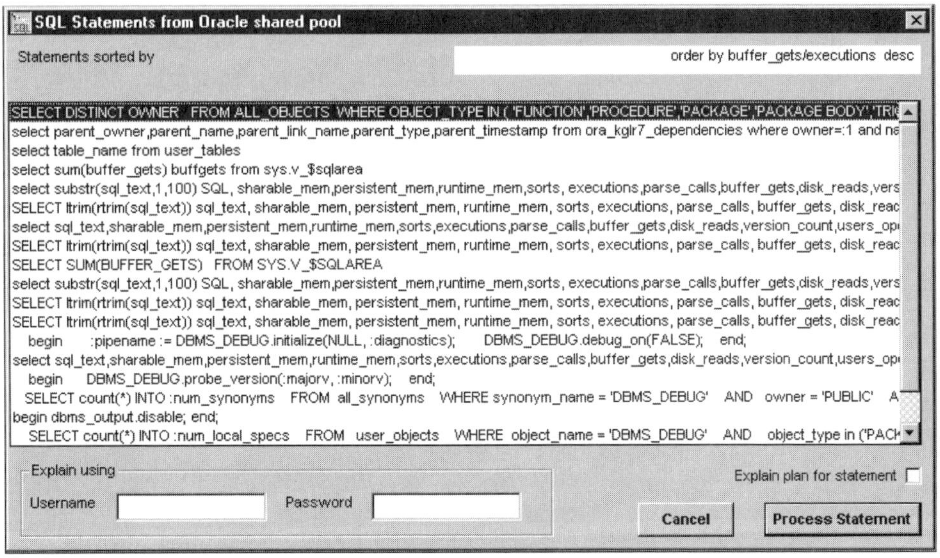

FIGURE 17.2 The SQL statements fetched from the shared pool

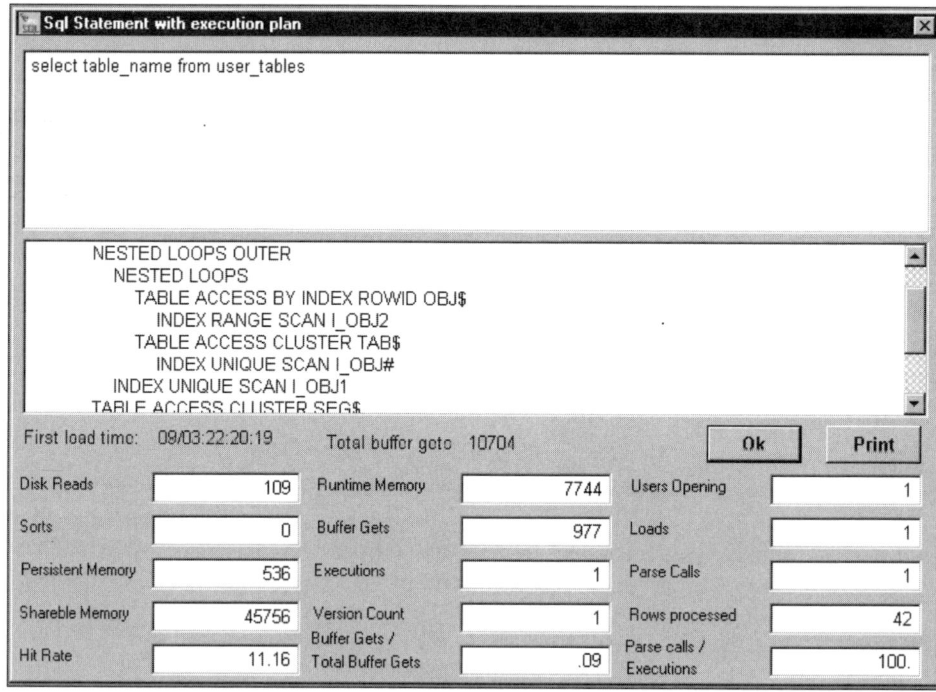

FIGURE 17.3 An Execution Plan Generated "on the Fly"

Relevant statement statistics taken from V$SQLAREA are displayed, together with the execution plan generated for the required statement.

Users can also request the displaying of statement statistics only, without the accompanying execution plan. In this case, the form hides the control that contains the execution plan, and an explain plan for the statement is not performed by ShrPool.

An application like ShrPool can be completed in a few hours of work, if a modern RAD tool is used for its development. Nevertheless, in spite of its simplicity, ShrPool can expose the key elements and characteristics of the tool used for its construction, such as the ability to use bind variables or the degree of control over cursor fetching given to developers.

17.2 ShrPool Source Code

The following sections will briefly discuss features and characteristics of each of the four RAD tools object of our analysis. The companion CD-ROM contains the source code of each implementation. A word of caution with regard to the source code must be said. Each implementation has been purposely kept as simple as possible; no advanced techniques have been used. The source code of ShrPool is by no means professionally written, production-ready code. The goal of the entire exercise is to allow IT professionals with either a general knowledge of the MS Windows environment or with specific skills in one of the tools analyzed here to be able to compare the four RAD tools and to read the source code used by each tool. This chapter is not about best practices and advanced techniques applied to each of the four RAD tools presented here.

Advanced Visual Basic developers would make more extensive use of classes, and would probably move application logic from .FRM files to module files, characterized by the .BAS extension. In the same manner, advanced Powerbuilder users would make use of user objects, using extensively window inheritance and other advanced object-oriented Powerbuilder features. Sophisticated naming conventions can also be adopted by advanced programmers, to be able to immediately recognize the type and the scope of each variable or object by its name. Unfortunately, professionally written code can usually be understood only by other professionals with at least the same level of competence in the same environment. For this reason, the source code presented here uses only very basic features, which don't require advanced skills to be understood. ShrPool is implemented using basically four windows:

1. Oracle connection Form
2. SQL statement fetch options
3. SQL statements from Oracle shared pool
4. Statistics and execution plan for each analyzed statement

In all versions of ShrPool presented in this chapter, source code has been attached to each menu option and each command button appearing in the application. Professionally written applications would rarely use this naïve technique. If object-oriented design patterns were adopted, each menu option would send a message to an application brain, possibly passing a reference to itself, allowing the application logic controller to detect the menu option chosen by the user.[1]

Each menu item would become an object, implementing specialized behavior carrying out the task specified by the menu option. The application brain would therefore receive an object of type *MenuItem*, invoking its *Execute* method. If state information is maintained through calls to the same menu option, an Undo feature can be easily implemented.

It is always a good idea to de-couple visual interface from application logic. If the application code that reacts to a click of the user to a command button is im-

---

[1] See the *Command Pattern* in Gamma, et al. *Design Patterns – Elements of Reusable Object-Oriented Software*, Boston: Addison Wesley, 1995.

plemented behind the command button, as done in ShrPool, there is no flexibility built in the application. That code will be meaningful only in the context of the command button attached to it. This is particularly limiting if development tools, such as Delphi or Powerbuilder, allow for window inheritance. Detaching application behavior from visual representation allows for code reuse and better use of polymorphism. ShrPool, on the contrary, has been intentionally kept simple and easy to understand by using straightforward techniques.

Each version of ShrPool presented in this chapter can be considered a *prototype* or *proof of concepts*, useful only to illustrate how to browse SQL statements from the Oracle shared pool in the simplest way. If you find ShrPool useful, and you want to improve it, you will probably end up rewriting ShrPool from scratch, using the advanced techniques supported by the IDE of your choice. There are at least two areas in which ShrPool must be improved to be able to compete with commercial software that performs the same task. One is printing, which, in the prototype, is very basic. The other weakness of ShrPool is the way it presents the execution plan (each line is indented in a listbox). Tools like SQL Navigator, by Quest Software, use a tree control that can be expanded and collapsed, numbering each sequential step, with a plain English explanation of each step (tables and indexes accessed, hints used, etc.) in a taskbar.

The rest of the chapter will illustrate all ShrPool implementations. Source code and application behavior will be discussed for each of the four windows comprising the tool. This will make the different development environments easier to compare.

17.3 ShrPool in Visual Basic

This version of ShrPool is developed in Visual Basic release 6, using the ActiveX Data Object (ADO) wrapper for the Ole DB provider for Oracle. The Ole DB provider for Oracle has been implemented by Microsoft using Oracle OCI (release 7), a great improvement over the older ODBC technology. We dare say that only with ADO/Ole DB Visual Basic can be proficiently used in an Oracle environment, without recurring to third party software for Oracle connectivity. The VB interface is very intuitive, and developers with no previous experience with the tool can quickly find their way without being forced to continuously consult either online or printed manuals. The two-way editing mechanism works without glitches, and allow developers always to be in control of all source code attached to the visual elements of the form. The same cannot be said, as we will see, for Powerbuilder or Oracle Developer.

Figure 17.4 shows the definition of the MDI main form of the application, together with the main menu, in the VB development environment.

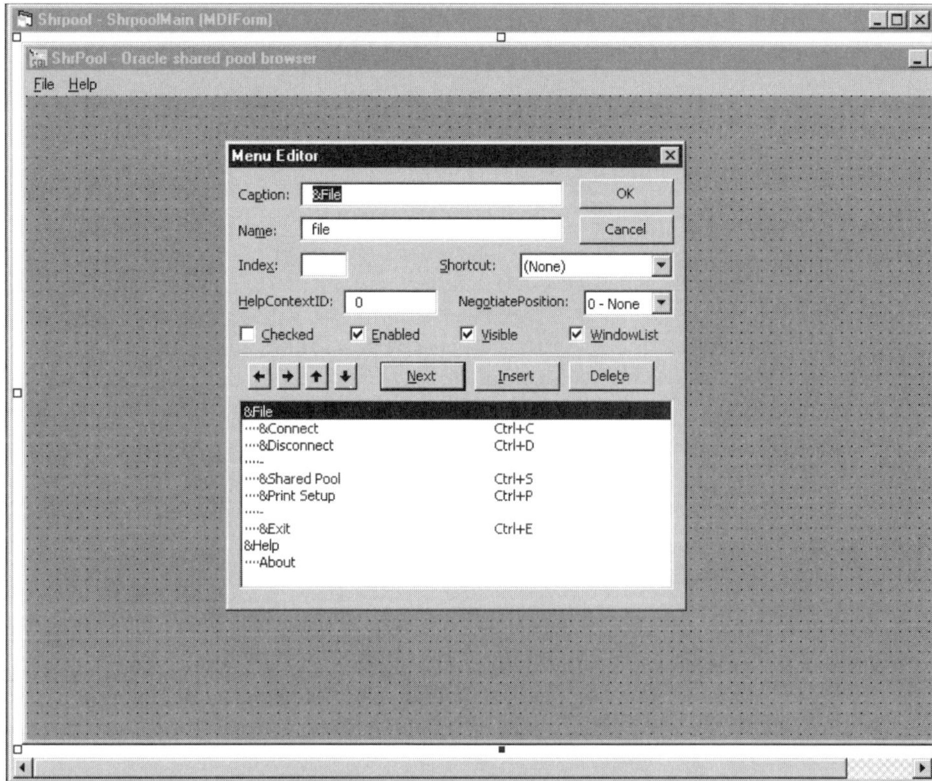

FIGURE 17.4 MDI Main Form and Menu Definition in VB ShrPool

The VB version of ShrPool includes six forms (.FRM files) and one module (.BAS file). The picture below shows the project applet containing all application components.

The only module used by ShrPool contains the definition of several global variables accessed throughout the application, the VB definition of 2 Windows APIs used by the connection form to read and write INI, the definition of the record (VB Type) used to fetch statement statistics from V$SQLAREA, and the definition of two functions used to enable/disable menu options.

Without any further ado, let us go straight to the application code. The MDI main form defines a menu that includes a few options. The source code behind the click event of each menu option is shown below.

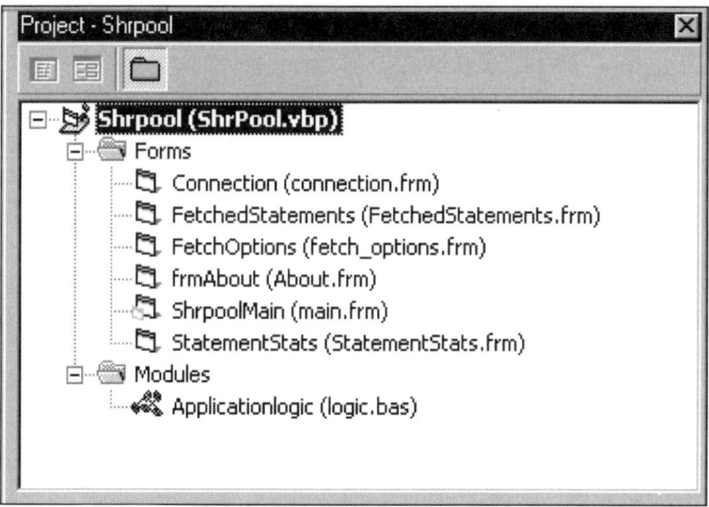

FIGURE 17.5 VB ShrPool Application Components

```
Main.frm:
Private Sub about_Click()
frmAbout.Show vbModal
End Sub
Private Sub connect_Click()
Connection.Show
End Sub
Private Sub disconnect_Click()
    If DBConnected Then
        cn.Close
        DBConnected = False
        menu_disable
    End If
End Sub
Private Sub exit_Click()
    disconnect_Click
    Unload Me
End Sub
Private Sub MDIForm_Load()
    DBConnected = False
End Sub
Private Sub print_setup_Click()
ShrpoolMain.PrintSetup.ShowPrinter
```

```
23: End Sub
24: Private Sub shared_pool_Click()
25:     FetchOptions.Show vbModal
26: End Sub
```

1–3 The about dialog is displayed when users click on the about option.

4–6 The connection form is displayed responding to the click event on the "Connect" menu option.

7 Logic behind the click event of the "Disconnect" menu option:

8–12 If the global variable DBConnected indicates that the application is currently connected, disconnect from Oracle and invoke the function that grays out the menu options that cannot be selected when the application is disconnected.

14–17 Logic responds to the click event of the "Exit" menu option. A disconnection from Oracle is attempted before closing the application.

18–20 Application logic triggered when the MDI main form is first loaded. Set the global variable DBConnected to FALSE.

21–23 Display the common dialog box for printer set up responding to the click event for the "Print Setup" menu option.

24–26 Application logic to respond to the click event of the "Shared Pool" menu option.

Following the logical flow of ShrPool, the next form the user requests interacting with the application is the Oracle connection dialog. To make ShrPool a little more user friendly, the VB version stores the user options in an INI file, and retrieves the last selected Oracle username and TNS connection string from the initialization file, leaving only the password field to be entered by the user. To implement this functionality, two Windows low-level APIs have been used. Figure 17.6 represents the connection dialog box. The VB source code follows.

```
Connection.frm:
Option Explicit
Private Sub b_cancel_Click()
Unload Me
End Sub

Private Sub b_ok_Click()
Dim ErrorRep As ADODB.Errors
Dim rel As ADODB.Recordset
Dim fld As ADODB.Field
Dim flds As ADODB.Fields
Dim release As String
Dim SinRel As Single

```

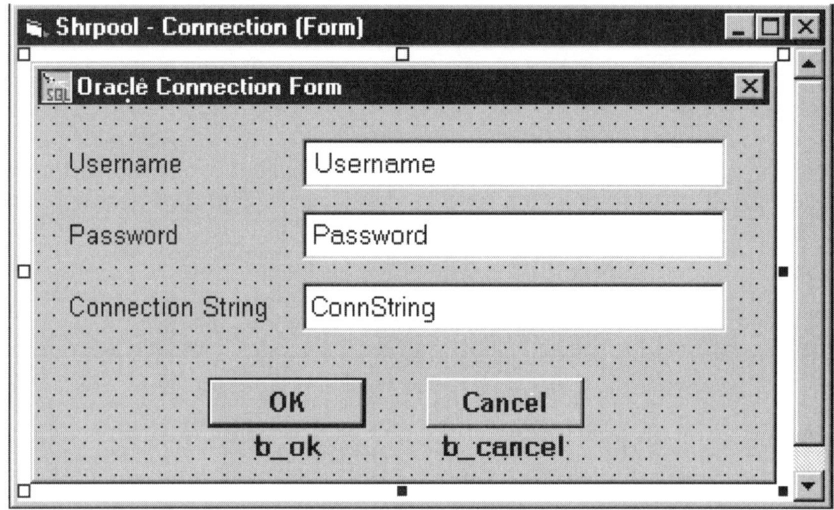

FIGURE 17.6 The Oracle Connection Dialog

```
Dim conn As String
Screen.MousePointer = vbHourglass
On Error GoTo AdoError
OraServer = ConnString.Text
OraSchema = Username.Text
conn = "provider=MSDAORA; Server=" + ConnString.Text + _
     ";User ID=" + Username.Text + ";Password=" + _
     Password.Text

cn.Open conn
'Determine if Oracle release is < than 7.2
Set rel = cn.Execute("select nvl(substr(value,1,3),'7.0') " _
        + "version from sys.v_$parameter where name='compatible'")
release = rel(0)
rel.Close
SinRel = Val(release)
InstanceRelease = SinRel * 10
DBConnected = True
WritePrivateProfileString "oracle", "username", _
        Username.Text, "shrpool.ini"
WritePrivateProfileString "oracle", "tns_string", _
     ConnString.Text, "shrpool.ini"
menu_enable
Unload Connection
```

```
38: Screen.MousePointer = vbDefault
39: Exit Sub
40:
41: AdoError:
42:     Dim SingleError As Error
43:     Dim ErrorString As String
44:     Set ErrorRep = cn.Errors
45:     For Each SingleError In ErrorRep
46:         ErrorString = ErrorString + SingleError.Description
47:     Next
48:     MsgBox "Oracle Error: " + ErrorString, vbExclamation, "Error"
49:     Exit Sub
50: End Sub
51:
52: Private Sub Form_Load()
53: Dim s_username As String * 128
54: Dim s_tns As String * 128
55: Dim l_len As Long
56:
57:
58: l_len = GetPrivateProfileString("oracle", "username", _
59:         "", s_username, 128, "shrpool.ini")
60: l_len = GetPrivateProfileString("oracle", "tns_string", _
61:         "", s_tns, 128, "shrpool.ini")
62: Username.Text = s_username
63: ConnString.Text = s_tns
64: If Len(Trim(Username.Text)) > 0 Then
65:     Show
66:     Password.SetFocus
67: End If
68:
69: End Sub
```

2–4 If the Cancel button has been clicked, the form is destroyed (unloaded).

6 Application logic responds to the click event of the Ok button.

7–14 A few variables are defined, mainly to support the ADO model for connectivity with Oracle.

15 The mouse pointer assumes the hourglass shape, to indicate a lengthy operation.

16 Exception handling diverts the code flow towards the section that deals with potential errors.

17–18 Two global variables are set to the content of the fields inputted by the user. OraServer (the TNS connection string) and OraSchema (the default schema) can be used later on by other components of the application. For this reason, they are defined as global.

19–23 The ADO connection object at work. The connection string is built from the form fields inputted by the user, and the Open method is called. If the connection to Oracle fails, the error handler will divert the flow to the label defined above.

24–28 The Execute method of the ADO connection object can generate a recordset, if the command passed to it is a SELECT. In this case, the query fetches the version of the Oracle engine. rel(0) is the content of the first field of the recordset. The recordset is destroyed after its content has been saved in a variable (release).

29–30 The string containing the Oracle release number is converted to a floating point number, which is multiplied by 10 to eliminate the decimal part from the number. The result of the conversion is stored in the global variable InstanceRelease, accessible throughout the entire application. It is important to know if we are connected to an old instance (prior to 7.2), which doesn't support the ROWS_PROCESSED field in the V$SQLAREA V$ view.

31–38 The DBConnected global variable is set to true, because at this point we have successfully established a connection to Oracle. The initialization file is updated with the connection values provided by the user, the form unloaded, and the mouse pointer changed back to the normal arrow shape.

41–50 This is the ADO error handler. If a connection to Oracle cannot be established, a message box displays an error string to the user, and the control goes back to the form.

52 Application logic is applied when the form is first loaded.

53–55 A few variables are defined. They will contain username and connection string as loaded from the initialization file.

58–63 The fields that will be displayed on the form are filled with the values taken from the ini file.

64–67 If the ini file provided a username, the field that will receive the focus when the form is displayed is the one requesting the password; otherwise, the field with focus will be the one requesting the username.

When users leave the connection dialog after having established a connection to Oracle, the main MDI menu displays options that were not previously available, such as "Disconnect" and "Shared Pool". Selecting "Shared Pool" causes the application to display the FetchOptions form, which allows users to enter selection criteria for the extraction of SQL statements from the Oracle shared pool. ShrPool dynamically builds an SQL statement from the options selected by the user interacting with this form. The source code associated with the FetchOptions form (Figure 17.7) is shown below.

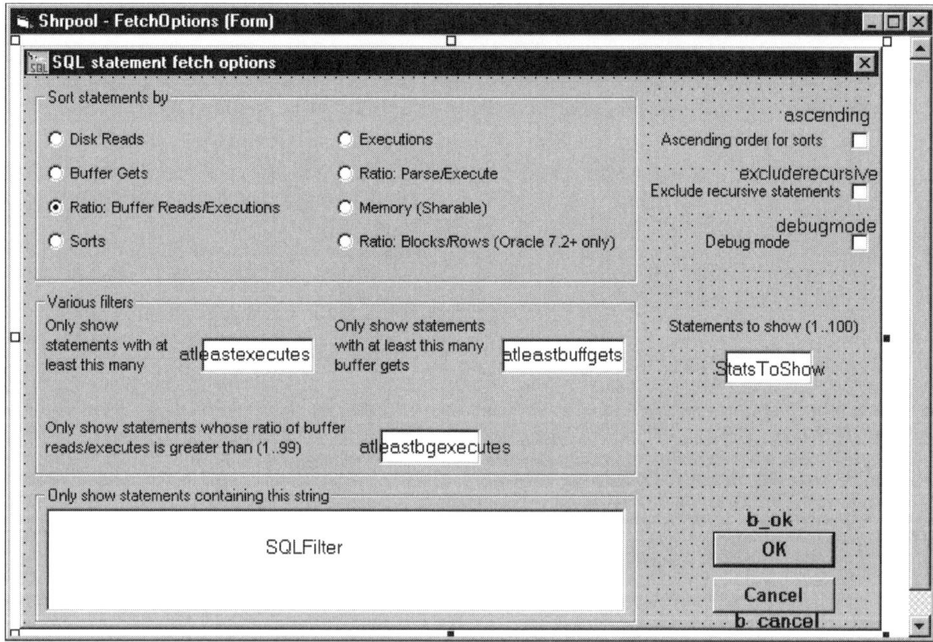

FIGURE 17.7 The FetchOptions Form

```
fetch_options.frm:
Dim OrderClause As String
Private Sub b_cancel_Click()
Unload FetchOptions
End Sub
Private Sub b_ok_Click()
Dim sts As Long
Dim ii As Integer
Dim ChosenOption As Integer
Dim main_select As String
Dim where_clause As String
Dim Cmd As New ADODB.Command

If InstanceRelease >= 72 Then
    main_select = "select sql_text,sharable_mem,persistent_mem," _
    + "runtime_mem,sorts,executions,parse_calls,buffer_gets," _
    + "disk_reads,version_count,users_opening,loads," _
    + "to_char(to_date(first_load_time,'YYYY-MM-DD/HH24:MI:SS')" _
 + ",'DD/MM:HH24:MI:SS') first_load_time,rawtohex(address)address" _
+ ",to_char(hash_value) hash_value,rows_processed from sys.v_$sqlarea"
```

```
Else
    main_select = "select sql_text,sharable_mem,persistent_mem," _
    + "runtime_mem,sorts,executions,parse_calls,buffer_gets," _
    + "disk_reads,version_count,users_opening,loads," _
    + "to_char(to_date(first_load_time,'YYYY-MM-DD/HH24:MI:SS')" _
+ ",'DD/MM:HH24:MI:SS') first_load_time,rawtohex(address)address," _
    + "to_char(hash_value) hash_value from sys.v_$sqlarea"
End If
For ii = 0 To 7
    If sortoption(ii).Value = True Then
        ChosenOption = ii
    End If
Next
Select Case ChosenOption
    Case 0: OrderClause = " order by disk_reads "
    Case 1: OrderClause = " order by buffer_gets "
    Case 2: OrderClause = " order by buffer_gets/executions "
    Case 3: OrderClause = " order by sorts"
    Case 4: OrderClause = " order by executions "
    Case 5: OrderClause = " order by parse_calls/executions "
    Case 6: OrderClause = " order by sharable_mem "
    Case 7: OrderClause = " order by buffer_gets/decode" _
        + "(rows_processed,0,1,executions) "
End Select

If ascending.Value = 1 Then
    OrderClause = OrderClause + " asc "
Else
    OrderClause = OrderClause + " desc "
End If
OrderByClause = OrderClause
where_clause = " where executions > 0 "
If excluderecursive.Value = 1 Then
   where_clause = where_clause + " and parsing_user_id != 0 "
End If
If Val(atleastbuffgets.Text) > 0 Then
where_clause = where_clause + " and buffer_gets > " _
    + atleastbuffgets.Text
End If
If Val(atleastexecutes.Text) > 0 Then
    where_clause = where_clause + " and executions > " _
    + atleastexecutes.Text
End If
If Val(atleastbgexecutes.Text) > 0 Then
```

```
64:     where_clause = where_clause + " and buffer_gets/executions > " _
65:     + atleastbgecutions.Text
66: End If
67: If Len(Trim(SQLFilter.Text)) > 0 Then
68:     where_clause = where_clause + _
69:     " and upper(sql_text) like upper('%" _
70:     + Trim(SQLFilter.Text) + "%') "
71: End If
72: FetchStatement = main_select + where_clause + OrderClause
73: If debugmode.Value = 1 Then
74:     Cmd.ActiveConnection = cn
75:     Cmd.CommandType = adCmdText
76:     Cmd.CommandText = "ALTER SESSION SET SQL_TRACE=TRUE"
77:     On Error Resume Next
78:     Cmd.Execute
79:     sts = MsgBox(FetchStatement, vbInformation + vbOKOnly, _
80:            "SQL statement")
81: End If
82: Unload Me
83: FetchedStatements.Show vbModal
84: End Sub
85: Private Sub Form_Load()
86:     excluderecursive.Value = 1
87:     sortoption(2).Value = True
88:     StatsToShow.Text = "20"
89: End Sub
90:
```

2–4 If the cancel button has been clicked, the form is destroyed.

5 Application logic responds to the click event for the Ok button.

6–9 Definition of a few variables used by the application logic. Note that the ADODB.command object, used to enable SQL tracing the debug mode option, has been chosen.

11–25 If the connected instance is of a release prior to 7.2, the SQL statement used to fetch the required SQL statements from the shared pool won't try to access the ROWS_PROCESSED column from V$SQLAREA. Otherwise, the dynamically built SQL statement will include that column.

28–43 An order by clause is derived from the selected radio button that prompts the user to choose an order criterion.

45–49 If the checkbox "Ascending order for sort" has been selected, the sort order will be ascending; otherwise, it will be descending (the default).

51–71 A where clause is worked out from the various selection filters chosen by the user.

72 The global variable FetchStatement is built by concatenating the main select clause with the where and order clauses derived from the form fields inputted by the user.

73–81 If the Debug mode option has been selected, the ADO command object is used to submit an ALTER SESSION command to Oracle, enabling SQL Trace. The SQL statement dynamically built by ShrPool is shown to the user in a message box (line 85).

82–83 The form is destroyed and the dialog showing the SQL statements fetched from the shared pool is displayed.

85–89 The form is initialized with a few default values each time it is loaded.

The source code that drives the FetchOptions form defines an ADO object, Command, which is used by ShrPool to submit a DDL statement (ALTER SESSION) to the Oracle engine. The ADO model is simple to use but powerful enough to support advanced features for SQL handling. On the negative side, the Value property of an OptionButton is a Boolean variable, while the Value property of a CheckBox can assume three values, 0 for unchecked, 1 for checked, and 2 for grayed. The two VB objects are very similar, yet the datatype specifying one of their most important properties is different. In Powerbuilder, for example, check boxes and radio buttons consistently define the checked property as a Boolean.

When the FetchOptions form completes its task, the application logic unloads it and the next form, shown in Figure 17.8, FetchedStatements is presented to the users.

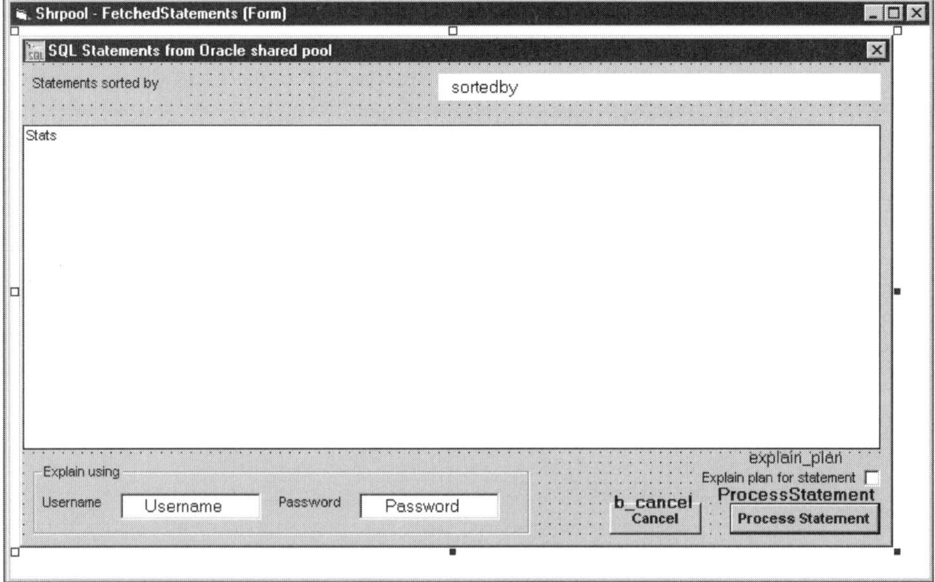

FIGURE 17.8 The FetchedStatements Form

60 lines of VB code attached to this form accomplish the following tasks:

- ❑ Submit the SQL statement built in the previous form to the engine.
- ❑ Fetch the required SQL statements from the shared pool.
- ❑ Store the statistics for each in an array residing in the local memory.
- ❑ Display the statements retrieved from the shared pool on the form.

The code could have been even more compact if a data aware control, say a grid, were used instead of programmatically populating the local array with statements and statistics from the recordset defined in ADO. The drawback of this approach is that it is hard to force the grid to display a limited set of SQL statements, as required by the users, rather than all statements identified by the where clause.

The source code defined in the FetchedStatements form follows.

```
Dim StatementNumber As Integer
Private Sub b_cancel_Click()
    FetchStatement = ""
    OrderByClause = ""
    Unload FetchedStatements
End Sub
Private Sub Form_Load()
    Dim SQLrs As New ADODB.Recordset
    Dim SQLTotBG As New ADODB.Recordset
    Dim ii As Integer
    Screen.MousePointer = vbHourglass
    sortedby.Text = OrderByClause
    StatementNumber = Val(FetchOptions.StatsToShow.Text)
    SQLrs.CursorLocation = adUseServer
    SQLrs.Open FetchStatement, cn, adOpenForwardOnly, adLockReadOnly
    SQLrs.MoveFirst
    ii = 0
    ReDim SQLStats(StatementNumber)

    Do While SQLrs.EOF <> True
        SQLStats(ii).sql_text = SQLrs(0).Value
        SQLStats(ii).sharable_mem = SQLrs(1).Value
        SQLStats(ii).persistent_mem = SQLrs(2).Value
        SQLStats(ii).runtime_mem = SQLrs(3).Value
        SQLStats(ii).sorts = SQLrs(4).Value
        SQLStats(ii).executions = SQLrs(5).Value
        SQLStats(ii).parse_calls = SQLrs(6).Value
        SQLStats(ii).buffer_gets = SQLrs(7).Value
        SQLStats(ii).disk_reads = SQLrs(8).Value
```

```
30:         SQLStats(ii).version_count = SQLrs(9).Value
31:         SQLStats(ii).users_opening = SQLrs(10).Value
32:         SQLStats(ii).loads = SQLrs(11).Value
33:         SQLStats(ii).first_load_time = SQLrs(12).Value
34:         SQLStats(ii).address = SQLrs(13).Value
35:         SQLStats(ii).hash_value = SQLrs(14).Value
36:         If InstanceRelease >= 72 Then
37:             SQLStats(ii).rows_processed = SQLrs(15).Value
38:         End If
39:         If ii >= StatementNumber Then
40:             Exit Do
41:         End If
42:         Stats.AddItem SQLStats(ii).sql_text, ii
43:         ii = ii + 1
44:         SQLrs.MoveNext
45:     Loop
46:     SQLrs.Close
47:     Stats.Selected(0) = True
48:     Set SQLTotBG = cn.Execute("select sum(buffer_gets) " _
49:                         + "buffgets from sys.v_$sqlarea")
50:     TotalBufferGets = SQLTotBG(0)
51:     SQLTotBG.Close
52:     Screen.MousePointer = vbDefault
53: End Sub
54: Private Sub ProcessStatement_Click()
55: StatementIndexChosen = Stats.ListIndex
56: StatementStats.Show vbModal
57: End Sub
58: Private Sub Stats_DblClick()
59:     ProcessStatement_Click
60: End Sub
```

2–6 Application logic responds to the click event on the cancel button. The form is unloaded and the global variables holding the fetch and order by clause of the statement built by the previous form are reset (i.e., set to NULL).

8–11 Click event for the Ok button logic—A few variables are defined, mainly two ADO recordsets that will hold the Oracle cursors needed to fetch the required statements from the shared pool and the sum of all buffer gets generated by the engine.

12–13 The sort option control is populated with the sort option used by the statement built by the previous form, taken from a global variable. The number of statements required by the user is taken from the parent form (FetchOptions).

14–16 The ADO recordset is initialized, and the SQL statement to get the required SQL statements from the shared pool associated with it. The statement is executed and the cursor pointer moved to the first entry of the cursor (MoveFirst).

17–18 The counter variable used to control the loop is initialized to 0, and the array that will receive SQL statement text and statistics is dimensioned to the number of statements required by the user.

20–45 The loop that fetches all selected rows from the server is started at line 20. The local array is populated with the data fetched from the cursor. If the connected Oracle engine is of a release greater than 7.2, the rows_processed statistics are fetched together with other relevant statistics. If the cursor fetches more rows than the ones requested by the user, the loop is interrupted, to avoid an array subscript range error. At line 42 the list item control displayed on the form is populated with the text of each SQL statement fetched from the shared pool.

46–47 The ADO recordset is destroyed, and the first row of the list item control is selected (i.e., highlighted).

48–51 The second ADO recordset is populated with the total number of buffer gets generated by the Oracle engine. The global variable TotalBufferGets receives that value, which will be displayed by the subsequent form.

54–57 These lines of code handle the click event for the "Process statement" button. The StatementStats form is displayed modally when the user clicks on the button.

58–60 These lines of code handle the double-click event on the list box item displayed on the form. Double-clicking on a selected statement in the list box is equivalent to selecting the statement and clicking on the "Process statement" button.

This form requires only 60 lines of code to perform a lot of tasks. This is truly remarkable, and shows one of the strongest points in favor of this development environment.

The last form displayed by ShrPool (Figure 17.9) is the one that shows all statement statistics and execution plan for the selected statement, if it has been required.

At this step of the application flow, all statement statistics have already been fetched from the server and are in the client memory. The first 1000 characters of the string containing the statement have already been fetched as well. Two operations must yet be performed by the application. First, the entire SQL statement being analyzed must be fetched from V$SQLTEXT. If an SQL statement is longer than 1000 characters, it must be built by concatenating the "pieces" stored in V$SQLTEXT. Second, if the user requested an execution plan, it must be generated and presented in the form. The problem here is presented by an annoying Oracle bug present in all releases from 7.3 to 8.0.4. The statement hash value,

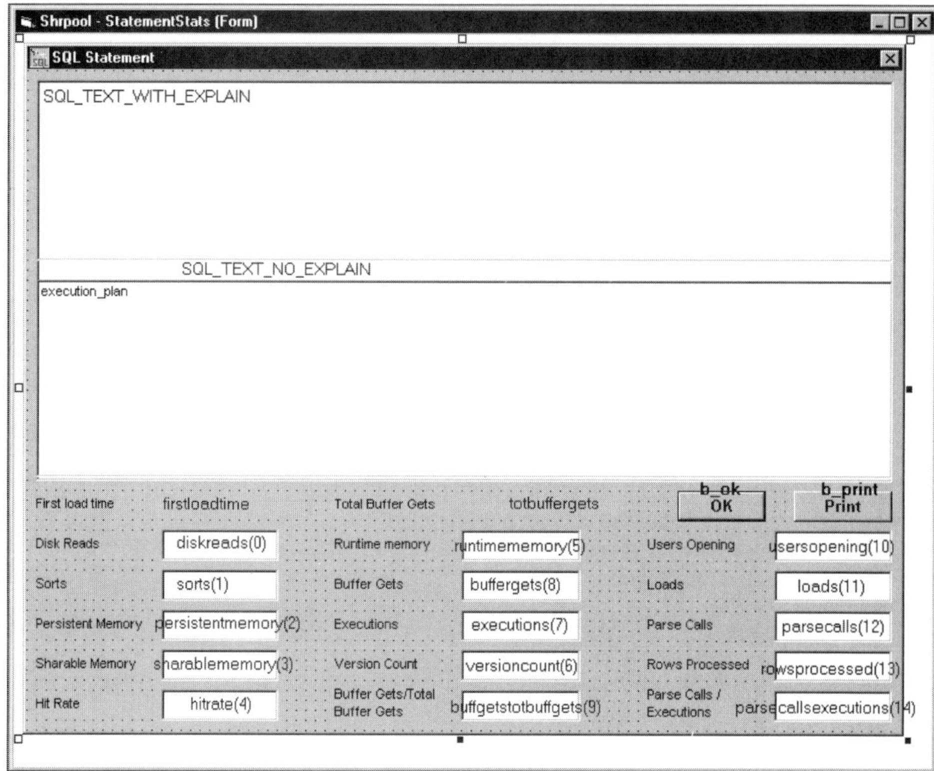

FIGURE 17.9 The StatementStats Form

used together with the address value to relate the statement statistics, held in V$SQLAREA with the statement string held in V$SQLTEXT, is an Oracle number that is internally cast by Oracle to a signed integer. The net effect of the casting is that the number often overflows, generating a negative number that makes relating the two tables impossible. ShrPool handles the problem by presenting the first 1000 characters of the statement if the fetch from V$SQLTEXT fails. This doesn't fix the problem if the statement is longer than 1000 characters, because the execution plan won't be built anyway, but at least something is displayed in the form. If an execution plan cannot be generated, a message box is displayed informing the user about the Oracle error, which prevents the displaying of the execution plan, but the form is displayed anyway, so that the statement statistics are always accessible.

This form is the most complex of the entire application. This fact is reflected by the number of lines of VB code attached to it (237). The complexity is given by the handling of the logic necessary to build an Oracle plan table in the user schema if a plan table is not already defined and by the option given to the user to explain the statement using a different Oracle account. The source code attached to the form is shown below.

```
StatementStats.frm:
Option Explicit

Private Sub b_ok_Click()
    Unload Me
End Sub

Private Sub b_print_Click()
    MsgBox "Make sure the printer is ready...", _
        vbInformation, "Printing SQL Analysis"
    Me.PrintForm
End Sub

Private Sub Form_Load()
Dim BuffGetsRatio As Single
Dim HitRatio As Single
Dim ParseExecsRatio As Single
Screen.MousePointer = vbHourglass
firstloadtime.Caption = CStr(SQLStats(StatementIndexChosen) _
    .first_load_time)
totbuffergets.Caption = TotalBufferGets
diskreads(0).Text = CStr(SQLStats(StatementIndexChosen) _
    .disk_reads)
sorts(1).Text = CStr(SQLStats(StatementIndexChosen) _
    .sorts)
persistentmemory(2).Text = CStr(SQLStats(StatementIndexChosen) _
    .persistent_mem)
sharablememory(3).Text = CStr(SQLStats(StatementIndexChosen) _
    .sharable_mem)
runtimememory(5).Text = CStr(SQLStats(StatementIndexChosen) _
    .runtime_mem)
buffergets(8).Text = CStr(SQLStats(StatementIndexChosen) _
    .buffer_gets)
executions(7).Text = CStr(SQLStats(StatementIndexChosen) _
    .executions)
versioncount(6).Text = CStr(SQLStats(StatementIndexChosen) _
    .version_count)
usersopening(10).Text = CStr(SQLStats(StatementIndexChosen) _
    .users_opening)
loads(11).Text = CStr(SQLStats(StatementIndexChosen) _
    .loads)
```

```
parsecalls(12).Text = CStr(SQLStats(StatementIndexChosen) _
    .parse_calls)
If InstanceRelease >= 72 Then
    rowsprocessed(13).Text = CStr(SQLStats(StatementIndexChosen) _
        .rows_processed)
End If
HitRatio = SQLStats(StatementIndexChosen).disk_reads * 100 _
    / SQLStats(StatementIndexChosen).buffer_gets
If TotalBufferGets > 0 Then
    BuffGetsRatio = SQLStats(StatementIndexChosen).buffer_gets _
        / TotalBufferGets
Else
    BuffGetsRatio = 0
End If
ParseExecsRatio = SQLStats(StatementIndexChosen) _
    .parse_calls * 100 / _
    SQLStats(StatementIndexChosen).executions
hitrate(4).Text = Format(HitRatio, "Fixed")
parsecallsexecutions(14).Text = Format(ParseExecsRatio, "Fixed")
buffgetstotbuffgets(9).Text = Format(BuffGetsRatio, "Fixed")
If FetchedStatements.explain_plan.Value = 1 Then
    SQL_TEXT_WITH_EXPLAIN.Visible = True
    execution_plan.Visible = True
    SQL_TEXT_WITH_EXPLAIN.Text = GetSqlText()
    compute_execution_plan
Else
    SQL_TEXT_NO_EXPLAIN.Visible = True
    SQL_TEXT_NO_EXPLAIN.Text = GetSqlText()
End If

Screen.MousePointer = vbDefault
End Sub
Private Function GetSqlText() As String
Dim sqltext As New ADODB.Recordset
Dim Cmd As New ADODB.Command
Dim prm1 As New ADODB.Parameter
Dim prm2 As New ADODB.Parameter
Dim BuiltText As String
Dim SQLTemp As String
Dim ErrorRep As ADODB.Errors

On Error GoTo AdoError
sqltext.CursorLocation = adUseServer
Cmd.ActiveConnection = cn
```

```
Cmd.CommandText = "SELECT SQL_TEXT FROM SYS.V_$SQLTEXT " _
    + "WHERE RAWTOHEX(ADDRESS) = ? AND TO_CHAR(HASH_VALUE)" _
    + " = ? ORDER BY PIECE"
Cmd.CommandType = adCmdText
Cmd.Prepared = True

Set prm1 = Cmd.CreateParameter("address", adVarChar, _
            adParamInput, 8)
Cmd.Parameters.Append prm1
Cmd("address") = Trim(SQLStats(StatementIndexChosen).address)
Set prm2 = Cmd.CreateParameter("hashvalue", adVarChar, _
           adParamInput, 10)
Cmd.Parameters.Append prm2
Cmd("hashvalue") = Trim(SQLStats(StatementIndexChosen) _
    .hash_value)
Set sqltext = Cmd.Execute
sqltext.MoveFirst
While sqltext.EOF <> True
    BuiltText = BuiltText + sqltext(0).Value
    sqltext.MoveNext
Wend
GetSqlText = BuiltText
Exit Function
AdoError:
    Dim SingleError As Error
    Dim ErrorString As String
    Set ErrorRep = cn.Errors
    For Each SingleError In ErrorRep
        ErrorString = ErrorString + SingleError.Description
    Next
    BuiltText = SQLStats(StatementIndexChosen).sql_text
    GetSqlText = BuiltText
End Function
Private Sub compute_execution_plan()
Dim create_table As String
Dim local_cn As New ADODB.Connection
Dim CreTab As New ADODB.Command
Dim Cmd As New ADODB.Command
Dim RecNum As New ADODB.Recordset
Dim ErrorRep As ADODB.Errors
Dim ExecPlan As New ADODB.Recordset
Dim OraMsg As String

create_table = "create table LOCAL_PLAN_TABLE (" _
```

```
                        + "statement_id     varchar2(30)," _
                          + "timestamp      date," _
                          + "remarks        varchar2(80)," _
                          + "operation      varchar2(30)," _
                          + "options            varchar2(30)," _
                          + "object_node    varchar2(128)," _
                          + "object_owner   varchar2(30)," _
                          + "object_name    varchar2(30)," _
                          + "object_instance numeric," _
                          + "object_type      varchar2(30), " _
                          + "optimizer        varchar2(255)," _
                          + "search_columns  numeric, " _
                          + "id         numeric," _
                          + "parent_id numeric," _
                          + "position  numeric," _
                          + "other     long)"

RecNum.CursorLocation = adUseServer
On Error GoTo ado_error_1
RecNum.Open "SELECT count(*) FROM LOCAL_PLAN_TABLE", cn, _
    adOpenForwardOnly, adLockReadOnly
On Error GoTo exit_label_2
Cmd.ActiveConnection = cn
Cmd.CommandText = "TRUNCATE TABLE LOCAL_PLAN_TABLE"
Cmd.CommandType = adCmdText
Cmd.CommandTimeout = 20
Cmd.Execute

If Len(Trim(FetchedStatements.Username.Text)) > 0 Then
    On Error GoTo exit_label_1
    local_cn.Open "provider=MSDAORA; Server=" + OraServer + _
    ";User ID=" + FetchedStatements.Username.Text + _
    ";Password=" + FetchedStatements.Password.Text
    On Error GoTo exit_label_2
    Cmd.ActiveConnection = cn
    Cmd.CommandText = "GRANT ALL ON LOCAL_PLAN_TABLE TO " _
        + FetchedStatements.Username.Text
    Cmd.CommandTimeout = 20
    Cmd.CommandType = adCmdText
    Cmd.Execute
    On Error GoTo exit_label_1
    Cmd.ActiveConnection = local_cn
    Cmd.CommandText = "EXPLAIN PLAN INTO " + OraSchema + _
        ".LOCAL_PLAN_TABLE FOR " + SQL_TEXT_WITH_EXPLAIN.Text
```

```
    Cmd.CommandType = adCmdText
    Cmd.Execute
    local_cn.Close
Else
    On Error GoTo exit_label_2
    Cmd.ActiveConnection = cn
    Cmd.CommandText = "EXPLAIN PLAN INTO LOCAL_PLAN_TABLE FOR " _
        + SQL_TEXT_WITH_EXPLAIN.Text
    Cmd.CommandType = adCmdText
    Cmd.Execute
End If
On Error GoTo exit_label_2
ExecPlan.CursorLocation = adUseServer
ExecPlan.Open "select lpad('',4*level)||operation||''||options||'" _
    + "'||object_name query_plan from local_plan_table " _
    + "connect by prior id = parent_id start with id=1", cn, _
    adOpenForwardOnly, adLockReadOnly
ExecPlan.MoveFirst
While ExecPlan.EOF <> True
    execution_plan.AddItem ExecPlan(0).Value
    ExecPlan.MoveNext
Wend
Exit Sub
ado_error_1:
    Dim SingleError As Error
    Dim ErrorString As String
    Set ErrorRep = cn.Errors
    For Each SingleError In ErrorRep
        ErrorString = ErrorString + SingleError.Description
    Next
    OraMsg = Left(ErrorString, 9)
    If OraMsg = "ORA-00942" Then
        CreTab.ActiveConnection = cn
        CreTab.CommandText = create_table
        CreTab.CommandTimeout = 15
        CreTab.CommandType = adCmdText
        CreTab.Execute
    End If
    Resume Next

Exit Sub
exit_label_1:
    Dim OraLocalError As Error
    Dim OraLocalString As String
```

```
217:     Set ErrorRep = local_cn.Errors
218:     For Each OraLocalError In ErrorRep
219:         OraLocalString = OraLocalString + OraLocalError.Description
220:     Next
221:
222:     MsgBox "Could not display execution plan" + OraLocalString, _
223:         vbInformation, "Oracle Error"
224:     Exit Sub
225: exit_label_2:
226:
227:     Dim OraGlobalError As Error
228:     Dim OraGlobalString As String
229:     Set ErrorRep = cn.Errors
230:     For Each OraGlobalError In ErrorRep
231:       OraGlobalString = OraGlobalString + OraGlobalError.Description
232:     Next
233:
234:     MsgBox "Could not display execution plan" + OraGlobalString, _
235:         vbInformation, "Oracle Error"
236:     Exit Sub
237: End Sub
```

3–5 The form is unloaded if the user clicks on the "Ok" button.

7–11 The form is dumped on the printer if the user clicks on the "Print" button.

13–17 Application logic governs the initial loading of the form. Three floating point variables are defined; they will hold the computation of the statement ratios such as parse calls over executions.

18–46 All statement statistics are displayed in their controls on the form. The values are taken from the array that has been previously filled with SQL statistics fetched from the Oracle engine.

47–60 The three statement ratios are computed, formatted, and displayed in their controls on the form.

61–69 This logic handles the user request of an execution plan. If the statement must be explained, the smaller TextBox is made visible, together with the ListBox that will contain the execution plan. Otherwise, the ListBox containing the execution plan is kept hidden and the larger TextBox is made visible. The visible TextBox is populated with the statement string generated by the form function GetSqlText(). If an execution plan has been requested, the compute_execution_plan form procedure is invoked.

71–72 These lines conclude the loading step of the form. The mouse pointer is changed from an hourglass shape to the default arrow.

73–80 The GetSqlText() function is defined. A few variables are defined here, mainly ADO objects to handle a parameterized query.

81–82 An error handler is established prior to perform ADO calls.

83–99 The ADO command object and two parameter objects are populated with the query parameters. This is the way ADO supports bind variables.

100–105 The ADO recordset is populated by executing the command object, which includes the query parameters. Each "piece" containing up to 64 bytes of SQL statement is fetched in a loop, and an SQL string is built concatenating all pieces.

106–107 The function returns the SQL statement built from V$SQLTEXT and exits.

108–117 This is the error handler that deals with errors generated by Oracle. If the statement cannot be generated out of V$SQLTEXT because of the Oracle bug mentioned above, the statement returned is the one taken from the array populated by FetchedStatements. In this case only the first 1000 characters will be displayed. If an error occurred, a message box informs the user of what happened.

118–126 The form procedure compute_execution_plan is created here. A few variables are defined, mainly ADO objects to handle a second connection and a few ADO recordsets needed to explain the statement and fetch all lines from the plan table.

128–144 The SQL statement that creates a explain plan table is defined here. If the user schema doesn't contain the plan table, it will be created the first time an explain plan is requested.

146–147 The ADO recordset is initialized and a specific error handler is established. If the SELECT COUNT(*) statement for the plan table fails with an ORA-00942 message, the plan table doesn't exist in the user schema, and must be created. This is done by the error handling code.

148–155 The rows in the plan table are counted. If the statement doesn't fail, we can proceed with the plan table truncation. In the SELECT COUNT(*) statement, the error handler will create the local plan table, and the execution will be resumed at line 150, which will establish a different, more generic error handler. The ADO command object, cmd, takes care of submitting the DDL statement that truncates the plan table to the engine.

157–176 If the user requested an explain plan under a different username, a second connection is arranged by the code in this section, which takes the TNS string from a global variable set by the Connection form. The plan table used to explain the statement will be the one in the default user schema, so all privileges are given to the second connection to be able to write in the local plan table. The EXPLAIN PLAN statement is built prefixing the plan table with the default schema owner. The statement is explained by the second connection, but the explain results will be stored in the main user schema. When the statement has been explained, the second connection is closed.

177–183 If the statement must be explained in the default user connection, the EXPLAIN PLAN command is built without prefixing the local plan table with a schema owner. The command is executed to populate the plan table with the execution plan for the statement.

185–194 The ExecPlan recordset is defined and created. Note the hierarchical fetching, which uses Oracle SQL extensions in the query. ADO is able to handle Oracle specific code without complaining. The strings containing the execution plan are fetched from Oracle and added, one by one, to the ListBox control displayed in the form (line 192).

196–211 The first of the three error handlers is defined in this form. This error handler contains specific code that will attempt the creation of the plan table in the user schema if the error returned by Oracle is 00942. This error handler is only established once in the form flow, just before attempting to count the number of rows in the plan table.

214–235 Two error handlers are defined, one that looks for errors in the default connection, and the other that looks for errors in the second connection, if the user requested to explain the statement using a different username.

The total number of lines of code required by the Visual Basic version of ShrPool is 521. This code can be further optimized, using advanced techniques. Visual Basic is simple to use and compact, yet powerful enough to allow for development of enterprise-class client/server applications, thanks to the ADO/OleDB pair. Another distinctive advantage of VB over tools like Oracle Developer and Powerbuilder is that the source code is saved in ASCII format files. This is true for both forms and VB code stored in modules. ASCII files are easy to deal with, especially when a version control system, such PVCS or MS Visual Source Safe, is used. On the negative side, the error handling mechanism is obsolete and naïve, good enough for an interpreted environment supporting a traditional language operating within the functional decomposition paradigm, such as GWBASIC in the old DOS era. A language based on the object-oriented paradigm, as VB claims to be, must support proper exception handling. Furthermore, VB should be extended to give more object-oriented features to the visual components, such as the possibility to inherit child forms from ancestor forms, like in Powerbuilder or Delphi. In spite of its deficiencies, Visual Basic release 6 has become a strong contender in the RAD tool market.

7.4 ShrPool in Oracle Developer

Oracle Developer shows its origins of form-displaying tool for data stored into relational tables in a character-based environment. Its character-based legacy is evident in the underlying philosophy that drives the behavior of the product and its interaction with the developer. Oracle Developer gives its best when data residing in Oracle tables must be presented to the user of the application for consultation and modification. The crucial object in an Oracle Developer application is the data block, or a set of columns taken from tables residing on the server and grouped together to be displayed and possibly modified in a visual environment. This visual environment is the canvas, which serves as a container for all data items, controls, text labels, labels and bitmaps that are visible in a form.

The navigation between fields displayed in the canvas, operated by users, causes triggers to fire. PL/SQL code found by Oracle Developer associated to triggers is executed. This model is very effective for data retrieval, displaying, data validation and storing back to the database table. Oracle Developer does an excellent job helping developers to easily define data blocks based upon complex master-detail relationships. Linking the data block to the displaying canvas is also easily accomplished, as well as enforcing business rules and validation logic in form-based triggers.

Unfortunately, applications that don't follow the data block–canvas–trigger model are difficult to implement in Oracle Developer. While it is possible to force the tool out of its natural model, doing so requires an intimate knowledge of the product and a much larger number of lines of code. Shrpool is definitely not suitable to be developed using Oracle Developer. The main reason is that the SQL statement that fetches the required SQL statements from the shared pool is built dynamically, according to the options chosen by the users. This prevents the definition of a well-defined, predetermined data block easily displayable in a canvas. Another issue is raised by the default behavior of Oracle Developer, which keeps synchronized the visual representation of the fields defined in the data block with the records stored in the database. Modifying a field in the canvas, even only programmatically, forces an internal SELECT… FOR UPDATE for the rows displayed in the form. Since it is not allowed to modify the data accessed through the V$ views, the default behavior of Oracle Developer must be overridden.

Oracle Developer allows for the definition of record groups, or memory only structures modeled after relational tables, but not necessarily synchronized with any of the real tables defined in the database. As soon as one starts using record groups instead of real data blocks, most of Oracle Developer's features and automatism are lost, and the amount of PL/SQL code required to perform even simple tasks soon becomes very large.

The ShrPool is the version developed in Oracle Developer that requires the highest number of lines of code. At the same time, it is the version that needs very little enhancements to become a "production" release. Without any further ado, let us delve into Oracle Developer forms and PL/SQL code.

The Object Navigator characterizes the development environment of Oracle Developer. It uses the popular tree visual metaphor to allow developers to access every object defined in the environment by expanding the relevant branches of the tree. In Figure 17.10, the Object Navigator displays all the objects built for the ShrPool application. The PL/SQL code needed for application processing is partially stored in form triggers and partially stored in a PL/SQL library called

SHRPOOL. This is one of the negative aspects of Oracle Developer, the exact opposite of the two-way editing mechanism typical of the modern RAD tools such as Delphi and Visual Basic.

The source code that drives the behavior of the application forms is scattered across many points in the object navigator. Developers can never see all source code governing a form at a glance, in one single window or dialog, like in VB or Delphi. The source code is instead broken down into bits, attached to triggers that can be defined at many levels (item – block – form) or contained in procedures and packages defined in PL/SQL libraries.

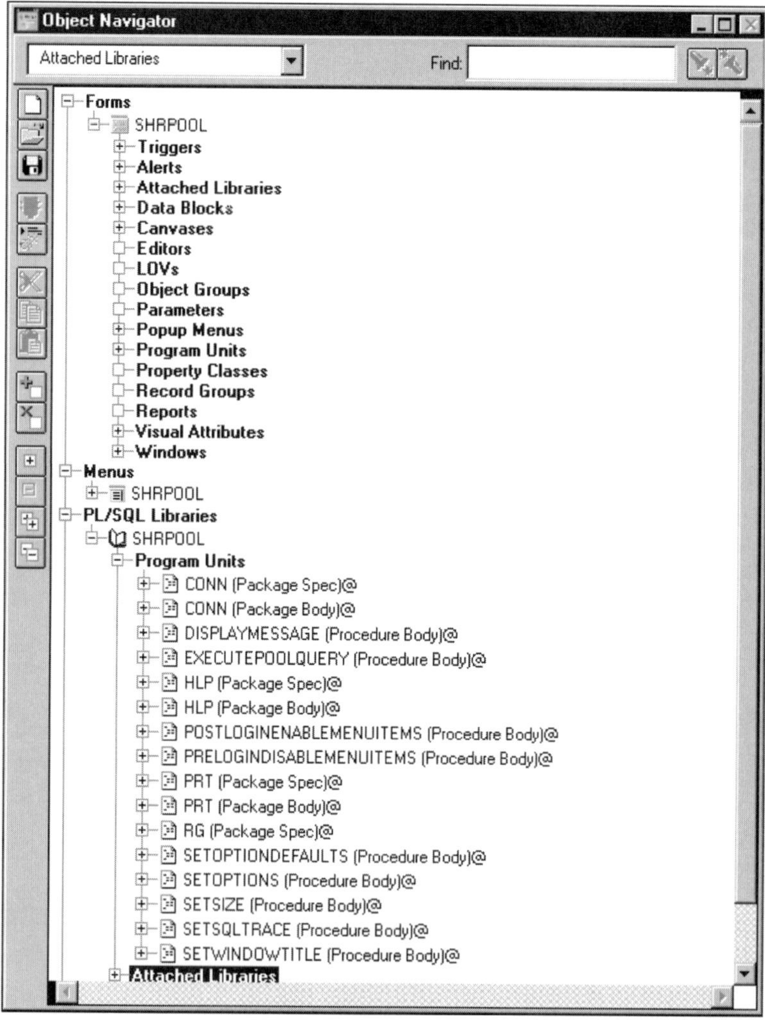

FIGURE 17.10 The Oracle Developer Object Navigator Showing ShrPool

Furthermore, it becomes sometimes difficult to track down the exact sequence of events that cause triggers to fire.

The knowledge required from developers and the number of notions they must remember in order to be proficient with Oracle Developer are comparatively much higher than what are required to use VB, Powerbuilder or Delphi. These tools obtain the same results as Oracle Developer without forcing developers to become intimately confident with the convoluted firing order of triggers.

The starting point of the Oracle Developer (OD) version of ShrPool is the connection form. In OD, the connection form is displayed by a built-in procedure, fired by the ON-LOGON trigger.

The PL/SQL source code that follows displays the form and is attached to the ON-LOGON trigger.

```
DECLARE
   vcEngVersion  varchar2(100);
   cOraSid       varchar2(30);
BEGIN
```

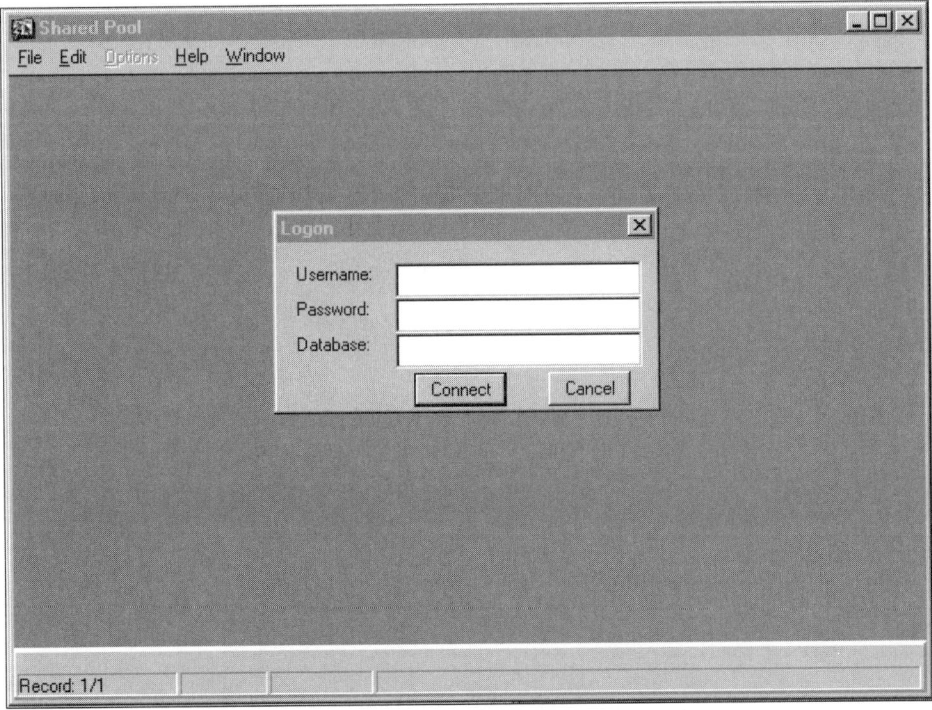

FIGURE 17.11 The Built-In Logon Screen

```
 5:     /*
 6:     ** If Forms startup is true then we suppress the default
 7:     ** login behavior but update the flag to false as now
 8:     ** forms is started.  Then the connect
 9:     ** menu item will cause this logon process to occur
10:     */
11:     IF rg.bFormStartUp THEN
12:         rg.bFormStartup := false;
13:     ELSE
14:       TOOL_ENV.GETVAR('ORACLE_SID', cOraSid);
15:       logon(null, null, true);
16:       -- let forms prompt for the answer
17:       IF form_success THEN
18:           BEGIN
19:              select substr(value,1,3) into vcEngVersion
20:              from sys.v_$parameter
21:              where name = 'compatible';
22:           EXCEPTION
23:              WHEN no_data_found THEN
24:                  vcEngVersion := '0.0';
25:           END;
26:           rg.nEngineVersion := to_number(vcEngVersion);
27:           PostLoginEnableMenuItems;
28:           message('Connected '|| get_application_property(datasource)
29:               ||' O(' || vcEngVersion ||') as '||
30:               get_application_property(username)|| '@' ||
31:               nvl(get_application_property(connect_string), cOraSid)
32:               ||' Version: ' || to_char(rg.nEngineVersion,'99.99'));
33:           Conn.bConnected := true;
34:           IF rg.nEngineVersion < 7.2 THEN
35:             set_item_property('v_$sqlarea.rows_processed',
36:                                   property_false);
37:           END IF;
38:       ELSE
39:           message('Login failure');
40:       END IF;
41:   END IF;
42: EXCEPTION
43:    WHEN others THEN
44:        message('Logon Exception Occurred');
45: END;
```

11–12 If the bFormStartup Boolean variable indicates that the application is in startup phase, we don't login but we set the variable to false and return.

14–15 The ORACLE_SID environment variable is read and the built-in connection form is invoked by calling logon and passing a null username and a null password and setting the logon_screen_ on_error variable to true.

17–25 If a connection to Oracle has been established, the engine version is read and stored in the vcEngVersion variable.

26–27 The engine version is converted into the package variable rg.nEngineVersion as a number and the menu items that allow users to access the application functions are enabled. The RG package defines only a few variables that will be accessed throughout the lifetime of the application by several modules.

28–32 The MDI toolbar message is built and displayed.

33–37 The Boolean variable bConnected defined in the conn package is set to true. If the connected Oracle engine is an old release, the rows_processed field in the v_$sqlarea data block is made ineffective by calling the forms built-in procedure set_item_property.

The form that is logically accessed just after a successful connection has been established (Figure 17.12) contains most of the complexity of the OD version of ShrPool.

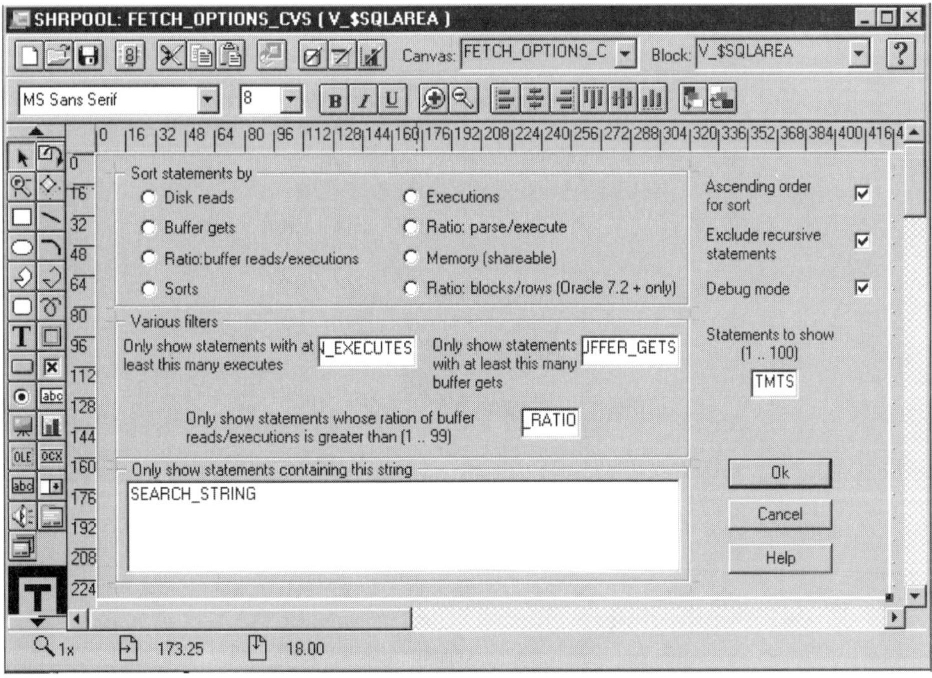

FIGURE 17.12 The Fetch Option Canvas

Before delving into the PL/SQL source code associated to the canvas, a few words to describe the sequence of events triggered by a click on the Ok button are in order. The Ok button fires a WHEN-BUTTON-PRESSED item-level trigger, which executes a procedure, *ExecutePoolQuery()*, defined in the SHRPOOL PL/SQL library. ExecutePoolQuery() starts the query event processing by issuing a *go_block()* built-in procedure. The data block made active is V$SQLAREA, and the query associated to the block is executed by issuing *do_key* built-in procedure. The canvas displaying the query result is made active by issuing a *go_item* built-in procedure that moves the focus to the SQL_TEXT field displayed on the canvas.

One of the weird features of OD is that moving the focus to a field makes the cursor appear at the end of the field, after the last displayed character. To force the cursor to appear at the beginning of the field an item trigger is defined for the text item SQL_TEXT, which fires on the WHEN-NEW-ITEM-INSTANCE event. This trigger uses a low-level MS Windows API function that sends the CTRL-HOME key to the text item control. This function is defined in the D2KWUTIL PL/SQL library, which must be deployed together with the application. When the query associated to V$SQLAREA is executed, a few events occur. The exact sequence is:

1. The query event processing starts with the KEY-EXEQRY trigger, which calls the built-in procedure *execute_query*.
2. The PRE-QUERY trigger fires. It displays the sort criterion chosen by the user and computes the total number of buffer gets generated by the engine.
3. An ON-SELECT trigger fires, creating a record group that will contain the data fetched from Oracle. It also fetches all rows from the cursor, storing the data in the record group.
4. An ON-FETCH trigger fires, creating a visual record to display the fetched data. Basically, it copies each row cell from the record group into the display field.
5. An ON-LOCK trigger is also defined, to prevent OD from attempting to lock the record in the data block when the content of the field is modified programmatically by the application.

WHEN-BUTTON-PRESSED trigger for the OPTIONS_OK_BTN button defined in the FETCH_OPTIONS_CTRL data block referred to by the Fetch Option canvas:

```
:v_$sqlarea_ctrl.execution_plan_cb := 'N';
ExecutePoolQuery;
```

ExecutePoolQuery procedure defined in the SHRPOOL PL/SQL library:

```
PROCEDURE ExecutePoolQuery IS
BEGIN
```

```
    IF Conn.bConnected THEN
        go_block('v_$sqlarea');
        IF form_success THEN
            do_key('execute_query');
            go_item('v_$sqlarea.sql_text');
        END IF;
    ELSE
        DisplayMessage('You are not connected -
                                please login first');
    END IF;
END;
```

KEY-EXEQRY trigger for the V$SQLAREA data block:

```
execute_query;
```

PRE-QUERY trigger for the V$SQLAREA data block:

```
:v_$sqlarea_ctrl.total_buffer_gets := nfGetTotalBufferGets;
:fetch_options.ordering :=
initcap(replace(
:fetch_options.sort_by,'_',' ')) || ' ' ||
lower(:fetch_options.ascending_sort) ||'ending';
```

ON-SELECT trigger for the V$SQLAREA data block:

```
DECLARE
  cSql  varchar2(1000);
  errno number;
BEGIN
  cSql := cfBuildSqlStatement;
  if checkbox_checked('fetch_options.debug_mode') then
      DisplayMessage(cSql);
      SetSqlTrace(true);
      :fetch_options.debug_mode := 'N';  – unset this
  end if;

  rg.rGid := find_group(rg.rgName);
  if id_null(rg.rGid) then
      rg.rGid := create_group_from_query(rg.rgName, cSql);
  end if;
  errno := populate_group_with_query(rg.rgName, cSql);
  if errno = 0 then
```

```
18:          rg.nRowsFetched := 0;
19:          rg.nRowsQueried := get_group_row_count(rg.rGid);
20:          message('Query returned '|| rg.nRowsQueried || ' row(s)');
21:    end if;
22: END;
```

5	The cfBuildSqlStatement is defined in the form program unit section of ShrPool. It builds the SQL statement by concatenating a fixed part (the main select) with the where clause containing the user defined filters and the order criterion chosen by the user.
6–10	If the user checked the "Debug mode" checkbox, the SQL statement just built is displayed in a message box, and the session is altered setting SQL_TRACE to true. SetSqlTrace is defined in the SHRPOOL PL/SQL library.
12	The record group ID is obtained by OD through the built-in call *find_group*.
13–16	If the record group does not yet exist, it is created by submitting the SQL statement built a few lines above. At line 16, the record group is populated fetching from the cursor defined by the built SQL statement.

ON-FETCH trigger for the V$SQLAREA data block:

```
DECLARE
  nRowsToFetch  number;
BEGIN
  nRowsToFetch :=
     Get_Block_Property(:system.current_block, RECORDS_TO_FETCH);
  if rg.nRowsFetched < rg.nRowsQueried THEN
   for i in 1..nRowsToFetch
    loop
     create_queried_record;
     :v_$sqlarea.sql_text :=
        get_group_char_cell(rg.rgName||'.sql_text', i);
     :v_$sqlarea.sharable_mem :=
        get_group_number_cell(rg.rgName||'.sharable_mem',i);
     :v_$sqlarea.persistent_mem :=
        get_group_number_cell(rg.rgName||'.persistent_mem', i);
     :v_$sqlarea.runtime_mem :=
        get_group_number_cell(rg.rgName||'.runtime_mem',i);
     :v_$sqlarea.sorts :=
        get_group_number_cell(rg.rgName||'.sorts',i);
     :v_$sqlarea.executions :=
        get_group_number_cell(rg.rgName||'.executions',i);
     :v_$sqlarea.parse_calls :=
        get_group_number_cell(rg.rgName||'.parse_calls',i);
```

```
24:        :v_$sqlarea.buffer_gets :=
25:           get_group_number_cell(rg.rgName||'.buffer_gets',i);
26:        :v_$sqlarea.disk_reads :=
27:           get_group_number_cell(rg.rgName||'.disk_reads',i);
28:        :v_$sqlarea.version_count :=
29:           get_group_number_cell(rg.rgName||'.version_count',i);
30:        :v_$sqlarea.users_opening :=
31:           get_group_number_cell(rg.rgName||'.users_opening',i);
32:        :v_$sqlarea.loads :=
33:           get_group_number_cell(rg.rgName||'.loads',i);
34:        :v_$sqlarea.parsing_user_id :=
35:           get_group_number_cell(rg.rgName||'.parsing_user_id',i);
36:        :v_$sqlarea.first_load_time :=
37:           get_group_char_cell(rg.rgName||'.first_load_time',i);
38:        :v_$sqlarea.address :=
39:           get_group_char_cell(rg.rgName||'.address',i);
40:        :v_$sqlarea.hash_value :=
41:           get_group_char_cell(rg.rgName||'.hash_value',i);
42:        if rg.nEngineVersion >= 7.2 then
43:            :v_$sqlarea.rows_processed :=
44:             get_group_number_cell(rg.rgName||'.rows_processed',i);
45:        end if;
46:        rg.nRowsFetched := rg.nRowsFetched + 1;
47:        EXIT WHEN rg.nRowsFetched = rg.nRowsQueried;
48:       end loop;
49:     end if;
50: END;
```

2–5 The variable containing the number of rows fetched from the shared pool is defined and then populated by querying a data block property.

7–8 A loop that traverses all rows fetched from the shared pool is started.

9 The built-in procedure create_quer_record is called to create a record in the block *waiting list*. The waiting list is an intermediary record buffer that contains records that have been fetched from the data source but have not yet been placed on the block's list of active records.

10–45 The value contained in the record group cells is copied in the record in the waiting list.

46–47 The counter variable controlling the loop is incremented and the loop is terminated when the number of rows fetched from the shared pool equals the number of statements required by the user.

ON-LOCK trigger for the V$SQLAREA data block:

```
/*
** Allow on screen updates but override change force
```

```
** the record be be marked as QUERIED.  This would
** not require a commit of changes.
*/
set_record_property(:system.cursor_record, :system.cursor_block,
                    status, query_status);
```

WHEN-NEW-BLOCK-INSTANCE trigger for the V$SQLAREA data block:

```
set_menu_item_property('file_menu.print', enabled, property_true);
```

An item-level trigger is defined for the SQL_TEXT text item and placed on the V$SQLAREA data block. The PL/SQL code executed when the trigger fires sets the Window title, moves the cursor caret at the beginning of the SQL-TEXT field and sets the current item on the window control as highlighted (blue background).

WHEN-NEW-ITEM-INSTANCE trigger for the SQL_TEXT text item defined in the V$SQLAREA data block:

```
SetWindowTitle(:system.cursor_item,
               'SQL Statements from Oracle shared pool');
KeyItemCtlHome;
set_item_instance_property(:system.cursor_item,
                           current_record, visual_attribute,
                           'blue_va');
```

The PL/SQL code executed when the ON-SELECT trigger fires calls two user-defined procedures/functions, *SetSqlTrace* and *cfBuildSqlStatement*. The source code for the user-defined procedures follows.

The **SetSqlTrace** procedure, defined in the PL/SQL library of shared code:

```
PROCEDURE SetSqlTrace (bTraceOn boolean := true) IS
BEGIN
     IF bTraceOn THEN
         forms_ddl('ALTER SESSION SET SQL_TRACE = TRUE');
     ELSE
         forms_ddl('ALTER SESSION SET SQL_TRACE = FALSE');
     END IF;
     IF NOT form_success THEN
        DisplayMessage('Alter Session set SQL Trace failed');
     END IF;
END;
```

The forms_ddl built-in procedure is used to issue a server side DDL statement.

The **cfBuildSqlStatement** function, defined in the program unit section of the form:

```
1: FUNCTION cfBuildSqlStatement RETURN varchar2 IS
2:    cSql  varchar2(1000);
3: BEGIN
4:    cSql := 'SELECT ltrim(rtrim(sql_text)) sql_text,
5:         sharable_mem, persistent_mem, ' ||
6:         'runtime_mem, sorts, executions,
7:         parse_calls, buffer_gets, ' ||
8:         'disk_reads, version_count,
9:         users_opening, loads, parsing_user_id, ' ||
10:        'to_char(to_date(first_load_time,''YYYY-MM-DD/HH24:MI:SS''),
11:        ''DD/MM:HH24:MI:SS'') first_load_time, ' ||
12:        'rawtohex(address) address, to_char(hash_value) hash_value';
13:   IF rg.nEngineVersion >= 7.2 THEN
14:      cSql := cSql ||', rows_processed';
15:   END IF;
16:   cSql := cSql || ' FROM sys.v_$sqlarea';
17:   /*
18:   ** Add the Conditions
19:   */
20:   cSql := cSql || cfBuildConditions;
21:   cSql := cSql || ' ORDER BY ' ||
22:          :fetch_options.sort_by || ' '||
23:          :fetch_options.ascending_sort;
24:   return(cSql);
25: END;
```

4–12 The fixed part of the dynamic SQL statement is built into the cSql VARCHAR2 variable.

13–15 If the engine supports the rows_processed field, the statement is concatenated to it.

16–20 The from clause of the statement is concatenated to the statement, and the where clause is built by invoking the cfBuildConditions function.

21–23 The sort criterion is appended to the statement. A nice feature of OD is that the selected radio button returns the strings associated to it. This avoids using a verbose and less efficient select case or cascading if to derive the chosen option from an index.

24–25 The built SQL statement is returned to the caller and the function ends.

CfBuildSqlStatement() calls cfBuildConditions() to work out a where clause. The source code of **cfBuildConditions** follows:

```
 1: FUNCTION cfBuildConditions RETURN varchar2 IS
 2:     cConditions  varchar2(1000) :=
 3:               ' WHERE executions > 0';
 4: BEGIN
 5:     cConditions := cConditions ||
 6:         cfAddCondition(:fetch_options.exclude_recursive,
 7:                        '<>', '0') ||
 8:         cfAddCondition('executions',
 9:                         '>',
10:                        :fetch_options.min_executes) ||
11:         cfAddCondition('buffer_gets/executions',
12:                        '>',
13:                        :fetch_options.min_buffer_gets) ||
14:         cfAddCondition('buffer_gets',
15:                        '>',
16:                        :fetch_options.min_buffread_ratio) ||
17:         cfAddCondition('sql_text',
18:                        'like',
19:                        :fetch_options.search_string, true) ||
20:         cfAddCondition('rownum',
21:                        '<=',
22:                        :fetch_options.nbr_stmts);
23:      RETURN cConditions;
24: END;
```

5–19 The cCondition VARCHAR2 variable is built by evaluating the content of each field displayed by the fetch_options canvas. The cfAddCondition() function is repeatedly called to work out the where clause.

20–22 The last condition limits the number of statements fetched from the shared pool. Only the number of statements required by the user and displayed by the fetch_options canvas will be fetched from the server.

The source code for the **cfAddCondition** function, called by cfBuildConditions(), is shown below.

```
FUNCTION cfAddCondition(cLhs  varchar2, cOper varchar2,
                        cRhs  varchar2,
                        bCaseInsensitive boolean := false)
                        RETURN varchar2 IS
   cCondition    varchar2(1000) := null;
BEGIN
    /*
    ** If input values for the left and right hand side
    ** of the condition are null then return without forming
```

```
    ** a condition string (return a null)
    ** otherwise build a new condition and prepend it with
    ** the "AND" operator.
    ** Also include checks for case insentive checks.
    */
    if (cLhs is not null) and (cRhs is not null) then
        if (bCaseInsensitive) then
            cCondition := ' AND upper(' || cLhs ||') ' || cOper;
            if lower(cOper) = 'like' then
                cCondition := cCondition ||'
                              upper(''%'|| cRhs || '%'')';
            else
                cCondition := cCondition ||' upper('|| cRhs || ')';
            end if;
        else
            cCondition := ' AND '||cLhs||' '||cOper||' '||cRhs;
        end if;
    end if;
    return cCondition;
END;
```

When the WHEN-NEW-ITEM-INSTANCE trigger fires, the PL/SQL executed invokes the KeyItemCtlHome procedure, to force the cursor caret to be positioned at the beginning of the field.

The source code of **KeyItemCtlHome** follows.

```
1: PROCEDURE KeyItemCtlHome IS
2:   nWindowHandle  pls_integer;
3: BEGIN
4:   nWindowHandle :=
5:    get_item_property(:system.trigger_item, window_handle);
6:   WIN_API_SHELL.SENDKEYS(nWindowHandle, '^{Home}', false);
7: END;
```

5–6 The window handle of the SQL_TEXT text item is obtained via the get_item_property built-in procedure, and passed as a parameter to the SENDKEYS procedure defined in the WIN_API_SHELL package, shipped with the D2KWUTIL.PLL library.SENDKEYS accepts three parameters, the window handle, the key or keys to be sent to the control, and a Boolean variable that makes the call generate an exception (TRUE) or the call ignore errors generated by the WIN API call (FALSE).

We are almost finished with the fetch_options form. A few more lines of code have been defined to execute at the firing of other triggers, but the core of the form behavior has been shaped by the PL/SQL code shown above. When the ExecutePoolQuery procedure terminates its execution, the canvas displayed to the user is SQL_POOL_CVS, made active by the go_item statement issued at line 7.

The user interacting with ShrPool can ask statistics to be displayed for a single statement, or for all statements fetched in the preceding steps. The execution plan can also be requested for either one or all statements, and the explaining schema can be different from the current connection.

All these alternatives are dealt with by the *ProcessAllStatements* procedure, which appears in the program units of the ShrPool application. The SQL_POOL_CVS canvas is shown in Figure 17.13.

ProcessAllStatements receives one optional parameter of Boolean type. If it is set to false, the default, the procedure processes only the statement currently selected (i.e., highlighted in blue). If the Boolean parameter passed to ProcessAllStatements equals to true, all fetched statements are processed by the procedure. The WHEN-BUTTON-PRESSED trigger defined for the "Process ONE Statement" button invokes ProcessAllStatements without parameters, defaulting to false. The same trigger defined for the "Process ALL Statements" invokes Pro-

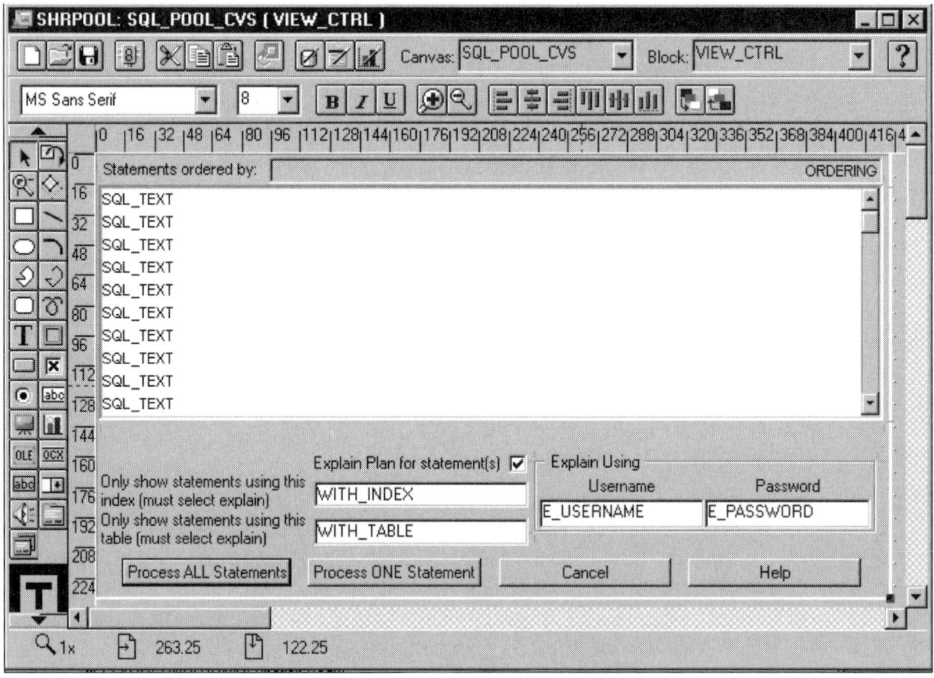

FIGURE 17.13 The SQL_POOL_CVS Canvas

cessAllStatements passing the Boolean value "true" as a parameter. The source code for the *ProcessAllStatements* procedure follows.

```
PROCEDURE ProcessAllStatements
         (bProcessAll boolean := false) IS
  eLoginFailed        exception;
  eExplainError       exception;
  bExplainPlanChecked boolean not null := false;
  cTempFile           varchar2(100) := 'shrpall.tmp';
  nTextLen            integer;
BEGIN
  rg.bProcessAll:= bProcessAll;
  bExplainPlanChecked :=
    checkbox_checked('v_$sqlarea_ctrl.execution_plan_cb');
  IF bExplainPlanChecked THEN
      set_item_property('v_$sqlarea.mirror_sql_text',
                        height, rg.nSqlTextHeight);
      set_item_property('v_$sqlarea.explain_plan',
                        visible, property_true);
      set_item_property('v_$sqlarea.explain_plan',
                        enabled, property_true);
  ELSE
      set_item_property('v_$sqlarea.mirror_sql_text',
                        height, rg.nSqlTextHeight*2);
      set_item_property('v_$sqlarea.explain_plan',
                        visible, property_false);
  END IF;

  IF bProcessAll THEN
      IF bExplainPlanChecked THEN
          set_item_property('v_$sqlarea.mirror_sql_text',
                             height, rg.nSqlTextHeight);
          set_item_property('v_$sqlarea.explain_plan',
                             visible, property_true);
          set_item_property('v_$sqlarea.explain_plan',
                            enabled, property_true);
          CreatePlanTable;
          explainAll(:v_$sqlarea_ctrl.with_index,
                     :v_$sqlarea_ctrl.with_table);
          DropPlanTable;
      END IF;
      prt.PrintSqlDetails(cTempFile, bExplainPlanChecked);
      ReadFile(cTempFile, 'view_ctrl.data');
      DeleteFile(cTempFile);
```

```
        set_menu_item_property('file_menu.explain_view',
                               visible, property_true);
        go_item('view_ctrl.data');
    ELSE  /* Process One */
        :v_$sqlarea.explain_plan := null;
        :v_$sqlarea.mirror_sql_text :=
                  fcGetSqlText(:v_$sqlarea.address,
                               :v_$sqlarea.hash_value);
        IF bExplainPlanChecked THEN
            IF :v_$sqlarea_ctrl.e_username is not null AND
                :v_$sqlarea_ctrl.e_password is not null THEN
                IF NOT Conn.ChangeLogon(
                       :v_$sqlarea_ctrl.e_username,
                       :v_$sqlarea_ctrl.e_password) THEN
                    DisplayMessage('Login failed for Username '||
                                   :v_$sqlarea_ctrl.e_username ||
                                   ' and the supplied password');
                    :v_$sqlarea_ctrl.e_username := null;
                    :v_$sqlarea_ctrl.e_password := null;
                    Conn.LastLogon;
                    raise eLoginFailed;
                END IF;
            END IF;
            CreatePlanTable;
            :v_$sqlarea.explain_plan :=
                 fcExplainQuery(:v_$sqlarea.mirror_sql_text);
            DropPlanTable;
            /*
            ** Reconnect as Last Logon, which will know if the login
            ** connect was changed with the ChangeLogon call.
            */
            Conn.LastLogon;
            :v_$sqlarea_ctrl.e_username := null;
            :v_$sqlarea_ctrl.e_password := null;
            IF substr(:v_$sqlarea.explain_plan, 1,4) = 'ORA-' THEN
                – raise eExplainError;
                :v_$sqlarea.mirror_sql_text := :v_$sqlarea.sql_text;
                :v_$sqlarea.explain_plan := :v_$sqlarea.explain_plan
                            || ' (Hash value overflow?)';
            END IF;
        END IF;
        nTextLen := NVL(LENGTH(:v_$sqlarea.mirror_sql_text),0);
        if nTextLen = 0 THEN
           :v_$sqlarea.mirror_sql_text := :v_$sqlarea.sql_text;
```

```
86:        end if;
87:        go_item('v_$sqlarea.mirror_sql_text');
88:    END IF;
89: EXCEPTION
90:    WHEN eLoginFailed THEN
91:        null;
92:    WHEN eExplainError THEN
93:        DisplayMessage('EXPLAIN Error: '||:v_$sqlarea.explain_plan);
94:    WHEN others THEN
95:        :v_$sqlarea.explain_plan :=
96:                  nvl(sqlerrm, nvl(error_text,dbms_error_text));
97:        DisplayMessage('OTHER Error:' ||:v_$sqlarea.explain_plan);
98: END;
```

2–7 Define exception and variables used by the procedure.

9–11 Store the received Boolean parameter in a packaged variable for later reference. Determine whether the user chose to display an execution plan for the statement.

12–24 According to the options chosen by the user, selected field in the V_$SQLAREA data block are either hidden or made visible.

26–27 If the user asked for all statements to be displayed, and also asked for an execution plan…

28–33 A few visual control get set (visible, enabled, height property modified)

34–37 An explain plan table is created, if it doesn't exist yet, by calling CreatePlanTable procedure defined in the program unit section. All statements are explained in a loop by the ExplainAll user-defined procedure. Finally, the explain table is dropped.

39–44 The PrintSqlDetails procedure, defined in the PRT package included in the PL/SQL library, explains all statements, filtering out the results if required. The user could have asked to explain all statements that refer to a particular table, or a particular index. The execution plan is temporarily stored in a file. The "data" field defined in the VIEW_CTRL canvas is populated with the content of the temporary file, which is erased from the disk. The VIEW_CTRL canvas is activated by the go_item built-in procedure.

45–49 If only one statement must be processed, the entire statement is fetched from V$SQLTEXT via the fcGetSqlText procedure, defined in the program unit section.

50–64 If an execution plan for the single statement has been requested, and the explain plan must be run under a different schema, the conn package ChangeLogon procedure is called to disconnect the current section and to re-connect using the schema owner specified by the user. If the second connection fails, ShrPool reconnects as the default user, giving an interactive feedback that explains what happened.

65–68 An explain plan table is created, the selected statement explained by calling the fcExplainQuery procedure, and the plan table is dropped.

76–81 If the request for a execution plan failed, the assumption is made that we incurred in the Oracle well known hash value bug. The string containing the SQL statement taken from the shared pool is built from V$SQLAREA, and a message is displayed in the execution plan listbox.

83–86 The same logic is cloned for statements that were not explained. If the hash value bug is detected, the SQL string is copied from V$SQLAREA and not derived from V$SQLTEXT.

87–88 The V$SQLAREA data block is made active by the go_item built-in procedure. The conditional processing that discriminates between one or many SQL statements ends.

ProcessAllStatements calls a few user-defined functions/procedures, which are included in the companion CD-ROM but omitted here. I believe that the goal of providing an overview of application development using Oracle Developer has been reached by the source code and forms shown above.

It is time to summarize our experience building ShrPool with Oracle Developer. The problem domain defined by ShrPool is less than ideal for a tool like OD, which prefers a more traditional environment where data stored in Oracle tables is visually accessed and modified by an interactive application. Doing dynamic SQL is not straightforward in Oracle Developer if you want to minimize impact on the server, as is one of the design goals of this application. This is needed to use the Developer record group mechanism to achieve dynamic query processing, which is limited by lack of control of the fetch processing. It is not possible to use reference cursors because they require static compile time checks. This latter problem can be overcome by rewriting this portion of the code to make use of the built-in server DBMS_SQL package to implement server-side dynamic SQL and row at a time fetching capabilities without requiring to create stored procedures.

The dynamic SQL processing required more programming effort to control Oracle Developer Forms query processing logic. This required the developer to control the query processing trigger event processing, that is, the ON-SELECT, ON-FETCH, and ON-LOCK triggers. ON-SELECT builds and executes the dynamic statement and fetches the rows into a record group. ON-FETCH creates the visible representation of the data in the GUI items for each field. ON-LOCK suppresses the default locking mechanism that Developer Forms uses when attempting to modify fetch fields.

An additional limitation affecting the use of multi-line text items is its 32K character limit, which requires the use of list items to allow for large amounts of textual display, limiting navigational capabilities to a line at a time. This lack of ability to edit the list item directly requires the addition of new components to provide editing features at the character level.

Furthermore, by default Oracle Developer places the cursor at the end of the text in a text item component after navigating to the field. This placement required the need to call the D2KWUTIL.PLL package, supplied with the Oracle Developer distribution, to allow the application to programmatically send a home key to the application after navigation to the field was successful, giving the effect that the cursor had been positioned before the first character in the text item. Using that package tightens our application into the MS Windows environment, requiring a porting effort if Apple Macintoshes or Motif-based workstations must also be supported. A few features of OD have been appreciated while developing our application. They are listed below.

1. Using the Value property of the Radio buttons to provide the value associated with the sorting order of the query avoided having to write a case statement (or cascading if statement).
2. The canvas structure of Developer/2000 and the ability to dynamically alter GUI item sizes allowed the developer to reuse a physical structure for two different views of the same data, one with execution plan and one without.
3. The default navigation features in Developer/2000 allowed the developer to add functionality to interface, allowing ALL processed statements to be viewed by scrolling through the processed statements with or without the explain plan.

Oracle Developer uses PL/SQL to accomplish all its tasks, and is shipped with a client-side PL/SQL engine. The executable image generated by OD is of p-code type, which runs slowly if compared to VB or Delphi. Oracle Developer is probably suitable for IT environments already strongly committed to Oracle technologies, where a good knowledge of PL/SQL is taken for granted. Server-side PL/SQL developers can start writing client-side GUI applications with little or no training. Oracle Developer is probably less appealing in environments where an Oracle database coexists with databases from other vendors, where a PL/SQL background is not shared among developers, and where client-side processing is very demanding, requiring the advantage of machine code executables, rather than interpreted environments.

7.5 ShrPool in Delphi

The Delphi version of ShrPool is a little different from the other versions, as it is implemented as a Windows Single Document Interface (SDI) application. Instead of an empty MDI frame, the Delphi version of ShrPool, after the startup phase, displays the form that allows users to specify the fetch options for the statements to be retrieved from the shared pool. The Ok button of the form is grayed out until a connection is made. The only way to be able to proceed with the application is by clicking on the menu options attached to the form, selecting the "Connect" option. Upon successful connection, the Ok button is enabled, allowing users to access the form that displays the SQL statements fetched from the shared pool.

Other features of ShrPool have been implemented slightly differently in the Delphi version. The user-entered filters that influence the where clause of the SQL statement dynamically built by ShrPool are spin controls instead of text boxes, and users cannot limit the SQL statements retrieved from the shared pool to a predetermined number. The statements selected according to the user-entered options and filters are displayed in a data-aware control. Limiting the statements displayed in the grid to a predetermined number would be difficult. To make the Object Pascal code more readable, we have omitted the feature present in other versions of ShrPool.

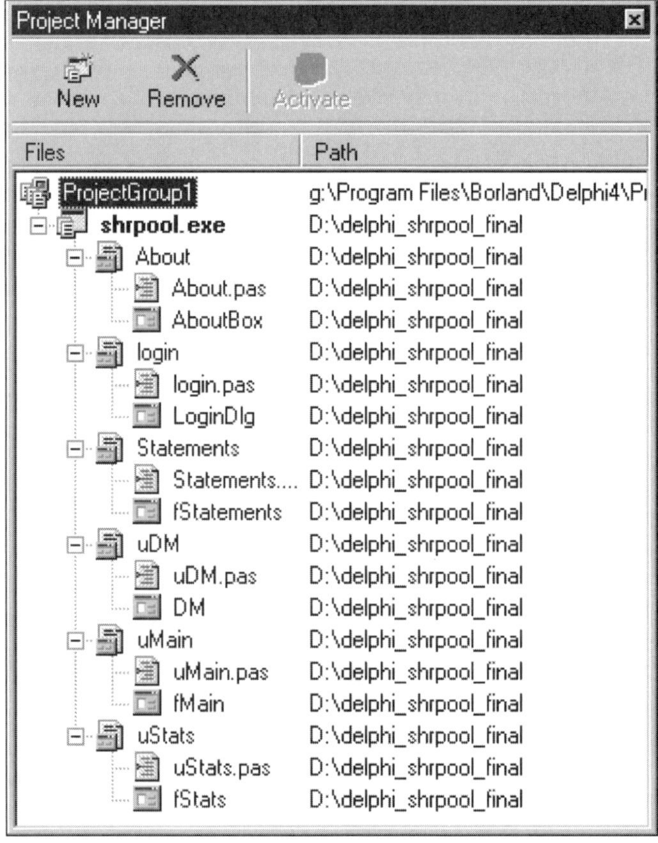

FIGURE 17.14 The ShrPool Objects Included in the Project

ShrPool developed in Delphi is the only version that uses an ODBC connection to Oracle. If you have access to a professional edition of Delphi, you can run the application, which doesn't require the more expensive Client/Server edition. Delphi ShrPool uses a data module class that groups together all data access logic. Modifying ShrPool to make it use a different connectivity model is greatly simplified by the data module approach. If you want to use low-level drivers to connect to Oracle, such as Allround Automations DOA or Borland.com SQL Links, the modifications required are minimal. This version of ShrPool includes six modules, the usual four forms (connection, fetch options, fetched SQL statements, and SQL statement statistics), plus a Data Module and an about dialog.

The main SDI form displayed by ShrPool at startup is shown in Figure 17.15.

The Object Pascal code that drives the behavior of the form follows.

```
unit uMain;

interface

```

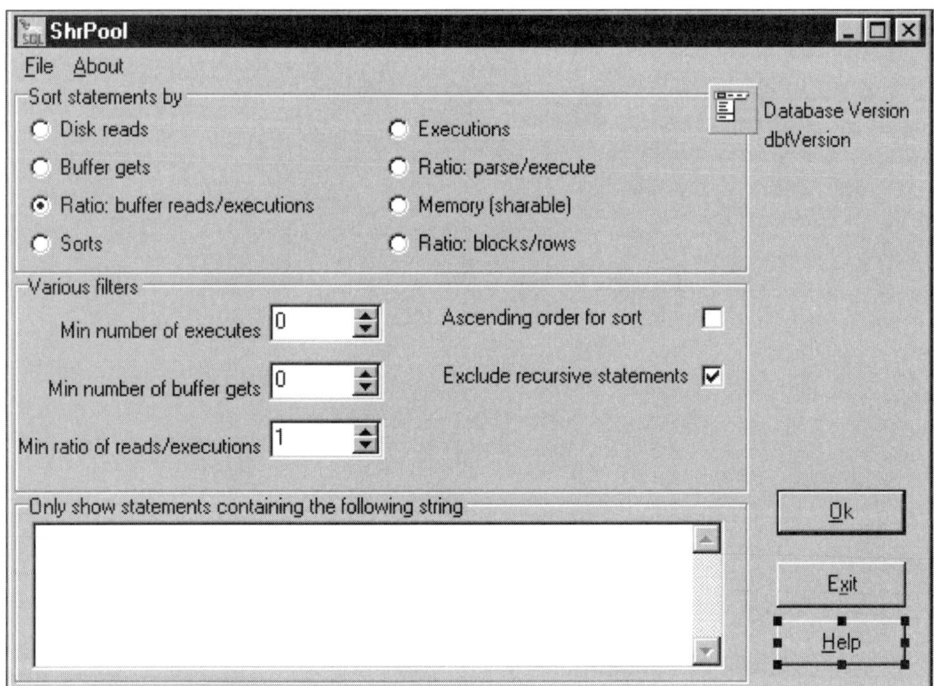

FIGURE 17.15 The Main SDI Window Shown at Application Startup

```
uses
  Windows, Messages, SysUtils, Classes, Graphics, Controls,
  Forms, Dialogs, Spin, StdCtrls, ExtCtrls, Menus, uDM,
  DBCtrls;
type
  TfMain = class(TForm)
    MainMenu1: TMainMenu;
    File1: TMenuItem;
    Connect1: TMenuItem;
    Disconnect1: TMenuItem;
    N1: TMenuItem;
    Exit1: TMenuItem;
    About1: TMenuItem;
    Panel1: TPanel;
    Panel2: TPanel;
    gbFilters: TGroupBox;
    gbFilterString: TGroupBox;
    rgSortBy: TRadioGroup;
    mFilter: TMemo;
    bOk: TButton;
    bExit: TButton;
    bHelp: TButton;
    seMinExec: TSpinEdit;
    seMinBuffGets: TSpinEdit;
    seMinReadtoExec: TSpinEdit;
    Label1: TLabel;
    Label2: TLabel;
    Label3: TLabel;
    cbSortOrder: TCheckBox;
    cbRecursive: TCheckBox;
    dbtVersion: TDBText;
    lDBVersion: TLabel;
    procedure Exit1Click(Sender: TObject);
    procedure bOkClick(Sender: TObject);
    procedure CheckNeg(Sender: TObject);
    procedure Connect1Click(Sender: TObject);
    procedure Disconnect1Click(Sender: TObject);
    procedure bHelpClick(Sender: TObject);
    procedure About1Click(Sender: TObject);
  private
    { Private declarations }
  public
    { Public declarations }
```

```
  end;

var
  fMain: TfMain;
  bNewVersion: boolean;

implementation

uses Statements, About;

{$R *.DFM}


procedure TfMain.Exit1Click(Sender: TObject);
begin
  Halt;
end;

procedure TfMain.bOkClick(Sender: TObject);
var
  SQLStatement : string;
  orderby: string;
begin
  // Do not allow sort on unavailable field
  if not(DM.bNewVersion) and (rgSortBy.ItemIndex = 7) then
  begin
    If MessageDlg
   ('Sorting by "Ratio: blocks/rows" is invalid for Oracle 7.0x. ' +
     'Sort will be set to "Ratio: buffer reads/executions"',
      mtWarning, [mbOK, mbCancel],0) = mrCancel  then
       exit
    else
       rgSortBy.ItemIndex := 2;
  end;
  // create the sql to retrieve the statements
  DM.qGetStatements.SQL.Clear;
  // create the Select portion
  SQLStatement := 'select substr(sql_text,1,100) SQL, ';
  SQLStatement := SQLStatement +
    'sharable_mem,persistent_mem,runtime_mem,sorts, ';
  SQLStatement := SQLStatement +
    'executions,parse_calls,buffer_gets,disk_reads,version_count, ';
  SQLStatement := SQLStatement +
    'users_opening,loads, ';
```

```
  SQLStatement := SQLStatement +
     'to_char(to_date(first_load_time,''YYYY-MM-DD/HH24:MI:SS''),' +
     '''DD/MM:HH24:MI:SS'') first_load_time, ';
  SQLStatement := SQLStatement +
     'rawtohex(address) address,to_char(hash_value) hash_value ';
  if DM.bNewVersion then
    SQLStatement := SQLStatement + ',rows_processed ';
  //from clause
  SQLStatement := SQLStatement + 'from sys.v_$sqlarea ';
  //where clause
  SQLStatement := SQLStatement + 'where executions > ' +
                 IntToStr(seMinExec.value) + ' ';
  if cbRecursive.checked then
    SQLStatement := SQLStatement +
                   'and parsing_user_id != 0 ';
  SQLStatement := SQLStatement + 'and buffer_gets > ' +
                 IntToStr(seMinBuffGets.value) + ' ';
  SQLStatement := SQLStatement + 'and buffer_gets/executions > '
                 + IntToStr(seMinReadtoExec.value) + ' ';
  if mFilter.Text <> '' then
    SQLStatement := SQLStatement
                   + 'and upper(sql_text) like upper(''%'
                   + mFilter.Text + '%'') ';
  // order by statement
  case rgSortBy.ItemIndex of
    0: orderby := 'order by disk_reads';
    1: orderby := 'order by buffer_gets';
    2: orderby := 'order by buffer_gets/executions';
    3: orderby := 'order by sorts';
    4: orderby := 'order by executions';
    5: orderby := 'order by parse_calls/executions';
    6: orderby := 'order by sharable_mem';
    7: orderby :=
       'order by buffer_gets/decode(rows_processed,0,1,executions)';
  end;
  if cbSortOrder.checked then
    orderby := orderby + ' asc'
  else
    orderby := orderby + ' desc';
  SQLStatement := SQLStatement + orderby;
  DM.qGetStatements.SQL.Add(SQLStatement);
  DM.qGetStatements.Open;
  fStatements.pSortType.Caption := orderby;
  fStatements.ShowModal;
```

```
end;

procedure TfMain.CheckNeg(Sender: TObject);
begin
  with Sender as TSpinEdit do
  begin
    if Value < 0 then
      Value := 0;
  end;
end;

procedure TfMain.Connect1Click(Sender: TObject);
begin
   DM.DB.AliasName := InputBox(
                   'Enter ODBC Alias for the Oracle database',
                   'ODBC Alias:', DM.DB.AliasName);
   DM.ExplainDB.AliasName := DM.DB.AliasName;
   try
     // open database
     DM.DB.Open;
     //get version
     DM.qVersion.Open;
     DM.bNewVersion :=
         not(AnsiPos('7.0',dbtVersion.Field.DisplayText) = 1);
     // enable/disable controls
     Connect1.Enabled := False;
     Disconnect1.Enabled := True;
     bOk.Enabled := True;
     bOK.SetFocus;
     // get instance name
     DM.qExec.SQL.clear;
     DM.qExec.SQL.Text := 'select global_name from global_name';
     DM.qExec.Open;
     Caption := 'ShrPool - ' + DM.qExec.Fields[0].AsString;
     DM.qExec.Close;
     // create plan table
     try
       DM.qMakePlanTable.ExecSQL;
     except
     end;
     try
       DM.qExec.SQL.clear;
       DM.qExec.SQL.Text :=
          'grant all on local_plan_table to public';
```

```
181:         DM.qExec.ExecSQL;
182:       except
183:         //error
184:       end;
185:
186:     except
187:       MessageDlg('Error While trying to open database',mtError,
188:                  [mbOK],0);
189:       caption := 'Share Pool';
190:     end;
191: end;
192:
193: procedure TfMain.Disconnect1Click(Sender: TObject);
194: begin
195:   DM.DB.Close;
196:   bOk.Enabled := False;
197:   Connect1.Enabled := True;
198:   Disconnect1.Enabled := False;
199:   Caption := 'ShrPool';
200: end;
201:
202: procedure TfMain.bHelpClick(Sender: TObject);
203: begin
204:   Application.HelpCommand(HELP_CONTEXT, 40);
205: end;
206:
207: procedure TfMain.About1Click(Sender: TObject);
208: begin
209:      AboutBox.ShowModal;
210: end;
211:
212: end.
```

1–61 This source code is automatically generated by Delphi while designing the form. At line 53 the Boolean variable bNewVersion is defined, to hold true if the connected Oracle engine is release 7.2 or greater and false otherwise.

62–65 This procedure stops the application when a click event is detected on the exit button.

67–70 The application logic that reacts to a click event on the Ok button is defined here. Two variables are initialized, SQLstatement to hold the dynamically built SQL statement and orderby, to temporarily store the order by clause of the dynamically built SQL statement.

72–82 This section prevents users from entering illegal options. If the connected engine older than 7.2, one cannot order by blocks read over rows_processed.

84–99 The select portion of the SQL statement dynamically built by ShrPool is assembled here.

100–115 The where clause of the statement is assembled by reading the options entered by the user in the fields displayed in the form.

117–127 The order by clause is derived from the radio button control currently active on the form.

128–131 These lines of code work out if the order clause is ascending or descending by reading the check box state displayed on the form.

132–136 The SQL statement is completed by concatenating the order clause. The query control that fetches the statements from the shared pool, stored in the data module, receives the dynamically built SQL statement and executes it. The fetched statement form is displayed modally after having set the order clause in the appropriate field.

139–146 The CheckNeg procedure is used by the spin control, triggered by the OnChange event, to check that negative numbers are not entered by the user.

148–149 Application logic that respond to the click event on the "Connect" menu option.

150–153 The ODBC alias is requested from the user and its value stored in the appropriate property of the database object stored in the data module form.

154–184 The database connection is open, the Oracle version of the connected engine is queried, the database name fetched, a plan table created if none exists and all privileges are given to PUBLIC, to allow other connection to be able to explain statements in the locally defined plan table. Additionally, the "Disconnect" menu option is enabled in case of a successful connection, and the "Connect" menu option grayed out, to prevent a second connection.

186–190 Catch-all exception defined for any of the exceptions possibly raised during the connection phase.

193–199 Application logic that responds to a click event on the "Disconnect" menu option. The database object defined in the data module form executes the close method to destroy the connection. The menu options are enabled/grayed out accordingly, and the caption of the main window is modified not to display the database name of the previously connected engine.

202–205 Application logic that responds to a click event on the "Help" button. The associated help file is opened, and the topic number 40 is displayed.

207–210 Application logic that responds to a click event on the "About" menu option. The about dialog is displayed modally.

The data access logic is conveniently self-contained in a data module. Data modules are one of the most innovative features of Delphi. Using data modules allows developers to de-couple data access logic from each individual form comprising the application. Data-aware controls can be kept synchronized with database changes when multiple forms are displayed concurrently on the screen. Data module forms can be seen only in the development environment at design time; they are not visible at run-time. Data-aware controls can be linked to data sources residing in data modules only if the form that contains them specifies the data module form in the *uses* clause, usually generated automatically by Delphi towards the beginning of the form source code. In our case the uDM data module form reference appears at line 7 in the source code of the main form.

If you have access to either a client/server edition of Delphi, or to the Direct Oracle Access (DOA) library, and you want to upgrade the Oracle connectivity layer from ODBC to a more efficient low-level driver, you would make your changes in the data module form, also amending the lines 150–153 of the source code contained in the main form. The data module form used by ShrPool is shown in Figure 17.16.

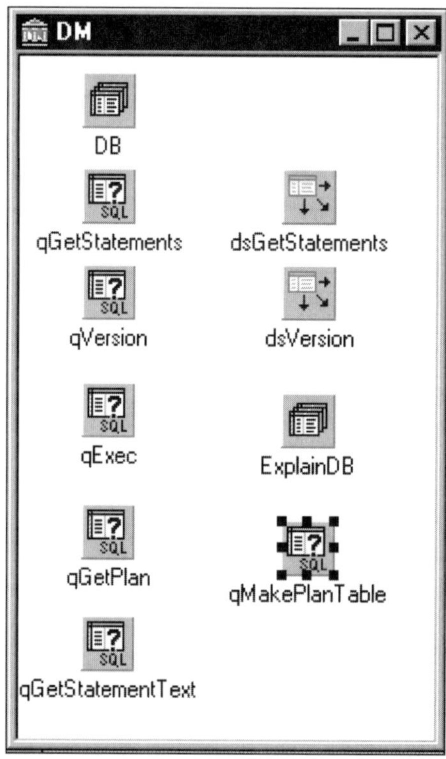

FIGURE 17.16 The Data Module Form Used by ShrPool

The source code associated to the data module form follows.

```
unit uDM;

interface

uses
  Windows, Messages, SysUtils, Classes, Graphics, Controls, Forms,
  Dialogs, Db, DBTables;

type
  TDM = class(TDataModule)
    DB: TDatabase;
    qGetStatements: TQuery;
    dsGetStatements: TDataSource;
    qVersion: TQuery;
    dsVersion: TDataSource;
    qExec: TQuery;
    qGetPlan: TQuery;
    qGetStatementText: TQuery;
    ExplainDB: TDatabase;
    qMakePlanTable: TQuery;
    procedure DBLogin(Database: TDatabase; LoginParams: TStrings);
  private
    { Private declarations }
  public
    { Public declarations }
    bNewVersion: boolean;
    sUserName: string;
  end;

var
  DM: TDM;

implementation

uses login;

{$R *.DFM}

procedure TDM.DBLogin(Database: TDatabase; LoginParams: TStrings);
begin
   LoginDlg.Password.text := '';
   if LoginDlg.ShowModal = mrOK then
```

```
43:     begin
44:       sUsername := LoginDlg.Username.Text;
45:       LoginParams.Add('USER NAME='+sUsername);
46:       LoginParams.Add('PASSWORD='+LoginDlg.Password.text);
47:     end;
48: end;
49:
50: end.
```

1–37	Source code automatically generated by Delphi. At line 35, the uses clause includes the login form, used by ShrPool instead of the built-in login dialog provided by the database component.
39–40	The DBLogin method is implemented.
41–43	The password text box in the login dialog is cleared and the login dialog is displayed modally to the user.
44–47	If the login dialog is dismissed by the user by pressing the Ok button, the content of the username and password fields is stored in the list of strings (LoginParams) received as a parameter.

After having established a successful connection to Oracle, clicking on the Ok button placed on main SDI form causes ShrPool to display the form that contains all SQL statements fetched from the shared pool. The main component of the form is a data-aware grid that is synchronized with the V$SQLAREA virtual table through the qGetStatements query component, which resides in the data module form. Figure 17.17 shows the statement form, which displays all SQL statements retrieved from the shared pool.

The source code associated to the form follows.

```
unit Statements;

interface

uses
  Windows, Messages, SysUtils, Classes, Graphics, Controls,
  Forms, Dialogs, ComCtrls, StdCtrls, ExtCtrls, uDM,
  DBCtrls, Grids, DBGrids;

type
  TfStatements = class(TForm)
    pHeader: TPanel;
    pControls: TPanel;
    Label1: TLabel;
    pSortType: TPanel;
    gbPlanOptions: TGroupBox;
```

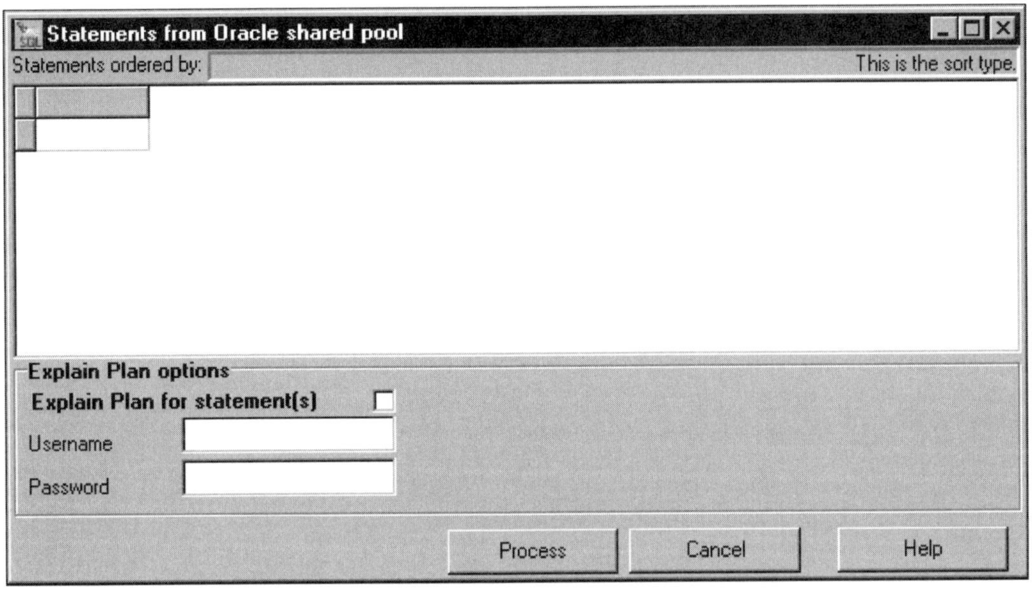

FIGURE 17.17 The Statements form Oracle Shared Pool Form

```
    Label2: TLabel;
    eUsername: TEdit;
    Label3: TLabel;
    ePassword: TEdit;
    DBGrid1: TDBGrid;
    Panel1: TPanel;
    cbExplain: TCheckBox;
    Panel2: TPanel;
    bCancel: TButton;
    bProcess: TButton;
    bHelp: TButton;
    procedure cbExplainClick(Sender: TObject);
    procedure bProcessClick(Sender: TObject);
    procedure bHelpClick(Sender: TObject);
  private
    { Private declarations }
  public
    { Public declarations }
  end;

var
  fStatements: TfStatements;
```

```

implementation

uses uStats;

{$R *.DFM}

procedure TfStatements.cbExplainClick(Sender: TObject);
begin
  eUserName.Enabled := cbExplain.Checked;
  ePassword.enabled := cbExplain.Checked;
end;

procedure TfStatements.bProcessClick(Sender: TObject);
var
  Statement : string;
  bStatementFound : boolean;
begin
  // Get the complete SQL statement
  DM.qGetStatementText.Params[0].Value :=
     DM.qGetStatements.FieldByName('address').value;
  DM.qGetStatementText.Params[1].Value :=
     DM.qGetStatements.FieldByName('hash_value').value;
  DM.qGetStatementText.Open;
  DM.qGetStatementText.First;
  Statement := '';
  bStatementFound := True;
  while not(DM.qGetStatementText.EOF) do
  begin
    Statement := Statement +
                 DM.qGetStatementText.Fields[0].asString;
    DM.qGetStatementText.Next;
  end;
  DM.qGetStatementText.Close;
  if Statement = '' then
  begin
    Statement :=
         DM.qGetStatements.FieldByName('SQL').AsString;
    bStatementFound := False;
  end;

  // Fill memo box
  fStats.mStatement.Text := Statement;

```

```
// Explain plan as required
if cbExplain.checked and bStatementFound then
begin
  if trim(eUsername.text) <> '' then
  begin
    DM.ExplainDB.close;
    DM.ExplainDB.params.clear;
    DM.ExplainDB.params.Add('USER NAME='+eUsername.text);
    DM.ExplainDB.params.Add('PASSWORD='+ePassword.text);
    DM.ExplainDB.Open;

    DM.qMakePlanTable.DatabaseName := 'ExplainDB';
    DM.qGetPlan.DatabaseName := 'ExplainDB';
    DM.qExec.DatabaseName := 'ExplainDB';
  end
  else
  begin
    DM.ExplainDB.params.clear;
    DM.qMakePlanTable.DatabaseName := 'DB';
    DM.qGetPlan.DatabaseName := 'DB';
    DM.qExec.DatabaseName := 'DB';
  end;

  // generate new plan
  DM.qExec.SQL.Clear;
  DM.qExec.SQL.Add(
      'explain plan set statement_id = ''ShrPool''');
  DM.qExec.SQL.Add(
       'into ' + DM.sUserName + '.local_plan_table for');
  DM.qExec.SQL.Add(Statement);
  DM.qExec.ExecSQL;

  // display plan
  DM.qGetPlan.SQL[2] :=
     'FROM '+ DM.sUsername + '.local_plan_table';
  DM.qGetPlan.Open;
  DM.qGetPlan.First;
  fStats.dbPlan.Lines.Clear;
  while not(DM.qGetPlan.EOF) do
  begin
    fStats.dbPlan.Lines.Add(DM.qGetPlan.Fields[0].asString);
    DM.qGetPlan.Next;
  end;
  DM.qGetPlan.Close;
```

```

    // tidy up
    DM.qExec.SQL.Clear;
    DM.qExec.SQL.Text :=
      'delete from ' + DM.sUsername +
      '.local_plan_table where STATEMENT_ID = ''ShrPool''';
    DM.qExec.ExecSQL;

    DM.qGetPlan.DatabaseName := 'DB';
    DM.qExec.DatabaseName := 'DB';
    if DM.ExplainDB.Connected then
       DM.ExplainDB.Close;
    fStats.mStatement.height := 120;
    fStats.dbPlan.visible := true;
  end
  else
  begin
    if cbExplain.checked then
       ShowMessage('Full statement not available.' +
         'Explain Plan not possible');
    fStats.mStatement.height := fStats.Panel1.height;
    fStats.dbPlan.visible := false;
  end;

  // fetch the total buffer gets
  DM.qExec.SQL.Clear;
  DM.qExec.SQL.Add('select sum(value) from v$sysstat');
  DM.qExec.SQL.Add(
     'where name in (''db block gets'', ''consistent gets'')');
  DM.qExec.Open;
  DM.qExec.First;
  fStats.lTotBuffGets.Caption := DM.qExec.Fields[0].asString;
  DM.qExec.Close;
  DM.qExec.SQL.Clear;

  // Calculate additional fields
  if DM.bNewVersion then
    fStats.dbeRows.DataField := 'rows_processed'
  else
    fStats.dbeRows.DataField := '';
  // Show the form
  fStats.eHitRate.Caption :=
         FloatToStrF((fStats.dbeBuffGets.Field.AsInteger-
         fStats.dbeReads.Field.AsInteger)
```

```
171:          /fStats.dbeBuffGets.Field.AsInteger * 100, ffFixed, 4,2);
172:    fStats.eRatioGets.Caption :=
173:          FloatToStrF(fStats.dbeBuffGets.Field.AsInteger /
174:          strtoint(fStats.lTotBuffGets.caption)* 100,
175:          ffFixed, 4,2);
176:    fStats.eRatioParses.Caption :=
177:          FloatToStrF(fStats.dbeParses.Field.AsInteger /
178:          fStats.dbeExecutions.Field.AsInteger,
179:          ffFixed, 4,2);
180:    fStats.ShowModal;
181: end;
182:
183: procedure TfStatements.bHelpClick(Sender: TObject);
184: begin
185:      Application.HelpCommand(HELP_CONTEXT, 60);
186: end;
187:
188: end.
```

1–44 Source code automatically generated by Delphi. The uses clause indicates that this form will call the uStats form to display the statistics for a selected SQL statement.

46–50 This code makes sure that username and password for the second connection can be entered only if the user asked for an explain plan.

52–53 Application logic to respond to the click event on the Process button.

54–55 Two local variables are defined, one to hold the SQL statement assembled from V$SQLTEXT and the other to flag if a statement has been found in V$SQLTEXT. This is needed to work the Oracle hash value bug. If an SQL statement cannot be assembled from V$SQLTEXT, this variable is set to false, and the first 1000 characters of the required SQL statement are fetched from V$SQLAREA.

57–61 Address and hash value are taken from qGetStatements and stored as parameters into qGetStatementText.

62–72 The cursor associated to the qGetStatementText is open, and all rows are fetched. The SQL statement is assembled from the 64 byte-long "pieces" stored in V$SQLTEXT. The loop appends each SQL piece at the end of the Statement string, until all rows have been fetched. The query is destroyed (closed) at the end of the loop.

73–78 If the string containing the statement is empty, the SQL statement lookup failed. Set the Boolean variable bStatementFound to false and copy the SQL portion of V$SQLAREA into the statement string.

80–82 Copy the statement string into the text box on the form.

84–85 If a statement has been found in V$SQLTEXT and the user asked for an explain plan . . .

86–97	If a username has been provided to explain the statement from a different user schema, a second connection is arranged and the data module queries to create and fetch from a plan table are set to point to the second connection.
98–104	Otherwise, the data module queries that create and fetch from a local plan table are set to point to the default connection.
106–113	The SQL statement that populates the plan table is assembled and stored in the query. The query is executed.
116–126	The content of the plan table is fetched from Oracle through the qGetPlan query and stored in the memo field displayed in the fStats form. When all rows have been fetched, the query is destroyed.
129–133	The plan table is emptied, that is, all rows are deleted from it.
137–140	If a second connection had been requested by the user, it is now closed. The visual controls are resized to make room for the execution plan, which is marked as visible.
143–149	This section takes care of the hash value bug. If a statement couldn't be found in V$SQLTEXT the user is informed, and the visual control that should display the execution plan made invisible.
151–160	The total number of buffer gets accumulated by the engine is fetched using the qExec query object. The result of the query is stored directly to the text label displayed in the fStats form. The query is closed.
168–180	The three ratios displayed in the fStats form are computed and stored in the visual controls.
183–186	Application logic to respond to the click event on the Help button. The help subsystem is called passing the topic number.

At this point, most of the work has been done. In this version of ShrPool, the SQL statement statistics are all stored in data-aware control displayed in the fStats form, with the exception of the three ratios, which have been computed at lines 168–180 in the Object Pascal code, which accompanies the fStatements form (see above).

Since most visual controls displayed by the fStats form are data-aware controls, the source code accompanying the form is reduced to a few lines. The fStats form (Figure 17.18) is shown with the source code.

Source code for the fStats form

```
unit uStats;

interface

uses
  Windows, Messages, SysUtils, Classes, Graphics, Controls,
  Forms, Dialogs, ExtCtrls, StdCtrls, Db, DBTables,
```

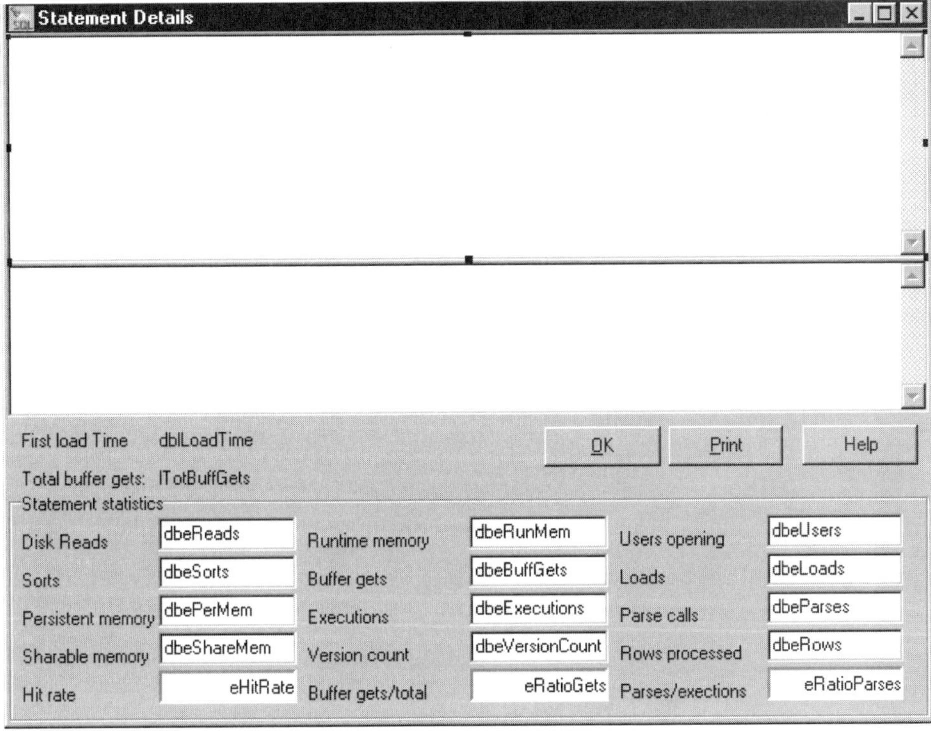

FIGURE 17.18 The Statement Details Form (fStats)

```
  DBCtrls, Mask, uDM;

type
  TfStats = class(TForm)
    Panel1: TPanel;
    mStatement: TMemo;
    Splitter1: TSplitter;
    gbStats: TGroupBox;
    Label1: TLabel;
    Label2: TLabel;
    Label3: TLabel;
    Label4: TLabel;
    dbeReads: TDBEdit;
    dbeSorts: TDBEdit;
    dbePerMem: TDBEdit;
    dbeShareMem: TDBEdit;
    Label5: TLabel;
```

```
    Label6: TLabel;
    dbeRunMem: TDBEdit;
    Label7: TLabel;
    dbeBuffGets: TDBEdit;
    Label8: TLabel;
    dbeExecutions: TDBEdit;
    Label9: TLabel;
    dbeVersionCount: TDBEdit;
    Label10: TLabel;
    Label11: TLabel;
    dbeUsers: TDBEdit;
    Label12: TLabel;
    dbeLoads: TDBEdit;
    Label13: TLabel;
    dbeParses: TDBEdit;
    Label14: TLabel;
    dbeRows: TDBEdit;
    Label15: TLabel;
    Panel2: TPanel;
    Label16: TLabel;
    dblLoadTime: TDBText;
    bOk: TButton;
    bPrint: TButton;
    bHelp: TButton;
    Label17: TLabel;
    lTotBuffGets: TLabel;
    eHitRate: TPanel;
    eRatioGets: TPanel;
    eRatioParses: TPanel;
    dbPlan: TMemo;
    procedure FormResize(Sender: TObject);
    procedure bOkClick(Sender: TObject);
    procedure bHelpClick(Sender: TObject);
    procedure bPrintClick(Sender: TObject);
  private
    { Private declarations }
  public
    { Public declarations }
  end;

var
  fStats: TfStats;

implementation
```

```
69:
70: {$R *.DFM}
71:
72:
73: procedure TfStats.FormResize(Sender: TObject);
74: begin
75:   if not(dbPlan.visible) then
76:     fStats.mStatement.height := fStats.Panel1.height
77:   else
78:   begin
79:     if mStatement.height > Panel1.Height then
80:       mStatement.height := Panel1.Height - 10;
81:   end;
82: end;
83:
84: procedure TfStats.bOkClick(Sender: TObject);
85: begin
86:   DM.qGetPlan.Close;
87: end;
88:
89: procedure TfStats.bHelpClick(Sender: TObject);
90: begin
91:      Application.HelpCommand(HELP_CONTEXT, 80);
92: end;
93:
94: procedure TfStats.bPrintClick(Sender: TObject);
95: begin
96:   Print;
97: end;
98:
99: end.
```

1–70 Code automatically generated by Delphi while designing the form.

73–82 Estethics adjustments operated at run-time if users resize the form by stretching the corners and dragging the edges. This code makes sure that the size ratio of the two major controls of the form remains unaltered.

84–87 Application logic to respond to the click event on the Ok button. The qGetPlan query object attached to the DM data module is closed. The form is closed.

89–92 The help subsystem is activated and the topic number 80 is displayed if the user clicks on the Help button.

94–97 The form is dumped on the default printer if the user clicks on the Print button.

With this form, the core of the Delphi version of ShrPool has been explored. A few other events triggers some other lines of Object Pascal code, but the bulk of the application is in the forms and source code presented above.

The Delphi environment is quite impressive. Its compiler speed and control over compiling optimization given to Delphi developers are unparalleled among the other RAD tools considered in this chapter. The data module form also contributes to give Delphi an edge over its competitors. Executable files produced by the compilation and linking of Object Pascal code, upon which the Visual Component Library (VCL) is built, are the smaller and faster of all RAD tools used in this chapter. If used together with the Direct Oracle Access low-level, OCI-based connectivity layer, Delphi is the environment of choice for traditional MS Windows based client/server applications.

The truly object-oriented features of Delphi, including its robust exception handling and support for function overloading introduced with release 4, contribute to promote Delphi as the more advanced development environment, from a purely technical point of view. As pointed out in chapter 10, this characteristic alone doesn't make Delphi the "best tool" in absolute terms. As an example, consider that Oracle Designer's code generation facility supports Visual Basic, and not Delphi. In IT environments committed to Oracle technologies, where Oracle Designer is probably the case tool of choice, this very fact can influence one to choose Visual Basic, instead of Delphi, as the client environment of choice for prototypes rapidly built out of Oracle Designer repositories, using the code generation facility.

The third party market of tools supporting Oracle development offers a few good examples of successful Delphi-based applications. Among the others, Quest Software TOAD and SQL Navigator are probably the most known tools, popular among the community of Oracle developers.

7.6 ShrPool in Powerbuilder

In spite of its decline in popularity, at the beginning of the new millenium Powerbuilder still has a considerable market share, rapidly accumulated at the beginning of the 1990s, when it was the only enterprise-class RAD tool to support the first wave of client/server applications. Even if from a purely technical point of view, Powerbuilder is definitely no longer the strongest contender, a few of its features are still unmatched by other competitors. Consider its multi-platform support, for instance, or the ability to deploy server-side Powerbuilder objects to create multi-tier applications. Unix/Motif versions of Powerbuilder are also available, making possible for developers with a PC-only background a smooth transition to an enterprise–class development environment through Powerbuilder for Unix.

The Powerbuilder version of ShrPool is modeled after the VB version. They are virtually identical, except for a major problem that affects the PB low-level Oracle connectivity drivers. Although Powerbuilder generally supports bind variables, it has been impossible to pass to a Powerbuilder data window that accesses the V$SQLTEXT table the ADDRESS field as a bind variable. I tried the HEXTORAW/RAWTOHEX Oracle functions on both sides of the where clause, as in:

```
select sql_text from V$SQLTEXT where
rawtohex(address) = <string_containing_address>;
```

or:

```
select sql_text from V$SQLTEXT where
address = hextoraw(<string_containing_address>);
```

No matter how hard I tried, I always received the Oracle error message "ORA-01460: unimplemented or unreasonable conversion requested." The problem appears to be related to the RAW datatype of the ADDRESS field, which is probably incorrectly internally converted by the PB low-level Oracle drivers.

The only way to force Powerbuilder to select from the V$SQLTEXT table has been to dynamically create a data window from Powerscript code, using the *SyntaxFromSQL* method of the connection object together with the data window control *create* method. Generating a data window on the fly has the unwanted side effect of submitting dynamic SQL to the Oracle engine, something that a tool like ShrPool should absolutely avoid.

The Powerbuilder version used in the example is 6.0, which has been followed by 6.5. I could not try the latest release of PB to verify if the bug has been fixed. The bug uncovered during the development of the Powerbuilder version of ShrPool would probably be very serious in a commercial environment, but doesn't defeat our purpose of demonstrating the PB features through a real application. We can live with the bug and the inefficient work-around for the sake of the example. If you are a Powerbuilder developer and you want to use the source presented here as the basis for your own version of ShrPool, consider further investigating the matter with Sybase/Powersoft, to find out if they have a fix available.

All objects comprising ShrPool are stored in a PBL library. The content of the PBL is shown in Figure 17.19.

The application comprises 1 menu, 4 application level functions, 8 data windows and 7 windows. Additionally, one mandatory application object must be present in the PBL. One project object, which instructs the Powerbuilder IDE on how to build the machine code executable, is also included.

Compared to the other versions of ShrPool, the PB version has one more window. This is because this version is the only one that allows users to see a

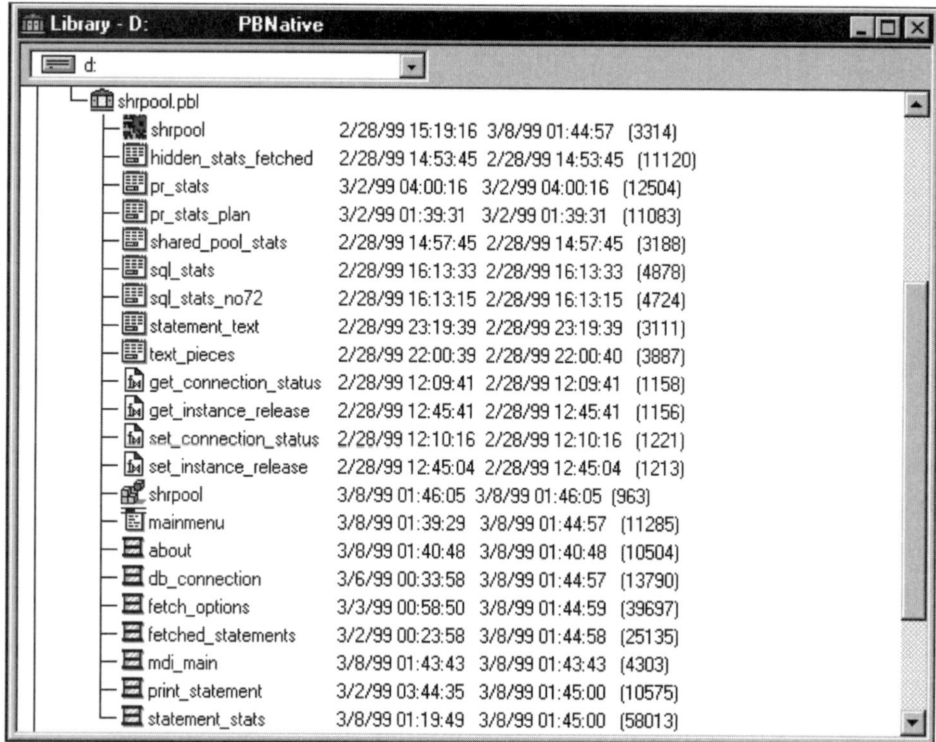

FIGURE 17.19 The PBL Library, which includes all Application Objects

print preview of the window that contains the SQL statement statistics and execution plan. Powerbuilder offers a very high-level development environment. Incorporating a print preview function in an application developed in Powerbuilder is a question of of one line of code:

```
<data window control>.modify( "DataWindow.Print.Preview=yes")
```

In other development environments, such as Delphi or Visual Basic, offering a print preview function requires a big effort.

The Powerbuilder IDE reflects its age. It shares similarities with Oracle Developer, for instance, in the way it organizes forms and source code, all stored in a binary format accessible only from within the IDE. In both IDEs, developers cannot access all source code attached to a form in one editing session, but they must search for lines of source code scattered in many places, such as behind controls, window functions, application functions, etc. For instance, globally-defined variables are stored in the application object, which provides a specific painter for them. Figure 17.20 shows the global variables defined in ShrPool as they appear in the painter.

The painter-centric environment is appropriate for the construction of visual elements, where you can physically drag and drop objects from toolbars into the form you are designing. The "painter visual metaphor" is much less appropriate for other objects, which are nonvisual by nature, like the application object. The application painter occupies one entire MDI sheet window only to display one little icon in the leftmost top corner.

To interact with the painter, developers must access the script painter, which allows them to access all the useful features provided by the application object, such as application level functions, structures and variables. The script stored behind the application object is run by the run-time system at application startup. The application script defined for ShrPool follows.

```
main_connection = CREATE TRANSACTION
alt_connection = CREATE TRANSACTION
open(mdi_main)
```

The script instantiates two connection objects, one used by the default connection and one to explain a statement using a different user schema, and creates an instance of the MDI main window. The MDI main window displays the appli-

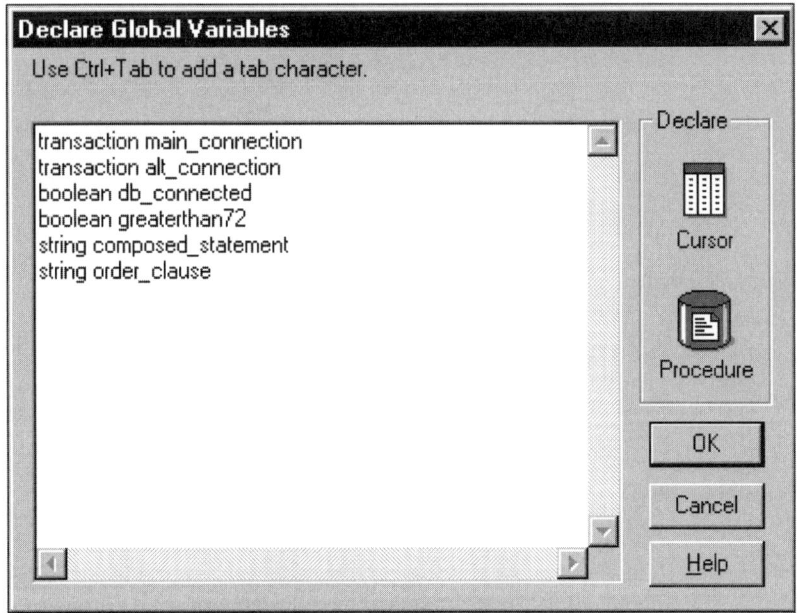

FIGURE 17.20 The Global Variables defined in ShrPool

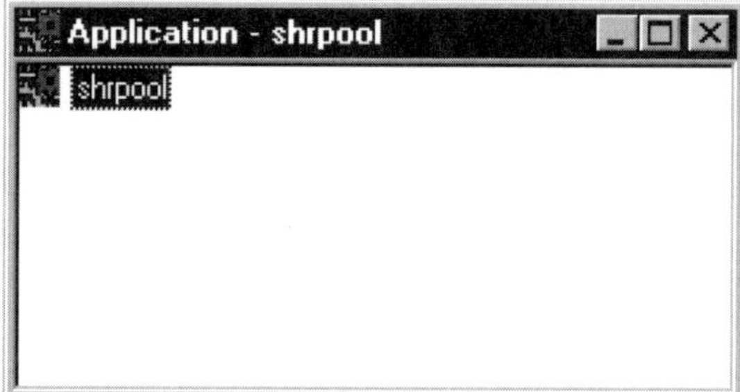

FIGURE 17.21 The Powerbuilder Application Painter

cation menu, which is initialized by the MDI window script that is executed at the opening of the window.

The MDI main window defines a window-level function, called menu_enable, which enables or disables the menu options accessible to the user at any one time. In Powerbuilder, it is possible to define window-level functions, structures, and local external functions (i.e., low-level calls to either MS Windows APIs or third party DLLs). A window can also receive parameters (!) and return values. The dot notation helps Powerscript, the Powerbuilder high-level language modeled after Basic and "C", to find the referenced object. For instance, if I define the menu_enable function in the MDI main window, called MDI_MAIN, I can invoke menu_enable from other application objects using MDI_MAIN.MENU_ENABLE(). Developers must make sure that the object exists, that is, the window is open, before invoking the function at run-time, otherwise an error occurs.

From the main menu attached to the MDI main sheet, users can click on the "Connect" menu option (Figure 17.22).

The relevant Powerscript code is stored behind the window control and behind the Ok button.

```
Open event of the form:
  1: sle_username.text = profilestring("shrpool.ini",&
  2:                       "oracle","username","")
  3: sle_connstring.text = profilestring("shrpool.ini",&
  4:                      "oracle","tns_string","")
  5: if len(sle_username.text) > 0 then
  6:  sle_password.setfocus()
  7: end if
```

1–4 Username and connection string are read from an initialization file (shrpool.ini) and stored in their respective visual controls.

5–7 If the ini file provided a username, the focus when the form is initially displayed will be on the password field. Otherwise, the focus will be on the username field.

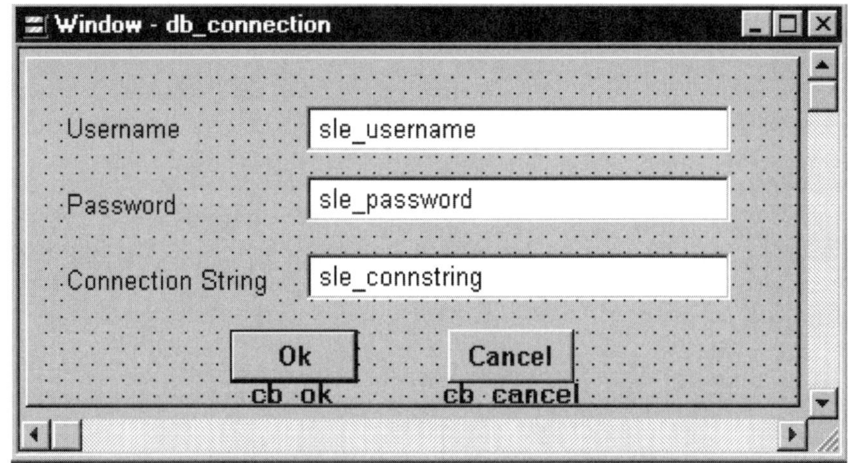

FIGURE 17.22 The Connection Form

Click event on the Ok button:

```
String s_ora_release
int    n_ora_release

setpointer(hourglass!)
main_connection.DBMS=profilestring("shrpool.ini",&
                         "Oracle","Server","OR8")
main_connection.servername=sle_connstring.text
main_connection.logid = sle_username.text
main_connection.logpass = sle_password.text
main_connection.AutoCommit = False
CONNECT USING main_connection;
if main_connection.sqlcode <> 0 then
 messagebox("Connection error",&
                "Could not connect to Oracle",Exclamation!)
 return
else
 mdi_main.menu_enable(true)
 set_connection_status(true)
 select nvl(substr(value,1,3),'7.0') into &
       :s_ora_release from sys.v_$parameter &
       where name='compatible' using main_connection;
 n_ora_release = integer(s_ora_release) * 10
 if n_ora_release >= 72 then
       set_instance_release(true)
 else
       set_instance_release(false)
```

```
27:   end if
28:   SetProfileString("shrpool.ini",&
29:         "Oracle","USERNAME",sle_username.text)
30:   SetProfileString("shrpool.ini",&
31:         "Oracle","TNS_STRING",sle_connstring.text)
32:   close(parent)
33:  end if
34:  return
```

1–4 One string and one integer variable are declared, to store the Oracle engine release number. The mouse pointer is set to the hourglass shape to inform the user that the application is processing.

5–10 The connection object used for the default connection is initialized with values stored in the ini file.

11–12 A connection is attempted. If the sqlcode property value is different from 0, the connection failed.

13–15 Inform the user through a message box that the application couldn't connect and go back to the connection window.

16–33 If the connection was successful, enable the menu options, retrieve the Oracle engine version number in a string, convert the release number into an integer, and evaluate its content. If the connected engine is greater than 7.2, call the set_instance_release function passing a boolean true; otherwise, call the function passing a Boolean false. Store the content of the username and connection string fields back into the ini file. Finally, destroy the connection window.

Like in all other versions of ShrPool, the user can now progress, asking ShrPool to display the fetch option window to select order criteria and filters for the SQL statements to be retrieved from the shared pool. The fetch option window is shown below, together with the source code that accompanies the window.

Open event of the form:

```
1: this.width=2725
2: this.height=1608
3: this.X=565
4: this.Y=228
5: rb_broverexecutions.checked=true
6: em_stats_to_show.text = string(20)
7: if get_instance_release() = false then
8:  rb_blockoverrows.enabled=false
9: end if
```

1–4 Size and position of the window are set.

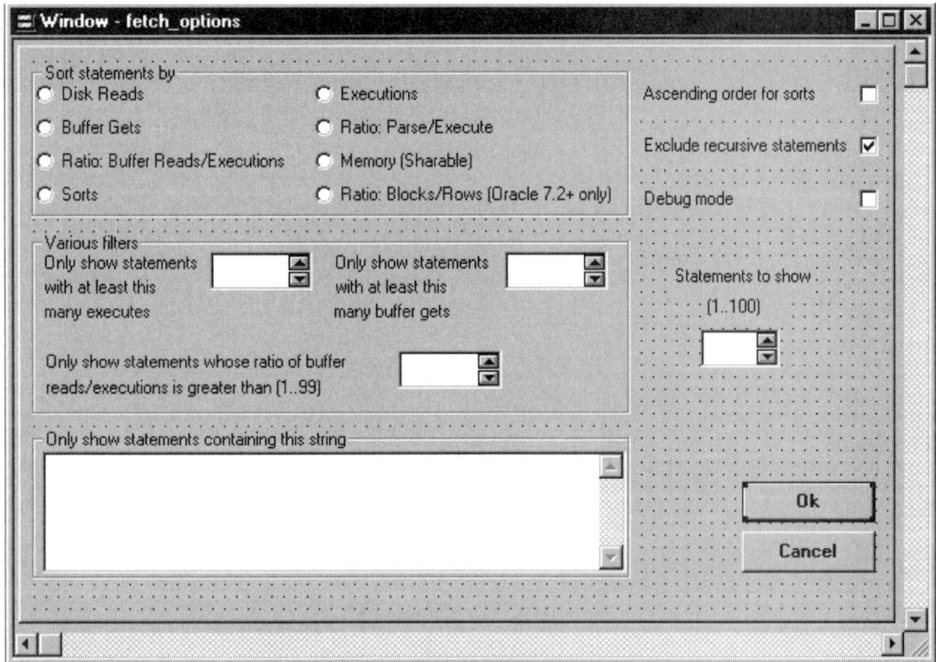

FIGURE 17.23 The Fetch Options Window.

5 – 7 The default order criterion is set to buffer gets over executions. The default number of statements to show is set to 20. If the connected engine is older than 7.2, the blocks over rows_processed ratio is made unavailable.

Click event on the **Ok** button:

```
 1: string main_select
 2: string where_clause
 3: string orderby_clause
 4: string sql_statement
 5:
 6: if get_instance_release() then
 7:   main_select="select sql_text,sharable_mem," &
 8:     +"persistent_mem,runtime_mem,sorts,executions," &
 9:            +"parse_calls,buffer_gets,disk_reads,version_count," &
10:     +"users_opening,loads,"&
11:     +"to_char(to_date(first_load_time,'YYYY-MM-DD/HH24:MI:SS')," &
12:    +"'DD/MM:HH24:MI:SS') first_load_time,rawtohex(address)address," &
13: +"to_char(hash_value) hash_value,rows_processed from sys.v_$sqlarea"
```

```
else
  main_select="select sql_text,sharable_mem,persistent_mem," &
     +"runtime_mem,sorts,executions,parse_calls," &
     +"buffer_gets,disk_reads,version_count,users_opening," &
+"loads,to_char(to_date(first_load_time,'YYYY-MM-DD/HH24:MI:SS')," &
 +"'DD/MM:HH24:MI:SS') first_load_time,rawtohex(address)address," &
 +"to_char(hash_value) hash_value from sys.v_$sqlarea"
end if
if rb_blockoverrows.checked then
  orderby_clause = " order by buffer_gets/decode" &
      +"(rows_processed,0,1,executions) "
end if
if rb_broverexecutions.checked then
  orderby_clause = " order by buffer_gets/executions "
end if
if rb_buffer_gets.checked then
  orderby_clause = " order by buffer_gets "
end if
if rb_diskreads.checked then
  orderby_clause = " order by disk_reads "
end if
if rb_executions.checked then
  orderby_clause = " order by executions "
end if
if rb_memorysharable.checked then
  orderby_clause = " order by sharable_mem "
end if
if rb_parseoverexecute.checked then
  orderby_clause = " order by parse_calls/executions "
end if
if rb_sorts.checked then
  orderby_clause = " order by sorts"
end if
if cbx_ascsrot.checked then
  orderby_clause = orderby_clause + "asc"
else
  orderby_clause = orderby_clause + "desc"
end if
where_clause = " where executions > 0 "
if cbx_excluderecusrsive.checked then
  where_clause = where_clause + " and parsing_user_id != 0 "
end if
if integer(em_buffgets.text) > 0 then
where_clause = where_clause + " and buffer_gets > "+em_buffgets.text
```

```
58: end if
59: if integer(em_executes.text) > 0 then
60:   where_clause = where_clause + " and executions > "+em_executes.text
61: end if
62: if integer(em_buffreadsoverexecutions.text) > 0 then
63:   where_clause = where_clause + &
64:           " and buffer_gets/executions > "+ &
65:           em_buffreadsoverexecutions.text
66: end if
67: if len(mle_string_filter.text) > 0 Then
68:   where_clause = where_clause + &
69:     " and upper(sql_text) like upper('%"+ &
70:       trim(mle_string_filter.text)+"%') "
71: end if
72: sql_statement = main_select + where_clause+orderby_clause
73: if cbx_debugmode.checked then
74:   messagebox("Fetch options selected",sql_statement,Information!)
75: end if
76: composed_statement = sql_statement
77: order_clause = orderby_clause
78: opensheet(fetched_statements,mdi_main)
79: close(parent)
```

6–21 If the Oracle engine release number is greater than 7.2, create a select statement that includes the rows_processed field; otherwise, omit the field in the select clause.

22–46 Work out the order criterion chosen by the user. Access all radio button controls and find out which one is checked.

47–51 Work out whether the user wanted an ascending or descending order by clause.

52–71 Build a where clause by accessing all filter fields. If filter options have been chosen, concatenate them to the where clause.

72–75 Build the SQL statement that will retrieve all statements from the shared pool by concatenating the select, where, and order by parts together. If the user selected the debug mode check box, display the dynamically built SQL statement in a message box.

76–78 Store the SQL statement just built into the composed_statement global variable and the order by clause into the order_clause global variable. Open the fetched_statements window as an MDI child sheet.

At this point, ShrPool has built the SQL statement that will be used to browse the shared pool from the user-entered options. The next step, carried out by the open event of the fetched_statements window, is to submit the statement to the Oracle engine and to fetch the results in a data window. The technique used by the fetched_statements window is as follows:

- One hidden data window is built dynamically using the SynatxFromSQL method provided by the connection object.
- Two other data windows are defined in the form, both made hidden at design time. One contains a reference to the rows_processed field, the second doesn't contain that reference.
- The correct data window is made visible according to the Oracle version number.
- The visible data window is populated with data by sharing the data store with the hidden data window dynamically built using SyntaxFromSQL.

The fetched_statements window is shown in Figure 17.24.

Open event of the form:

```
string dw_sqlsyntax
string errors
string presentation_str
int n_rows
long sum_buffgets
```

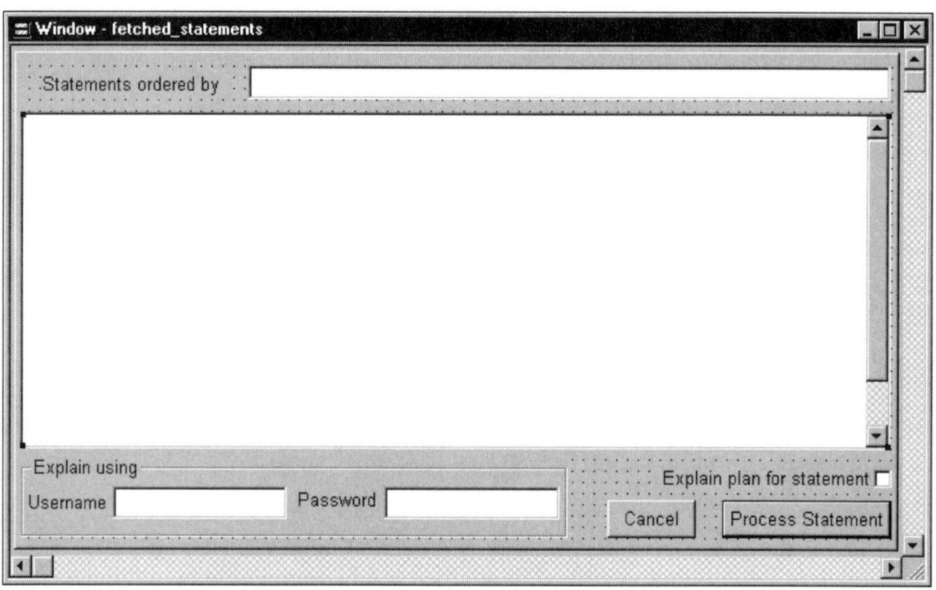

FIGURE 17.24 The fetched_statements Window

```
 6:
 7: this.width=2981
 8: this.height=1508
 9: this.X=400
10: this.Y=300
11: sle_orderby.text = order_clause
12: presentation_str="style(type=tabular)"
13: dw_sqlsyntax = main_connection.SyntaxFromSql&
14:  (composed_statement,presentation_str,errors)
15: if len(errors) > 0 then
16:  messagebox("DW Error",errors,exclamation!)
17:  return
18: end if
19: dw_fetchall.create(dw_sqlsyntax,errors)
20: dw_fetchall.SetTransObject(main_connection)
21:
22: n_rows = dw_fetchall.retrieve()
23: if get_instance_release() then
24:  dw_statements_all.visible=true
25:  dw_statements_all.enabled=true
26:  dw_fetchall.Sharedata(dw_statements_all)
27:  dw_statements_all.selectrow(1,true)
28:  dw_statements_all.setfocus()
29:  l_rownum=1
30: else
31:  dw_statements_no_rows.visible=true
32:  dw_statements_no_rows.enabled=true
33:  dw_fetchall.Sharedata(dw_statements_no_rows)
34:  dw_statements_no_rows.selectrow(1,true)
35:  dw_statements_no_rows.setfocus()
36:  l_rownum=1
37: end if
38: SELECT sum(buffer_gets) INTO :sum_buffgets &
39:         FROM V$SQLAREA USING main_connection;
40: set_tot_buffgets(sum_buffgets)
```

7–11 Window size and position are set by the opening script. The Order by field is populated with the content of the order_clause global variable.

12–22 The hidden main data window is dynamically created, a transaction object is associated with it, and the rows are selected by the associated SQL statement fetched.

23–37 According to the Oracle engine release number, the appropriate data window is made visible and populated by sharing the rows contained in the main data store.

38 – 40 The total number of buffer gets generated by the engine is fetched from Oracle and stored in a locally defined variable by calling the set_tot_buffgets() window function defined in fetched_statements.

Click event on the **Ok** button:

```
 1: long statement_number
 2:
 3: setpointer(hourglass!)
 4: if get_instance_release() then
 5:    statement_number = dw_statements_all.getselectedrow(0)
 6: else
 7:    statement_number = dw_statements_no_rows.getselectedrow(0)
 8: end if
 9: OpenSheetWithParm(statement_stats,statement_number,mdi_main)
10: if get_instance_release() then
11:    dw_statements_all.setfocus()
12: else
13:    dw_statements_no_rows.setfocus()
14: end if
```

3–8 The mouse pointer changes its shape into an hourglass. If the Oracle release is greater than or equal to 7.2, get the currently selected row from the dw_statements_all data window. Otherwise, get the currently selected row from the dw_statements_no_rows data window. Store the number corresponding to the selected row in a local variable.

9 Open the statement_stats MDI child window passing the variable, which stores the currently selected row as a parameter.

10–13 Set the focus on the appropriate data window. The effect of this statement will be visible when the user closes the statement_stats window.

The statement_stats window (Figure 17.25) displays SQL statement statistics and, if requested by the user, an execution plan for the statement currently being analyzed.

Open event of the form:

```
long l_statement_nbr
string dw_syntax
int n_how_many
string sql_addr
string trunc_table
string explain_stat
string expl_line
string grant_privs
string filter_1
```

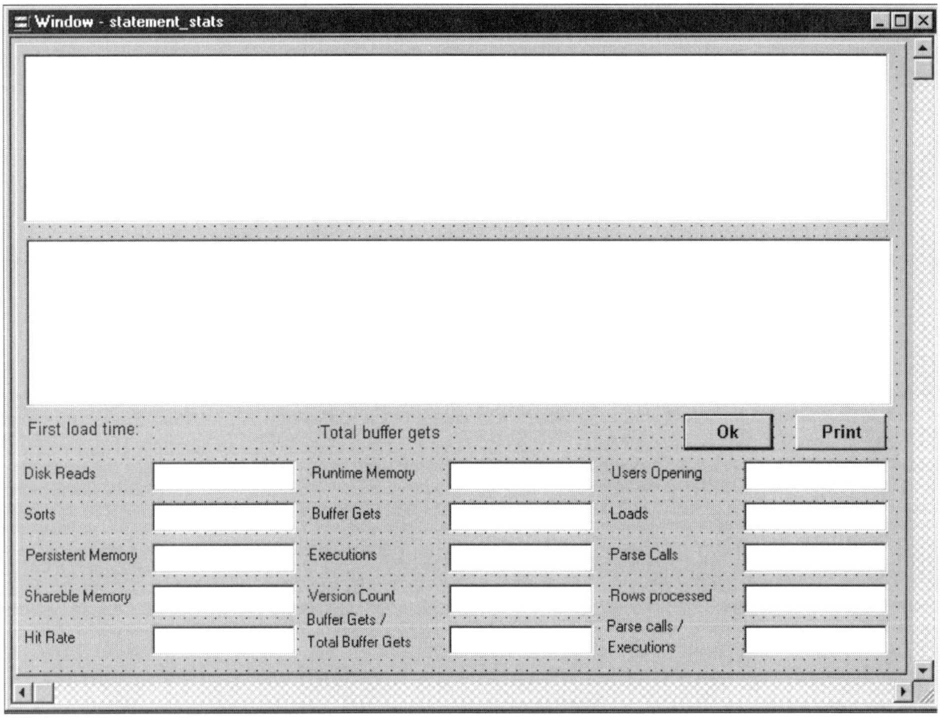

FIGURE 17.25 The statement_stats Window

```
int    sql_pieces
real   hit_rate
real   buff_gets_rate
real   parse_execute_rate
int    ii
boolean cannot_explain
string errors
String sql_text_piece
string create_table
String   sql_hash

this.width=3150
this.height=1956
this.X=200
this.Y=150

setpointer(hourglass!)
l_statement_nbr=Message.doubleParm
```

```
cannot_explain = false
sql_addr=fetched_statements.dw_fetchall.getItemString &
    (l_statement_nbr,"address")
sql_hash=fetched_statements.dw_fetchall.getItemString &
    (l_statement_nbr,"hash_value")

dw_syntax=main_connection.SyntaxFromSQL(&
   "SELECT SQL_TEXT FROM V$SQLTEXT WHERE ADDRESS " &
   +"= HEXTORAW('"+sql_addr+"') AND HASH_VALUE = " &
   +"TO_NUMBER('"+sql_hash+"') ORDER BY PIECE",&
    "style(type=tabular)", errors)

dw_all_statement.create(dw_syntax,errors)
dw_all_statement.SetTransObject(main_connection)
sql_pieces=dw_all_statement.retrieve()

if sql_pieces > 0 then
  for ii = 1 to dw_all_statement.RowCount()
  sql_text_piece = sql_text_piece + &
         dw_all_statement.getitemstring(ii,"sql_text")
  next
else
  sql_text_piece=fetched_statements.dw_fetchall.getitemstring &
    (l_statement_nbr,"sql_text")
end if
if fetched_statements.cbx_explain.checked then
  mle_sql_with_explain.text =sql_text_piece
  mle_sql_with_explain.visible=true
  lb_explain_plan.visible=true
  this.title = this.title + " with execution plan"
else
  mle_sql_no_explain.text = sql_text_piece
  mle_sql_no_explain.visible=true
end if
st_total_buffer_gets.text=string( &
   fetched_statements.get_tot_buffgets())
st_firstloadtime.text=&
   fetched_statements.dw_fetchall.getitemstring( &
   l_statement_nbr,"first_load_time")
sle_buffgets.text =string(&
   fetched_statements.dw_fetchall.getitemnumber &
   (l_statement_nbr,"buffer_gets"))
sle_diskreads.text = string(&
   fetched_statements.dw_fetchall.getitemnumber &
```

```
   (l_statement_nbr,"disk_reads"))
sle_executions.text = string(&
   fetched_statements.dw_fetchall.getitemnumber &
   (l_statement_nbr,"executions"))
sle_loads.text = string(&
   fetched_statements.dw_fetchall.getitemnumber &
   (l_statement_nbr,"loads"))
sle_parse_calls.text = string(&
   fetched_statements.dw_fetchall.getitemnumber( &
   l_statement_nbr,"parse_calls"))
sle_persmem.text = string(&
   fetched_statements.dw_fetchall.getitemnumber &
   (l_statement_nbr,"persistent_mem"))
sle_runtimemem.text = string(&
   fetched_statements.dw_fetchall.getitemnumber( &
   l_statement_nbr,"runtime_mem"))
sle_sharemem.text = string(&
   fetched_statements.dw_fetchall.getitemnumber &
   (l_statement_nbr,"sharable_mem"))
sle_sorts.text = string(&
   fetched_statements.dw_fetchall.getitemnumber &
   (l_statement_nbr,"sorts"))
sle_usersopening.text = string(&
   fetched_statements.dw_fetchall.getitemnumber &
   (l_statement_nbr,"users_opening"))
sle_version_count.text = string(&
   fetched_statements.dw_fetchall.getitemnumber &
   (l_statement_nbr,"version_count"))
if get_instance_release() then
  sle_rows_processed.text=string(&
       fetched_statements.dw_fetchall.getitemnumber &
       (l_statement_nbr,"rows_processed"))
end if
hit_rate = integer(sle_diskreads.text) * 100 / &
    integer(sle_buffgets.text)
sle_hitrate.text = string(hit_rate,"###.##")
buff_gets_rate = integer(sle_buffgets.text) /&
    integer(st_total_buffer_gets.text)
sle_buffgetsovertotbuffgets.text = string(buff_gets_rate,"###.##")
parse_execute_rate = &
   integer(sle_parse_calls.text) *100/ integer(sle_executions.text)
sle_parsecallsoverexecution.text= &
    string(parse_execute_rate,"###.##")
if fetched_statements.cbx_explain.checked then
```

```
 SELECT count(*) INTO :n_how_many FROM LOCAL_PLAN_TABLE &
    USING main_connection;
if (main_connection.sqlcode <> 0) then
     if (main_connection.sqldbcode = 942) then
          create_table = "create table LOCAL_PLAN_TABLE (" &
                 +"statement_id    varchar2(30)," &
               +"timestamp          date," &
               +"remarks            varchar2(80)," &
               +"operation          varchar2(30)," &
               +"options            varchar2(30)," &
               +"object_node        varchar2(128)," &
               +"object_owner       varchar2(30)," &
               +"object_name        varchar2(30)," &
               +"object_instance numeric," &
               +"object_type     varchar2(30), " &
               +"optimizer       varchar2(255)," &
               +"search_columns  numeric, " &
               +"id          numeric," &
               +"parent_id   numeric," &
               +"position    numeric," &
               +"other               long)"

        EXECUTE IMMEDIATE :create_table USING main_connection;
        if (main_connection.sqlcode <> 0) then
           cannot_explain = true
           messagebox(&
            "Oracle Error","Could not create PLAN table. Error: " &
            +main_connection.sqlerrtext,exclamation!)
        end if
    else
        cannot_explain = true
        messagebox(&
           "Oracle Error","Could not access PLAN table. Error: " &
               +main_connection.sqlerrtext,exclamation!)
        goto display
    end if
else
  if (len(trim(fetched_statements.sle_username.text)) > 0) Then
        alt_connection.DBMS = main_connection.DBMS
        alt_connection.servername=main_connection.servername
        alt_connection.AutoCommit = False
        alt_connection.logid = fetched_statements.sle_username.text
        alt_connection.logpass = fetched_statements.sle_password.text
        CONNECT USING alt_connection;
```

```
          if alt_connection.sqlcode <> 0 then
                messagebox("Oracle error","Could not login as "+&
                fetched_statements.sle_username.text+"~nError: "+&
                alt_connection.sqlerrtext,Exclamation!)
                  DISCONNECT USING alt_connection;
                 goto display
          end if
      end if
   trunc_table = "truncate table local_plan_table"
   EXECUTE IMMEDIATE :trunc_table USING main_connection;
   explain_stat="EXPLAIN PLAN INTO "&
      +trim(main_connection.logid)+ &
         ".LOCAL_PLAN_TABLE FOR " + sql_text_piece
   if (len(trim(fetched_statements.sle_username.text)) > 0) Then
       grant_privs="GRANT ALL ON LOCAL_PLAN_TABLE TO "&
          +fetched_statements.sle_username.text
       EXECUTE IMMEDIATE :grant_privs USING main_connection;
       if main_connection.sqlcode <> 0 Then
          messagebox(&
          + "Oracle error","Cannot explain statement~nOracle error: "&
          + main_connection.sqlerrtext, exclamation!)
          goto display
       end if
       EXECUTE IMMEDIATE :explain_stat USING alt_connection;
       if alt_connection.sqlcode <> 0 Then
           messagebox(&
           "Oracle error","Cannot explain statement~nOracle error: "&
            +alt_connection.sqlerrtext, exclamation!)
           DISCONNECT USING alt_connection;
           goto display
       end if
       DISCONNECT USING alt_connection;
   else
      EXECUTE IMMEDIATE :explain_stat USING main_connection;
      if main_connection.sqlcode <> 0 Then
          messagebox(&
           "Oracle error","Cannot explain statement~nOracle error: "&
            +main_connection.sqlerrtext, exclamation!)
          goto display
      end if
   end if
   DECLARE rec_curs CURSOR FOR
   select lpad(' ',4*level)||operation||' '||options||' '||object_name
         query_plan from local_plan_table connect by
```

```
204:    prior id = parent_id start with id=1 USING main_connection;
205:    OPEN rec_curs;
206:    DO
207:            FETCH rec_curs INTO :expl_line;
208:            lb_explain_plan.additem(expl_line)
209:    LOOP WHILE main_connection.sqlcode = 0
210:    CLOSE rec_curs;
211:    lb_explain_plan.deleteitem(lb_explain_plan.totalitems())
212:   end if
213: end if
214: display:
215: cb_ok.setfocus()
216:
```

21–24 Size and position of the window are determined here.

26–32 Mouse pointer changes into a hourglass. The window parameter is read from the application message queue and stored into a variable of type long. Address and hash values are taken from the fetched_options window by accessing the dw_fetchall data window directly, using the received parameter as a line number.

34–42 The data window that will contain the SQL statement retrieved from V$SQLTEXT is built dynamically. This step generates dynamic SQL on the server. The main transaction object is associated with the newly created data window and an attempt to fetch the rows from Oracle is made.

44–52 If the fetch operation is successful, the entire statement is built by concatenating SQL “pieces” together into a string. Otherwise, the SQL statement is taken from V$SQLAREA.

53–61 Visual controls are made visible or invisible according to the options chosen by the user. If an execution plan has been requested, the caption of the window is changed to signal that the window contains an execution plan.

62–104 All visual controls displaying SQL statement statistics are populated with the values fetched by the fetched_statements window.

105–114 The three ratios are computed and displayed in the appropriate visual controls.

115–117 A Select count(*) of all rows contained in the LOCAL_PLAN_TABLE is issued with the purpose to determine if the local_plan_table exists in the user schema.

118–119 If oracle returns an ORA-00942 error, the local plan table doesn’t exist.

120–136 A string containing the SQL statement to create a plan table is initialized.

138–144 A DDL command is issued to the server to create the plan table. If an error occurred, inform the user and continue processing.

145–150 If the error returned by the select count() is not ORA-00942, inform the user and stop processing. The control returns to the form.

153–167 If the user requested an execution plan for a different user schema, arrange a second connection, attempt to connect, and, in case of failure, alert the user and stop processing. The control returns to the form.

168–200 The plan table if truncated if an explain has been requested for the default connection. If the explain plan has been requested for a second connection, the rows are deleted from the plan table. In this case, the default connection grants all privileges to the alternate connection, to allow the second connection to store data in the local plan table.The EXPLAIN PLAN statement is executed, and in case of failure, the user is alerted and the script stop processing.

201–210 A cursor is defined to fetch the rows stored by Oracle in the plan table. The cursor is open and in case of success, all rows are fetched, using the specific Oracle syntax for hierarchically selecting records of the same table in a parent-child kind of relationship. Each row fetched from the cursor is appended to the list box displayed in the form. At the end of the loop the cursor is closed.

Clicking on the "Print" button of the statement_stats window causes the print_statements window to be displayed. This window shows a print preview of what will be dumped on the default printer if the "Print" button is clicked. The print_statements window contains a data window that is populated with data fetched from the statement_stats window. This is done to exploit the powerful printing capabilities built in the data window objects. The open event of the form performs a copy from the visual controls holding SQL statistics displayed in the statement_stats window to the data window that will present the print preview to the user. The print_statement window is shown in Figure 17.26 and the script triggered by the open event follows.

Open event of the form:

```
long l_row
string ex_plan
int    i_lb_items
int         ii

this.width=3803
this.height=1812
this.x=1
this.y=50
dw_print.InsertRow(0)
l_row = dw_print.RowCount()
if statement_stats.lb_explain_plan.visible=false then
```

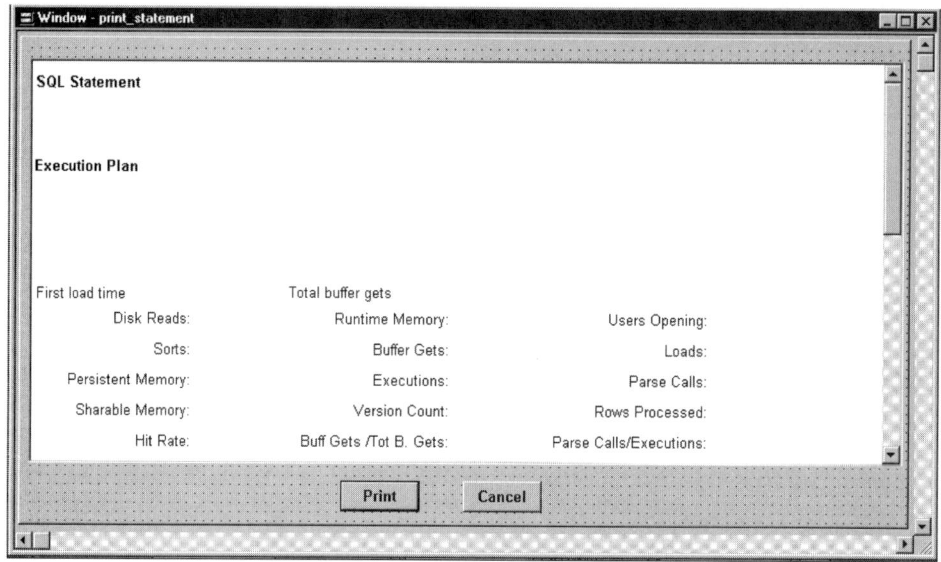

FIGURE 17.26 The print_statement Window

```
   dw_print.modify("explain_plan.visible=0")
   dw_print.modify("exection_plan.visible=0")
   dw_print.SetItem(&
      l_row,"SQL_TEXT",&
      statement_stats.mle_sql_no_explain.text)
else
   i_lb_items = statement_stats.lb_explain_plan.totalitems()
   ex_plan="|"
   for ii = 1 to i_lb_items
      ex_plan = ex_plan + &
      statement_stats.lb_explain_plan.text(ii) + "~n|"
   next
   dw_print.SetItem(l_row,"explain_plan",ex_plan)
   dw_print.SetItem(&
     l_row,"SQL_TEXT",&
           statement_stats.mle_sql_with_explain.text)
end if
dw_print.SetItem(l_row,&
    "FIRST_LOAD_TIME",statement_stats.st_firstloadtime.text)
dw_print.SetItem(l_row,&
    "TOTAL_BUFF_GETS",statement_stats.st_total_buffer_gets.text)
dw_print.SetItem(l_row,&
```

```
35:     "DISK_READS",statement_stats.sle_diskreads.text)
36: dw_print.SetItem(l_row,&
37:     "SORTS",statement_stats.sle_sorts.text)
38: dw_print.SetItem(l_row,&
39:     "PERSISTENT_MEMORY",statement_stats.sle_persmem.text)
40: dw_print.SetItem(l_row,&
41:     "SHARABLE_MEMORY",statement_stats.sle_sharemem.text)
42: dw_print.SetItem(l_row,&
43:     "HIT_RATE",statement_stats.sle_hitrate.text)
44: dw_print.SetItem(l_row,&
45:     "RUNTIME_MEMORY",statement_stats.sle_runtimemem.text)
46: dw_print.SetItem(l_row,&
47:     "BUFFER_GETS",statement_stats.sle_buffgets.text)
48: dw_print.SetItem(l_row,&
49:     "EXECUTIONS",statement_stats.sle_executions.text)
50: dw_print.SetItem(l_row,&
51:     "VERSION_COUNT",statement_stats.sle_version_count.text)
52: dw_print.SetItem(l_row,&
53:     "buffer_gets_tot_buffgets",&
54:     statement_stats.sle_buffgetsovertotbuffgets.text)
55: dw_print.SetItem(l_row,&
56:     "USERS_OPENING",statement_stats.sle_usersopening.text)
57: dw_print.SetItem(l_row,&
58:     "LOADS",statement_stats.sle_loads.text )
59: dw_print.SetItem(l_row,&
60:     "PARSE_CALLS",statement_stats.sle_parse_calls.text )
61: dw_print.SetItem(l_row,&
62:     "ROWS_PROCESSED",statement_stats.sle_rows_processed.text)
63: dw_print.SetItem(l_row,&
64:     "parse_calls_execs",&
65:     statement_stats.sle_parsecallsoverexecution.text)
66: dw_print.modify("DataWindow.Print.Preview=yes")
```

6–9 Size and position of the window are set here.

10–11 Insert an empty row in the print data window, and obtain a pointer to it.

12–17 If an execution plan has not been requested, prevent the printing of an empty execution plan.

19–24 If an execution plan must be printed, work out the plan from the list box displayed in the statement_stats window. A little trick must be used here, to prevent Powerbuilder from automatically trimming the leading tabs, which would lose the indenting of the execution plan. A pipe sign (|) is displayed at the beginning of each row, forcing powerbuilder to maintain the correct indenting for the execution steps.

25–65 The data window method SetItem is repeatedly used to copy all statement statistics from the statement_stats window into the local data window that will be dumped on the default printer.

66 The data window populated by the previous step is shown to the user as a print preview. If the user clicks on the print button, the form is sent to the default printer.

With the print_statement window, we are finished with the Powerbuilder version of ShrPool. Powerbuilder can produce a machine code executable file, through a laborious and cumbersome procedure. The executable file is an order of magnitude slower than Delphi or Visual Basic, and the size of the run-time DLLs that must be shipped together with the application is considerable. In spite of these disadvantages, Powerbuilder is a powerful development environment, which can be appealing for developers who must support multi-platform applications.

Summary

This chapter focused on client-side development tools. One application has been developed using the four most popular RAD tools currently used to access Oracle databases located in the back-end, using the traditional client/server paradigm. The four RAD tools considered in this chapter were MS Visual Basic, Oracle Developer, Borland.com Delphi, and Sybase/Powersoft Powerbuilder. The application developed, called ShrPool, is an Oracle-shared pool browser, used to analyze SQL statements submitted to the Oracle engine. ShrPool can generate execution plans for selected SQL statements, which are useful to pinpoint inefficient or untuned statements.

Developing the same application in the four different environments allowed for comparing advantages and drawbacks of each tool. The four versions of ShrPool can be found in the accompanying CD-ROM. When the source code is not natively available in ASCII format, as in the case of Oracle Developer or Powerbuilder, a subdirectory called *source* can be found, which contains all source code extracted from the internal format used by the tool and saved in ASCII format. This is useful if you don't have access to Oracle Developer or Powerbuilder, but you are interested in examining the source code anyway.

Chapter 18

ORACLE PERFORMANCE TUNING

This chapter illustrates OPERA (**O**racle **P**erformance **E**valuator and **R**eal-time **A**nalyzer). OPERA is a software tool that simplifies the preliminary analysis needed to improve the performance of Oracle databases. Tuning a running Oracle instance is an intrinsically difficult task, which requires not only a great deal of competence, but also a very good memory by the Database Administrator, who has to remember many parameters, performance ratios and SQL statements by heart. OPERA helps automate many of the tasks required for the tuning effort. Furthermore, OPERA is the only currently available tool able to run from a WEB browser.

The chapter starts with an overview of the performance issues usually associated with Oracle databases. The second section deals with the generic requirements that an Oracle performance monitoring tool should have in order to be effective. The third section illustrates the design of OPERA, and how the requirements identified by the second section are taken into account by the OPERA design. The fourth section lists the relevant parts of the Java client source code. Section five describes the key aspects of the source code of the server-side Opera process, to help developers who want to customize and enhance the product to their requirements; this section also lists the possible enhancements that can be incorporated in future releases of OPERA.

18.1 Two Areas Where Oracle Performance Can Fail

The performance problems generally found when dealing with an Oracle environment stem from two different key causes:

- ❑ SQL Statements sent to the engine are not properly formulated or tuned.
- ❑ Oracle engine is not properly tuned and/or startup parameters are wrongly set.

There is a third area, the host operating system where Oracle runs, which can affect the overall performance of the engine, but this is out of the OPERA scope.

18.1.1 POORLY FORMULATED SQL STATEMENTS

The overall Oracle Architecture is heavily influenced by the design decision made by the Oracle engineers to have a global memory region that is shared across all the Oracle components (user processes, background processes, etc). This memory region is called SGA (System Global Area).

When a user performs an operation involving any database activity, the SQL statement issued by that user is put in a sub-part of the SGA, called the Shared Pool. This part of the statement processing (called parse) is very expensive in terms of computing resources. If the same user, or every other user, reissues the same SQL statement soon after, the Oracle engine realizes that the statement is already in the Shared Pool, and does not reparse it, therefore gaining in performance.

The words "soon" and "after" have been used. They imply a very important concept: the SQL statements are put in the Shared Pool, but they are also thrown away to make room for new SQL statements sent by the Oracle users. There is a LRU type of algorithm (Least Recently Used), which keeps track of all those statements that have been issued once and not reissued for a while, marking them good candidates for being thrown away as soon as the engine must process new SQL statements and the space in the Shared Pool has become scarce.

It is possible for a DBA to intervene in this mechanism in order to fix certain statements in the Shared Pool irrespective of the frequency at which they are being accessed. Experience shows that even very complex applications (particularly in the OLTP field) have a limited amount of core SQL statements, issued by most users repetitively. By default, Oracle would keep the most used statements in the Shared Pool, therefore avoiding the continuous reparse.

The above statement is correct only if the SQL statements use "bind" variables. If the SQL statement sent to the engine contains literal strings in the where clause, it must be reparsed every time the where clause changes. See Chapter 5, section 5.4.3 for a detailed discussion about bind variables.

In order to be efficient when evaluating the statements in the Shared Pool, the Oracle engine performs a very simple comparison (based on hash keys) between the SQL statement just received and all the statements residing in the pool. This implies that the two following statements:

- SELECT * FROM EMP WHERE NAME = :MY_NAME
- SELECT * FROM EMP WHERE NAME = :SURNAME

are considered different by the engine, even if they use bind variables.

18.1.2 ENGINE POORLY CONFIGURED

There are several components in every Oracle system:

- Files

  Control files: these define the location of all the database files and also have information about all the checkpoints performed by the engine

  Database files: these contain the tables, indexes, and the segments which make up the database

  Redo log files: these contain the details of transaction data

- Segments and tablespaces. Segments are logical subdivisions of homogeneous data and are contained within physical boundaries (tablespaces). A popular way to structure the database is according to the Optimal Flexible Architecture (OFA), a set of guidelines published by Oracle Corporation with the goal of standardizing the database layout. The OFA defines a minimum of seven tablespaces:

  System—for storing the data dictionay tables

  Data—for storing tables

  Indexes—for storing indexes

  Tools—for storing SQL*Forms, CASE and third party tools

  Rbs—for storing the rollback segments

  Temp— for storing temporary segments created dynamically by Oracle (for instance during large sorting operations)

  Users—for storing each individual user's object

- System Global Area. The SGA is an area of shared memory. It is further subdivided in three homogeneous sub-areas:

  Buffer Cache: it caches blocks of data taken from the database tables

  Shared Pool: it contains data dictionary information and cached SQL statements

  Redo Buffers: they are memory buffers for the redo logs processes

One can logically group the Oracle processes in three different categories:

1. Oracle background processes, which perform services needed by the engine (for instance, LGWR performs all the writes in the Redo log files and keeps synchronized the Redo log buffers in the SGA with the physical Redo log files)
2. User processes, for example, an executable written in PRO*C and running on the server machine
3. Server processes, which perform database operations on behalf of individual users (also called "shadow" processes)

Every running Oracle engine has at least four background processes:

- ❑ DBWR
- ❑ LGWR
- ❑ SMON
- ❑ PMON

In addition, if the database is running in ARCHIVELOG mode (that is, automatic archiving), one more background process is required (ARCH).

Starting with Oracle version 7, two major features have been added to the engine. The first is the ability to parallelize the engine processes and the execution of a single SQL statement (Oracle Parallel Server and Parallel Query Option). The second is the ability to enable server processes that can serve multiple users through the use of dispatchers, therefore minimizing the active Oracle connections (Multi-Threaded Server or MTS).

The introduction of these new features has made the entire Oracle Architecture much more complex, and also increased the number of different background processes. If using the MTS options, one will find at least one dispatcher process per network protocol used to connect to the instance (Dnnn) and at least one server process (Snnn, where nnn is the sequential number assigned by Oracle while creating the process). If the Parallel Server option is enabled, additional processes can be found, all identified by the prefix LCK. They are used for inter-instance locking, and are crucial for synchronizing the database activity between different machines which share the disks where the Oracle files are stored.

It is also possible to enable two more background processes, the first for carrying out the task of resolving the potential failures involved in distributed transactions (the RECO process) and the second for sending a signal to DBWR at checkpoint time, updating the headers of Control Files and data files (CKPT). By default, these operations are performed by the process LGWR, but if there are many data files making up the database, the LGWR performance could suffer.

Additional background processes can be found when Oracle instances implement advanced replication, Advanced Queuing (AQ) and Oracle cartridges, such as Oracle ConText.

In such a complex architecture, made up of so many composite components that must interact with each other so closely, it is very easy for some parameters to be incorrectly set, thus affecting the performance of the entire engine. Oracle makes available its own internal memory structures in the form of tables. The X$ prefix characterizes these pseudo-tables, which contain fields whose name is generally not meaningful or self-explanatory. For this reason there exists a set of views, characterized by the V$ prefix, which organize the information contained in the pseudo-tables in a more comprehensible manner.

The process of tuning Oracle mainly involves performing queries against the relevant V$ views, and in a few cases the X$ tables, with the goal of finding clues that can identify the Oracle parameter, or set of parameters, incorrectly set.

Remembering the name and the meaning of every V$ view is a daunting task, even for the consummate DBA. Oracle8i has 175 V$ views defined, to expose its internal memory structures. An Oracle7 engine would have less V$ views, far too many anyway to be remembered by heart. A DBA would have to consult a manual (or a set of manuals) to fine tune the database. A tool like OPERA can simplify the DBA's life, carrying the burden of remembering the meaning of all the relevant tables and drawing the DBA's attention to those values that exceed specific thresholds, thus pinpointing an abnormal behavior.

18.2 The Tool DBAs Need

There are three main areas of interest for performance tuning:

1. Memory allocation
2. Input/Output
3. Resource Contention

To complete the tuning process, one should also consider sort areas, free list contention, and checkpoints. Inevitably, every tool that helps in tuning performance is biased towards a specific tuning method, and OPERA is no exception. The way to mitigate this sort of built-in bias is to simply declare explicitly the tuning method for which the tool, in this case OPERA, has been designed. The following section will describe in detail the method chosen to conduct a tuning session using OPERA.

18.2.1 OPERA AND ITS TUNING METHOD

The method followed by OPERA is essentially inductive (top-down). The main tuning window should provide a set of critical ratios covering the three delicate areas where performance generally suffers. The user should be able to access further windows that display in detail all values related to the specific part of the engine that made the ratio have an unsatisfactory value in the first place.

A list of tuning ratios follows:

MEASURE	DESCRIPTION
Buffer Cache Hit Ratio	Percentage of time required data blocks are found in cache. Should be > 90%.
Library Cache Get Hit Ratio	Percentage of time SQL issued is found in cache. Should be > 90%. Low values indicate dynamic SQL.
Library Cache Exec Hit Ratio	Percentage of time SQL executed is found in cache. Should be > 99%. Low values indicate Shared Pool is too small.
Dictionary Cache Hit Ratio	Percentage of time data dictionary information is found in cache. Should be > 99%. Low values indicate Shared Pool is too small.
Worst Latch Hit Rate	All latch hit rates should be > 99%. Meaning of low values depends on latches involved.
Disk Sort Ratio	Proportion of sorts that could not be performed in memory. High values may indicate that sort_area_size is too low.
Indexed Fetch Ratio	Proportion of rows that were gotten via rowid (index). Should be > 80%. Low values may indicate excessive table scans, missing indexes, etc.
Parse/Execute Ratio	Number of parses per SQL execution. Should be < 10%. Higher values may indicate poor cursor reuse inside the application.
Recursive Call Ratio	Percentage of calls generated by ORACLE. Should be < 20%. Can indicate free space fragmentation, dynamic SQL, Shared Pool too small.
Commits/Transactions	Percentage of transactions that were committed. The aim is to avoid rollbacks, which are very expensive from a performance point of view. Should be > 90%.

Investigating the engine waits is also an important aspect of the tuning process. It is crucial to understand what parts of the engine were idle, waiting for something to happen before being able to restart processing.

In general, events commencing with "db file" and "log file" account for almost all waits in a well-tuned system. The ratio between "db file" and "log file" waits is typically 80% to 20%. These waits are indicative of I/O being done on behalf of the client and as such can be regarded as "healthy". The following waits can indicate bottlenecks in the application/database, and should be displayed in a specific OPERA window.

OPERA should also allow the user to monitor latches, which are Oracle internal locks placed by the engine to protect memory structures in the SGA. The SGA can be concurrently accessed by different processes, several CPUs, and even

MEASURE	DESCRIPTION
Buffer Busy Waits	Should be negligible. High values can indicate rollback segment or free list contention. Analysis of SESSION_WAITS may be necessary.
Free Buffer Waits	Should be negligible. High values are often due to excessive sorts and inode contention on the temporary table space.
Latch Wait	Should be negligible. Otherwise, need to check latch window.
Enqueue	High values can occur due to a single process being locked. Consistently high values may indicate contention for locks.
Write Complete Waits	Should be negligible. High values may indicate insufficient db_writers or _db_write_batch is too high.

different machines (Oracle Parallel Server). In order to maintain consistency and avoid corruption, every relevant memory structure, before being modified, must be locked. Those locks, in Oracle parlance, are "latches". If the "Latch Free Waits" ratio displayed in the main tuning window is negligible, the person conducting the tuning exercise can safely ignore latches. If that ratio is not negligible, on the other hand, one should examine the latch statistics in detail. OPERA should provide one window that will group together all the different types of latches.

The Oracle provided tool to monitor database locks is not very effective. In fact, the SQL script UTLLOCKT.SQL is slow and acquires locks itself, and is a classic example of an observer that modifies the observed world with its presence. The output produced by the script is a lock tree, which displays sessions holding locks, and sessions that are waiting for those locks. OPERA should provide a similar report in a window, but the process used to gather lock information should not acquire any lock, and should display additional information (Oracle Session Id, OS Id, and type of lock, etc).

Finally, OPERA should give the user the ability to display in an ancillary window all the SQL statements stored in the Shared Pool, in descending order by resource consumption. In other words, the most expensive statement will be at the top of the list. Selecting the chosen statement will cause the opening of a window to show the execution plan for the statement in question.

Experience shows that a proper formulation of SQL statements is essential for optimal performance of Oracle engines. In other words, a perfectly tuned engine could be brought to its knees by a small set of poorly designed SQL statements, especially if they perform unwanted full table scans or are continuously re-parsed. Browsing the Shared Pool and being able to access the execution plan of each selected SQL statement is as important as, if not more important than, being able to fine-tune the instance parameters. Chapter 17 showed several implementations of ShrPool, a utility written to browse the SQL statements parsed in the shared pool. The same functionality should be part of a tool like OPERA.

18.3 OPERA Design

Oracle Corporation provides an Enterprise Manager add-on, called Tuning Pack, which offers capabilities similar to, and possibly more advanced than, those of OPERA. Why did I bother to spend so much of my spare time building a tool like OPERA? First of all, only by understanding the Oracle internals, and programming using OCI, can one get a full comprehension of the Oracle architecture. Designing and coding OPERA has been fun and thoroughly instructive. I invite advanced Oracle developers and professionals to use OPERA as a starting point, and build extensions and enhancements upon the basic infrastructure provided in this chapter (and in the accompanying CD-ROM).

Second, OPERA is free, with its source available for modifications. The Tuning Pack is proprietary and closed, and requires a PC running MS Windows to work. This is particularly annoying for somebody like myself (and many other professionals I know), who feel much more comfortable in more stable environments, like OpenVMS or Unix. Oracle Corporation will probably port the Tuning Pack to Java, but the source code won't be available.

Third, OPERA doesn't require SQL*Net/Net8 to work. OPERA uses TCP/IP sockets for interprocess communication, and only requires a "C" compiler on the back-end machine. A WEB browser is all that is needed on the client side to display the Oracle performance statistics. I have used OPERA in the most disparate environments, Siemens/Pyramid machines running DC/OSx, OpenVMS VAX and Alpha, Solaris (several releases, from SunOS to Solaris 7), HP/UX (9 to 11), IBM AIX. Using OPERA I was able to monitor the performance of Oracle engines from release 7.0.16 to Oracle8i.

Thanks to its open architecture, OPERA can be easily customized to specific environments. An example of how to enhance OPERA will be given further ahead in the chapter. OPERA was conceived when the "current" release of the database server was 7.3.2. Oracle8 was shipped, and with it Oracle Advanced Queuing. With Oracle 8.0.4, a new V$ view has been made available to monitor the queuing performance. I added the window that displays Advanced Queuing performance parameters in less than 15 minutes. It is possible that the "standard" release of OPERA, shipped with this book, doesn't cover areas that you would like to see covered. If the preconfigured set of performance ratios or raw statistics presented by OPERA doesn't satisfy you, just customize it to fulfill your needs. On the server side you need just an editor (like the good old vi) and a "C" compiler (obviously, you must link the OPERA object files to the Oracle OCI libraries, so you need Oracle installed on the machine). On the client side you need a Java compiler and one KLG component (the LiveTable class). This component is shipped with the professional editions of most Java IDEs (Borland JBuilder, Sybase PowerJ++, Oracle JDeveloper 1.0–1.1, etc). If you don't have access to the LiveTable component, with little effort, you can modify the source code to use a different grid.

18.3.1 A THREE-TIER ARCHITECTURE

OPERA is based on a three-tier architecture, where the Oracle instance being monitored plays the role of the first tier, the OPERA server process, which performs all data gathering, plays the role of the second tier, and the Java client, providing presentation services, is the third tier.

The OPERA component that runs on the server side uses the OCI7 to interact with Oracle instances. The OCI7 is now in the "obsolescent" state, which means that it is not leading edge technology. The advantage of using the OCI7 is in its compatibility with both Oracle7 and Oracle8. When the OCI7 will make the transition from "obsolescent" to "obsolete", a new version of OPERA, which will use the OCI8, will be promptly released.

18.3.1.1 Data Gatherer The core of the OPERA functionality resides in the server process, which runs as a daemon, waiting for socket connections from the Java clients. When a connection is established, the server process "forks," spawning a child process that will serve all requests coming from the connected client, while the parent is listening again for additional, incoming connections.

The Java client implements the GUI interface that allows users to interact with the data gatherer and uses TCP/IP sockets to connect to the server process. The starting point for a performance analysis is given by a set of key ratios that should give, at a glance, an overall impression of the running of the Oracle engine being observed.

The Java client provides a menu option that allows users to display a dialog reporting 25 ratios computed from the values taken from the Oracle memory structures, published through the V$ views.

18.3.1.2 Engine Performance Ratios The following table lists the ratios, providing the SQL statements used to compute them.

PERFORMANCE RATIO	SQL STATEMENT
Overall Hit Ratio	`Select round(( congets.value + dbgets.value - physreads.value) *100/(congets.value + dbgets.value),4) "HIT RATE" from v$sysstat congets, v$sysstat dbgets, v$sysstat physreads where congets.name='consistent gets' and dbgets.name = 'db block gets'and physreads.name = 'physical reads'`
Recursive Calls / User Calls	`select (rc.value/(rc.value+ uc.value)) *100 from v$sysstat rc, v$sysstat uc where rc.name = 'recursive calls' and uc.name='user calls'`
Connected Users	`select count(*) from sys.v_$session where username is not NULL`
Active Users	`select count(*) from sys.v_$session where username is not NULL and status ='ACTIVE'`

(*cont.*)

PERFORMANCE RATIO	SQL STATEMENT
Dictionary Cache Hit Rate	`select sum(gets-getmisses) *100/ SUM (GETS),3 from sys.v_$rowcache`
Short/Total Table Scan Ratio	`select sc.value /(sc.value+ls.value) *100 from sys.v_$sysstat ls, sys.v_$sysstat sc where sc.name=' table scans (short tables)' and ls.name=' table scans (long tables)'`
Disk Sort Ratio	`select ds.value/ decode( (ds.value +ms.value) ,0,1,(ds.value+ms.value)) *100 from sys.v_$sysstat ds, sys.v_$sysstat ms where ms.name=' sorts (memory)' and ds.name= 'sorts (disk)'`
Buffer Busy Wait Ratio	`select (bbw.total_waits* 100/ (cg.value+dbg.value)) from sys.v_$system_event bbw, sys.v_$sysstat cg, sys.v_$sysstat dbg where bbw.event='buffer busy waits' and cg.name= 'consistent gets' and dbg.name='db block gets'`
Free Buffer Wait Ratio	`Select (bbw.total_waits* 100/ (cg.value+dbg.value)) from sys.v_$system_event bbw, sys.v_$sysstat cg, sys.v_$sysstat dbg where bbw.event='free buffer waits' and cg.name= 'consistent gets' and dbg.name='db block gets'`
Overall Library Cache Hit Ratio	`select sum(gethits)*100/sum(gets) from sys.v_$librarycache`
Library Cache Pin Hit Ratio	`select sum(pinhits)*100/sum(pins) from sys.v_`
Block Changes Per Transaction	`$librarycache select bc.value/t.value from sys.v_$sysstat bc, sys.v_$sysstat t where`
Calls Per Transaction	`bc.name='db block changes' and t.name='user commits' select c.value/t.value from sys.v_$sysstat c, sys.v_$sysstat t where c.name='user calls' and t.name='user commits'`
Rows Per Sort	`select r.value/decode( (d.value +m.value) ,0,1, (d.value+m.value) ) from sys.v_$sysstat r,sys.v_$sysstat d, sys.v_$sysstat m where r.name=' sorts (rows)'and d.name='sorts (disk)'and m.name='sorts (memory)'`
Consistent Change Ratio	`select (cg.value-cc.value) *100 /cg.value from sys.v_$sysstat cg, sys.v_$sysstat cc where cg.name=' consistent gets' and cc.name=' consistent changes'`
Redo Space Wait Ratio	`select (sw.value)*100/lw.value from sys.v_$sysstat sw, sys.v_$sysstat lw where sw.name=' redo log space requests' and lw.name='redo writes'`
Chained Rows Encountered Rate	`select rfcr.value*100 / (tsrg.value +tfbr.value) from sys.v_$sysstat rfcr, sys.v_$sysstat tsrg, sys.v_$sysstat tfbr where rfcr.name='table fetch continued row'and tsrg.name='table scan rows gotten and tfbr.name='table fetch by rowid'`

PERFORMANCE RATIO	SQL STATEMENT
Parse/Execute Ratio	`select pc.value*100/(ec.value) from sys.v_$sysstat ec, sys.v_$sysstat pc where ec.name='execute count' and pc.name='parse count'`
Enqueue Success No Wait Ratio	`select 100-(ew.value*100/er.value) from sys.v_$sysstat ew, sys.v_$sysstat er where ew.name=' enqueue waits' and er.name='enqueue requests'`
Enqueue Wait No Timeout Ratio	`select 100-(ew.value*100/er.value) from sys.v_$sysstat ew, sys.v_$sysstat er where ew.name=' enqueue timeouts' and er.name='enqueue requests'`
Overall Latch Get Rate	`select (sum(gets)-sum(misses))*100 sum(gets) from sys.v_$latch`
Worst Latch	`select substr(name,1,25),(gets-misses) *100 /gets from sys.v_$latch where (gets-misses)/gets= (select min((gets-misses)/gets) from sys.v_$latch where gets!= 0 and name!= 'redo copy') and gets!= 0`
Rows From Indexes/ Total Rows Ratio	`select (r.value/ (r.value+s.value)) *100 from sys.v_$sysstat r, sys.v_$sysstat s where r.name='table fetch by rowid' and s.name='table scan rows gotten'`
Commits/Transactions Ratio	`select (c.value/ (r.value+c.value)) *100 from sys.v_$sysstat r, sys.v_$sysstat c where r.name='user rollbacks' and c.name='user commits'`
Cursors/Transactions Ratio	`select oc.value/(r.value+c.value) from sys.v_$sysstat c,sys.v_$sysstat r,sys.v_$sysstat oc where c.name='user commits' and r.name='user rollbacks' and oc.statistic# = 2`

Figure 18.1 shows the Java client that displays the performance ratios computed by the OPERA server process.

The dialog that displays the performance ratios should indicate to the DBA analyzing the instance the area or areas requiring attention. If the number of waits is abnormally high, one should look at the dialog displaying detailed statistics on engine waits. Accordingly, if latch contention is detected when looking at the overall ratios, the appropriate dialog that displays latch statistics should be requested.

18.3.1.3 The Engine Statistics Menu Figure 18.2 shows the options available from the "Engine Statistics" menu, displayed by the Java frame.

By clicking on the "Lock Analysis" menu option OPERA, users can see a dialog that displays two grids: on the left-hand side, a list of all engine locks, and on the right-hand side, a list of SQL statements responsible for causing locks.

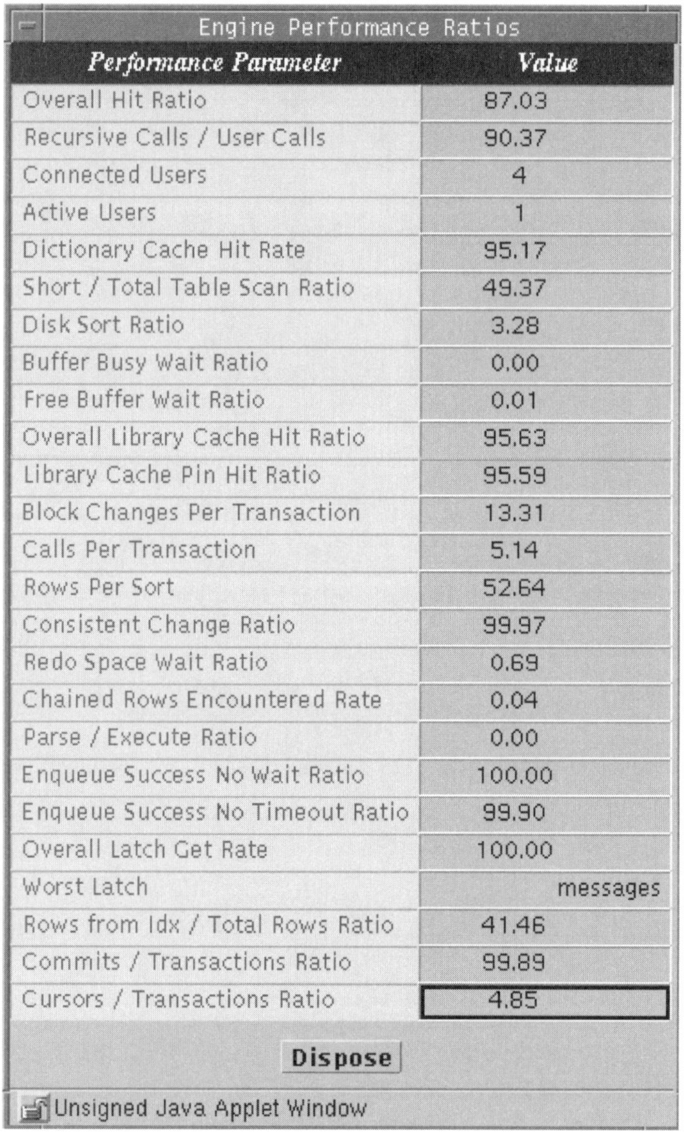

Engine Performance Ratios

Performance Parameter	*Value*
Overall Hit Ratio	87.03
Recursive Calls / User Calls	90.37
Connected Users	4
Active Users	1
Dictionary Cache Hit Rate	95.17
Short / Total Table Scan Ratio	49.37
Disk Sort Ratio	3.28
Buffer Busy Wait Ratio	0.00
Free Buffer Wait Ratio	0.01
Overall Library Cache Hit Ratio	95.63
Library Cache Pin Hit Ratio	95.59
Block Changes Per Transaction	13.31
Calls Per Transaction	5.14
Rows Per Sort	52.64
Consistent Change Ratio	99.97
Redo Space Wait Ratio	0.69
Chained Rows Encountered Rate	0.04
Parse / Execute Ratio	0.00
Enqueue Success No Wait Ratio	100.00
Enqueue Success No Timeout Ratio	99.90
Overall Latch Get Rate	100.00
Worst Latch	messages
Rows from Idx / Total Rows Ratio	41.46
Commits / Transactions Ratio	99.89
Cursors / Transactions Ratio	4.85

Dispose

Unsigned Java Applet Window

FIGURE 18.1 The Client Dialog Displaying the Performance Ratios

OPERA provides data dictionary statistics, available from the "Engine Statistics" menu. The content of the data dictionary window is shown in Figure 18.4.

In order to find out if the load on the Oracle instance is spread evenly across different disks, it is important to evaluate the data file statistics.

The "Data File Stats" (Figure 18.5) option presents a grid in a window, which shows absolute numbers and percentages of reads and writes performed on each datafile comprising the database.

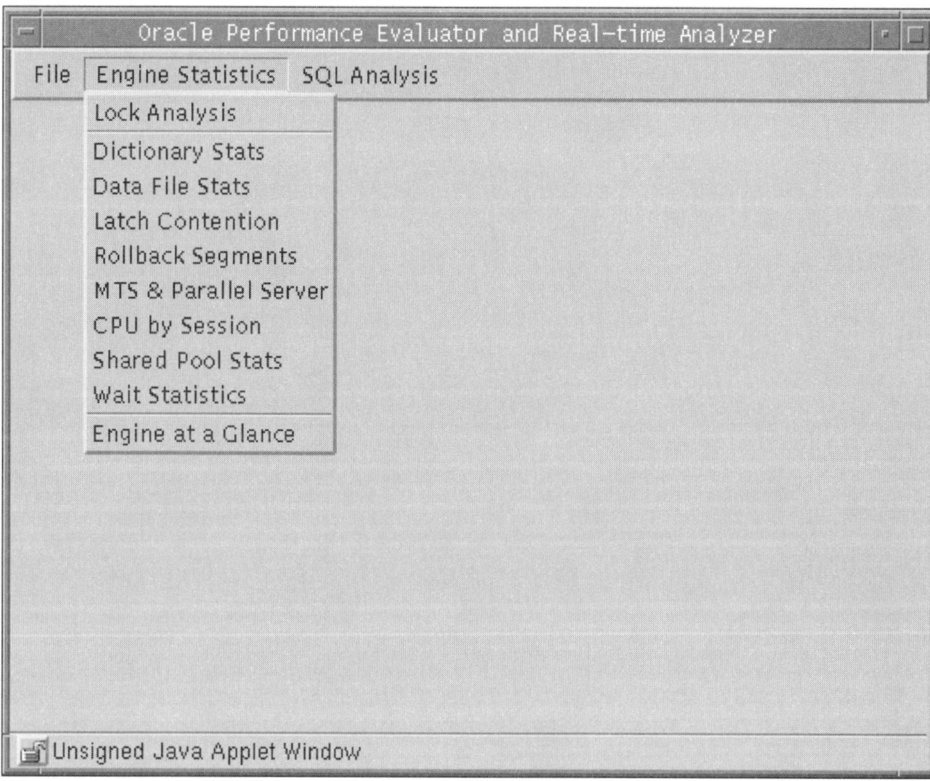

FIGURE 18.2 Engine Statistic Options Provided by OPERA

The next option in the "Engine Analysis" menu is "Latch Contention." For each significant latch type, the grid displays a set of seven statistics, formatted in seven columns. They are: number of gets and their percentage over the overall total gets; number of misses and their percentage over the overall total misses; number of sleeps and their percentage over the overall sleeps, and sleep rate. A few words will help to explain the meaning of these statistics.

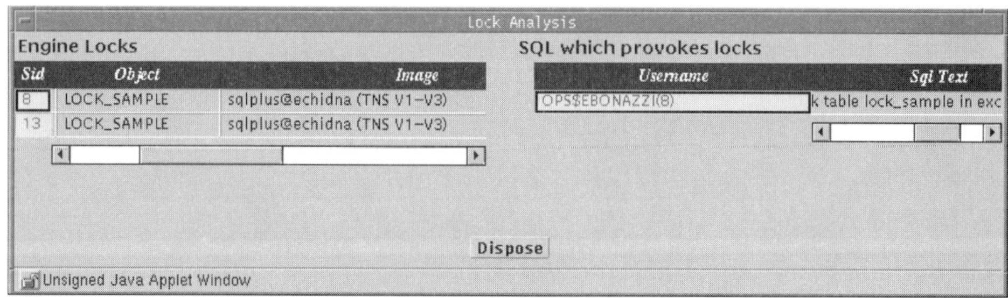

FIGURE 18.3 Lock Analysis performed through OPERA

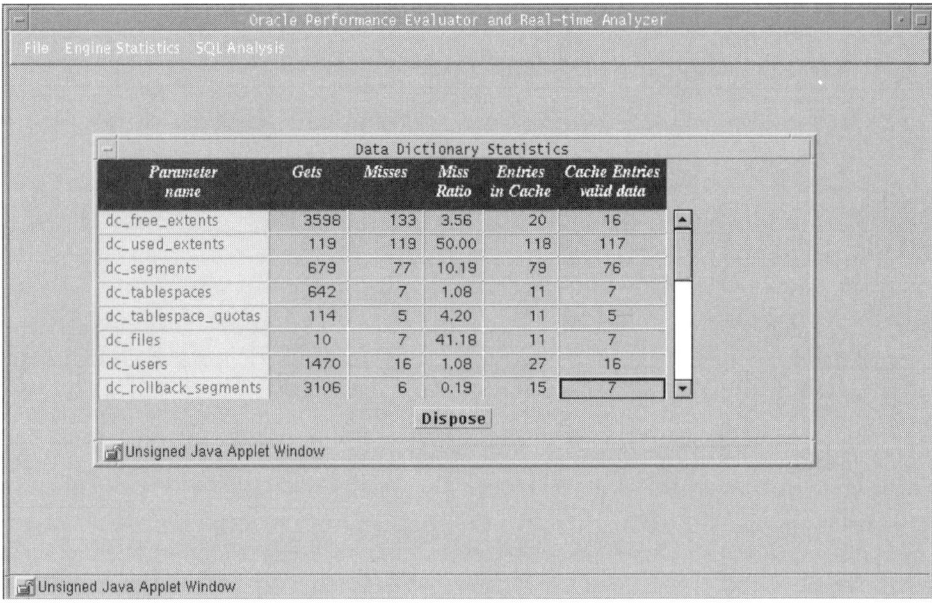

FIGURE 18.4 Data Dictionary Statistics

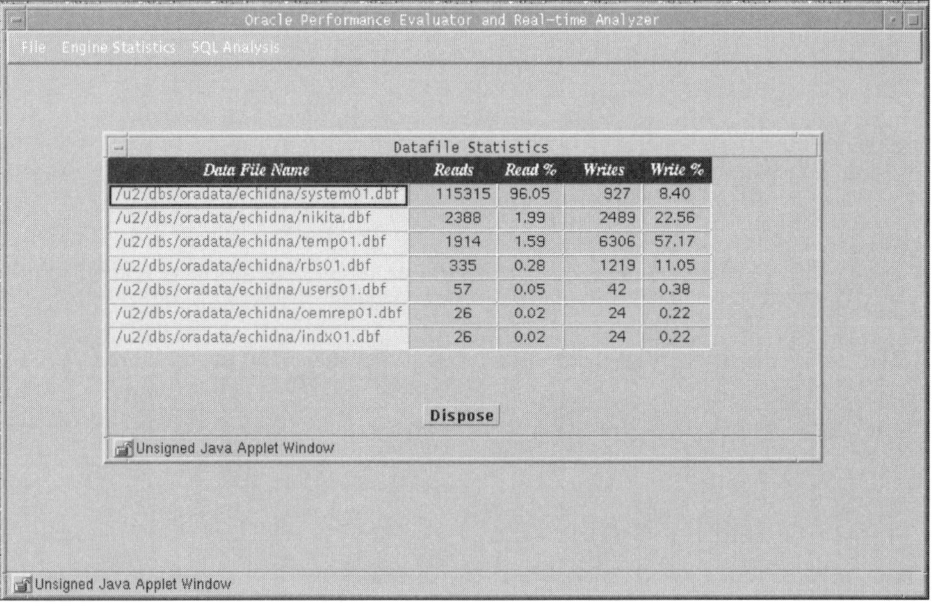

FIGURE 18.5 Data File Statistics

A latch can be requested with a willing-to-wait type of request. If the latch cannot be granted by Oracle, the process requesting the latch misses the request and sleeps for a little while, in order to submit another request when the sleep period has expired. It is easy to understand that the goal is to minimize the number of times a process must wait because its request to acquire a latch couldn't be satisfied by the engine. Basically, if the ratio of misses to gets exceeds 2%, latch contention is occurring in the database being monitored, and should be addressed.

The next option allows OPERA users to display statistics about rollback segments and their activity. Figure 18.7 shows what OPERA offers in this area.

If the Oracle Multi-Threaded Server option has been enabled, it is important to find out if an adequate number of servers and dispatchers have been allocated. Accordingly, if the Parallel Server option is enabled, OPERA users can see its specific parameters in a grid. What follows is a screen snapshot of the window displayed by OPERA when the "MTS & Parallel Server" option is selected (Figure 18.8).

If the TIMED_STATISTICS engine parameter has been set to TRUE, statistics related to time are gathered by the Oracle engine, and can be seen in a window displayed by OPERA when the "CPU by Session" option is requested, as in Figure 18.9.

The "Shared Pool Stats" (Figure 18.10) option displays two grids. On the left-hand side are shown the engine parameters affecting the shared pool; on the

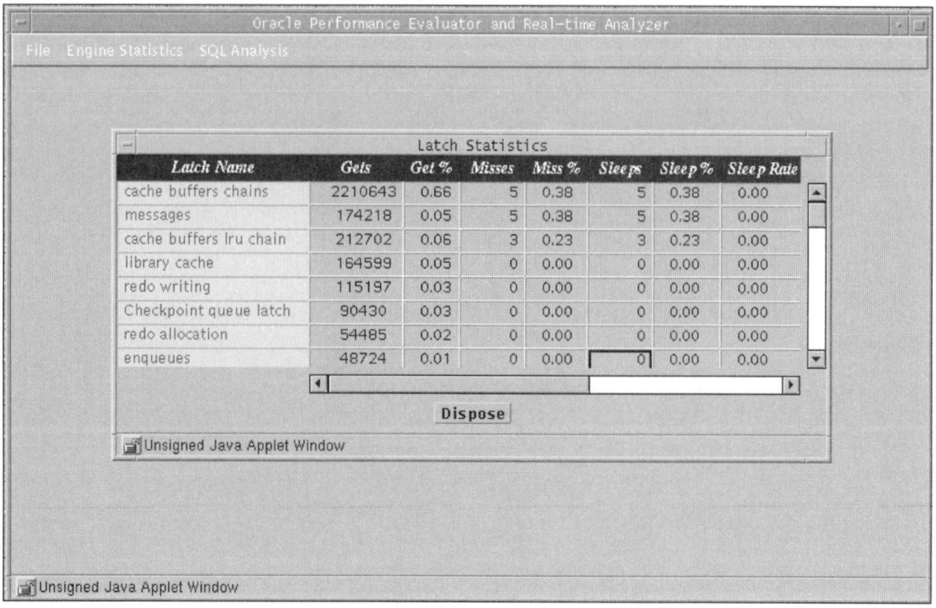

Oracle Performance Evaluator and Real-time Analyzer

File Engine Statistics SQL Analysis

Latch Statistics

Latch Name	Gets	Get %	Misses	Miss %	Sleeps	Sleep %	Sleep Rate
cache buffers chains	2210643	0.66	5	0.38	5	0.38	0.00
messages	174218	0.05	5	0.38	5	0.38	0.00
cache buffers lru chain	212702	0.06	3	0.23	3	0.23	0.00
library cache	164599	0.05	0	0.00	0	0.00	0.00
redo writing	115197	0.03	0	0.00	0	0.00	0.00
Checkpoint queue latch	90430	0.03	0	0.00	0	0.00	0.00
redo allocation	54485	0.02	0	0.00	0	0.00	0.00
enqueues	48724	0.01	0	0.00	0	0.00	0.00

Dispose

Unsigned Java Applet Window

Unsigned Java Applet Window

FIGURE 18.6 Latch Statistics

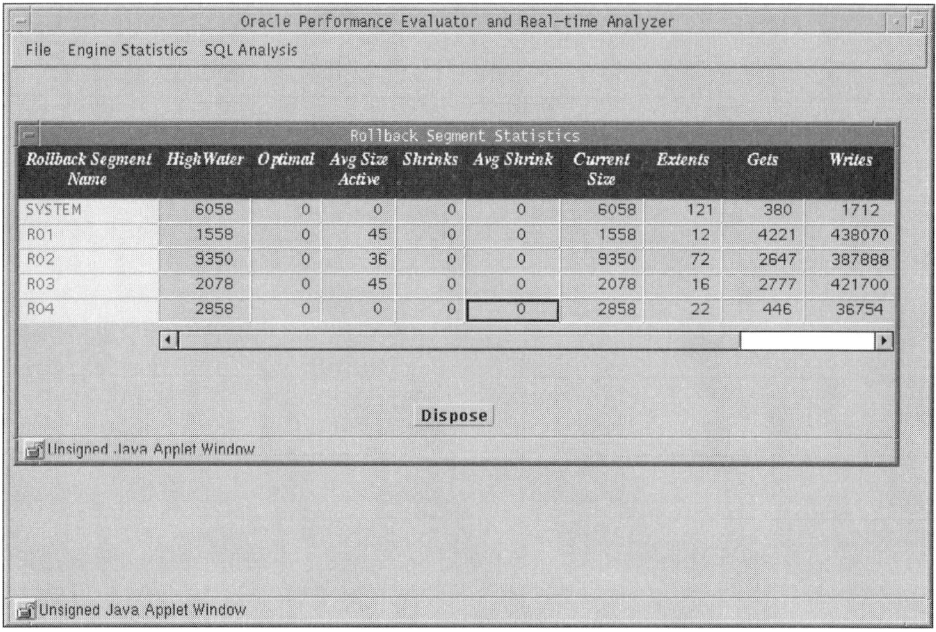

Oracle Performance Evaluator and Real-time Analyzer

File Engine Statistics SQL Analysis

Rollback Segment Statistics

Rollback Segment Name	HighWater	Optimal	Avg Size Active	Shrinks	Avg Shrink	Current Size	Extents	Gets	Writes
SYSTEM	6058	0	0	0	0	6058	121	380	1712
R01	1558	0	45	0	0	1558	12	4221	438070
R02	9350	0	36	0	0	9350	72	2647	387888
R03	2078	0	45	0	0	2078	16	2777	421700
R04	2858	0	0	0	0	2858	22	446	36754

Dispose

Unsigned Java Applet Window

Unsigned Java Applet Window

FIGURE 18.7 Rollback Segment Statistics

Oracle Performance Evaluator and Real-time Analyzer

File Engine Statistics SQL Analysis

MTS & Parallel Server Statistics

Parameter Name	Value
(ADDRESS= dispatcher busy%	0.00
(ADDRESS= dispatcher busy%	0.00
COMMON queue avg wait %	0.00
DISPATCHE queue avg wait %	0.00
Parallel Query Servers Highwater	0.00
mts_max_dispatchers	5.00
mts_max_servers	20.00
mts_servers	1.00
parallel_max_servers	5.00
parallel_min_servers	0.00

Dispose

Unsigned Java Applet Window

Unsigned Java Applet Window

FIGURE 18.8 MTS and Parallel Server Statistics

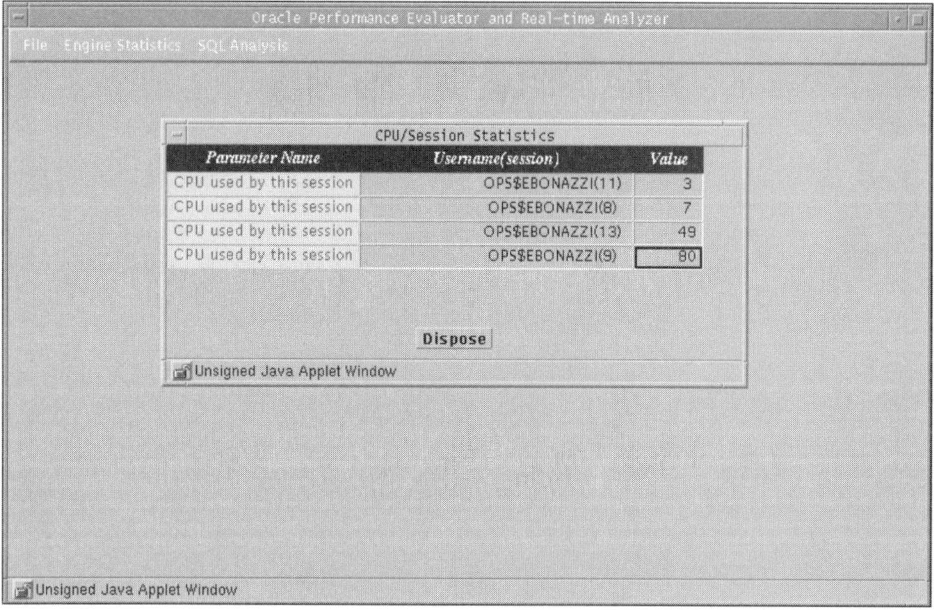

FIGURE 18.9 CPU by Session Statistics

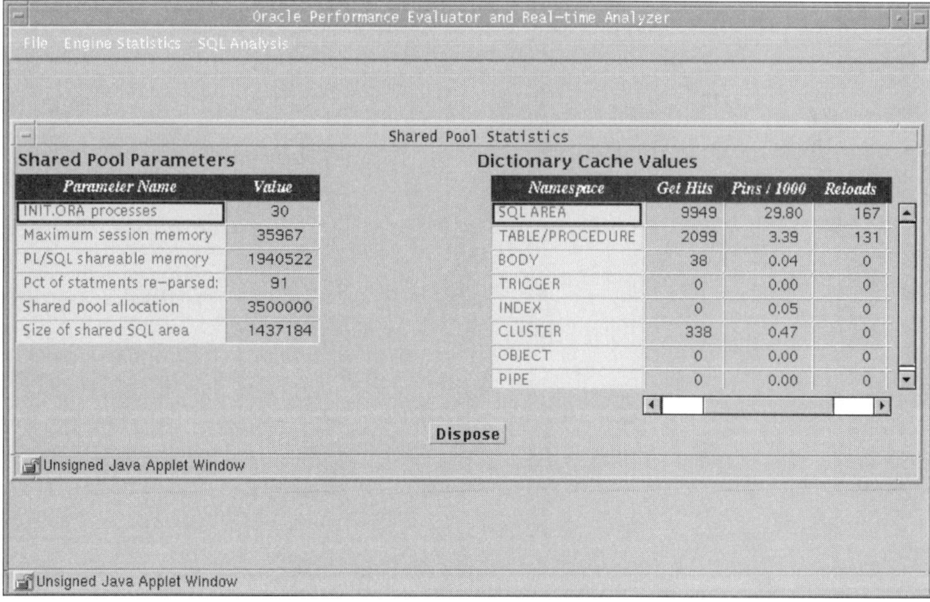

FIGURE 18.10 Shared Pool Statistics

right-hand are side several statistics that can be useful to fine-tune the shared pool are displayed.

The analysis of the engine waits is important to pinpoint potential bottlenecks that can adversely affect a smooth running of Oracle. OPERA provides a window that displays detailed information about engine waits (Figure 18.11), on the left-hand side grid, and miscellaneous waits on the grid located on the right-hand side of the window.

As already stated in a preceding section of this chapter, a tool such as OPERA cannot possibly satisfy all users, being useful for all instances. It is likely that all advanced users will sooner or later feel the need for enhancements and customizations. Everybody is welcome to participate with original contributions, in the true open source spirit, to build the "ultimate" performance monitoring tool.

18.3.1.4 SQL Analysis The remaining part of OPERA is a replica of the functionality offered by ShrPool (see Chapter 17), customized to fit into the OPERA architecture. The first screen, shown in Figure 18.12, allows OPERA users to enter selection criteria for the SQL statements to be analyzed. The sort criterion can be chosen from a set of criteria, organized on the screen as a radio-button checkbox group. Other filters can be applied to the SQL statements fetched from the shared pool, for instance, to identify specific statements based on keywords.

Clicking on the OK button provokes the selection criteria to be sent to the server. The server OPERA process evaluates the criteria, builds an SQL statement

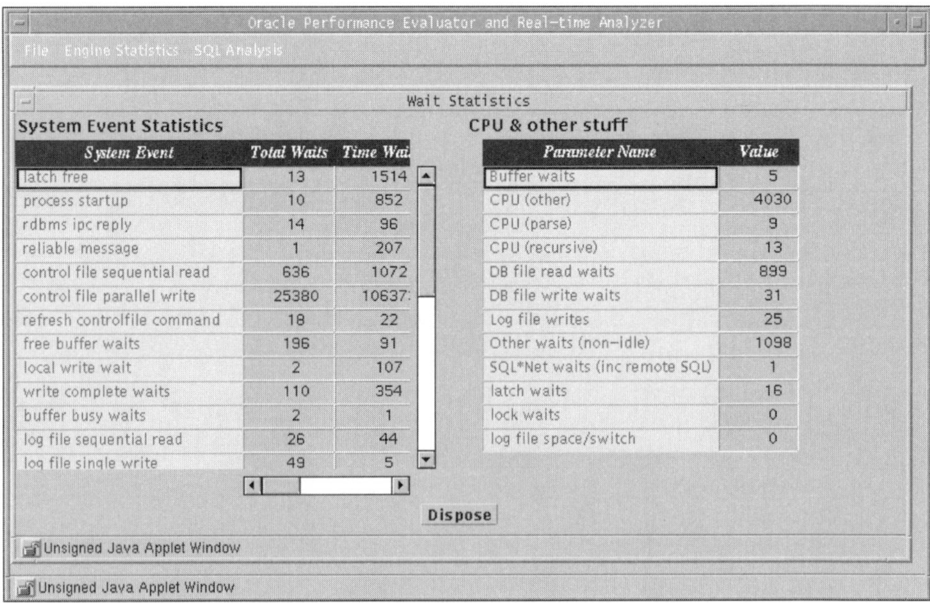

FIGURE 18.11 Wait Statistics

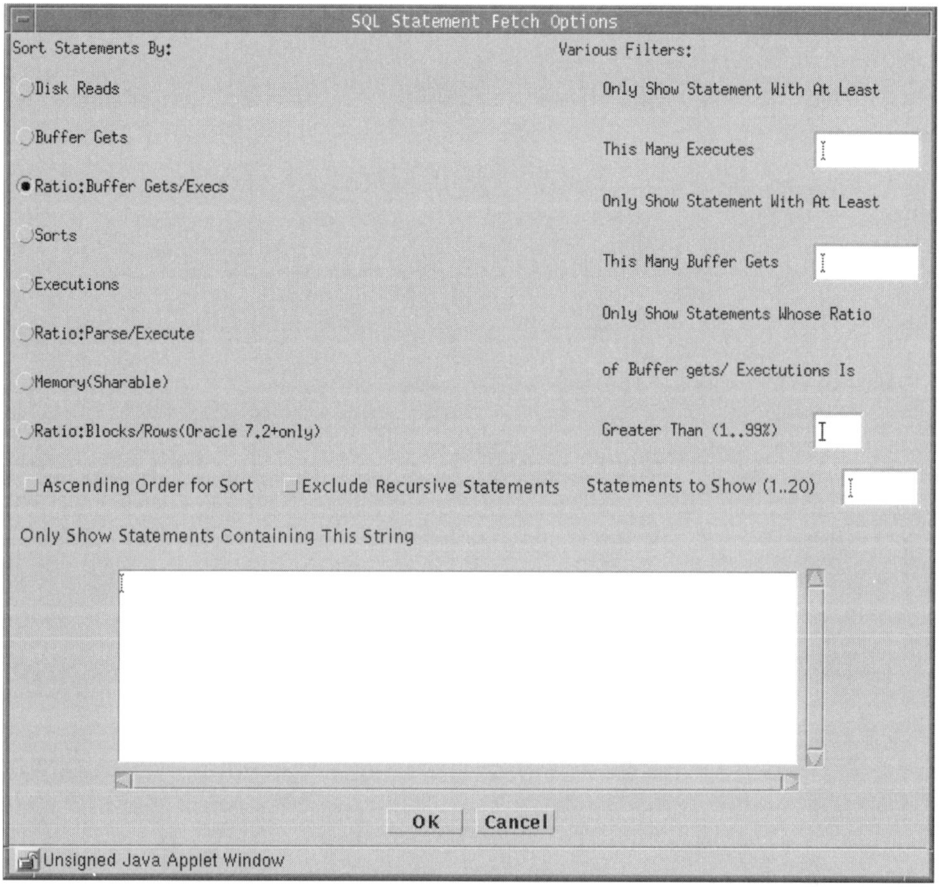

FIGURE 18.12 The SQL Statements Fetch Options Window

that fetches the SQL statements from the shared pool according to the user-entered criteria, and executes the statement dynamically built. The server then queues the results into a linked list, and sends them through the socket channel. The Java client reads the statements from the socket channel, and displays them in a listbox.

Users can then ask OPERA to produce an execution plan on the fly, if they have the necessary privileges on the objects accessed by the SQL statement being analyzed. Alternatively, the single SQL statement can be displayed without execution plan, but with all associated statistics.

If the Oracle engine being analyzed is very active, the statement being analyzed can be aged out of the shared pool after it has been displayed by OPERA in the window shown in Figure 18.13, but before the detailed analysis has been performed. In this case, an appropriate message is displayed by OPERA, informing

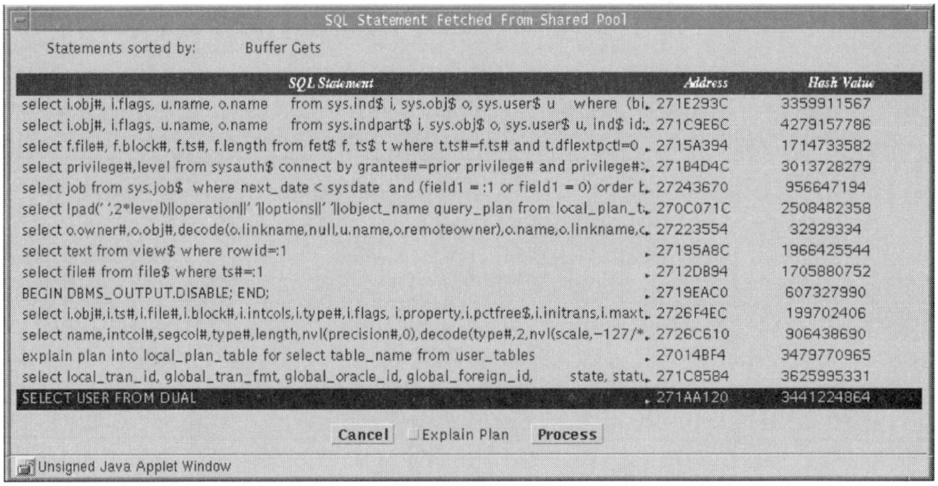

SQL Statement Fetched From Shared Pool

Statements sorted by: Buffer Gets

SQL Statement	Address	Hash Value
select i.obj#, i.flags, u.name, o.name from sys.ind$ i, sys.obj$ o, sys.user$ u where (bi,	271E293C	3359911567
select i.obj#, i.flags, u.name, o.name from sys.indpart$ i, sys.obj$ o, sys.user$ u, ind$ id:,	271C9E6C	4279157786
select f.file#, f.block#, f.ts#, f.length from fet$ f, ts$ t where t.ts#=f.ts# and t.dflextpct!=0 ,	2715A394	1714733582
select privilege#,level from sysauth$ connect by grantee#=prior privilege# and privilege#:,	271B4D4C	3013728279
select job from sys.job$ where next_date < sysdate and (field1 = :1 or field1 = 0) order t,	27243670	956647194
select lpad(' ',2*level)||operation||' '||options||' '||object_name query_plan from local_plan_t,	270C071C	2508482358
select o.owner#,o.obj#,decode(o.linkname,null,u.name,o.remoteowner),o.name,o.linkname,c,	27223554	32929334
select text from view$ where rowid=:1 ,	27195A8C	1966425544
select file# from file$ where ts#=:1 ,	2712D894	1705880752
BEGIN DBMS_OUTPUT.DISABLE; END; ,	2719EAC0	607327990
select i.obj#,i.ts#,i.file#,i.block#,i.intcols,i.type#,i.flags, i.property,i.pctfree$,i.initrans,i.maxt,	2726F4EC	199702406
select name,intcol#,segcol#,type#,length,nvl(precision#,0),decode(type#,2,nvl(scale,-127/*,	2726C610	906438690
explain plan into local_plan_table for select table_name from user_tables ,	27014BF4	3479770965
select local_tran_id, global_tran_fmt, global_oracle_id, global_foreign_id, state, statu,	271C8584	3625995331
SELECT USER FROM DUAL ,	271AA120	3441224864

Cancel | Explain Plan | Process

Unsigned Java Applet Window

FIGURE 18.13 The SQL Statements Fetched From the Shared Pool

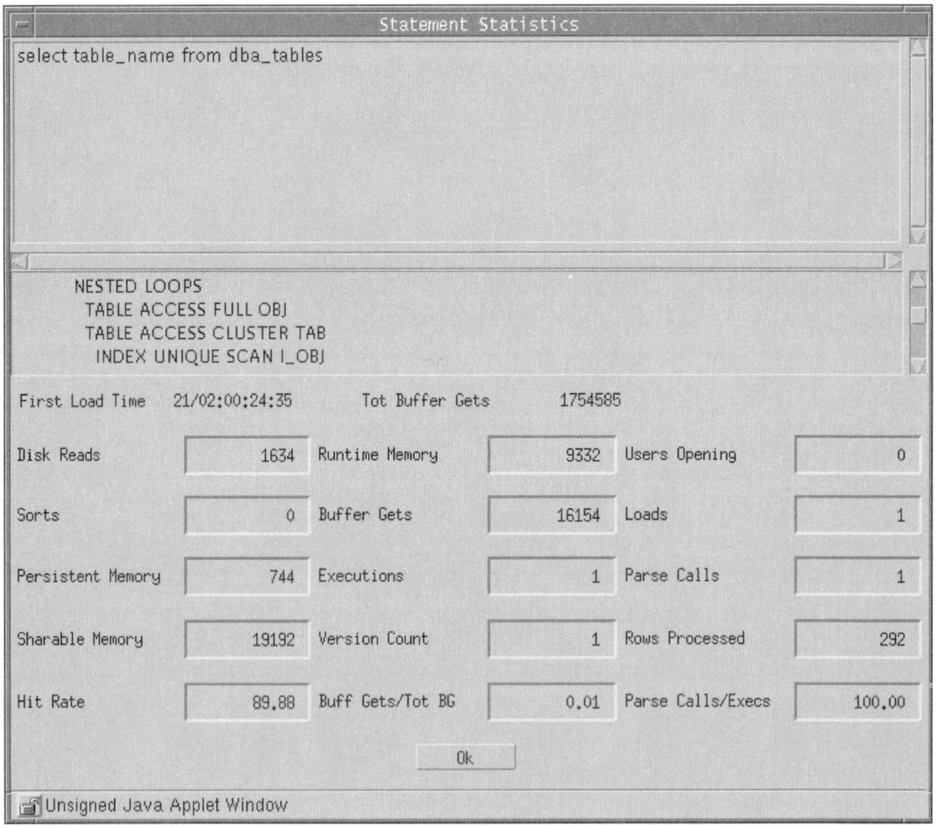

Statement Statistics

select table_name from dba_tables

NESTED LOOPS
 TABLE ACCESS FULL OBJ
 TABLE ACCESS CLUSTER TAB
  INDEX UNIQUE SCAN I_OBJ

First Load Time 21/02:00:24:35 Tot Buffer Gets 1754585

Disk Reads	1634	Runtime Memory	9332	Users Opening	0
Sorts	0	Buffer Gets	16154	Loads	1
Persistent Memory	744	Executions	1	Parse Calls	1
Sharable Memory	19192	Version Count	1	Rows Processed	292
Hit Rate	89.88	Buff Gets/Tot BG	0.01	Parse Calls/Execs	100.00

Ok

Unsigned Java Applet Window

FIGURE 18.14 The Statement Statistics Window

the user that the statement cannot by analyzed any further. The window that displays the statement statistics computes three statement-level ratios, hit rate, buffer gets over total buffer gets, and parse calls over executions. Figure 18.14 shows the statement statistics window.

18.4 The OPERA Java Client

The client component of OPERA is designed to be small, or *thin*. It doesn't perform any computation or statistical analysis, but provides only presentation services. Its basic functionality is to request data by submitting requests to the server through a socket channel, to read the data formatted in records having each field delimited by the pipe sign (" | ") from the socket channel, and to display the received data in Java AWT frames.

OPERA client has been designed to be a Java applet, run from a WEB browser. The screen snapshots presented in the preceding section have been taken while running Netscape 4.5 on a Sun Solaris workstation. OPERA client can also be run as a Java application, as it contains startup code for running either as an applet or an application.

The jar file containing all Java code needed to run OPERA client is approximately 280 KB large. When used in an intranet environment, OPERA client loads and starts running in a handful of seconds. When downloaded over a telephone line it takes little more that a minute, if using a 33.6 Kbits modem.

In order to keep the jar file as small as possible, only standard AWT graphical components have been used. It is easy to be tempted to use the more sophisticated Java beans usually shipped with the Java IDE, for instance, the JBCL library shipped with Borland JBuilder and Oracle JDeveloper. The problem associated with third party Java beans is that they add a lot to the size to the final jar file. Furthermore, the commercial Java IDEs tend to encourage the use of graphical layouts that use absolute component positioning (the XYLayout). While they greatly simplify the design of forms during development, absolute layouts are not easily portable across MS Windows and Motif.

OPERA client comprises a set of 14 Java classes. the following table lists the Java classes, providing an explanation for each.

JAVA CLASS	PURPOSE
CommandControl.java	the application brain, which contains all logic needed to handle menu selections by users
ConnectToHost.java	implements the socket connection to a listening server
ConnectToDB.java	database connection dialog and logic

(*cont.*)

JAVA CLASS	PURPOSE
CustomDialog.java	subclasses the standard AWT dialog implementing OPERA specific functionality
DisplayFetchedStatements.java	displays the SQL statements fetched from the shared pool
DisplayInFrame.java	interface between CommandControl and DisplayStats or DisplayTwinStats
DisplaySQL.java	displays the analyzed SQL statement, together with statistics and, if requested, execution plan
DisplayStats.java	displays server generated statistics in one grid
DisplayTwinStats.java	displays server generated statistics in two grids
HostConnection.java	implements socket calls and connection logic to the remote host
MessageBox.java	emulates an MS Windows Message Box
Opera2Applet.java	applet startup code
Stage2MainFrame.java	implements the main Java frame containing the menu presented to the users
StatementFetchOptions.java	displays the dialog that allows users to define selection criteria for fetching SQL statements from the shared pool

The applet startup code in Opera2Applet.java creates an instance of the main visual frame (Stage2MainFrame). Each menu option is processed by CommandControl.java, instantiated by Stage2MainFrame. The source code follows.

Opera2Applet class, jbinit() method:

```
public void jbInit() throws Exception
{
    this.setBackground(Color.lightGray);
    this.setLayout(Layout1);
    Stage2MainFrame St2MF = new Stage2MainFrame();
    St2MF.setTitle("Oracle Performance Evaluator and Real-time
               Analyzer");
    Dimension d = Toolkit.getDefaultToolkit().getScreenSize();
    St2MF.setLocation((d.width - St2MF.getSize().width) / 2,
          (d.height - St2MF.getSize().height) / 2);
    St2MF.setVisible(true);
}
```

jbinit() is called by init(), the standard method invoked by Java during the applet start-up phase. Stage2MainFrame creates instances of two important classes, HostConnection and CommandControl.

```
public class Stage2MainFrame extends Frame
{
  HostConnection HC = new HostConnection();
  CommandControl ComCon = new CommandControl(this);
  BorderLayout borderLayout1 = new BorderLayout();
  MenuBar menuMainBar = new MenuBar();
  Menu File = new Menu();
  .. omitted lines ..
}
```

Stage2MainFrame also defines and instantiates a menu bar with all the menu options needed by OPERA. Additionally, it creates all required listeners to be able to process the events generated by clicking on the menu options. Consider, for instance, the "Dictionary Stats" option. The source code that implements the menu option and the event listener is shown below.

```
In the class constructor:
…omitted lines …
MenuItem mDictSts = new MenuItem();
…omitted lines …
In jbinit():
…omitted lines …
mDictSts.setLabel("Dictionary Stats");
mDictSts.addActionListener(new
                  Stage2MainFrame_mDictSts_actionAdapter(this));
…omitted lines …
     mEngineAnalysis.add(mDictSts);
…omitted lines …
void mDictSts_actionPerformed(ActionEvent e)
{
    ComCon.mEval(mDictSts);
}
```

The mDictSts_actionPerformed() method is activated by the menu option listener when users click on the "Dictionary Stats" option. The CommandControl class implements an mEval() method, that recognizes the menu option chosen by the user.

```
CommandControl class:
      …omitted lines …
public void mEval ( MenuItem MI)
  {
      String sChoice = new String(MI.getLabel());
      if (sChoice.equals("Dictionary Stats"))
```

```
        {
                String clabels[] = { "Parameter\nname",
                        "Gets","Misses","Miss\nRatio",
                        "Entries\nin Cache", "Cache Entries\nvalid data"};
                DisplayInFrame DIF = new DisplayInFrame(parentFrame,
                                   "0006","Data Dictionary Statistics",
                                   clabels,6,83);
            return;
        }
                }
...omitted lines ...
```

The mEval() method of the CommandControl class receives a reference to a MenuItem as a parameter and invokes the AWT call getLabel() to obtain the string containing the menu option chosen by the user. The string is used to recognize the option and to call the corresponding routine.

The DisplayInFrame class implements two constructors: the first receives six parameters and drives the creation of a dialog displaying one grid; the second receives 11 parameters and drives the creation of a dialog displaying two grids. The first constructor creates an instance of the DisplayStats class; the second constructor creates an instance of the DisplayTwinStats class.

When the CommandControl.mEval() method calls DisplaInFrame() passing six parameters, as in the case of the data dictionary statistics, a dialog containing one grid is displayed. An example follows:

```
DisplayInFrame DIF = new
        DisplayInFrame(parentFrame,
                          "0006","Data Dictionary Statistics",
                          clabels,6,83);
```

The first parameter is a reference to the main OPERA frame. The second parameter is the code to be sent to the server to ask for data dictionary statistics, and the third is the title of the dialog to be created. The fourth parameter is an array of strings containing the labels for each column in the grid. The fifth parameter is the number of column displayed in the grid, and the last parameter is the number of bytes sent by the server for each data block received through the socket channel.

When a dialog displays two grids, for instance, when the “Wait Statistics” menu option is selected, DisplayInFrame() receives 11 parameters. The first parameter is again the reference to the main OPERA frame, and the other 10 specify server codes, column labels, and line length in bytes for two grids. An example follows.

```
String c1labels[] = { "System Event","Total Waits","Time Waited",
                      "Average Wait","Event Waits /\nSystem Waits",
```

```
                        "Event Time Waited /\nSystem Time Waited"};
String c2labels[] = { "Parameter Name","Value"};
DisplayInFrame DIF = new DisplayInFrame(parentFrame,
                             "0013","Wait Statistics",
                             c1labels,6,89,
                             c2labels,2,41,
                             "System Event Statistics",
                             "CPU & other stuff");
```

The last two parameters specify the caption label for each of the grids displayed in the dialog.

The logic that populates the grids in the dialogs presented to the users is implemented in CustomDialog(). The CustomDialog class creates two instances of the JCTable class (a Java bean provided by the KL group and shipped with Oracle JDeveloper and other popular Java IDEs).

To populate the JCTable with data received from the server, a JCVector and a JCConverter are created by the FillTable() methods defined in CustomDialog. JCVector is a specialized version of a Java vector used by the JCTable and is a helper class that facilitates data conversion into JCVectors. The toVector() method defined in JCConverter converts a string containing delimited fields into JCVector elements. This method is used to convert each data block sent by the server in a JCVector that is passed to the addRow() method of the JCTable class. The following example shows this technique.

```
public  void FillTable1(int Bytes)
{
    String stNum = new String();
    stNum=parentFrame.HC.read(4);
    int nNum = Integer.parseInt(stNum);
    for (int ii=0;ii<nNum;ii++)
    {
        String lSt = new String();
        JCVector lJCV = new JCVector();
        JCConverter  JCConv = new JCConverter();
        lSt=parentFrame.HC.read(Bytes);
        lJCV = JCConv.toVector(this,lSt,'|',false);
        jCTable1.addRow(JCTblEnum.MAXINT,null,lJCV);
    }
}
```

The first socket read call obtains the number of lines (or data blocks) that the server will send. The string containing the number in ASCII is converted into a Java integer, and a loop from 0 to the number of lines is entered.

The second socket read call receives a data block into a string. The string is converted into a JCVector, which is passed to the addRow() method of the JCTable bean. The data block length is passed from CommandControl.mEval() to DisplayInFrame(), which creates and instance of DisplayStats() and calls the FillTable1 method directly. The source code of DisplayInFrame() is shown below.

```
DisplayInFrame class constructor:
...omitted lines ...
DisplayStats DS = new DisplayStats(frame,sStats,true);
DS.setTableLabels(cLabels);
DS.setTableAspect();
DS.setTableColNum(nColNum);
DS.FillTable1(nBytes);
DS.centre();
frame.setCursor(cDefault);
DS.show();
...omitted lines ...
```

In order to be able to extend OPERA to include additional functionality, you should be familiar with Opera2MainFrame() and CommandControl(). In Opera2MainFrame, you will add new menu options and relative listeners; in CommandControl, you will modify the mEval() method, adding if statements that will recognize the new options, instantiating the corresponding classes. See Section 18.5.2 for an example on how to extend OPERA with additional functionality.

18.5 OPERA Server Source Code

The OPERA server is implemented as a daemon that listens for incoming connections and forks child processes that serve data requests coming from Java clients. Each client connects to the database only once, and stays connected for the entire duration of the performance analysis. The server process maintains a connection state throughout the lifetime of the interaction with the client.

All database activity is performed using OCI7 calls. The OCI library is shipped with the Oracle server at no additional cost. One of the requirements of OPERA was its ability to be used in environments that didn't include a Pro*C (or Programmer 2000) license. Using OCI keeps the operating requirements of OPERA to a minimum, just a "C" compiler and TCP/IP. I used OPERA in an OpenVMS environment that didn't have a Java virtual machine, by connecting to the VAX my laptop using OpenVMS UCX as TCP/IP layer and running a Java virtual machine under Linux. In environments where the computer hosting the Oracle instance being monitored also offers a Java virtual machine, the performance analysis can be conducted on the same server. The screen snapshots shown in the preceding sections were all taken from Netscape, on a Sun computer running both Oracle and the WEB browser. A PC running MS Windows can also be used to display the statistics gathered from the back-end server. In order to avoid data marshaling and unmarshaling, all data exchanged by client and server is converted into ASCII characters at both ends.

18.5.1 *OPERASVR* SOURCE CODE

The OPERA server daemon, *OperaSvr*, requires one command line parameter, the TCP/IP port number used by the listener to accept socket connections. Two environment variables can be set to control the verbosity of the DBUG package. They are DBUG_FLAG, which stores the DBUG flag string, and TIMING, which controls the time stamping up hundredths of second. Setting TIMING to 1 enables time stamping, if this environment variable is either not set or set to 0 time stamping won't occur.

OperaSvr comprises 23 "C" files that implement all OPERA server functionality. The following table lists all required files to build server side OPERA.

"C" FILE	PURPOSE
OperaSvr.c	implements main(), signal handling routines and socket read and write
AncillaryFunctions.c	implements ancillary functions such as daemon initialization and local assert
AncillaryOraFunctions.c	implements Oracle ancillary functions, such as connection, disconnection and oracle error message handling
DictSts.c	implements the gathering of data dictionary statistics
FileStats.c	implements the gathering of datafile statistics
LatchStats.c	implements the gathering of latch statistics
LockSql.c	implements the identification of the SQL statements provoking instance locks
RbsStats.c	implements the gathering of rollback segment statistics
SessCpu.c	implements the gathering of data showing CPU consumption per session
SvrStats.c	implements the gathering of MTS and parallel server parameters and statistics
WaitStats.c	implements the gathering of instance wait statistics
AllLocks.c	implements the identification of instance locks

(*cont.*)

"C" FILE	PURPOSE
StatGather.c	implements the gathering of instance wide performance ratios
OperaRatios.c	implements the cursor definitions, variable binding and data fetching for instance wide performance ratios
ShrPoolStats.c	implements the gathering of shared pool statistics
OperaSock.c	implements the selector function, interprets the function code sent by the client, and invokes the corresponding routine
dbug.c	the Fred Fish's package for internal debug instrumentation
now.c	implements OPERA server time stamping
ShrPool.c	creates the SQL statement that browses the shared pool, and executes the SQL statement built, fetching data from V$SQLAREA
OperaStatsParse.c	parses all statements comprising the instance wide ratios
GetSqlStatement.c	computes statement statistics for explained statements
fdreopen.c	implements the reopening of a stream without an associated file name
SqlInteract.c	processes interactive requests from users asking for statements to be explained

Once invoked, OperaSvr becomes a daemon by forking and forcing the father to terminate. The child process detaches itself from the terminal, becoming owned by root. It then performs all needed TCP/IP and socket initializations and, if everything is OK, listens to the port number specified on the command line for incoming connections. When a socket connection is requested from a Java client, OperaSvr() forks again. The father closes the socket channel used by the child and resumes listening for additional socket connections, while the child closes the socket channel used by the father and performs a blocking read on the newly created socket. The chil d server process blocks until the client sends a function code, requesting for specific services. The function code is interpreted and the corresponding routine is invoked. When all data has been sent to the client, the subroutine returns and the process reenters the loop that starts with a blocking read, waiting for the next request. The source code that implements what we have just described follows.

main() function:

```
...omitted lines ...

    /* DBUG PACKAGE Initialization */
    DBUG_ENTER("main");
    DBUG_PROCESS(argv[0]);
    memset(szPort,'\0',sizeof(szPort));
    if (argc < 2)
    {
            fprintf(stdout,"Usage: OperaSvr <TCP Port>\n");
            DBUG_EXIT(-1);
```

```
    }
    /* Environment variables to control DBUG verbosity */
    szDebugFlag=(char *) getenv("DBUG_FLAG");
    strcpy(szPort,argv[1]);
    szMicro=(char *) getenv("TIMING");
    if(szMicro != NULL)
            Micro = atoi(szMicro);
    nPort=atoi(szPort);
    /* If we have a DBUG flag, let us issue it */
    if(szDebugFlag != NULL)
    {
            DBUG_PUSH(szDebugFlag);
    }
    DBUG_MAIN;
    DBUG_PRINT("OPRSVR",("Socket Port: %d",nPort));
    DBUG_PRINT("OPRSVR",("Debug string: %s",szDebugFlag));
    /*
    ** Call to DaemonInit,
    ** which forks and forces the parent
    ** to exit
    */
    if ( nDaemonInit() != OP_STG_2_STATUS_OK )
    {
#ifdef ULTRIX
                openlog("OPERA Daemon ", LOG_PID);
#else
                openlog("OPERA Daemon ", LOG_PID, LOG_LOCAL0);
#endif
                syslog(LOG_ERR,"Could not run as a daemon  %m");
                abort();
    }
    /* Signal Handling */
    signal(SIGPIPE,pipe_handler);
    signal(SIGHUP, closedown);
    signal(SIGTERM, clientclose);
    /* Reliable signal initialization */
    sigemptyset(&allzero);
    sigemptyset(&blockmask);
    sigaddset(&blockmask,SIGPOLL);
    sigprocmask(SIG_BLOCK,&blockmask,&allzero);
    DBUG_PRINT("Main",("Initialiasing..."));

    signal(SIGCHLD, SIG_IGN);
    /* Socket Creation */
    if ((sockfd = socket(AF_INET, SOCK_STREAM, 0)) < 0)
```

```
        {
                  perror("socket_create");
                  DBUG_EXIT(1);
        }
        /* Network initialization */
        memset(&serveraddr,'\0',sizeof(struct sockaddr_in));
        serveraddr.sin_family       = AF_INET;
        serveraddr.sin_addr.s_addr = htonl(INADDR_ANY);
        serveraddr.sin_port         = htons(nPort);
        reuse = 0;
        setsockopt(sockfd, SOL_SOCKET, SO_REUSEADDR, (void *) &reuse,
                                                          sizeof(reuse));
        l.l_onoff = 1;
        l.l_linger = 0;
        /* Setting socket options */
        setsockopt(sockfd, SOL_SOCKET, SO_LINGER, (void *) &l,
                                                          sizeof(l));
        /* Socket bind */
        if ( bind(sockfd,(struct sockaddr *)&serveraddr,
                   sizeof(struct sockaddr_in)) < 0)
        {
                  perror("socket_bind");
                  DBUG_EXIT(2);
        }
        /* Socket Server definition */
        listen(sockfd, 8);
        DBUG_PRINT("OPRSVR",("Listening on port: %d",
                                    serveraddr.sin_port));
       while(1)
       {
         if ((sockcli = accept(sockfd,
             (struct sockaddr *) &clientaddr,
            &clientaddrlen)) < 0)
         {
             if (errno == EINTR)
             {
                 printf("Bye...\n");
                 DBUG_EXIT(0);
             }
             else
             {
                  perror("socket_accept");
                         DBUG_EXIT(3);
             }
         }
```

```
    printf("Forking for client socket %d parent socket %d\n",
                                  sockcli, sockfd);
      lPid = fork();
      switch(lPid)
      {
        case -1:        /* error */
          perror("dosession_fork");
          break;
        default:
          printf("In parent closed sockcli %d\n", sockcli);
          if (close(sockcli) < 0)
             printf("Failed to close sockcli\n");
          break;
        case 0:         /* child */
          DBUG_PRINT("MAIN",("Child closing socket"));
          printf("In child closing sockfd %d\n", sockfd);
          reuse = 0;
          l.l_onoff = 1;
          l.l_linger = 0;
          setsockopt(sockfd, SOL_SOCKET, SO_LINGER,
                                (void *) &l, sizeof(l));
           setsockopt(sockcli, SOL_SOCKET, SO_REUSEADDR,
                         (void *) &reuse, sizeof(reuse));
          if (close(sockfd) < 0)
             printf("Error closing socket sockfd\n");
          while(1)
          {
              /*
              ** Call to function selector. It performs a
              ** blocking read as first call.
              */
              nSts=nProcessRequest();
              if (nSts == 1)
                  break;
              else if (nSts == -1)
              {
                 DBUG_PRINT("MAIN",
                 ("nProcessRequest failed!"));
              }
              else if (nSts == -2)
              {
                  DBUG_PRINT("MAIN",
                         ("Breaking endless loop!"));
                   break;
              }
```

```
                }
                printf("In child closing sockcli %d\n", sockcli);
                if (close(sockcli) < 0)
                    printf("Error closeing down client\n");
                exit(0);
            }
        }
        DBUG_RETURN(0);
}
```

The nProcessRequest() routine is coded in the OperaSock.c file. It interprets the requests received from the Java clients and invokes the routines that implement the services requested. The source code follows.

OperaSock.c:

```
int nProcessRequest(void)
{
    int      nRequestNum=0;
    int      nFuncSts;
    int      sts;
    static int nCounter=0;
    int      nBytesRead=0;
    char     szRequest[5];

    DBUG_ENTER("nProcessRequest");
    memset(szRequest,'\0',sizeof(szRequest));
    /* Blocking read from socket channel */
    if( (nBytesRead=Read(szRequest,4)) < 4 )
    {
        DBUG_PRINT("RCV_ERR",
               ("Could not receive message through sockets"));
        nCounter++;
        if (nCounter > 3)
        {
               DBUG_RETURN(-2);
        }
        else
        {
               DBUG_RETURN(-1);
        }
    }
    nCounter = 0;
    szRequest[4]='\0';
    DBUG_PRINT("PRCREQ",("Option Requested: %s",szRequest));
```

```
nRequestNum=atoi(szRequest);
switch(nRequestNum)
{
      case 0:
         if ( (nFuncSts=nOracleConnect()) != 0)
         {
               DBUG_PRINT("OPR_ERR",("nOracleConnect failed!"));
               DBUG_RETURN(-1);
         }
         break;
      case 1:
          if ((nFuncSts=nAllLocks()) != 0)
          {
                DBUG_PRINT("OPR_ERR",("nAllLocks failed!"));
                DBUG_RETURN(-1);
          }
          break;
      case 2:
      case 3:
      case 4:
      case 5:
         if ( (nFuncSts=nLockSql()) != 0)
         {
                 DBUG_PRINT("OPR_ERR",("nLockSql failed!"));
                 DBUG_RETURN(-1);
         }
         break;
      case 6:
         if ( (nFuncSts=nDictSts()) != 0)
         {
                DBUG_PRINT("OPR_ERR",("nDictSts failed!"));
                DBUG_RETURN(-1);
         }
         break;
    …omitted lines …
      case 24:
      case 30:
         break;
      case 998:
         if ( (nFuncSts=nOracleDisconnect()) != 0)
         {
             DBUG_PRINT("OPR_ERR",("nOracleDisconnect failed!"));
             DBUG_RETURN(-1);
         }
```

```
            break;
        case 999:
            DBUG_RETURN(1);
            break;
    }
    DBUG_RETURN(0);
}
```

Apart from the SQL analysis and execution plan displaying routines, which follow their own specific patterns, all server functions that show engine-related statistics are coded according to the following model:

1. A "C" structure that represents a linked list node containing a "line of data" gathered from Oracle is defined.
2. A "C" string containing the SQL statement used to fetch performance data from Oracle is defined.
3. Memory is allocated for the root node of the linked list.
4. OCI API(s) to parse and execute the SQL statement. The return status of every OCI call is checked, and, if an error occurred, the "ERROCI" message is written to the socket channel back to the client, and the control is passed back to the main selector function.
5. If the SQL statement has been successful, and one or more rows have been fetched from the database, one linked list node per row is allocated, and the Oracle performance data is copied in the appropriate location within the node.
6. Once all the rows have been fetched and the linked list has been totally built, the message "OPEROK" is sent back to the client through the socket channel.
7. A counter is incremented every time a new node is inserted into the linked list. The counter is converted in ASCII and sent to the client, which reconverts the number from ASCII into integer. The client then loops from 1 to the number of rows to be received. The server traverses the linked list, writing the content of the Oracle rows to the socket channel.
8. When all the rows fetched from Oracle and stored into the linked list have been sent, the list is traversed again, and every node is destroyed (i.e., released from memory).
9. The server passes the control of the execution back to the main selector function, which is an endless loop that performs as first instruction a blocking read from the socket channel, waiting from a new request from the client.
10. The client displays the information received from the server, and waits for input by the user, to reinitiate the information fetching cycle.

The following pseudo-code explains the above more formally. The pseudo-code is for any of the server functions that use OCI library to fetch performance data and store every row coming from the database in a linked list. The linked list is then traversed and all the "rows" are sent through the socket channel.

```
allocate a string to host the SQL statement
allocate all the variables needed to fetch the wanted columns out of
      Oracle (in arrays of 10 position, since the host array feature
      will be used)
define a structure which represent a node of a linked list, containing a
      string and a pointer to the next node
define a few pointer of the type of the structure just defined
copy the SQL statement into the defined string
call the OCI function to parse the SQL statement
if the oparse() function returns an error
      send the ERROCI message to the socket channel
      exit from the routine back to the endless loop (selector function)
end if
for all the output variable of the select statement
      call the OCI function to bind the output variable to the select
      statement
                                                            (odefin())
      if the odefin() function returns an error
            send the ERROCI message to the socket channel
            exit from the routine back to the endless loop (selector
            function)
      end if
end for
for all the input variables of the select statement (the parameters of
                                                         the where clause)
      call the OCI function to bind the output variable to the select
      statement
      (obndrn())
      if the obndrn() function returns an error
            send the ERROCI message to the socket channel
            exit from the routine back to the endless loop (selector
            function)
      end if
end for
call the OCI function to open the defined SQL cursor (oexec())
if oexec() returns an error
      send the ERROCI message to the socket channel
      exit from the routine back to the endless loop (selector function)
end if
```

```
allocate memory for the root node of the linked list
for (endless) /* Until all data is fetched from Oracle */
        initialize all the output variables (memset to NULL)
        call the OCI function to fetch from the loop 10 rows at any
                                                        one time (ofen())
        if the error returned from ofen() is different from
                NO_MORE_DATA_TO_BE_FETCHED
                send the ERROCI message to the socket channel
                de-allocate the memory holding the root node of the linked
                list
                exit from the routine back to the endless loop
                                                        (selector function)
        end if
        keep a row fetched counter
        for all the rows fetched from Oracle (up to 10 at any pass)
        allocate one more node in the linked list
                copy the fetched values from the output variables in the
                        string within the node of the linked list
                if there are no more rows fetched from the cursor
                        exit from the endless loop
                end if
        end for
end endless for /* All data fetched from DB */
if no rows where fetched from the cursor
        send the ERRNOD (NO data) message to the socket channel
        de-allocate the memory holding the root node of the linked list
        exit from the routine back to the endless loop (selector function)
end if
convert the row counter from integer to ASCII string
write to the socket channel the message "OPEROK"
write to the socket channel the ASCII string representing the number
                                of rows to be sent to the client
for loop to traverse the linked list
        get the next node in the linked list
        write the string containing all the values fetched from Oracle
                to the socket channel
end loop which traverses the linked list
traverse the linked list using a for loop
        get the next node in the linked list
        de-allocate the memory holding the previous node in the linked
        list
end loop which traverses the linked list
de-allocate the root node of the linked list
exit from the routine back to the main function selector
```

To illustrate how the concepts shown in the pseudo-code work, the source code of the functions that implements the gathering of data dictionary statistics is presented below. Getting familiar with this function is the first step for anybody who wants to extend OPERA to include additional functionality.

DictSts.c:

```
#include <string.h>
#include <stdlib.h>
#include <stdio.h>
#include <sys/errno.h>

/* OCI includes */
#include "oratypes.h"
#include "ocidfn.h"
#include "ociapr.h"
#include "ocidem.h"

/* DBUG package include */
#include "dbug.h"

/* OPERA includes */
#include "OperaStg2.h"
#include "OperaSvr.h"

int nDictSts(void)
{
/************************<DICT_STS>**********************/
/*   Dictionary Cache statistics                        */
/*   array size: 83 bytes                               */
/********************************************************/
char    szSqlStmt[212]; /* SQL Statement */

/*
** Output variables taken from v$rowcache:
** PARAMETER     VARCHAR2(32)
** GETS          NUMBER,
** GETMISSES     NUMBER,
** USAGE         NUMBER
** Host arrays are used. We fetch 10 rows at a time.
*/
char    szParameter[10][33];
float   fMissRatio[10];
int     nGets[10];
int     nMiss[10];
```

```
int     nCount[10];
int     nUsage[10];
char    szRowNum[5];
int     nn,
        nRowsDone,
        ii,
        sts,
        nStatementsProcessed=0;
/*
** the following structure represents each node
** in the linked list.
*/
typedef struct tagDictSts
{
        char    szLine[84];
        struct  tagDictSts *pNext;
}DICT_STS;
DICT_STS *pDictSts=NULL, *pDictStsCur=NULL,
   *pDictStsPrevious=NULL, *pDictStsLast=NULL;
BOOL    bFirstTime=TRUE;

/* The function starts here */
DBUG_ENTER("vDictSts");

/* SQL Statement definition */
strcpy(szSqlStmt,"select parameter, gets, getmisses, decode \
(getmisses,0,0,round((getmisses/(gets+getmisses) )*100,2) ),\
count, usage from sys.v_$rowcache");

/* OCI call to parse the SQL statement */
if (oparse(&CursCda,(text *) szSqlStmt,-1,1,2))
{
   DBUG_PRINT("ORA_ERR",("%s",GetOraMsg(&CursLda,CursCda.rc)));
   if( (sts=SendToClient("ERROCI",6)) == -1)
   {
        DBUG_PRINT("SND_ERR",
           ("Could not send message through sockets"));
        DBUG_RETURN(-1);
   }
   DBUG_RETURN(0);
}
/*
** The statement doesn't contain bind variables, so
** we can define all output variables.
```

```
*/
if (odefin(&CursCda,1,(ub1 *) szParameter, 33, STRING_TYPE,-1,
       (sb2 *) 0,(text *) 0,-1,-1,(ub2 *) 0,(ub2 *) 0))
{
    DBUG_PRINT("ORA_ERR",
       ("%s",GetOraMsg(&CursLda,CursCda.rc)));
    if( (sts=SendToClient("ERROCI",6)) == -1)
    {
        DBUG_PRINT("SND_ERR",
       ("Could not send message through sockets"));
        DBUG_RETURN(-1);
     }
     DBUG_RETURN(0);
}

if (odefin(&CursCda,2,(ub1 *) nGets , sizeof(int),
    INT_TYPE,-1,sb2 *) 0,(text *) 0,-1,-1,(ub2 *) 0,(ub2 *) 0))
{
     DBUG_PRINT("ORA_ERR",
       ("%s",GetOraMsg(&CursLda,CursCda.rc)));
     if( (sts=SendToClient("ERROCI",6))== -1)
     {
        DBUG_PRINT("SND_ERR",
       ("Could not send message through sockets"));
        DBUG_RETURN(-1);
     }
     DBUG_RETURN(0);
}
if (odefin(&CursCda,3,(ub1 *) nMiss, sizeof(int), INT_TYPE,
       -1,(sb2 *) 0,(text *) 0,-1,-1,(ub2 *) 0,(ub2 *) 0))
{
   DBUG_PRINT("ORA_ERR",
       ("%s",GetOraMsg(&CursLda,CursCda.rc)));
   if( (sts=SendToClient("ERROCI",6)) == -1)
   {
      DBUG_PRINT("SND_ERR",
       ("Could not send message through sockets"));
      DBUG_RETURN(-1);
   }
   DBUG_RETURN(0);
}
if (odefin(&CursCda,4,(ub1 *) fMissRatio, sizeof(float),
       FLOAT_TYPE,-1, (sb2 *) 0, (text *) 0,-1,-1,(ub2 *) 0,
       (ub2 *) 0))
```

```
{
   DBUG_PRINT("ORA_ERR",
       ("%s",GetOraMsg(&CursLda,CursCda.rc)));
   if( (sts=SendToClient("ERROCI",6)) == -1)
   {
       DBUG_PRINT("SND_ERR",
         ("Could not send message through sockets"));
       DBUG_RETURN(-1);
   }
   DBUG_RETURN(0);
}
if (odefin(&CursCda,5,(ub1 *) nCount, sizeof(int), INT_TYPE,-1,
       (sb2 *) 0,(text *) 0,-1,-1,(ub2 *) 0,(ub2 *) 0))
{
   DBUG_PRINT("ORA_ERR",("%s",GetOraMsg(&CursLda,CursCda.rc)));
   if( (sts=SendToClient("ERROCI",6)) == -1)
   {
       DBUG_PRINT("SND_ERR",
           ("Could not send message through sockets"));
       DBUG_RETURN(-1);
   }
   DBUG_RETURN(0);
}
if (odefin(&CursCda,6,(ub1 *) nUsage, sizeof(int), INT_TYPE,-1,
       (sb2 *) 0,(text *) 0,-1,-1,(ub2 *) 0,(ub2 *) 0))
{
   DBUG_PRINT("ORA_ERR",
       ("%s",GetOraMsg(&CursLda,CursCda.rc)));
   if( (sts=SendToClient("ERROCI",6)) == -1)
   {
      DBUG_PRINT("SND_ERR",
            ("Could not send message through sockets"));
      DBUG_RETURN(-1);
   }
   DBUG_RETURN(0);
}

/*
** All variables have been defined, we can now execute
** the statement.
*/
if (oexec(&CursCda))
{
   DBUG_PRINT("ORA_ERR",("%s",GetOraMsg(&CursLda,CursCda.rc)));
```

```
   if( (sts=SendToClient("ERROCI",6)) == -1)
   {
      DBUG_PRINT("SND_ERR",
        ("Could not send message through sockets"));
      DBUG_RETURN(-1);
   }
   DBUG_RETURN(0);
}

/*
** We successfully executed the statement. We can now
** allocate the root node of the linked list.
*/
pDictSts=(struct tagDictSts *)
      malloc(sizeof(struct tagDictSts));
/*
** An endless loop starts, to fetch all rows
** from the OCI cursor.
*/
for (nRowsDone = 0 ; ;)
{
    /* All variables are initialized to NULL */
    memset(nGets,'\0',sizeof(nGets));
    memset(nMiss,'\0',sizeof(nMiss));
    memset(szParameter,'\0',sizeof(szParameter));
    memset(fMissRatio,'\0',sizeof(fMissRatio));
    memset(nCount,'\0',sizeof(nCount));
    memset(nUsage,'\0',sizeof(nUsage));
    /*
    ** We ask Oracle to fetch in lots of 10 rows.
    */
    if (ofen(&CursCda,10))
    {
        if (CursCda.rc != NO_DATA_FOUND)
        {
           DBUG_PRINT("ORA_ERR",
           ("%s",GetOraMsg(&CursLda,CursCda.rc)));
            free(pDictSts);
            if( (sts=SendToClient("ERROCI",6)) == -1)
            {
               DBUG_PRINT("SND_ERR",
                  ("Could not send message through sockets"));
               DBUG_RETURN(-1);
            }
```

```
            DBUG_RETURN(0);
         }
    }
    /* We find out how many rows we fetched in the last pass */
    nn = CursCda.rpc - nRowsDone;
    nRowsDone += nn;
    /*
    ** We loop through each fetched row,
    ** storing the data in linked list nodes created
    ** on the fly.
    */
    for ( ii = 0; ii < nn; ii++)
    {
       if (bFirstTime)
       {
          pDictStsCur=pDictSts;
          memset(pDictStsCur,'\0',sizeof(DICT_STS));
          bFirstTime=FALSE;
       }
       else
       {
          pDictStsCur->pNext=
          (struct tagDictSts *) malloc(sizeof(struct tagDictSts));
          if (pDictStsCur->pNext == NULL)
          {
             if( (sts=SendToClient("ERR999",6)) == -1)
             {
                DBUG_PRINT("SND_ERR",
                ("Could not send message through sockets"));
                DBUG_RETURN(-1);
             }
             DBUG_VOID_RETURN;
         }
         pDictStsCur=pDictStsCur->pNext;
         memset(pDictStsCur,'\0',sizeof(DICT_STS));
      }
      nStatementsProcessed++;
      /*
      ** We store the content of the ith element of
      ** output variables into the node of the
      ** linked list created by the preceding statements.
      */
      sprintf(pDictStsCur->szLine,
              "%32s|%10d|%10d|%6.2f|%10d|%10d",
```

```
            szParameter[ii],nGets[ii],nMiss[ii],
            fMissRatio[ii],nCount[ii],nUsage[ii]);
    }/* End for all fetched rows */
    if (CursCda.rc == NO_DATA_FOUND) break;
}/* End endless for */

/*
** If the SQL statement didn't find any row,
** we communicate to the client that we won't
** be sending anything. We can return to the
** selector function safely.
*/
if (nStatementsProcessed == 0)
{
   free(pDictSts);
   if( (sts=SendToClient("ERRNOD",6)) == -1)
   {
      DBUG_PRINT("SND_ERR",
      ("could not send message through sockets"));
      DBUG_RETURN(-1);
   }
   DBUG_RETURN(0);
}
/*
** The following statement formats the number of
** lines found into a string of or chars. Note that
** the number will have leading zeros. This is done to
** simplify the Java conversion. The Java method
** Integer.parseInt(String) fails to convert into
** a number a string that begins with spaces. To avoid
** trimming the string in Java before converting it,
** we send a string with leading zeros.
*/
sprintf(szRowNum,"%04d",nStatementsProcessed);
/*
** We inform the client that on the server side
** everything was OK and we are now ready to
** send the data fetched.
*/
if( (sts=SendToClient("OPEROK",6)) == -1)
{
    DBUG_PRINT("SND_ERR",
       ("Could not send message through sockets"));
    DBUG_RETURN(-1);
```

```
}
/*
** The next statement sends the number of lines
** (or data blocks) that will be sent to the client
*/
if( (sts=SendToClient(szRowNum,4)) == -1)
{
    DBUG_PRINT("SND_ERR",
       ("Could not send message through sockets"));
    DBUG_RETURN(-1);
}
/*
** The following loop traverses the linked list and
** sends all data blocks through the socket channel.
*/

for(     pDictStsCur=pDictSts;
         pDictStsCur != NULL;
         pDictStsCur = pDictStsCur->pNext)
{
   if( (sts=SendToClient(pDictStsCur->szLine,83)) == -1)
   {
      DBUG_PRINT("SND_ERR",
          ("Could not send message through sockets"));
      DBUG_RETURN(-1);
   }
}
/*
** The following loop traverses the linked list freeing
** all nodes.
*/
bFirstTime=TRUE;
for(     pDictStsCur=pDictSts;
         pDictStsCur != NULL;
         pDictStsCur = pDictStsCur->pNext)
{
   if (bFirstTime)
   {
           pDictStsPrevious = pDictStsCur;
           bFirstTime = FALSE;
   }
   else
   {
       free(pDictStsPrevious);
```

```
            pDictStsPrevious=pDictStsCur;
    }
    pDictStsLast = pDictStsCur;
}
free(pDictStsLast);
DBUG_RETURN(0);
} /* End function */
```

18.5.2 EXTENDING OPERA: AN EXAMPLE

The OPERA infrastructure can be used as a skeleton, upon which new and extended features are built. It requires a few steps and a relatively small amount of new source code to display additional statistics gathered from an Oracle instance being monitored. In this section, we will create a new option that displays information about Oracle processes. The V$ view that provides this information is V$PROCESS. Its structure is shown below.

```
SQL> desc v$process
 Name                              Null?    Type
 --------------------------------- ------   ------------
 ADDR                                       RAW(4)
 PID                                        NUMBER
 SPID                                       VARCHAR2(9)
 USERNAME                                   VARCHAR2(15)
 SERIAL#                                    NUMBER
 TERMINAL                                   VARCHAR2(10)
 PROGRAM                                    VARCHAR2(48)
 BACKGROUND                                 VARCHAR2(1)
 LATCHWAIT                                  VARCHAR2(8)
 LATCHSPIN                                  VARCHAR2(8)
```

We want to fetch and display the following fields:

```
ADDR
SERIAL#
PID
SPID
USERNAME
TERMINAL
PROGRAM
BACKGROUND
```

First, we work out the SQL statement needed to retrieve the required information.

```
select rawtohex(addr),serial#,pid,spid,username,
decode(background,1,'Background','Interactive'), terminal,
program from v$process;
```

The next step is to compute the number of bytes of each data block sent to the client. This is given by the following formula:

```
sum(max(characters of each field)) + number of fields -1
```

The following table shows the space required by each field.

FIELD	LENGTH
USERNAME	15
ADDR	8
PID	6
SPID	9
SERIAL#	8
TERMINAL	10
BACKGROUND	12
PROGRAM	48
Number of fields –1	7
Total	123

The length of a few fields has been arbitrarily assigned. For instance, the ADDR field will be retrieved via the SQL function *rawtohex()*, which will expand its length to eight characters. PID is a number, and we arbitrarily decide that we won't display more than six digits on the client, which should be enough under most circumstances.

Once we have formulated the SQL statement and worked out the length of the data block to be transmitted to the server, a few other steps are required to plug in the new function into the OPERA environment.

1. A "C" file containing the new function must be coded.
2. The nProcessRequest() function, residing in OperaSock.c, must be amended to add one more branch to the switch statement that evaluates the function codes received from the client.
3. Compile and link logic for the new "C" file must be added to the makefile.

Step 1 can be simplified by cloning an existing file, say DictStats.c, modifying the source code to reflect the new variables and structures needed by the added function.

To display the data fetched from V$PROCESS, we must change the variables cloned from DictStats.c into the following set:

```
char     szUsername[10][16];
char     szAddr[10][9];
int      nPid[10];
char     szSpid[10][10];
int      nSerial[10];
char     szTerminal[10][11];
char     szBackground[10][13];
char     szProcess[10][49];
```

We call the new function *nProcSts()*. The "C" structure used to define each node of the linked list must be modified as follows:

```
typedef struct tagProcSts
{
        char    szLine[124];
        struct  tagProcSts *pNext;
}PROC_STS;
PROC_STS *pProcSts=NULL,          *pProcStsCur=NULL,
          *pProcStsPrevious=NULL, *pProcStsLast=NULL;
```

The entire section that associates the output variables with the OCI cursor must be modified to reflect the new variable names and the changed datatypes. The sprintf() function that formats each line containing data to be sent to the Java client must also be modified as follows:

```
sprintf(pProcStsCur->szLine,
        "%15s|%8s|%6d|%9s|%8d|%10s|%12s|%48s",
        szUsername[ii],szAddr[ii],nPid[ii],
        szSpid[ii],nSerial[ii],szTerminal[ii],
        szBackground[ii],szProgram[ii]);
```

The find-and-replace function of the editor can be used to change all occurrences of pDictsSts into pProcSts, to efficiently modify all source code that traverses the linked list repeatedly. The line that sends the fetched data through the socket channel must be changed from:

```
if( (sts=SendToClient(pDictStsCur->szLine,83)) == -1)
```

into:

```
if( (sts=SendToClient(pProcStsCur->szLine,123)) == -1)
```

We now must add an additional branch to the switch coded in *nProcessRequest()* to allow OPERA to call *nProcSts()* when the appropriate function code is received from the client. We arbitrarily decide the the code associated with *nProcSts()* is 21. The following code is added to nProcessRequest() to make the function selector aware of the newly added routine:

```
case 21:
        if ( (nFuncSts=nProcSts()) != 0)
        {
              DBUG_PRINT("OPR_ERR",("nProcSts() failed!"));
              DBUG_RETURN(-1);
        }
        break;
```

We now have to edit the makefile to add one more target and to add the new "C" file to the target that links together all modules. We launch OPERA compilation and linking, perhaps fixing a few overlooked things that slipped through the editing process, until we can successfully build the new OPERA executable that contain nProcSts().

We must now modify the Java client to add one menu option and the logic required to send the new function code to the server. We start by editing Stage2MainFrame.java. A new menu item must be added to the Stage2MainFrame class. We add the following line at the beginning of the class definition:

```
MenuItem mProcStats = new MenuItem();
```

The following lines must be added to the jbInit() method:

```
mProcStats.setLabel("Process Stats");
mProcStats.addActionListener(
      new Stage2MainFrame_mProcStats_actionAdapter(this));
```

And, a few lines below:

```
mEngineAnalysis.add(mProcStats);
```

We must add the action listeners, towards the end of the Stage2MainFrame file. The source code is shown below.

```
class Stage2MainFrame_mProcStats_actionAdapter implements
java.awt.event.ActionListener
{
  Stage2MainFrame adaptee;

  Stage2MainFrame_mProcStats_actionAdapter
```

```
        (Stage2MainFrame adaptee)
    {
      this.adaptee = adaptee;
    }
    public void actionPerformed(ActionEvent e)
    {
      adaptee.mProcStats_actionPerformed(e);
    }
}
```

We are almost done with Stage2MainFrame. The last remaining bit is to add the adapter method that sends a reference of the chosen menu item to *CommandControl.mEval()*.

```
void mProcStats_actionPerformed(ActionEvent e)
{
    ComCon.mEval(mProcStats);
}
```

This completes our amendments to the Stage2MainFrame class. We must now add a little bit of logic to CommandControl.java, to send the function code that requests nProcSts() to be executed on the server and to display the data received. The following lines of Java code do the job:

```
if (sChoice.equals("Process Stats"))
{
    String clabels[] = { "Username","Address","Pid",
                         "Server Pid","Serial#","Terminal",
                         "Process Type","Program Run"};
    DisplayInFrame DIF = new DisplayInFrame(parentFrame,
                              "0021","Process Statistics",
                              clabels,8,123);
    return;
}
```

Et voila! We recompile our Java classes, we produce a new Jar file containing the new bytecodes, and we can test the new function just added to OPERA.

Summary

This chapter introduced and illustrated OPERA, an Oracle performance monitoring tool that allows DBAs and developers to rapidly identify performance problems affecting running Oracle instances. The source code is freely available and comes with the companion CD. The chapter explained the concepts behind the design and implementation of OPERA and showed how to extend the basic functionality of the package, so that OPERA users can customize the software to better fulfil their needs. The OPERA presentation services are implemented in Java, allowing users to monitor Oracle from a WEB browser. A server process written in "C" and OCI7 generates the database statistics. Communication between the Java client and the server running on the back-end computer occurs through TCP/IP sockets.

GLOSSARY

Abstraction A mental tool that allows designers to perceive real-world problems, re-elaborating their basic elements according to varying degrees of detail, ranging from high-level to low-level.

ACID, ACID message Acronym that defines the four basic characteristics of transactionally enabled messages: atomicity, consistency, isolation and durability.

Advanced replication A complex method that allows data residing in databases to be copied to multiple locations to support distributed applications. Advanced replication does not enforce a hierarchical relationship among the participating nodes/ databases (peer-to-peer, update anywhere model).

Algorithm A programmatic recipe that implements a systematic approach for the resolution of a computational problem.

API See *Application programming interface.*

Application programming interface A standardized library of function calls used by software developers to write applications that interface with external services or software modules.

ASCII Abbreviation/acronym for American Standard Code for Information Interchange. A set of 8-bit binary numbers representing the alphabet, punctuation, numerals, and other special symbols used in text representation and communications protocol.

ATMI Application-to-Transaction Monitor Interface. The TUXEDO API that provides the programming interface for applications that interface with the TUXEDO system.

Atomicity One of the four properties of a transaction. It means that either all actions delimited by the transaction boundaries occur, or none of them occur.

Attribute A named property of a class describing a data value held by each object of the class.

Autotrace Feature provided by recent releases of Oracle SQL*Plus. It allows users to display useful SQL tracing information while submitting SQL statements to the Oracle engine.

Bandwidth The throughput capacity. The bandwidth of a bus is the maximum rate at which data can be transferred across the bus.

Basic replication A simple method that allows data residing in databases to be copied to multiple locations to support distributed applications. Basic replication enforces a hierarchical relationship among the participating nodes/databases, where one node is elected to be the master node, which coordinates the activities of all nodes participating in the distributed database (Master/slave model). Normally, only the master node has read-write privileges on the data that is transferred. Slave nodes can only read the distributed data.

Binary format A software entity, generally a file, which is formatted as a collection of ones and zeros. Its specific format is only intelligible to the application that created it and deals with it. A typical example is the file created by a word processor such as MS Word. A DOC file is only readable by Word, and not freely displayable on the screen by using OS commands.

Bind variables Allow the variable portions of an SQL statement, such as data values to be inserted or a search key, to be defined as "parameters" to the SQL statement The use of bind variables allows SQL statements to be re-executed without re-parsing the SQL statement. The alternative approach, where substitution variables are embedded as literals within the SQL statement requires that the SQL statement be re-parsed when re-executed.

Black-box testing techniques When applied to software modules under test, they are aimed at proving that input is correctly verified and either accepted or refused, that output is coherently and consistently produced according to the given input and that the overall integrity of information processed by the module is preserved.

Branch In version control, a separate line of development consisting of one or more revisions.

Business logic A set of business rules, expressed in computer terms, grouped together to accomplish a business task.

Cardinality A measure of the number of unique values within a column or an index. The higher the cardinality of the index, the fewer the number of rows which will be returned by an exact lookup of a key value and hence the more useful the index will be.

CASE Acronym for *Computer Aided Software Engineering.*

Cda In OCI, the cursor data area. Memory structure holding cursor-related parameters.

CMS Code Management System. The source code control software shipped by DEC/Compaq for the OpenVMS operating system.

Code-and-Fix The SDLC model that is characterized by an absolute absence of a structured approach to software project-related activities such as designing, coding, documenting and debugging. It can be said that it represents the negation of an SDLC.

Code coverage The percentage of source code of a software program exercised by the battery of tests applied to it.

Cohesion The ability of a software module/entity to group together related and homogeneous elements, excluding the unrelated and extraneous ones.

Complexity reduction Intellectual tool commonly used by high-level designers who strive to simplify a real-world problem by breaking its components down into smaller and more manageable units.

Composition In OO, an implementation mechanism defined when an object, responding to an operation on itself, forwards the operation to another object. This technique is also called *delegation.*

Conceptual model A very high-level definition of a business domain, where the participating elements are not described in detail.

Configuration management Management of the typical activities concerning source code control, version control and deployment control. Under the configuration management umbrella are source control, dependency checking, bug tracking, automated testing and customer installation.

Conflicts In an Oracle replication context, conflicts arise when multiple sites change the same data during the latency period. DBAs can establish policies for an automatic resolution of potential conflicts.

Connection concentration Multiplexing techniques are used to combine the network traffic from several or many clients onto a single physical network connection to the server. A client connection is guaranteed never to be dropped.

Connection pooling Allows a limited number of physical, transport-level connections to be shared among a greater number of logical network connections. Idle transport connections can be temporarily released, provided that their network sessions are maintained. With this approach, a client connection can be dropped and re-established when required. If all logical connections are taken by other clients, the connection that was temporarily dropped could experience a noticeable delay while waiting for a logical slot to become available.

Consistency One of the transaction properties, which states that the transaction as a whole represents a correct transformation of the resource managers involved, that is, it takes the database from a consistent state to another consistent state.

ConText Oracle add-on to the database server, focused on text management. It offers excellent text retrieval capabilities, based on sophisticated algorithms that implement pattern matching, sound-like searches, proximity searches, and fuzzy logic.

CORBA Acronym for Common Object Request Broker Architecture. Industry standard for distributed-object programming.

Coupling Represents the degree to which a software entity is connected to other entities. Strong coupling means that software modules are heavily dependent on one another, and cannot be used in isolation. Loose coupling describes the opposite situation, in which software modules do not rely on other participating modules to be able to provide their services.

Cron A UNIX system utility that allows tasks to be executed at regularly scheduled intervals.

Cursor variable In Pro*C, a memory handle or pointer to an area that holds cursor related information. The cursor is opened on the server side, typically by a PL/SQL statement, and the memory holding the cursor information is then made available to the client program, written in Pro*C.

CVS Acronym for Concurrent Version System. Source code control software implemented as a front-end to RCS. CVS offers more sophisticated capabilities, such as code merging and check-in/check-out coordination, useful when the same source code is worked upon by large teams of developers.

Daemon A UNIX term for a program that runs constantly, listening for requests for a particular connection or service (which it will answer and then spawn off a child process to fulfill).

Data-flow diagram A graphical representation of the functional model, showing dependencies between values and the computation of output values from input values without regard for when or if the functions are executed.

Data consolidation Technique used in basic replication. Each peripheral node has read-write access to data that is replicated and transferred to a central site, which has read only access over the shared data. According to this model, multiple master nodes convey information to a single slave node.

Data convergence Term used in data replication, it is the goal of the replication process. It means that ultimately all sites will have the same content for any given row. Data convergence is usually reached at a later stage, that is, there is a latency period between the change applied to the data and its consistent propagation to all participating sites, until convergence is achieved.

Data-dependent routing In TUXEDO, assignment of a request to a server offering the requested service based on the values of the data within the message.

Data dissemination Technique used in basic replication. A single master node, having read-write access, propagates data that must be shared to multiple slave nodes, which can access it in read-only mode.

Data independence The ability to access and update data without knowing the underlying storage formats or offsets.

Data replication Encompasses the analysis, design, implementation, administration, and management of a service that guarantees data consistency across multiple resource managers in a distributed environment.

Datafile File used by Oracle to store data or indexes. Oracle deals with three different types of files: datafiles, redo log files, and control files.

Datatype equivalencing In Pro*C, arbitrary equivalence established by developers between Oracle internal datatypes and host language supported datatypes.

DCE RPC Remote procedure calls defined according to the standard established by DCE, which stands for Distributed Computing Environment. DCE is about middleware software, developed by the OSF, that includes communications, security, time, and file system services. Contrast with ONC RPC, remote procedure call standard defined by Sun Microsystems.

Deferred integrity In a distributed environment, database integrity that is eventually reached at a postponed point in time, that is, when data across the various sites become reconciled.

Delegation See *Composition.*

Denormalization The process of re-introducing redundant or derived information into a data model with an aim to improving performance.

Diff An OS provided command that allows for quick comparison of the content of two or more files, flagging eventual differences found in the process. The analog MS Windows command is *comp*, available from the command line interface.

Dispatcher In an Oracle multi-threaded environment, the process that links user connections to server processes, lessening the number of processes required to run on the host computer to support a large user population.

Distributed lock manager In a distributed database, the software utility that regulate the access of Oracle engines residing on different nodes to the same data block shared among the database engines. A distributed lock manager can be provided by the operating system, but Oracle 8 ships with a bundled distributed lock manager that is normally more effective, because it is implemented directly in the Oracle kernel.

DLM See *Distributed lock manager.*

Domain The set of legal values for an attribute in a database.

Driving table The driving table is the table that is accessed first in a table join. Choosing the best driving table is a key decision when optimizing join order.

DTD Acronym for Document Type Definition. An SGML specification that defines the markup elements, their content-models, and other aspects of a markup language.

Durability One of the properties of a transaction. It means that the effects of a committed transaction survive failures.

Dynamic load balancing Assignment of multiple, concurrent requests to service dispatchers performed in a manner that optimizes throughput by evenly distributing the request load among the cooperating dispatchers. This assignment occurs at run-time, and is subject to constant modification, according to factors such as the number of requests and the current load on each dispatcher.

Dynamic SQL SQL statements built and submitted to the Oracle engine dynamically, i.e. at run-time. Because of historical reasons, dynamic SQL is often used to indicate SQL statements that contain literals instead of bind variables in the where clause. This is not correct, because it is possible to build SQL statements dynamically, which use bind variables.

Easy retrieval One of the basic requirements for project documentation. It means that facilities should be provided by the document management system in order to allow project members to easily retrieve, assess, and compare different versions of the same document.

Encapsulation A modeling and implementation technique that separates the external aspects of an object from the internal implementation details of the object. Also called *information hiding.*

ER diagram A graphical representation that shows entities, drawn as rectangular boxes, and the relationships between them, drawn as connecting lines.

Explain plan Oracle DML command that provides an indication of the execution plan chosen by the optimizer to satisfy a given SQL query.

FIFO Acronym for first-in, first-out. A queuing technique in which the next item to be retrieved is the item that has been in the queue for the longest time.

FML Acronym for field manipulation language, a TUXEDO interface for maintaining buffers with field/value pairs.

Foreign key A column or columns within one table which relate to the primary key of a "master" or "parent" table. These matching foreign and primary key columns can be used to join the two tables.

Formatter Software tool that gives typographical formatting to SGML documents, interpreting the various document elements and formatting them according to the typographical conventions of a specific target.

Full table scan Sequential read of data blocks from disk to SGA performed to fetch data by an Oracle engine. It is generally the least efficient execution path for data retrieval for small result sets. If the result set is large, say more than 20%, often a full table scan becomes more efficient than an indexed lookup.

Generalization The relationship between a class and one or more refined or specialized versions of it.

Grep Unix utility that allows users to scan one or more file looking for specific content, specified on the command line. If a specific file contains the required string or strings, its name, and optionally, the line numbers, are displayed by grep on the standard output.

HDA In OCI, the host data area, or an area of memory holding information about the host where the database resides.

Hot standby Technique used to provide fault tolerance in sites where the Oracle parallel server option is not used. A second database mirrors the main database by sharing the redo log files. If the main instance crashes, the backup database becomes the main instance in very little time, simply by recovering the last redo-log files produced by the main instance just prior to the crash. Database down-time is only procrastinated, and not avoided, because a complete database cold backup is required to reach again the initial situation, where the second instance actively mirrors the main instance.

IDEF1X methodology Data modeling methodology developed by Robert Brown in the late 1970s. Its graphical notation is supported by most data modeling tools available on the market.

Impedance mismatch Term borrowed from electronics. When two devices operate at different electrical impedance, it becomes difficult to connect them, unless their incompatibility is somehow mitigated or prevented. OO theoreticians often use this term to underline that it is difficult to seamlessly integrate the simple relational datatypes with complex objects, when objects must be given persistence. Objects must be decomposed into simple dataypes before they are stored into the database, and recomposed when retrieved from the database. Object-oriented databases are able to store objects in their entirety, without decomposing them, therefore preventing impedance mismatch from occurring.

Indicator variable In embedded SQL, an optionally enabled variable that stores information about the value contained in its associated column. If the latter contains a null value, the indicator variable contains –1. If the associated column contains a value, which has not been truncated during the fetch operation, the indicator variable contains 0. Finally, if the associated column contains a value which has been truncated during the database fetch, perhaps to accommodate a host variable shorter in size than the database column, the indicator variable contains a number, corresponding to the last successful byte read before the truncation.

Information Engineering (IE) methodology Data modeling methodology conceived by James Martin [1990]. In IE every relationship between entities is binary and involves either two entities or one only entity if the relationship is reflexive.

Information hiding Technique that strives to avoid global publishing of data, which could be inadvertently modified by modules that do not have logical ownership over it.

Instrumentation The act of appending either debug or performance-related information to source code or object files, so that they can produce trace information. The freely available DBUG package requires developers to instrument their source code to produce trace statistics. Pure Coverage, a commercially available product by Rational Software, instruments the object files produced by the compiler, in a far less intrusive manner.

Interconnect Communication facility between the various nodes in a MMP or clustered environment. Typically implemented through Ethernet, FDDI, or other proprietary protocols.

ISO International Standards Organization. Entity that supervises, enforces, and controls international standards.

Isolation One of the four properties of a transaction. It ensures that concurrent operations on the underlying data do not interfere with each other.

Lda In Oracle OCI, the logon data area, a memory structure that holds information on a specific Oracle session.

LOB Object type supported by Oracle8. There are four basic LOB datatypes: BFILE, BLOB, CLOB, NCLOB. A BFILE is a LOB whose content is stored in an external file, residing on the OS. A BLOB is a LOB that contains binary data. A CLOB is a LOB that contains single-byte character data, and a NCLOB is a LOB that contains multi-byte character data.

Localization Dynamically adjusting software modules in order to make them aware of locale-specific punctuation, currency symbols, date displaying conventions, etc. Technique used in software internationalization, where the same software module appears to "speak" different languages, simply by dynamically modifying its locale.

Logical data access layer Software layer that groups together logical data access functions. The logical data access layer does not contain embedded SQL, but organizes the data fetched from the physical access layer in a more convenient manner for the business logic layer.

Logical model In data modeling, a model that logically describes a database definition. A logical model is independent from any vendor-specific implementation, and could theoretically be suitable for any target RDBMS. Contrast with physical data model.

LONG Oracle-specific datatype. Used to store unstructured, binary data up to two gigabytes in size. Superseded by the new family of large objects, or LOBs, introduced by Oracle8.

Loosely coupled systems Parallel hardware configurations that share disks. They are characterized by having one or more CPUs, which do not share memory between them. Each node shares disks (and possibly other resources) with the other nodes. Communication occurs over high-speed Interconnects.

Massively parallel processing hardware Parallel hardware configuration where each processor (or node) has its own portion of memory.

MDI Acronym for Multiple Document Interface. A particular way to implement MS Window-based applications, where a parent window, the MDI frame, can optionally contain one or more child windows, called sheets. This way to organize the visual desktop is particularly useful for applications that open a large number of different, but similar objects, such as a word processor that opens multiple documents and keep them in the user's reach.

Message oriented middleware Middleware that supports a publish-and-subscribe or broadcast metaphor. IBM MQ Series is an example of MOM.

Metadata Data about data. Data structure used to define the format of other data. The Oracle data dictionary is an example of metadata: the data dictionary tables, owned by the user SYS, contain the definition of all user-defined data.

Method The implementation of an operation for a specific class.

Middleware Software that runs on a server, and acts as either an application processing gateway or a routing bridge between remote clients and data sources or other servers, or any combination of these.

MOM See *Message-oriented middleware.*

MPP See *Massively parallel processing.*

MTS See *Multi-threaded server.*

Multi-threaded server Oracle configuration in which multiple user sessions are connected to a restricted number of dispatchers, which are in turn served by a number of shared servers. The goal that this architecture strives to achieve is lessening the number of processes required on the host machine to serve client requests.

Mutating table Side effect due to the Oracle implementation of triggers. When the application logic contained in a trigger that fired from a table performs a lookup operation on the same table, Oracle issues a mutating table error.

Network computer architecture Architecture that promotes a wide use of thin clients, connected to a few, centralized, and powerful servers. A network computer is a diskless workstation only capable of running a WEB browser and a few other applications, such as terminal emulators. The goal that the NCA strives to achieve is to lessen the administrative burden associated with the management of many small intelligent devices, physically located in geographically dispersed locations, by centralizing all administration in a single point.

Normalization In database modeling, the process of making all entities adhere to the normal form rules, established by E. F. Codd in the 1970s.

Null values They indicate that a value is missing, unknown or inapplicable. The use of NULL values extends the normal two valued logic to a three-valued logic. NULL values are important in SQL tuning because they are not generally stored in indexes and therefore present unique tuning problems.

OCI See *Oracle call interface.*

OLTP Acronym for on-line transaction processing. OLTP databases typically have a very high rate of update and query activity. OLTP is typified by high rates of index lookups, single-row modifications and frequent commits.

ONC RPC Acronym for Open Network Connectivity Remote Procedure Call. Sun Microsystems' specifications for the RPC paradigm.

OPS See *Oracle parallel server.*

Optimistic locking A locking strategy based on the assumption that a row is unlikely to be changed by another session between the time the row is queried and the time it is modified. Optimistic locking minimizes the lock duration but requires that the transaction be aborted if the row is changed by another session.

ORACA Oracle communication area. Memory structure optionally enabled in Pro*C, useful to collect extended information about errors and cursor efficiency.

Oracle call interface One of the interfaces provided by Oracle to allow developers to interact with the database. It is a very low-level interface, which gives a lot of control to developers. In exchange, it is more complex to use than, say, Pro*C. A few programming techniques are only available through the use of OCI, for instance callback functions activated by the arrival of a message on an advanced queue.

Oracle Open Gateways Oracle middleware used to transparently connect Oracle instances to a variety of databases from other vendors. Using the open gateway technology it is possible, for example, to join an Oracle table with a table stored in an IBM DB2 database.

Oracle Parallel Server An add-on package to the Oracle RDBMS that allows for multiple systems to share a common database. Each systems runs its own instance, but the database tables are shared.

OTT See *Oracle type translator.*

Oracle type translator Utility provided by Oracle that maps object definitions stored in the database to "C" structures. Used by Pro*C developers to interact with the object-relational interface provided by Oracle8.

Parallel Query Option An add-on package to the Oracle RDBMS that allows for concurrent processing of some query-related functions. Pre-requisite for its use is a host computer with SMP capabilities.

Parsing The process of preparing a SQL statement for execution. This involves checking the statement for syntax errors, checking for a matching statement in the shared pool and determining the optimal execution plan. Parsing can contribute significantly the processing overhead, especially in OLTP like environments.

Parser In SGML, a software tool that verifies the correctness of an SGML document against the DTD that describes the content of the document.

Passthrough SQL In ODBC, an SQL statement that is not parsed by the ODBC layer but passed without any further processing directly to the back-end engine.

Persistence The ability for data to survive across different runs of applications (or sessions) that make use of it. Languages such as C++ and Java use the notion of streamable objects. An object, seen as a complex datatype, can be saved as a file and subsequently rebuilt by reading the file. This action is commonly called "giving persistence to the object".

Pessimistic locking A locking strategy based on the assumption that a row might be changed between the time it is fetched and the time it is updated. Pessimistic locking involves locking the row when it is selected to prevent any concurrent updates.

Physical data access layer Software layer that groups together physical data access functions. This layer contains embedded SQL, and supervises all database lookups and insertions, passing the data back to the logical data access layer.

Physical model In data modeling, a model of the database which reflects implementation characteristics of the target database chosen for application implementation. A physical data model defining entities stored in an Oracle database can legitimately refer to Oracle specific datatypes, such as ROWID, and Oracle specific storage definitions, such as tablespaces.

PL/SQL Oracle-proprietary extension to SQL. Loosely based on ADA, PL/SQL implements procedural logic, such as IF..ELSE..ENDIF and loop controls. Initially introduced by Oracle Corporation to implement triggers and stored procedures, it has rapidly become one of the most common means to interact with an Oracle database. Many built-in features offered by Oracle today are implemented in PL/SQL, through the use of standard packages.

Postscript A page description language defined by Adobe Systems, used by printers, plotting devices, and occasionally by monitors (Postscript displays). It is a procedural markup language, which defines attributes and position in the page of all text and graphic elements comprising a document.

PQO See *Parallel query option.*

Primary key A column or columns which uniquely identify a row in a table.

Pro*C An Oracle product. Is a pre-compiler that transforms "C" files containing embedded SQL into plain "C" containing calls to the SQLLIB, a library that encapsulates SQL primitives directly callable from the "C" language.

Procedural markup A way of describing document contents and layout that emphasizes the *how* of display, rather than the structural elements embodied in the document. Procedural markup is common in proprietary document formats such as Postscript and RTF, since they are concerned with telling a single program how to display (or print) a file.

Profiler Software tool that allows developers to trace applications with the purpose of pinpointing performance bottlenecks. It operates by collecting statistics on function calls and time spent by each function.

Program control logic Used when applying software-layering techniques. The program control logic includes the main entry point for the process. It usually initializes the processing environment, handles fatal errors, and provides the process exit status. After startup, control is passed to the business logic layer.

Promotional group Promotion is the process of moving software forward from one stage of its life cycle to the next. A promotional group represents each stage.

PVCS Commercial product offered by Intersolv. It is a multi-platform version control system, available for the major Unix platforms and MS Windows.

RCS Acronym for Revision Control System. A Unix-based source code control system used to manage the software development process.

Referential integrity Referential integrity ensures that foreign keys correctly map to primary keys. A referential constraint will prevent the insert or update of foreign keys for which there are no matching primary keys and will either prevent the deletion of primary keys if foreign keys exist or delete these foreign key rows (delete cascade). Referential integrity can result in table-level locking if there are no indexes on the foreign keys.

Remote Procedure Call A procedure call that is executed in a non-local program or address space.

Replication catalog A set of data dictionary tables and views that maintains information about replicated objects and replicated groups at every site.

Replication group A set of related replication objects that are grouped together to facilitate administration and management. A replication object can be a member of one replication group only.

Replication Object A database object existing on multiple servers in a replicated database system.

Replication Site A database node participating in a replicated database environment. There are two different types of replication sites: a *master site* maintains a complete copy of all objects in a replication group, while a *snapshot site* supports read-only and updateable snapshots of the table data residing in an associated master site.

Repository A place where data is kept, like a file archive, database server, document management system, etc.

Resource manager A module or collection of modules, the most common of which are databases, that maintain the state of an application.

Revision In source code control, each configured change to a managed file is referred to as a revision.

Rich text format Microsoft standard for document interchange, based on a procedural markup language that uses an ASCII representation to describe the rendering of a document produced using a word processor such as MS Word.

RTF See *Rich text format.*

ScaleUp Factor that expresses how much more work can be done in the same time period by a larger (i.e., parallel) system.

SCCS Source code control system. A standard source code control system generally available with the Unix distribution kit.

SDI Acronym for Single Document Interface. GUI-based application that allows users to interact with a main window, which can open other windows.

SDLC See *Software development life cycle.*

Server In TUXEDO, a software module that accepts requests from clients and other servers and return replies. More generally, a data station that provides facilities for other stations, for example, mail servers, print servers, etc.

Service In TUXEDO, the name given to an application routine available for request by a client in the system with well-defined inputs, outputs, and processing.

SGML Acronym for Standard Generalized Markup Language. Is a metalanguage suitable for describing all kinds of markup languages, such as HTML or XML.

Shadow process In many environments, the Oracle program runs in a separate process from the client program (i.e., SQL*Plus). This "server" process is referred to as the shadow process.

SMP Acronym for Symmetric Multiprocessing. A form of mulitprocessing that allows the operating system to execute on any available processor or on several available processors simultaneously.

Software contract A software contract specifies the behavior of a software entity and its associated routines and sub-routines, outlining the responsibilities of both the user of the software entity and the software entity itself.

Software development life cycle Well defined set of stages or phases that a software product goes through during its lifetime, from its inception—analysis of requirements—to its completion—release into production and maintenance.

Source code control Set of procedures, techniques, and tools whose purpose is to ensure management and control over the production of source code.

Specialization The creation of subclasses from a superclass by refining the superclass.

SpeedUp Extent to which more hardware can perform the same task in less time than the original system.

Spiral model A software life-cycle model that supposes incremental development, using the waterfall model for each step, with the aim of managing risk. In the spiral model, developers define and implement features in order of decreasing priority.

SQLCA SQL communication area. Pro*C provided data structure that contain information pertaining to errors, warning, and status information. The SQLCA reflects the outcome of the most recently executed SQL statement.

Sqlda SQL descriptor area. Used when submitting to an Oracle engine SQL statements dynamically built at run-time. It is a host-defined data structure that holds descriptions of select-list items and input host variables.

Static SQL SQL statements statically defined at compile time. Contrast with Dynamic SQL.

Symmetric multi processing hardware Hardware configuration in which multiple processors share the same memory resource.

Synonym In Oracle, an alias for a table, view, sequence, or program unit.

Tablespace In Oracle, a logical structure that consists of one or more datafiles. Tables, clusters, and indexes are logically contained in a tablespace.

Tightly Coupled Systems Parallel hardware configurations that share memory. They are characterized by having multiple CPUs sharing memory, each CPU having full access on shared memory through a common bus.

Tip In source code control, the most recent revision of a branch.

Tkprof Oracle software tool that provides formatting for trace data accumulated during a database session, after the "alter session set sql_trace=true" command has been issued. The raw trace data file is processed by tkprof, which produces a file containing intelligible information about SQL statement execution.

TMIB In TUXEDO, a set of classes of objects with attributes within an application, describing the topology of the application components and the computers hosting the application.

TNS See *Transparent network substrate.*

TP monitor Software product used to create, execute, and manage transaction-processing applications. Popular TP monitor systems are Bea Systems TUXEDO, IBM-Transarc Encina, and Microsoft Transaction Server (MTS).

Traceability The ability for files and documents to be accessible by their users in all versions produced. When a document is traceable, it is possible to see the incremental changes occurred during its entire lifespan.

Transaction bracketing Establishing the boundaries of a transaction by using programmatic instructions to delimit the beginning and the ending of the transaction.

Transaction coordinator Software module that directs the execution of the commitment algorithm.

Transaction infection In TUXEDO, the passing of transaction properties from one module to another. When one module, which has been transactionally enabled, includes another module in its processing, it infects the second module. That is, the second module becomes part of the on-going transaction.

Transaction initiator The application software module that begins a transaction.

Transaction terminator The application software module that ends a transaction.

Transparent network substrate Oracle networking technology that provides a single application interface to all industry-standard networking protocols.

Trigger A mechanism that executes PL/SQL procedures or packages whenever a DML command is issued against a table or a view. Triggers are generally used to enforce integrity constraints and to implement customized behavior when data is inserted, deleted or modified in the database.

Troff A Unix text formatting utility that uses procedural markup.

Trunk In source code control, the main development branch.

Two-phase commit / presumed abort (2PC-PA) protocol Algorithm used to ensure the atomicity of a committing transaction.

Typed buffer A memory area, allocated by the TUXEDO system, which has an associated data type and subtype or format.

VIEW A typed buffer format in which the data is composed of one or more fields similar to a "C" structure or a Cobol record.

Visual source safe Microsoft product that implements a source code control system.

Waterfall model Model of SDLC that assumes software development to proceed in discrete stages, from analysis of requirements through specifications, design, coding testing, to release into production. This model represents the first serious attempt to a scientific approach to software engineering. The waterfall model has been recently criticized and its effectiveness questioned.

White-box testing techniques Testing techniques that try to prove that all independent paths of a software module have been utilized, all logical decisions have been taken in both directions and all loops have been tested using both minimum and maximum allowed values for the controlling variable. White-box testing pertains to the internal functioning of a module.

Workload partitioning Data replication technique that avoids conflicts by assigning logical ownership of data to users, who are not allowed to access in read-write mode data that doesn't logically belong to them.

XA The X/Open transaction manager to resource manager interface. Used by TP monitors and queuing systems to drive Oracle transactions using the two-phase commit protocol.

XML Acronym for eXtensible markup language.

BIBLIOGRAPHY

Andrade, Juan et al. 1996. *The TUXEDO System.* Addison Wesley.

BEA Systems, Inc. 1997. *BEA TUXEDO Application Development Guide.*

BEA Systems, Inc. 1997. *BEA TUXEDO Administrator's Guide.*

BEA Systems, Inc. 1997. *BEA TUXEDO Application Development Guide.*

BEA Systems, Inc. 1997. *BEA TUXEDO FML Programmer's Guide.*

BEA Systems, Inc. 1997. *BEA TUXEDO Programmer's Guide.*

Berard, E. 1992. *Essays on Object-Oriented Software Engineering*. Prentice Hall.

Bernstain, Philip and Newcomer, Eric. 1997. *Principles of Transaction Processing for the Systems Professionals.* Morgan Kaufmann.

Bloomer, John. 1992. *Power Programming with RPC.* O'Reilly & Associates.

Boehm, Barry. 1988. "A Spiral Model of Software Development and Enhancement," *IEEE Computer*, vol.21, #5, May 1988: 61–72.

Booch, Grady. 1994. *Object Oriented Analysis and Design: With Applications,* 2d ed. Benjamin/Cummings.

Brooks, Frederick Jr. 1987. "No Silver Bullits—Essence and Accidents of Software Engineering", IEEE Computer, April 1975: 10–19.

Brooks, Frederick Jr. 1975. *The Mythical Man-Month.* Addison Wesley.

Bruce, Thomas. 1995. *Designing Quality Databases with IDEF1X Information Models.* Dorset House.

Chen, Peter. 1976. "The Entity Relationship Model - Toward a Unified View of Data," *ACM Transactions on Database Systems,* Volume 1, No. 1: 9–36.

Codd, E. 1990. *The Relational Model for Database Management*. Addison-Wesley.

Date C. 1995. *An Introduction to Database Systems.* Addison-Wesley.

DeGrace, Peter and Stahl, Leslie. 1990. *Wicked Problems, Righteous Solutions.* Yourdon Press.

Dynamic Information Systems, LLC. 1998. *Oracle WEB Application Server Handbook.* Osborne: McGraw Hill.

Ensor, Dave and Stevenson, Ian. 1997. *Oracle8 Design Tips*. O'Reilly & Associates.

Feuerstein, Steven. 1995. *Oracle PL/SQL Programming*. O'Reilly & Associates.

Gamma, Erich et al. 1995 *Design Patterns: Elements of Reusable Object-Oriented Software*. Addison Wesley.

Gray, Jim and Reuter, A. 1992. *Transaction Processing: Concepts and Techniques*. Morgan Kaufmann.

Gurry, Mark and Corrigan, Peter. 1996. *Oracle Performance Tuning*, 2d Ed. O'Reilly & Associates.

Harrison, Guy. 1997. *Oracle SQL High Performance Tuning*. Prentice Hall.

Henderson-Sellers, Brian. 1992. *A Book of Object Oriented Knowledge*. Prentice Hall.

Henderson-Sellers, Brian and Edwards, J. 1993. "The Fountain Model for Object-Oriented System Development" *Object Magazine*, 3 (2): 71–79.

Henderson-Sellers, Brian and Edwards, J. 1994. *BOOKTWO of Object-Oriented Knowledge: The Working Object*. Prentice Hall.

Hobuss, James. 1998. *Building Oracle WEB Sites*. Prentice Hall.

IBM Corporation. 1997. *MQ Series for Sun Solaris Quick Beginnings*. GC33-1870-00.

IBM Corporation. 1997. *MQ Series Application Programming Guide*. SC33-0807-07.

IBM Corporation. 1997. *MQ Series Application Programming Reference*. SC33-1673-03.

IBM Corporation. 1997. *MQ Series Planning Guide*. GC33-1349-05.

IBM Corporation. 1997. *MQ Series System Administration*. SC33-1873-00.

Lewis, Bil and Berg, Daniel. 1996. *Threads Primer. A Guide to Multi-Threaded Programming*. Prentice Hall.

Lulushi, Albert. 1996. *Developing Oracle Forms Applications*. Prentice Hall.

Lulushi, Albert. 1998. *Inside Oracle Designer/2000*. Prentice Hall.

Lynch, Nancy et al. 1994. *Atomic Transactions*. Morgan Kaufmann.

Maguire, Steve. 1993. *Writing Solid Code*. Microsoft Press.

Martin, James. 1990. *Information Engineering*. Prentice Hall.

McConnell, Steve. 1996. *Rapid Development*. Microsoft Press.

Royce, Winston. 1970. "Managing the Development of Large Software Systems: Concepts and Techniques." *Proceedings WESCON*, August 1970.

Rumbaugh, James et al. 1991. *Object-Oriented Modeling and Design*. Prentice Hall.

Stallings, William. 1995. *Operating Systems*, 2d Ed. Prentice Hall.

Tittel, Ed, et al. 1995. *Foundations of World Wide Web Programming With HTML & CGI*. IDG Books.

Whalen, Edward. 1996. *Oracle Performance Tuning and Optimization*. Sams Publishing.

INDEX

Abstraction, 50
ACID (atomic, consistent, isolated, durable), 576–577
ActiveX Data Objects (ADO), 294
ADO object model, 320–322
Advanced Queuing (AQ), 290, 541, 553–563
  advanced features of, table, 554–555
  basic terms, table, 553–554
  using, 556–563
Advanced queuing (OCI), 474–476
Agent (AQ), 554
Alias libraries, 528
ANSI SQL, Oracle extension to, 497–498
Application event logging, 175–180
  application monitoring—operator alerts, 179–180
  problem escalation, 180
Application objects owner, 269–271
Archive, 184
Array enabled OCI calls with scalar counterpart, table, 456
ATMI (TUXEDO), 577
Attributes, 428
Authentication, 3
Automatic code generation, 121, 159–160
Automatic generation of electronic forms, 121–122
AUTOTRACE, 219–223

Bandwidth, 63
Batch (array), 108
BEA Systems TUXEDO, 577–597
  architecture, 584–585
  data conversion, 582–584
  MIB, 579–581
  servers and services, 581–582
  support for middleware paradigms, 585–593
  tips and tricks, 595–597
  transactions and Oracle, 593–595
BFILE, 427
Bind variables, 104–107
Black-box testing, 235
BLOB, 427
Block chaining, 110
Blocking timeouts, 587
Borland Database Engine (BDE), 299–302
Branch, 184, 185
Build it twice process, 17
Bundle, 186
Business logic and PL/SQL, 498–504
Business logic layer, 143
Business (or application) logic, 91

C++, support for, 394–399
Callback functions (OCI), 473
Call descriptor, 587
CASE tools, 121–138
C++ Builder, 297
  summary, 303–304
Centralized logging facility, 178
CHAR and VARCHAR2 data types, 109–111
Client, developing, 276–330
  connecting to Oracle, 313–327
    Inprise BDE/SQL Links, 323–324
    Microsoft connectivity, 317–322
    native drivers/third party OCI drivers, 314–317
    Oracle Objects for OLE, 324–327
  major client-server providers
    Inprise/Borland.com, 296–304
    Microsoft, 291–296
    Oracle, 280–291
    Sybase/Powersoft, 304–313
  no "best tool," 276–279
  software engineering focus, 328–330
Client development tools, using, 611–702
  ShrPool, Oracle shared pool browser, 612–616
  ShrPool in Delphi, 659–680
  ShrPool in Oracle Developer, 640–659
  ShrPool in PowerBuilder, 680–702
  ShrPool in Visual Basic, 618–640
  ShrPool source code, 616–618
Client-server application, software engineering focus of, 328–330
Client-server model, 90
  traditional, 278
CLOB, 427
Code-and-fix, 12
Cohesion, 51–52
Column groups, 79
Column objects, 430, 438
Common object request broker architecture (CORBA), 94
Complexity reduction, 52
Composition in object-oriented environments, 160–168
Configuration management, 183
Connection concentration, 567, 568
Connection pooling, 567, 568
CORBA, 291
Country kits, 239
Coupling, 51
Cursor variable, 374

Daemon, 178
Dangling REF, 431
DataBase Driver (DBD), 564
DataBase Interface (DBI), 564
Database triggers, 504–509
Data consolidation approach, 74, 76
Data Definition Language (DDL) statements, 447
Data dissemination approach, 74, 75
Data logic, 91
Data Manipulation Language (DML) statements, 447
Data mining, 86
Data modeling and CASE tools, 113–140
  CASE tools, 121–138
    ER/Studio, 135–138
    ER/Win, 129–131
    Oracle Database Designer (ODD), 128–129
    Oracle Designer, 122–128
    PowerDesigner, 131–135
  data modeling methodologies, 114–120
  design deliverables, 138–140
  repository, importance of, 120–121
Data modeling methodologies, 114–120
Date and currency, 237
DBArtisan, 251–252
DBMS_ALERT package, 542–545
  procedures and functions, table, 544
DBMS_JOB, 520–522
  methods, table, 522
DBMS_OUTPUT, 525–526
DBMS_PIPE package, 545–547
  modules, table, 545–546
DBMS_SESSION, 523–524
DBMS_SHARED_POOL, 524–525
  methods, table, 524
DBMS_SQL, 517–520
DBTools.h++, 477
De-coupling, 51
Deferred transaction queue, 78
Delphi, 297, 328
  summary, 303–304
De-normalization, 61
Deployment nightmare, 92–93
Dereferencing, 438
Design deliverables, 138–140
Designing an Oracle application, 49–87
  for distribution and replication of data, 72–81
  for flexibility, 53–59
  intellectual tools, 49–53
  for performance, 59–62
  for reliability, 70–72
  for scalability, 62–70
  for very large database/data warehouse, 81–86
Detailed design, 88–112
  application architecture paradigms, 90–94
  choosing development environment/language, 89–90
  issues, 96–111
    bind variables, 104–107
    CHAR and VARCHAR2 data types, 109–111
    host arrays, 108–109
    null values and indicator variables, 97–102

referential integrity, 102–104
rapid application development tools: compatibility and performance issues, 94–96
Dimension table, 84
Directives, 255
Direct Oracle Access (DOA), 314–316
nonvisual components of, table, 314–315
Disabling instrumentation in production code, 200–202
Distributed lock manager (DLM), 63
Distribution and replication of data, 72–81
DML statements with a returning clause (OCI), 473–474
Documentation, 30–48
HTML, 39–41
project deliverables as documents, 47–48
three fundamental requisites, 30–38
easy retrieval, 31, 41–43
synchronization, 31, 44–46
traceability, 31, 32–38
using Oracle ConText to manage project documentation, 41–44
XML, 38–39
Domains, role of, 118–120
Driving table, 213
DTD editor, 35
Duration events, 488
Dynamic queue creation (MQ series), 601
Dynamic SQL in Pro*C, 401–409
Dynamic SQL processing (OCI), 470–472

Easy retrieval, 31, 41–43
using Oracle ConText, 31, 41–43
example of, 43–44
features, 42–43
managing project-related documentation, 41–42
Embarcadero SQL-Sombrero, 328
Entera, 297
Entity relationship (ER) model, 114–115
Environment setup, 272–274
Epilogue script, 236
Error/exception handling, 168–174
in "C," 170–173
in OO languages, 173–174
Error handler, building, in Pro*C, 340–365
Error handling
in OCI, 449–456
table, 449
in Pro*C, 332–365
Error storms, 179
ER/Studio, 135–138
ER/Win, 129–131
Evolutionary prototyping model, 18, 19
Exemplars, 255
EXPLAIN PLAN, 215–225
Extensible markup language (XML), 38–39
External procedures, 526–533

Fact table, 84
Fan-out parallelism, 588
Field Manipulation Language (FML), 582
File management, 184–186
Flexibility, 53–59
Flushing, 438
FML (TUXEDO), 577
Foreign currency, 239
Foreign grammar, 238
Formatter, 35
Form Builder, 280
Fountain model, 24–27
Freeing, 438

Generalization, 50
Getting data in/out of Oracle, 541–566
advanced queuing, 553–563
communicating with external world, 541–566
Oracle PIPEs and ALERTs, 541–547
PLEX, 547–553
Perl—OraPerl/PerlDBI, 564–565
Granularity, 490

Host array processing, 365–372
Host arrays, 108–109
Hot standby database, 71

IBM MQ series, 597–610
MQI interface, 604–609
objects, 599–601
and Oracle, 601–604
IDEF1X methodology, 115
Impedance mismatch, 16, 429
Independence, 83
Information engineering (IE) methodology, 115
Information hiding, 51
Inprise BDE/SQL Links, 323–324
Inprise/Borland.com, 296–304
Integration, 236, 237
Integration testing, 246
Interconnect, 63
Interfaces, 429
Internal debuggers, 193–200
Internalization issues, 237–241
Intranet, 94
Items, 488
resource, 488–489
table, 489

Jaguar CTS, 304
Java, 278–279
Job queue mechanism, 78

Lag time, 575
Large object management (OCI), 472
functions, table, 472
Large Objects (LOB), handling in Pro*C, 427–428
Latency, 63
Layers, communication between—parameters and return values, 145
Listener load balancing, 567, 568
List Of Value items (LOV fields), 281–282
Literal strings or numbers, use of, 4
LOB locators, 427
Logical data access layer, 143
Logical data model, 117
Loosely coupled systems, 63
LRU (least recently used) algorithm, 704

Marking, 438
Markup language, 34
descriptive, 34
procedural, 34
Massively parallel processing hardware (MPP), 63
Merging, 185
Message (AQ), 553
Message-oriented middleware (MOM) products, 572–573
Metadata, 53
Metalanguage, 34
Methods, 428
Microsoft, 291–296
Microsoft connectivity, 317–322
Microsoft Data Access Components (MDAC), 319–320
MIDAS, 297
Middleware paradigms, 573–577
conversation based, 573, 574
event based, 573, 575–576
queue based, 573, 574–575
request/response, 573–574
Model queues (MQ series), 601
MQI APIs, table, 604
MQI data structures, table, 605
Multiple environments, managing, 242–275
application objects owner, 269–271
development, test, production, 242–247
environment setup, 272–274
Oracle security model, 262–269
synchronizing environments, 247–262
Multi-threaded applications, developing, 415–427
Multi-Threaded Server (MTS), 290
Mutating, 505

National Language Support (NLS) subsystem, 239
Native drivers/third party OCI drivers, 314–317
NLOB, 427
Normalization, 60
NT threads, 421–427
Null values and indicator variables, 97–102

Object level privileges, 264
Object navigational and associative interfaces, 437–444
Object navigational new keywords, table, 439
Object navigation (OCI), 475–476
Object oriented (OO) paradigm, 22–24
Object-relational paradigm, 428–434
Object tables, 430
OCI
and C++, 476–477
data structures, 446–447
table, 446
handles, 457–459
table, 458
release 8, 456–467
OCI/Oracle interaction sequence, table, 448
ODBC connectivity, 317–319
OleDB consumers, 319
OleDB for Oracle, 328

OleDB providers, 319
One thread-one session context model, 415
One-to-one relationship, 62
Operator alerts, 179–180
Optimal Flexible Architecture (OFA), 272
Oracle 8, 290
Oracle, connecting to, 313–327
  Inprise BDE/SQL Links, 323–324
  Microsoft connectivity, 317–322
  native drivers/third party OCI drivers, 314–317
  Oracle Objects for OLE (OO4O), 324–327
Oracle Call Interface (OCI), 445–478
  advantages of, 467–476
    advanced queuing, 474–475
    DML statements with a returning clause, 473–474
    dynamic SQL processing, 470–472
    large object management, 472
    object navigation, 475–476
    schema metadata querying and reverse engineering, 468–470
  OCI and Pro*C, 476–477
  release 7, 446–456
    cursors, 447–448
    error handling, 449–456
    OCI data structures, 446–447
  release 8, 456–467
Oracle ConText, 41–44
  example of, 43–44
  managing project-related documentation, 41–42
  text retrieval features, 42–43
Oracle Corporation, 280–291
Oracle Database Designer (ODD), 128–129
Oracle Designer, 122–128
Oracle Developer, 279, 280
  summary, 289–291
Oracle Enterprise Manager (OEM), 480
Oracle Intelligence Agent, 479
Oracle objects, table of terms, 438
Oracle Objects for OLE (OO4O), 324–327
Oracle Performance Evaluator and Real-time Analyzer (OPERA), 703–752
  data gatherer, 711
  engine performance ratios, 711
    table, 711–713
  engine statistics menu, 713–720
  Java client, 723–728
    classes, table, 723–724
  server source code, 728–751
    required files, table, 729–730
  SQL analysis, 720–723
  tuning ratios, table, 708
Oracle performance tuning, 703–752
  areas where Oracle performance can fail, 704–707
    engine poorly configured, 705–707
    poorly formulated SQL statements, 704–705
  OPERA design, 710–723
    three-tier architecture, 711–723
  OPERA Java client, 723–728
  OPERA server source code, 728–751
  tools needed by DBAs, 707–709
    OPERA and its tuning method, 707–709
Oracle projects
  SDLC in, 27–28
  software engineering in, 1–10
    mid-range: domain of rightsizing, 1–3
    mistakes to avoid, 3–5
    structure of book, 5–10
      design and documentation, 6–8
      development environment, establishing, 8–9
      Oracle and third party development tools, 9
      projects ancd practice, 9–10
Oracle security model, 262–269
Oracle tools: Pro*C/C++, 331–444
  developing multi-threaded applications, 415–427
    NT threads, 421–427
    Sun threads, 420–421
  dynamic SQL in Pro*C, 401–409
  error handling in Pro*C, 332–365
    building an error handler in Pro*C, 340–361
    Oracle Communication Area (ORACA), 361–365
  handling LOB types in Pro*C, 427–428
  host array processing, 365–372
  interfacing Pro*C to OCI, 409–415
    to OCI release 7, 409–411
    to OCI release 8, 411–415
  object navigational and associative interfaces, 437–444
  object-relational paradigm, 428–434
  Oracle Type translator (OTT), 434–437
  precompiler options, 399–401
  Pro*C and PL/SQL, 372–393
  support for C++, 394–399
Oracle Trace, 210–211, 225–233, 479–495
  APIs, 490–493
    calls, table, 492
  Collection Services, 479
  components, 479–487
    client side, 481–487
    server side, 480–481
      executables, table, 480
      required files, table, 480–481
  formatting and analyzing data, 493–494
  using—what to sample, 487–490
Oracle Type Translator (OTT), 434–437
OTL, 477

Packages, 515–516
  body, 515
  definition, 515
  procedure/function overloading, 516
Parallelism, 63–70
Parsing, 704
Partitioned views, 82
Password aging mechanism, 268
Performance, 59–62
Performance tuning, 707
  input/output, 707
  memory allocation, 707
  resource contention, 707
Perl—OraPerl/PerlDBI, 564–565
Physical access data layer, 143–144
Physical data model, 117
Pinning, 438
PIPEs and ALERTs, 542–547
PLEX (PL/SQL Extender), 547–553
PL/SQL
  hiding code, 533–534
PL/SQL as query helper, 510–515
Point events, 488
Power++, 304
Powerbuilder, 304
PowerDesigner, 131–135
PowerJ++, 304
Precalculated fields, 62
Precompiler options, 399–401
Presentation logic, 91
Problem escalation, 180
Pro*C, interfacing to OCI, 409–415
  release 7, 409–411
  release 8, 411–415
Pro*C and PL/SQL, 372–393
Procedural code layering, example in "C," 146–159
Procedural SQL, 496–540
  business logic and PL/SQL, 498–504
  database triggers, 504–509
  external procedures, 526–533
  hiding PL/SQL code, 533–534
  Oracle extension to ANSI SQL, 497–498
  packages, 515–516
  PL/SQL as query helper, 510–515
  supplied packages, 516–526
    DBMS_JOB, 520–522
      methods, table, 522
    DBMS_OUTPUT, 525–526
    DBMS_SESSION, 523–524
    DBMS_SHARED_POOL, 524–525
    DBMS_SQL, 517–520
  third party tools, 534–540
Product, 186
Product definition file, 481
Profilers, 202–205
Programmatic object support, 437
Project Builder, 280, 281
Prologue script, 236
Promotional group, 184
  models, 188–190
Public synonym, 243
Publish-and-Subscribe paradigm, 474–475, 562
Purity level, 432, 514

Query optimizer, 212
Queue (AQ), 553
Queue control structure, 590
Queue Monitor (AQ), 554
Queues and events, potential uses of, table, 562–563
Queue Table (AQ), 554

Rapid application development (RAD) tools, 95
Redundant array of independent disks (RAID), 70–71

Referential integrity, 102–104
Refreshing, 438
Regression testing, 236
Release building, 190–193
Reliability, 70–72
Remote procedure call (RPC), 571
Replication
catalog, 78
conflicts, types of, 78–79
group, 78
object, 78
site, 78
Reports and Graphics, 287–289
Repository, importance of, 120–121
Reverse engineering process, 248
Revision, 184
Roman alphabet, 238
Row-level trigger, 505
Row objects, 430, 438
Run-time error detection, 208–210

Sashimi model, 18
Scalability, 62–70, 236–237
ScaleUp, 63
Schema, 243
Schema metadata querying and reverse engineering (OCI), 468–470
Script debugging capabilities, 236, 237
Security, 3
Server, communicating with, 567–610
middleware and ACID messages, 572–610
BEA Systems TUXEDO, 577–597
IBM MQ series, 597–610
middleware paradigms, 573–577
SQL*Net/Net8, 567–570
when not to use SQL*Net, 570–572
SQL*Net alternatives, 571–572
Server-centric, dumb terminal based architecture, 90
Server code, how to structure, 141–181
application event logging, 175–180
application monitoring—operator alerts, 179–180
problem escalation, 180
beyond Oracle manuals, 142
error/exception handling, 168–174
in "C," 170–173
in OO languages, 173–174
procedural code and error handler function, 143–160
automatic code generation, 159–160
business logic layer, 143
communication between layers—parameters and return values, 145
logical data access layer, 143
physical data access layer, 143–144
procedural code layering, example in "C," 146–159
using composition in OO, 160–168
Server (TUXEDO), 578
Service (TUXEDO), 578
SGML editor, 35
SGML parser, 35
SGML retrieval system, 35
Shared pool browser application, ShrPool, 611–702
in Delphi, 659–680
in Oracle Developer, 640–659
in PowerBuilder, 680–702
source code, 616–618
in Visual Basic, 618–640
Snowflake star, 85
Software development life cycle (SDLC), 11–29, 12
different methodologies, same development paradigm, 22–24
object orientation and fountain model, 24–27
in Oracle projects, 27–28
risk analysis, prototyping, and spiral model, 19–22
traditional approach, 11–12
waterfall model, 12–19
issues and problems associated with, 15–19
use in large corporations, 14–15
Software engineering essentials, 182–241
internalization issues, 237–241
release building, 190–193
source code keywords, 191–192
trouble shooting faulty builds, 192–193
testing strategies, 233–237
test techniques, 234–237
tools for better code, 193–211
disabling instrumentation in production code, 200–202
internal debuggers, 193–200
Oracle Trace, 210–211
profilers, 202–205
run-time error detection, 208–210
test coverage monitoring, 205–208
version control, 183–190
file management, 184–186
products and bundles, 186–188
promotional group models, 188–190
writing performance conscious SQL statements, 211–233
EXPLAIN PLAN, 215–225
Trace and TKPROF, 225–233
Software engineering practices for Oracle projects, table, 271
Source code control, 183
Source code keywords, 191–192
Specialization, 50
SpeedUp, 63
Spiral model, 19–22
SQLCA, 333–335
SQLCODE, 333
SQL Navigator, 249–251, 534, 538–540
SQL*Net alternatives, 571–572
remote procedure call (RPC), 571
straight sockets, 571–572
SQL-Programmer, 534–538
SQLSTATE, 333
SQL statements, writing performance conscious, 211–233
Staged delivery model, 18–19
Standard generalized markup language (SGML), 34–38
environment, components of, 35–38
Star queries, 84
Stateless, 573
Statement-level trigger, 505
Straight sockets, 571–572
Sun threads, 420–421
Sybase/Powersoft, 304–313
Symmetric multiprocessing hardware (SMP), 63
Synchronization, 44–46
of environments, 247–262
through change management, 46
System privileges, 264

Tablespace fragmentation, 272–273
Test coverage monitoring, 205–208
Testing strategies, 233–237
Test script, 235
Test verification, 236, 237
Tightly coupled systems, 63
Tip, 184, 185
Tip revision, 185
TKPROF, 225–233, 511–514
TMIB (TUXEDO), 578
Tool for Oracle Application Developers (TOAD), 248
Traceability, 32–38
through HTML, 39–41
through SGML, 34–38
Transaction bracketing (TUXEDO), 578
Transaction coordinator (TUXEDO), 578
Transaction infection (TUXEDO), 578
Transaction initiator (TUXEDO), 578
Transaction terminator (TUXEDO), 578
Transaction time-out, 587
Transient copy of persistent objects, 437
Transparency, 83
Trigger types, table, 504
Trouble shooting, 192–193
Trunk, 184, 185
TUXEDO, 577–597
Two-phase commit, presumed abort (2PC-PA) (TUXEDO), 578
Two-phase commit protocol, 72
Typed buffer (TUXEDO), 578

Unmarking, 438
Unpinning, 438
User feedback, 236, 237

Version control, 183–190
Very large database/data warehouse, 81–86
VIEW (TUXEDO), 578
Visual Basic, 291–296, 328
Enterprise, 291
summary, 296

Waterfall model, 12–19, 233
White-box testing, 234–235
Workload partitioning model, 75–76, 77
Wrapping, 533

LICENSE AGREEMENT AND LIMITED WARRANTY

READ THE FOLLOWING TERMS AND CONDITIONS CAREFULLY BEFORE OPENING THIS CD PACKAGE. THIS LEGAL DOCUMENT IS AN AGREEMENT BETWEEN YOU AND PRENTICE-HALL, INC. (THE "COMPANY"). BY OPENING THIS SEALED CD PACKAGE, YOU ARE AGREEING TO BE BOUND BY THESE TERMS AND CONDITIONS. IF YOU DO NOT AGREE WITH THESE TERMS AND CONDITIONS, DO NOT OPEN THE CD PACKAGE. PROMPTLY RETURN THE UNOPENED CD PACKAGE AND ALL ACCOMPANYING ITEMS TO THE PLACE YOU OBTAINED THEM FOR A FULL REFUND OF ANY SUMS YOU HAVE PAID.

1. **GRANT OF LICENSE:** In consideration of your purchase of this book, and your agreement to abide by the terms and conditions of this Agreement, the Company grants to you a nonexclusive right to use and display the copy of the enclosed software program (hereinafter the "SOFTWARE") on a single computer (i.e., with a single CPU) at a single location so long as you comply with the terms of this Agreement. The Company reserves all rights not expressly granted to you under this Agreement.

2. **OWNERSHIP OF SOFTWARE:** You own only the magnetic or physical media (the enclosed CD) on which the SOFTWARE is recorded or fixed, but the Company and the software developers retain all the rights, title, and ownership to the SOFTWARE recorded on the original CD copy(ies) and all subsequent copies of the SOFTWARE, regardless of the form or media on which the original or other copies may exist. This license is not a sale of the original SOFTWARE or any copy to you.

3. **COPY RESTRICTIONS:** This SOFTWARE and the accompanying printed materials and user manual (the "Documentation") are the subject of copyright. The individual programs on the CD are copyrighted by the authors of each program. Some of the programs on the CD include separate licensing agreements. If you intend to use one of these programs, you must read and follow its accompanying license agreement. You may not copy the Documentation or the SOFTWARE, except that you may make a single copy of the SOFTWARE for backup or archival purposes only. You may be held legally responsible for any copying or copyright infringement which is caused or encouraged by your failure to abide by the terms of this restriction.

4. **USE RESTRICTIONS:** You may not network the SOFTWARE or otherwise use it on more than one computer or computer terminal at the same time. You may physically transfer the SOFTWARE from one computer to another provided that the SOFTWARE is used on only one computer at a time. You may not distribute copies of the SOFTWARE or Documentation to others. You may not reverse engineer, disassemble, decompile, modify, adapt, translate, or create derivative works based on the SOFTWARE or the Documentation without the prior written consent of the Company.

5. **TRANSFER RESTRICTIONS:** The enclosed SOFTWARE is licensed only to you and may not be transferred to any one else without the prior written consent of the Company. Any unauthorized transfer of the SOFTWARE shall result in the immediate termination of this Agreement.

6. **TERMINATION:** This license is effective until terminated. This license will terminate automatically without notice from the Company and become null and void if you fail to comply with any provisions or limitations of this license. Upon termination, you shall destroy the Documentation and all copies of the SOFTWARE. All provisions of this Agreement as to warranties, limitation of liability, remedies or damages, and our ownership rights shall survive termination.

7. **MISCELLANEOUS:** This Agreement shall be construed in accordance with the laws of the United States of America and the State of New York and shall benefit the Company, its affiliates, and assignees.

8. **LIMITED WARRANTY AND DISCLAIMER OF WARRANTY:** The Company warrants that the SOFTWARE, when properly used in accordance with the Documentation, will operate in substantial conformity with the description of the SOFTWARE set forth in the Documentation. The Company does not warrant that the SOFTWARE will meet your requirements or that the operation

of the SOFTWARE will be uninterrupted or error-free. The Company warrants that the media on which the SOFTWARE is delivered shall be free from defects in materials and workmanship under normal use for a period of thirty (30) days from the date of your purchase. Your only remedy and the Company's only obligation under these limited warranties is, at the Company's option, return of the warranted item for a refund of any amounts paid by you or replacement of the item. Any replacement of SOFTWARE or media under the warranties shall not extend the original warranty period. The limited warranty set forth above shall not apply to any SOFTWARE which the Company determines in good faith has been subject to misuse, neglect, improper installation, repair, alteration, or damage by you. EXCEPT FOR THE EXPRESSED WARRANTIES SET FORTH ABOVE, THE COMPANY DISCLAIMS ALL WARRANTIES, EXPRESS OR IMPLIED, INCLUDING WITHOUT LIMITATION, THE IMPLIED WARRANTIES OF MERCHANTABILITY AND FITNESS FOR A PARTICULAR PURPOSE. EXCEPT FOR THE EXPRESS WARRANTY SET FORTH ABOVE, THE COMPANY DOES NOT WARRANT, GUARANTEE, OR MAKE ANY REPRESENTATION REGARDING THE USE OR THE RESULTS OF THE USE OF THE SOFTWARE IN TERMS OF ITS CORRECTNESS, ACCURACY, RELIABILITY, CURRENTNESS, OR OTHERWISE.

IN NO EVENT, SHALL THE COMPANY OR ITS EMPLOYEES, AGENTS, SUPPLIERS, OR CONTRACTORS BE LIABLE FOR ANY INCIDENTAL, INDIRECT, SPECIAL, OR CONSEQUENTIAL DAMAGES ARISING OUT OF OR IN CONNECTION WITH THE LICENSE GRANTED UNDER THIS AGREEMENT, OR FOR LOSS OF USE, LOSS OF DATA, LOSS OF INCOME OR PROFIT, OR OTHER LOSSES, SUSTAINED AS A RESULT OF INJURY TO ANY PERSON, OR LOSS OF OR DAMAGE TO PROPERTY, OR CLAIMS OF THIRD PARTIES, EVEN IF THE COMPANY OR AN AUTHORIZED REPRESENTATIVE OF THE COMPANY HAS BEEN ADVISED OF THE POSSIBILITY OF SUCH DAMAGES. IN NO EVENT SHALL LIABILITY OF THE COMPANY FOR DAMAGES WITH RESPECT TO THE SOFTWARE EXCEED THE AMOUNTS ACTUALLY PAID BY YOU, IF ANY, FOR THE SOFTWARE.

SOME JURISDICTIONS DO NOT ALLOW THE LIMITATION OF IMPLIED WARRANTIES OR LIABILITY FOR INCIDENTAL, INDIRECT, SPECIAL, OR CONSEQUENTIAL DAMAGES, SO THE ABOVE LIMITATIONS MAY NOT ALWAYS APPLY. THE WARRANTIES IN THIS AGREEMENT GIVE YOU SPECIFIC LEGAL RIGHTS AND YOU MAY ALSO HAVE OTHER RIGHTS WHICH VARY IN ACCORDANCE WITH LOCAL LAW.

ACKNOWLEDGMENT

YOU ACKNOWLEDGE THAT YOU HAVE READ THIS AGREEMENT, UNDERSTAND IT, AND AGREE TO BE BOUND BY ITS TERMS AND CONDITIONS. YOU ALSO AGREE THAT THIS AGREEMENT IS THE COMPLETE AND EXCLUSIVE STATEMENT OF THE AGREEMENT BETWEEN YOU AND THE COMPANY AND SUPERSEDES ALL PROPOSALS OR PRIOR AGREEMENTS, ORAL, OR WRITTEN, AND ANY OTHER COMMUNICATIONS BETWEEN YOU AND THE COMPANY OR ANY REPRESENTATIVE OF THE COMPANY RELATING TO THE SUBJECT MATTER OF THIS AGREEMENT.

Should you have any questions concerning this Agreement or if you wish to contact the Company for any reason, please contact in writing at the address below.

Robin Short

Prentice Hall PTR

One Lake Street

Upper Saddle River, New Jersey 07458

About the CD-ROM

The CD-ROM included with *Software Engineering with Oracle* contains … It can be used on Microsoft Windows® 95/98/NT®.

License Agreement

Use of *Software Engineering with Oracle* is subject to the terms of the License Agreement and Limited Warranty, found on pp 770–771.

Technical Support

Prentice Hall does not offer technical support for any of the programs on the CD-ROM. However, if the CD-ROM is damaged, you may obtain a replacement copy by sending an email that describes the problem to: disc_exchange@prenhall.com